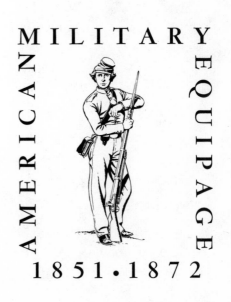

AMERICAN MILITARY EQUIPAGE

1851 · 1872

AMERICAN MILITARY EQUIPAGE

1851 . 1872

A description by word and picture of what the American soldier, sailor and marine of these years wore and carried, with emphasis on the American Civil War.

By Frederick P. Todd

In collaboration with George Woodbridge,
Lee A. Wallace, Jr., and Michael J. McAfee

original illustrations by George Woodbridge

With additional illustrations by
Michael J. McAfee and others.

Originally published in 3 volumes by
The Company of Military Historians,
Westbrook, Connecticut

CHARLES SCRIBNER'S SONS · NEW YORK

Copyright © 1974, 1977, 1978 Maria Todd Damerel
First published by Charles Scribner's Sons 1980

Library of Congress Cataloging in Publication Data

Todd, Frederick P
  American military equipage, 1851-1872.

  Includes bibliographies and index.
  1. United States—Armed Forces—Uniforms—History. 2. United States—Armed Forces—
  Equipment—History.
I. Title.
UC463.T62   355.8'1'0973   80-39749
ISBN 0-684-16862-6 (v. 1)

1 3 5 7 9 11 13 15 17 19   Q/C   20 18 16 14 12 10 8 6 4 2

Printed in the United States of America

AMERICAN MILITARY EQUIPAGE

1851 • 1872

VOLUME I

AMERICAN MILITARY EQUIPAGE

1851 • 1872

A description by word and picture of what the American soldier, sailor and marine of these years wore and carried, with emphasis on the American Civil War.

VOLUME I

PREFACE

Fig. 1. Recommendations for improving the Army uniform made by Lieutenant George H. Derby ("John Phoenix, Esq., The Veritable Squibob") in August 1851. It is one of a number of ludicrous drawings submitted by this Army humorist in response to an appeal for new ideas from the Secretary of War. (Courtesy of the Bancroft Library, University of California.)

Proposed amendments to the New Uniform, Respectfully referred Aug. 1851
1. *Cap. To be of dark blue paper as per pattern; possessing all the grace, and beauty of outline of the regulation cap, it is far lighter, and may be obtained for a trifle at any grocery.*
2. *Shoulder Knots. To be hair and clothes brushes, thus combining ornament and utility. A soldier may employ his epaulettes to advantage upon his own head and his officer's clothing.*
3. *Pantaloons. To have a star of gold embroidery or yellow metal upon the seat, with a brass hook in the centre. The star is highly ornamental and the use of the hook in transporting small articles upon a march is rendered apparent by reference to Fig. 2.*

   As a human contrivance, in doing away with "Bucking" it is to be recommended, as by attaching the hook to a stationary staple the soldier would be effectually secured without doing violence to his feeling of self respect.

Acknowledgments

This book is the work of many persons. While the authors alone accept responsibility for what appears in text and pictures—and for all errors and omissions—the book began as a cooperative venture and continued as such over the twelve and more years of its preparation. The assistance and advice given by scores of persons has been generous and widespread.

In acknowledging this debt and rendering thanks, the authors have, for convenience, recorded assistance given on a specific chapter in the chapter itself. Here we desire to pay homage to those associates and friends whose aid has embraced the book as a whole.

First, we should record our indebtedness to The Company of Military Historians, which has encouraged and supported the enterprise from the start and graciously agreed to publish the finished work. Every word has been read by its Board of Review, and to this eminent body—Henry I. Shaw, Jr., Harold L. Peterson, H. Charles McBarron, Jr., and the late Robert L. Miller—we are immensely beholden for numerous suggestions and criticisms.

To Maria P. Todd, who has typed the entire manuscript, not once but two or three times over, we owe an everlasting debt.

To Colonel John R. Elting, former Deputy Director of the course on the history of the art of war at the United States Military Academy, who has read the manuscript from beginning to end, we are indebted for many improvements.

Mrs. John Nicholas Brown, former President of The Company of Military Historians and one of the world's leading authorities in military equipage, has been unstinting in the assistance and encouragement she has offered.

H. Michael Madaus, scholar extraordinary, has given invaluable assistance in such disparate areas as corps flags, imported firearms, and zouave uniforms.

Many others deserve thanks as much for their display of patience and understanding as for outright help, notably our respective families and the staffs of the West Point Museum and the National Park Service. Mrs. Leona Patton and the late Gerald C. Stowe of the first institution were unfailing in their loyalty. Special appreciation is due William K. Kay, Lee J. Miller, and Herbert L. Ganter for services far beyond the call of friendship.

As detailed below, our basic source of manuscripts has been the National Archives. Effective use, over the years, of its holdings was made possible through the informed assistance of its staff, notably Elmer O. Parker, Mrs. Sara D. Jackson, Milton K. Chamberlain, and the late David C. Haase. In the Library of Congress we received cordial cooperation from the late Hirst D. Milhollen, Milton Kaplan, Carl E. Stange, and others.

Museums and repositories used outside Washington are acknowledged individually later, but the staff of one—the Museum of the Confederacy in Richmond, Va.—must be singled out for special thanks in this section. Miss India Thomas, Director Emeritus, and Miss Eleanor S. Brockenbrough, Assistant Director, have given help graciously and effectively.

Finally, to the Company's Board of Publication and to Mowbray Company-Publishers go our thanks for a painstaking job of book making.

Fig. 2. Drawing of the 1st Virginia Cavalry in the field, probably in September 1862, by Alfred R. Waud (Library of Congress) and a wood engraving based on it, from *Harpers Weekly*, 27 September 1862.

Notes on Sources

Four distinct categories of source material have been available in preparing this study: published works, manuscripts, graphic materials, and artifacts or actual objects, all requiring balanced and critical use.

For a number of reasons—space being the most compelling—the individual citation of sources has not been practical. To compensate for this, a list of the over-all sources for each chapter is included at its end, with special consideration given to published works that are reasonably accessible. The more general sources of information, including some of the strengths and weaknesses of each, are worthy of initial examination.

Published Books

The literature of the American Civil War and the surrounding years is immense. In 1960 the New York Public Library estimated it held more than 18,000 books on the war with new volumes appearing almost daily. It is, therefore, fortunate that only a small percentage of this output has been found to be essential or even useful to this study. Great areas of writing—books about battles and campaigns, biographies, and narrative histories, for example—as a rule have little or nothing to offer. Their place has been taken by a handful of carefully compiled reference works, the most important being:

Frederick H. Dyer, *A Compendium of the War of the Rebellion*, Des Moines, Iowa, 1908; reprinted, 3 vols., New York, 1959.

Francis B. Heitman, *Historical Register and Dictionary of the United States Army from its Organization . . . to 1903*, 2 vols., Washington, D.C., 1903; reprinted, Urbana, Ill., 1967.

Vincent J. Esposito, Chief Ed., *The West Point Atlas of American Wars*, 2 vols., New York, 1959.

William F. Fox, *Regimental Losses in the . . . Civil War*, Albany, 1898.

Mark M. Boatner, III, *The Civil War Dictionary*, New York, 1959.

R. Ernest Dupuy and Trevor N. Dupuy, *The Compact History of the Civil War*, New York, 1960.

U.S. War Department, *List of Regiments and Battalions in the Confederate States Army 1861-1865*, Washington, D.C., n.d.

The vast number of books in recent years about the Civil War has been made possible in large measure by the publication of what is conceded to be the most important documentary military history ever produced: *The War of the Rebellion: A Compilation of the Official Records of the Union and Confederate Armies.* Begun in 1864, compiled nominally by the War Department but actually as a distinctive governmental activity, and completed in 1927, the series comprises 128 volumes plus 1,006 maps and sketches in a separate 3-volume atlas of 175 plates. A comparable naval history, *Official Records of the Union and Confederate Navies,* was published 1894–1922. Impressive as are these series in terms of size, their comprehension and relative impartiality form the real reason for their fame. While the biographer and student of military operations must use them with some caution, the worker in the field of military equipage can count quite surely on their overall accuracy and honesty.

Official Publications: The starting point for most research into military equipage is contemporary printed government documents, either those of the general governments* or those of the states. They include periodic reports; regulations and

---

* A central government—in this case, the U.S.A. and the C.S.A.

manuals; orders, circulars, and memoranda; registers and troop lists. These documents are mentioned when applicable in the chapters that follow.

It was customary for a military officer to make some sort of report to his immediate superior, usually annually. Reports from the higher levels of command were consolidated by the ranking executive officer—normally the President of the United States or the governor of a state—and submitted to the controlling legislative body in printed form. Thus the papers of these bodies contain a large amount of information not always published separately. Indeed, the practice of printing separate annual reports of the state adjutants general did not commence in most states until the late 1850's or the 1860's.

For the student of military uniforms and insignia the various published dress regulations are of great importance, yet all must be used with caution. This is especially true with the two regulations that play leading roles in this period: The U.S. Army dress regulations of 12 June 1851 (GO 31) and those of the Confederate States dated 6 June 1861 (GO 9). The former were designed primarily for the use of officers and for the firms (like William H. Horstmann & Sons who published an illustrated edition) that provided them with uniforms. In the main, only those articles of enlisted men's wear which were of the new pattern are mentioned, and those were all for full dress. Nowhere is a word said about fatigue clothing since those garments were manufactured by the Army in its own shops.

The artist who drew the Horstmann colored plates apparently had little or no contact with the Ordnance Office, which issued belts, cartridge boxes, and the like, all of which are loosely added and in some cases positively incorrect. Worst of all, the orders specified that articles of the old uniform had to be exhausted before the new pattern could be issued. We know now that it took some regiments four years to draw the new pattern clothing, by which time later patterns had been substituted. Thus an uncritical use of the 1851 regulations can easily lead the student into misunderstandings and errors.

A word should be said about the dress regulations of 29 January 1850 which, in fact, introduced the radical changes usually associated with the following year. In a preamble to the regulations the Secretary of War frankly admitted they came as a result of the appeals of more than half of his officers for "a uniform less expensive, less difficult to procure, and better adapted to campaign and other service." The dress and insignia prescribed as a result are interesting—but were never worn. On 23 August 1850 the orders were suspended and completely rewritten for publication the following year.

The 1861 Confederate regulations will be found to possess many of the same shortcomings as their U.S. counterpart. The uniform prescribed for enlisted men, for example, was rarely if ever worn and, apparently, seldom even seriously considered. This problem will be discussed at length in the chapter on Confederate dress. It will suffice here to say that the only positive result of these orders was to establish gray as the color of coats and lay down a novel system of commissioned rank insignia.

Dress regulations issued by states usually turn out to be slightly modified copies of the U.S. Army regulations. In such cases they should be treated with great caution; usually one can find a statement exempting militia organizations already uniformed from their provisions, and the chances are that such exemptions include the entire state volunteer militia force.

The illustrated Horstmann regulations mentioned above were very popular in their day and were reprinted as late as 1857. This led the Adjutant General of Ohio to write (Ohio, *General Regulations*, 1859):

> The Ohio volunteers are cautioned with regard to a volume of plates issued by Horseman [sic] & Sons, of Philadelphia; otherwise they may be led into error.
>
> The book was issued in conformity to the army regulations of 1851. It still is a valuable book of reference. The date of 1857 being upon the title page of the recent reprints, might induce the impression, however, that the plates represent the U.S. army uniform of 1857. Reference to army regulations of that year will show discrepancies in respect to cap, coat, pantaloons and ornaments.

An interesting offshoot of the Horstmann regulations is a copy published in 1857 by Robert Weir, "Army, Naval and Civic Costumer" of Boston. This purports to bring the 1851 orders up to date and to include details of the dress of the volunteer militias of the several states. A copy can be found in the War Records Office of the Adjutant General of Massachusetts, State House, Boston. Unfortunately, it falls far short of its purpose.

Collections of general orders and circulars of the U.S. and C.S. armies can be found without too much trouble. Those published by the major army field and geographic commands (such as the Army of the Potomac) are harder to locate. And general orders issued by the adjutants general of the various states are usually impossible to find save in isolated copies.

The principal dress regulations of the U.S. Army in this period are listed in Chapter 8.

Memoirs and Regimental Histories

Histories of one sort or another exist for perhaps a quarter of the regiments that served in the Civil War and extensive use has been made of these. Many contain detailed descriptions of clothing, arms, and even accouterments, and all are useful in discovering the story of the unit covered as well as the minutiae of soldier life. Even the books that say nothing about uniforms or arms are of value, if only as negative evidence. An author naturally tends to neglect the commonplace in all areas, just as he makes special mention of the extraordinary. Thus it is fairly safe to assume that a regiment whose uniform, weapons, and other gear are not described was issued only run-of-the-mill equipage.

The inherent defect of this class of literature—its partiality and narrow judgement—need not concern us too greatly, but it is important to remember that many histories were written long after the events described, when memories of details tend to fade. Regimental histories are rarely cited, but for those interested in locating specific books the *Bibliography of State Participation in the Civil War, 1861–1866,* 3rd edition, published by the War Department in 1913, is a valuable tool covering both sides of the conflict. An up-to-date and far more exhaustive listing of regimental histories has now been prepared by Charles E. Dornbusch: *Military Bibliography of the Civil War,* 3 vols., New York, 1961–1967. This bibliography also lists regimental publications for both North and South, as well as biographies and general works.

More valuable than regimental histories are several books that set out to describe in detail the daily life of the common soldier. The classic example is John D. Billings, *Hardtack and Coffee, or the Unwritten Story of Army Life . . .,* Boston, 1887, which is profusely illustrated and covers all aspects from rations to insignia, mules to wood ticks. Of the same importance, but covering the Western armies, is Wilbur F. Hinman, *Corporal Si Klegg and His "Pard,"* 12th ed., Cleveland, 1900; and Leander Stillwell, *The Story of Army Life in the Civil War, 1861–1865,* 2nd ed., Erie, Kansas, 1920. Carlton McCarthy's *Detailed Minutiae of Soldier Life in the Army of Northern Virginia, 1861–1865,* Richmond, 1882, does much the same for the Confederate soldier. And there are others. Valuable for furnishing the same sort of human-interest information are Bell I. Wiley's *The Life of Johnny Reb,* New York, 1943, and *The Life of Billy Yank,* New York, 1951, especially in that each contains detailed bibliographic notes.

Newspapers and Magazines

No research can be more laborious or frustrating, and none more rewarding, than working with contemporary newspapers. Frequently the newspaper is the only available source of information on the history and appearance of state military companies. Indeed, some subjects that follow are based almost entirely on details gleaned from three- or four-line notices in the daily or weekly press of the period.

Here and there one can find useful compilations of clippings, and this is why scrapbooks should be thoughtfully inspected. In the days of the Works Progress Administration an exhaustive compilation was made of articles and notices in the New Orleans press on military subjects; the entries cover our entire period and many years on both sides. More recently a dedicated student combed the New York and other big-city papers for similar material. In judging the value of this source of data on military dress it should be recalled that Charles M. Lefferts based his classic volume on the American uniforms of the Revolution almost exclusively upon newspapers.

Contemporary illustrated magazines are an excellent if obvious source. There were four of importance to this study, all weeklies published in the North: *Gleason's* (later *Ballou's*) *Pictorial Drawing-Room Companion* (1851–1859), *Frank Leslie's Illustrated Newspaper* (1855 on), *Harper's Weekly* (1857 on), *New York Illustrated News* (1859–1864). Among several other illustrated weeklies which existed briefly in the period, the *Southern Illustrated News* was published in Richmond but was illustrated in title only and has little to offer the researcher. Often the foreign illustrated magazines, notably the *Illustrated London News,* contained pictures of American military events.

The medium of illustration in all these magazines was the woodcut. Its limitations are discussed later, but what the weeklies lacked in quality they made up in quantity. The editor of *Leslie's* estimated at the end of 1864 that his magazine had published nearly 3000 pictures of the war and had employed over eighty artists since 1861; he then had twelve correspondents at the front. Used in conjunction with other research, these illustrations are of first-rate importance.

Complete runs of these illustrated magazines can be found today only in the larger libraries, although scattered copies are fairly common. Much of the graphic information they contained must therefore be gleaned from the pictorial histories issued after the Civil War that reprinted the woodcuts. The more important ones are:

Benjamin LaBree, ed., *The Pictorial Battles of the Civil War* . . ., 2 vols., New York, 1885.

Alfred H. Guernsey and Henry M. Alden, eds., *Harper's Pictorial History of the Great Rebellion,* Chicago, 1866–1868.

Fig. 2

Paul F. Mottelay, ed., *The Soldier in Our Civil War* . . ., 2 vols., New York, 1884–1885 (also a later edition).

The paper in some of these histories, inferior to that used in the Civil War, is rapidly crumbling, but fortunately we have more recent reprints like Fletcher Pratt's *Civil War in Pictures*, New York, 1955, and the centennial reprinting, week by week, of *Harper's* by Living History, Inc.

One work attempted to do for the Confederacy what the others did for the Union:

Benjamin LaBree, ed., *The Confederate Soldier in the Civil War, 1861–1865*, Louisville, 1897.

Another useful class of magazine is the military journal. The *Military Gazette*, published in Albany, 1858–1861, is an excellent source for the New York state militia, while the *Army and Navy Gazette* (1862–1863) and its highly important successor, the *United States Army and Navy Journal*, contain much of value on the war as a whole, especially articles on weapons and accouterments. To these should be added a vast if very different class of magazine that followed the Civil War, the veteran's journals. And finally, *The Scientific American* is of first-rate importance in the study of Civil War weapons and equipment among other subjects.

Manuscript Sources

Manuscript materials of interest to military collectors and historians lie almost wholly in official archives and in the larger historical societies. The National Archives in Washington houses the Federal military records and is a large and professionally run establishment. Its *Guide to Federal Archives Relating to the Civil War* and *Guide to the Archives of the Government of the Confederate States of America*, published in 1968, are useful aids. In every state there is at least one comparable agency and these vary widely in size, coverage, and professional attainments. When dealing with state troops it is essential that local archives be examined and this can only be done effectively in person. It is this requirement for extensive travel—impossible for most—that has kept books on the uniforms, arms, and devices of the several states to a minimum. It is also a reason why this volume will be found to have serious limitations in some areas.

Fortunately, there need be no question about the location and general contents of local records repositories. The American Association for State and Local History biennially publishes a *Directory of Historical Societies and Agencies in the United States and Canada* which is an excellent locator, and Philip M. Hamer, ed., *A Guide to Archives and Manuscripts in the United States*, New Haven, 1961, is the first place to check as to their contents. Almost all repositories have access to photostat and microfilm facilities and the majority offer easy access to documents. It remains, then, for the researcher in military matters to get to the agency and to know as far as possible what he is looking for and how to go about finding it. In many instances this will require a real outlay of patience, imagination, and persuasiveness. Military records are so rarely used that their keepers have had little occasion to become familiar with them.

There is no standard arrangement of material in local archives and historical societies, and a recommended research procedure for one would not apply to another. The authors' checklist of things to ask for first included the following, and was often presented to the custodian in advance of the visit.

1. Letters, orders, and reports of the adjutants general of the state and sub-

ordinates, if any, such as quartermasters general.

2. Personal papers of the governors and of military officers, especially scrapbooks.

3. Collections of papers of or about state military corps.

4. Collections of military photographs and pictures.

5. Registers of the officers and military organizations of the state.

6. Collections of state flags.

7. Any material on state contracts for military supplies.

8. Any military artifacts that might also be in the institution.

Other manuscript sources examined (although not as thoroughly as the authors would have liked) were unpublished regimental histories and other historical studies, collections of transcripts of newspaper articles and notices, and museum card files.

Original Drawings and Paintings

Military painting and drawing is a branch of genre art. It demands realism, accuracy of detail and an appreciation of military affairs. Its authenticity depends upon first hand observation. If the artist has not been able to work from life, only the most exhaustive and dedicated study can fit him for the task of recreating a military scene. Only a few artists in the world can be said to have attained this state of perfection, examples including Jean Meissonier, Edouard Detaille, and Alphonse DeNeuville in France; Anton Hoffman and Carl Röchling in Germany; and Vassili Vereschagin in Russia. Few American artists have reached this rank although several have tried.

One of the accomplishments requisite in a military artist is that he be thoroughly aware of the soldier's uniforms, arms, and equipments. His expert portrayal of these things, therefore, gives us one of our best sources. Between 1851 and 1861 there were only two men working in America whose pictures are of importance in this direction.

Otto Boetticher (1816–?), a German military artist and lithographer, as well as soldier, came to America about 1850. He was the only artist of any standing who pictured military uniforms *per se*, and his series of eighteen lithographs showing volunteer militia regiments of New York City is outstanding for its accuracy and beauty. He made a number of larger plates, especially of the 7th Regiment, N.Y.S.M. Boetticher was an officer of the 68th New York Volunteer Infantry, 1861–1864, and was captured in 1862. Nothing is known of his later life. Apparently he specialized in transferring photographs to prints, which gives his work an unusual touch of authenticity.

The second pre-Civil War artist is James Walker (1819–1889). By 1861 he had achieved a modest reputation for his paintings of Scott's campaign in Mexico, especially his "Battle of Chapultepec" mural in the U.S. Capitol. He had a studio in New York City and during the Civil War made a number of paintings, probably on commission. These include battle scenes in the Gettysburg, Chattanooga, and Atlanta campaigns, and possibly others. Whether he was actually present in the field on any of these occasions is difficult to say, but his paintings are filled with details that had to meet the critical eyes of participants. Walker had a keen sense for uniforms and accouterments and took pains to present a diversity of both. At the same time he doubtless maintained a collection of studio props which he used over and over again, perhaps not always with discretion. On the whole his pictures have been found to be quite trustworthy and informative.

The Civil War, of course, stimulated a demand for military pictures "fresh from the front." As mentioned earlier, the illustrated weekly newspaper had made its appearance a few years earlier and these papers hired numerous "special artists" to accompany the armies and send back pictorial reports of newsworthy episodes and scenes of human interest. Most of these drawings were reproduced as woodcut prints, but several large collections of the original sketches survive, notably in the Library of Congress. In addition, some of these artist-reporters worked on their own to produce drawings, paintings, and prints of unusual merit. As source material these pictures vary widely, but all deserve attention.

Among the scores of artists of one sort or another who left contemporary and reliable evidence on how the soldier looked in the Civil War, the most important are listed below.

A fine artist who left an unusually vivid and detailed portfolio of the Civil War —and later continued on to international fame—was Winslow Homer (1836–1910). He made his start in Boston by drawing for lithography and woodcut reproduction, striking out for himself as a free lance in New York in 1859. *Harper's Weekly* sent him on various trips to the front during the war, from which came not only oil paintings and pencil drawings, but numerous small sketches containing a wealth of color and detail. Many of these are owned today by the Cooper-Hewitt Museum of Decorative Arts and Design in New York City.

Another careful reporter of the military scene was Thomas Nast (1840–1902), the son of a German soldier, born in a regimental barracks. He joined the staff of *Leslie's* magazine about 1855 and subsequently worked for other illustrated papers. Before he turned to cartooning he had done many military scenes, including a large painting of the departure of the 7th Regiment, N.Y.S.M. for the Civil War.

Edwin Forbes (1839–1895) was another staff artist for *Leslie's,* serving throughout the war. At the same time he made sketches for himself which were the basis of a portfolio of etchings, published in 1876 and titled *Life Studies of the Great Army.* Forbes' work is filled with homely details of army life but he had no eye for distinctions of dress and accouterments. His soldiers become stereotypes despite their patent authenticity. In addition to *Life Studies,* Forbes published several other illustrations of the Civil War, much in the same vein. The bulk of his sketches, copper plates, and other material is in the Library of Congress.

Almost the only artist of note to work in the South during the War was Conrad Wise Chapman. About thirty-one of his oils can be seen in the Museum of the Confederacy at Richmond. The man who shared honors with him was Frank Vizetelly (1830–1883), English war artist for *The Illustrated London News,* who had established his reputation in Sicily and Italy before he was sent to America in 1861 to cover the Civil War. He opened his career by describing the First Battle of Bull Run in terms quite unfavorable to the Union command and, as a result, decided to picture the war from the Confederate side. Most of his original sketches were destroyed during World War II but a collection of twenty-eight are in the Harvard College Library.

The field sketches and watercolors of Adolf Metzner (1834?–1917) have only recently come to light. Metzner was an officer of the 32nd Indiana Volunteers, an all-German regiment, and an indefatigable recorder of the humor, daily life, and horrors that came his way. Over a hundred of his drawings were displayed in 1961 by the Kennedy Galleries in New York City.

Certainly the most prolific war artist was Alfred R. Waud (1828–1891), an

Fig. 2 Englishman, who came to America in 1858 and quickly got a job as a staff artist with *Harper's*. Some 344 of his drawings were published during the war. His brother, William (?–1878), came over at the same time and worked for both *Leslie's* and *Harper's*. Two bulky albums in the Library of Congress contain the battlefield sketches sent back by these men, very few of which have been published save through the medium of the woodcut.

Julian Scott (1846–1901) was a soldier turned painter. His work consists almost entirely of Civil War scenes which, although done after the war, are based upon personal observation. Two other soldiers who painted were Confederates. One was Allen C. Redwood (1844–1922) of Baltimore. No other artist has left us such a large stock of drawings of Confederate soldiers as he; many of them are reproduced in *Battles and Leaders of the Civil War*. Redwood seems to have done his drawings many years after the war and some feel he dressed up his Confederates unnecessarily—probably an unjust conclusion. William L. Sheppard (1833–1912) of Richmond, also worked considerably after the conflict. A series of his watercolors of life in the Confederate army hang in the Museum of the Confederacy.

The Civil War momentarily attracted the interest of numerous other contemporary painters whose work deserves mention. Among these were Sanford R. Gifford, Thomas Waterman Wood, David G. Blythe, Albert Bierstadt, Eastman Johnson, George Caleb Bingham, Edward Lamson Henry, Alessandro E. Mario, Enoch Wood Perry, Jr., James Hope, and many others. Additionally, a fair number of American marine painters pictured the naval side of the war, while probably all contemporary portrait painters tried their hands at military men in uniform. Almost without exception (and for obvious reasons) these men painted only the higher-ranking officers on the Union side; Confederate generals rarely sat for their portraits and enlisted men of both sides virtually never did.

This brief review should dispel any illusion that the Civil War was inadequately covered by the artist. Quite the contrary, it was plentifully covered although, as has been suggested, not always in a way that has left source material for this study. To all the above must be added those artists like Gilbert Gaul, Thure de Thulstrup, Rufus Zogbaum, and E. A. Trego who, while not first-hand observers, worked in an era when enough veterans were alive to lend considerable validity to their art. These men were, in fact, almost the only true "military artists" to cover the war.

Lithographs and Woodcuts

So far we have considered merely the artists and their original drawings or paintings. Far more plentiful, in one form or another, are the prints made from many of these originals. All of the artist-correspondents and some others drew primarily for reproduction. During the Civil War the demand for portraits of leaders and for battle scenes was enormous, and print firms like Currier & Ives joined with the illustrated weeklies to fill it. As a result the Civil War, of all major world conflicts, is the one best recorded by the graphic arts.

Viewed solely as sources for this study, the prints of the period 1851–1872 fall into three rough classifications. First come a limited number of carefully executed lithographs, based upon sound contemporary paintings or photographs. Although all too few deliberately set out to illustrate uniforms, this category as a whole can be trusted. With it we can include the military music cover, so important a source for uniform data a generation earlier but going out of fashion by 1861.

Fig. 3. Sketch by Winslow Homer of a Union cavalry-man, made in the field in 1862. (Cooper-Hewitt Museum of Decorative Arts and Design).

Fig. 4. "Traffic Between the Lines," an etching by Edwin Forbes in his *Life Studies of the Great Army* (1876), based on sketches and notes made in the field.

At the other extreme is the great mass of lithographic prints published during the war and for decades afterward. This includes virtually all issued by Currier & Ives, by Kurz & Allison, Rosenthal, and L. Prang & Co. Almost without exception these prints, hastily prepared for the popular market, and based largely on the lithographer's imagination, are useless as sources. They can usually be identified by their straight lines of well-uniformed men, their saber-waving generals, and their pervasive lack of realism.

Somewhere in between lie the woodcut prints of the illustrated weeklies. These were news pictures based upon sketches by first-hand observers. They were intended to be accurate and factual and their artists at least tried to make them so. The problem lay in the speed with which they had to be produced in order to qualify as news. The correspondent could not take time to make a finished picture. The bulk of Waud's drawings, for example, are little more than hasty sketches with written instructions on details. From these the woodblock carver had to work with equal rapidity in order to meet his deadlines. Even at the most rapid pace these prints tended to appear some three or four weeks after the events pictured. There is little wonder that some of the spontaneity and much of the detail of the field sketches were lost or obscured in the process; the real wonder is that so much of both remained. In the final reckoning these woodcut prints—by their sheer volume alone—remain one of our most helpful guides to military dress.

The outstanding collection of military prints, of this and all other eras of world history, is in private hands, owned by Mrs. John Nicholas Brown, of Providence, R.I. An extensive collection of American prints is in the Library of Congress, and smaller collections may be found in many local historical societies.

Photographs

Up to 1851 photography was accomplished mainly by the daguerreotype process, with an impression taken upon a silvered copper plate sensitized by iodine and developed by vapor of mercury. The process produced only one impression from each operation of the camera. The exposure time of a daguerreotype was twenty to forty seconds, or even more, depending upon the light—the sole source of which was a skylight—and this time necessitated the use of a clamp to prevent movement of the sitter's head. The finished picture, which could be developed in a few minutes, was a negative and had to be held to the light in a certain way in order to be seen.

In addition to being a negative, the daguerreotype image was reversed, that is, it was a mirror image—what the sitter wore on his right side appeared in the picture to be on his left. While this was of small importance in civilian photography it created a problem with the soldier whose sword, for example, appeared to be on the wrong side. Some studios had their military sitters reverse their accouterments as best they could, which led to incongruous arrangements (like upside down belt plates) and inconsistencies. A daguerreotype should always be examined carefully with these possibilities in mind.

The daguerreotype was mounted for sale in an ornamental case and the name of the sitter was at times—unfortunately, only too rarely—noted on the rear of the copper plate. While only one picture resulted from an exposure, various methods of copying were soon perfected. Rephotography was, of course, often used. Pictures were transferred to lithographic plates by hand, reproduced by an India ink process, or made the basis of a steel engraving. But printing was possible only through the medium of the hand-cut wood block, mechanical reproduction coming long after the period of our study.

In the year 1851 a practical method of photography was perfected in England whereby a negative image was formed within the camera on a sensitized glass plate. This method, soon to be known as the "wet-plate process," revolutionized photography in the course of the next five years. Its importance lay in the ability of the photographer to secure from the negative plate any number of positive impressions (or "prints") on paper. The fact that the prints came on a material as light and flexible as paper, and were positives, lent added merit to the process. The wet-plate process was in general use by 1860 and remained the common method throughout our period, although the equally revolutionary "dry plate" had been invented by the 1870's.

About 1854 the ambrotype was commercially perfected, its development coinciding with that of the wet plate, which process it resembled in some respects. In this method the impression was taken on a glass plate coated with collodion, resulting in a negative image. By placing a piece of black paper on the rear of the plate, or painting the rear black, the image became positive as far as black and white are concerned. Ambrotypes were easier to make than daguerreotypes and took less time. However, the limitations of this process were those of the daguerreotype in that only one impression could be secured from each exposure, and the image was reversed. The tintype, developed in 1856, was still another process whose resultant picture closely resembled an ambrotype. Again the image was reversed.

While this brief review greatly oversimplifies the numerous processes being tried out in these early days of photography, it gives a basis for investigating the potentials of the photograph as a source of information in our field. It is, on the whole, a research tool of the greatest importance although, as will be seen, its usefulness depends on certain vital conditions.

All photography made in the years 1851–1872 by whatever process, was essentially commercial in origin; there were no amateur cameramen in those days. The vast bulk was portrait photography, although the work of a few enterprising men outside the studios—among whom Mathew B. Brady stands head and shoulders above the rest—tends to capture most of the attention today. Brady himself was primarily a portrait photographer and, as documents, the pictures he and his operators made inside the studio are every bit as valuable to us as those they made in the field, remarkable as were the latter.

In 1851, as noted, the daguerreotype was in universal use in American photographic studios. Although the process was barely ten years old, there were about 100 such studios in New York City alone, and a newspaper of that day estimated that no less than 10,000 daguerreotypists were at work in the United States. The output of photographs was, therefore, immense and it continued steadily to grow. Brady's studio in New York alone was making over 30,000 portraits each year, at a cost of from one to thirty dollars apiece. Naturally, an appreciable number of these were of men in military uniform.

Despite a few earlier attempts, the movement of the camera from the studio into the open air—from the realm of portraiture to news photography—really began about 1850. By then exposure time had been so reduced that, with sufficient light, a daguerreotypist could sometimes succeed in making a street scene that showed people in sharp detail. Ten years later it was possible to capture the image of people and things in moderate motion.

The advent of the wet-plate process brought the advantage of limitless reproduction, but required that the plate be processed immediately before exposure and developed immediately afterward. The time usually allowed for the entire process was ten minutes. Exposure time was about the same as the daguerreotype and depended, again, on natural light. Thus the head clamp remained in use. No advance had been made in the processes of reproduction by the printing press.

The work done during the Civil War by Mathew B. Brady deserves special mention although it must be limited to a few words. For those interested, the story of his ambitious and costly project to picture the war, his struggles to sell his "War Views," and the final disposition of his negatives is told in Roy Meredith's, *Mr. Lincoln's Camera Man: Mathew B. Brady*, New York, 1946. Brady was not the first war photographer. Roger Fenton, an Englishman, undertook a very similar, if more restrained, series during the Crimean War in 1855, and even he was not the first man to make photographs in the field. Nor were Brady and his crews the only photographers working near the Civil War battle lines. For mere volume of documentary pictures, however, (as early as August 1862 Brady had operators working out of thirty-five centers in all theatres of war) he was unsurpassed for many years to come.

Fig. 5 One of the most important results of the wet-plate process for the student of military dress was the carte-de-visite. This was a small photographic portrait mounted on a card about 2.5 x 3.5 inches. It was usually produced with a special camera which took four to eight exposures at a time, and prints were made on albumen paper which was exposed to sunlight. A final gold chloride toning gave them their familiar brownish look. By this method the cost per photograph was greatly reduced and as many as ten or fifteen could be sold for a dollar.

The carte-de-visite came into popularity about 1857 and at once became the stock in trade of all photographers and the only size taken by many. Its ostensible purpose was to serve as a visiting card—a person could add his name to the back or leave merely his picture—but its use was far wider. Soldiers going off to war and loved ones left behind had cartes made of themselves for exchange and for inclusion in specially designed albums. Untold thousands must have been printed during the war years and these form a source of great importance for the student of military dress. Shortly after the war ended, the carte-de-visite disappeared as quickly as it had appeared.

The carte-de-visite was inexpensive and within the reach of everyone, hence we find them of privates as well as generals. Many show men in rough and informal clothing and these were probably made in the army camps by traveling photographers. Other cartes indicate definite dressing up, a process in which the studio could play a part by providing sitters with swords, capes, gauntlets, and other props that lent glamor to the photograph.

By and large, photography multiplied sources of information on military dress and accouterments a hundredfold. Its usefulness, however, can be overvalued. Whereas its spread probably did not lead to less drawing or painting, it did reduce our knowledge of and interest in the work of the artist. Worse yet, its entirely black-and-white result has tended to dull our sense of color in military clothing. We cannot help but visualize the Civil War uniform as uninteresting when compared to periods that provide us with drawings of military dress in color. The reds, greens, and yellows on American uniforms are lost in the photograph. Wesley Webber's 1865 painting of the 16th Maine, for example, shows the men in scarlet pants; to judge by photographs they are dressed like the rest of the Union Army.

The two most important collections of Civil War photographs are today in the National Archives and the Library of Congress. Both of the collections originated with negatives made by Mathew Brady and to a large extent they duplicate one another. Many of the pictures were included in 1911 in the ten-volume *Photographic History of the Civil War*, one of the most comprehensive pictorial records of a war ever published. This valuable work has recently been reprinted, while several pictorial histories have supplemented its photographic coverage of the period.

Even today the photograph, except in very limited areas, has not surpassed the products of the artist as a method of detailing uniforms, arms, and accouterments, especially when reproduced in printed form.

An unusual and valuable photographic source is a series of forty-five official pictures of enlisted men, made in Philadelphia for the Quartermaster General in 1866. At least one set was hand colored. In 1961 the Smithsonian Institution published thirty-six of the photographs in a booklet titled *Uniform Regulations for the Army of the United States, 1861.*

Each picture shows a single figure in the full uniform and accouterments of an enlisted man of the regular army. There is one or more for each branch of the service and for most of the NCO grades. Pictures cover both dress and fatigue uniforms. One man, a sad-faced, full-bearded fellow, posed for all the shots and the temporary character of his assignment is proved by the fact that his chevrons are merely pinned to his sleeve.

Fig. 6

Despite their official character the photographs contain a number of curious mistakes. The infantry musician is shown wearing an NCO's sword instead of a musician's sword. The types were quite similar, to be sure, and some musicians may well have been so armed, but they were different swords nevertheless. The cavalry musician is shown blowing an infantry bugle, the cap cords of the light artilleryman are incorrectly arranged, and, perhaps strangest of all, all dress hats are shown pinned up on the left side despite the clear statement in regulations that mounted men would wear theirs pinned up on the right. Equally contrary to regulations is the method shown of hooking the saber on the waist belt with its hilt to the front. Certainly this was often done, as other Civil War photographs show, but it is not the method prescribed in *Cavalry Tactics* (Plate 5, "The Sabre hooked up."). Worst of all, the carbine and haversack are shown slung on the wrong side.

This series is the basis of the six colored drawings of Union Army soldiers in the atlas to the *Official Records* (Plate CLXXII), but some of the errors were corrected before inclusion in the atlas. Another official compilation of uniform photographs entitled "Uniforms of the Army Prior and Subsequent to 1872," was made in 1875.

Artifacts

The physical object, whether it be a weapon, a uniform, a cartridge box, or a piece of insignia, would seem to be the ultimate of sources. And it is, provided the object can be identified and authenticated. Unfortunately, this process is not as easy as some collectors have been wont to assume.

Artifacts form the basis of most military collections, in private hands and in museums. Lack of precise knowledge is characteristic of both areas, only with the former it takes the guise of misinformation and guesswork while in the latter one tends to find apathy and the baneful influence of family legend. Only in the field of weapons, where a sizable body of literature exists, can the col-

22

Fig. 5. Col. John J. Cladek, 35th New Jersey Volunteer Infantry, 1863 or 1864. (New Jersey Historical Society Collection). Example of an identified carte-de-visite photograph.

Fig. 6. Pioneer of U.S. Artillery, 1866. One of the series of colored official photographs taken at the Philadelphia Depot and forwarded to the Quartermaster General. (Quartermaster Center Library, Fort Lee, Va.).

lector or the curator identify his specimens with any surety.

Nowhere in military collecting is skepticism in greater need than with the identification of artifacts. Some of the guidelines the authors have tried to keep in mind are:

1. Guessing is easy since there are few people to check the guesser, and it is very human to want objects to be old and rare.

2. Family legends are just that and can rarely be trusted. The background story given by an actual user of an object can be most worthwhile, but second- and third-hand histories are usually inaccurate and must be carefully sifted.

3. Faking is growing more and more common as military items rise in value. Examples are noted throughout this book but new ones are appearing every year. Furthermore, fraudulent military artifacts are nothing new. There is an intriguing story about the citizens of Harpers Ferry in 1859 and 1860 selling imitation John Brown pikes to curiosity seekers who got off the B & O trains there long enough to visit the scene of the raid.

4. More common than the complete reproduction is the object that has been altered to appear older or more valuable. Gun collectors have a rigid code about alteration but much of it goes on nevertheless. In considering the subject of alteration it should be remembered that military objects of all sorts have been changed, not only by collectors in recent years but by their users generations ago. Civil War saddles, for example, are rarely found with all of their original fittings. Most were altered during the years following the war to suit personal needs. Old uniforms saw later service as theatrical costumes; cartridge boxes were changed to accept new model ammunition; firearms were frequently altered from military to sporting types; and so forth. The possibility of such alteration should always be borne in mind.

5. Battlefield pickups furnish valuable evidence of an article having been used in a specific battle but beyond that it is unsafe to go. Furthermore, it is wise for a collector to be cautious unless he, personally, has been the finder. Like family heirlooms, battlefield relics tend to attract legends, and natives sometimes have not been above manufacturing and rusting objects for sale to the incautious.

6. Finally, the specialized private collection would appear to be a splendid source of information, as it is. But even here there are dangers to be avoided. Specialized collectors are forced to limit and define their fields and this often makes for artificial and misleading categories. Collectors of "Confederate arms," for example, are less interested in types of weapons carried in the South than in actual specimens that can be proven to have been. A well known collector of "powder containers" arbitrarily eliminated all cartridge boxes from his collection. Enthusiasts for insignia are especially fond of arbitrary break-off dates and limiting definitions.

While it would be helpful to list the military museums in this country which contain material from the years 1851–1872, and to discuss their contents, such a review would exceed the limits of this chapter. Most of the local museums and historical societies consulted will be mentioned in their proper places further along. The larger, general collections like the National Museum in Washington, the Museum of the Confederacy in Richmond, and the West Point Museum at the U.S. Military Academy are sufficiently well known to require no introduction.

TABLE OF CONTENTS

Abbreviations

Abbreviations used in the body of the narrative and in the descriptions of equipage are those in common use and require no explanation. Extensive use, however, is made of specialized abbreviations in the orders of battle, and these are explained below.

AC	Army Corps	HQ	Headquarters
a.d.	African Descent		
AG	Adjutant General		
AGO	Adjutant General's Office	in	inch or inches
		inf	infantry
ANV	Army of Northern Virginia		
A of P	Army of the Potomac	M	Model
arty	artillery	Mil Div	Military Division
		mos	months
bn	battalion		
brig	brigade	organ	organized or organization
btry, btrys	battery, batteries		
		QMG	Quartermaster General
c.	circa, about		
cal	caliber		
cav	cavalry	redesig	redesignated
Cir	Circular	reg	regulation
comp, comps	company, companies	regt	regiment
consol	consolidated, consolidation	reorgan	reorganized, reorganization
CS	Confederate States		
CSA	Confederate States of America	serv	service
		Smith.	Smithsonian Institution
dept	department		
disb	disband, disbanded	US	United States
div	division	USA	United States of America
D of Ark	Department of Arkansas		
D of Cum	Department of the Cumberland	U.S.C.T.	United States Colored Troops
D of Ohio	Department of Ohio		
D of WVa	Department of West Virginia	vol	volunteer
		WDGO	War Department General Orders
EM	enlisted man or men		
		WDSC	War Department Signal Corps
Fed	Federal	WPM	West Point Museum
		yrs	years
GHQ	General Headquarters		
GO	General Orders		

INTRODUCTION

Fig. 7. Full dress uniforms of the 7th Regiment, New York State Militia, 1853–1861. These illustrate the swallow-tailed dress coat and shako of the first half of the 19th century. At the same time, the Band here has been uniformed in frock coats. The regimental uniforms are grey with black trim and gold lace; white pompons. All leather is black, all metal yellow. The bandsman's uniform comprises a dark blue coat with scarlet collar, cuffs and plastron; sky blue pants; cap with a gold lace band around the top and half way down the front, and scarlet cord and pompon. The drum major's coat is also blue, trimmed with scarlet; he has no plastron. He wears the grey pants of an officer, with gold lace stripes; his baldric is scarlet, edged with gold lace, with brass fittings; his bearskin bag is scarlet with gold cord trim, and the feather is white with red top.

Influences, Civil & Military

Any study of the military dress and equipment of the American Civil War must necessarily include the ten years prior to the conflict, since it was in those years that the basic styles evolved, as well as the several years following the war when the vast stocks of clothing and accouterments on hand were still being worn. Yet the period 1851–1872 has a validity all its own, and witnessed trends in dress and armament quite distinct from the years on either side; its terminal dates are important signposts in the history of American military uniforms, arms, and equipments—far more so than the beginning and end of the Civil War itself.

Passing of the conservative uniform: In 1848, scarcely more than a decade before the Civil War, Europe had been shaken by revolts against the conservative social system which had reigned there since 1815. These volcanic eruptions managed to destroy many a symbol of absolutism before they were quelled. One such symbol was the common military uniform which had long represented repression: the tight, swallow-tailed dress coat and tall, hard shako. By 1848 *Fig. 7* these were as redolent of conservatism as the white coat and *culottes* had seemed to the revolutionary of 1792. In the train of these revolts came a radical change in military dress; within a few years all European armies were clothed in the frock coat, a garment introduced earlier by the French army and more in keeping with liberal and national ideals. Our own regular army changed over in 1851, and Great Britain, last of all, in 1855.

Not everywhere, however, was this change in uniform greeted with joy. Resistance and ridicule often came from soldiers themselves. Although a popular American magazine of 1852 called the change "important" and claimed to be "most heartily tired of the swallow-tailed coats that have so long prevailed," ridicule was heaped upon the new styles by Lieutenant George H. Derby (the *Fig. 1* Army's satirical cartoonist and writer) giving some idea of the soldier's attitude. Old conservative militia outfits like the 7th and 8th New York or the Washington Light Infantry of Charleston, S.C., retained the swallow-tail as a dress uniform to the Civil War and after, but newer units and those in closer touch with the common man were quick to adopt the new style.

Changing ordnance and tactics: The decades of the 1850's and 1860's witnessed a revolution in ordnance, and especialy in small arms; the Civil War came at its climax. In normal infantry weapons this represented a movement from the muzzleloading smoothbore to the breechloading rifle and metallic cartridge; in terms of arms carried by officers and civilians, it moved even further into the repeating rifle and revolver. With changes in weapons came corresponding changes in accouterments.

The American infantryman of 1850 was armed and accoutered (as well as uniformed) much as he had been forty years before. Within five years there had come a marked change following the introduction of the rifled musket with its Minie ball cartridge and black leather equipment. The end of our period, in 1872, saw an infantryman whose arms and accouterments differed in almost every detail from the soldier of 1850. One of the tasks of this study will be to trace these changes as they occurred within the different arms of the service and the states of the Union.

In terms of infantry tactics, the two decades saw a persistent attempt to get away from the ponderous linear formations of the old "infantry of the line" school as laid down by General Winfield Scott. Scott's *Infantry Tactics* had been adopted in 1835, with revisions and reprints appearing as late as 1861. Its first serious challenger was *Rifle and Light Infantry Tactics*, by Lieutenant Colonel William J. Hardee, published in 1855. The innovations of Hardee's system over Scott's are not overly clear to the reader of today. The manoeuvres and words of command were much the same and both sought to establish the line of battle. But Hardee accomplished this with greater speed than Scott. Indeed, many officers at the time felt he demanded a rapidity of movement possible only with highly disciplined troops.

The rigid line of battle, in which the infantryman stood upright while in action, was still required by the weapons of that day, whose slow rate of fire could only produce effective volume in this manner. Furthermore, it was simply impractical to load a muzzleloader while lying down or even kneeling. This line of battle lasted throughout the period and for years afterward, and as long as it did there could be no concern about protective coloration of uniforms —that would be a thing of the future for most soldiers.

Following Hardee came others who challenged, if they could not entirely change, the older systems of tactics. Much of their inspiration stemmed from France, where a constant search was being made for more deployed formations and rapid movements. Captain George B. McClellan reported favorably on the French zouave drill he had witnessed in Europe and found a convert in Elmer E. Ellsworth, who formed and trained the first zouave company in America. Thus when the Civil War broke out American soldiers were being trained under several general systems, all of which led up to the establishment of a line of battle but accomplished it in somewhat different ways.

The systems of Scott and Hardee were largely reconciled by General Silas Casey in his *Infantry Tactics*, first published in 1862. It became the most widely used manual of the Civil War and largely standardized the drill of the foot soldier. Finally, in 1867, an entirely new and simpler system of drill was adopted and as our period ends we enter the era of the manual of General Emory Upton.

Fig. 20; see also 9th U.S. Infantry, 1858

While it cannot be said that each tactical system itself produced new styles in uniforms, arms, or accouterments, it is evident that with each came a type of soldier who was dressed and armed in what was felt to be the appropriate style. Scott's "heavy infantry" was evident at the start. Hardee's system produced the *"chasseur"* with his pleated uniform and radically new belts. As the fashion for light infantry increased among the volunteer militia we find more and more commands aping the French chasseur battalions, and the War Department itself came within an inch of adopting the chasseur uniform for all the army. The zouave drill brought the well-known zouave dress, and it is possible that the adoption in the end of a distinctively American system of tactics had something to do with the widespread standardization of state military dress in the 1870's.

Military eminence of France: Under the superficial brilliance of Napoleon III, the French army had gained an eminence in military matters which rivaled that held under the First Empire. It had fought two successful and highly publicized wars as well as numerous colonial campaigns. Still ahead lay the disastrous defeats of 1870–1871. It is safe to say that for perhaps fifteen years prior to 1861 the French army served as a model for all the military virtues.

All students of the Civil War have been struck by the persistent influence of French military doctrine and tactics upon American thinking and action. The armies of Great Britain and Prussia seem scarcely to have existed. From grand strategy to the arrangement of buttons we looked to France for guidance, much as we had done, indeed, since the American Revolution.

In the matter of military clothing, it is true, the French were well in advance of other countries by 1860. The long frock coat, which most armies had just *Fig. 8* adopted, had been replaced by a tunic with short skirts, low collar, and a minimum of buttons. For field service the French soldier wore a soft, low cloth cap and loose, comfortable trousers. The much more baggy zouave trousers, just coming into fashion in America, were not worn by the bulk of the French infantry because of their excessive weight when wet. Even the Imperial Guard had discarded its heavy, confining cross belts, so common elsewhere. All French troops had received a black leather waist belt which carried the cartridge box and bayonet scabbard and was supported by light shoulder straps. Experiments were being carried out with breechloading weapons which led to the adoption of the Model 1866 "Chassepot." These and other modernities of dress and accouterments were all reflected to some degree in this country and we must return to the subject later.

An American observer wrote in 1861:

> The equipment of the soldier is made a perfect study in France, and there was not a strap or button that did not receive [the Emperor's] personal attention, and his questions to the soldiers were innumerable as to the improvements sought to be established, to make them easy and comfortable under arms.

Little wonder Americans were impressed!

The clothing industry: The year 1851 is significant in the story of ready-made clothing for it was in that year that Isaac Singer's sewing machine was introduced in England and its potential began to be realized. Even army clothing had been manufactured by machine in France before this time, but it was not until after 1851 that the impact of this development was felt in America.

By 1860 the manufacture of ready-made clothing had become a great industry in the United States. Carroll D. Wright, tracing our industrial evolution, has said, "The revolution in the tailoring industry that followed upon the invention of the sewing machine, resulting in the combination of the small shops and the organization of large establishments for the manufacture of wearing apparel for sale ready-made, was practically complete by 1860." This development had occurred almost exclusively in the North. More than half of all the men's clothing made in the country in 1860 came from the four cities of Boston, New York, Cincinnati, and Philadelphia. Naturally this trend was stimulated by war orders with the result that ready-made clothing, a comparative rarity before, became a commonplace of retail trade in the North after the war was over.

Closely allied were the numerous conditions surrounding the fabrication of military clothing at this period. The use of analine dyes was in its infancy; indigo blue was an imported color and always fast, but was difficult to work with; light-blue shades could be produced by weaving blue and white threads together —these and other conditions, far too complex to list, rendered uniforms of dark blue more expensive than light blue, and grey the least expensive of all. All of the factors above played a part in determining what uniforms were worn, usually a more important part than the decisions of boards of officers, the desires of soldiers, or even tradition.

To these background factors which influenced the development of military dress in America after 1851 one other purely domestic condition should be added. Our regular army in the years before the war was so tiny, so widely scattered along the Indian frontier, that it might seem to have exerted very little influence on military clothing. Each state, and there were thirty-four of them at this period, had its own uniformed volunteer militia. These volunteers as a rule existed as independent companies, and most of the companies were authorized to select a distinctive dress for their members. Only in a few large centers like New York were all companies of a regiment or battalion uniformed alike. In 1860, at a conservative estimate, there were some 1200 volunteer companies in cities from the eastern seaboard to beyond the Mississippi, and most wore a distinctive garb traversing the scale of costume from Continentals to Scottish Highlanders, from wide-brimmed frontier hats to bearskins.

Despite this bewildering variety of dress it is still apparent that most states patterned a considerable portion of their dress regulations upon those issued by the U.S. War Department. In many instances the prescribed state uniform resembled that of the regular army in all but minor details. Even if most of its volunteer militia companies were exempted, the state would have its staff officers and the less gaudy units in regulation uniform. Every year of the 1850's saw more and more state corps adopt uniforms essentially similar to those of the regulars, making the uniforms prescribed by the War Department within this period an important factor despite the obvious independence of the several state forces.

Trends in civilian fashion: The fashionably dressed man of the 1850's had moved away from the rather effeminate styles of the previous decade. He no longer wore a tail coat pinched in at the waist and curved over the chest and hips, trousers slimmed down to the ankle, and a wide expanse of shirting. By 1860, except for evening wear, he had abandoned the tail coat entirely and was wearing a fairly tight frock coat with slightly flaring skirts and flat collar. This he often left open to display a waistcoat whose style varied much during the period. Under these was a white shirt with large sleeves and dropped shoulders, starched and pleated in front.

Fig. 9

For informal or sports wear there was the short "sack coat," which by 1860 had become an important garment, widely worn in America. Pants, held up by braces, maintained a "stove pipe" style throughout the 1850's and were neither creased nor cuffed. The high, stiff felt hat, flaring somewhat at the top in the 1850's and almost straight sided in the next decade, was the common headdress of the man of affairs. Bowlers and low-crowned hats were worn on informal occasions and stiff straws in the hot weather. The 1860's brought longer, heavier, and more shapeless coats, while sleeves and trousers became wider and waistcoats declined somewhat in importance.

As one moved toward the Western frontier, civilian costume, of course, grew more utilitarian and primitive. Soft felt hats with wide brims, short coats, and shirts worn as outer garments were common. Fringed buckskin clothing was now rarely worn, even in the Indian country. Boots were a familiar sight on men working in the fields and forests of both East and West, but their wear was by no means universal.

Many civilian styles exerted profound effect on the tailoring and especially on the wearing of military dress. The wide use of the brimmed soft hat led to its adoption as both a formal and an informal army headdress, probably equalling, during the Civil War, the use of the more military cap.

It was customary during the 1860's to encase the neck in a cravat with ends sometimes a foot across in front. Since this ornament was hidden under a military coat collar, it became the practice to unbutton the coat, or at least the top buttons, to display the cravat. As the unbuttoned frock coat was fashionable in

Fig. 8. Private, 83rd Pennsylvania Volunteer Infantry, wearing one of the chasseur uniforms imported from France in 1861. Blue jacket with yellow braid and yellow worsted epaulets; medium blue pants with yellowish leather greaves and white leggings; black leather cap with brass plate and black cocks feather plume; white metal buttons. Standard infantry accouterments. (By Frederick T. Chapman after photograph).

civilian life, the mode was adopted by all whose rank and position gave them opportunity to defy regulations.

Men's clothing of the period tended toward somber colors; blue, black and shades of gray predominating. After 1860 black was the only color used for dress wear in the evening. This restrained range made the change to less gaudy clothing by the heretofore brilliantly garbed militia more palatable. Conversely, it caused some corps to adopt reds, bright blues, and gold braid as a contrast.

One of the most significant adoptions by the military was the sack coat, discussed more fully below, especially since it became the pattern for uniforms of the future. Another was the woolen shirt. Volunteer firemen had worn red merino shirts as an outer garment for two decades and their wide adoption by military companies in 1860 and 1861 was a natural step in selecting a colorful, inexpensive, and readily obtainable garment. The pleated smock was, apparently, a development by itself with origins in European styles.

Against the backdrop of these many and varied circumstances came the Civil War. The changes it produced in military dress and equipment were profound—as profound, perhaps, as the changes it wrought in all aspects of the science of warfare. But none of the changes can be laid solely to the War; all had their origins in earlier years and in the broad social, industrial, and military conditions of that day.

PART ONE

THE UNITED STATES ARMY

CUT-AWAY COAT
C.1850 —

WORN AS BOTH
MORNING AND
EVENING SUIT.

FROCK COAT SUIT
OF THE
1860'S

LABORER, C.1860

SACK COAT
OF THE 1860'S,
WORN ON
INFORMAL
OCCASIONS.

OVERCOAT —

Fig. 9. Civilian clothing of the 1850's and 1860's.

CHAPTER I

Clothing

Procurement and Issue of Clothing in the U.S. Army

The procurement and issue of clothing for enlisted men and, to some extent, officers of the United States Army was, throughout the period 1851–1872 as it is today, a function of the Quartermaster General. On 18 December 1851 Brevet Major General Thomas Sidney Jesup, who had been Quartermaster General since 1818, described the system to a Senator.

All clothing for the Army is made at the U.S. Arsenal on the Schuykill near Philadelphia, under the direction of an Officer of the Quartermaster Department, the operatives being employed and paid by the Government, the material, only, being furnished by contract. This system is the result of experience, and has proved to be the best, most satisfactory, and in the end most economical. The same system prevails at the Military Academy at West Point, and by it the Cadets are now clothed at a trifling expense beyond cost.

On examining the Contract Book I find that the principal supplies of Cloth & Kersey, samples of which are enclosed for Colonel Johnson's examination, have been furnished latterly by the "Wool Growers Manufacturing Company," of Little Falls, Herkimer County, NY, and by the "Utica Steam Woollen Company" of Utica N.Y.

A copy of the new Uniform of the Army, illustrated, is herewith sent for the Library of the Kentucky Military Institute.

Should Colonel Johnson desire more particular information as to the Clothing System of the Army, he will obtain it by addressing Major Geo. H. Crosman, Quartermaster, at Philadelphia, in charge of the Clothing establishment near there.

The "U.S. Arsenal" mentioned in the letter housed the Army Clothing Establishment, also known by its more formal title, Office of Army Clothing and Equipage.

The clothing authorized for an enlisted soldier was regularized and published in *Army Regulations*. For a five-years enlistment an infantryman in 1857 was allowed:

7 dress caps	15 flannel shirts
2 pompons	11 pairs flannel drawers

2 eagles and rings	20 pairs of bootees (shoes)
5 cap covers	20 pairs of stockings
8 frock coats	2 leather stocks
13 pairs of trousers	1 great-coat
2 blankets	

Mounted men could draw 1 pair of boots and 2 pairs of shoes a year instead of 4 pairs of shoes, and they were authorized 2 washable stable frocks per enlistment. Special fatigue overalls were allowed Engineer and Ordnance troops, but no other fatigue clothing was listed. These, with sashes for first sergeants, knapsacks and other accouterments, insignia, and all camp and garrison equipage were, in effect, company property and were issued to the men as needed.

Each item of authorized clothing had a fixed money value and the soldier was given a clothing allowance which permitted him to draw the items. At the outbreak of the Civil War the figure was $30.00 a year for a dismounted man and $36.00 for one who was mounted. Should a man's clothing allowance be insufficient to get him through that period he drew what he required. Such extras were charged against his clothing account and deducted from his pay at the end of the year. If, by some infrequent chance, a soldier did not overdraw his allowance he received the difference in cash. Clothing lost due to no fault of the soldier was usually writen off.

Officers, then as now, purchased their own uniforms from civilian sources. Late in 1851 the Secretary of War authorized officers to purchase kersey and wool overalls at cost from the Army Clothing Establishment. Jefferson Davis, when he became Secretary, withdrew this privilege, but Secretary Floyd restored it by permitting officers at remote stations to purchase enlisted men's clothing and other items at reasonable prices. By and large, the officer traded with the several military furnishers of the period like William H. Horstmann & Sons in Philadelphia or Baker & McKenney in New York.

Uniforms for both officers and men were specified in considerable detail in the dress regulations already mentioned. These were laid down mainly for the use of officers and the private firms who supplied them; enlisted men's clothing was given less attention and some items were omitted altogether. Patterns of all items were kept at the Clothing Establishment in Philadelphia for government tailors as well as outside contractors to inspect. No elaborate system of inspection was necessary since the Army made its own garments.

General Jesup died in June 1860 and was succeeded by Brigadier General Joseph E. Johnston of Virginia. At that time his department contained, beside himself, 36 officers and 7 military storekeepers, scattered in posts throughout the country. The Civil War broke and on 22 April 1861 General Johnston resigned to enter the Confederate service. Over a month passed before Colonel Montgomery C. Meigs, an army engineer, was appointed in his stead. Meigs reached his office on 13 June to find it, as might be expected, swamped by the work at hand. In the hectic interim the acting chief had been Major Ebenezer S. Sibley, a West Pointer of the class of 1827 (*not* the inventor of the Sibley tent). Meigs, however, was a competent administrator and his record in this emergency guaranteed him this post until 1882.

The Army Clothing Establishment at Philadelphia had for some years been under the direction of Colonel Charles Thomas, Assistant Quartermaster General, an older officer who had entered the Army as a 3rd Lieutenant of Ordnance in 1819. To judge from correspondence, the sudden shift from the sleepy and punctilious procedures of 1860 to the mad scramble of 1861 was more than difficult for Colonel Thomas. Although he remained at his post throughout the War, a Deputy Quartermaster General was sent to Philadelphia about August of 1861 to supersede him. By the end of that year contracts for clothing were being let by Quartermasters at the principal depots, of which Philadelphia was only one. The Clothing Establishment continued to play a significant part in our story throughout the War, but its unique importance ended after the summer of 1861.

When, on 15 April 1861, President Lincoln issued his call for 75,000 infantry to serve for three months, the War Department had no idea what accouterments the states could supply for these regiments. But not many hours passed before its worst fears were realized. On the 17th the Quartermaster General directed Colonel Thomas to procure by contract, as rapidly as possible, a large list of equipment for these men, ranging from knapsacks to tents. On the following day he wired Thomas to dispense with the customary advertising for bids. By the 20th it was apparent that many state regiments lacked not only equipment but clothing as well, and further telegrams sped to the worried chief of the Clothing Establishment: "Direct all your energies to the preparation of fatigue clothing for the Volunteers," and "Issue [them] such articles of clothing as may be required and that can be spared."

On 23 April Secretary of War Cameron formally authorized the issue to state regiments of the less expensive and simpler items: "forage caps, infantry trousers, flannel sack coats, flannel shirts, bootees, stockings, great coats, blankets, . . ." But authorization was a long way from procurement and delivery. A week later Cameron was still trying to answer the question: Who was going to uniform state volunteers? His reply was now evasive. "Clothing is sometimes issued to volunteers. Just at present we have not the supplies, but they are being prepared as rapidly as possible. The soldier receives a monthly allowance for clothing in addition to his pay." In view of these conditions he recommended the states furnish clothing and be reimbursed for so doing by the U.S. Government. The clothing allowance, then fixed at $2.50 a month for infantry and $3.00 for cavalry, was soon boosted to $3.50 for both if not furnished in kind. Thus was the clothing of the first 75,000 infantry dumped into the laps of the states.

From the beginning the states had provided their regiments with what clothing was available and now they undertook to contract for the additional equipments necessary. Some acted carefully, some less so. Charles Olden, Governor of New Jersey, reported in early June that his "troops will be equipped in two weeks in a manner which has been approved by an inspector sent from Philadelphia by General Thomas . . ." But other states were less fortunate. The uninspiring story of the fraud and inefficiency that prevailed all too generally in 1861 has been told many times and need not be repeated. The point to remember, so far as uniforms are concerned, is that each state was a separate story, for each solved the problems of those frantic first months in its own way, as best it could. The result, naturally, was a medley of uniforms.

By early May it was obvious that the War would outlast the three-month regiments then in service, and the President called upon the states for thirty-nine regiments of volunteer infantry and one of cavalry to serve three years, and, in addition, accepted thirty-eight regiments of volunteer infantry from New York for two years. On 15 May the Secretary of War ordered that no more Federal clothing be issued the three-month regiments. Even by then Colonel Thomas had been unable to accomplish very much in the way of procurement and the states continued to equip, or attempt to equip, their regiments. Then the tide began to turn, and by August the War Department felt able to assume more responsibility. On the 19th of that month it requested the governors of nine states who were having trouble outfitting their troops to send on all regiments accepted by Federal authorities "whether provided with equipments or uniforms or not," with the promise they would be uniformed at Washington.

During this period, of course, and for some while afterward, the Federal quartermasters were forced to compete with the states, and to purchase cloth of all colors and qualities designed for the civilian market, often knowing it to be inferior. The records are filled with the clamor for uniforms and dire predictions of what would happen to health and morale if they were not received. And there is an equally large volume of complaints about the clothing which finally did arrive. One regimental uniform lasted only ten days, so poorly was it made, and even in late 1861 sentinels walked about Washington "in freezing weather in their drawers, without trousers or overcoats." To such obvious causes as lack of cloth and the time it takes an industry to shift over to war production, must be added poor methods of distribution, inferior workmanship, untrained inspection, and wasteful methods of the soldiers themselves, the last an all-too-common trait in any period.

The remarkable part of this story is the rapid recovery made by the Northern clothing industry and by the Quartermaster General. Large importations of cloth had been made from abroad in the early months, but when General Meigs planned to continue this practice in the fall of 1861 he received a formal complaint from the Board of Trade of Boston, pointing out that American factories could now handle the job by themselves. This prediction proved true; uniforms of blue cloth sufficient to clothe the Union Army—now 550,000 strong—were produced by the end of the year—and more. Nothing can give a better idea of the fullness of this accomplishment than a glance at the reports of the clothing on hand in depots.

On hand in clothing depots	Dress Coats	Trou-sers	Fatigue Sack Coats	Jackets	Dress Hats	Forage Caps	Great Coats	Flannel Shirts
15 January 1862	220,439	696,203	159,166	236,528	180,657	570,444	479,646	773,841
28 July 1862	636,000	636,000	?	300,000	?	550,000	405,000	380,000

In February 1862 the direct issue of uniforms by states to their regiments that had been mustered into active Federal service was ordered discontinued. No longer were volunteer officers allowed to requisition from both state and Federal quartermasters and thus secure clothing in excess of the regulation allowance (GO 18). Between then and July the states were requested to turn the clothing they had purchased into U.S. Quartermaster depots with only the stipulation that "as far as possible . . . supplies provided by the States [would be issued] to the troops of the same." In this way the War Department hoped even to take over the soldier's initial outfit.

For various reasons the new method of supply was not everywhere popular and in July 1862 the War Department decided to permit those states which desired to resume direct issue of uniforms to their troops, prior to muster into Federal service, to do so. A number so elected. These took back the stocks of clothing recently handed over to the Federal quartermasters and continued to procure and issue uniforms to newly organized regiments until 1864, when once again the U.S. Army assumed the entire responsibility.

However it was handled, by mid-1862 the clothing battle was won in the North. With requisitions filled, there was a supply of all items sufficient to fill the Army's needs for six months ahead. And the fact should not be missed that "all items" included the complete outfit for full dress as well as the clothing more usually worn in the field. Even General Meigs had to admit in August that his stock of clothing was "extraordinarily large." Complaints still reached him, of course, but by now the principal difficulty was distribution. Some idea of this difficulty can be appreciated by reading General George B. McClellan's reports to the War Department on the Antietam Campaign. In time this problem, too, was largely overcome and the Union soldier could find little to complain about in the matter of clothing and equipment after mid-1862.

The list of clothing authorized an enlisted man in the 1850's, mentioned above, had by late 1861 been somewhat modified. As prescribed in *Revised Army Regulations* of 1861 and GO 95 of that year it included, for a five-years enlistment:

5 dress hats with trimmings
5 forage caps
5 frock coats (or jackets)
13 pairs of trousers
10 sack fatigue coats
2 blankets
2 stable-frocks (for mounted men)

15 flannel shirts
11 pairs flannel drawers
20 pairs of bootees
20 pairs of stockings
2 leather stocks
1 great-coat

Each of these items will be considered in detail below; here it will be sufficient to note that this list, which remained substantially the same until 1872, recognized the need of a regular issue of fatigue clothing.

Materials

We should look briefly at this point at the fabrics from which uniforms were made. Except for soldiers stationed in hot climates, the common military suit the world over, down to the 20th century, was made of wool, or of wool mixed with cotton or flax. During the first half of the 19th century the U.S. Army had regularly issued linen or cotton fatigue clothing to all troops, but procurement of this material ceased about 1853 and only occasional issues were made after 1855. All U.S. regulation clothing (except certain specialized articles like canvas overalls and stable frocks) during the period 1853–1872 was made of wool. On the other hand, such was not the case with state troops or those in the Confederate service.

The cheaper uniform fabrics of the mid-19th century were jean, linsey-woolsey, satinet, and kersey. All except kersey normally contained some cotton or flax. Better grade coats were made of cassimere and officers purchased uniforms of broadcloth or serge, which were more likely to be 100 percent wool. As the war developed, flannel became a common fabric in the Union Army due to the extensive use of the sack coat. Cloth made of shoddy achieved some notoriety in 1861, but it was not long before the Army inspectors had learned how to eliminate it.

Cotton played an important role in military clothing during the actual war years, especially in the South. Many a Confederate soldier was clad entirely in some cotton fabric during the final two years. The twilled cotton cloth called jean was extensively used as a substitute for wool in 1861; many early Civil War units wore uniforms made of jean.

Linsey-woolsey (commonly called linsey) was a relatively coarse material of inferior wool woven upon a cotton or linen warp. By this period the word itself had come to signify "vile, mean, of different and unsuitable parts." Many of the uniforms made in 1861 were of linsey but, so far as is known, it was never accepted for U.S. Army clothing.

Kersey was another rough, coarse cloth, but woven of wool, used chiefly for enlisted men's trousers and overcoats. It was usually ribbed. This was a common material throughout the period and was used extensively for regular army clothing.

Satinet (or satinette) was woven with a cotton warp and woolen weft, and had a satin-like surface. It was made into uniforms in 1861 and possibly at other times.

Broadcloth was the quality fabric for men's garments. It was a fine cloth, plain-woven and dressed, and quite often heavy. When the term "cloth" was used in dress regulations it meant broadcloth, or at least a fabric of wool in contradistinction to one made of some other material. In 1853 the War Department convened a Board to select the coat cloth for NCO's and privates of the Army. This Board fixed the standard weight of the dark blue cloth at 21 ounces per yard.

Cassimere (often incorrectly called "kerseymere") was also a quality cloth, made of wool and twilled, and lighter than broadcloth. Serge was a very durable twilled cloth of worsted, or with the warp of worsted and the weft of wool. Both cassimere and serge were widely used for officers' coats. This kind of serge should not be confused with silk serge, which was a twilled, silk fabric used for coat linings.

Flannel was a soft woolen cloth of loose texture. Its military use for outer garments was comparatively new at this time due to its formless appearance. Flannel shirts and undergarments, on the other hand, were articles of common issue to soldiers of the regular service as well as the state forces.

We sometimes read of fustian being worn for both trousers and coats. This was also made of cotton, a coarse twilled stuff with a short pile. The term, even then an ancient one, also embraced corduroy and velveteen.

Color

"Dark blue is the national color." Such are the opening words of the uniform regulations of 1821, and they expressed a tradition which endured for over a century and became for some officers a matter of deep faith and concern. With but few exceptions the U.S. Army wore dark blue coats throughout the period 1851–1872, and for a brief time in 1858–1861 dark blue trousers as well. Yet that was only part of the story; there were other occasions when light or sky-blue was as widely used, and in the Mexican War the common fatigue suit of the foot soldier had been almost entirely sky-blue. Finally, just as the British army had its critics of scarlet, so the American service contained officers who viewed dark blue with less than pleasure.

It is not possible here to go into the background of the controversy between proponents of the two blues, but the nub seems to be that dark blue cloth implied a relatively expensive, smooth, finely woven broadcloth, dyed in the cloth, while sky-blue meant a much cheaper, rougher material, often dyed in the thread and woven afterward. Dark blue, in some minds, stood for formal dress parades whereas sky-blue meant field soldiering. Sky-blue also was much easier to procure and much less expensive.

Prior to 1861 the matter of which blue to use was fairly academic, but thereafter it became a matter of great moment. The Army Clothing Establishment estimated on 7 December 1861 that the substitution of sky-blue kersey for dark blue cloth in trousers alone would save the government $750,000 a year. A week later, on the 16th, the War Department ordered the trousers of regimental officers and enlisted men to be made of "sky-blue mixture." Still the Clothing Establishment did not rest its case. It pointed out that the substitution of a light blue kersey jacket at $5.10 for the dark blue frock coat at $7.12 would save $4,848,000 in five years. In a memorandum to General McClellan, the Quartermaster General commented:

> The change here recommended from dark to light blue has been effected from the necessity of the case in a very large portion of the Vol. army. I think that it would be well to return to the old color (light blue) as the established uniform and to substitute for the frock coat, a light blue jacket made like the French jacket lately imported. The scale on the Infy uniform should be discarded . . . .

This plan was one of several put before a Uniform Board appointed in 1862. It was not endorsed by that body for they preferred adoption of a French jacket in dark blue. Neither plan was carried out in the end, but sky-blue jackets were issued to the Invalid Corps when it was formed in 1863.

The term "sky-blue" was used in the U.S. Army dress regulations of 1851 and in all others issued throughout the Civil War period. The color was considered at the time to be a pure blue color like that of the sky in daylight. Actually the samples of sky-blue examined are considerably darker than normal sky and have a somewhat greenish cast. There is nothing of the slate or baby blue about the color.

In practice, the color "sky-blue" was not consistent. Whereas the kersey trousers and overcoats of the soldiers remained relatively light in shade, the trousers worn by officers usually were dark enough to deserve the term "medium blue."

For a time between 1851 and 1854 the branch color for Infantry was described as "Saxony blue." This was a bright shade formed from a solution of indigo in concentrated sulphuric acid, very popular as a dye in the 1840's. There is no evidence that this color was used other than in facings and pipings. It was abandoned in 1854 for reasons unknown, possibly because of the difficulty of maintaining a consistent shade.

Since kersey garments were the ones usually colored sky-blue it would be well to see how the color was achieved. The dress regulations of 1851 and 1857 refer to the color as "white and light blue mixed, commonly called sky-blue mixture." This meant a cloth woven from yarn containing both white and light blue. None of the Civil War sky-blue kersey garments examined, however, were made this way. All were woven from wool dyed sky-blue in the yarn or in the bolt.

Gray played a role in the Northern uniform during the early days of the Civil War when the problem of what blue to adopt was overshadowed by that of securing clothing of any kind. The Quartermaster General later summarized the situation, describing how his officers were forced to buy

> . . . materials manufactured for the ordinary clothing of the people . . . In some cases these articles were redyed, of the uniform colors, light and dark indigo blue, but the greater part of the gray, brown, and black cloths purchased were made up in these colors . . . When these troops came into contact with the enemy on thickly wooded fields mistakes occurred. The rebel forces were generally clothed in gray, and our troops in some cases fired into each other. This caused orders to be issued, both by the Eastern and Western commanders, prohibiting the issue or use of clothing of any

but the established uniform colors, light and dark blues. As fast as uniform clothing could be obtained the irregular clothing was withdrawn from service . . . There is still on hand a considerable stock of this clothing . . .

The Quartermaster General, however, tells only half the story. It would appear that gray was the color often deliberately selected by states for clothing their newly formed regiments. It was, of course, in all its shades more common in the trade than blue. Furthermore, there was a tradition in many states that gray was the color for state troops. Indeed, it appears to have cut even deeper in some areas. There is a suggestive story in the history of the 2nd Massachusetts Volunteers, a fine three-year regiment raised among the elite of Boston and commanded by Colonel George H. Gordon, a West Pointer of the Class of 1846, breveted for gallantry at Cerro Gordo, and prior to 1861 commander of the New England Guards.

> The clothing [for the regiment] was procured, by contract, from Whiting, Galloupe & Bliss, of Boston, and was the best the regiment ever had. Strong efforts were made to have "gray" adopted; But Colonel Gordon was firm, —and the opinion of Lieutenant-Colonel [George L.] Andrews [another West Pointer, Class of 1851] supported him,—that the army uniform must be had . . . A general said, "He hoped never to see the Massachusetts soldier clothed in the uniform of the regular army. Such an attempt had nearly caused a mutiny in a Massachusetts regiment in Mexico."

No matter the reason for its choice, protests against the use of gray in the field by Union regiments soon were heard. General McClellan took the lead in this fight, requesting Secretary Cameron as early as 25 August 1861 to order that no more regiments be uniformed in gray, "that being the color generally worn by the enemy." A letter to this effect was addressed to the governors of the states on 23 September, recommending a dark blue uniform instead, as being "readily distinguishable from that of the enemy." But huge stocks of black, dark, and mixed gray uniforms and overcoats had just been acquired, and for a while the Quartermaster General attempted to send them to Western armies where opposition was not so pronounced. Finally, General Orders 59, Department of the Missouri, 10 March 1862, forbade all wearing of "gray or mixed clothing" on the pain of arrest, and blue once more became the army color.

One other color, dark green, was adopted by the War Department during this period. It was supplied to the two regiments of U.S. Sharpshooters. It was a forest green, dark in shade but not as dark as, say, the Russian uniform of the late 19th century.

Styles and the Influence of France

Any discussion of fashion in American military clothing in the 1850's and 1860's must, to be intelligible, contain a resumé of several developments in the French military service during the two decades previous.

The increasing importance of light infantry tactics, particularly as required by her colonial wars, induced France as early as 1830 to form two specialized kinds of foot soldier. In that year a Corps of Zouaves was organized, and eight years later a provisional battalion of *Chasseurs a pied* (Foot Chasseurs) came into being, specifically to replace the old Light Infantry which by then in no way differed from the Infantry of the Line. Both of these new corps were distinguished from the rest of the army by their dress, as well as by their arms, equipment, and tactics. The Zouave wore a loose, flashy Oriental outfit while the French Foot Chasseurs in 1838 were the first corps to wear the frock coat as a regular military garb. It was dark blue in color and was worn with blue-gray trousers, a blue cloth cap, and black leather equipment. As the size of these corps increased, and as stories of their unique styles of fighting spread, they naturally found imitators in other armies. The uniforms adopted by the U.S. Army in 1851 followed closely upon the original chasseur pattern and color.

In 1845 the frock coat was given to all the French infantry at which time the officers of the Foot Chasseurs received a new style of frock coat having skirts attached to the body with pleats 1.2 inches wide. The style seems to have become popular for it was adopted for American infantry in 1855 and lasted several years.

In 1860 occurred another radical change in the uniform of the French infantry. Always *avant garde* in military dress, France abandoned the frock coat for a middle length jacket with short, flaring skirts. Very full trousers, tucked into duplex zouave gaiters, replaced the long trousers, and the tall cloth cap shrunk to a low *kepi*. This was the smart, "modern" military style at the outbreak of our Civil War, and units who were wealthy enough to keep up to the minute tried to adopt it, usually in the chasseur colors of dark blue coat and light blue trousers. An example is that of the 12th Regiment, N.Y.S.M., then commanded by the enterprising Colonel Daniel Butterfield, and there were many others, from Massachusetts to South Carolina.

Fig. 8

The trend for what had come to be called the "chasseur" uniform was not confined to militia and volunteers. On 9 August 1861 the Federal Quartermaster General placed an order with M. Alexis Godillot of Paris for complete equipments for 10,000 men "to be uniformed as the chasseurs a pied." These uniforms arrived in November and were distributed throughout the army.

On 11 February of the following year a board of officers was appointed to consider changes in the Army uniform. On it was Daniel Butterfield, now a brigadier general, together with such prominent regulars as George Sykes, W. S. Hancock, Irvin McDowell, and Philip Kearney. Its deliberations lasted until 8 March; every aspect of the uniform and insignia of the Army, and much of its personal equipment was considered. Virtually every item then in use was found wanting and voted out—a suggestive feature in itself—and in their place was proposed the chasseur uniform.

It has been impossible to trace the final correspondence in this matter, or to find out precisely who turned down the Board's proposal, but it is clear that the U.S. Army came within a narrow margin of adopting the chasseur uniform for

Fig. 10. 5th New York Volunteer Infantry (Duryea's Zouaves). Medium or dark blue jacket and vest trimmed with red, full red trousers trimmed with blue, red sash edged with blue, red fez with blue tassel, sky blue chevrons, yellow leather greaves and white gaiters; standard infantry accouterments with "SNY" belt plate. Officers in dark blue coats with red pants and caps, trimmed with gold lace. Dark blue cloak-coat trimmed with black.

48

the rest of the Civil War.

It is difficult to say for certain what regiments wore the 10,000 chasseur uniforms secured from France in 1861, but probably very few did. When the order was placed, apparently, the relative size of Frenchmen and Americans was overlooked; the uniforms that arrived were generally too small. One thousand were issued the 83rd Pennsylvania who wore them during the winter 1861–1862. A shipment offered to the State of Missouri was returned reluctantly on 25 March 1862 with the comment that the "French clothing . . . was of the best quality and style [but was] entirely too small for our service." Two years later the Army Clothing Establishment was still trying to dispose of "French zouave clothing, too small for issue." It had outfitted several bands of the U.S. Colored Troops with the French uniforms, but the numerous suits that remained were fit only for boys.

Fig. 8

Although never worn by troops of the general government, the various sorts of zouave uniforms seen during the Civil War should be mentioned. The French Corps of Zouaves had by 1859 achieved a renown almost unequalled in military history, yet its uniform—due perhaps to its bizarre character or to an erroneous belief that it was worn by Moslems*—had rarely been copied by other armies and never in the United States except perhaps in New Orleans. Its sudden adoption and subsequent craze on this side of the Atlantic was due entirely to Ellsworth's Zouave Cadets, a militia company of Chicago. Formed in 1859 through the chance association of a penniless law clerk and a French sword-master who had once served in the Corps of Zouaves, this company became so expert in drill that it was able to tour the East in 1860 and compete with all comers. The flashy dress and rapid drill captured the fancy of Americans both North and South, just at a time when hundreds of new volunteer companies were being formed or considered. This was the immediate cause, but it is doubtful if Ellsworth's company would have exerted the influence it did on American military dress without the vast reputation of the Corps of Zouaves behind it.

As an estimate, some thirty-five regiments, and easily as many more separate companies, of the Union and Confederate armies wore the zouave uniform at one time or another. A considerable percentage maintained their uniform throughout their entire war service. In some cases the zouaves were issued additional fatigue clothing and by the middle of the war were reserving their zouave uniforms for formal occasions. Yet the often repeated comment that zouave dress was abandoned early in the war is not true. On one occasion it was issued to an entire brigade as late as 1863 as a mark of commendation. Most Union zouaves enjoyed the uniform's comfort and color, and this last feature particularly appealed to staff officers and provost marshals who welcomed ways of distinguishing one regiment from another. The relatively few zouaves in the Confederate

* General Lew Wallace wrote concerning a zouave uniform he designed: "There was nothing of the flashy, Algerian colors in the uniform . . . no red fez, a headgear exclusively Mohammedan and therefore to be religiously avoided by Christians . . .," Lew Wallace, *An Autobiography*, 2 vols., New York, 1906, I, 270.

service were unable to replenish their supply of French jackets and trousers, and the uniform seems to have disappeared there by 1862.

The true zouave uniform of 1859 consisted of a soft red fez with blue tassel; blue collarless vest, trimmed around the neck and down the front with red braid; blue jacket, also collarless, worn open and trimmed on edges and seams with red braid; very full, distinctively cut Arab trousers of red with a small amount of black cord piping; wide, light blue sash; russet leather leg cuffs (*jambières*) trimmed with black leather, extending from knee to ankle and covered at the bottom by white canvas gaiters. The entire dress was Arab in origin and style. Around the fez, for parade, was worn a green (later white) turban. On each side of the jacket front was a distinctive device formed by red braid, the circle of which was the *tombo,* a sort of false pocket whose color (red, white, or yellow) distinguished the regiments of the Corps of Zouaves. The uniform had no visible buttons except at the cuffs. It was very loose and comfortable except in a rain storm, when the full trousers became unpleasantly heavy.

Fig. 10

Replicas of the zouave dress seen in America varied from almost exact copies to types scarcely recognizable as such. Some were really based upon French infantry, chasseur, or African tirailleur uniforms, and their wearers should never have been called "zouaves." The 14th New York Militia, for example, wore a distorted version of the 1860 French infantry garb. Some regiments, like the 11th New York and the 11th Indiana, adopted gray zouave clothing at the very start. The 9th New York's initial kit was fairly authentic except that its trousers were of the chasseur pattern and dark blue instead of red, while the 10th New York's final zouave uniform, by force of circumstances, consisted of brown jackets and light blue trousers. The regiment which most faithfully followed the original zouave styles was the 5th New York, or Duryea's Zouaves.

Fig. 10

Among the common domestic modifications of the zouave uniform were the use of red firemen's shirts instead of vests, variously colored caps for the fez and turban, and russet leather leggings for the true Arab leg covering. Rarely were the trousers as full as the originals found in Africa. Such substitutions were the result both of preference and circumstances, usually the latter. Yet it was no more costly to secure a zouave outfit than a regulation one, and quite permissible, as the following letter, written 13 August 1861 to Captain Charles H.T. Collis of Philadelphia by the Quartermaster General, will indicate.

> Having this day been authorized to raise a company called Zouaves d'Afrique provided it be ready for marching orders within twenty days, you are informed that if you succeed in making arrangements for the supply of your uniforms though different in style from the Regulation uniform, they will on application to Col. Charles Thomas & exhibition of this authority be inspected by a sworn U.S. inspector & if of quality equal to the Regulation standard will be paid for at prices not to exceed the U.S. regulation prices by him.

Although its real popularity was gained during the war years, zouave dress continued in use here and there for years afterward. Moreover, zouave veteran societies were formed which continued to wear the same uniform. Uniforms made for these post-war commands and societies can easily be confused with Civil War issues.

In the years following the Civil War, from 1865 to 1872, the U.S. Army attempted to live off the vast stocks of clothing remaining in its warehouses. Some idea of the poor quality of these uniforms may be gained from the *Medical Report*, cited below. This frank study was based upon the reports of 168 Army surgeons stationed throughout the country and, of course, reflected the character of clothing worn during the war itself.

> The most general subject of complaint, [reads this *Report*] is [about] its quality. The same article appears to vary in character at different posts, but each is condemned by some one or another, and the more important by all. Equally prominent is the shameful carelessness in the cut and make . . . All who allude to it regard it as a serious hygienic defect that the men cannot be reasonably comfortable until the clothing provided by the government is remade or substituted by other at their personal (and often great) expense . . . The men become dissatisfied, consider they are neglected and defrauded, positive hatred of the service is sometimes engendered, and the discipline and morale of the army are materially impaired.

One other interesting fact is brought out by this report. Soldiers discharged after the Civil War were permitted to keep their uniforms and many, from necessity or desire, continued to wear parts or all of a suit in their daily occupations. The man still in the service came in time to resent seeing "laborers in the streets and hackmen on their boxes clothed in his own garb. The universal use of military clothing destroys the caste feeling in the soldiery which is essential to the highest development of martial qualities . . . This is a legitimate subject for legislation."

Coats and Jackets

A soldier's coat is the garment upon which his uniformity of appearance chiefly depends. It is, thus, the most important single article of clothing and the most difficult to manage. How to preserve uniformity and how to enhance the soldier's appearance, without sacrificing his comfort and efficiency is the problem that has faced every designer of military coats.

Fig. 7   The oldest style of upper garment to be used in the period 1851–1872 was the dress coat or "swallowtail," prescribed by the U.S. Army until 1851 and by many Federal and state regiments for years thereafter. It went by many nicknames, among them "spiketail," "clawhammer," "tail coat," and "steelpen." Worn open in front, it was the evening dress of the male civilian and, of course, remains so today.

Fig. 11   The tail coat (it will be so called hereafter to avoid the confusion inherent in the term "dress coat") was in this period a formal garment, at times padded over the chest, cut off in front at or just below the waist, with long skirts in rear. Its standing collar was at least 2 inches high. In the 1870's and 1880's the collar was lowered to about an inch and this difference is a useful guide in identifying a tail coat. Facings were usually provided for the skirts and it was customary to decorate the collar, cuffs, and skirts with patches of color or loops of braid. Tail coats could be single or double breasted; if the former they might have one or three rows of buttons. Very frequently the three rows were connected by worsted braid (still called "false buttonholes"), and often the shoulders were adorned by epaulets.

Shell or Fatigue Jacket

Next in point of age was the shell jacket, an offshoot of the tail coat since in tailoring it was a tail coat without tails. When first adopted by the U.S. Army in the early 19th century it was called a "roundabout"—a single-breasted garment with sleeves, reaching an inch or so below a man's waist, and usually cut straight around. For more than a generation before 1851 it had served enlisted soldiers as a fatigue and field service garment, being universally worn by them throughout the Mexican War. As issued it tended to be a little looser in fit than the tail coat and rarely contained padding. It could be made of wool, cotton, or linen. Issue of the fatigue jacket ended in the U.S. Army in 1857 but the garment saw extensive use thereafter by state troops and in the Confederacy.

Fig. 12

The fatigue jacket of 1851 carried a standing, hooked-up collar about 3 inches high. By 1861 its collar was reduced to barely 1.5 inches and was open in front. It was commonly fitted with cloth shoulder straps and sometimes with cloth belt loops at the sides. There were from eight to twelve small buttons down the front, and two on the cuff of each sleeve. Originally these cuffs had been slashed—thus the buttons—but by 1861, with wider sleeves in vogue, the slash was often sewn up for much of its length.

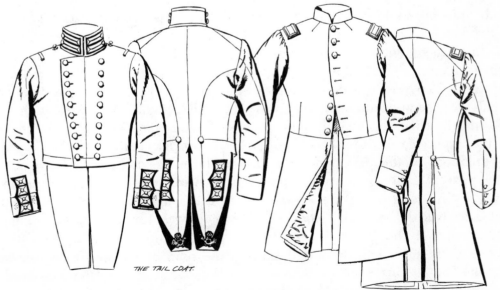

THE TAIL COAT.

FROCK COAT WORN BY OFFICERS BELOW FIELD GRADE.

Fig. 11A. Coats.

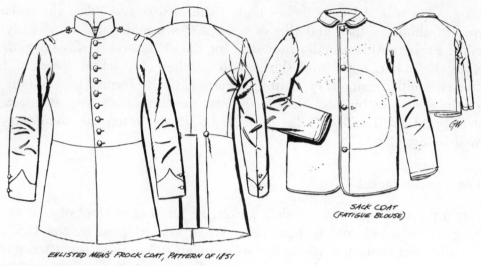

ENLISTED MEN'S FROCK COAT, PATTERN OF 1851

SACK COAT
(FATIGUE BLOUSE)

Fig. 11B Coats.

Most fatigue jackets had lace binding on collar, shoulder straps, and outer edges. Outer pockets were sometimes introduced into one or the other side of the front, over the breast or abdomen, and it is not uncommon to find two outer pockets in Confederate jackets. Originally a pocket on the lower right side had been intended to hold percussion caps and it may well have served this purpose in the Confederate infantry.

Polka-Skirted or Uniform Jacket

Fig. 12

The disadvantage of the shell jacket lay in its extreme shortness, which caused it to ride above the trouser top and leave an unsightly gap, plus the considerable number of buttons needed to hold it together evenly in front. At the same time, some shortness was an advantage to the man in a saddle, a fact that became most obvious when the long-skirted frock coat was introduced in the U.S. Army for all branches in 1851. The result was a compromise on a garment called the "uniform jacket," developed by the War Department in 1853 and prescribed for issue to all mounted men on 20 January 1854 (GO 1).

As its name implied, the uniform jacket was designed for dress wear, not for fatigue, and was intended to replace the frock coat in all mounted services. To enhance the appearance, it was provided with a high collar, fitted with brass scales on the shoulder, and liberally decorated with lace. It was cut rather full. But its basic departure from the shell jacket lay in its greater length.

Regulations of the period describe the uniform jacket in several ways, and it is apparent that there were a number of variant styles, but all unite in calling it "cut long in the waist." To secure this length tailors first resorted to what was called the "polka style skirt" which was formed by lowering the bottom edge of the jacket 5 to 6 inches without introducing a seam at the waist, and by slitting the resultant skirt in the rear, or on both sides. In some early models pockets were introduced into the skirts on the front, covered by three-pointed flaps. Many uniform jackets were supplied with belt loops.

The uniform jacket produced at the Army Clothing Establishment, at least after 1860, had no slits. Instead, it was pointed in front and rear and thus shorter over the hips. It used twelve small buttons down the front, one or two on each side of the collar, and two on each pointed cuff. On the rear were two belt-rest pads (which became, interestingly enough, a fine place to hide money while a prisoner of war).

The uniform jacket was adopted by several states after 1854, as much for infantry as for mounted troops. New York called it a "fatigue jacket" and it is clear the differentiation between these two styles was never too sharply drawn. Indeed, the U.S. Army in 1857 drew out its entire stock of uniform jackets to outfit the Utah Expedition, infantry as well as mounted troops. It proved to be a light and serviceable garment, superior to the more expensive frock coat on this sort of campaign.

Officers' Fatigue Jackets

Officers never seem to have worn the uniform jacket. Indeed, their use of shell and fatigue jackets was fairly limited although authorized by dress regulations from 1851 on. Officers' jackets were made of broadcloth (or linen if in summer) and commonly had low collars. Quite apparently, many were frock coats with the skirts cut off.

Chasseur Jacket

In using the term "chasseur" we must distinguish between the earlier *chasseur a pied* style of frock coat and long pants worn by the U.S. Army about 1855–1858, and the later style that bore the same name, introduced in 1860, which included a jacket.

Fig. 12

This latter chasseur jacket (the *habit-tunique* of the French) was a moderately well fitted garment, single-breasted with usually nine large buttons in front, and seamed at the waist. Below the waist was a five- to six-inch skirt, slit in the rear and on both sides, with two buttons on the rear above ¾-inch pleats. Most such jackets were fitted with belt loops and shoulder straps, and some had pockets cut into the breast. Chasseur jackets were commonly edged with cord or lace.

Special Jackets

Before leaving this subject, mention should be made of an unusual and only partially explained adaptation of the jacket to special dress purposes. This seems to have taken place in the Department of the Gulf during the latter half of 1863, or at least in the 3rd Division, 13th Army Corps. The Division contained regiments from Illinois, Indiana, Iowa, Ohio, and Wisconsin. One of the regiments, the 11th Indiana, had worn a partial zouave dress since its muster in, which by 1863 had been simplified to merely a blue jacket with a sky blue front "that buttons up close which makes it look like a vest," as Corporal Sylvester C. Bishop

Fig. 13

54

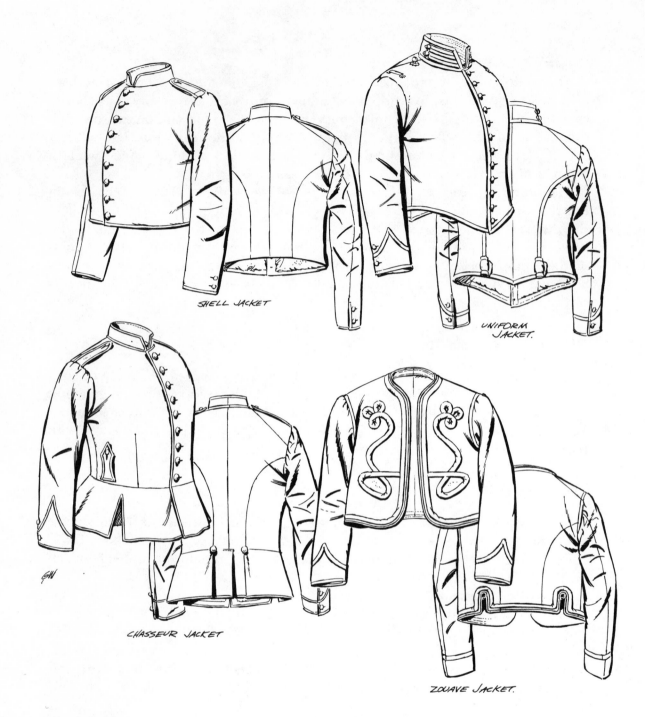

SHELL JACKET

UNIFORM JACKET.

CHASSEUR JACKET

ZOUAVE JACKET.

Fig. 12. Jackets.

wrote his mother.

Bishop was wounded at Vicksburg and when he returned to the Division, then in southern Louisiana, he was indignant at the change he found. On 26 August 1863 he wrote again,

> I hardly know our regiment any more by their dress. Nearly every regiment in our division have got our suits, besides regiments in other divisions . . . But wearing our suit is not so much but they use it to hide the meanness of their own regiment. They will do some scabby trick, get caught, and then say they belong to the 11th Indiana . . .

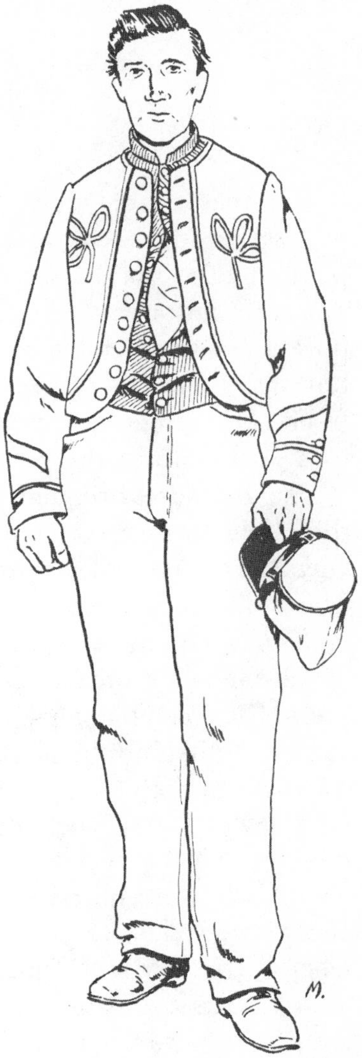

Fig. 13. Private, 34th Indiana Veteran Volunteer Infantry, 1864, in dress uniform. Dark blue semi-zouave jacket with sky blue false vest, sky blue trefoils on front, blue vest and cap, sky blue pants. Half chevrons of sky blue on each arm indicating membership in a re-enlisted regiment. This illustrates the special jacket worn in the 3rd Division, 13th Army Corps. (By Michael J. McAfee, after photograph).

Photographs bear out Corporal Bishop's observation although not the reason he suggests for the change. Higher authority must have felt the need for more color in the uniform and arranged to have jackets issued with strips of sky blue cloth sewn down either side of the front, 2 to 3 inches wide. The result was to create a sort of plastron.

Frock Coats

The frock coat was the characteristic formal garment of the period under consideration. It was the everyday coat of the civilian of even moderate means and the standard uniform coat of the military. Its use was worldwide and probably developed out of the light overcoat or *redingote* of the early years of the century. American army officers had worn the frock coat for field service and undress since about 1829, but its use by enlisted men was a new departure.

Fig. 11A

The military frock coat was what the French called a *tunique,* a fitted garment with body and skirts cut separately except for the center of the back. The skirts could be as wide or long and the waist as narrow as desired. The coat was double breasted for field and general officers, with the two rows of buttons arranged in patterns to indicate the rank of the wearer, and single breasted for all others.

56

The rear skirts were divided from the waist seam down and one pocket was set inside each skirt. Outside each rear skirt on an officer's coat was a pointed false pocket set in under a pleat. Each pleat was headed by a large uniform button and in the regulation version another button held the false pocket. In some styles of frock coat the false pockets had two points and two buttons. Hence there were at least four large buttons on the tails of an officer's frock coat; sometimes six. Enlisted men's coats commonly had only the two buttons at the top of the pleats and no false pockets.

The 1851 dress regulations called for the skirts "to extend from two-thirds to three-fourths of the distance from the top of the hip [waist] to the bend of the knee" in the case of officers. Enlisted men's coats extended half of this distance. These dimensions remained regulation throughout the period considered. In the civilian world, however, the coat grew in length during the 1850's and photographs showing officers during the Civil War with skirts reaching to the knees are not uncommon. This length was achieved by lowering the waistline as much as by lengthening the skirts. The distances in front from collar to waistline, and waistline to bottom edge, remained normally in the proportion 17.5 to 19 inches.

Officers' frock coats prior to 1851 tended to have 2.5-inch cloth stand-up collars, lined with velvet and fastened straight up with two pairs of hooks and eyes. Cuffs were round and 3.25 inches high, of double thickness, slashed on the outside and closed by three small uniform buttons. There was no piping anywhere. The 1851 coat introduced an open collar, held by one hook at the bottom. Collars decreased in height until, by 1865, the usual was 1.5 inches. Cuffs after 1851 were single weight unless covered with velvet, but the slash and buttons remained. One noticeable change between 1851 and 1865 was the increasing fullness of the sleeves. Commencing with about 14 inches of cloth at the elbows, sleeves grew in width to the neighborhood of 17 inches by 1861 and some fashionable officers wore as large as 20 before the war ended. Sleeves of these dimensions had to be gathered considerably when set into the arm holes.

Enlisted men's frock coats were plainer than officers' in most respects. Their skirts were shorter and less full, their sleeves narrower, and there were no false pockets set into the skirts. Enlisted men's cuffs were pointed and slashed, yet fastened with two buttons only. From 1851 to 1854 both collar and cuffs were supposed to be made of cloth of branch color, but thereafter they were dark blue edged with a cord or piping of branch color. As pointed out later, most units did not receive the new pattern uniforms for two or three years and the use of the colored cuffs and collar must have been very limited.

In 1855 the War Department ordered (GO 4) that the frock coat for all dismounted troops (and the uniform trousers for all troops) be cut on the "chasseur-a-pied" pattern, and this pattern was based on an actual uniform imported from France in 1854. No American coats of this pattern are known to have survived but there are ample pictures of the French originals. The new coat was about the length of the older style, but it had considerably fuller and more flaring skirts, gathered evenly at the waist in a series of short pleats. It was issued until 1858. The officers' version of this coat was even more exaggerated in width of skirt and narrowness of waist. In the French original the officer's skirts were gathered evenly into the coat body in long folds and it is possible that American officers followed this style. The rear of the French chasseur pattern frock coat was very plain, consisting merely of the slit in the skirts and two closely-spaced buttons at the waistline.

Assessing the extent the frock coat was worn in the Union Army during the Civil War, John D. Billings in *Hardtack and Coffee* (p. 316) says, "many regiments never drew a dress coat after leaving the state, the blouse [sack coat] serving as a substitute for that garment." Clothing records do not entirely bear out this statement. It seems more likely that dress coats were issued and then worn in winter encampments after which they were turned in or discarded by the men, to be drawn again after the year's campaigns were over. In *Corporal Si Klegg* the author tells of an Indiana regiment, late in 1862, drawing its dress coats some weeks following muster-in, after all other clothing and equipage had been received. The coats were stiff and formal and were rarely taken into the field. "On the first hard march the dress coats disappeared rapidly. They were recklessly flung away to lighten knapsacks and ease aching shoulders, or were traded off to Negroes for chickens and other eatables" (pp. 96–97). The common notion that the frock coat was rarely worn after 1861 is distinctly incorrect.

Sack Coats

About 1840, men of fashion began to wear a coat called the "paletot" for informal occasions. It differed radically in tailoring from what was then usual in that it had no seam at the waist, the skirt and body being in one piece. By 1851 this garment was being called a "sac," "sack coat" or, sometimes, "blouse." Its chief feature was looseness, since it was not shaped to the figure but hung more or less straight from the shoulders. It came in different styles, lengths, and weights and by 1860 its most usual civilian form was that of an overcoat.

Fig. 11B

In 1857 the War Department decided to abandon the use of the jacket for fatigue wear and to adopt in its place (first for mounted men and then, in 1858, for all troops) a dark blue flannel sack coat. This essentially utilitarian garment was loose and formless, extended half way down the thigh, had a simple turnover collar and four large uniform buttons. It was issued with sleeve and body lining to recruits, and without lining as a fatigue coat.

The U.S. Army sack coat carried no braid nor decoration of any sort; it even lacked shoulder straps. Its greatest assets were comfort, simplicity of manufacture, and cheapness. Costing $2.10 compared with $6.56 for the frock coat, it was produced in only three or four sizes and could be manufactured in large numbers. Practically every Union soldier owned one and wore it frequently. The sack coat was never intended to be worn in the field, but in 1861 when clothing was short, it was so widely produced and distributed that it gained a popularity never lost during the war.

Fig. 16

Sack coats were also purchased by officers for wear off duty. These tended to be longer than the regulation model, often falling the same length as the frock coat and being, in essence, overcoats. Since they were controlled neither by regulation nor custom, these officers' coats took several forms. The most common, perhaps, was a four-buttoned flannel coat which looked like an oversized version of the enlisted man's. Another and more formal style, often seen on New York officers, was a dark blue cloth coat with *five* buttons and 6-inch pockets on either side in the front. Collar, front and bottom edges, as well as pockets, were edged with half-inch black mohair braid.

Zouave Jacket and Vest

Fig. 12

Entirely different from all of the garments just described was the zouave jacket, introduced earlier in this chapter. It took many and bizarre forms in the American service but the traditional and most commonly found jacket was short, collarless, rounded in front at the waist, and designed to be hooked or buttoned only at the very top. Blue was the most usual color, varying in shade from light to dark. Almost all jackets were trimmed with lace or cord along the rear and outer seams, on the cuffs, and over the chest. This last embellishment often followed the original French design of a curving twist of lace forming the *tombo* and a crows-foot on top.

Zouave vests normally had the same material and lace as the jackets, and were fastened on the side by ties or buttons. In some American adaptations the vest was merely two strips of cloth sewn to the inside of the jacket and then hooked or buttoned down the front. Some jackets and vests were heavily decorated with small brass bullet buttons. Firemen's shirts often did duty as vests.

It should be added that zouave units almost always carried their accouterments on waist belts fastened underneath the jacket.

Trousers

Fig. 14

With all of the coats and jackets mentioned above, except the chasseur and zouave jacket, the enlisted soldier wore straight, cuffless "stove pipe" trousers, fairly full. Creasing was unknown in those days and trousers were pressed round, if pressed at all. Mounted men were issued trousers reinforced by extra pieces of material on the insides of the legs, sometimes called "saddled" trousers.

U.S. Army issue trousers were made of sky-blue kersey save for the years 1858–1861 when dark blue uniform cloth was used. Normaly they were given two "frog pockets" in the front with two-sided openings formed by buttoned flaps. However, pockets varied in type; a pair of cavalry or horse artillery trousers in the West Point Museum has a single horizontal pocket on the right side without a button, and vertical or side pockets are found on French peg top and chasseur styles. All trousers had fly fronts. Trousers for dismounted men had one-inch slits at the bottom to assist in passing the straight bottoms over heavy shoes. Mounted ones often had two pairs of suspender buttons inside the bottoms for instep straps.

The trousers were provided with suspender buttons but suspenders were not always worn. The Army issued a narrow, black buff leather belt to wear with trousers, but how it functioned is somewhat of a mystery since belt loops were never provided. In the rear of each pair was a slit some 4 inches long, held together by a string or thong at the top. This permitted an adjustment of waist size of as much as 3 inches, while the cut of the trousers enabled them to derive support from the hip bones. The waist belt may have been intended merely as a secondary means of support.

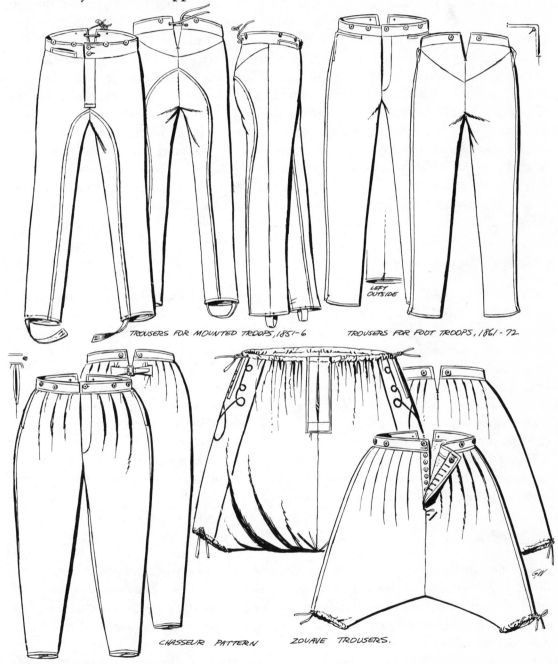

TROUSERS FOR MOUNTED TROOPS, 1851-6   TROUSERS FOR FOOT TROOPS, 1861-72

CHASSEUR PATTERN   ZOUAVE TROUSERS.

Fig. 14. Trousers.

The *Medical Report* of 1868 mentions "the undeviating thickness of heavy trousers . . . is a source of severe complaint throughout the entire warm season. Equally is it dificient for health and comfort during exposure to the piercing winter winds of the plains [because of] the criminal inferiority of the cloth now supplied."

Officers' trousers were made of softer, finer materials than those worn by enlisted men—often of cassimere. In cut they tended to follow civilian or French military fashions. In 1851 they were relatively straight, becoming fuller, especially over the hips and knees, during the next decade and a half. The extreme of this development were the "peg-top" trousers which were very full in the center but reduced to small openings at the ankles. A pair worn by an officer of the 165th New York (2nd Duryea Zouaves) was pleated at the waist and had vertical side pockets. This style was left to officers of Volunteer units wearing French uniforms. Yet ordinary trousers were often as wide over the hips as peg-tops.

The first *chasseur a pied* pattern trousers to be adopted for enlisted men and worn by them in the U.S. Army between 1855 and 1858 were long, straight, and only a little fuller than what had been worn before. French Chasseur officers, however, were wearing peg-top trousers in 1855 and it is probable that American officers did in these years wear pants that were much fuller than before.

Chasseur Trousers

Fig. 14 The trousers worn with the French 1860 pattern chasseur uniform (the "chasseur jacket" has been described above) were full but cut in the conventional manner. They were gathered at the waist with pleats, and below the knee into wide cuffs fastened by buckles or buttons. They were always worn with gaiters of some sort.

It was common to decorate the fronts of chasseur trousers with knots made of cord or lace, and to run stripes of the same down each side. Normally the material of which these trousers were made was the same as in the jacket, although sky blue in color.

Full trousers, cut generally along these lines, were worn by many volunteer regiments, and the great majority of zouave corps were given this sort of garment rather than the actual zouave pattern.

Zouave Trousers

Fig. 14 The genuine zouave trousers were like nothing normally tailored in this country. They can best be likened to a flaring skirt that falls well below knee level and whose bottom is sewn together except for holes large enough to admit the leg at either end. These trousers, naturally extremely full, were gathered at the waist with pleats.

Only a few American regiments wore such trousers, the chasseur pattern sufficing for the rest. In the descriptions that follow, however, any sort of full trousers worn with gaiters that were part of a zouave costume will be referred to as "zouave trousers."

Headdress

For dress purposes the common military headwear of the 1850's was a rigid, visored cap made of felt or of cloth laid over a stiff cardboard or papier-mache cylinder. The visor was constructed of leather or patent leather and the better caps had leather crowns and bands. A few models were constructed entirely of leather. The crown was smaller than the head band and was tilted somewhat forward, standing, in the mid-1850's, about 6 inches high in front and 7 inches in the rear. The visor projected straight forward, was usually more square than round, and varied from 2 to 3 inches in width at the center, although 2 inches was most common.

Fig. 15

Invariably this cap, also called a "dress hat" and known as a *shako* in France, carried an insignia of some sort attached to its front, while a plume or pompon projected above. Most models had patent leather chinstraps attached by two side buttons. The cap had been introduced in the French army in 1837 where it remained in essentially the same form until 1856. In that year a lower style with a more forward projecting crown was adopted. This was, in turn, replaced in 1860 by an all leather shako of the same form, which gave way in 1868 to an even lower, cloth model. By this time the average height in front was 4.5 inches and, in rear, about 5.5. These dates are of some importance in this study, since all the dress hats worn in America have their origins in one or another of these styles.

The cap adopted by the War Department in 1851 was the simplest and cheapest of the types mentioned above. It was made of dark blue cloth over a cardboard frame, with no further support, no waterproof crown, and no reinforcing bands of leather. How it could have survived a single hard rain storm defies the imagination. To prevent such a calamity the soldier was given a waterproof cap cover which he kept handy at all times. In the mid-1850's experiments were conducted with a cloth-covered gutta percha dress cap—three examples are in the National Museum—but apparently this new material did not measure up to expectations.

Although War Department policy did not permit new pattern uniforms to be issued until stocks of the old were exhausted, it so happened that the supply of old pattern dress hats ran out soon after 1851. Rather than manufacture more, the Quartermaster General authorized the issue of new pattern cloth caps with old pattern uniforms.

The U.S. Army dress cap at first carried a cloth band, pointed up in front, of branch coloring. In January 1854 this band was ordered removed and replaced by a narrow cord or welt in the branch color. The reason for the change is not clear but it seems to be connected with a problem of over-supply in the Army Clothing Establishment and a consequent attempt to render caps and other items more readily exchangeable between branches. This simplified blue cloth dress hat was worn by all U.S. Army regiments except the 1st and 2nd Cavalry until 1858 when the black felt hat was substituted for dress wear.

The Dress or "Hardee" Hat

Fig. 15

The introduction into the regular army of a full brimmed felt hat was a tradition-defying move and gave us one of the few native American articles of clothing used during the Civil War. Its introduction in 1855 was closely associated with Jefferson Davis, then Secretary of War, and Captain William J. Hardee, 2nd Dragoons—to such an extent that thereafter it was sometimes called the "Jeff Davis" or the "Hardee" hat—but its origins are probably earlier. During the Mexican War Colonel Timothy P. Andrews, commanding the Regiment of Voltigeurs, devised and actually ordered a brimmed hat for his command. The war ended before the hats reached the regiment and they went into storage.

About 1853 the stock was discovered by Colonel William S. Harney, commanding the 2nd Dragoons, then in Texas, who had the hats issued to his men on an experimental basis. The hat was of soft felt, pearl or stone gray in color, with a wide brim capable of being looped up in much the same fashion as the old chapeau bras. Ventilation holes were introduced on two sides. The hat was worn exclusively on scouting expeditions where shade from the Texas sun was needed. Its use was a decided success and probably led to the adoption of the Model 1855 felt hat for the two new cavalry regiments raised that year (GO 13).

In 1858 a very similar headdress was authorized as the dress hat for the entire army and was worn throughout the Civil War. The difference between the two patterns could not have been great and no distinction will be made herein. However, it is probably more correct to use 1858 as the date of the model.

The Model 1858 hat was made entirely of black felt of a good grade with a 3-inch brim, looped up by regulation on one or the other side. The edge of the brim was bound with silk braid for officers and stitched for others. A medium size crown was 6 inches high with insignia of branch and regiment worn on the front. From one to three black ostrich feathers were fastened to the side not looped up and a cord ending in acorns or tassels, at first of black and yellow and later of various colors, encircled the hat. A brass device representing the national seal, called an "eagle," fastened the brim to the crown.

When issued to the 1st and 2nd Cavalry in 1855 the hat was looped up on the right side by all ranks, and this arrangement was confirmed in the dress regulations of 1857. When the hat was given to all the Army in 1858 it was specified that general officers, staff officers and officers of all the staff corps including engineers, and officers and men of all mounted regiments would loop it up on the right side. Officers and men of infantry and artillery—the dismounted arms—were ordered to loop the hat on the left (GO 3). In February 1861 this arrangement was changed. All officers were ordered to loop on the right, together with

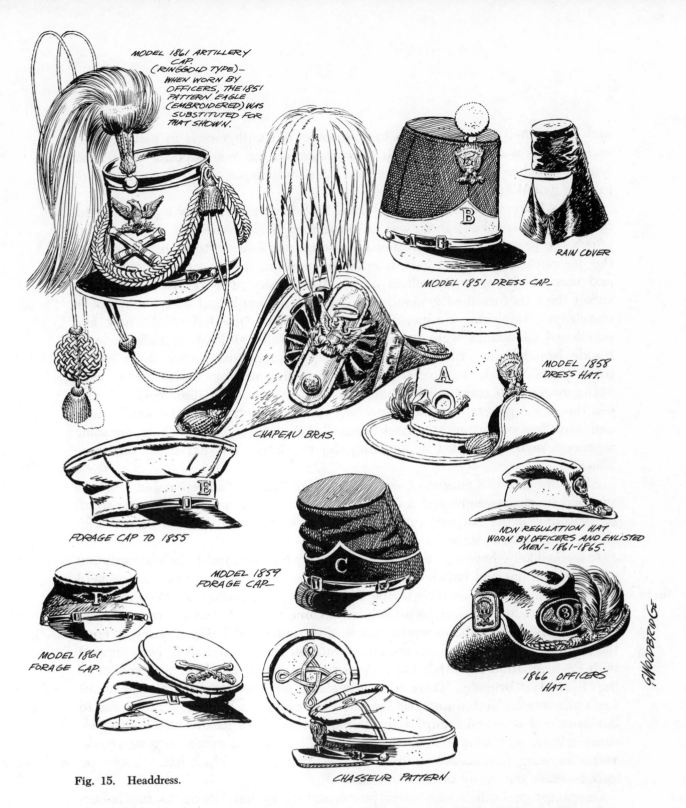

MODEL 1861 ARTILLERY CAP. (RINGGOLD TYPE)— WHEN WORN BY OFFICERS, THE 1851 PATTERN EAGLE (EMBROIDERED) WAS SUBSTITUTED FOR THAT SHOWN.

MODEL 1851 DRESS CAP.

RAIN COVER

CHAPEAU BRAS.

MODEL 1858 DRESS HAT.

FORAGE CAP TO 1855

MODEL 1859 FORAGE CAP.

NON REGULATION HAT WORN BY OFFICERS AND ENLISTED MEN — 1861-1865.

MODEL 1861 FORAGE CAP.

CHASSEUR PATTERN

1866 OFFICER'S HAT.

G. WOODBRIDGE

Fig. 15. Headdress.

mounted enlisted men; foot soldiers only looped on the left (GO 4). This distinction was a practical one, due to the fact that the saber was carried in the right hand by officers and mounted men, while the habitual method of carrying the musket was in the left hand at either shoulder or support arms.

The Model 1858 hat gave us the hat cord, so long a feature of the American uniform. The cords first worn by the cavalry in 1855 were of gold for officers and yellow worsted for the men. On the Model 1858 hat the cord for general officers was gold with acorn shaped ends; for other officers, black silk and gold;

64

and for enlisted men, "of colors to suit corps and with tassels in lieu of acorn ends." Cords were first worn with their tassels on the side opposite the feather but the practice of having them on the front must have come into vogue early in the Civil War.

It must be remembered that the Model 1858 hat was primarily a parade head-dress. Strictly speaking, there was no prescribed field service hat. The extent to which the dress hat was converted for use in the field, or to which it inspired the use of other black felt hats, is open to question. It was a fairly popular hat and was widely worn. An officer of the 1st Cavalry at Fort Washita in 1859 called the hats furnished generally too large and complained about the lack of chinstraps "which are indispensible." But he found "the felt of the new Hat excellent." Chinstraps were furnished to the cavalry at least in 1859. Later a Rhode Island light artilleryman summed up his reactions to the dress hat in these words: "While they were useful in protecting us from the sun, they were not convenient to carry on the march, and they were soon discarded." Doubtless this was a general reaction, especially among infantrymen, who would have had even less opportunity to pack around these non-collapsible hats. In some regiments men specialized in lowering the regulation felt hat to a "one-story affair."

After the war the Surgeon General declared the hat "objectionable from its size and its great weight and want of ventilation . . . at nearly every post south of Washington the hat and cap give place in warm weather to a lighter substitute, generally of straw."

It seems likely, however, that the Model 1858 hat, lowered in height, stripped of its decorations and battered in about the crown, was widely worn in the field by all ranks. In the early days of the war it tended to distinguish Western regiments, but gradually, by order or fashion, it came to denote the veteran infantryman. General John Gibbon wrote that in the summer of 1862, in order to have the regiments of his brigade in the same uniform, he "ordered all to be equipped with the regulation black felt hats." As a result his command became known as the "Black Hat Brigade." There is an interesting but unsubstantiated story about Lee's advance to Gettysburg. His leading division saw a body of infantry far to the front and attacked immediately, thinking they were hastily raised Pennsylvania militia. The blue line, however, met them with a savage counterattack, and a knowing Confederate called out, "See them damn black hats—they're no militia—that's the Army of the Potomac!"

On campaign both armies wore practically every hat known to the haberdasher. Black felts were seen on Confederate soldiers, but more common with them were soft brimmed hats of various shades of brown and drab. "Shapes," Professor Wiley writes, "varied from high-crowned 'beegums' to low-topped bowlers." Straws were common in the deep South.

The black felt hats purchased by Union officers during the Civil War came in various patterns. One style had a 3.5-inch loose brim, bound with black silk braid, with a 6-inch crown, rounded on top and usually worn dented from front to rear. Another, with a 4- or 5-inch crown and called the "Burnside Pattern,"

Fig. 16

was illustrated in Schuyler, Hartley & Graham's catalog. Still another style was quite rigid, with a low (3-inch) crown, fully rounded, and a 2.5-inch brim curled over on opposite sides.

When the war ended the regulars did not, apparently, return to the Model 1858 hat. Instead the officers, at least, adopted a lower hat, something like the last one described. It had about a 4-inch crown, dented from front to rear, and a brim that was curled up on both sides. Insignia, cord, and feathers were as prescribed but the "eagle" was omitted as unnecessary.

Forage Caps

The forage cap worn by all regular troops in 1851 was the one commonly associated with the Mexican War, a dark blue cloth cap with a soft crown that was wider than the band, a leather visor, and chinstrap. The cap was often Fig. 15 trimmed with a colored band or piping. It was issued until 1855 during which time its band heightened and its crown diminished somewhat in size.

From 1855 to 1859 the Model 1851 dress cap or the new felt hat served for fatigue wear as well as dress, the soldier wearing out his previous year's head-dress in this way. During this period only the engineer soldiers were given (1857) a special forage cap. In November 1858 the Secretary of War announced his desire to introduce a new forage cap for enlisted men and several styles were considered. The one selected was essentially a non-rigid version of the Model 1851 dress cap with only the top of the crown stiffened. This was first is-sued with a welt of branch color above the band. Unassigned recruits received one without the colored welt and in 1861 this simpler kind was given everyone. In 1859 the Secretary directed that the remaining Model 1851 caps would be is-sued as forage caps, presumably with stiffening removed.

The earliest Model 1858 forage cap had a stiff horizontal visor, but this dis-appeared with the mass produced caps of 1861 and later, whose visors were roughly cut pieces of leather that rapidly assumed a curved shape and were forced to point down or up when worn. The usual height of the cap in front was 5.5 inches but this varied considerably. The sides collapsed so that the top tended to incline forward.

It was fashionable early in the war, especially for the mounted services, to wear caps with crowns 6.5 inches high in front, and these as a result projected forward well over the visor. This was sometimes called the "cadet pattern." One variant form was given a sharply sloping visor, another (more common in the South) had a very small top. In one style or another the cap lasted through the war and for years afterward.

Oil-cloth covers were often worn on forage caps and, in the summer of 1861, the wearing of white linen or cotton covers with "havelocks" had a wide if momentary vogue. These relics of British service in India were invariably sewn by ladies at home and reflected a romantic approach to the war which dis-appeared soon after First Bull Run. Occasionally one sees caps having crowns made of glazed cloth, apparently waterproof.

With the chasseur uniform came a distinctive form of the forage cap, lower than the regulation pattern and without its fullness. The visor was straight and thick, being made of two pieces of leather over some sort of a stiffener, and the top of the crown was usually countersunk. This chasseur pattern became the officer's forage cap of the period and was worn throughout the rest of the century. The chasseur cap normally had vertical piping on four sides and around the band, but it could be plain.

Officers of chasseur and zouave corps wore a similar cap that was, in fact, a copy of the French officer's *kepi* of the day. Somewhat the same style was prescribed for C.S.A. officers in January 1862. The crown and sides were usually red but could be of other colors; the band was most often dark blue or black. Above the band one or more horizontal stripes of quarter-inch gold braid circled the cap; above them similar stripes rose vertically to a circle of braid around the top of the crown, inside which was a Hungarian knot of the same braid.

Rank was determined by the number of stripes: usually 1 for lieutenants, 2 for captains, 3 for field officers, and 4 for generals.

Fig. 16. An Ohio Volunteer Infantryman, 1863–1865. Blue flannel blouse, sky blue pants, black felt hat. (By Michael J. McAfee, after photograph).

Other Headdress

The chapeau bras or cocked hat, traditional formal headdress of general officers and their staffs, was eliminated by the dress regulations of 1851 but authorized again in 1859. The next year a lighter model of the "French chapeau, either stiff crown or flat" was designed and made regulation for general and field officers. The use of this hat was always optional and very limited.

Fig. 15

Companies of light artillery managed to retain throughout much of the period the dress cap with red horsehair plume, cords, and tassels they had worn before 1851. This cap will be described under light artillery in Chapter 8.

The fez most commonly worn by zouave corps was a North African style, made of semi-stiff red felt, about 6.5 inches high in the center, with a tassel of blue silk. The zouave wore it on the back of his head. If a turban was attached it was rolled and sewed together beforehand.

Shirts and Waistcoats

The shirts worn by men in the 1850's and 1860's fell broadly into three kinds: dress shirts, undershirts, and fireman's shirts. The first kind were normally made of linen, were carefully tailored, and came in white and various colors. Sometimes they were pleated down the front, in which case they unbuttoned all the way, but less formal patterns were fastened by 4 buttons and slipped over the head. Most had low turnover collars but some carried only the band to which a collar had to be attached. Shirts with full fall sleeves were still to be found, but by 1860 had largely been replaced by the sleeve as we now know it. This kind of shirt, in all its variety, was the sort worn by gentlemen, normally over an undershirt.

Fig. 17

The second kind was the pull-over shirt issued to the soldier and worn widely by the working man. It normally had a simple turnover collar fastened by a single button, and sleeves with or without cuffs. In design it differed little from some styles of dress shirt, but it was cruder in workmanship and usually made of flannel. It was actually an undershirt since it was not intended to be worn as an outer garment. With it the soldier wore long drawers, often provided with cords at the bottom to tie under his insteps.

In 1852 the U.S. Army stopped the issue of cotton shirts, and thereafter the regulation was made of flannel, usually white in color. During the Civil War some soldiers received coarse shirts of bluish gray flannel and others got shirts of the same color but made of coarsely knit wool. There were frequent complaints in hot weather about the excessive weight and roughness of issue shirts which were worn, of course, next the skin.

The third kind was the "fireman's" shirt. This immensely popular garment was usually made of red flannel or merino, but it did come in dark blue, white, or gray. It was essentially an outer garment and almost always worn as such. It had long tails covering the hips and was usually trimmed square at the bottom so that it could be worn outside the trousers.

The fireman's shirt was double breasted and fitted with a wide neck and broad falling collar. As a point of style its buttons were often of white bone or other fancy makes like mother of pearl. It was frequently worn over another shirt.

The advantages of a flannel or merino shirt were obvious at the time—its conduction of heat and its superior absorption of moisture. It also gave the warmth necessary in cool weather, and by wearing two or three shirts at one time the soldier could better withstand real cold. But there were also disadvantages. It was uncomfortably warm in hot weather and difficult to wash. Furthermore, vermin appeared to propagate in wool far more rapidly than in cotton. As a result, in the Civil War wool shirts were gradually discarded in favor of cotton ones and it is said that plain white cotton became the most popular kind with enlisted men, in the Confederacy at least.

Homespun shirts came in any of these three styles and were of all materials, many being woven in plaid designs.

Off duty it was both comfortable and fashionable to unbutton the coat or jacket. This called for a vest, and in 1851 one was authorized for officers which continued in use through 1872. It was buff, white, or dark blue in color, with small brass buttons denoting corps, regiment, or department.

To judge from commercial photographs of Union soldiers in the years 1861–1865 enlisted men also wore vests, but it is quite probable that some of these were props furnished by the photographer to enhance the appearance of his sitters. Others were the personal property of the men and doubtless were useful garments. So far as can be told, all vests were sleeveless.

Stocks and Cravats

Officers alone were authorized in all dress regulations from 1851 to 1863 to wear ties or cravats. If worn, however, "the tie [was] not to be visible at the opening of the collar." Among state troops prior to the Civil War the exposure of the bow tie was a commonplace, especially off duty and when posing for photographs. Bows of six and eight inches across can be seen in cartes de visite, worn outside the coat, usually an inch wide and always black. Their wear in combat, however, was limited.

Black leather stocks were prescribed for enlisted men in all dress regulations and a patent was taken out for a new style as late as 1858. There is evidence that some were worn during the Civil War, especially on formal dress parades. But by the war's end the leather stock had been so generally discarded that it was rarely commented upon by Army medical officers in the 1868 survey of clothing. The few who did speak of it refer scathingly to its great inconvenience and the frequent injury it did to the men.

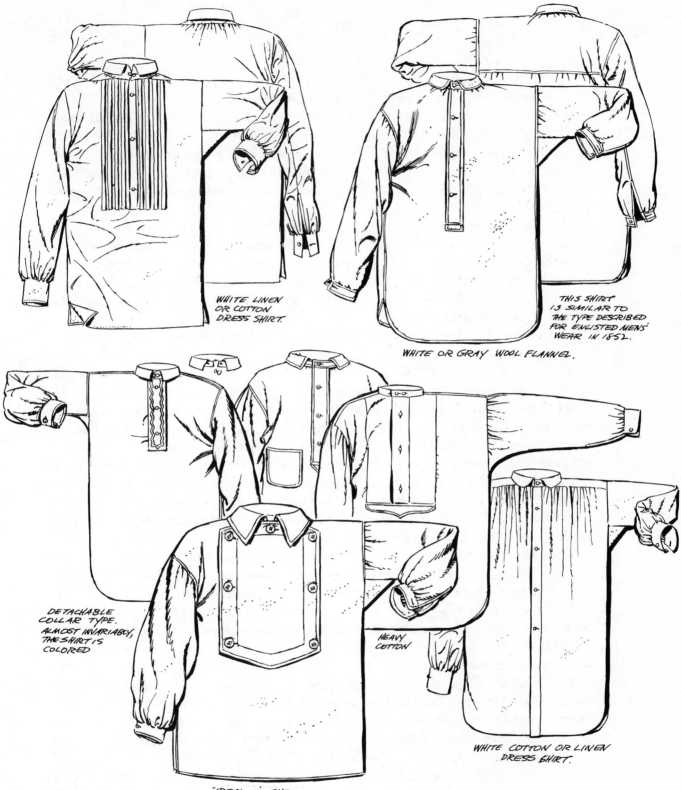

WHITE LINEN
OR COTTON
DRESS SHIRT.

THIS SHIRT
IS SIMILAR TO
THE TYPE DESCRIBED
FOR ENLISTED MENS'
WEAR IN 1852.

WHITE OR GRAY WOOL FLANNEL.

DETACHABLE
COLLAR TYPE.
ALMOST INVARIABLY,
THE SHIRT IS
COLORED

HEAVY
COTTON

WHITE COTTON OR LINEN
DRESS SHIRT.

FIREMAN'S SHIRT

Fig. 17. Shirts.

Footwear

Fig. 18

The terminology for military boots and shoes of the 1850's and 1860's is far from clear and even seems to have caused some confusion in the period itself. In 1854 the Quartermaster General determined that the footwear intended for the mounted service would be called the "boot," while that for the foot service would be called the "bootee." The word "shoe" was rarely used in military writing, being apparently confined to ladies' footwear and to the lower or lighter styles worn by men.

Dress regulations throughout the period, on the other hand, mention only the "ankle boot" and the "Jefferson boot." Both types were prescribed for officers and the mounted service, while the foot service received only the Jefferson boot. It can be concluded that the ankle boot was a medium height riding boot, without lacing, and otherwise called a "half boot," while the bootee or Jefferson meant a high quarter shoe or, in its rougher forms, a "brogue" or "brogan." These, of course, were only general categories; within each there must have been considerable variation in manufacture and style.

Every year after 1850 saw a greater number of bootees and shoes manufactured by machinery for the ready-made markets, but it was not until after the Civil War that the hand-made shoe became a rarity. In the period under study even the cheapest shoes came in pairs made on right and left lasts. The characteristic vamp or front of the military bootee ran straight from the instep to a soft, low toe; quarters were moderately high with from two to five pairs of eyelets for laces. Soles were sewn to uppers or fastened by pegs, nails, and occasionally rubber. Heels tended to be rather high on officers' bootees, but this was a matter of style. U.S. Army boots and shoes were invariably made of black leather, the latter with the flesh or rough side out.

Since the mounted man's boots (if he wore such instead of bootees) were, by regulation, covered by his trousers, and since no detailed description of them has been found, it is difficult to be certain just what they were like. Doubtless they varied in type over the years of the 1850's and 1860's, but in general they must have been medium in height, of plain calf with straps, and of the Wellington pattern. How often they were worn, in contrast with bootees, has not been determined.

The coming of the Civil War added new and more military looking riding boots. The most common style, privately purchased and, in all probability, issued as well, were rather heavy and rigid boots coming to just below the knees and rising slightly in front. Officers wore somewhat taller ones of the same style, or a more expensive kind of softer leather which came well over the knee all around. These last were either held up by straps around the upper legs or permitted to droop. The German name for such boots was *Stulpstiefel* or "top boot." All of these boots were worn over the trousers as often as under them; apparently this was a matter of regimental authority.

Many infantrymen wore boots. It must be remembered that a low leather boot was the common footwear of the farmhand of this period and many pre-

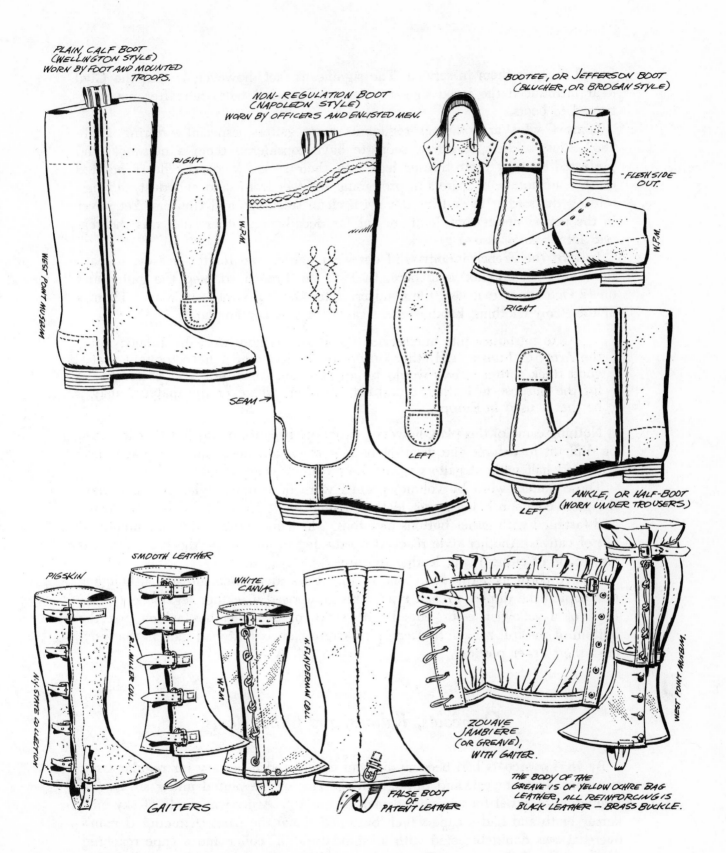

PLAIN, CALF BOOT
(WELLINGTON STYLE)
WORN BY FOOT AND MOUNTED
TROOPS.

RIGHT.

WEST POINT MUSEUM

W.P.M.

NON-REGULATION BOOT
(NAPOLEON STYLE)
WORN BY OFFICERS AND ENLISTED MEN.

SEAM →

LEFT

BOOTEE, OR JEFFERSON BOOT
(BLUCHER, OR BROGAN STYLE)

-FLESH SIDE
OUT.

W.P.M.

RIGHT

ANKLE, OR HALF-BOOT
(WORN UNDER TROUSERS)

LEFT

PIGSKIN

SMOOTH LEATHER

WHITE
CANVAS.

N.Y. STATE COLLECTION

R.L. MILLER COLL.

W.P.M.

N. FLAYDERMAN COLL.

GAITERS

FALSE BOOT
OF
PATENT LEATHER

ZOUAVE
JAMBIERE
(OR GREAVE),
WITH GAITER.

WEST POINT MUSEUM.

THE BODY OF THE
GREAVE IS OF YELLOW OCHRE BAG
LEATHER, ALL REINFORCING IS
BLACK LEATHER — BRASS BUCKLE.

Fig. 18. Footwear.

ferred to wear them in service. The significant fact, however, is that the Civil War introduced the laced shoe to many a farm lad who thereafter never returned to boots.

Some Civil War volunteer regiments wore gaiters, especially during 1861–1862. Most soldiers, however, seem to have considered them a nuisance, and preferred to tuck their trouser legs into their socks. Medical officers pointed out the advantage of gaiters in protecting the feet from sand and dust and permitting the soldier to end his day with clean stockings and trousers. Yet never in the period under consideration, nor for decades on either side, was the regular infantryman issued gaiters.

In 1851 the French infantry did not wear gaiters and for this reason, in part, they were not adopted over here. In 1860 the French adopted the gaiter and on 12 October of that year the Quartermaster General wrote to Colonel Thomas of the Army Clothing Establishment saying it was contemplated

> . . . to introduce into our service the *gaiter* as now worn by Infantry in the Army of France, and other European services, and I have thought that good thick cotton canvas would be an excellent substitute, and preferable, for the purpose to leather, or artificial leather, whatever the material may be that is used in Europe.

Nothing came of this plan, however, probably because it was felt that it would be difficult to enforce the wearing of gaiters on all men, and a regiment half with and half without gaiters would be too unpleasant a sight.

Those gaiters worn by volunteer units were of various styles and materials, the most common being russet leather, rising about 12 inches above the instep and fastened with either buttons or talons. The same pattern was manufactured out of canvas. Another style reached up the leg to just below the knee and was also made of either russet leather or canvas.

Zouave corps as a rule wore one of the styles mentioned already although a few copied the duplex French type. This comprised a leather leg piece (*jambiere*) of a yellowish color, edged with strips of black leather, which met the bottom of the full zouave trousers, plus white canvas buttoned gaiters that covered their lower portion.

Overcoats, Talmas, and Other Items

By 1851 overcoats had become an item considered necessary for regular issue to troops. In that year, and throughout the rest of the period under study, the regulation overcoat for an enlisted man of the U.S. Army was made of sky-blue kersey cloth and had a cape which buttoned down the front. A mounted man's overcoat was doublebreasted with a "stand-and-fall" collar and a cape reaching to the cuffs of the sleeves. For dismounted men it was single breasted, with a standing collar and a cape falling only to the elbow. With a few exceptions

Fig. 19

these two models were worn in all the Union Army throughout the Civil War.

The prescribed overcoat for officers was a quite different affair, a "cloak coat" of dark blue cloth, closed in front by four frogs and loops of black silk cord. A black silk braid bound all edges and formed several loops at appropriate places. This cloak coat had first been prescribed in 1851 and is illustrated in Plate 20 of the Horstmann edition of the dress regulations of that year. It was a direct steal from the French—even the Horstmann illustration is lifted unaltered from the official French uniform plates of 1845. A long, dark blue cape, and even a hood, could be attached to the cloak if desired.

The extent to which this cloak was worn is not clear. Late in 1861 officers of infantry, cavalry, and artillery were authorized to wear an enlisted man's mounted model "in time of actual field service" (GO 102), but photographs of officers so dressed are rare. The cloak coat was regulation for many years after the war and it seems safe to assume that one was the property of most officers of the Union Army.

Rank was indicated on the sleeves of the cloak coat by knots of one to five lines of black silk braid. Colored linings were not prescribed for the capes of either officers or enlisted men but there is some indication that a few units may have worn them. In writing of a grand review at Bailey's Cross Roads, Va., in November 1861, the historian of the 1st New York Cavalry says "the artillery wore their over-coats with capes buttoned back, showing the red lining." It should also be recalled that prior to 1851 officers had been permitted "cloaks" which were lined with cloth of distinctive colors.

The American soldier was not provided with any special clothing (except a cap cover) for use in wet weather until about 1857, when an experimental issue of a garment called a "talma" was made to the 1st and 2nd Cavalry Regiments. The other mounted regiments complained of this partiality and the dress regulations of March 1861, as a result, authorized "a gutta percha talma, or cloak extending to the knee, with long sleeves" for all types of cavalry (GO 6).

The talma was cut very full and had large, loose sleeves but no cape. The few photographs of it in use show it coming down almost to the knees. Apparently arms and accouterments were worn underneath the talma whereas they were invariably worn outside the regulation enlisted overcoat.

The need of foot soldiers for some comparable sort of protection against the rain led the Secretary of War on 1 November 1861 verbally to authorize the issue to all soldiers of "waterproof blankets." These were either "painted" or "rubber," the latter being more expensive. About the same time mounted men began to be issued ponchos, waterproof blankets slit in the center for wear as a cape, of the same two materials. This left the question of continuing the issue of talmas to cavalrymen up to the Quartermaster General. General McClellan preferred the poncho for use by all troops, and in this opinion he was supported by Generals Stoneman and Meigs. As a result the issue of talmas was suspended by the U.S. Army in 1862 and in their place the cavalry was issued the poncho. Colonel Sibley, Deputy QMG, cautioned the Clothing Establishment in December 1861 that these ponchos "should not be less than the tente abri in size."

74

CAPE REMOVED TO SHOW CONSTRUCTION.

OFFICER'S CAPED GREAT COAT.

OFFICER'S CLOAK-COAT.

INFANTRY ENLISTED MEN.

MOUNTED ENLISTED MEN'S GREATCOAT.

TALMA

PONCHO

GW

Fig. 19. Overcoats, talma and poncho.

Thus the talma was gradually replaced in the mounted service by the poncho, despite the former's greater popularity. A monthly return of clothing for the 2nd Iowa Cavalry for March 1865 shows rubber and painted blankets, as well as rubber ponchos, but no talmas.

Whether infantrymen were issued ponchos is open to question. An Indiana regiment was issued blankets made of India rubber in late 1862. "Its official name was the 'poncho,'" wrote an Indiana soldier, "but this word had no meaning to the boys . . . and they always called it the 'gum blanket.'" After a time, half the blankets had checker-boards and the other figures needed for games like chuck-a-luck, sweat, and Honest John, painted on the inside.

Special winter clothing was on occasions authorized and fabricated for campaigns conducted in cold weather. For the Indian campaign in Oregon and Washington Territory during the winter of 1858–1859 the following clothing was provided:

    3000 Great Coats, with capotes & hoods
    3000 Prs. Cavalry boots (for Infantry Service)
    3000 Caps with ear-pieces (old pattern Forage, or the last pattern cap)
    3000 Worsted throat Mufflers (of some uniform dark color)
    5000 Prs Mittens, buckskin, lined with flannel or other warm material
        (to come up over the cuff)

Throughout the period the Army issue blanket was made of gray wool and had the letters "U.S." hand-stitched in black outline, 4 inches long, in the center. It was 7 x 5.5 feet in size, and weighed 5 pounds.

Mounted men were issued washable stable frocks, made of linen or cotton, and described as being "white and made like dusters." They were very full and hung straight from the shoulders to within three or four inches of the knees. Three bone buttons held this single-breasted frock together. With it could be worn a pair of wide trousers of the same material.

Gauntlets appear to have been privately purchased by men as well as officers and were not an item of issue. Their use was normally confined to mounted men, although examples of infantry officers and NCO's wearing them are known.

SOURCES

U.S. Army dress regulations, especially the illustrated edition of the June 1851 regulations published by William H. Horstmann & Sons, Philadelphia, 1851, usually referred to as the "Horstmann edition." For discussion of these regulations see Chapter 8.

MS records and correspondence of the Quartermaster General in the National Archives, Washington, D.C., especially "Clothing Series" letter books, 1851-1861, and proceedings of boards of officers convened in 1851 and 1862 to revise the army uniform. Useful summaries of Quartermaster equipment can be found in *Official Records*, series 3, vol. II, pp. 615-616; vol. IV, pp. 907-909; vol. V, pp. 275-278.

U.S. Surgeon General, *A Medical Report upon the Uniform and Clothing of the Soldiers of the U.S. Army*, Washington, D.C., 1868 (referred to as *Medical Report*).

U.S. Quartermaster General's Office, *A Sketch of the Organization of the Quartermaster's Department* . . ., Washington, D.C., 1876.

Russell F. Weigley, *Quartermaster General of the Union Army: A Biography of M.C. Meigs,* New York, 1959.

Erna Risch, *Quartermaster Support of the Army: A History of the Corps, 1775-1939,* Washington, D.C., 1962.

John D. Billings, *Hardtack and Coffee,* Boston, 1887.

Wilbur F. Hinman, *Corporal Si Klegg and His "Pard,"* 12 ed., Cleveland, 1900.

Perry Walton, *The Story of Textiles,* New York, 1936.

Arthur H. Cole, *The American Wool Manufacture,* 2 vols., Cambridge, Mass.

Edgar M. Howell and Donald E. Kloster, *United States Army Headgear to 1854, . . ., Volume 1,* Washington, D.C., 1969.

The outstanding collection of original United States Army uniforms of this period is in the Museum of History and Technology, Smithsonian Institution. These date back to about 1845 and there is good reason to believe that the collection originated with pattern uniforms kept at the Office of Army Clothing and Equipage in Philadelphia. We are greatly indebted to Major Edgar M. Howell, Curator of Military History, and his staff for permitting us to examine these uniforms in detail.

The larger collections of contemporary photographs have already been mentioned and these have been especially useful in preparing this and later chapters. We thank the staff of the Prints and Photographs Division, Library of Congress, and especially Miss Josephine Cobb of the National Archives for help in making these materials available.

CHAPTER II

Insignia and Decorations

The contents of this chapter are confined to insignia authorized and worn by the U.S. Army in the period 1851–1872 and, as a result, worn by a large segment of state troops during the same period. It contains no mention of distinctive state or regimental insignia, nor does it discuss naval or Confederate devices, all of which will be covered further along in this book.

The primary effort here, as elsewhere in the study, has been to arrange the objects into logical categories—in the main the categories established by army regulations. Variations within these categories may be mentioned but no attempt has been made to treat them in detail unless they represent a significant change of pattern. Actually, almost all of these variations had their origin in commercial manufacture as a result of accident or design, and played no part in distinguishing one type of soldier from another.

The year 1851 saw several radical changes made in the U.S. system of military insignia. It marked the end of the two-metal system (white for infantry, yellow for artillery, etc.), the formal adoption of distinctive colors for the branches of the service and the regularizing of their distinctive devices, and the establishment of the modern system of rank insignia for both officers and enlisted men.

The chapter will be divided into five sections, as follows:

1. *General Service Insignia.* Devices that were worn by the army at large, usually as an element of an accouterment to identify the wearers as U.S. troops.

2. *Insignia of Branch and Unit.* A large grouping that includes the semi-official insignia of the larger tactical commands of the Civil War, plus regimental devices of the standardized sort.

3. *Insignia of Rank, Function, and Long Service.*

4. *Buttons.*

5. *Medals and Decorations.*

U.S. Army insignia, furthermore, was divided another way: by the War Department agency that prescribed and issued it. Items attached to accouterments related to a soldier's weapons, such as belt and cartridge box plates, were the province of the Ordnance Department; items related to a soldier's clothing came under control of the Quartermaster Department. Semi-official insignia like corps devices were at first procured locally, although the Quartermaster Department came in time to recognize and even issue them.

General Service Insignia

The "Eagle" Cap and Hat Ornament. This device, introduced for wear on all caps in 1851, was made of gold embroidery for officers and yellow metal for men. The latter was a thin stamping of the arms of the U.S., the national eagle being 1.75 inches between wing tips and the entire device slightly under 2.5 inches high. The device is described in heraldic terms in *Army Regulations* (for example, on page 435 of the 1857 *Regulations*). Those designed for use on the hat had two brass wires or a hook-and-eye device soldered on the back for fastening. On the earlier dress cap the eagle was soldered directly to one of two long brass wires integral with the pompon. The eagle did not function as a plume socket.

The officers' eagle was embroidered on a black velvet oval, numerous variations of embroidery being used. The velvet was sewn over a tin plate to which two wire loops were brazed for fastening to the cap.

When the dress hat was introduced the eagle was utilized to hold up the brim. Again two wires were used, but to the rear of some eagles was soldered instead a small iron hook which engaged an eye sewn to the brim of the hat.

The use of a national eagle on headdress was, of course, nothing new in 1851 and the practice has continued in one form or another to the present day. But the eagle in the specific form referred to above is confined to the years of this study, 1851–1872. In both officers' and enlisted men's models the eagle may look to the right or to the left. The black velvet base of the officer's device was usually an oval but examples are known which are almost square. None of these variations have any significance, nor are they of help in determining dates.

The Sword Belt Plate. Since the first years of the century American officers had worn rectangular sword belt plates bearing the arms of the United States. The dress regulations of 1851, however, established a new pattern of this plate for officers and enlisted men that was to endure until World War II with only minor modification. It was prescribed as

> . . . gilt, rectangular, two inches wide, with a raised bright rim; a silver wreath of laurel encircling the "Arms of the United States;" eagle, shield, scroll, edge of cloud and rays bright. The motto, "E PLURIBUS UNUM," in silver letters, upon the scroll; stars also of silver; according to pattern.

No record of the "pattern" has survived and the plate illustrated in the Horstmann edition of these regulations is somewhat misleading. It is 2.75 inches long, which is correct enough, but it shows a fixed extension forming a brass slot on each end. It also shows the eagle looking to sinister. In actual practice the slot on the left side (right as one looks at the plate) was a separate piece which was attached permanently to the belt end, while the eagle—in all but one example known to have been produced in this period—looks to dexter.

Methods of attaching this plate to the sword belt differed but all methods had two things in common. The right end of the belt always passed through a slot cut in the right side of the plate, and at or near the left end of the belt was

Fig. 22

Fig. 23

attached a brass loop so designed that when engaged over the hook on the rear of the plate it matched the slot on the right. Furthermore, on most sword belt plates in this period the hook brazed on the rear was narrow (.5–1.25 inches). By these details the plates of the period can be recognized; after 1872 the slot on the right side was replaced by a long loop on the rear and the hook was widened to almost 2 inches.

The design of the sword belt plate quoted above remained unchanged until after 1872, yet one finds considerable variation in detail and quality, the results of commercial manufacture. Belts sold to officers, of course, were of finer quality than those manufactured under contract for enlisted men. Some plates were cast, others stamped, and one example of thin stamped brass had a lead-filled back to give it body. Belt plates issued enlisted men by the Ordnance Department had the silver wreath applied separately, while those purchased individually, as a rule, had the wreath cast as an integral part of the plate and silvered later. Examples with silvered motto and stars are very rare.

Sword belt plates manufactured by contract can often be distinguished by the presence of a serial number (1 to 999) stamped on the rear and on the separate brass loop. This number served to relate the right loop to a belt plate since, it will be recalled, the loop had to fit snugly to the plate as well as engage the hook on its rear.

The two pieces of insignia just mentioned were specified in dress regulations although only the eagle hat ornament was an article of Quartermaster issue. The next two pieces to be described were Ordnance items, worn only by enlisted men, and are described nowhere in dress regulations. To learn about them one must turn to *Ordnance Manuals* where they are covered in some detail.

The Eagle Shoulder Belt Plate. The leather shoulder belt that held the foot soldier's cartridge box from about 1845 to 1872 was decorated with a circular brass plate having a raised rim and an eagle holding three arrows and an olive branch. The plate was of thin stamped brass with lead-filled back, into which were imbedded the devices for fastening it to the belt. As used non-functionally on the cartridge box belt, the plate had fasteners of iron wire. However, when used on sergeants' shoulder sword belts consisting of two branches, the plate was employed to join the branches. For this purpose it was fitted with three "arrowhead" hooks, or hooks of bent wire.

The shoulder belt plate had a prescribed diameter of 2.5 inches which remained unchanged throughout the period, virtually without exception. There were numerous die variations but, again, the basic design stayed constant.

The "US" Plates. Ordnance Department regulations prescribed that one oval "US" plate be affixed to the flap of the cartridge box and another to the foot soldier's waist belt. This "US" plate dates back at least to the 1840's and, with one unexplained exception, came in two sizes. Both were made of stamped sheet brass with soft solder filling. The two kinds of fastening devices are described under Accouterments; we need here merely review the use given the two sizes, which were 3.5 x 2.2 inches and 2.8 x 1.6 inches:

Infantry cartridge box plate, 1841–c.1865: large (Thereafter sometimes replaced by the same design pressed into the leather flap.)

Infantry waist belt plate, 1841–1857: small

Infantry waist belt plate, 1857–c. 1872: large

Rifle (Mounted) cartridge box plate, 1841–1856: small

Rifle (Mounted) cartridge box plate, 1856–1861: large

Rifle (Mounted) waist belt plate, 1841–1861: large

Dragoon cartridge box plate, 1841–c.1856: small

Dragoon cartridge box plate, c.1856–c.1861: large (Thereafter special boxes which carried no plate came into general use.)

Dragoon waist belt plate, 1841–c.1855: large (Thereafter sword belt plate worn.)

Cavalry cartridge box plate, 1855–c.1861: large (Thereafter special boxes which carried no plate came into general use.)

Cavalry waist belt plate: sword belt plate worn

Foot Artillery cartridge box, 1841–c. 1863: large

Foot Artillery waist belt plate, 1841–1857: 2-piece pattern

Foot Artillery waist belt plate, 1857–c.1872: large

Mounted (Field) Artillery cartridge box plate: usually no box worn

Mounted (Field) Artillery waist belt plate, 1841–c.1855: 2-piece pattern (Thereafter sword belt plate worn.)

Both large and small oval "US" plates were worn in the Civil War although, of course, the former were far more common. The large plates were in the main fabricated at government armories although the Army purchased 257,726 of them from private contractors during the Civil War period. The die variations in this relatively simple device are numerous but there is no indication of a change in specifications during the period.

In addition to the one-piece oval "US" plate, there was a circular, cast-brass, two-piece belt plate prescribed by the 1841 *Ordnance Manual* for use on the white buff leather belt that carried either the artillery sword or saber. The outer diameter of the outside clasp was 1.95 inches, while that of the inside was 1.4 inches. The "US" is .5 inches high, as contrasted with 1.125 inches on the larger oval plate and .825 on the smaller. As noted in the list above, this plate was given up about 1855–1857 in favor of other patterns, although it still saw use in the Civil War.

Insignia of Branch and Unit

Figs. 24 and 26 As has been said above, the dress regulations of 1851 officially inaugurated the system of branch devices which has continued in all essentials to the present day. This is not to say that branch insignia was unknown before; far from it, devices like the infantry bugle and the artillery crossed-cannon were in use prior to 1851. But in that year they were made part of the first regularized

Fig. 20. U.S. Army staff officer in full dress, 1855–1858. Blue frock coat of the *chasseur à pied* pattern, dark blue pants with buff welts, dark blue cap with embroidered devices: gold "eagle," gold wreath with silver "US." The pompon is colored according to the staff department. Gilt buttons, epaulets, belt plate, and gold lace sword knot. Crimson silk net sash.

arrangement of devices embracing all branches. The various insignia are well illustrated in the Horstmann edition of the dress regulations.

Command and Staff. General officers and officers of staff departments (except engineers, topographical engineers, and ordnance) were given an embroidered cap insignia: a silver "U.S." in old English characters, within a golden laurel wreath. Until 1858 the staff departments were, in dress uniform, also distinguished by two-color pompons described below. General officers wore an acorn-shaped pompon of gold on their dress caps.

Fig. 21. Captain Louis Johnes Lambert, Assistant Adjutant General of Volunteers, 1865 (?). A Frenchman by birth, this staff officer won the brevet rank of colonel in March 1865 by repeated acts of gallantry in the field. Here he poses in unusually full dress, including a "light French chapeau", a baldric, gauntlets and epaulets. These last have the half-inch bullion fringe of a field officer although only the two silver bars of a captain—an interesting interpretation of the dress regulations (par. 183, GO 6, 1861). (Library of Congress).

General and staff officers also were identified by various distinctions of uniform and accouterments, listed elsewhere, but by no other kind of insignia unless we include the chapeau device authorized in 1859. This was a 6.5-inch strap of gold braid that was fastened over the black silk cockade of the chapeau. It was 2.5 inches wide, edged with a rope of gold braid, and had fastened to it a large General Staff button, a brass national eagle (very erect and regular in shape), with a silver ribbon above him bearing "E PLURIBUS UNUM."

Dragoons, Mounted Riflemen, and Cavalry. The cap insignia established for dragoons in 1851, besides an orange pompon, was the crossed-sabers, a relatively new device at the time. Previously the six-cornered star and the Napoleonic eagle had been the distinctive insignia of the two regiments. These crossed-sabers were of gold, sheathed, and had their edges upward. The regimental number in silver was placed in the upper angle. They were normally embroidered on the cloth of the cap but brass sabers designed to imitate embroidery were also used. The width of the device seems to have been 3.75 inches.

The crossed-sabers were prescribed only for officers; enlisted dragoons were ordered to wear a brass company letter (and probably the number of their regiment in the case of regimental staff sergeants), one inch high. This cap insignia, except in the case of officers, was not generally worn in the regiments until 1854, when the new model caps began to be issued.

Distinctive dragoon insignia appeared elsewhere than on the cap. Officers wore a 1.75-inch circle of orange cloth within the crescent of their epaulets, edged with silver embroidery and with a gold embroidered regimental number. Enlisted men had orange colored lace or facings and brass 1-inch regimental numbers on each side of their collars. These last could hardly have been in general use with dragoons more than a year or two at the most and some companies probably never received them.

When the two regiments were ordered to wear felt hats on 24 March 1858 (GO 3), the officers' cap insignia was transferred to the hat. Now, however, it was placed "on black velvet ground." This was an oval of velvet (about 2.5 x 4 inches) with a narrow embroidered border and a tin back, fitted with wire loops for easy removal. By these same orders enlisted men also received the crossed-sabers but in yellow metal with a company letter instead of the regimental number, or sometimes both, in the upper angle.

This remained the dragoon and, after 1861, the cavalry hat insignia until 1872. Officers commonly wore small crossed-sabers (1.75–2 inches wide), of metal or embroidered on black or dark blue cloth, on the front of forage caps. Enlisted men often attached their insignia to the top of their caps, and officers at times did likewise. Finally, volunteer cavalrymen wore the same insignia as the regulars, in all its variety, or plain crossed-sabers without further identification.

Mounted Riflemen. Although mounted rifleman insignia were actually regimental devices, they will be included here if for no other reason than that the rifles were considered a branch of the service, to which additional regiments could be added. In 1850, in the tradition of the light corps, the regiment was given the trumpet as a device (GO 2, 13 Feb. 1850). As reaffirmed the next year

(GO 31, 12 June 1851), officers were authorized to wear the trumpet "embroidered in gold, with the number of the regiment in silver, within the bend," standing about 2.5 inches high. Enlisted men wore brass company letters in common with other branches. Facings were "medium or emerald green." Officers had a 1.75-inch circle of this color containing the number "1" inside the crescent of their epaulets, while enlisted riflemen wore "1" on a green collar until about 1854. Pompons, worn until 1858, were emerald green.

In 1858 the officer's trumpet was prescribed as "gold embroidered . . . on a black velvet ground," omitting the regimental number, while enlisted men were given the "trumpet, perpendicular" in brass. The first pattern trumpet was about 3.3 inches high with two crooks on the right. Sometime before the Civil War a smaller pattern was introduced—2.5 inches high, with a single crook on the left. These devices were worn by the rifles until, in 1861, the regiment was redesignated the 3rd Cavalry and given cavalry devices.

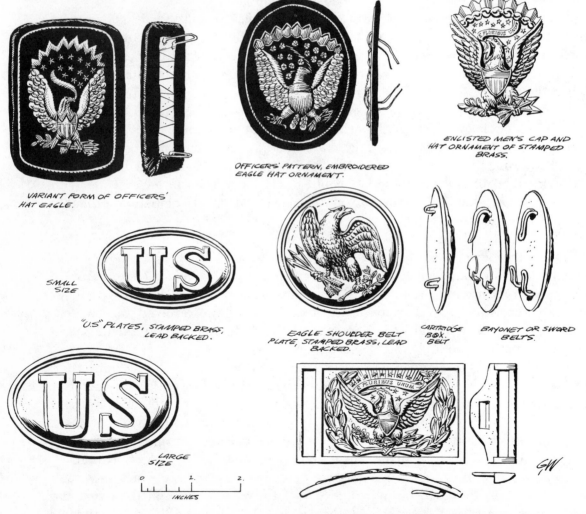

VARIANT FORM OF OFFICERS' HAT EAGLE.

OFFICERS' PATTERN, EMBROIDERED EAGLE HAT ORNAMENT.

ENLISTED MEN'S CAP AND HAT ORNAMENT OF STAMPED BRASS.

SMALL SIZE

"U.S" PLATES, STAMPED BRASS, LEAD BACKED.

EAGLE SHOULDER BELT PLATE, STAMPED BRASS, LEAD BACKED.

CARTRIDGE BOX BELT

BAYONET OR SWORD BELTS.

LARGE SIZE

CONTRACT SWORD BELT, 1861-1865; CAST BRASS WITH SEPARATELY APPLIED WREATH OF SILVER.

Fig. 22. General Service insignia, U.S. Army.

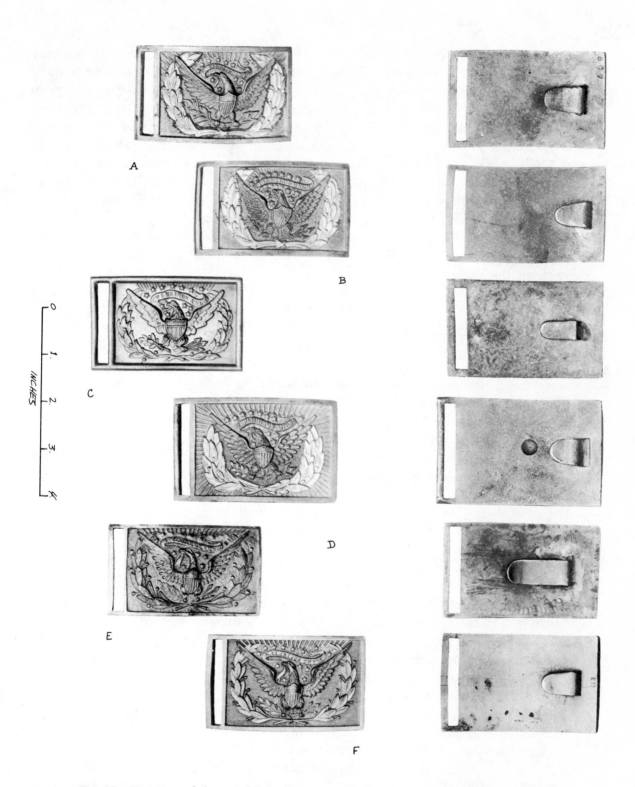

Fig. 23. Variations of the sword belt plate: A. Contract, issue plate, 1861–1865; cast brass with separately applied silvered wreath in three parts; serial no. 567. B. Similar to A but from a different die; serial no. 986. C. Pre-1861 issue plate; thin brass stamping with lead-filled back; no part silvered; no serial number. D. Plate sold to officers, 1861–1865; cast brass with separately applied silvered wreath; no serial number. Note the short wreath and fully rayed background—both non-regulation features. E. Probably a pre-1861 officer's plate; solid brass stamping, hand-burnished, no part silvered; no serial number. F. Contract, issue plate, 1861–1865; solid brass stamping, no part silvered; serial no. 31. (All Smithsonian Institution).

Cavalry (1855–1861). During their first three years or so the two cavalry regiments wore no distinctive insignia, merely company letters and regimental numbers. In 1858, however, they were authorized the same device as dragoons except that the number or letter was placed in the lower angle (GO 7, 24 June). It is possible that, for a time, cavalry officers wore a device with saber edges down, since an example exists and the insignia was briefly regulation.

The regiments were given yellow (rather than orange) trimmings when formed and this they continued to wear. This color appeared on the braiding of jackets, on officers' epaulets, enlisted men's hat cords (after about 1860), etc. In 1861 all mounted troops were designated cavalry and given yellow as their branch color. At the same time all cavalry regiments were given the old dragoon insignia, that is, crossed-sabers with the number or letter, or both, in the upper angle of the sabers.

Artillery. This branch has worn crossed-cannon as its insignia from 1836 to the present day. The 1851 regulations gave officers "gold embroidered cross cannon, with number of the regiment in silver, above the intersection." As with other branches, this device was also manufactured in gilt metal to imitate embroidery. The embroidered cannon came with somewhat different shapes and embellishments but a feature in common was that their muzzle ends were longer than their breech ends. Normally the extreme width was about 2.5 inches, but examples as small as 2 inches are known. Pompons, worn until 1858, were scarlet.

Enlisted men were given only company letters on their caps until 1858. In that year (GO 3) they were authorized as hat insignia a brass crossed-cannon resembling the one worn on the pre-1851 dress caps. With it came a brass regimental number, .625 inches high, and a company letter, 1 inch high, placed over the device. The 1858 pattern crossed-cannon, which can be distinguished from the earlier one by being flatter and having slimmer and longer barrels, was worn, essentially without change, through 1872. Artillerymen put it on top of their forage caps as well as on the front of dress hats. Any combination and placement of the letter and number seems to have been possible.

In 1858 the artillery officer's cap device was changed to a black velvet oval bearing a gold embroidered crossed-cannon, with the regimental number "in silver at the intersection" of the cannon, or in other words, on top of them. This number was embroidered on a black base within a small circle of gold embroidery. As a rule the artillery officer's black velvet oval was a little smaller than that worn by cavalry, from 2.5 x 3.5 to 2.25 x 3 inches. An even smaller or "miniature" size (about 1.5 x 2 inches) was sold commercially for wear on caps, and small embroidered crossed-cannon without the oval were also worn.

Near the close of the Civil War the horse artillery officers of the Army of the Potomac adopted a distinctive badge. No order authorizing it has been found but it is described as a pin with a ribbon showing a laurel wreath and horse, with crossed-cannon, inscribed "Horse Artillery" suspended below the ribbon.

Infantry. The bugle (the round hunting horn of the French *voltigeurs*) was made the infantry device in 1836. In 1851 its metal was changed from silver to gold and infantry officers were authorzied to wear on their caps "a gold em-

broidered bugle, with the number of the regiment in silver, within the bend."
This device was about 2 x 3 inches in size. It went through all the permutations
described above for officer's hat insignia and was widely worn in large and small
sizes throughout our period. Some "ovals" were far from being that shape and
now and then one finds examples with light blue cloth inside the bend. Infantry
pompons were light blue.

After wearing only the company letter, in 1858 the infantry enlisted man also
received the bugle, made of brass, about 3.5 inches wide. As a rule, the regimental number was placed inside the bend with the company letter above the
bugle, but to judge from Civil War photographs the number was at times worn
below the bugle with the letter inside the bend, etc.

Corps of Engineers and Topographical Engineers. The familiar "turretted
castle" device of the engineers was first used on the forage cap and epaulets of
engineer officers in 1840, then on the dress cap of U.S. Military Academy cadets
in 1842. Four years later the same device was given to the Company of Engineer Soldiers at its formation. In the meanwhile engineer officers continued to
wear on the collars of their dress coats the star within a wreath of laurel and
palm, all in gold embroidery, which had long been the insignia of the corps.

The 1851 regulations made the castle the official device of all engineers. Officers wore it, in silver metal, within a gold laurel and palm wreath (about 3
inches overall width). Engineer soldiers continued to wear the brass castle given
them in 1846, which was about 1.75 inches wide. These, with slight modification,
remained the hat insignia of the corps throughout our period. The officers' device
was placed in a black velvet oval in 1858 (GO 3) and in some cases a gold embroidered "US" was placed over the castle (perhaps by U.S. Army officers to
distinguish them from state engineer officers). The pompon prescribed in 1851
for engineer enlisted men was yellow, while engineer and topographical engineer
officers wore a buff one with black top.

Engineer officers wore white metal castles (1.75 inches wide) in the crescents
of their epaulets after 1840, and from 1854 until about 1858 engineer soldiers
wore a brass castle on each side of the collars—the same device worn on their
caps. These brass castles, varying a little in size, were worn during the Civil
War on forage caps and informal field service hats.

A badge described as "two oars crossed over an anchor, the top of which is
encircled by a scroll surmounted by a castle," is illustrated in several sources.
There is no record that this device was ever worn or, for that matter, ever made.

In 1851 officers of the Corps of Topographical Engineers were given a gold
embroidered national shield within a similar wreath of oak leaves, long the corps'
insignia. The shield itself, above the letters "T.E." in silver old English characters,
was embroidered in the epaulet crescent. With the usual changes this remained
the insignia of this tiny group of officers until they were merged with the Corps
of Engineers in 1863.

Although not strictly related to the Corps of Engineers, note should be made
of an interesting badge prescribed for the officers of the Pioneer Brigade, Department of the Cumberland, on 26 April 1864 (GO's 62 and 63, D of Cum).

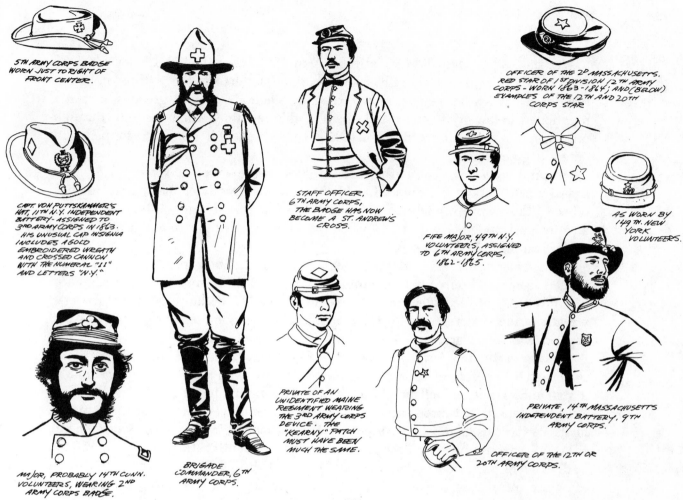

5TH ARMY CORPS BADGE WORN JUST TO RIGHT OF FRONT CENTER.

CAPT. VON PUTTSKAMMER'S HAT, 11TH N.Y. INDEPENDENT BATTERY - ASSIGNED TO 3RD ARMY CORPS IN 1863. HIS UNUSUAL CAP INSIGNIA INCLUDES A GOLD EMBROIDERED WREATH AND CROSSED CANNON WITH THE NUMERAL "11" AND LETTERS "N.Y."

MAJOR, PROBABLY 14TH CONN. VOLUNTEERS, WEARING 2ND ARMY CORPS BADGE.

BRIGADE COMMANDER, 6TH ARMY CORPS.

STAFF OFFICER, 6TH ARMY CORPS, THE BADGE HAS NOW BECOME A ST. ANDREW'S CROSS.

PRIVATE OF AN UNIDENTIFIED MAINE REGIMENT WEARING THE 3RD ARMY CORPS DEVICE. THE "KEARNY" PATCH MUST HAVE BEEN MUCH THE SAME.

OFFICER OF THE 2D MASSACHUSETTS. RED STAR OF 1ST DIVISION 12TH ARMY CORPS - WORN 1863-1864; AND (BELOW) EXAMPLES OF THE 12TH AND 20TH CORPS STAR

FIFE MAJOR, 49TH N.Y. VOLUNTEERS, ASSIGNED TO 6TH ARMY CORPS, 1862-1865.

AS WORN BY 149TH NEW YORK VOLUNTEERS.

OFFICER OF THE 12TH OR 20TH ARMY CORPS.

PRIVATE, 14TH MASSACHUSETTS INDEPENDENT BATTERY, 9TH ARMY CORPS.

Fig. 25.   Corps badges worn in the field.

It consisted of crossed hatchets, probably of enamel on metal in the colors of the divisions to which these officers were assigned, worn on top of the cap.

Ordnance Department.   The "shell and flame" device, associated with the department since about 1833, was made its exclusive insignia in 1851. It was worn by officers in gold embroidery on their dress and forage caps and in silver embroidery on the epaulet crescents. Ordnance enlisted men wore a somewhat similar brass shell and flame on collars and caps. The officers' device was placed on black velvet in 1858 and the soldiers' collar devices were given up. No further changes were made. Ordnance enlisted men wore at first a crimson pompon, officers one of buff topped with crimson.

Left, Fig. 24.   Insignia of branch and unit: A. Command and Staff (embroidered); B. 2nd Dragoon officers (embroidered); C. 2nd Cavalry officers (embroidered); D. Mounted Riflemen enlisted men (first stamped brass pattern); E. Mounted Riflemen officers, 1858 (embroidered); F. Mounted Riflemen enlisted men (second stamped brass pattern); G. Dragoon or Cavalry officers (stamped brass imitating embroidery); H. Dragoon or Cavalry enlisted men, 1858; I. Artillery officers (embroidered); J. Artillery officers (stamped brass imitating embroidery); K. Artillery enlisted men, 1858 (stamped brass); L. Infantry officers (embroidered); M. Infantry officers (stamped brass imitating embroidery); N. Infantry enlisted men, 1858 (stamped brass); O. Corps of Engineers enlisted men (stamped brass; or in silver or white metal if worn by officers); P. Topographical Engineer officers (embroidered); Q. and R. Corps of Engineers officers (embroidered); S. Ordnance Department officers (embroidered); T. Ordnance Department enlisted men (stamped brass).

Medical Department.   Medical officers in 1851 wore the "U.S." device of the staff on their caps but the silver embroidered letters "M.S." with a gold embroidered wreath in their epaulet crescents. Their distinctive green silk sash is mentioned below. With the usual changes this remained their insignia throughout the period. Medical officers in 1851 were given buff pompons topped with emerald green.

Hospital stewards, first authorized in 1856, were given a silver "U.S." in a brass wreath (about 2 inches wide) for their caps and, later, hats. Like medical officers, they wore miniatures of this device on forage caps. Their distinctive arm insignia, together with those worn by other medical personnel, are described under uniforms in Chapter 8.

Pay Department.   This department, so far as military personnel were concerned, contained only officers. From 1851 to 1872 they wore the hat insignia of a staff officer but the silver embroidered letters "P.D." within a gold embroidered wreath inside the crescents on their epaulets. Their pompon until 1858 was buff topped with olive green.

Quartermaster Department.   Like the Pay Department, the military personnel of this staff department consisted solely of officers, who wore the cap insignia of a staff officer with a buff pompon topped with light blue. But during the Civil War the department hired thousands of civilian employees, many of them blacks, at its various installations. To identify these persons the Quartermaster General, in May 1863, approved a design for a badge of identification, and some 20,000 badges were produced under contract. It was a disk, 1.75 in. in diameter, made of white metal and perhaps gilded. In the center was the national eagle and around the edge ran the words "UNITED STATES QUARTER MASTER'S DEP'T." Six holes were provided to permit sewing the badge to clothing. In some instances it was worn on a red background.

Signal Corps.   In 1864 this corps was given its first insignia (GO 36, WDSC, 22 Aug. 1864), a hat device for officers and an arm device for enlisted signalmen. These are described in Chapter 8.

U.S. Military Academy.   Devices worn by cadets, bandsmen, and the teaching staff are described in Chapter 8.

Distinctive Branch Colors.   These colors are detailed in Chapter 8 covering the uniforms of U.S. Army regiments and corps. Yet a few words could be said here about the origins of these branch colors which, formally established in 1851, remain in large measure in effect today.

Dragoons were given yellow trimmings in 1833 but these could hardly be called distinctive since artillerymen were already using yellow at times. However, for reasons not known, dragoon officers were given sashes of "a deep orange color." This seems to have led to the adoption of orange as a distinctive color for dragoons (but not for the mounted arm as a whole) in 1851. When the two cavalry regiments were formed in 1855 it was felt necessary to give them different facings, and yellow—having been largely given up for artillery (see below)—was selected arbitrarily. Six years later all mounted regiments were standardized and a single branch color had to be selected. Apparently orange tended to fade and look like yellow anyway, so the latter was selected. Or, since "cavalry" was the name adopted for everyone, the cavalry color was chosen.

Mounted riflemen, who were always considered more a dismounted than a mounted corps (and had largely been employed on foot in the Mexican War), received green which, for centuries in most countries, had been the accepted color of the rifleman and hunter (note *chasseur, jaeger, cicciatore,* etc.). Why green facings were not given to the 9th and 10th Infantry when they were formed in 1855 to be foot riflemen is not known. Doubtless the exponents of standardization of that day prevailed.

Artillery received scarlet as its branch color, with which it had long been associated. The color certainly went back to the scarlet facings of the Royal Artillery, adopted formally by our Continental Artillery in 1779. When the War Department restored the "Revolutionary Army facings" to the U.S. Army uniform in 1832, scarlet naturally was further formalized.

The association of the artillery with yellow metal, and hence yellow as a color, was equally ancient. But when everyone was given yellow metal in 1851 this distinction was lost. The color ultimately went to cavalry although artillery did not give up its yellow regimental flags until long after the Civil War.

Infantry facings in the American Revolution began as regimental distinctions, then changed to represent brigades or sections of the country. Finally one—white —was adopted for all the infantry. In 1832 white was brought back as its branch color and remained exclusively so until 1851. Apparently the fact that white soiled so easily led to a change and light blue was adopted instead, with dark blue replacing it when necessary.

The other colors adopted in 1851 seem to be the result of compromise or sheer arbitrary decision. Engineer soldiers were given yellow, for example, possibly due to their one-time association with artillery.

Green was selected as the color to distinguish officers of the Medical Department in 1851 by providing them—alone of all the army—with a green silk sash. Green also was used on pompons and later on the sleeve insignia of hospital orderlies, but these men also wore crimson piping and stripes and it can hardly be said that green—also used for mounted riflemen—was a branch color. Yet it was not entirely discarded by the Medical Department until 1901 when maroon was adopted.

Pompons. All ranks wore colored pompons on their dress caps until 1858. Those for enlisted men and usually officers of the main branches (dragoons, artillery, infantry, mounted riflemen, engineers, and ordnance) were in solid branch colors. The others, worn by staff officers, were usually in two colors—the lower two-thirds buff and the top third as follows.

Adjutants General: white
Inspectors General: scarlet
Subsistence Department: ultramarine blue
Quartermasters: light blue
Medical Department: emerald green
Pay Department: dark olive green

Engineers and Topographical Engineers: black

Ordnance: crimson

Aides-de-camp wore all buff pompons, and Judge Advocates, all white.

These pompons were permanently attached at the base to a gold netted circular ring and an "Eagle" of embroidery or stamped brass, which in turn was attached to the cap front.

Hat Cords. When the Model 1858 felt hat was first introduced (GO 3, 24 March 1858) a hat cord of black and yellow mixed was prescribed for all arms. On 8 May of the same year the Adjutant General ordered that all cords be made of branch color and be fitted with tassel ends, but the order does not seem to have been carried out until about 1860. In this manner were cords of branch color introduced into the army.

Fig. 26. Drum Major Henry S. Peck, 20th Connecticut Volunteer Infantry, 1862. His office on the NCO Staff of the regiment (which appears to have entitled him to an officer's sword and belt, red sash and the unusual chevrons with tasselled arc) was abolished in December of that year. He seems to wear an all dark blue uniform with officer's trousers; sky blue chevrons and trousers welts, probably gold fringe on chevrons. (By Michael J. McAfee, after photograph).

Corps and Division Badges

The desire of a body of soldiers to fight under a distinctive emblem or device of some sort is as old as history, and in this respect there was nothing novel in the widespread adoption of corps badges during the Civil War. What was novel was the transfer of the symbolism, as it were, from the regimental level to a higher one. The reasons for this are clear: a great number of new regiments without traditions, a rapid dwindling of regimental strengths and hence individual significance in combat, and a new feeling of permanence given the higher commands from 1863 on.

Fig. 25

Corps and division insignia, as we shall see, were in the main official and regulated. During the war period they were displayed principally in two ways: as devices on headquarters flags and as badges on clothing. The former use will be described in some detail in the chapter on Army Colors and Flags and there it is pointed out that the history of these flags is confused and often legendary. The same can be said for corps badges. It is difficult now to say which of the two came first, but there can be little doubt that the badge worn on the uniform played a far greater role in the life of the common soldier than did the flag, which he rarely saw.

Corps badges at first took the form of distinctive shapes cut out of colored cloth—red for a 1st division, white for a 2nd, blue for a 3rd. Such a badge was unmarked and roughly sewn to a hat or coat. In all ways it was simple to procure and apply in the field. Gradually more sophisticated badges made their appearance, especially among officers, either embroidered or, more commonly, made of metal with enamelled designs. Finally, following the war, these badges were manufactured in metallic form and in large quantities for veteran societies with the result that today we can distinguish those used during the war only with great difficulty.

The corps badge was a mark of the combat soldier and was worn proudly as such. By 1864 probably two-thirds of the fighting men of the Union Army wore a badge of some kind. A few corps failed to adopt badges and perhaps some organizations wore them without our knowledge today. The badges we know about and how they appear to have been worn are listed below in condensed form with no pretense that the list is comprehensive. The order of divisional colors is always red-white-blue unless noted otherwise.

The first actual use of an identifying patch occurred in Major General Philip Kearny's 3rd Division, 3rd Corps. The usual story is that Kearny, mistakenly reprimanding some officers of another division, determined to find some way of identifying his own officers in the field. On 28 June 1862 he ordered that "a piece of red flannel (2) two inches square" be sewn to the top of their caps. After his death in September of that year his successor, General D.B. Birney issued an order which read in part:

> To still further show our regard [for the memory of General Kearny], and
> to distinguish his officers as he wished, each officer will continue to wear

on his cap a piece of scarlet cloth or have the top or crown-piece on the cap made of scarlet cloth.

It seems clear that this first badge was intended only for wear by officers and was not thought of as a mark of esprit de corps. But Kearny was a gallant and popular leader and soon the enlisted men of his command, without sanction of orders, cut out their own cap badges. Quickly the device became known as the "Kearny Patch" and today is even better known by its fictitious name, "The Red Badge of Courage." No doubt many of these homemade badges were anything but square, which has led some historians to write that the patch was round or just a piece of red cloth. Kearny is said to have given up his own red blanket to be cut into the first patches and any sort of red fabric must have been used for the others.

The next instance of a corps badge was a square or diamond patch adopted by the 1st Division, 9th Corps in February 1863 and described below. We have no idea to what extent this patch (seemingly the same as the Kearny patch) was worn or for how long. On 19 March the 9th Corps was removed from the Army of the Potomac and ordered to the Department of the Ohio. As a result it was not included in the general assignment of corps badges made two days later by the Army of the Potomac.

It is with this assignment of badges on 21 March 1863 (Circular, A of P) that the real story of the devices begins. Major General Joseph Hooker had become commander of the Army of the Potomac on 26 January 1863 and he sought ways to bolster its sagging morale. He must have recalled the Kearny Patch and realized it was more than a mark of identification. In his imaginative Chief of Staff, Major General Daniel Butterfield, he had the ideal man to carry out a plan to give comparable devices to the Army of the Potomac. This task Butterfield accomplished, and history has, with apparent justice, given him much of the credit for the plan.

Below are listed the known corps badges, when they were adopted, and how they were usually worn. Most, but not all, were colored to designate the divisions within the corps. It must be borne in mind that here we shall speak only of badges worn on uniforms; corps flags are detailed in Volume II.

1st Army Corps, Army of the Potomac (12 Sept 1862–24 March 1864). Disk or circle (sometimes called "the full moon"), prescribed 21 March 1863 (Cir A of P). Worn on the top of the cap or front of the hat by enlisted men and commissioned officers. When the corps badge was worn on the straw hat it was placed in front on the ribbon of the hat, the bow of the ribbon on the left side. When the 1st Corps was merged into the 5th Corps its men were allowed to keep the circle device, sometimes adding a Maltese cross inside.

1st Army Corps, Veteran Volunteers (28 Nov 1864–11 July 1866). Septagon sunburst, prescribed 18 June 1865 (GO 6, 3rd Brig, 1st AC). Worn on the top of the cap or front of the hat by enlisted men and commissioned officers. When hats were worn the corps badge was placed in front with the number of the regiment in white metal in the center of the badge. Same rule applied when the corps badge was worn on the top of the cap.

2nd Army Corps, Army of the Potomac (3 March 1862–28 June 1865). Trefoil (three-leaf clover called "clubs" by its wearers), prescribed 21 March 1863 (Cir A of P). Worn on the top of the cap by enlisted men and commissioned officers. 1st Division orders directed that when the badge was worn on top of the cap, the number of the regiment was placed below it and the letter of the company above.

3rd Army Corps, Army of the Potomac (3 March 1862–24 March 1864). Square adopted 28 June 1862 by Kearny's 3rd Division (see above); worn on top of cap by company officers and many enlisted men, and on front of cap by field officers. Lozenge (diamond) prescribed 21 March 1863 (Cir A of P). Worn on the top of the cap, or front or side of the hat, by enlisted men and commissioned officers. The badge of the artillery was multi-colored. The arrangement of the colors denoted the divisional assignment. Although GO 3, Hqrs. 3rd Army Corps, 6 Sept. 1863, directs that the badge be worn on the top of the cap or front of the hat, some historians claim it was generally worn on the left side of the cap.

When broken up in 1864 it is believed the men of the 1st and 2nd Divisions were permitted to continue wearing the diamond on their caps.

4th Army Corps, Army of the Cumberland (28 Sept 1863–1 Aug 1865). Equilateral triangle, prescribed 26 April 1864 (GO 62, D of Cum). Worn on the top of the cap or front of the hat by enlisted men and commissioned officers.

5th Army Corps, Army of the Potomac (18 May 1862–28 June 1865). Maltese cross, prescribed 21 March 1863 (Cir A of P). Worn on top of the cap and on the right side of the hat. Also known to have been worn on left side of hat.

6th Army Corps, Army of the Potomac; Army of the Shenandoah (18 May 1862–28 June 1865). Greek cross, prescribed 21 March 1863 (Cir A of P). Worn on top of the cap, and when officers wore a hat it was usually placed on the right side. Photographs also show it pinned on the left of the coat.

The badge was first worn as a Greek cross; later orders of various divisions authorized its wear as the St. Andrews cross in conjunction with a regimental number.

7th Army Corps, Dept of Arkansas (6 Jan 1864–1 Aug 1865). Inverted crescent with star, prescribed 1 June 1865 (Cir D of Ark). Order did not specify where badge was to be worn, but a photograph shows it pinned on left breast.

The frontier cavalry of this corps wore a spur device with shank bent to the shape of a "7", curb chain, and crescent and star suspended. Probably pinned on breast.

8th Army Corps, Middle Dept (22 July–1 Aug 1865). Six pointed star said to have been worn, but no order was published and nothing is known about manner of wearing badge.

9th Army Corps, Army of the Potomac; Dept of the Ohio; Dept of Washington (22 July 1862–1 Aug 1865). Square or diamond prescribed for 1st Division, 10 Feb 1863 (Cir 1st Div, 9th AC). Worn on the top of the cap as a square by field officers, and as a diamond by staff officers. Worn as a square on the front of the cap by line officers, on the right side by non-commissioned officers, and on the left side of the cap by privates. Possibly not worn in the West.

When the corps returned to the East it adopted, 10 April 1864 (GO 6, 9th AC), a shield with foul anchor crossed with a cannon, sometimes bearing the figure "9." Worn on the top of the cap or left side of hat by enlisted men and commissioned officers. Orders also authorized the wearing of this badge as a medal if so desired. The medal could be manufactured of gold, gilt, silver, or white metal, bronze or copper. It was to be attached to the left breast of the coat as a pin or suspended by a red, white, and blue ribbon. References indicate the general and his staff wore quite expensive badges of great appeal. There are at least four variations of this shield.

Probably because of the expense, a plain cloth shield was authorized 23 Dec 1864 (GO 49, 9th AC; GO 66, 1st Div, 9th AC, 28 Dec 1864). Worn on the top of the cap by enlisted men and commissioned officers. Worn on the left side of the hat by commissioned officers. Enlisted men were directed to wear the plain cloth shield. However, they were authorized to wear the more ornate shield with embroidered cannon and anchor if they desired. This corps for a time had a 4th Division whose badge was green.

10th Army Corps, Army of the James (28 April–3 Dec 1864). Four-bastioned fort, prescribed 25 July 1864 (GO 18, 10th AC). Worn on the top of the cap and the side of the hat by enlisted men and commissioned officers.

11th Army Corps, Army of the Potomac; Dept of the Cumberland (12 Sept 1862–14 April 1864). Crescent, prescribed 21 March 1863 (Cir A of P). Worn on top of cap. Probably retained by 1st Div when transferred on 3 Sept 1863 to 10th Corps. It is said that elements of this corps retained the crescent by combining it with the star after merger into the 20th Corps.

12th Army Corps, Army of the Potomac; Army of the Cumberland (12 Sept 1862–4 April 1864). Five-pointed star, prescribed 21 March 1863 (Cir A of P). Worn on top of cap, front of hat, or pinned on left breast by officers; on side of hat and elsewhere by enlisted men. This badge was continued by the 20th Army Corps.

14th Army Corps, Army of the Cumberland; Army of Georgia (24 Oct 1862–1 Aug 1865). Acorn, prescribed 26 April 1864 (GO 62, D of Cum). Worn on the top of the cap or the left side of the hat by enlisted men and commissioned officers.

15th Army Corps, Army of the Tennessee (18 Dec 1862–1 Aug 1865). Cartridge box with words "40 ROUNDS," prescribed 14 Feb 1865 (GO 10, 15th AC). The order directed that the badge be worn on hat or cap without specifying position. The 4th Division wore a yellow badge and corps HQ wore one including the four colors. Effort was made by the corps commander to have every soldier wear the badge.

16th Army Corps, Army of the Tennessee; Army of the Gulf (18 Dec 1862–20 July 1865). Circular Maltese cross ("A.J. Smith Cross"), said to represent a circle with four Minie-balls, points toward the center, cut out of it. No order for adoption found, and no clear record that badge was ever worn.

17th Army Corps, Army of the Tennessee; Army of the Gulf (18 Dec. 1862–1 Aug 1865). Following the use of another device so far not identified, arrow, prescribed 25 March 1865 (GO 1, 17th AC). Divisions wore an arrow 2 inches long, corps HQ, 1.5 inches long. Orders specify only that the badge was to be worn on the hat or cap by enlisted men and commissioned officers. A painting by James E. Taylor in *Campfire and Battlefield* shows an officer wearing the badge on the left side of the hat.

18th Army Corps, Dept of North Carolina; Army of the James (24 Dec 1862–3 Dec 1864). Cross-bottony, prescribed 7 June 1864 (Cir 18th AC). This circular prescribed a complex system of badges and their wear. General and staff officers were to wear gilt metal crosses suspended by a tri-colored ribbon from the left breast, line officers by a ribbon of divisional color. The badge for division commanders had a triangle superimposed on it, brigade commanders had their brigade number on the badge, and cavalry and artillery officers had further distinctions. Enlisted men were given plain crosses of cloth sewn to the left breast.

This system was somewhat simplified by General E.O.C. Ord (GO 108, 18th Corps, 25 Aug 1864) by requiring line officers and enlisted men to wear plain crosses of divisional color, officers on the left breast and enlisted men on the top of the cap or front of the hat.

19th Army Corps, Army of the Gulf; Army of the Shenandoah (14 Dec 1862–20 March 1865). Fan-leaved cross, prescribed 17 Nov 1864 (GO 11, 19th AC). The coloring prescribed is unusual in that it ran *red* for 1st Div, *blue* for 2nd, and *white* for 3rd. Cloth badges for enlisted men, metallic for officers. Worn on the top of the cap or side of hat by enlisted men and on the left breast by commissioned officers.

20th Army Corps, Army of the Cumberland (4 April 1864–1 June 1865). Five-pointed star, previously worn by 12th Army Corps, continued in use (GO 62, D of Cum, 26 April 1864). Worn on top of the cap or left side of the hat, although photographs exist showing it pinned on the left breast.

22nd Army Corps, Dept of Washington (2 Feb 1863–11 June 1866). A quinque foliate device (pentagonal cross) worn on top of the cap; apparently adopted without orders.

23rd Army Corps, Army of the Ohio; Dept of North Carolina (27 April 1863–1 Aug 1865). Shield, prescribed 25 Sept 1864 (Spec Field O 121, D of Ohio). The order directs that the badge worn by enlisted men was to be an inch and a quarter in width. It does not say where it was to be worn or whether officers were required to wear it.

24th Army Corps, Army of the James (3 Dec 1864–1 Aug 1865). Heart, prescribed 18 March 1865 (GO 32, 24th AC). The order does not specify where the badge was to be worn. Available sketches of the period show it was worn on the top of the cap.

25th Army Corps, Army of the James; Army of Occupation in Texas (3 Dec 1864–8 Jan 1866). Square prescribed 20 Feb 1865 (Orders, 25th AC). The order does not specify where the badge was to be worn. A photograph of an officer shows the badge on the front of the cap.

Army of West Virginia (28 June 1863–27 June 1865). Eagle adopted 3 Jan 1865 (GO 2, D of W Va). The department order directs that all officers and enlisted men wear the department badge, but orders only the enlisted men to wear it upon the hat or cap. It is assumed from this that the officers were to wear it upon the breast.

[Sheridan's] Cavalry Corps, Army of the Potomac (Feb 1863–May 1865). Glory in silver surrounding an oval of division color, on which are gold crossed-sabers; device adopted in late 1864; no order published. Available samples of this badge show it could be worn as a pin although photographs show it suspended on the left breast from a ribbon. Few, if any, enlisted men wore this badge. Apparently most common with blue center although red is known.

The 3rd Division of this corps, commanded by General Custer, March–May 1865, adopted their leader's symbol, a red kerchief. A photograph of Custer in the uniform of a major general shows this kerchief, which is pinned by an unusual insignia, a five-pointed star above a Maltese cross lacking the top portion.

[Wilson's] Cavalry Corps, Military Division of the Mississippi (29 Oct 1864–26 June 1865). Spencer carbine with swallow-tailed guidon suspended below, adopted in June 1865; no order published. It is assumed this was worn on the breast since the carbine was worn as a pin with a ribbon the color of the division suspended below.

Insignia of Rank, Function, and Long Service

This category of insignia can conveniently be divided into the epaulets, shoulder straps, and cuff braids of officers; the epaulets and brass scales of enlisted men; chevrons and half chevrons; plus a small group of furnishings that served the purpose of insignia of function. While most of the devices here mentioned also indicated the wearer's branch of service, their primary task was to show rank.

Epaulets and Shoulder Straps for Officers

The officer's epaulet established in 1851 differed only in details from the preceding model. It is well illustrated in the Horstmann edition and remained unchanged until 1872. It was made of gold lace with a solid gilded brass crescent, rigid strap topped by an appropriate small button, and "dead and bright" gold bullion fringe. Each pair contained a right and a left, with straps shaped to fit the shoulders. It tended to differ from earlier types by having an ornate roll of gilt thread embroidery around the outer edge of the crescent, by employing "straight" rather than "broken" cords of gilt lace on the strap, and by greater use of patent fasteners and leather rather than silk linings. *Fig. 27*

So called patent fasteners had been used on epaulets since the 1830's. A common form utilized an open brass strap on the underside which passed through cloth loops on the shoulder of the coat and was secured to the epaulet button by a spring clip. Another comprised a brass channel on the underside that slid over a stud near the arm seam of the coat and a spring mounted hook that fastened to the button. Prior to the Civil War it was usually possible to mount shoulder straps in the same loops or studs for undress wear, but after 1861 epaulets were so rarely worn that straps were sewn directly to the shoulders.

Epaulets came with three sizes of bullion fringe. For general and field officers it was 3.5 inches long and .5 inch in diameter; for captains it was 2.5 inches long and .25 inch in diameter; for lieutenants, the same length but only .125 inches in diameter. The ends of the fringes were sewn together in this period but only in examples purchased abroad were they fastened to a stiff inner lining.

The strap of the epaulet carried the insignia of rank in silver metal and (except for general officers) the area inside the crescent held a regimental or corps device. The rank devices in 1851 were

> *General in Chief (Winfield Scott himself).* Three silver embroidered stars in graduated sizes, the largest inside the crescent, 1.5, 1.25 and 1.125 inches in diameter.
> *Major General.* Two silver embroidered stars, 1.5 and 1.25 inches in diameter.
> *Brigadier General.* A single 1.5-inch star.
> *Colonel.* Silver embroidered eagle.
> *Lieutenant Colonel.* Silver embroidered oak leaf.
> *Major.* No insignia.
> *Captain.* Two silver embroidered bars.
> *1st Lieutenant.* One silver embroidered bar.
> *2nd Lieutenant.* No insignia (he was distinguished from a major by the smaller size of his bullion).

Epaulets were widely worn by officers, regulars and state troops alike, before 1861. Thereafter they were almost entirely replaced by shoulder straps. Following the Civil War epaulets enjoyed a partial revival but their high cost rendered them increasingly unpopular and in 1872 they were given up (except for general officers) by the regular army and most state corps.

Shoulder straps were worn when the epaulet was not; that is, for all occasions except full dress. There was no difference in the regulation size of shoulder straps *Fig. 29* (1.375 x 4 inches) and all had borders of gold embroidery. These borders were .25 inches by regulation but it was possible to buy straps with wider borders. The "extra rich" border was .375 inches wide, which reduced the inside dimensions, while straps with two or three rows of border could reach an overall size of 2 x 4.75 inches.

The gold embroidered border in 1851 was sewn on cloth of branch coloring for dragoons, mounted riflemen, artillery, and infantry; all others used dark blue. In 1855 shoulder straps of yellow cloth were added for officers of cavalry (GO 4) and in 1861 the dragoon's orange and rifleman's green was removed from the list. No other changes were made in these colors.

The rank devices on shoulder straps were the same as on epaulets with four exceptions. General officers' stars were made the same size (except those of the

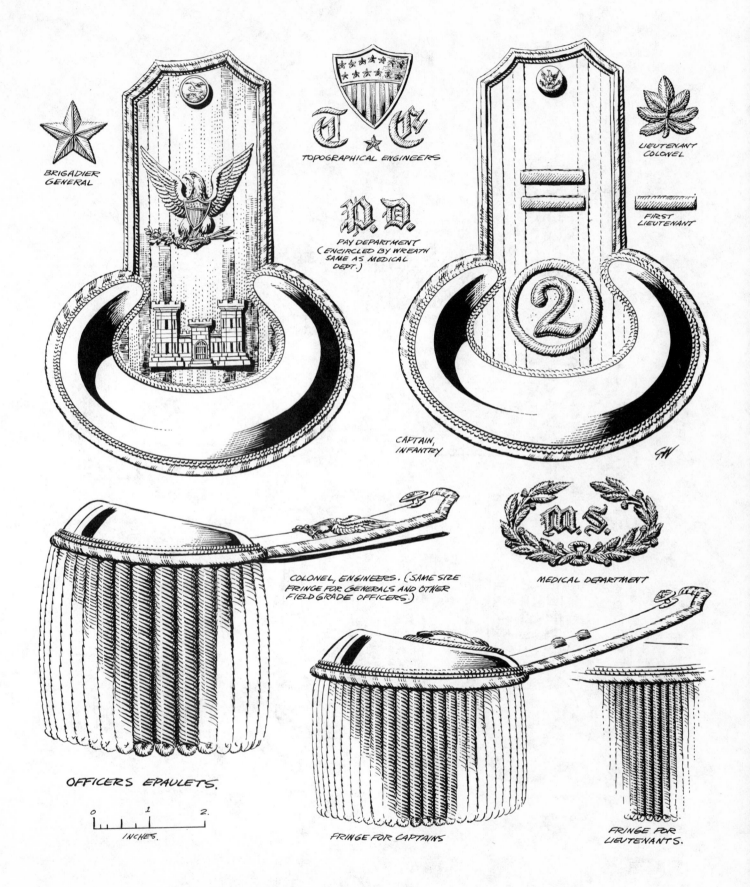

Fig. 27. Officers' epaulets, U.S. Army.

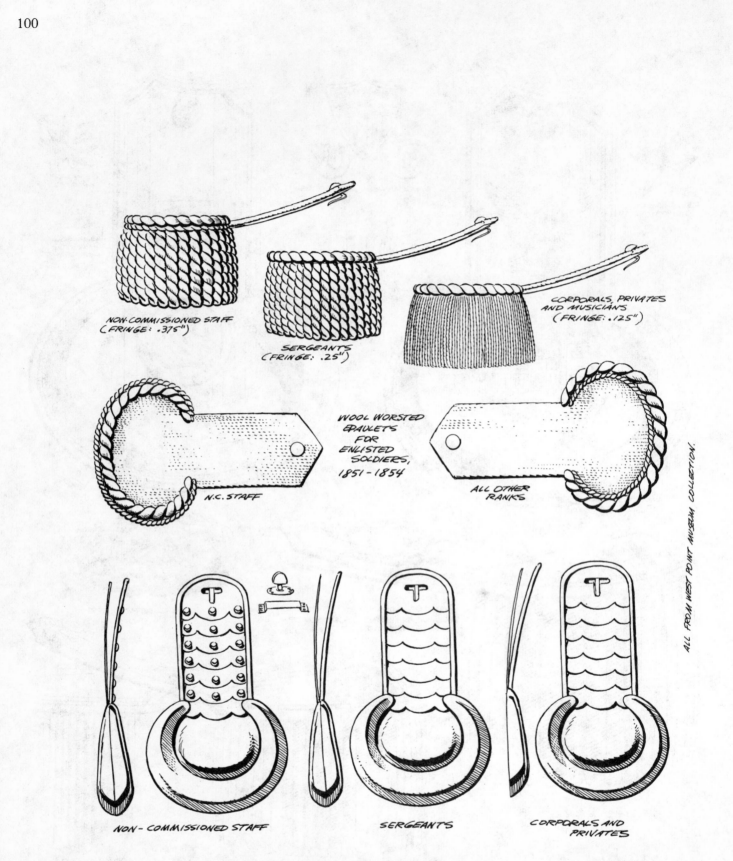

NON-COMMISSIONED STAFF
(FRINGE: .375")

SERGEANTS
(FRINGE: .25")

CORPORALS, PRIVATES
AND MUSICIANS
(FRINGE: .125")

WOOL WORSTED
EPAULETS
FOR
ENLISTED
SOLDIERS,
1851-1854

N.C. STAFF

ALL OTHER
RANKS

ALL FROM WEST POINT MUSEUM COLLECTION.

NON-COMMISSIONED STAFF

SERGEANTS

CORPORALS AND
PRIVATES

BRASS SCALES FOR ENLISTED SOLDIERS,
1854-1872

Fig. 28 Enlisted men's epaulets and brass scales, U.S. Army.

Major General Commanding the Army, later Lieutenant General, whose center star was slightly larger than the others. The colonel's eagle was more flatly shaped to fit the strap. A pair of gold embroidered oak leaves was given the major, who no longer had an epaulet fringe to distinguish him from a 2nd lieutenant.

Two new rank insignia came as a result of the Civil War. The medical cadet, established in 1861, was given a strip of gold lace, 3 inches long and .5 inches wide, on a patch of green cloth 3.75 x 1.25 inches. And the rank of general was created in 1866 (GO 75), indicated by four silver embroidered stars of equal size on the shoulder straps.

Cuff Braids. Rank was indicated on the cuff of the officer's cloak coat by knots of flat black silk braid, .125 inches wide. The 2nd lieutenant's sleeve was bare; other officers up to generals wore a "single" knot of three loops composed of from one to five braids as follows.

Fig. 29

> *1st Lieutenant.* 1 braid
> *Captain.* 2 braids
> *Major.* 3 braids
> *Lieutenant Colonel.* 4 braids
> *Colonel.* 5 braids

General officers wore a "double" knot of five loops and five braids.

These knots should not be confused with those worn by Confederate officers, which were all double knots of from one to four gold lace braids. Nor should they be confused with the non-regulation gold braid knots worn by officers of zouave regiments, based usually on French patterns.

Epaulets and Scales for Enlisted Men

Between 1851 and 1854 dismounted men were given worsted epaulets of branch color as follows.

> *Artillery.* Scarlet
> *Infantry.* Light or Saxony blue
> *Engineers.* Yellow
> *Ordnance.* Crimson
> *Mounted Rifleman.* Medium or emerald green

Fig. 28

In addition to indicating thus a soldier's branch, these epaulets showed his rank by the size of their 3-inch twisted worsted fringes. For the non-commissioned staff the fringe width was .375 inch; for sergeants, .25 inch; for corporals, privates, and musicians, .125 inch.

These epaulets had two double twisted worsted cords for crescents; straps of coarse twill weave over tinned plate, pointed at the top; three rows of fringes 3 inches long on the outside and often held in place at the bottom by a cord which ran through their lower ends. They were fastened to the coat by means of a hook at the pointed end of the strap and a loop of cloth on each shoulder through which the strap was passed. Although a uniform button was still sewn to the strap, it had ceased to be functional after 1851.

In 1854 (GO 1) all worsted epaulets were withdrawn and replaced by brass scales, which had been worn only by mounted men up to that time. Scales were known by several names. The 1851 regulations called them "shoulder knots," but by 1854 the official term was usually "metallic scales." The name "shoulder straps (brass)" is also found in correspondence of the Quartermaster General in the early 1850's.

Prior to 1851 or 1852 brass scales seem to have been issued in two patterns, one for the non-commissioned staff and the second for other enlisted men of dragoons and light artillery. The latter pattern is probably the one illustrated in the Horstmann regulations—about 6.5 inches overall length, with a strap 2.5 inches wide with clipped corners, and a crescent, half-round in profile. The former is more difficult to identify. It could have had a brass replica fringe, 1.9 inches long, or it could have been fitted with wire clips underneath to hold a real fringe. Examples of both of these types have survived.

Beginning in 1855 correspondence about clothing consistently mentions three patterns of brass scales, and these patterns appear to have continued in use throughout the rest of our period. A shipment to the newly organized 10th Infantry in April 1855 will give an idea of the relative numbers of each pattern issued:

"4 pairs   NCS scales
40 pairs   Sergeants scales
800 pairs   Privates scales."

The private's scale (the pattern commonly found today) had seven scalloped surfaces on a strap 2.2 inches wide with rounded end and a half-round, 4-inch wide crescent. The strap was edged all around. The sergeant's scale had the same strap but its crescent was slightly larger (4.5 inches) and fully rounded in profile. The non-commissioned staff scale was similar to the sergeant's except that on six of the scallops are three small round-head rivets, making eighteen in all. These patterns can be detected in Quartermaster series of photographs, mentioned in the Preface, although there are inconsistencies in their use. Specimens of the private's scale exist with a covering of brass soldered to the underside of the crescent, probably for reinforcement.

Scales were attached by means of open brass straps that passed through cloth or brass loops on the shoulder and over brass staples sewn on near the collar. These staples fitted through T-shaped holes in the strap of the scales and were capable of being "locked" in place.

Chevrons

The chevron, used as a cloth insignia on the arm of a uniform coat, was introduced into the French army in 1771 as a mark of long service, and retained this significance for over a century. It was adopted by the British army as a badge of rank in 1802, and first appeared in the American service in 1817 on the arms

Fig. 29

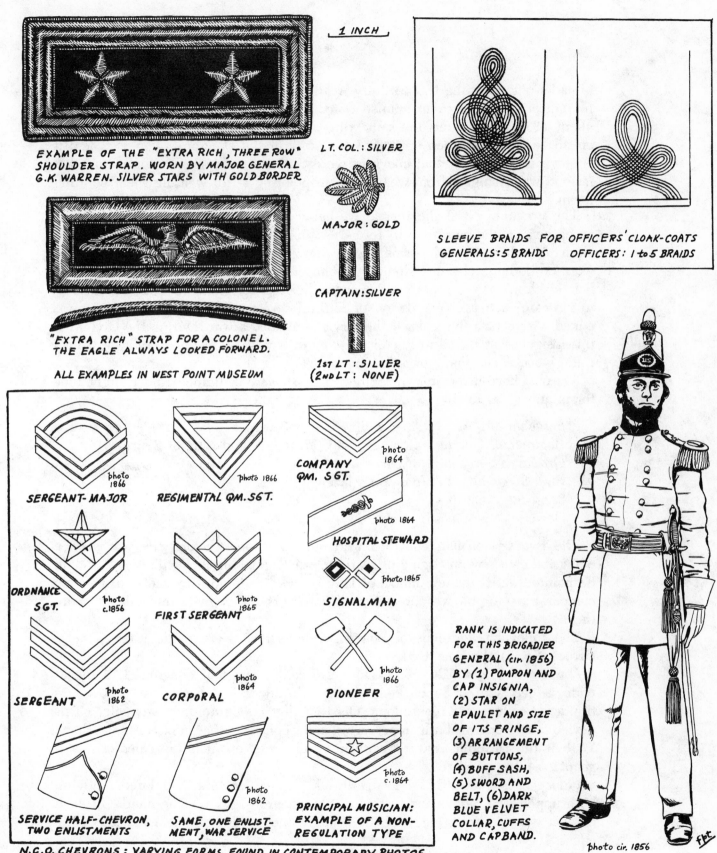

103

EXAMPLE OF THE "EXTRA RICH, THREE ROW" SHOULDER STRAP. WORN BY MAJOR GENERAL G.K. WARREN. SILVER STARS WITH GOLD BORDER

"EXTRA RICH" STRAP FOR A COLONEL. THE EAGLE ALWAYS LOOKED FORWARD.

ALL EXAMPLES IN WEST POINT MUSEUM

1 INCH

LT. COL.: SILVER

MAJOR: GOLD

CAPTAIN: SILVER

1ST LT: SILVER
(2ND LT: NONE)

SLEEVE BRAIDS FOR OFFICERS' CLOAK-COATS
GENERALS: 5 BRAIDS   OFFICERS: 1 to 5 BRAIDS

SERGEANT-MAJOR   REGIMENTAL QM. SGT.   COMPANY QM. SGT. photo 1864

photo 1866   photo 1866

HOSPITAL STEWARD photo 1864

ORDNANCE SGT. photo c.1856   FIRST SERGEANT photo 1865   SIGNALMAN photo 1865

SERGEANT photo 1862   CORPORAL photo 1864   PIONEER photo 1866

SERVICE HALF-CHEVRON, TWO ENLISTMENTS   SAME, ONE ENLISTMENT, WAR SERVICE photo 1862   PRINCIPAL MUSICIAN: EXAMPLE OF A NON-REGULATION TYPE photo c.1864

N.C.O. CHEVRONS: VARYING FORMS FOUND IN CONTEMPORARY PHOTOS

RANK IS INDICATED FOR THIS BRIGADIER GENERAL (cir. 1856) BY (1) POMPON AND CAP INSIGNIA, (2) STAR ON EPAULET AND SIZE OF ITS FRINGE, (3) ARRANGEMENT OF BUTTONS, (4) BUFF SASH, (5) SWORD AND BELT, (6) DARK BLUE VELVET COLLAR, CUFFS AND CAPBAND.

photo cir. 1856

Fig. 29. Insignia of rank, U.S. Army.

of cadet officers at the U.S. Military Academy. The U.S. Army adopted chevrons for officers and non-commissioned officers in 1821, abolished them for officers about 1830, and around the same time authorized a long service chevron for enlisted men. From then until 1851 the story of the chevron is confused and it is only possible to say that chevrons were confined to fatigue uniforms and that fashion was changing from wearing them pointing up to wearing them pointing down.

The system of NCO chevrons as we know it today began in 1851. With a few exceptions all chevrons used in 1851–1872 pointed down, were of branch-colored cloth, .5 inch wide, with a small space between stripes. Chevrons of rank were worn on both upper arms, extending from seam to seam. In addition, a "diagonal half chevron" of the same width was authorized for wear on both lower arms to indicate each five-year period of faithful service, and this half chevron was edged with contrasting color if the service included a war. During the Civil War this insignia was issued to re-enlisted men of a veteran regiment and was sometimes worn in the shape of a "V" on the left coat sleeve.

The six chevrons of rank prescribed in 1851 were of branch colors (light blue for infantry), as follows.

> *Sergeant Major.*   3 stripes and an arc of 3 stripes
> *Regimental Quartermaster Sergeant.*   3 stripes and a tie of 3 stripes
> *Ordnance Sergeant.*   3 stripes and a star
> *First Sergeant.*   3 stripes and a lozenge
> *Sergeant.*   3 stripes
> *Corporal.*   2 stripes

The two service half chevrons were also of branch colors, the war service being indicated by an edging of scarlet cloth (light blue for artillery). It should be pointed out that these marks of long service were worn by enlisted men; no comparable insignia was prescribed for officers although a few officers wore them.

The following additions or changes in chevrons were made after General Orders No. 31, 12 June 1851.

● *Hospital Steward (GO 53, 1851).*   Emerald green half chevron, 1.75 inches wide, edged with .125-inch yellow silk embroidery and bearing a yellow embroidered caduceus, 2 inches long. Occasionally the embroidery was gold. (This device was worn on both upper arms and replaced other rank insignia there. With it the Hospital Steward wore, for full dress, epaulets or scales of a sergeant.)

● *Pioneer (GO 53, 1851).*   Two crossed hatchets in branch colored cloth on both upper arms, above and resting on the chevrons, if any. The handle of each hatchet was 4.5 inches long and the heads, 2 inches long and 1 inch wide at the edges.

● *Hospital and Ambulance Personnel (1862–1865).*   Various chevrons and half chevrons of green, the former having points toward the shoulder. Each Federal field army tended to establish its own system.

● *Signalmen (GO 36, WDSC, 1864 and GO 88, AGO, 1868)*. Crossed signal flags, red and white, on dark blue cloth, worn on both upper arms and above the chevrons, if any (see Chapter 8).

● *Company Quartermaster Sergeant (CO 100, 1866)*. Three stripes and a tie of one stripe. Worn as early as 1864, according to contemporary photographs.

● *Regimental Commissary Sergeant (GO 40, 1867)*. Three stripes and "an angular tie (vertex pointing upwards)" of three stripes. This insignia was abolished by 1872 but evidence of its use has been found.

● *Regimental Hospital Stewards (GO 40, 1867)*. Three stripes and an oval, with a caduceus embroidered in dark blue silk in the center of the oval. This insignia was abolished in 1872 and no evidence of its use has been found.

Normally chevrons were made of silk or worsted binding sewn on backgrounds of uniform cloth prior to issue. Photographs indicate, however, that some were merely cut out of cloth and sewn on the sleeves directly, especially in the early days of the Civil War and in the Confederacy. In such cases the spaces between stripes could easily equal the width of the stripes.

Certain non-regulation sleeve devices made their appearance among the state regiments which will be mentioned in the appropriate places. Sometimes a single knot of lace was added to a chevron to indicate the commissary sergeant; drum majors might add a fringe to their stripes; and chevrons pointing upward are occasionally found.

Other Insignia of Rank and Function

Aiguillettes were twisted gold, or gold and silver, cords terminating in "tags" or points, worn suspended from the right shoulder under the epaulet. Prior to 1851 they were worn by certain general and regimental staff officers and especially by aides-de-camp in full dress. The points had originally contained pencils which were thus conveniently suspended on the officer's breast permitting note-taking or order-writing in the field. U.S. Army dress regulations between 1851 and 1872 did not prescribe the wearing of aiguillettes, although they could be found in some of the states. The insignia was again prescribed in 1872 for wear by aides-de-camp.

Another insigne of the staff officer was the baldric, an example of which is illustrated in the Schuyler, Hartley & Graham *Catalogue*, page 47, under the description of "gold and silk belt and cartridge-box for staff officers." The baldric was a leather shoulder belt, sometimes covered with gold lace of various designs, to the front of which was fastened a lion's head of gilded brass. From the lion's mouth hung three brass chains, terminating in pins that fitted behind a shield of the same metal. Suspended by rings from the belt was a small brass-mounted leather box. The length of the belt was adjusted by a brass buckle with brass tip and loop. By this period the baldric was purely ornamental, but earlier the pins had served as pencils or prickers for pistol touch holes, and the box to hold cartridges.

Figs. 21 and 62

Another form of baldric was worn by drum majors and is mentioned briefly in Chapter 4.

Cords for dress hats also indicated rank, and they have been mentioned above in Chapter 1. General officers' cords were all gold and ended in acorns. The cord was looped twice around the hat, passing through a slide kept at the front of the hat. Cords for all other officers had the same shape but were made half of gold and half of black silk, either "machined" to form a zig-zag pattern of lace or "twisted" to resemble a rope. Enlisted men were issued worsted cords of branch color with tasselled ends.

Rank among general officers was also indicated by the grouping of buttons on their frock coats. This is described under "General Officers" in Chapter 8.

Finally, the size of trouser stripes also indicated the rank of the wearer. General officers wore plain trousers; other officers had one-eighth inch cords or welts of gold or branch color; sergeants, stripes 1.5 inch wide; and corporals, stripes .5 inch wide. Privates went without stripes.

Buttons

Fig. 30

Military buttons constitute a separate field of collecting which the novice rightfully enters with hesitation. Nevertheless, buttons are an integral part of military clothing and an important tool in its identification, and must be included in this work if only in broad terms. Here and in subsequent chapters we will record the principal button patterns and types that were worn, giving the authority for their devices, who their wearers were, and their general period of use. No attempt will be made to single out the varieties of any distinctive pattern.

Virtually all military buttons of this period were machine-made by mass production methods, and virtually all were made of a yellow metal with gilt or plated surface. The gilding could be anything from yellow lacquer to pure gold of various karats and depths, and button makers advertised the quality of this surfacing by marking on the rear "Double Gilt," "Treble Gilt," etc.

With two exceptions, all U.S. Army uniform buttons were the built-up, three-part "shell" type patented by R. Sanders in 1823 and named after him by modern collectors. Distinctive devices were pressed between a pair of matching dies on the front portion, the manufacturer's name and other information was inscribed on the rear, and the shank was brazed on. An outgrowth of the Sanders type was a four-part shell button. Produced at the Scovill factory in the early 1830's, by 1851 it was being worn by General and General Staff officers. Known to collectors as the "Staff" type, it became the most widely worn military button in America after our period.

Buttons normally came in two sizes, the larger for fastening the coat and the smaller for use on collars, cuffs, vests, etc. However, small buttons were also worn on the front of jackets and large on the rear of frock coats. Officers' buttons as a rule differed in size from those worn by enlisted men of the same

Fig. 30. U.S. Army buttons, letters and numbers.

branch, averaging .875 inch (⅞ inch or 23 mm) and .5 inch (14 mm), as against .75 inch (20 mm) and .55 inch (15 mm). Button makers of this period used the "line" as a measurement of size—a measurement exclusive to their trade in which forty lines equalled an inch. Modern button collectors use the millimeter scale.

Numerous minor variations can be found in most patterns of military buttons, resulting from the initial designing and quality of die work used by the different button manufacturers. These variations are often useful in dating buttons, especially when studied in conjunction with the information on the rear.

The dress regulations of 1851 (GO 31) prescribed eight patterns of buttons. Each came in a large and small size and for five there were distinctions in type between those worn by officers and men. All were gilt and all, save those for the Ordnance Department, had essentially the same device.

● *General and General Staff Officers.* "Staff eagle" device. Sizes .875 and .5 inch. Same pattern as worn before 1851; continued in use until about 1872 when stars were added to shield. Thick, fully domed "Staff type" construction. As many as sixteen varieties identified.

● *Corps of Engineers.* Eagle-scroll-fort-rising sun device, being the same pattern as worn before 1851; continued in use after 1872. Officers' pattern had bright rim; enlisted Engineer troops probably without rim. Sizes (officers) about .9 and .55; (EM) about .75 and .6. Two-piece construction. About eleven varieties identified.

● *Corps of Topographical Engineers.* Shield and "TE" device, as worn before 1851. Convex, solid type specified in regulations, but two-piece construction also used. Sizes .875 and .5. Probably not worn after 1863.

● *Ordnance Department.* Crossed cannon-garter-flaming bomb device, newly authorized. Johnson believes this device was slightly modified in 1860 to make the cannon cross at right angles. No EM's version known. Sizes .875 and .5, two-piece with rim.

● *Artillery.* Eagle device with "A" on recessed shield, as worn prior to 1851; same worn after 1872 except shield was raised and stippled. Two-piece type without rim. Sizes (officers) .875 and .5, (EM) .75 and .55. As many as twenty-two varieties identified.

● *Dragoons.* Same as artillery but letter "D" on shield. Not regulation after 1861. About eight varieties identified.

● *Regiment of Mounted Riflemen.* Same as artillery but letter "R" on shield. Not regulation after 1861. About fifteen varieties known. This button was probably worn by U.S. Sharpshooters in 1861–1865.

● *Infantry.* Same as artillery but letter "I" on shield. Numerous varieties known, since this was the second most widely worn button in this period.

After 1851 only three significant changes were made in U.S. Army buttons. The first came as a result of orders issued 20 January 1854 (GO 1), the same orders that brought wide changes to the uniform as a whole:

The same button will be used for all corps, to wit: that now used for the Infantry, omitting the I on the shield.

The button so introduced is now called the "general service button"; it applied only to enlisted men. Doubtless several years passed before the old buttons were exhausted and, indeed, there is ample evidence that enlisted men wore buttons marked with "A" and "I" during the Civil War. For a time general service buttons were issued with, literally, a blank shield (Johnson No. 259), but soon the shield was given horizontal and vertical lines and the device came to look much like that worn by the command and staff although, of course, the two buttons differed in size and shape. This is the most common button found in the period and many varieties have been identified.

The second button change was the authorization in 1857 and possibly as early as 1855 of a distinctive pattern for officers of cavalry. It had the same design worn by dragoon officers but with a "C" on the shield. In 1861 this button became the sole pattern worn by officers of the mounted arm. Some twenty varieties of this button have been identified. It continued in use after 1872.

When a uniform was prescribed for chaplains in 1861 (GO 102) and 1864 (GO 247) they were given "black buttons." Neither size nor construction were specified but it is clear that common civilian buttons covered with black cloth were intended and worn.

Medals and Decorations

At the outbreak of the Civil War there was no American medal authorized as a reward for gallantry or distinguished conduct. Long service in the U.S. Army was indicated by half chevrons on the uniform of enlisted men, and gallantry by officers was rewarded by brevet rank or by individual medallions specially presented by Congress, the only official forms of award in use at the time. The Civil War, however, was to change our outlook on decorations despite the misgivings of older officers.

Figs. 31 and 32

The single decoration formally established by the general government prior to 1872 was the Medal of Honor. It was authorized by Congress for enlisted men of the army on 12 July 1862 and on 3 March 1863 was extended to include commissioned officers. Actually at the time there were two Medals of Honor, a Navy Medal and an Army Medal. The former was the first to be established, President Lincoln signing the bill on 21 December 1861, two months before any action had been taken to introduce the bill for the Army Medal in Congress.

Designs for the new models were submitted by the Director of the U.S. Mint at Philadelphia and the navy approved one of them on 9 May 1862. In November of that year the War Department contracted with the firm of William Wilson & Son, Philadelphia—where the Navy Medal was being made—for 2,000 of the same type for the army. The only difference between the two medals was that the army version was attached to its ribbon by an American eagle and crossed cannon device instead of by an anchor and star.

The Army Medal of Honor hung from a ribbon of 13 alternating vertical stripes of red and white, with a solid blue stripe on top. The pin to which this

Fig. 31. Individual decorations of the Civil War: Obverse, left to right: Fort Sumter Medal, 4th Class; Fort Pickens Medal, 4th Class; Kearny Cross (bronze); Fort Pickens Medal, 3rd Class; Butler's Medal for Colored Troops; 17th Army Corps Medal; Kearny Medal (gold). (John Wike, in *Military Collector & Historian*, V, 60).

Fig. 32. Individual decorations of the Civil War: Reverse of medals shown in Fig. 31.

was attached was decorated with a small U.S. shield. The medal itself was a five-pointed bronze star bearing on its obverse a female warrior representing the "Union" holding her shield against an attacker bearing snakes in both hands. Thirty-four stars encircle the figures. The reverse of the medal was left blank, and on this the name of its holder and the date and place of his deed, were inscribed.

The first Army Medals of Honor were awarded on 25 March 1863 to six soldiers who had survived the celebrated Andrews Raid. Over 2,100 were issued during the Civil War and a considerable number between 1865 and 1872. About one third of these were revoked in 1917.

During the course of the Civil War a number of other medals were proposed, and some actually adopted, by higher army commands, state governments, and other civil bodies. The medals of which we have record (exclusive of any state decorations that may have appeared after the war and before 1872) are as follows. The first two medals were not strictly decorations since they could not be worn on the uniform.

● *Sumter Medal.* Issued by the New York State Chamber of Commerce to officers and men who had defended Fort Sumter in 1861. Approved by the Chamber 6 June 1861 and medals issued in May 1862. Four classes were struck, all bronze, for award to General Anderson, commissioned officers, non-commissioned officers, and privates. All bore the profile of Anderson on the obverse. A total of 168 of this medal and the Pickens Medal, below, were issued.

● *Pickens Medal.* Same details as the Sumter Medal except they were issued to Major Adam J. Slemmer and the defenders of Fort Pickens, Fla.

● *Kearny Medal.* Issued semi-officially by officers of the command of the late Major General Philip Kearny (3rd, later 1st Division, 3rd Corps, Army of the Potomac) to officers and soldiers who had served honorably in battle under Kearny. Adopted 29 Nov 1862 and about 317 medals distributed. Gold, maltese cross under a circle bearing the words "Dulce et decorum est pro patria mori." Colored ribbon. Made by Ball, Black & Co., New York.

● *Kearny Cross.* Authorized 13 March 1863 (GO 25, 1st Div, 3rd Corps) as a "cross of valor" for enlisted men by Brigadier General D. B. Birney, Kearny's successor in command. It supplemented the Kearny Medal, and a soldier could not receive both. Bronze "cross pattee" with "Kearny Cross" on one side and "Birney's Division" on the other; suspended from a colored ribbon. Two women were awarded this decoration.

● *17th Army Corps (McPherson) Medal.* Authorized 2 October 1863 (GO 30, 17th AC) as a reward for gallantry by officers and men of that corps. Gold or silver star suspended from a semicircle-shield-wreath combination, over a red-white-blue ribbon. Made by Tiffany & Co, New York.

● *Gillmore Medal.* Authorized 28 October 1863 (GO 94, Dept of the South) as a medal of honor for gallant and meritorious conduct during the operations before Charleston, S.C., July–September 1863. Bronze, round, suspended from a bronze bar bearing the recipient's name. A representation in relief of Fort Sumter in ruins on obverse; General Gillmore's signature and other lettering on reverse. Made by Ball, Black & Co. There were 400 medals struck.

● *Butler Medal for Colored Troops.* Established about October, 1864 by Major General Benjamin F. Butler for award to Negro soldiers of the 25th Corps for valor displayed during the storming of New Market Heights and at Chaffins' Farm, in September, 1864. Bronze, round, suspended from a red-white-blue ribbon bearing an oak leaf with inscription "Army of the James." Obverse showed a bastioned fort being attacked by Negro soldiers, and the motto "Ferro iis libertas preveniet"; reverse bore the words "Distinguished for Courage" and "Campaign before Richmond 1864." Made by Tiffany & Co. and Ball, Black & Co. Butler ordered 200 medals struck and distributed.

● *Other Decorations.* Two other forms of decoration issued during the Civil War were the red ribbon, tied in a button hole or pinned over the left breast, believed to have been worn by Roll of Honor men of the Army of the Cumberland in mid-1863 and later, and the special signal flag with a star denoting skill and bravery in action by a signal officer (see Chapter 8).

In addition to these decorations an officer or soldier in uniform might have worn prior to 1872 any one of the following badges which roughly correspond to modern service medals

Aztec Club of 1847
Military Order of the Loyal Legion of the U.S.
Society of the Army of the Tennessee
Society of the Army of the Potomac
Grand Army of the Republic
Society of the Army of the Cumberland

SOURCES

U.S. Ordnance Dept., *The Ordnance Manual for the Use of the Officers of the United States Army,* 1st ed., 1841; 2nd ed., 1850; 3rd ed., 1862.

U.S. Army dress regulations cited above, especially the Horstmann edition of 1851.

Schuyler, Hartley & Graham, *Illustrated Catalogue of Arms and Military Goods . . .,* New York, 1864. (Reprinted 1961 by Norm Flayderman.)

David F. Johnson, *Uniform Buttons: American Armed Forces, 1784–1948,* 2 vols., Watkins Glen, N.Y., 1948.

Alphaeus H. Albert, *Record of American Uniform and Historical Buttons . . . 1775–1968,* Hightstown, N.J., 1969.

Eugene Zieber, *Heraldry in America,* 2nd ed., Philadelphia, 1909.

William G. Gavin, *Accoutrement Plates, North and South, 1861–1865,* Philadelphia, 1963.

Frank C. Townsend and Frederick P. Todd, "Branch Insignia of Regular Cavalry, 1833–1872," in *Military Collector & Historian,* VIII (1956), 1–5.

John W. Wike and Frederick P. Todd, "'Shell and Flame': The Story of the Ordnance Corps Insignia," in *Military Collector & Historian,* V (1953), 91–94.

John W. Wike, "The Wearing of Army Corps and Division Insignia in the Union Army, 1862–1865," in *Military Collector & Historian,* IV (1952), 35–38.

John W. Wike, "Individual Decorations of the Civil War and Earlier," in *Military Collector & Historian,* V (1953), 57–64.

John D. Billings, *Hardtack and Coffee . . .,* Boston, 1887, pp. 250–268.

J. Duncan Campbell and Edgar M. Howell, *American Military Insignia 1800–1851,* United States National Museum Bulletin 235, Washington, 1963.

Marius B. Peladeau and Roger S. Cohen, Jr., "Corps Badges of the Civil War," in *Military Collector & Historian,* XXIII, 103–112.

Special thanks are due to Colonel J. Duncan Campbell for his great help over a long period of time, especially for use of material from his personal collection of American military insignia, one of the largest in private hands. Major Edgar M. Howell and his staff of the Museum of History and Technology, Smithsonian Institution, also gave real assistance by making the W. Stokes Kirk Collection available for use. This unique assembly of military insignia was begun in 1878 and enlarged by two generations of the Kirk family of Philadelphia until acquired by the Smithsonian Institution in 1959.

Others whose help and advice on this chapter are gratefully acknowledged include the late Captain Frank C. Townsend and John W. Wike. The section on corps badges is based largely on Mr. Wike's research. Finally, Major William G. Gavin—another eminent collector—read the MS in draft and offered numerous suggestions.

CHAPTER III

Small Arms

On no branch of American military equipage has as much attention been showered by collectors and writers, professional and amateur, as upon that of weapons, and especially portable firearms. In this area of research and writing Americans appear to lead the world, and specialists abound for almost every aspect of the field.

Without attempting to compete in such a heavily endowed study area, some coverage must be provided by this work if a picture of the complete soldier is to be presented. This chapter, while comprehensive, is necessarily too brief and general to be aimed at the close student of American arms or the advanced collector.

The purposes of the chapter are to list all patterns of weapons carried by a significant number of soldiers in the period, to describe each kind in enough detail to permit an actual example to be identified, to picture an example and describe its size and coloration as an aid to artists*, to place weapons in their correct historical and tactical perspective, and, so far as possible, to associate weapons with the regiments that used them.

Muskets and Rifles

In 1851 the foot soldier of the U.S. Army carried the U.S. Musket, Model 1842, a smoothbore, percussion cap muzzleloader of caliber .69, firing a round lead ball. It was the first standard percussion or "cap lock" musket and the last standard smoothbore. It had a contemporary in the U.S Rifle, Model 1841, also percussion, of caliber .54 and firing a round, patched ball—the last model to do so. This rifle was carried by the Regiment of Mounted Riflemen and many state rifle corps.

From 1842 on, experiments had been conducted with an eye to adopting the rifle as a standard arm. By 1853, following the designs of James Henry Burton,

---

* Only imported long arms, purchased abroad by Union and Confederate agents, plus a few other pieces, are actually illustrated as such. Most weapons are shown in the hands of soldiers in subsequent volumes. References made in the margins to regiments indicate those places in later volumes where the weapon is best delineated.

the cylindro-conoidal Minie (actually "Minié") bullet was being tested, and intensive experiments were under way to determine the optimum caliber for a proposed new line of small arms designed to use it. This line was adopted in 1855 with a standard caliber of .58, and gave the army a "rifle musket," a rifle (differing chiefly in external form and length), and a rifled "pistol-carbine." The rifle musket, with only minor variation, remained the standard infantry weapon to within a few years of the end of our period. During the Civil War alone approximately 1,500,000 rifle muskets were made at Springfield Armory or purchased from contractors.

The widespread use of rifling was only one of several significant advances in military firearm design made in this period. Breechloading was another, although long before 1851—in fact, in 1824—the first breechloading arm had been introduced into the United States service. This was the Hall rifle which, while it saw use in the field, was not an unqualified success and had been withdrawn by 1851. By then, however, other breechloaders, chiefly experimental carbines, were being offered to the army for trial. They met with fairly consistent resistance from both army and navy officials, and not until 1859 could the Secretary of War write favorably of the breechloading principle. The outbreak of the Civil War forced the army to buy breechloaders, and others were purchased by states or by regiments themselves. The majority were carbines and their variety offered a serious problem: several calibers, some using paper, some linen, and others metallic cartridges. In all, thirty-one American makes of carbine, plus several foreign types, were purchased by the United States during the war. A few infantry commands carried breechloaders during the war, and after it ended one breechloading system (Allin's) was accepted by the army. In 1866 the army issued its first breechloaders to infantry, obtained by converting old muzzle-loading rifle muskets.

Among the breechloading rifles tested by the army in 1861 were the Henry and the Spencer, both magazine arms destined to become the outstanding systems of the period. Both were rejected by the Chief of Ordnance as uncertain of operation, heavy, and expensive. Despite this rebuff the Spencer had made its reputation before the end of the war and more carbines of this make were purchased by the government than any other kind of breechloader. The lever-action Henry was never welcomed wholeheartedly into the service, although later an improved pattern manufactured as the Winchester won great fame as a civilian weapon.

The accumulation of stocks of obsolete firearms caused by this adoption of new models after 1855, and later the great demand for serviceable weapons at the outbreak of the Civil War, led the general government and some of the states to alter or "convert" older patterns into more modern ones. The conversion of flintlocks to percussion arms had begun as early as 1843, and in 1850, for example, 56,134 flintlock muskets were so converted. Large numbers of these "conversions" were issued to the states in the 1850's. Following the Civil War, as has been said, many muzzleloaders were converted to breechloaders. Other pre-war and wartime alterations consisted of transforming smoothbore muskets into rifled arms, of changing arms of smaller calibers (.54) to a standard caliber of .58 in order to facilitate ammunition supply, of adding Maynard primers, improving sights, etc. For convenience, the word "conversion" will be used hereafter to indicate a change in ignition system, while "alteration" will encompass all other changes.

All infantry weapons produced in this period except the Model 1841 rifle were equipped with a bayonet. Even the 1841 rifles were altered to take bayonets. There were two principal types, the "socket" or "triangular" bayonet, vastly in the preponderance, and the "sword" or "saber" bayonet that came with some of the shorter pattern rifles. Occasionally a sliding bayonet was used which fitted under the barrel, and a rather distinctive pattern of sword bayonet, longer and more sword-shaped than normal, was provided for the U.S. Sappers and Miners Musketoon, Model 1847.

The general government at this period maintained armories for the manufacture of small arms at Harpers Ferry, Virginia, and Springfield, Massachusetts. These two armories were easily able to sustain the peacetime needs of the regular army and navy, but there were other troops that had to be supplied. Under an act of Congress in 1808 a total of $200,000 worth of ordnance material was distributed annually to the states, prorated according to reported militia strengths, specific items being requisitioned by governors according to their needs. Muskets and rifles were by far the items most commonly demanded and accounted for a very large share of the supply provided by the general government. Of the more than 93,500 Model 1841 percussion rifles manufactured in government armories or purchased from contractors, for example, hardly five percent could have found their way to the regulars.

Inability of government armories to keep pace with the needs of the states, especially during the Civil War, led the War Department to resort to contracting for small arms. This was, of course, an accepted practice, as it is today, dating back to the founding of the Republic. During the period 1851–1872 at least twenty-three firms accepted government contracts for the manufacture of regulation muskets and rifles alone, to say nothing of those that supplied their own patented weapons or those that made weapons for the Confederacy. In addition, several states contracted for rifles and muskets on their own.

The principal muskets and rifles used by the United States forces during our period are described briefly below, arranged in this fashion: a) regulation models, b) commercial breechloaders and repeaters, c) converted flintlocks and altered muzzleloaders, and d) foreign purchases.

The Regulation Models, 1851–1872

● *U.S. Musket, Model 1842.* Percussion muzzleloader, cal .69, smoothbore, 57.75 in. overall. Socket bayonet, 18 in. blade, clamping band (locking ring) on socket. Barrel and iron furniture, bright finish. Marked on lock plate with eagle over "U.S." and "SPRING/FIELD" over year; or same eagle and "U.S." with "HARPERS/FERRY" over year. Produced 1844–1855 at Springfield and

Fig. 10

118

Harpers Ferry Armories. Between 1856 and 1859 14,182 of these muskets were rifled and equipped with long range rear sights.

Plate XIV

● *U.S. Rifle, Model 1841.* Percussion muzzleloader, cal .54, rifled with 7 grooves, 48.75 in. overall. No bayonet provided. Barrel browned; lock and hammer case-hardened in mottled colors; blued trigger; brass furniture, polished bright; brass patch box in stock, 7.7 in. long. Markings on lock plate same as musket above.

Some 25,296 were made at Harpers Ferry Armory Rifle Works, 1846–1855, and possibly 3,200 at Springfield Armory in 1849. In addition, over 68,000 were made under contract by E. Remington & Son, 1845–c.1850; Robbins, Kendall & Lawrence, 1845–1849; George W. Tryon, 1844–c.1850; and Eli Whitney, 1842–1855. The lock plates of these rifles were marked, respectively as follows:

"REMINGTON'S/HERKIMER/N.Y." and "U.S." over year

"ROBBINS/KENDALL/&/LAWRENCE/U.S." and "WINDSOR VT" over year; and after about 1846, "ROBBINS/&/LAWRENCE/US" and "WINDSOR VT" over year

"TRYON/US" and "PHILADA/PA" over year

"E. WHITNEY/U.S." and "N. HAVEN" over year

Between 1855 and 1862 many of this model were re-rifled to caliber .58, equipped with longer range sights, and provided with bayonet attachments and saber bayonets, three methods of attachment being tried. After 1859 some were given socket bayonets instead. This popular weapon was usually called the "Mississippi" or "Jaeger" rifle, and after being altered, the "long range rifle."

See 10th Regt., NYSM

● *U.S. Rifle Musket, Model 1855.* Percussion muzzleloader, cal .58, rifled with 3 grooves, 56 in. overall. Socket bayonet, 18 in. blade with clamping band on socket. Barrel and iron furniture bright; brass or iron stock tip. Lock fitted with a Maynard tape primer magazine. Swell in ramrod near front. This was one of the first three U.S. arms specifically designed for use of the Minie bullet. The barrel had an adjustable leaf sight until 1858 when a smaller 2-leaf sight was introduced. Stock originally made plain, but in late 1859 a small iron patch box was added.

This model was made at Springfield Armory (47,115 during 1857–1861) and at Harpers Ferry (12,158 during 1859–1861). Lock plate marked "U.S./SPRING-FIELD" or "U.S./HARPERS FERRY", with eagle on tape box cover and year at rear end.

The 1855 rifle musket was also manufactured by Eli Whitney, Jr., with a lock plate marked "E. WHITNEY/N. HAVEN", eagle on tape box cover, and "1857", "1858" or undated.

See 9th U.S. Inf., 1857

● *U.S. Rifle, Model 1855.* Percussion muzzleloader, cal .58, rifled with 3 grooves, 49.4 in. overall. Originally equipped with adjustable slide leaf, folding rear sight; in 1858 replaced with two-leaf sight. Saber bayonet with brass hilt, 21.5–21.75 in. blade; engaged a lug on right side of barrel near muzzle. Manufactured only at Harpers Ferry Armory from 1857 until April 1861. Barrel and iron furniture bright on arms made 1859–1861, iron patch box in stock. The 1857–1858 rifles had browned barrels and brass furniture. Same lock plate, primer magazine, and markings as above; sometimes refitted with Springfield locks. Arms made 1857–1858 had a separate "crosshair" type front sight which could be slipped over the barrel.

This pattern was often called the "long-range rifle" in official reports. During the Civil War it was sometimes referred to as the "zouave rifle," possibly because of its saber bayonet.

● *U.S. Rifle Musket, Model 1861.* Percussion muzzleloader, cal .58, rifled with 3 grooves, 56 in. overall. Socket bayonet, 18 in. blade, with locking ring. Barrel and iron furniture bright. Tape primer magazine and patch box in butt omitted. Marked on lock plate "U.S./SPRINGFIELD" and year. A total of 265,129 of this model were made at the Springfield Armory alone during 1861–1863.

See 7th Regt., NGSNY, 1865–1868

Rifle muskets of Model 1861 were also produced under contract for the War Department by the firms noted below in the years 1861–1865, a total of 643,439 being delivered. Still others were manufactured under state contracts. Those made by the first three firms listed below differed in several ways from the regulation—such as bands held by screws, no clean-out screw, outward curving or "S"-shaped hammer, and straight ramrod held by "spoon" (spring)—and were referred to as the "Colt Pattern" or "Special Model 1861." All bore distinctive markings on their lock plates, which are given *in part* below. These contracts are discussed in Edwards, *op. cit.*, pp. 25–59:

Amoskeag Mfg. Co., Manchester, N.H. ("AMOSKEAG MFg Co")
Colt Arms Mfg. Co., Hartford, Conn. ("COLTS Pt F.A. Mfg. Co.")
Lamson, Goodnow & Yale, Windsor, Vt. ("WINDSOR VT")
Addison M. Burt, Trenton, N.J. ("TRENTON")
Eagle Mfg. Co., Mansfield, Conn. ("EAGLEVILLE")
C.B. Hoard, Watertown, N.Y. ("WATERTOWN")
James T. Hodge, Trenton, N.J. ("TRENTON")
Alfred Jenks & Son, Philadelphia and Bridesburg, Pa. ("PHILADELPHIA" or "BRIDESBURG")
William Mason, Taunton, Mass. ("Wm MASON")
James D. Mowry, Norwich, Conn. ("JAs. D. MOWRY/NORWICH CONN.")
William Muir & Co., Windsor Locks, Conn. ("Wm Muir & CO/WINDSOR LOCKS, CT.")
James Mulholland, Reading, Pa., ("PARKER, SNOW & Co"?)
Norwich Arms Co., Norwich, Conn. ("NORWICH")
Parker, Snow & Co., Meriden, Conn. ("PARKER, SNOW & Co.")
Providence Tool Co., Providence, R.I., ("PROVIDENCE TOOL Co")
E. Remington, Ilion, N.Y. ("REMINGTON'S")
E. Robinson, New York, N.Y. ("E. ROBINSON")
Sarson & Roberts, New York, N.Y. ("NEW YORK")
Savage Revolving Firearms Co., Middletown, Conn. ("SAVAGE R.F.A. Co")
Caspar D. Schubarth, Providence, R.I. ("C.D. SCHUBARTH")
William W. Welch, Norfolk, Conn. ("NORFOLK")
Eli Whitney, Whitneyville, Conn. ("WHITNEYVILLE" or "E. WHITNEY")

The Model 1861 rifle musket was also manufactured under state contracts, S. Norris and W. T. Clements, for example, making them for Massachusetts. Finally, a small number were manufactured in Suhl, in Prussia. These interesting weapons were exact copies of the regulation rifle except for their markings: eagle, "US" and "1861" on the lock plate; "US" on the barrel; and "SUHL" underneath the barrel.

● *U.S. Rifle Musket, Models 1863 and 1864.* The Model 1863 is basically the same as the Model 1861 with the following changes: screw-held oval bands; no clean-out screw in cone seat, which was reduced, flattened, and stamped with eagle; straight ramrod held by ramrod spoon (spring); case-hardened lock, and new hammer shape. Total of 273,265 produced at Springfield Armory.

Model 1864 was basically the same as Model 1863 with the following changes: band springs re-introduced, ramrod head knurled and slotted, and rear sight with only one leaf; 255,040 produced at Springfield Armory.

● *U.S. Rifle, Model 1863 (Remington).* Percussion muzzleloader, cal .58, rifled with 3, 5, or 7 grooves, 49 in. overall. Saber bayonet, brass hilt, blade approx. 20 in. Engaged a stud on the right side of the barrel. Barrel finished blue, lock case-hardened in mottled colors, brass furniture; oval bands. Marked on lock plate "REMINGTON'S/ILION, N.Y." with "U.S." and year. 10,000 manufactured by Remington in 1863. Commonly referred to today as the "Remington Zouave." While manufactured during the Civil War, none of these arms were issued into the service; they were sold as a lot after the war.

● *U.S. Double Rifle Musket, Model 1863 (Lindsay).* This weapon can readily be distinguished by its twin hammers. It was an unsuccessful experimental arm, only 1,000 being made. It is described in Gluckman, *Muskets*, pp. 246–248. It was used by the 16th Michigan only during the battle of Peebles Farm, Va., in 1864.

● *U.S. Rifle, Model 1865 (Allin Conversion).* Basically a U.S. rifle musket of the Model 1861 altered to breechloader by a mechanism designed by Erskine S. Allin, Master Armorer of Springfield Armory. This system employed a rising breech-block hinged at the front, unlatched by a thumb piece, and a short, cal .58 rim-fire, copper-case cartridge. Springfield Armory altered about 5,000 weapons to this system.

● *U.S. Rifle, Model 1866 (Allin Conversion).* Generally similar to the Model 1865 except that the caliber was reduced to .50, the mechanism improved, and a center-fire copper-case cartridge used in place of rim-fire. About 25,000 muzzle-loaders were converted to this system; "1866" is marked on the breech-block.

● *U.S. Rifle, Models 1868 and 1870.* Metallic cartridge, breechloading, cal .50, rifled with 3 grooves, 52 in. overall. These and the preceding model used 50-70 center-fire, copper-case cartridge of two types, both manufactured at Frankford Arsenal. Socket bayonet, 18 in. blade with a locking ring on the socket. Barrel and iron furniture, bright finish. Although new barrels were made, many of these models used Civil War type rifle-musket lock plates and other components.

* The Allin Conversions were popularly termed the "trap door" Springfields.

These models were still experimental although they foreshadowed the infantry weapon used by the regular army for 30 years thereafter; relatively few appear to have been made. The Model 1870 included a few minor changes and was .25 in. shorter. The models were distinguished by "1868" and "1870" on the breech-block.

● *U.S. Cadet Rifle, Model 1868.* Similar to Model 1868 except for shortened barrel and proportionately reduced size. Overall size 51.8 in., furniture bright, 2 bands. Issued to cadets of U.S. Military Academy.

The Commercial Breechloaders and Repeaters, 1855–1872

● *Colt-Root Model 1855 Percussion Repeating Rifle.* Percussion, loading like a revolver into a cylinder; produced in cal .40 through .64 with .44, .50, and .56 most common; rifled with 7 grooves; lengths vary from 49.5 in. to 56.5 in. overall. On cal .56 rifles and larger only five shot cylinders used. Fired nitre-treated, self-consuming paper cartridges. All metal blued except hammer and loading lever which were case-hardened. Usually marked on strap over cylinder: "COL. COLT HARTFORD CT. U.S.A." and "COLT'S PATENT NOV. 24th 1857." *See 1st Regt., Conn. Militia*

About 7000 were sold to the general government or to the states. Also called the "Army Pattern Revolving Rifle." A number of minor changes were made in these arms over the years. The cal .56 rifle was the weapon first issued the 1st U.S. Sharpshooters.

(*Jenks Breechloading Percussion Rifle.* See "U.S. Navy")

(*Maynard Breechloading Rifle "First Model."* See *Maynard Breechloading Carbine*)

● *Merrill Breechloading Percussion Rifle.* Cal .54, rifled with 3 grooves, 48.5 in. overall. Saber bayonet 24.1 in. overall with slightly recurved blade. Barrel usually browned, all furniture brass, lock case-hardened, patch box in butt. Breech loaded by lifting a lever latched under the rear sight base. Lock plate marked "J.H. MERRILL BALTO./PAT. JULY 1858/APL. 8, MAY 21-28–61." Manufactured by Merrill, Thomas & Company (later Merrill's Patent Firearms Company) of Baltimore, Md., 1861–1863. More than 770 rifles were sold, their production being overshadowed by that of the Merrill carbine, *q.v.*

● *Sharps Breechloading Rifle Musket, New Model 1859.* Percussion, vertically sliding breech-block manipulated by the trigger guard, cal .52, side hammer, rifled with 6 grooves, 53 in. overall. Used paper or linen wrapped cartridge and primers fed mechanically by magazine fitted into the forward vertical edge of the lock plate. Two types of saber bayonet furnished with this model. Patch box in stock; 3 bands with sling swivel on middle band, rear swivel on butt near toe. All furniture bright. Marked on right of lock plate: "R.S. LAWRENCE PAT./ APRIL 12th 1859" and "C. SHARPS' PAT./OCT. 5th 1852"; and on left of frame: "C. SHARPS' PAT./SEPT. 12th 1848." Other markings include "NEW MODEL 1859" on top of barrel in rear of rear sight. No cleaning rod.

● *Sharps Breechloading Rifle, New Model 1859.* Similar to the rifle musket of this model except overall length was 47 in. Saber or socket bayonet. This was *Plate V* the weapon issued the U.S. Sharpshooter regiments; some 2,000 were purchased by the general government in the spring of 1862. Some rifles came equipped with "set" triggers.

● *Sharps Breechloading Rifle, New Model 1863.*   Similar to the New Model 1859 except in minor details, being marked "NEW MODEL 1863." Socket bayonet. Blued metal except for lock plate, patch box, butt plate, bands, nose cap, and hammer, which were case-hardened in mottled colors. Some 6,000 purchased by the general government late in the Civil War.

● *Sharps Single-Shot Cartridge Rifle.*   Frame and mechanism similar to models above but adapted to metallic cartridge. Cal .50, center-fire, side hammer, rifled with 3 grooves, 52 in. overall. No patch box. Forearm held by 2 bands. Socket bayonet, 18 in. blade, using front sight as stud. All furniture bright. Markings on lock plate and frame same as New Model 1859 Rifle; none on barrel. Had cleaning rod. This pattern was altered at the Springfield Armory about 1870, 1,000 being produced for trial. Fired cal .50-70 government cartridge.

The Sharps Rifle Manufacturing Company also converted many of its percussion rifles to use the cal .50-70 government ammunition.

● *Peabody Single-Shot Cartridge Rifle, Model (1867 ?).*   Tipping breech-block manipulated by trigger guard, cal .433, side hammer, rifled with 3 grooves, 51.5 in. overall. Used center-fire metallic cartridge. U.S. regulation socket bayonet, 18 in. blade. Two bands, with sling swivel on lower; lower swivel on butt stock. Cleaning rod. Marked on left of breech frame: "PEABODY'S PAT./JULY 22, 1862/MAN'F'D BY/PROVIDENCE TOOL CO./PROV., R.I." Barrel and band browned, frame case-hardened.

Adopted by militia of Connecticut and Massachusetts after the Civil War on an experimental basis, but replaced by the Springfield breechloader in both states. This rifle was also manufactured in cals .45 and .50, but these models saw no significant military use in America. The Peabody was widely used abroad. See also Peabody cartridge carbine.

● *Sharps & Hankins Single-Shot Breechloading Army Cartridge Rifle, Model 1862.*   Sliding barrel action, manipulated by trigger guard, cal .52, center hammer, rifled with 6 grooves, 42 in. overall. Used rim-fire and later center-fire metallic cartridge. No bayonet. Made without forestock. Frame marked on left "SHARPS/PATENT/1859" and on right "SHARPS/&/HANKINS/PHILADA." Barrel blued, frame case-hardened, brass butt plate. (Naval version described under U.S. Navy)

See 1st D.C. Vol. Cal. ● *Henry Repeating Cartridge Rifle.*   Sliding block action manipulated by trigger guard lever, cal .44, center hammer, octagonal barrel rifled with 6 grooves, 43.5 in. overall. Used a rim-fire cartridge, carried in a magazine running under the full length of the barrel, loading near the muzzle, and holding 15 cartridges. Barrel and magazine, lever and hammer, iron blued; brass breech frame and butt plate. Sling swivels on left of barrel and of stock. Marked on barrel "HENRY'S PATENT. OCT. 16. 1860/MANUFACT'D BY THE NEW HAVEN ARMS CO. NEW HAVEN. CT." Production commenced in 1862.

● *Spencer Repeating Cartridge Rifle.*   Dropping breech-block manipulated by trigger guard, cal .52, side hammer, rifled with 6 grooves, 47 in. overall. Used a *See 42nd Penn. Vol. Inf.* copper .56-56 rim-fire cartridge, carried in tubular magazine passing through the butt of the stock and holding 7 cartridges. Socket bayonet, 18 in. blade. Three bands with sling swivel attached to center band; lower swivel attached to butt stock. No cleaning rod. Barrel blued; receiver and other metal parts case-hardened. Marked on top of receiver: "SPENCER REPEATING-RIFLE CO. BOSTON, MASS. PAT'D MARCH 6, 1860."

A total of 12,471 Spencer rifles of all models were furnished the War Department, exclusive of carbines.

● *Spencer Repeating Cartridge Rifle, Model 1865.* Similar to previous except cal .50, using a copper .56-52 rim-fire cartridge. Manufactured by the Spencer Co. and by the Burnside Rifle Co. in slightly different patterns. Rifles made by former had 6 grooves; by latter, 3 grooves. Both had 2 bands, with swivel on upper one, and cleaning rod. Cut-off inside trigger guard. Sling ring on bar sometimes attached to small of the stock on left. Marked on top of receiver same as previous, adding "MODEL/1865." Rifles made in Providence, R.I. marked "SPENCER REPEATING-RIFLE/PAT'D MARCH 6, 1860/MANUF'D AT PROV, R.I./BY BURNSIDE RIFLE CO." and "MODEL 1865."

Converted Flintlocks and Altered Muzzleloaders

Mention has been made that as early as 1843 the War Department began to convert its stock of regulation flintlock muskets to the percussion or cap lock system. This process continued with interruptions until the end of the Civil War, the weapons being issued to the several states upon requisition. The muskets converted were mainly those made from 1821 to 1844. They are referred to hereafter collectively as "conversions." Between 1856 and 1859 a number of Model 1822 and Model 1842 muskets also were rifled and sighted with a long range folding leaf rear sight. This produced the "cal .69 rifle musket" referred to in subsequent chapters.

Three methods of conversion appear to have been used in government armories. These are described and illustrated in Hick, *Notes,* I, 79–80 and plates 45 and 49; and Gluckman, *Muskets,* pp. 189–190. Some muskets were given the Maynard tape lock system by mounting an entirely new lock, and in 1854 a contract was let to the Remington Arms Company of Ilion, N.Y. for the conversion of 5,000 Model 1822 muskets on the Maynard plan, a new lock being substituted. Some of these muskets were also rifled and sighted.

Following the outbreak of the Civil War, several states undertook conversion of their stocks of flintlocks. It should also be borne in mind that some of the muskets and rifles imported from Europe, and next to be described, were conversions or alterations in one form or another, the work being done either in Europe or in this country.

After the Civil War, several firms (as well as Springfield Armory) undertook to convert muzzleloading arms to the breechloading cartridge system. Examples pertinent to this study are mentioned in the appropriate places.

Foreign Purchases (Including Carbines)

Both the Union and the Confederacy entered the Civil War with a totally inadequate supply of weapons. One obvious remedy was to purchase arms abroad and, after some hesitation here and there in high circles, a race began in which both the general governments and several of the states took part.

Among the Union officials to seek arms directly in Europe were General John C. Frémont, Colonel George L. Schuyler, and Marcellus Hartley (of the firm of Schuyler, Hartley & Graham), and the ministers to Belgium and France: Henry S. Sanford and William L. Dayton, respectively. The Confederate States relied largely on the efforts of Majors Caleb Huse and Edward C. Anderson, Commander James D. Bullock, and Captain James H. North. Numerous Northern firms and individuals undertook to import small arms on their own, among them Herman Boker & Company; Josiah Heddon and John Hoey; Thomas Poultney; Kruse, Drexel & Schmidt; A. Moller & Company; Tomes, Son & Melvain; Tiffany & Co.; and Charles A. Bulkley. Others, notably Courtney & Tennant of Charleston, S.C.; S. Isaacs, Campbell & Company of London; and Nelson Clements of Texas, acted as agents and importers for the South.

Various state agents roamed Europe, among them James L. Peyton of North Carolina and F.B. Crowninshield and William F. McFarland of Massachusetts. Most American agents abroad carried in their pockets orders and letters of credit from several state governments, all desperate for arms. Eventually the general governments succeeded in withdrawing these state agents.

In quality the foreign arms varied from useless to excellent. Many were overpriced and charges of fraud or incompetence followed some of the contracts. But, by and large, the purchases were well worth making if for no other reason than quantity. Even the poorer weapons permitted the raw recruit to learn something about soldiering and, if in so doing he damaged the weapon, it was no great loss. It has been estimated that half of the Union regiments that went into battle before the fall of 1862 were armed with foreign rifles or muskets. Many kept them willingly throughout their entire service.

Some of the arms purchased came directly from government arsenals, others from the hands of dealers in obsolescent material, or simply speculators who counted on procuring them, whereas a substantial proportion was manufactured specifically for exportation. Due to the immense demand in America, the bulk of the weapons had to be accepted as is, but here and there contracts called for alterations which were more or less faithfully carried out.

All told, the story of our purchase of arms abroad is confusing and little known. The guns themselves do not interest many American collectors, in part because of the difficulty of distinguishing between a weapon imported for use in the Civil War and one brought over later. Yet it is an integral part of the story of American arms in our period and must be included. Several chapters in William B. Edwards' *Civil War Guns* are devoted to the topic and deserve the close scrutiny of anyone seeking further information .

The types of imports will be arranged below according to their country of origin and, within that, their dates and patterns. Since relatively few carbines were imported they will be included here with muskets and rifles. The descriptions that follow, of course, relate alike to weapons used in the North and South during the Civil War.

British Muskets, Rifles, and Carbines

Of all the firearms imported from abroad, those obtained from England were the most significant in both quantity and quality, and this statement applies alike to the Union and Confederate armies. Although this reputation rests primarily on the Enfield rifle musket and rifle, a few earlier model firearms were sent over and thus a brief review of British service muskets and rifles from the introduction of cap lock arms to the first model of the Enfield may be helpful.

Figs. 33, 34, 35

One of the characteristics of British service small arms of the 1830's and 1840's was their variety. An official statement of the percussion weapons in use in December 1841 listed eleven types, including four patterns of musket, three of carbine, and four sea service arms. Among these was the "Musket for Regiments of the Line, Pattern of 1839," which had been adopted after almost a decade of experimentation. It was not the first cap lock weapon to be officially adopted, nor even to be issued, but it was the most common type in use at the time.

● *Muskets, Patterns 1839 and 1842.* The Pattern 1839 was actually a converted flintlock. It was caliber .753, smoothbore, 55 inches overall, and took a socket bayonet (held by a spring under the barrel) with a 17 inch blade. It had no bands; its furniture was brass and its barrel browned. Open rear sight. This same weapon was newly manufactured as the Pattern 1842, the only significant changes being in the brass furniture and in the lock, which foreshadowed in its design all Enfield locks to come for over two decades. Its plate was marked with a crown over "VR", a crown-and-broad-arrow, the year of manufacture, and the word "ENFIELD." Although considered "4th class" by U.S. Ordnance standards, more than 4,000 were imported by Charles A. Bulkley for sale to the North. The Confederacy also purchased these patterns.

● *Rifles, Patterns 1837 and 1847 (Brunswick Rifles).* In the meanwhile, the Brunswick percussion rifle had been adopted for rifle regiments in 1837, the invention of a Captain Berners of the German state of Brunswick, hence the name. Its most distinctive feature was that it was rifled with only two fairly deep grooves and used a belted spherical ball. Its length was 46 inches, its caliber .704, and it was sighted for 300 yards. The Brunswick was given a cross-handled sword bayonet, held by a strong bar on the right side of the 30-inch barrel. A few thousand of these rifles were imported into the western Confederate States.

The rifle was issued in 1839 as the first service percussion arm to be tried out, but it soon came to be thought of as one of the worst weapons of its time. It underwent numerous alterations in design and by 1854 had been replaced by the Rifled Musket, Pattern 1851, which was based on the Minie system.

● *Rifled Musket, Pattern 1851.* The Rifled Musket, Pattern 1851, was a cumbersome and not wholly satisfactory arm, probably considered as a temporary

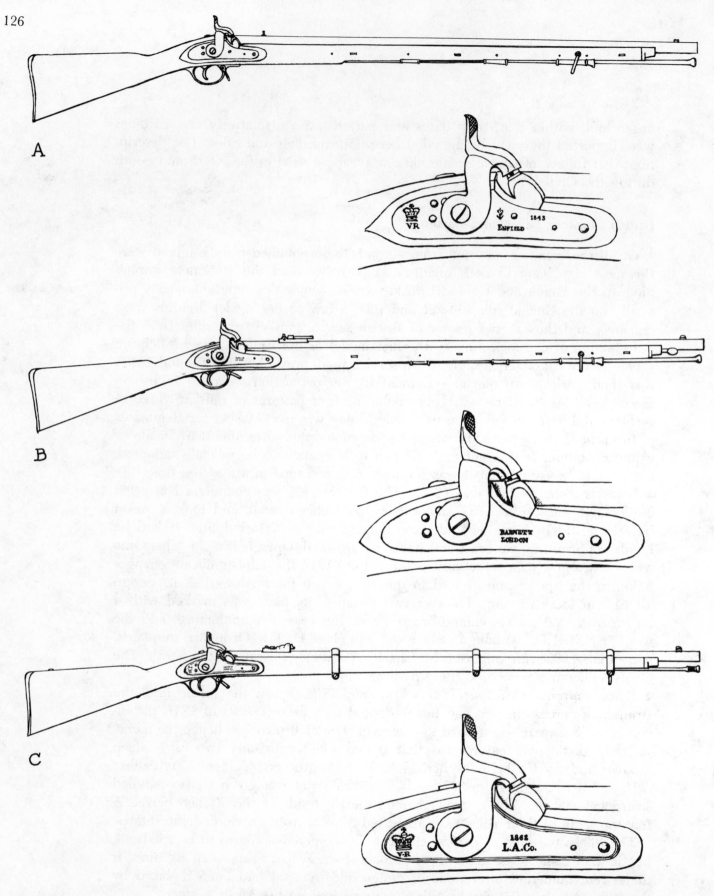

Fig. 33.   Imported British firearms: A. Pattern 1842 musket (Springfield Armory); B. Pattern 1851 rifled musket (Springfield Armory); C. Pattern 1853 rifled musket (West Point Museum). (Drawings by Walter J. Nock).

expedient. It replaced both the Brunswick rifle (in the hands of rifle regiments) and the service musket (either percussion of the Pattern 1842, or converted, or still flintlock) of the infantry. It closely resembled the Pattern 1842 in appearance having an overall length of 55 inches, but its caliber was .702. Its 39-inch barrel was rifled with four grooves.

The bulk of the British infantry sailing for the Crimea in 1854 were armed with the Pattern 1842 smoothbore musket; slowly these were replaced by the 1851 Minie rifle. But by this time a new and far superior model, the Enfield rifled musket Pattern 1853, had been adopted and a complete re-equipment of the army with the Pattern 1851 was never undertaken. It is believed that about 9,000 of these arms were imported in 1861 by John Hoey.

● *Rifled Musket, Pattern 1853, and modifications.* The Enfield rifled musket was adopted in 1853 following a series of experiments and a very considerable expansion of the Royal Small Arms Factory at Enfield, from which the pattern derived its name. New machinery had been supplied by Robbins & Lawrence of Windsor, Vermont, and the Ames Manufacturing Co. of Chicopee Falls, Mass. The Enfield first saw service in the Crimea in 1854–1855.

● The Enfield Pattern 1853 rifled musket underwent several alterations in the course of its life, especially in its rifling and ammunition. Earlier models were found to vary considerably in the size of their parts (lack of interchangeability was a common complaint of American users) and this was never completely corrected except perhaps in government armory-made weapons, which never reached this country.

Equally pronounced are the variations found today in the types in use at one time; details such as sights, bands, bayonet studs, and metal finish; as well as in the multiplicity of marks stamped into each weapon. Much of this variation can be laid to the fact that the Enfield imported to America was not the government armory-made weapon but one manufactured by several commercial houses in London and Birmingham, whose manufacture included much hand-fitting.

One feature of the Enfield was that its nominal caliber was only three-thousandths of an inch smaller than that of the Springfield, the difference being sometimes small enough to permit both to use each other's ammunition. All told, the United States purchased over 500,000 Enfields in 1861–1863, during which period the Confederacy acquired some 400,000. Although fifty importers sold Enfields to the U.S. government, seven of these (Howland & Aspinwall; Marcellus Hartley; John P. Moore; Naylor & Co.; Schuyler, Hartley & Graham; George L. Schuyler; and Tomes, Son & Melvain) accounted for 80 percent of these arms.

The more common and significant patterns of Enfield's imported during the Civil War were as follows:

● *Enfield Rifled Musket, Pattern 1853.* Percussion muzzleloader, cal .577, rifled with 3 grooves, 55 in. overall; after 1859 shortened to 54 in. Paper cartridge of cylindrical form having stiff paper insert (see Lewis, *Small Arms*, pp. 193–199). Socket bayonet, 17.5 in. blade, with locking ring on socket. The 39-in. barrel and three iron bands blued; lock plate bright or case-hardened in mottled colors; brass butt plate, trigger guard, and nose cap. Sliding leaf rear sight. This early model can be distinguished by its use of spring bands and swelled ramrod.

Commencing in 1856 the spring bands were eliminated in favor of screw-fastened ones, and the swell in the ramrod was discontinued in favor of a spring retainer. The ramrod head was slotted and knurled for a cleaning rag, and the piece was equipped with a nipple protector. This model remained the principal British service rifle until the conversion to a breechloader, known as the Snider, in 1867. As noted below, several shorter versions were produced for sergeants, for naval use, mounted men, and the like. The full story of the Enfield and its derivatives is told in C.H. Roads, *The British Soldier's Firearm, 1850–1864.*

The Pattern 1853 was manufactured at the Royal Small Arms Factory at Enfield, and by Belgian and English contractors. About 16,000 were also manufactured by Robbins & Lawrence, Windsor, Vermont. These had a crown on the lock plate with the word "WINDSOR" forward of the hammer under a year. Some of the Windsor Enfields were never shipped to England and saw service in the Civil War.

Lock plates of Enfield-made weapons intended for the British regular establishment bore the word "ENFIELD" under a year, plus the broad arrow. As has been said, these were never imported to the United States. Lock plates of weapons made by the London Armoury Company bear the letters "L.A.Co." under the year, as well as names of individual makers. Those made in Birmingham have the word "TOWER" under the year. Belgian-made arms were marked with a script date. All bore a crown over "VR" or the crown alone.

Barrel markings are numerous and complex, but usually include the London, Birmingham, or Liége view and proof marks on the upper surface, and the maker's name with the inspector's initials beneath.

● *Enfield Sergeants and Naval Rifles (or Rifled Muskets), Patterns 1856, 1858, and 1860.* Percussion muzzleloaders, cal .577, rifled: sergeants patterns 1856 and 1858 with 3 grooves; sergeants pattern 1860 and naval rifle with 5 grooves. Overall length 48.75 in. These patterns had 2 bands, screw fastened. Lug for saber bayonet on the barrel except in the case of the sergeants pattern 1858 which carried it on a reinforced front band. Used same ammunition as the rifled musket. Saber bayonet of yataghan style, 22.75-in. blade, with wood or hard rubber grips. On the sergeants rifles the rear sling swivel screwed into butt, while the naval rifle had its rear sling swivel attached to the trigger guard bow; front swivel on upper band. Same sight as rifled musket.

Barrel and bands blued, lock plate similar to rifled musket. Furniture brass on naval rifles, but bright iron on sergeants. Furnished with nipple protector. These rifles were sometimes advertised in America as used by English volunteer corps, in which case the wrist and forestock were usually checkered.

These arms were hand manufactured by private gun makers in London and Birmingham and consequently were non-interchangeable. A variety of lock plate markings will be found, together with minor differences in furniture. Approximately 8,000 of these short rifles were imported by the U.S. government during the war, better than half by Samuel Colt and by Schuyler Hartley & Graham.

● *Enfield Volunteer Rifle.* In most respects similar to the rifled musket as far

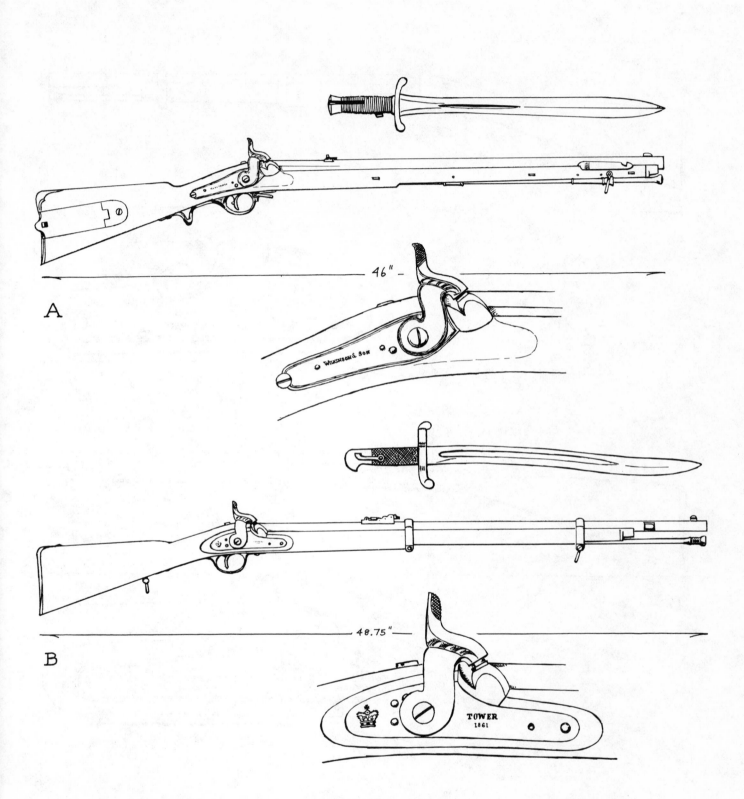

Fig. 34. Imported British firearms: A. Pattern 1837 rifle (Brunswick Rifle) and bayonet (Springfield Armory); B. Sergeants Pattern 1856 rifle and bayonet (West Point Museum). (Drawings by Walter J. Nock).

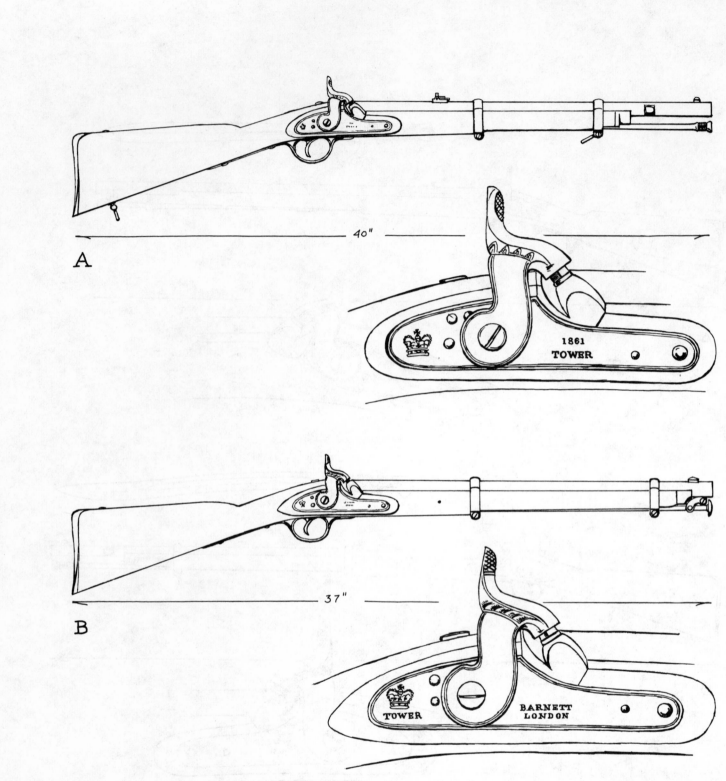

Fig. 35. Imported British firearms: A. Pattern 1858 artillery musketoon; B. Pattern 1858 cavalry carbine (both Springfield Armory). (Drawings by Walter J. Nock).

forward as the rear band, but approx. 50 in. overall and having only 2 bands. Same socket bayonet as rifle musket. Lock plate engraving varies. Many of these rifles were given as prizes and in some examples the grip was checkered and other changes occurred.

● *Enfield Artillery Musketoon (Carbine), Pattern 1858.* Percussion muzzle-loader, cal .577, rifled with 3 grooves, 40 inches overall. Same paper cartridge as Enfield rifle musket. Two bands and lug for saber bayonet on barrel. Saber bayonet with 22.8 in. yataghan blade and checkered leather grips. Small three-leaf rear sight. Butt plate, trigger guard, and nose cap brass; barrel and bands blued; lock plate case-hardened. Sling swivel on upper band and another screwed into butt near its toe. Same markings on lock plate as rifle musket. Some 500 were imported for use in the North, primarily by Naylor & Co. They also saw service in the South.

● *Enfield Cavalry Carbine, Pattern 1858.* Percussion muzzleloader, cal. .577, rifled with 3 grooves; 37 in. overall. Same paper cartridge as Enfield rifle musket. Two bands, the upper one placed close to the muzzle; sling swivels on upper band and trigger guard or sling rod and ring on left side. Ramrod fixed by a swivel attachment. Barrel and bands blued; butt plate, trigger guard, and nose cap brass; other metal usually case-hardened in mottled colors. Various markings on lock plate including crown and "BARNETT/LONDON." Although only 200 were imported for the Union, the Confederacy is known to have purchased significant numbers.

Austrian Muskets and Rifles

In terms of numbers received, the weapons imported from Austria-Hungary stood second in importance to British long arms. The U.S. Ordnance Bureau categorized these arms into eighteen types, graded as 2nd, 3rd, or 4th class, but initially they fell into two broad categories as far as ignition systems and calibers were concerned. Weapons made before 1854 were caliber .70 (16.9 mm) and had a tube-primer, while those made after that year were caliber .54 (13.9 mm) and used a conventional cone and percussion cap. Most imported Austrian weapons were altered in one way or another.

Figs. 36, 37, 38

Until 1842 the regulation Austrian infantry musket was a flintlock. In that year a new pattern rifle musket was adopted which employed the Augustin tube-lock. A similar ignition system invented by Giuseppe Console had been used since 1835 to convert some flintlocks. As late as 1854 the bulk of Austria's foot troops were armed with smoothbores converted to Augustin locks. Sixteen or twenty selected men of each company (*Karabiniers*) were issued rifles. Both were caliber .70. Since the tube-lock ammunition had the detonator rolled into each cartridge, there was no need to provide the soldier with a cap pouch on his belt.

Jaeger battalions after 1842 carried a short rifle (*Stutzen*) with the Augustin tube-lock, as well as a long rifle (*Karabiner*) and a Delvigne chambered rifle (*Kammer-Buechse*), with similar ignition. The short rifle was not fitted with a

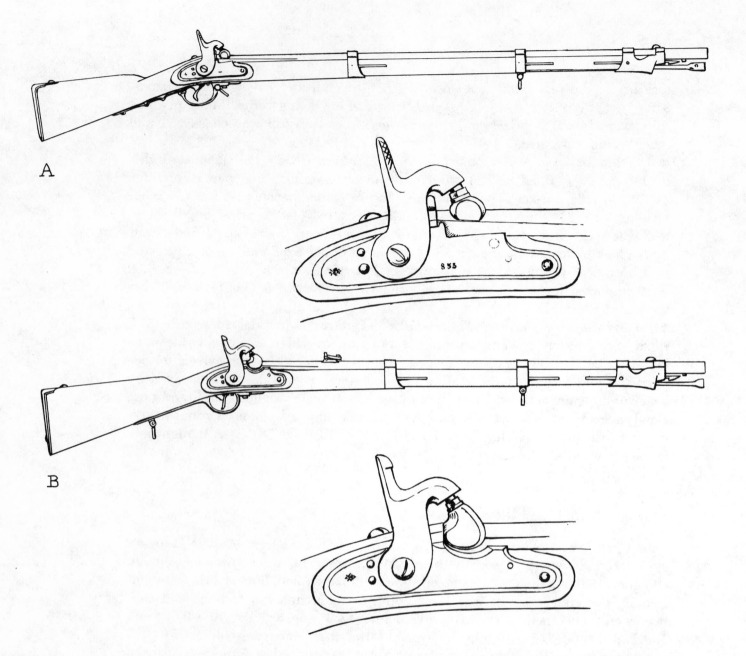

Fig. 36. Imported Austrian firearms: A. Converted and rifled Augustin musket, Model 1842 (West Point Museum); B. Converted Augustin short (Engineer) musket, Model 1842 (Springfield Armory). (Drawings by Walter J. Nock).

ramrod, this being suspended from one of the jaeger's belts. About 1848–1849 the short rifle was given up and the *Kammer-Buechse* redesigned; the latter had both ramrod and bayonet.

In 1854 the Austrian army adopted the percussion-cap system, bringing out a rifle musket and two types of rifled carbine. The latter two took bayonets but had no ramrods. The new pattern, called the "Lorenz," was caliber .54 throughout. Cap pouches were issued and worn over the chest on one of the cross belts. These arms were used in Austria's conflict in 1859 with France and Italy. An Austrian decision to switch to a gun-cotton propellant, requiring a stronger mechanism, made these arms available for sale in large numbers.

In 1861 agents from both the North and South combed Austria for serviceable weapons. Over 300,000 of the Model 1854 alone were exported to America, secured from the government arsenal in Vienna and from various gunmakers and entrepreneurs. Many were rebored to calibers as large as .60, supposedly to accept U.S. regulation ammunition. Slightly more than 25,000 of the tube-lock models were exported to the North only, for the Augustin tube-lock presented insurmountable difficulties for the Confederate ordnance authorities. All but 15,000 of these were converted from tube-lock to percussion and rifled in order to facilitate their use over here. Thousands of Austrian tube-lock arms were converted to percussion in Europe for sale to the United States. The converted tube-lock weapons were often called "Boker" models, after Herman Boker & Company, and included conversions of Austrian flintlocks dating back to the Model 1798.

The principal Austrian weapons imported to America were as follows:

● *Converted Infantry Musket, Models 1798, 1807, and 1828.* Percussion, muzzle-loader, rifled with 4 grooves, cal .71. Overall length 57.75 in. Paper cartridge with conical ball. Lock and furniture bright or brass, depending on model. Three bands with upper band double-strapped; all flattened on bottom. Nipple inserted on top right of barrel. Folding leaf rear sight, graduated to 1000 meters, or simple notch on barrel tang. Sling swivels on center band and trigger guard. Quadrangular socket bayonet, 18.75 in. blade, fastened by lug or spring catch under barrel. Lock plate plain; marked on trigger guard with small Austrian eagle in oval and year of manufacture (first number omitted).

● *Augustin Musket, Model 1842.* Augustin pattern tube-lock, muzzleloader, cal .70, smoothbore. Overall length 57.75 in. Paper cartridge with round ball. Quadrangular socket bayonet retained by two types of spring clamp beneath muzzle; blade length 18–18.75 in. Three bands flattened on bottoms, with upper band double-strapped. Furniture usually iron, bright; some examples had brass trigger guard, bands, and butt plate. Simple notched rear sight on barrel tang, not adjustable. Front sight partially enclosed by upper strap of forward band. Sling swivels on trigger guard and center band. Marked on lock plate with small Austrian eagle and year of manufacture (the first number omitted). Others marked on top of barrel with "R. S. HERETTA" and "IB" in oval, etc. Most of these muskets converted to percussion lock in 1861, the cone seat being forged into the top of the barrel; many were rifled with four grooves and given the 1000 meter leaf rear sight described above. Some 10,000 of this model were converted and rifled in Cincinnati for General Frémont; these had the cone tapped directly into the barrel and some were given U.S. pattern long range sights.

Two shorter versions of the Model 1842 were also imported. The first had an overall length of 52.5 in. and the heel of the butt was almost squared; otherwise similar. (In the example inspected, the conversion was accomplished by inserting the cone seat into the side of the barrel and notching—rather than cutting away—the top of the lock plate. The hammer is primitive with square sides. No significant markings found. Not rifled.) This variant was known in Austria as the cadet musket.

The second shortened variant was converted from an Augustin tube-lock muzzleloader issued in Austria originally to engineer troops, cal .70; its 33.5-in. barrel was rifled with 4 grooves. Overall length 48.5 in. Paper cartridge with ball wrapped separately from powder. Quadrangular socket bayonet retained by spring clamp beneath muzzle (or possibly, at times, by a lug), blade length 18.5 in. Three bands. Leaf rear sight like Lorenz rifle musket, graduated to 900 meters. Furniture bright or brass, bright lock plate and hammer. Sling swivels on center band, and underneath butt or on trigger guard tang. Lock plate markings: year and eagle as on musket. Converted to cap lock as described in Model 1849, below.

● *Augustin Long Rifle (Kammer-Buechse), Model 1842.* Tube-lock, muzzleloader, cal .71. Rifled with 12 grooves. Overall length 47.5 in. Paper cartridge. Three bands; sling swivel on center band and trigger guard tang. Fitted with wooden patch box until 1847. Brass furniture and butt plate; bright hammer and lock plate. Cheek piece on stock. Trigger guard extended in rear to form grip for second finger. Unusual sword bayonet without guard or hilt, attached by means of sleeve that engaged a spring underneath the barrel in front of the band. Blade 23.5 in.; 1.3 in. wide at base. Marked with year and double-headed eagle and some examples stamped "BENTZ" on top of barrel.

This rifle was converted to cap lock in the same manner as described for the Model 1849, below. It can readily be distinguished by its trigger guard and its single-branch upper band, which was fitted around the blade front sight. Equipped with a 2-leaf rear sight. This rifle was sometimes called the "Garibaldi" pattern. Because of its Delvigne chamber it was considered 4th class by the U.S. Ordnance Department; nevertheless nearly 6,000 were sold to the U.S. by George Hoydecker.

● *Augustin Long Rifle (Kammer-Buechse), Model 1849.* Similar to 1842 pattern except a single front band only; no patch box; rifled with 12 grooves; trigger guard extended in rear to form a hand grip. Overall length 48.3 in. Slightly longer bayonet, 24-in. blade, having a slotted sleeve that engaged a lug on the right side of the barrel near the muzzle, plus a locking ring. Brass trigger guard and butt plate, other metal bright. Lock plate marked with year and eagle, and name of maker on top of barrel. Barrel octagonal in rear. Cheek piece on stock. Upper sling swivel inserted into stock 14 in. from muzzle; lower swivel on rear of trigger guard. Converted to cap lock by inserting cone seat on top of barrel and cutting a circular or square notch in lock plate, or by adding a cone seat having a curved bottom to the side of the barrel. Leaf rear sight with three holes. This rifle, also called the "Garibaldi," was originally issued to sailors of the Danube *Flottillen-Corps.* Nearly 20,000 were imported by Charles Bulkley and George Ramsdell.

● *Augustin Carbine (Kammer-Karabiner), Model 1842.* Augustin pattern tube-lock, muzzleloader, cal .71, rifled with 12 grooves. Overall length 30 in. with 14.5-in. barrel. No bayonet. Single iron band. Double sling ring on left-side held by bar near small of stock. Trigger guard formed into partial grip. Metal bright. Open notch rear sight on breech plug tang. George Schuyler purchased 10,000 of these carbines in 1861 and brought them into the United States after conversion to percussion.

● *Lorenz Rifle Musket, Model 1854.* Percussion, muzzleloader, cal .54, rifled with 4 grooves; overall length 52.75 in. The Austrian cardboard and paper cartridge with Wilkinson cylindro-ogival ball was not used in this country. Quadrangular bayonet with spiralling slot and lock ring; 18.75-in. blade. Furniture all iron of originally grey finish. Lock plate usually bright. Three bands, the front band being single-strapped and dished on top in front. Both leaf and block rear sights used, the leaf sights having two peeps and sighted to 900 meters. Sling swivels on trigger guard and center band. Barrel octagonal in rear. Lock plate marked with small Austrian eagle and year of manufacture (the first number omitted). Manufacturer's markings on barrel, such as "ANN J. OSTERLEIN," "ZEILINGER," "PIRKO IN WIEN," "CARL HEISER," etc.

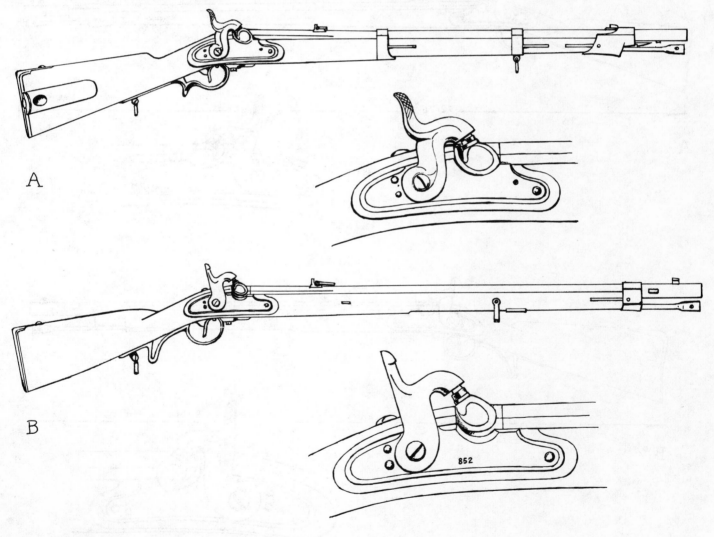

Fig. 37. Imported Austrian firearms: A. Converted Augustin long rifle (*Kammer-Buechse* or "Garibaldi"), Model 1842, markings obliterated (Springfield Armory); B. Converted Augustin long rifle (*Flottillen-Corps Kammer-Buechse* or "Garibaldi") Model 1849, markings partially obliterated (West Point Museum). (Drawings by Walter J. Nock).

The major importers of this model in the North were Herman Boker, S. Dingee & Co., Guiterman Bros., Marcellus Hartley, L. Marx & Co., G. Schuyler, and Samuel Smith. Huse purchased large numbers for the Confederacy.

● *Lorenz Jaeger Short Rifle, Model 1854.* Percussion muzzleloader, cal .54, rifled with 4 grooves; overall length 43.25 in. Same cartridge as rifle musket. Unusual sword bayonet without guard or hilt, attached by means of a sleeve cut with a spiralling slot that engaged both front sight and lug; locking ring; blade 23.5 in., 1.3 in. wide at base.

Octagonal barrel to within 4 in. of muzzle; all furniture bright iron. No bands; sling swivels 10.5 in. from muzzle and 4.5 in. from toe to butt. Walnut stock had

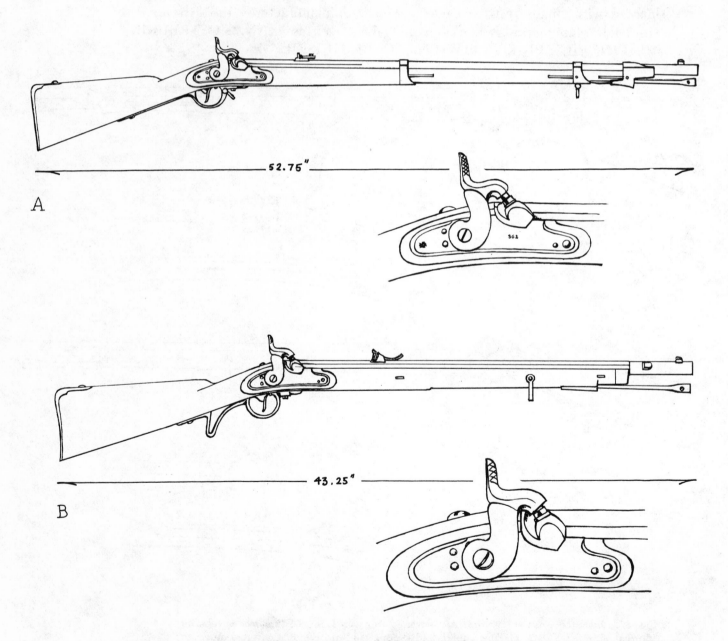

Fig. 38. Imported Austrian firearms: A. Lorenz rifle musket Model 1854; B. Lorenz Jaeger short rifle Model 1854 (both Springfield Armory). (Drawings by Walter J. Nock).

cheek piece and trigger guard tang formed a hand grip. Curved rear leaf sight which elevated, held by wing nut. The Austrian original had no fitting for ramrod but all export weapons had their stocks bored and fitted with them. Eagle and date sometimes on lock plate; manufacturers' names like "BENTZ," "FERD FRUWIRTH," etc. inscribed on top of barrel. P.H. Tuska and Herman Boker imported over 2,500 of these rifles.

Prussian Muskets and Rifles

Experiments with percussion weapons began in Prussia as early as 1826 and a short percussion jaeger rifle was issued in 1835. In 1839 the army decided to convert all flintlocks to the percussion system and to issue a new model infantry musket with this type of ignition.

Fig. 39

In the meanwhile, Prussia had been engaged in other experiments: with the Thouvenin "tige,"* with rifling, and with breechloading. One result was the decision to rifle its stock of old conversions and to manufacture all new Model 1839 weapons thereafter as rifle muskets on the Minie system. Another was the issue of the Model 1841 breechloading infantry rifle, or "needle gun."

By 1855 one battalion of each line infantry regiment and all the guard infantry were armed with the breechloader, and it was planned to increase this percentage gradually. Other line infantrymen carried the percussion rifle musket while the arsenals were stocked with everything from converted smoothbores to new rifle muskets. As more breechloaders were issued, these stocks grew in size.

Prussian jaegers carried the Model 1835 short rifle adapted to the tige in 1847; gradually these were replaced by breechloaders. Pioneers carried a converted musketoon until these, too, were replaced.

When American agents reached Prussia in 1861 and 1862 they found the government willing to sell a portion of its surplus of long arms. When they could purchase the rifled musket, they secured a well made gun, often little used, whose only serious limitation was its large caliber. Breechloaders, of course, were not to be had at any price.

The four patterns of Prussian weapon imported to this country in any number appear to have been:

● *Prussian Musket, Model 1809.* Converted to percussion, with curved cone seat forged onto side of barrel. Muzzleloader, cal .72, smoothbore. Overall length 56.6 in. Paper cartridge with round ball. Triangular socket bayonet with unslotted sleeve, attached by spring lock beneath barrel; blade 19.2 in. Three bands; sling swivel on center band and trigger guard. Barrel, lock plate, and butt plate usually bright; brass bands, trigger guard, and sometimes butt plate. Markings on lock plate: Potsdam," "Saarn," or "Neisse" under crown, or "Sp/Suhl," etc. Various other markings were used, especially on the rear of the barrel, such as

* A type of muzzleloading rifle invented by Col. Thouvein of the French artillery: a pin (*tige*) projected from the bottom of the breech, causing the bullet to expand when it was rammed home.

"FW" under crown, year of manufacture or conversion, and regimental designation. These conversions can be distinguished from later patterns by the distinctively 3-pointed ends of the trigger guard and heel of the butt plate. Stock notched for cheek; simple notch rear sight on barrel tang. Hammer thumb piece cross hatched.

The cones on these muskets were altered to accept the U.S. regulation cap. Some appear also to have been altered to cal .69. All were rated as 3rd class weapons. Major importers included Herman Boker & Co., Heddon & Hoey, A. Moller & Co., James B. Taylor, and Sarson & Roberts.

● *Prussian Musket, Model 1839.* Percussion, muzzleloader, cal .70/.71, smoothbore. Overall length 57 in. Paper cartridge with round ball. Socket bayonet attached by spring catch, or set over lug with locking ring; blade 19.2 in. Three bands; sling swivel on center band and trigger guard. Bands and trigger guard (sometimes butt plate) brass; other parts iron, bright. Cheek rest on stock. Simple notched rear sight on barrel tang. Cone seat fitted to a patent breech that could be unscrewed from barrel. Markings on lock plate: crown above place of manufacture: 'SUHL/S&C," "Zella," "Potsdam," etc., with year of manufacture sometimes under that; crown and cypher on top of barrel at breech; small crown and letter or serial number on other parts. Rear of lock plate rounded. Upper band varied in size (possibly later models had smaller type although these may have been fitted only to rifle muskets of the Model 1839).

Many of these muskets were rifled in cals .69–.72 and equipped with leaf rear sight.

● *Prussian Rifle Musket, Model 1839/55.* Same as musket, but rifled with 4 grooves in cal .69, and fitted with leaf rear sight. All bayonets for this pattern appear to have been fitted with locking ring which secured the socket to a stud under the barrel.

● *Prussian Jaeger Short Rifle, Model 1835/47.* Percussion (with hair trigger and safety lock), muzzleloader. Cal .58, rifled with 8 grooves and fitted with a patent breech. Overall length 43.8 in. Octagonal barrel, no bands, wooden patch box in stock. Mountings of brass, with trigger guard formed into a grip. Paper cartridge. Hunting pattern sword bayonet, fitting onto barrel by slide on right side; blade 21.2 in.; rear sight with two leaves, the larger one pierced for ranges up to 700 paces (580 yards). Markings on lock plate: a crown over "Potsdam/G.T," "SUHL/S&C," etc.

Commercially-Made Arms from Suhl

The city of Suhl, in the Thuringian province of Prussia, and its satellite cities, Zella, Mehlis, and St. Blasien, provided the German states with a private armsmaking complex that rivaled those of Liége and Birmingham. A number of Northern merchants entered into agreements with the Suhl gunmakers to provide weapons for the Union. Prussian pattern M1839/55 arms were the main types produced; however, a number of special types were also manufactured. The main types were:

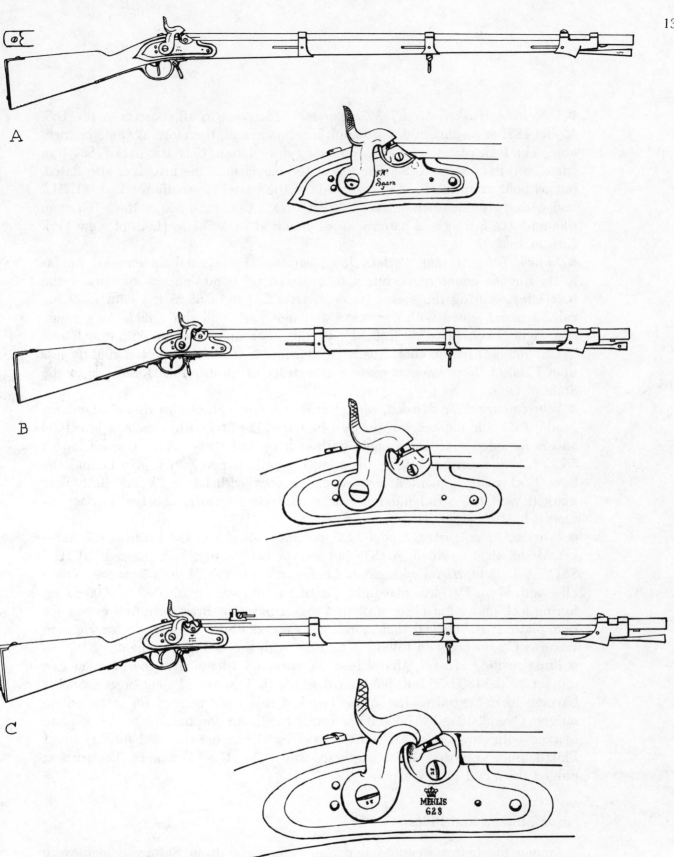

Fig. 39. Imported Prussian firearms: A. Converted infantry musket, Model 1809 (Springfield Armory); B. Infantry musket, Model 1839, markings obliterated (West Point Museum); C. Rifle musket, Model 1839/55, commercially manufactured at Suhl (West Point Museum). (Drawings by Walter J. Nock).

● *U.S. Rifle Musket, Model 1861, variant.* Identical in all respects to the U.S. Model 1861 as to dimensions although handmade and, therefore, not interchangeable. The lock plates bear no contractor's designation, only the date "1861," an eagle, and the letters "U.S." The top of the barrel near the breech is also dated, but without proof marks. The underside of the barrel is usually marked "SUHL" and with the name of the maker, "CH. FUNK." Less than 500 of these "German rifle-muskets, Springfield pattern" were imported by William Hahn of New York City in 1862.

● *Enfield Rifle Musket, Pattern 1853, variant.* In external appearance similar to its English counterpart, but with brass barrel bands and a stud under the barrel for securing the socket bayonet. Overall length 55.25 in., with a 39 in., cal .58 barrel, rifled with 3 grooves and mounted with the Enfield long range rear sight. Lock plate of Enfield pattern either unmarked or with the letters "VCS" forward of the cock. Schuyler, Hartley, & Graham imported slightly less than 1,700 of these arms as part of a contract to furnish 10,000 Enfields to the State of Ohio.

● *Wurtemburg Rifle Musket, Model 1857, variant.* Similar to the Wurtemburg Model 1857 rifle musket, but the 39.4 in. barrel is rifled with 3 grooves in cal .58 and is mounted with the Enfield pattern long range rear sight. Overall length 55.25 in. All furniture bright; the trigger guard shaped into a grip behind the bow. Lock plate is marked forward of the cock with letters "VCS." Butt plate marked with the serial number; various inspection marks. Socket bayonet attached to stud under barrel.

● *Prussian Rifle Musket, Model 1835, variant.* Similar to the Prussian rifle musket Model 1839 as rifled in 1855 but with a back action lock marked "SUHL/ S&C." A 41.25 in. barrel with patent breech; rifled in cal .72 with 5 grooves. Overall length 57 in. Two-leaf rear sight, the larger with slide graduated to 1000 paces. Spring lock under barrel for unslotted socket bayonet. Brass furniture except for butt plate. It is believed that more than 4,000 of these were made for Herman Boker & Co., in order to fulfill his contract with the U.S. government.

● *Prussian Rifle Musket, Model 1835/55, variant.* Identical to the Prussian rifle musket Model 1839/55 but rifled in cal .615 with 4 grooves. Patent breech. Socket bayonet locks to stud under barrel. Two-leaf rear sight pierced for intermediate ranges. Overall length 57 in. Brass furniture except for butt plate. Lock plate marked with crown over "MEHLIS," over serial number. In 1862 John Hoey of Philadelphia imported 1,700 of these arms. The U.S. Ordnance Department judged them 2nd class weapons.

Saxon Muskets and Rifles

Among the better weapons imported were those from Saxony, which were purchased in Dresden and often carried that name in America. The Saxon army had received the percussion musket in 1836 and in 1859–1860 its infantry was rearmed with rifle muskets using projectiles of the Austrian pattern. Prior to 1859 its four jaeger battalions had been using a short rifle, adapted to the tige

Figs. 40 and 41

in 1849, and during the same period many of the smoothbore percussion muskets in stock had been rifled. Furthermore, it appears that the first rifle muskets secured in 1851 had the Thouvenin system *à tige* which the Saxon war minister had, by 1861, decided to replace with plain chambered rifles. In any event, a quite considerable stock of reasonably serviceable weapons were available in Dresden.

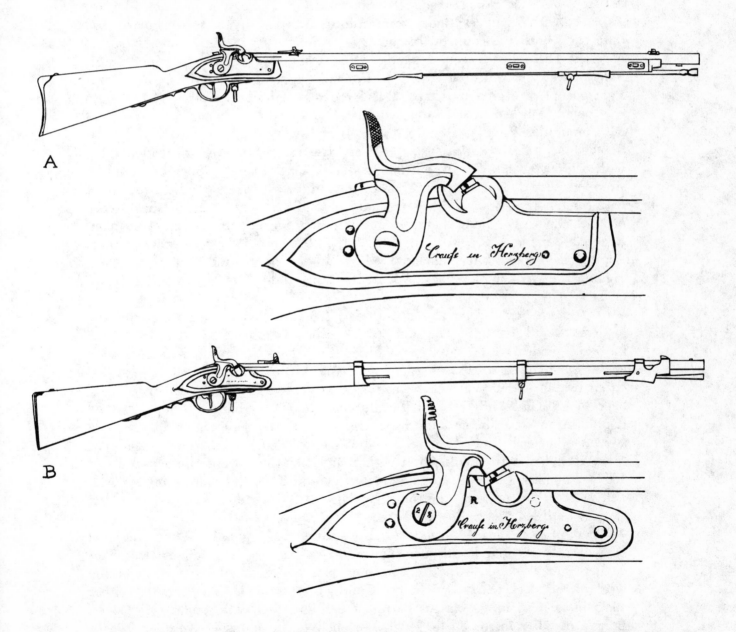

Fig. 40. Imported Saxon firearms: A. Infantry musket, Model 1835 (rifled) (West Point Museum); B. Rifle musket, Model 1852 (?), some parts replaced (Springfield Armory). (Drawings by Walter J. Nock).

The more usual Saxon weapons imported were:

● *Saxon Infantry Musket, Model 1835 (rifled).* Percussion, muzzleloader, cal .70, smoothbore. No bands, stock held by 3 large pins fastened through rectangular brass escutcheons. Two brass trumpets for ramrod; sling swivels fitted to upper trumpet and trigger guard. Part brass trigger guard; brass foretip on stock; barrel browned, other parts bright. Overall length 55.5 in. Bayonet lug on bottom of barrel for socket bayonet. Lock plate with squared front; marked in script "Crause in Herzberg," monogram "T" and "S", or letter "R" in several places.

Also rifled with 4 narrow grooves and fitted with leaf rear sight with 3 holes.

● *Saxon Infantry Musket, Model 1852(?) (rifled).* Percussion, muzzleloader, cal .71, rifled with 5 grooves; tige screwed into breech pin. Bands, trigger guard, and butt plate brass; other metal bright. Overall length 55.75 in. Triangular socket bayonet. Three bands, upper band double-strapped of French trumpet shape. Sling swivels on center band and on front of trigger guard. Original open rear sight occupied all of barrel tang; 3-leaf rocking rear sight added, graduated to 600 meters. Marked in script on lock plate "Crause in Herzberg" and on barrel with proof marks and small crown over "L."

● *Liége-made Saxon Rifle Musket, Model 1844.* Percussion, muzzleloader, rifled with 5 grooves, cal .71. Overall length 57 in. Three bands, upper one double-strapped; sling swivels on center band and front of trigger guard. Leaf rear sight with three holes. Bands and trigger guard brass; other metal bright. Cheek piece on stock. Lock plate had squared front resembling Saxon pattern. Socket bayonet. Lock plate marked "P.J. MALHERBE/A LIEGE" and "W" under crown; others are known marked only with letters "B.F." under crown, and with Ohio markings on the wrist of the stock. Apparently still others had "A.F." under crown on lock plate.

● *Liége-made Saxon Rifle Muskets, Models 1851 and 1857.* Percussion, muzzleloaders, overall lengths 53 in. and 56 in., respectively with 37.12 in. and 40.25 in. barrels, rifled with 4 grooves in cal .58. Both have 200 paces rear sight with leaves for 400 and 600 paces. Liége proof marks on barrel. Socket bayonet secured by lug under barrel. Back action lock marked "PJ MALHERBE & Cie." over "A LIEGE," and "JH." All furniture bright. Three bands; trumpet shaped double strap front band and distinctive double-strapped center band. Sling swivels attached to middle band and butt stock. Cheek rest. (The longer barreled version was originally fitted with a tige, but these were eliminated about 1857). Purchasing agent George Schuyler secured 27,000 of these arms in Dresden in 1861 for the U.S. government, whose Ordnance officials rated them 1st class in both lengths.

● *Rifled Musket, Saxon Manufacture, nicknamed "Cyclops".* While this arm has not been identified with any known foreign pattern, its origin is clear. Percussion, muzzleloader with a center-hung hammer, secured by a strap at the wrist of the stock marked in script "Crause in Herzberg." Two lengths, either 49.25 in. or 55.5 in. Damascus barrel of cal .70 rifled with 4 narrow grooves. Barrels of 33.12 in. or 39 in. length fastened to stock respectively by two or three wedges. Patent breech with cone inset into rear. Stud under barrel secures

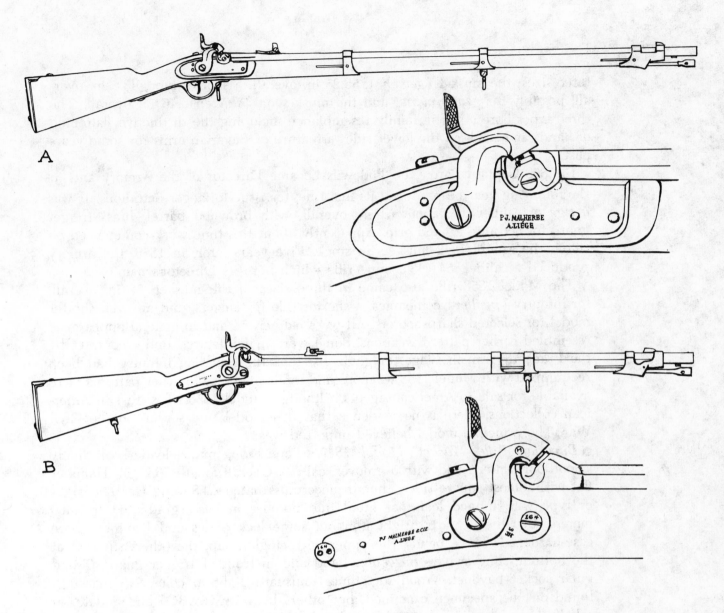

Fig. 41 Imported Saxon firearms of Liége manufacture: A. Rifle musket, Model 1844 (West Point Museum); B. Rifle musket, Models 1851 and 1857 (Springfield Armory). (Drawings by Walter J. Nock).

a triangular bayonet. Rear sight is a hole through the center of the hammer (hence the nickname "cyclops"). Brass nosecap, trigger guard bow, and ramrod pipes; iron butt plate. Cheek rest in stock.

Bavarian Muskets and Rifles

The Bavarian army introduced cap lock weapons in 1839, commencing with the conversion of existing reserves. Considerable experimentation had preceded this step, and a special force of artisans was assembled to carry it out. In 1842 the royal armory at Amberg issued its first standard cap lock musket, and it is with this pattern that we are chiefly concerned; only a few earlier conversions could have reached America, if any at all. The Model 1842 was produced in

Fig. 42

three sizes: the musket (*gewehr*), 56.25 in. overall; a shorter type, 48.5 in. over-all, possibly for *gendarmerie*; and the musketoon (*stutzen*), 46 in. overall. The three types bore a strong family resemblance including the distinctive flattening of bands and stock on the lower side—a feature of Bavarian arms for some years past.

In 1853 Captain Baron von Podewils became Director of the Armory and in the following year he produced its first rifle, for issue to jaeger battalions. It was *à tige* of caliber .67, about 51 in. overall, with browned barrel, brass trigger guard formed into a hand grip. Apparently about this time work commenced on rifling the Model 1842 muskets in stock. Five years later, in 1858, the armory produced a caliber .54 (13.9 mm) rifle which bore its Director's name.

The Model 1858 rifle also came in three sizes: a rifle-musket, 52 in. overall, for infantry (*fusilier*) companies, a shorter rifle for jaegers, and an even shorter model for selected sharpshooters. All were caliber .54 and in general appearance resembled earlier pattern weapons. Some were manufactured under contract by the Francotte firm in Liége, Belgium. By 1862 the Bavarian infantry had been reequipped with Model 1858 weapons and a fair number of earlier patterns were available for sale to American agents. Although Model 1858 rifles exist in American collections, there is no evidence that this model saw service in the Civil War. The principal model believed imported was:

● *Bavarian Rifle Musket, Model 1842.* Percussion, muzzleloader, originally smoothbore, later rifled with 5 grooves, cal .70. Overall length 56.25 in. Hammer flat with almost square sides; thumb piece cross hatched. Sliding leaf rear sight or type with hinged leaf that fitted into notches in base, graduated to 1400 meters. Usually all parts bright iron but some lock plates and hammers were case-hardened. Three bands, the upper with single strap, the others squared at the bottom; sling swivels on center band and in front of trigger guard. Triangular socket bayonet. Wood sometimes unusually light in color. No markings found on one specimen examined, but others bear "AMBERG" and a date, in a half circle over crown. Rated 3rd class by U.S. Ordnance Department.

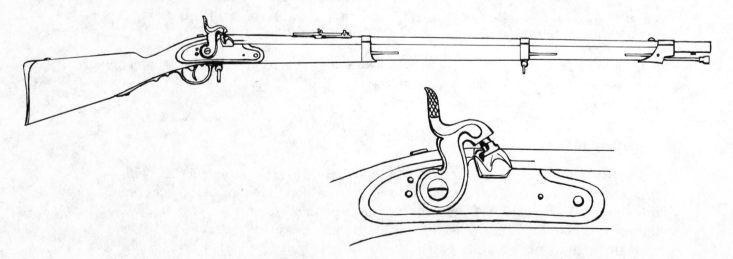

Fig. 42.   Imported Bavarian firearms: Rifle musket Model 1842 (West Point Museum). (Drawing by Walter J. Nock).

French Muskets and Rifles

The French army adopted the percussion system in 1840 for all of its services and at once began to convert its flintlock infantry muskets, reaching back to the Model 1822. The conversions of 1840, as well as the new models adopted that year, utilized a patent breech. By 1842 this breech had been replaced throughout by a forged bolster. Both converted and new muskets came in two overall lengths (57.9 in. and 55.9 in. for the former, 56.9 in. and 54.5 for the latter), the longer for grenadiers and fusiliers, the shorter for voltigeurs. The caliber of the new model was .71, and the conversions were enlarged to this caliber from their original .69. The Model 1842 had a back-action lock which was somewhat altered in design in 1847. Small alterations were made six years later, but there was no noticeable change in exterior appearance except in the bolster.

Figs. 43 and 44

In the meanwhile, experiments had been conducted with rifling, which led to the issue of three experimental rifled percussion weapons, utilizing Delvigne's reduced chamber and all firing a spherical ball: the "Carabine à la Pontcharra" Model 1837, the Light Rampart Rifle Model 1838, and the "Carabine de munition" Model 1840. The Rampart Rifle was modified slightly in 1840. These and later models, through 1842, were issued for trial, principally to the newly formed battalions of Foot Chasseurs.

The next development came in 1846 when the chamber of the Model 1842 Chasseur "carabine" (or rifle) was replaced by a tige, developed by Colonel Thouvenin. And finally, with the introduction of the pointed bullet with a hollow base by Captain Minié, a new line of rifled weapons was adopted during the years 1853–1857.

The "System of 1853" included a musket for infantry, one for the navy, another for dragoons, and a musketoon for gendarmerie. A modified rifle or "carabine" was also authorized that year and in 1854 some infantry muskets and gendarmerie musketoons were rifled and issued to the Imperial Guard.

In 1857 the French army adopted its first standard rifle musket and what turned out to be its last muzzleloader. It came in a single length for all branches and closely resembled the Model 1853 infantry musket. A new gendarmerie musketoon along the same lines was also issued, and in 1859, a new "carabine" or rifle. Models going back to 1840 were altered to conform to the new rifle musket. These were the chief weapons in the hands of the French army at the outbreak of the American Civil War.

The result of these frequent changes of model, and even more frequent alteration of older models, was a bewildering assortment of weapons often differing only slightly in external appearance. Examples of as many as thirty variant forms, dating from the twenty years or so before the Civil War, can be found today in this country in a single collection.

Not only was the stock of French arms well assorted in 1861, but it was very large. The Emperor Napoleon III at first did not favor the sale of arms to either of the American belligerents, but his objections could not prevail for long. During 1861 and 1862 large quantities of the obsolescent French muskets and rifles found their way into the hands of Union and Confederate agents and speculators.

Federal ordnance officers divided these imported French arms into seven categories, arranged into four classes on the basis of their serviceability. For practical purposes the seven categories can be reduced to three, especially in terms of their external appearance.

● *Converted Infantry Musket, Model 1822.* Percussion, muzzleloader, cal .69 or .71, smoothbore or rifled with 4 grooves. Overall length 57.9 in. or 55.8 in. Small open rear sight on barrel tang, or folding leaf rear sight graduated to 1,000 meters if rifled. Three bands; upper band of characteristic "trumpet" type with two straps; sling swivels attached on center band and in front of trigger guard. All metal bright, Model 1822 socket bayonet; blade c. 15 in., with locking ring. Cone seat either set into top of barrel or (in the case of some Liége conversions) placed on right, with clean-out screw.

Markings on these conversions varied but all had the name of the royal arsenal on the lock plate ("Mre. Rle. de Tulle," ". . . de Charleville," ". . . de Mutzig," or ". . . de St. Etienne"); "M1822" (or an even earlier date) was on the barrel tang; the date of conversion was stamped on the barrel, coupled with proof marks and indications of caliber in millimeters.

(Examples of converted Model 1816 French infantry muskets exist. The differences between Models 1816 and 1822 were slight, and except in length the details above apply to both.)

● *Infantry Musket, Models 1842, 1853, and 1857.* Percussion, smoothbore, or rifled muzzleloader, cal .71 or .70. Back-action lock of the Models 1840 or 1847; nipple screwed into shoulder. Paper cartridge with round ball. Small open rear sight on barrel tang. Three bands; upper band of characteristic "trumpet" type with two straps; sling swivels attached on center band and in front of trigger guard. Overall lengths: 56 in. and 58.2 in. Metal usually bright, Model 1822 socket bayonet; c. 15 in. blade, with locking ring. Markings on lock plates, as with Model 1822, indicated the manufacturing armory—"Royale" before 1848, "Nationale" ("Nle") 1848–1852, "Imperiale" after 1852, as for example: "Mre. Rle./de St. Etienne." Most were dated and all bore proof marks and other symbols. The model year was marked on the barrel tang. A distinctive feature of these muskets was the three-sided escutcheon on the left side, opposite the lock plate.

In 1847 the interior arrangement of the lock was altered without exterior change. A new Model 1847 bayonet was provided, differing only in a reinforced shoulder from the previous pattern. Minor alterations followed in 1853 but the general appearance remained almost unchanged. After 1857 many of these infantry muskets were rifled in either cal .69 or .71, and given a leaf or curved rear sight. If rifled, they were rated in America as 2nd class weapons; smoothbore, as 3rd class.

The Model 1857 was a rifle musket, but it retained the outward appearance of the Model 1842, except the octagonal breech was extended forward and the cone seat made heavier. It was rifled with 4 grooves and used a paper cartridge with the pointed Minie ball, hence its ramrod also differed. It came in only the shorter length, 56 in. overall.

(A version of the shorter infantry musket was manufactured for naval use; differences will be found in the use of brass and method of attaching sling. No record has been found of naval muskets or rifle muskets being imported.)

● *Dragoon Musket, Models 1842 and 1857.* Similar to the infantry muskets in all details except overall length, which was 48.8 in. Like the musket, early models were later rifled, apparently in cal .71, and given folding leaf rear sights. All carried the same socket bayonets as the infantry muskets. Some of the Model 1842 were manufactured under contract and are marked on lock plate "PALIARD V F/A St ETIENNE."

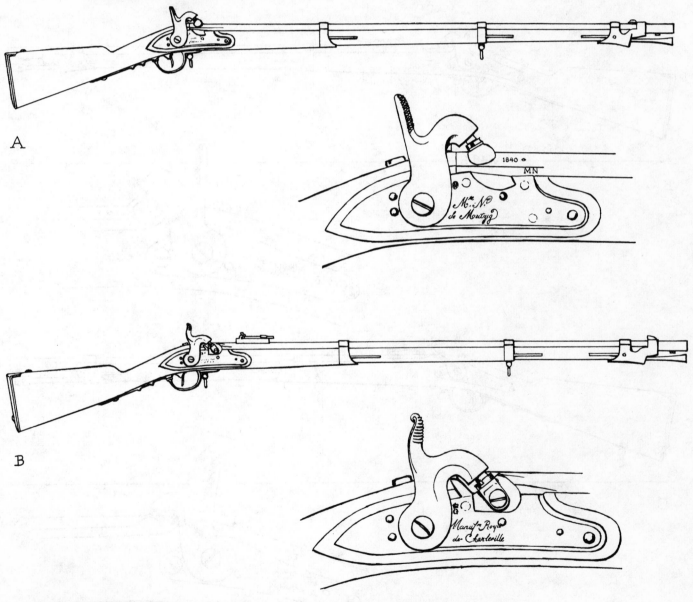

Fig. 43. Imported French firearms: A. Converted infantry musket, voltigeur length, Model 1822 (?); B. Infantry musket Model 1822, converted and rifled in Liége, grenadier length (both Springfield Armory). (Drawings by Walter J. Nock).

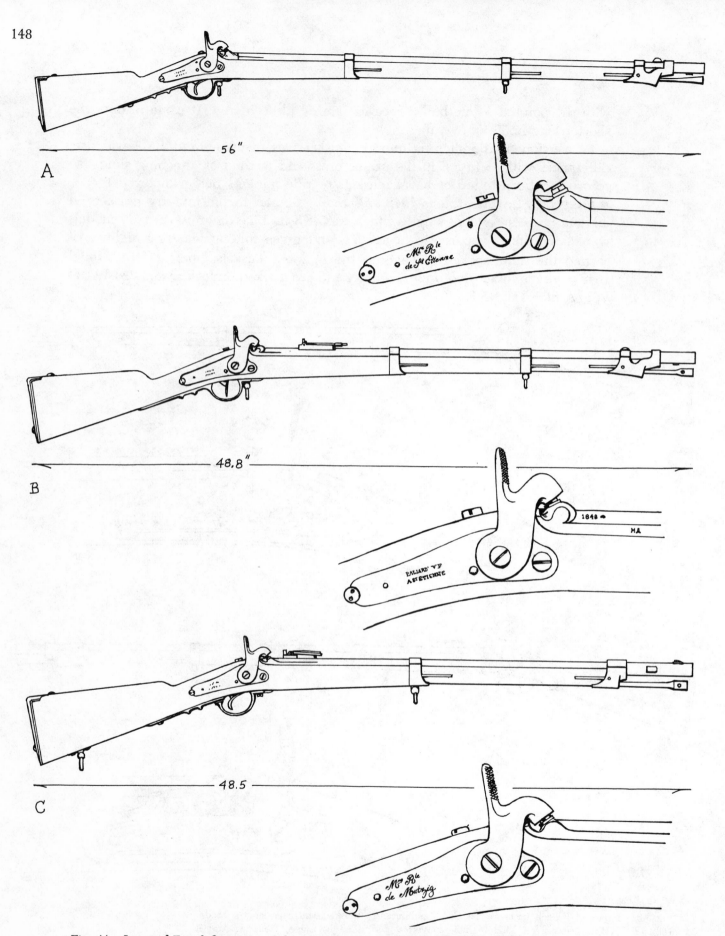

Fig. 44.   Imported French firearms: A. Infantry musket, Model 1842; B. Dragoon rifle musket, Model 1857; C. Short rifle (*carabine à tige*), Model 1846. (All West Point Museum.) (Drawings by Walter J. Nock).

● *Short Rifle (Carabine), Model 1842; Short Rifle (Carabine a tige), Models 1846 and 1853; Short Rifle (Carabine de Vincennes), Model 1859.* Percussion, muzzleloader, cal .69 or .70, rifled with 4 grooves. Nipple screwed into shoulder. Back-action lock like the musket; two bands with sling swivels on lower band and stock near toe of butt. Overall length 48.5–50.5 in., the Model 1842 being longer because of a contoured butt plate. Furniture bright. Folding leaf rear sights: Model 1842, fixed base with leaf containing a single hole; Models 1846 and 1853 with leaf graduated to 1,000 meters, and a slide; Model 1859 with leaf graduated to 1,100 meters. All except Model 1859 took a paper cartridge with a round ball. Markings on these models same as found on muskets, above, so far as the lock plates were concerned. Barrel tangs plain, with date of manufacture stamped on right side of barrel.

The Models 1842 and later were given a new brass-handled saber bayonet with a 22.7 in. yataghan blade and iron guard. In all the models above, the bayonet was attached by a lug and slide on the right side of the barrel. The Model 1842 bayonet was given a catch with a flat spring and push button and a groove cut into the back of the hilt.

In the Model 1859 short rifle the tige was eliminated and the ramrod was made slightly longer. This weapon took a paper cartridge with pointed Minie ball. The saber bayonet was also slightly changed for this model, being given a double-spring catch instead of a flat spring.

The short rifles, depending upon their model, age, and condition, were classed as 2nd or 4th class weapons; Models 1846 and 1853 received the poorest rating. Nevertheless, Boker was able to import 25,000 of the Model 1842 over the objections of Ordnance officials.

The short rifle was probably the best known weapon imported from France. It often went under the name of the Chasseur de Vincennes rifle. Its Liége-made commercial counterpart, of course, shared this fame.

Liége-made Commercial Muskets and Rifles

Belgium was the source of many imported arms, and in Liége both Hartley and Huse found new and used weapons in considerable variety offered for sale. Later, American ordnance officers arranged these Belgian guns into five categories and rated them from 1st to 3rd class, but this does not help much in discovering what they really were like in type and appearance.

Figs. 45 and 46

Major Mordecai, in reporting on his 1855 visit to the small arms manufacturing at Liége, had this to say. "At Liége an immense number of arms are made for foreign governments and for the trade, and the rooms of the large manufacturers . . . present models of almost every invention in this line of business. The barrels of all these arms are inspected and proved at the government proof-house . . . The report of arms proved at Liége in 1854 . . . contains the names of ninety manufacturing houses for whom arms were presented for proof." During the Crimean War the British government had been one of the largest purchasers of arms from Liege, the Pattern 1853 Enfield rifled musket being produced there

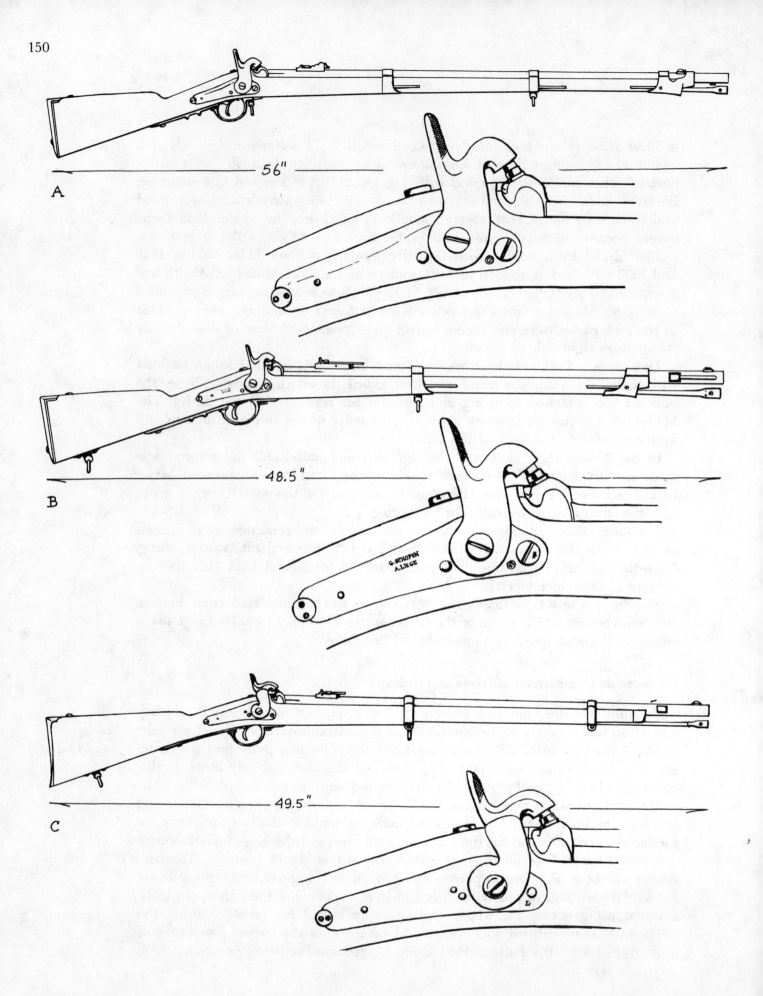

56"

A

48.5"

B

G. SCHOPEN
A. LIEGE

49.5"

C

L

in 1854–1856.

The actual firearms used in the Belgian army closely resembled those issued French troops, but it is not with these that we are concerned; it is to the commercially-made models that we must look. They were often fabricated out of available parts and took all sorts of forms, but the models believed to have been imported in any number were:

● *Liege-made French Infantry Musket, Models 1842 and 1857.* Similar to their French armory-made prototypes except as to markings. Lock plates were usually plain; barrels stamped "E/LG/*" in oval and with proof marks; stocks sometimes stamped with Liége devices. Some with leaf rear sights graduated to 1,000 meters. No escutcheon opposite plate.

● *Liege-made French Short Rifle (Carabine), Model 1859.* Similar to the French armory-made prototype, with folding leaf rear sight graduated to 1,000 meters. Markings similar to Liége-made French muskets but back-action lock usually marked with manufacturer's name such as "G. Schopen/A.Liege." Saber bayonet with yataghan blade (type probably varied), attached by a lug and slide on right side of barrel. U.S. Ordnance rated these arms as 2nd class.

These Liége-made "Chasseur de Vincènnes" rifles were imported in far larger quantities than their French prototypes. John Hoey, H. Hothansen, and George Schuyler were responsible for the majority received in the North.

● *Liege-made French Short Rifle, variant.* Percussion, muzzleloader, rifled with 4 grooves, cal .61. Overall length 49.5 in. Two bands, sling swivels on lower band and under stock near butt. Sliding leaf rear sight graduated to 700 meters. Back-action lock. Barrel and bands blued; lock plate and hammer case-hardened; other metal bright. Ramrod head pierced for cleaning rag. Lock plate plain except for small "L"; Liége proof marks on barrel. Saber bayonet retained by slide and lug on right side of barrel. John Pondir of Philadelphia is believed to have contracted for and delivered more than 10,000 of this type in 1862.

● *Liege-made Brazilian Short Rifle.* Percussion, muzzleloader, rifled with 3 grooves, cal .577. Overall length 48.25 in. Enfield-type lock plate. Folding leaf rear sight, graduated to 500 meters. Two bands; sling swivels fitted to lower band and to butt stock. Brass butt plate and trigger guard, blued barrel, lock plate furniture case-hardened in mottled colors. Usually took the straight sword bayonet made by Schnitzler & Kirshbaum of Solingen, brass hilted, attached to right of barrel by a lug and slide; no provision for bayonet on some examples. Serial number on bayonet lug; some marked on lock plate, barrel, stock, etc. with an anchor flanked by letters "D" and "G". Brass escutcheons bearing U.S. eagle screwed into stock behind barrel tang on most specimens.

The weapon (according to Edwards, *op. cit.*, p. 266) was being manufactured in Liége for the Brazilian government when purchased by American agents. C. K. Garrison delivered 6,000 of them in late 1861 to fulfill his contract to deliver "Minie rifles of Liége pattern with saber bayonets."

Fig. 45. Imported Liége-made firearms: A. French infantry rifle musket, Model 1857; B. French short rifle (*carabine*), Model 1859; C. French short rifle of variant pattern (all West Point Museum). (Drawings by Walter J. Nock).

Fig. 46. Imported Liége-made firearms: A. "Brazilian" short rifle; B. "U.S. Springfield" rifle musket, an unidentified type of mixed ancestry made by A. Francotte for the American market (both Springfield Armory). (Drawings by Walter J. Nock).

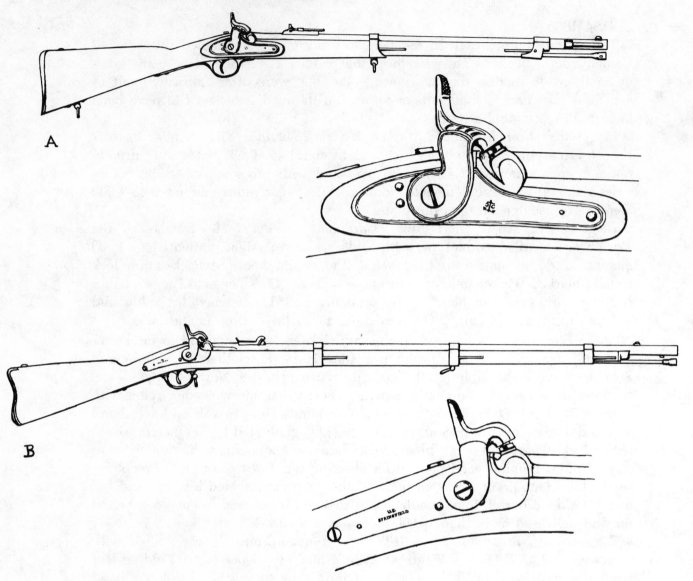

Carbines and Musketoons

In transferring our attention from American muskets and rifles to carbines, we move from the firearm of the foot soldier to that of the mounted man; from relatively standardized and often arsenal-made weapons, produced in large numbers, to a long list of models manufactured by numerous firms, frequently in small lots, and, generally speaking, from muzzleloading to breechloading weapons. The reasons for these differences will become clearer if we examine briefly the background of the carbine.

Cavalry of the mid-19th century was still classed as heavy, light, and dragoons, but the distinctions between the three types had become blurred, certainly so far as armament was concerned. All were armed with sabers, most with pistols or revolvers, and an increasing number with carbines. Each of these kinds of weapon had its advocates—in America as well as Europe—and immediacy was lent to the arguments of each group by the obvious necessity of reducing the load of arms and ammunition carried on a horse.

We read that the traditional American cavalryman was the dragoon, trained to travel on horseback and fight on foot. This definition actually fits the mounted rifleman and does not reflect the doctrines of most American cavalry leaders of the mid-19th century. In the Confederacy, especially, there were several distinctive schools: Stuart's troops used equally the carbine, saber, and revolver; Morgan's and Mosby's men relied heavily on the revolver; whereas Forrest's horsemen did most of their fighting on foot with the carbine or rifle. The fact is that the U.S. War Department was faced throughout the period with uncertainty as to the correct weapon for the cavalryman. This left the field far more open for experimentation than in the case of the foot soldier, for whom repeating arms at least were usually ruled out officially.

American inventors and arms manufacturers were quick to seize the opportunity to produce breechloading, and later repeating, weapons with which to arm the soldier on horseback. The more promising systems were tried out by the government, commencing as early as 1839 and continuing after 1872. Some systems were actually adopted as standard, but official resistance on the grounds of expense, uncertainty of operation, potential wastage of ammunition, and other reasons kept the breechloader out of the government arsenal. When the Civil War broke out, the emphasis had to be placed on arsenal-manufactured weapons for the foot soldier, and the cavalryman could only be supplied with commercial carbines. Numerous inventors of breechloaders clamored for orders, and at first almost any arm that would work was purchased. Although in the end several patterns, notably the Sharps and then the Spencer, became appreciated above others, they were not recognized as standard, nor did they entirely replace other types.

The fact that far fewer carbines were required than rifle muskets conditioned the supply of the former which was, furthermore, never as important or decisive a weapon in battle. All of these factors, then, played a part in making the carbine an advanced arm of frequent and ever changing design.

The breechloader, and especially the repeating rifle, did not assume its ultimate efficiency until the perfection of the metallic cartridge that combined powder, ball, and ignition system in one rigid case. The road toward this end was lined with a variety of intermediary processes which cannot be treated here. The reader is recommended to Colonel Berkeley R. Lewis' *Small Arms and Ammunition,* Chapter V, for a competent treatment.

The metallic cartridge period is characterized by an often confusing terminology used by manufacturers to describe the size and other characteristics of their ammunition. A brief explanation of this matter might be useful.

In the beginning, a simple caliber and maker's name such as ".58 Joslyn" would suffice to identify a cartridge. Such a round would have a bullet fifty-eight hundredths of an inch in diameter, adapted to the Joslyn carbine of this size. As the number of cartridge types and loadings increased, a second number was added giving the weight of the charge of powder. Thus a .50-60 Peabody designation meant a fifty caliber cartridge containing sixty grains of powder adapted to the Peabody rifle.

As the number of cartridges and loadings continued to increase, particularly in the center-fire era, a third number was added to the name representing the bullet weight in grains. A .50-70-450 Springfield meant a cartridge with a caliber .50 bullet, a powder charge of 70 grains and a bullet weight of 450 grains. Where necessary, the term rim-fire or center-fire was added to avoid confusion. Unfortunately, not all cartridge makers followed these rules, and probably the most notable exception was found in the Spencer series.

The original Spencer cartridge was known as the .56 Spencer. During the Civil War, the rush to produce large quantities of Spencers forced the use of existing caliber .52 barrels and rifling machinery. To produce the necessary ammunition for such weapons, the regular caliber .56 Spencer case was slightly necked down to take a .52 bullet, the resulting cartridge being called the .56-.52 Spencer, or in other words the .56 reduced to .52. After the war, when U.S. ordnance authorities declared fifty caliber as military standard, the .56 Spencer was further reduced to .50, resulting in the .56-.50 cartridge. A .56-.46 Spencer cartridge was also made for sporting use. In retrospect, for uniformity, the original .56 Spencer cartridge was renamed the .56-.56.

U.S. Muzzleloading Carbines and Musketoons

Plate 1 ● *U.S. Artillery Musketoon, Model 1847.* Percussion, cal .69, smoothbore, using a paper cartridge with round ball. Overall length 41 in. Model 1842 socket bayonet, 18 in. blade, fitted with locking ring. All metal bright. No rear sight; two bands, the upper being a two-strap trumpet shape. Sling swivels on lower band and on butt stock on some examples; none on others, which were converted cavalry musketoons. Marked on lock plate "SPRING/FIELD" above year, and "US" under eagle.

Springfield Armory produced 3,359 of this model in 1848–1859.

● *U.S. Sappers and Miners Musketoon, Model 1847.* Identical to the artillery musketoon, above, except a bayonet stud was fixed on the right side of barrel to take a special brass-handled Roman sword-type bayonet, with 21.75 in. double-edged blade. A total of 830 of these musketoons and bayonets were manufactured at Springfield Armory in 1847–1856. They were withdrawn from service by an order of the Secretary of War, 5 July 1855.

See U.S. Dragoons ● *U.S. Cavalry Musketoon, Model 1847.* Identical to the artillery musketoon except in these particulars: furniture was brass; there was no bayonet stud or bayonet, and no sling swivels; instead, a sling rod and ring were attached on the left; the ramrod was connected with a stud under the barrel by two short curved arms and so kept from being lost; the upper band was differently shaped and the lower band held an end of the sling rod.

This musketoon was altered in 1852 by replacing the swivel ramrod attachment by a sleeve chain. The barrels of some were rifled and equipped with leaf rear sights of several types. In some cases the sling rod was removed and sling swivels provided, or provision was made for bayonet attachment. A total of 6,703 were manufactured at Springfield Armory by 1854.

● *U.S. Cavalry Rifled Carbine, Model 1855.* Percussion, cal .54, rifled with 3 grooves, using a paper cartridge with Minie ball. Overall length 36.75 in. No bayonet. Metal was iron, polished bright, except brass fore end tip. Barrels were sometimes browned. Open or two-leaf rear sight graduated to 700 yards. Fore-arm held by one band; ramrod held by oval loop swivel. Sling ring attached to rear of trigger guard bow on some examples; to front on others. Marked on lock plate "SPRING/FIELD" over year, and "US" under eagle.

During 1855 and 1856 a total of 1,020 of these arms were manufactured at Springfield Armory. It appears to have been a somewhat extemporized weapon, originally planned for the two new cavalry regiments. It was probably replaced by the pistol-carbine and by experimental breechloading weapons after about 1857.

(For the *U.S. Percussion Pistol-Carbine, Model 1855* see section following on Pistols and Revolvers.)

U.S. and Contract Breechloading Percussion Carbines

● *U.S. Carbine, Models 1840, 1842, and 1843 (Hall-North and Hall).* Percussion, smoothbore, cal .52, overall length 40 in. No bayonet. Finished lacquer brown, ramrod bright. Breech opened on Model 1840 by an "elbow (later modified to 'fish tail') catch" underneath. The Model 1842 had brass furniture and was made with bayonet support lug. The Model 1843 breech opened by lever on right side; all raised the front of the hinged receiver. Fixed "V" notch rear sight; two bands; sling ring under small of stock or a sling bar and ring on left side.

See Missouri, Frémont Hussars, 1862

These were the final models of a line of carbines which began in 1833. At Harpers Ferry, 1,001 Model 1842 carbines were manufactured and were usually marked on the breech-block "H. FERRY/US/1842." Under contract by Simeon North of Middletown, Conn., 6,501 Model 1840's and 11,000 Model 1843's were made and were marked "US/S.North/MIDLtn/CONN" and with the year. Later examples were inscribed "STEEL" on the barrel. Although this carbine was not used by regulars after 1851, it was in the hands of some state mounted commands as late as the Civil War.

The Hall carbine is also included because some 5,000 of them were purchased from the War Department in 1861, rifled and sold at considerable profit to General John C. Frémont. The transaction subsequently achieved immense notoriety as "The Hall Carbine Affair." A detailed account under this title, by R. Gordon Wasson (New York, rev. ed., 1948) has all the charm of a detective story.

● *Burnside Breechloading Carbine (1st and 4th Models, 1856–1864).* Percussion, using a special rearward-tapering brass cartridge and separate percussion cap placed on the cone of the breech-lock. Cal .54; conical ball rifled with 5

See 1st R.I. Vol. Cav.

grooves. Overall length 40 in. No bayonet. Brass butt plate; barrel blued and frame and lock case-hardened. Action was unlocked by a spring lever-latch against the trigger guard, and breech-lock dropped by lowering the trigger guard. Sliding leaf rear sight. No forearm on 1st and 2nd Models; 4-in. sling rod and ring on left side. Frame marked on top "BURNSIDE'S/PATENT/MARCH 25th/ 1856" and serial number; lock plate not marked.

The 2nd (1860) Model had an improved locking system and a two-leaf open rear sight. Marked on trigger guard latch "G.P. FOSTER PAT/APRIL 10th 1860." Lock plate inscribed "BRISTOL FIREARM CO." and later "BURNSIDE RIFLE Co/PROVIDENCE-R.I."

The 3rd (1861) Model was given a wooden forearm held by a single band, and the hammer slightly changed. Marked on barrel "CAST STEEL 1861."

Fig. 47

The 4th (1864) Model was given an improved breech action and altered in several other ways. Overall length 39.5 in.; leaf, peep, and open rear sight; sling swivel on the butt and a sling rod and ring on left side. Barrel and trigger guard blued; curved steel butt plate, and other furniture case-hardened in mottled colors. Marked on top of frame "BURNSIDE PATENT/MODEL OF 1864" and serial number.

A small number of the 1st Model were purchased by the War Department and issued experimentally, probably in 1858. Over 55,500 carbines, chiefly of the 3rd and 4th Models, were purchased during the Civil War.

● *Colt Repeating Carbine, Model 1855.* Percussion, loading like a revolver into a 5-shot cylinder; cal .56, side hammer; rifled with 5 grooves. Overall length 36.5 in. Used nitre-treated, self-consuming paper cartridge with conical ball. Steel butt plate, barrel dull blue, frame and loading lever bright or case-hardened; trigger guard usually brass. Two-leaf rear sight. Sling ring on left side of frame, or sling swivels on butt stock and loading lever catch. Marked on frame "COL. COLT HARTFORD CT. U.S.A." and "COLT'S PATENT/NOV. 24th 1857." A bullet mould, screw driver, and nipple wrench were usually furnished with each carbine.

See 2nd Mich. Vol. Cav.

The Colt carbine was manufactured also in cals .36 and .44, in different lengths, and with a 6-shot cylinder; some were rifled with 7 grooves. The model described, however, is believed to be the usual military style and the one experimented with by the War Department in 1859. It was never a U.S. regulation weapon, although adopted by volunteer units and militia of several states. It was also carried as a private arm by some officers during the Civil War.

(*Cosmopolitan: see Gwyn & Campbell*)

● *Gallager Breechloading Carbine, Model 1860.* Percussion, using a Poultney foil and paper cartridge and conical ball. Cal .50, rifled with 3 grooves, overall length 39.2 in. No bayonet. Side hammer; broke like a shot gun by unlatching and depressing trigger guard. Barrel dark blue, other metal usually case-hardened in mottled colors. Steel butt plate and patch box containing extra cone. Rear sight varied, usually open, sometimes three-leaf graduated to 500 yards. No forearm. Sling bar with ring on left side. Marked on lock plate "GALLAGER'S PATENT/ JULY 17th 1860" and "MANUFACTd BY/RICHARDSON & OVERMAN/PHIL-

See 1st Tenn. Mounted Regt. (Union)

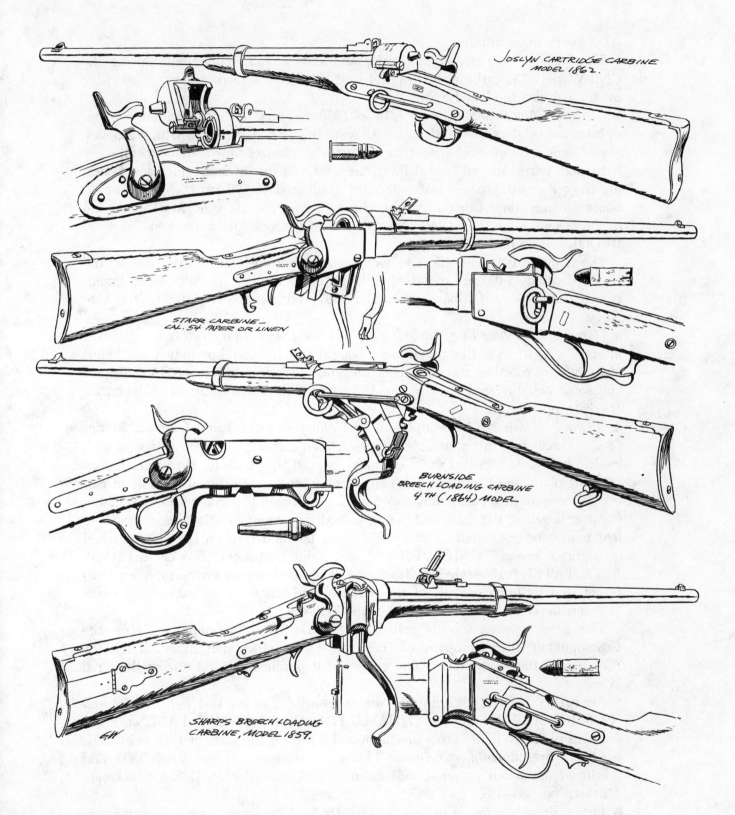

JOSLYN CARTRIDGE CARBINE
MODEL 1862.

STARR CARBINE
CAL. 54 PAPER OR LINEN

BURNSIDE
BREECH LOADING CARBINE
4TH (1864) MODEL

SHARPS BREECH LOADING
CARBINE, MODEL 1859.

GW

Fig. 47. Some American breechloading carbines.

ADA" with serial number.

The Gallager was issued to regular and state cavalry commands during the Civil War; 17,782 carbines were purchased by the War Department. A cartridge model was also produced in 1865.

● *Gibbs Breechloading Carbine, Model 1856.* Percussion, using either a paper or linen cartridge of special design with conical ball. Cal .52, rifled with 6 grooves, overall length 39 in. No bayonet. Steel butt plate; barrel blued; other metal case-hardened. Barrel moved forward and breech tilted up by unlatching and lowering trigger guard. Open 3-leaf rear sight graduated to 500 yards. Side hammer. Short forearm, nose cap only. Sling bar with ring on left side. Marked on top of breech "L.H. GIBBS/PAT'D/JANY 8 1856"; lock plate marked "Wm F. BROOKS/MANFr NEW YORK."

The Gibbs was not an effective weapon and saw only limited use during the Civil War; only 1,052 are recorded as being purchased by the War Department. It was tested by an Ordnance Board in 1857 and, apparently, also by the U.S. Navy.

● *(Greene Breechloading Carbine, Models 1854 and 1857,* saw no significant military use. In 1855 the government bought 200 for test but they were found to be inferior to other makes. Greene carbines were purchased by Great Britain and some possibly sold back to the U.S. during the Civil War. See Gluckman, *Muskets,* pp. 380–382.)

See 5th Ill. Vol. Cav.

● *Gwyn & Campbell (Cosmopolitan or Union) Breechloading Carbine, Model 1862.* Percussion, using either a paper or linen cartridge of special design with conical ball. Cal .52, rifled with 3 grooves, overall length 39 in. No bayonet. Barrel, butt plate, and breech tang blued; other parts case-hardened in mottled colors (some were given a tin finish for navy use). Breech-block lowered by unlatching and lowering trigger guard. Long-arched side hammer. No forearm. Sliding leaf rear sight graduated to 600 yards. Sling bar and ring on left side. Marked on right of breech "UNION/RIFLE" and behind hammer "GWYN & CAMP-BELL/PATENT/1862/HAMILTON, O." The second pattern carbine was differentiated by minor details of the hammer and trigger guard/operating lever. It seems never to have been used in the Civil War.

This carbine was variously called the "Union," the "Cosmopolitan" (for the Cosmopolitan Arms Company of Hamilton, Ohio, which manufactured it), the "Ohio," and the "Grapevine." The government purchased 9,342 during the Civil War.

An earlier pattern, differing in many details, was marked behind hammer "COSMOPOLITAN ARMS CO/HAMILTON O. U.S/GROSS' PATENT/1859" and was probably limited to a production of 1,140 for the state of Illinois in 1861.

● *(Jenks Breechloading Carbine.* This early weapon, in use since 1839 and produced in various patterns, was essentially obsolete by 1851. See Gluckman, *Muskets,* pp. 384–386.)

● *Joslyn Breechloading Carbine, Model 1855.* Percussion, using a paper cartridge of special design with conical ball. Cal .54, rifled with 3 grooves, overall length 38 in. No bayonet. Barrel browned or blued, with frame and hammer case-hardened in mottled colors; sometimes given a tin finish for navy use. Side hammer; loaded by unlatching and raising a long breech lever, the action of the hammer being controlled by a safety device. Short forearm with a single brass band. Open, sliding rear leaf sight graduated to 800 yards. Sling bar and ring on left side. Marked on lock plate "A.H.WATERS & CO/MILBURY." Some marked on top of breech lever "PATd BY/B.F. JOSLYN./AUG. 23. 1855."

The inefficient paper-cartridge Joslyn was greatly overshadowed by the later model metallic cartridge carbine (q.v.). Only about 860 were sold to the War Department.

● *Lindner Breechloading Carbine, Model 1859.* Percussion, using a special nitre-treated paper cartridge. Cal .58, rifled with 3 grooves, overall length 38.75 in. No bayonet. Steel butt plate, metal bright finished. Side hammer; loaded by means of an upward tilting breech held in place by a turning cover. Short forearm, no band. Two-leaf rear sight. Fixed sling ring on left side. Marked on top of breech-block EDWARD LINDNER'S/PATENT./MARCH 29, 1859," and those produced after 1863, on lock plate, "AMOSKEAG MFG CO./MAN-CHESTER, N.H." with an eagle and year.

The Lindner was not an especially effective weapon and only 892 were purchased by the War Department.

● *Maynard Breechloading Carbine, "Second Model".* Percussion, using a special wrapped foil (later brass or tinned) unprimed cartridge with a broad rimmed base and a pointed- or flat-nosed bullet. Cal .50, rifled with 3 grooves, overall length 36.875 in. No bayonet. Steel butt plate, barrel, and hammer blued, frame and trigger guard lever case-hardened in mottled colors. Central hammer; lowering the trigger guard tilted up the barrel. Used a conventional percussion cap. No forearm. Open 3-leaf rear sight graduated to 500 yards. Sling bar and ring on left side. Marked on left of frame "EDWARD MAYNARD/PATENTEE/MAY 27, 1851/DEC. 6, 1859," and on right "MANUFACTURED BY/MASS. ARMS CO/CHICOPEE FALLS."

See Georgia, Cobb's Legion

The Maynard was one of the earliest capping, metallic cartridge arms and saw wide military use; over 20,000 were purchased by the War Department. The "First Model," which was manufactured in cals .35 and .50, underwent several changes in the 1850's, being produced both as a carbine and a rifle. It was tape-primed and had a unique butt plate with rounded toe and heel; a patch box in the butt held extra rolls of Maynard tape primers. Apparently neither the rifle nor the carbine was fitted for a sling. In 1857 the War Department bought 400 of these First Model carbines, while 1,000 rifles and carbines were contracted for by Georgia in 1860.

● *Merrill, Latrobe & Thomas Breechloading Carbine, Model 1855.* Percussion, using a paper cartridge with pointed bullet. Cal .58, rifled with 3 grooves, overall length 38 in. No bayonet. Brass butt plate, patch box trigger guard, and band; blued lock and receiver; blued or bright barrel. Tape primer magazine of the Maynard type on right of lock. Side hammer; breech was opened by unlatching and lifting a long, hinged lock lever and so rotating a pivotal shaft. Short forearm with single band. Sliding leaf rear sight. Sling bar and ring on left side. Marked on lock plate "S. REMINGTON/ILION N.Y." and on receiver "MERRILL, LA-TROBE & THOMAS/BALTIMORE MD./PATENT APPLIED FOR."

This was not a successful carbine and its principal interest lies in the fact that 170 were issued in 1855 to two companies of the newly formed 1st Cavalry for trial. In 1858 James H. Merrill, its inventor, patented a simpler and more practical mechanism which is described next.

Plate XIX

● *Merrill Breechloading Carbine, Model 1858 (Improved 1861)*. Percussion, using a nitre-treated paper cartridge with pointed bullet. Cal .54, rifled with 3 grooves, overall length 37.25 in. No bayonet. Brass patch box in butt. All furniture of some examples brass, tinned, or nickled; in others barrel and furniture blued with frame and lock case-hardened in mottled colors. Side hammer; loaded by unlatching a lever fastened under rear sight base and raising it backwards, exposing the breech. Used conventional percussion cap. Three-leaf open rear sight graduated to 500 yards. Sling rod and ring on left. Short forearm and single brass band. Lock plate marked "J.H. MERRILL BALTO./PAT. JULY 1858/APL. 9 MAY 21–28–61," and on top of lever marked "J.H. MERRILL, BALTO./PAT. JULY 1858."

A new model was produced in 1863 that differed in several particulars: no patch box, smaller lever latch, wider band, etc. The lock plate of these was marked with "1863" and a small eagle.

The War Department purchased 14,695 of these carbines during 1861–1866.

● *Perry Breechloading Carbine, Model 1855.* Percussion, using a combustible paper or linen cartridge. Cal .54, rifled with 7 grooves, overall length 39 in. No bayonet. Steel butt plate, barrel blued, frame and hammer case-hardened in mottled colors. Loaded by depressing oval ring end of trigger guard, revolving breech-block centrally, and tilting the breech upwards. Side hammer; used conventional percussion caps carried in a long 50-cap tube extending through the butt and fed automatically to the cone. Open rear sight; forearm held by one band. No sling bar. Marked on breech-block "A.D. PERRY/PATENTED" and within the block "PERRY PATENTED ARM/NEWARK, N.Y."

The Perry proved unsuccessful. The War Department in 1855 issued 200 to two companies of the newly formed 2nd Cavalry for trial. Others were purchased by the Navy for experiment.

● *Sharps Breechloading Carbine, Model 1852.* Percussion, using special linen cartridge with paper base or conventional paper cartridge, both with pointed bullet. Cal .52, rifled with 6 grooves, overall length 37.75 in. No bayonet. Brass butt plate, patch box, and mountings (iron on some examples); blued barrel, frame case-hardened in mottled colors. Side hammer and sloping breech-block; loaded by unlatching and depressing trigger guard which dropped the breech-block. Used patent pellet priming device. Various kinds of rear sight; short forearm with single brass band. Sling bar and ring on left. Marked (in part) on lock plate "SHARPS/PATENT/1852" and on barrel tang "SHARPS/PATENT/1848." Some had the manufacturer's name on the barrel.

Among the most successful and celebrated firearms of the period, the Sharps was manufactured as a rifle, rifle musket, and carbine, and in several models of each. The model above followed one or two prototypes, the earliest dating from 1848, and was probably the first martial carbine to be sold to the Army. The War Department purchased 200 in 1854 for experiment.

● *Sharps Breechloading Carbine Model 1853.* Basically as the above with sliding leaf rear sight, changes in breech lever pin. Retained the pellet primer device. This is the model carbine used by abolitionist John Brown at Harpers Ferry. An extreme few of this model (as well as the Model 1859) had a coffee mill inserted in the stock with a detachable handle run through the patchbox.

See Kansas Free-State Vols., 1856

● *Sharps Breechloading Carbine, Model 1855.* Similar to the above except equipped with a Maynard primer device. It used only the special Sharps linen cartridge. Only about 400 of this rare model were purchased by the government in April 1855, an amount which may constitute the entire production of these arms. The 1st U.S. Dragoons were still using this carbine in February, 1858.

See 1st U.S. Dragoons

● *Sharps Breechloading Carbine, Model 1859.* Similar to the above except the breech-block was vertical instead of sloping and the pellet primer was substituted for the Maynard. Overall length 39.13 in. Lock plates marked "C. SHARPS' PAT/OCT. 5th 1852" and "R.S.LAWRENCE PAT/APRIL 12th 1859," the latter referring to a patent pellet cut-off to enable the use of percussion caps. Increasing use was made of iron bands, trigger guards, and butt plates.

See 3rd Ind. Vol. Cav.

The Model 1859 carbine was the one most extensively used in the Civil War; some 50,000 of this model and a "New Model 1859" were produced. The "New Model 1859" featured patented gas-escape check devices as the basis for the "New Model" designation. The patch box was now eliminated. This is the most common of the Sharps models and was the most widely used. In 1863 the manufacturer began to stamp the barrels with "NEW MODEL 1863." The only difference between the "New Model 1863" carbine and the "New Model 1859" was an increase in the size of the clean-out screw in the breech block and the utilization of iron furniture. After the Civil War the Sharps Company commenced altering existing carbines to accept a cal .50 center-fire cartridge. This and subsequent changes are described later.

● *Smith Breechloading Carbine.* Percussion, using a special rubber cartridge with pointed ball (heavy paper and foil cases were also used, as well as patented metallic ones). Cal .50, rifled with 3 grooves, overall length 39.5 in. No bayonet. Blued barrel, breech latch, trigger guard, and furniture; frame and hammer casehardened in mottled colors. Side hammer; loaded by unlocking catch inside trigger guard, raising a long spring latch on top of the barrel, and then breaking the carbine like a shotgun. Used conventional percussion cap. Sliding leaf rear sight; short forearm with one band. Sling bar and ring on left. Marked on left of frame: "ADDRESS/POULTNEY & TRIMBLE/BALTIMORE, U.S.A." and "SMITH'S PATENT/JUNE 23 1857" and "MANUFACTURED BY/MASS. ARMS CO./CHICOPEE FALLS" or "MANUFACTURED BY/AM'N M'CH'N WKS./SPRINGFIELD, MASS."

See 1st Mass. Vol. Cav.; Ohio Union Light Guard

The Smith proved to be a moderately successful carbine and over 30,300 were purchased by the government in 1860–1865. Note, however, that the historian of the 1st Massachusetts Cavalry termed it "not a good weapon," condemned in his regiment.

● *Starr Breechloading Carbine.*   Percussion, using a linen cartridge with pointed ball. Cal .54, rifled with 5 grooves, overall length 37.5 in. No bayonet. Brass butt plate; blued barrel; frame, lock, and trigger guard case-hardened in mottled colors. Side hammer; loaded by unlatching and lowering trigger guard which depressed the breech-block. Used conventional percussion cap. Open leaf rear sight with three adjustments. Short forearm with single brass band. Fixed sling ring on left. Marked on barrel and lock plate "STARR ARMS Co., YONKERS, N.Y."; and on breech tang "STARR'S PATENT/SEPT. 14th 1858."

See Ark. Vol. Cav. (Union); Fig. 47

The War Department purchased 20,601 Starr carbines during the Civil War. The company, with plants in Yonkers, Binghamton, and Morrisania, N.Y., also made revolvers.

A version of the Starr modified to take a rimfire cartridge was produced in 1865. This model was made in cal .52, using the Spencer No. .56-.52 rimfire cartridge. About 5,000 of these cartridge models were sold to the War Department in 1865, but evidently never saw use in the field.

● (*Union*: see Gwyn & Campbell)

U.S. and Contract Metallic Cartridge Carbines

● *U.S. Carbine, Model 1870.*   Cal .50, single-shot, using a .50-70 government center-fire cartridge. Rifled with 3 grooves. Overall length 41.3 in. No bayonet. Steel butt· plate; all metal bright. Side hammer; rising breech-block hinged at front, unlatched by thumb piece on right. Folding slide-leaf rear sight. Short forearm held by single band. Sling bar and ring on left. Marked on lock plate with eagle, "U.S. SPRINGFIELD," and year, usually "1864" or "1865" since old lock plates were used. Breech-block dated "1870" together with a month.

Only 313 of this model were made for trial. In 1873 the caliber was reduced to .45 and other modifications followed in the production of this, the basic U.S. army carbine for twenty years.

● *Ball Repeating Carbine.*   Cal .50, 7-shot using .56-70 Spencer rim-fire cartridge (although a shorter Ball cartridge was made). Rifled with 5 grooves; overall length 37.5 in. No bayonet. Blued barrel, frame and butt plate case-hardened in mottled colors. Side hammer; lowering trigger guard operated mechanism, drawing cartridge from a tubular magazine under barrel. Open leaf rear sight. Long forearm held by 2 bands. Sling bar and ring on left. Marked on receiver "E.G. LAMSON & CO./WINDSOR, VT./U.S./BALLS PATENT./JUNE 23, 1863,/ MAR. 15, 1864."

This repeater emerged late in the Civil War when 1,002 were delivered to the War Department. It is doubtful if any saw service in combat.

● *Ballard Cartridge Carbine.*   Cal .54, single shot, using rimfire cartridges or combustible cartridges. Rifled with 5 grooves; overall length 38 in. No bayonet. Steel butt plate; barrel blued, frame and furniture case-hardened. Centrally set hammer; some with percussion nipple set in breech block for use with combustible cartridges. Operated by lowering the trigger guard which dropped the

See 13th Ky. Vol. Cav. (Union)

breech mechanism. Open leaf rear sight graduated to 500 yards. Short forearm held by one band. Sling swivels on band and under butt stock; no sling ring. Marked on frame "MERWIN & BRAY/AGTS N.Y." and "BALLARD'S PATENT/ Nov. 5, 1861."

The Ballard was also made in cal .44. During the Civil War the government purchased 1,509 Ballard carbines and appendages, all believed to have been cal .54. In 1864 the state of Kentucky contracted for 15,000 Ballard rifles and carbines, which were probably delivered after the war.

● *Gallagher Cartridge Carbine, Model 1865.* Cal .50, single-shot using a special "50 Gallager All Metal Case" cartridge with a round nosed bullet, or more frequently a .56-.52 Spencer rimfire cartridge. Rifled with 6 grooves, overall length 39 in. No bayonet. Steel or case-hardened butt plate; breech tang and trigger guard finished in bright blue, barrel in dull blue, other parts case-hardened in mottled colors. Side hammer; action similar to percussion model—unlatching and lowering trigger guard swung the barrel forward and downward on the frame. Three-leaf rear sight graduated to 500 yards. No forearm. Sling bar and ring on left. Marked on lock plate "GALLAGER'S PATENT/JULY 17th 1860" and "MANUFACTd BY/RICHARDSON & OVERMAN/PHILADA" with serial number.

The War Department purchased 5,000 of this model in 1865, but the weapon was not popular with soldiers.

● *Joslyn Cartridge Carbine, Models 1862 and 1864.* Cal .52, single-shot, using .56–.52 Spencer rim-fire cartridge. Rifled with 3 grooves, overall length 38.75 in. No bayonet. Brass butt plate and trigger guard, blued barrel, other parts case-hardened in mottled colors. Side hammer; loaded by raising a knob on the right of the swinging breech-block and throwing it over to the left. Three-leaf open rear sight. Short forearm held by one brass band. Sling bar and ring on left. Marked on lock plate "JOSLYN FIRE ARMS Co/STONINGTON/CONN" and patent information on rear of block.

See 1st N.Y. Dragoons, 1863; Fig. 47

In the Model 1864 the breech-block was made heavier, a spring release replaced the knob, and a circular shield was placed about the firing pin. All metal except the barrel was either bright or case-hardened. The War Department purchased 11,060 of these during the Civil War. The Joslyn company also produced a converted Springfield rifle with the same mechanism, and after the Civil War continued to improve its rifles and carbines.

● *Peabody Cartridge Carbine 1862.* Cal .50, single-shot, using the special Peabody .50-50 rim-fire cartridge, or .56-.50 Spencer rim-fire. Rifled with 3 grooves, overall length 39 in. No bayonet. Case-hardened butt plate; barrel blued and receiver case-hardened in mottled colors. Side hammer; same tipping breech-block mechanism as the Peabody cartridge rifle (*q.v.*), manipulated by depressing trigger guard. Short forearm held by single band. Sling ring fixed on left. Two-leaf rear sight. Marked on left of breech frame "PEABODY'S PAT./JULY 22, 1862/MAN'F'D BY/PROVIDENCE TOOL CO./PROV. R.I."

The Peabody rifle in its several forms and calibers was one of the most successful weapons of the immediate post-Civil War period, especially in European armies. About 1871 the carbine was chambered for the government cal .50-70, but neither before nor after this date did it receive any significant military usage in America.

9th U.S. Cavalry, 1871

● *Remington Cartridge Carbine.* Cal .50, single-shot, using .56-.50 and .56-.52 Spencer rim-fire cartridges. Rifled with 3 grooves, overall length 34 in. No bayonet. Case-hardened butt plate; barrel blued, frame case-hardened in mottled colors. Central hammer; "split breech" pattern, loaded by cocking the hammer and pushing back a thumb piece to open the breech. Short forearm held by one band. Two-leaf rear sight graduated to 500 yards. Fitted either with sling ring on left, or sling swivels under the band and on butt stock. Marked on breech tang "REMINGTON'S ILION, N.Y./PAT. DEC. 23, 1863, MAY 3 & NOV 16, 1864."

A quantity of this model was manufactured in cal .46, using a .46 long rim-fire cartridge, with minor mechanical differences. Markings were the same as above. The War Department procured 15,000 of the cal .50 and 5,000 of the cal .46 in 1865–1866. Only a few of the latter could have seen service in the Civil War.

In addition to this carbine, Remington within the 1851–1872 period produced several kinds of muzzleloaders, a wide variety of revolvers, six or more models of rifle for foreign governments, carbines and rifles for the U.S. navy, and the "rolling block" army rifle and carbine (called the Model 1870) chambered for the .50-70 government cartridge. The muzzleloaders and revolvers are covered elsewhere in this study; the later rifles and carbines appeared just as the period was ending and do not properly belong herein.

● *Sharps Cartridge Carbine.* Used an experimental cal .52 Sharps center-fire cartridge. Rifled with 3 grooves, overall length 39.25 in. No bayonet. Barrel and furniture blued, frame case-hardened in mottled colors. Used the frame and mechanism of the earlier Sharps percussion carbine (*q.v.*), altered to use a metallic cartridge. Sliding leaf rear sight. Short forearm held by one band. Sling bar and ring on left. Markings similar to percussion types, especially Model 1859.

Sharps introduced new model carbines in 1867, 1869, and 1870 which still were alterations of the earlier percussion frame. Some had their barrels relined and rebored to cal .50, to accept a .50-70 government center-fire cartridge. These were issued to the U.S. cavalry for trial in 1871. The Model 1867 was chambered for a special .52 Sharps rim-fire cartridge and was marked on barrel: "NEW MODEL 1867."

See 11th N.Y. Vol. Cav.

● *Sharps & Hankins Cartridge Carbine, Model 1862.* Cal .52, single-shot, using No. 56 Sharps & Hankins rim-fire cartridge. Rifled with 6 grooves, overall length 38.75 in. No bayonet. Brass butt plate; made in both blued and tinned finish. No forearm. Open and leaf rear sights, moveable and graduated to 800 yards. Central hammer; loaded by unlocking and depressing trigger guard. Sling swivel on butt stock and fixed sling ring on left. Marked at first "C. SHARPS & CO, PHILADA" on frame; after 1863 marked "SHARPS/&/HANKINS/PHILADA." and "SHARPS/PATENT/1859."

For navy use the barrel was covered with leather held by an iron ring at the muzzle; the butt plate was brass and the frame was tinned. Some 1,450 were purchased by the War Department in 1862–1865 and the carbine is known to have been carried by the 11th New York Cavalry.

● *Spencer Repeating Carbine.* Cal .52, 7-shot, using .56-.52 Spencer rim-fire cartridge (and other models, see below). Rifled with 3 or 6 grooves, overall length 39 in. No bayonet. Blued barrel, all other parts case-hardened in mottled colors. Short forearm held by one band. Side hammer; loaded by depressing trigger guard which moved a cartridge from a tubular 7-shot magazine passing through the butt of the stock. Sliding leaf rear sight. Sling bar and ring on left. Marked on breech "SPENCER REPEATING/RIFLE CO. BOSTON, MASS/PAT'D MARCH 6, 1860." The Spencer Company called this model its "Heavy Carbine." *See 2nd N.Y. Vol. Cav.; 17th Ind. Vol. Inf.*

Carbines sold in 1865 and after were equipped inside the trigger guard with the Stabler cut-off, permitting the arm to be used as a single loader. In 1864 the introduction of the Blakeslee Patent Box (see Fig. 52) allowed the soldier to carry first 6, then 10 thin detachable magazine tubes, each holding 7 rounds. This device considerably augmented the rapidity of fire of the Spencer.

Spencer carbines were also made in 1865 by the Burnside Rifle Company of Providence in cal .50, using a .56-.50 Spencer rim-fire cartridge. These had an overall length of 37 in. but were otherwise similar in appearance to the earlier model. They were marked on top of the frame "MODEL 1865" and "SPENCER REPEATING RIFLE, PATENTED MARCH 6, 1860, MANUFD AT PROV. R.I, BY BURNSIDE RIFLE CO." This carbine was sometimes called the "Indian Model."

The Spencer Company itself manufactured a cal .50 carbine in and after 1865, having the general dimensions of the Burnside version. It also produced during the Civil War a navy rifle with saber bayonet, and two patterns of army rifle; following the war it continued to manufacture military carbines and rifles in cal .50 until 1869. These later versions incorporated various minor modifications.

The Spencer was considered by most soldiers to be the best arm used during the Civil War. It did not begin to reach troops until 1863, yet by 1866 the general government had purchased and received over 77,000 heavy carbines, almost 30,500 of the Burnside type, and 3,000 of the cal .50 Model 1865, not to mention the rifles purchased. Many thousands more were procured by states. The Spencer rifle was issued to the Michigan Cavalry Brigade in January 1863 and to Wilder's Lightning Brigade about three months later. These were later replaced by Spencer carbines.

● (*Starr Cartridge Carbine, Model 1865.* Described under percussion carbines, above.)

● *Warner Cartridge Carbine, Model 1864.* Cal .50, single-shot, using the Warner rim-fire cartridge, and later altered to take the .56-.50 Spencer cartridge. Rifled with 3 grooves, overall length 37.5 in. No bayonet. Breech, trigger guard, and butt plate of brass; barrel and band bright. Short forearm held by one band. Loaded by half-cocking the centrally-hung hammer, unlocking and swinging the brass breech over to the right. Open leaf rear sight. Fixed sling ring on left. Marked on breech "JAMES WARNER, SPRINGFIELD MASS/WARNER'S *See 1st Wisc. Vol. Cav.*

PATENT." A similar carbine, but with significant variations, was produced by the Greene Rifle Works, Worcester, Massachusetts. It was based on Warner's patent and is often called the "Warner-Greene" carbine. In 1864 the War Department bought 1,501 using the Warner cartridge and in 1865 an additional 2,500 chambered for the Spencer cartridge. These were sold off in 1871.

See 11th Ohio Vol. Inf.

● *Wesson Cartridge Carbine, Model 1862.* Cal .44, single-shot, using a special rimfire cartridge. Rifled with 5 grooves, overall length 39.5 in. No bayonet. No forearm. Blued octagonal barrel. Breech frame, trigger guard, and butt plate plated. Loaded by half-cocking centrally-hung hammer, pulling back on the forward of two triggers which dropped the barrel downward and exposed the breech. Open leaf rear sight. Sling swivels under barrel and butt stock. Marked on top of barrel "F. WESSON'S PATENT OCT. 25, 1859 & Nov. 11, 1862" and "B. KITTEREDGE & CO./CINCINNATI, O."

Only 151 of this carbine were purchased by the War Department for trial. However, 1,366 were bought by Kentucky, 760 by Indiana, and more by individual military commands during the Civil War.

Pistols and Revolvers

The story of the military hand gun during the period 1851–1872 is largely that of the percussion revolver, and this story is dominated—certainly in the earlier years—by the figure of Colonel Sam Colt of Hartford, Conn. There had been revolvers with automatically rotating cylinders before Colt, and numerous other kinds of repeating arms, but to him must go the credit for perfecting and producing the first popular firearm equipped with a mechanically operated cylinder; indeed, of producing the first really practical repeater of any sort. This he accomplished in 1836, fifteen years before the period under study commenced.

The Colt percussion revolver was in full production by 1851 and serious competition was forestalled until 1856, when the basic Colt patents expired. Thereafter the field of revolver manufacture burgeoned, other firms offering products that ranged from improvement over the Colt design to absolute imitation of it. The Civil War, of course, greatly stimulated the production; about 374,000 revolvers of various makes were purchased by the United States alone. Private buying must have accounted for almost as many, and in the South numerous small plants produced revolvers (chiefly copies of the Colt cal .36 navy model) to supplement hand weapons imported from Europe.

Although occasionally a tricky and unreliable weapon, the martial revolver played a larger role in warfare in this era than, perhaps, in any other period of history. Certainly it was more relied upon in America than in Europe, and especially by the Confederate cavalryman. While he fought a good deal on foot with carbine or rifle, he greatly preferred working mounted with a "pair of Navy sixes." Yet the revolver was never produced in a U.S. government armory during the period. Indeed, the War Department had always preferred to secure its pistols and revolvers through contract, less than one percent of arsenal-made weapons up to 1860 being pistols. To some extent this was because the revolver was the personal weapon of the officer, purchased by him, and individual preference always played a dominant role. It was also the weapon of the cavalryman and, like the carbine, its tactical employment was open to much discussion. Then too, the government may have been anxious—or under pressure—to encourage the continuation and development of revolver manufacture by private firms. Surely one reason was the reluctance of army officers in the 1850's and 1860's to sanction too formally the use of multi-fire weapons of any sort.

At all events, the percussion revolver was adopted for the regular mounted arm about 1851, having been widely used by officers and by some mounted commands long before then. Despite attempts to return to a single-shot cartridge pistol in 1869–1871, the percussion revolver remained the standard army hand weapon until our period closed. Its naval employment, on the other hand, was more limited, despite the wide use of "navy model" revolvers. The navy had begun experimenting with revolvers in 1845 and some naval officers championed their employment by seamen in boarding operations. But, as is explained in detail later, the official naval hand weapon in 1871 was the single-shot cartridge pistol.

The pistols and revolvers described below are those that saw significant military service in the U.S. Army and by state forces. Confederate revolvers and those enjoying significant naval use are listed in the appropriate sections. It should be stressed again that the revolver was an officer's personal weapon and he could have carried one of several types not covered here.

Single-Shot Pistols

● *U.S. Pistol, Model 1842.*   Single-shot, percussion, smoothbore, cal .54. Overall length 14 in.; swivel ramrod. Mountings brass; bright barrel and lock, blued trigger. Paper cartridge with spherical ball. Manufactured entirely by contract. Marked on lock plate "US/H. ASTON"   and "MIDDtn/Conn." with the year; or "H. ASTON   & CO."; or "I.N. JOHNSON." (See Gluckman, *Pistols*, pp. 78–83, for detailed coverage of markings.) Pistols made for the navy had an anchor stamped on the barrel.

The Model 1842 was regarded as the best martial pistol of its time. A total of over 15,000 were produced. The pistol was first issued for service in 1845, in time for the War with Mexico. Many survived for use in the Civil War.

● *U.S. Pistol, Model 1843 (Box-lock).*   Single-shot, percussion, smoothbore (some made by Deringer were rifled with 7 grooves and given rear sights), cal .54. Overall length 11.75 in. Barrel lacquered brown, lock and hammer case-hardened, mountings brass. Swivel ramrod; hammer inside lock plate. Paper cartridge with spherical ball. Marked on lock plate "N.P. AMES/SPRINGFIELD/MASS," or "US/DERINGER/PHILADELa," or "RP" only; occasionally unmarked. Pistols made for the navy were stamped "USN" on the lock plate; those for Revenue Service use, "USR."

This model was actually the first regulation percussion pistol to be issued. It was manufactured by N.P. Ames of Springfield, Mass., and Henry Deringer, of Philadelphia. About 3,000 were produced. It is now generally believed that Deringer failed to complete his contract with the navy and sold the pistols commercially.

● *U.S. Pistol-Carbine, Model 1855.* Single-shot, percussion, cal .58, rifled with 3 grooves. Overall length without stock, 17.75 in.; with stock, 28.25 in. Paper cartridge with a lightweight Minie bullet. Equipped with Maynard primer. Three-leaf rear sight graduated to 400 yards. All mountings brass; steel was bright. Furnished with a brass mounted, detachable stock to fit on butt against steel back-strap, tightened by a round nut. Sling swivel on band of pistol and on stock; ring on butt cap. Marked on lock plate "U.S./SPRINGFIELD" and year. Eagle on primer door.

The pistol-carbine was produced at Springfield Armory, about 4,000 being made. It was one of the line of cal .58 weapons authorized in 1855 and was issued to both dragoons and cavalry in 1856. Its component parts could be conveniently carried in two saddle holsters.

U.S. Revolvers

A few general remarks about revolvers should be made at the outset. Most were single-action, that is the hammer had to be cocked by hand, which action turned the cylinder one chamber. Most had visible and external center hammers. Most used standard percussion caps and self-consuming cartridges wrapped in a combustible paper or fabric, but all percussion models could accept loose powder and ball. Thus each chamber of the cylinder had to be loaded by means of a loading lever which rammed home the charge. Many were altered later to accept self-contained metallic cartridges, but this development came after the Civil War.

The Smith & Wesson was the only metallic cartridge revolver of significance used during the period, enjoying this monopoly until the expiration of the Rollin White patents in 1869. But even before this date percussion revolvers, notably Colts, began to be altered to the use of the cartridge. The alteration was carried out individually by gunsmiths or systematically by the Colt factory after 1868.

Most Civil War revolvers found today have lost their original factory finish. Needless to say, many were refinished in later years and not always according to the original plan. A few revolvers were plated all over with nickel, tin, or silver at the time of their manufacture.

It must be repeated that the terms "army model" and "navy model" did not mean that these types were exclusively designed for or used by these services.

● *Adams Navy Revolver.* Five-shot, double-action, percussion, rifled with 3 grooves, cal .36. Overall length 11.5 in. Octagonal barrel. Metal parts blued, although hammer sometimes case-hardened; checkered walnut grips with hole for lanyard. Self-consuming combustible cartridge. Marked on top of frame "MANUFACTURED BY/MASS. ARMS CO./CHICOPEE FALLS"; "ADAM'S PATENT./MAY 3, 1858." and "PATENT/JUNE 3, 1856" on sides of frame; "KERR'S PATENT/APRIL 14, 1857" on distinctive loading lever along left side of barrel.

The Adams revolver was manufactured under license by the Massachusetts Arms Company. It was patented in England as early as 1851 and manufactured there in several sizes and styles. Both imported and locally-made types were carried by officers. (See also under "Foreign Revolvers.")

● *Allen & Wheelock Army Revolver, Model 1858.* Six-shot, single-action, percussion, rifled with 6 grooves, cal .44. Overall length 12.5 in. Barrel part round, part octagonal. Barrel and cylinder blued; frame, trigger guard, and hammer case-hardened in mottled colors; varnished walnut grips. Self-consuming combustible cartridge. Trigger guard, when released by a catch, dropped and operated rammer. Marked on left of barrel "ALLEN & WHEELOCK WORCESTER MASS. U.S./ALLEN'S PT'S JAN. 13 DEC. 15 1857. SEPT. 7, 1858."

About 600 of this model were manufactured, but only 198 were purchased by the War Department. Later changed to a cartridge arm with a different cylinder and hammer, and the introduction of a loading gate; the hinged trigger guard then operated the ejector.

● *Allen & Wheelock Navy Revolver, Model 1858.* Six-shot, single-action, percussion, rifled with 6 grooves, cal .36. Total length varied but usually was 13.5 in. Octagonal barrel. Barrel, frame, and cylinder blued; trigger guard and hammer case-hardened; cylinder engraved with a forest scene; varnished walnut grips. Trigger guard operated as in army model. Side hammer on right side. Self-consuming combustible cartridge. Marking almost identical to army model.

This revolver saw relatively little use, even by officers. It was also manufactured in a center hammer model and with various barrel lengths.

● *Beals (or Remington-Beals) Navy Revolver, Model 1858.* Six-shot, single-action, percussion, rifled with 5 grooves, cal .36. Overall length 13.375 in. Octagonal barrel. Barrel, frame, and cylinder blued; hammer case-hardened; trigger guard brass; walnut grips. Self-consuming combustible cartridge. Marked on barrel "BEALS PATENT SEPT. 14, 1858. MANUFACTURED BY REMINGTONS ILION NEW YORK."

This was the first of the famous line of Remington revolvers; 12,251 Beals revolvers of this and the following model were purchased by the War Department. Manufactured 1860–1862.

● *Beals (or Remington-Beals) Army Revolver, Model 1858.* Similar in all respects to the navy model except that the caliber was .44, the frame slightly larger, and the overall length was 13.75 in.

● *Butterfield Army Revolver, Model 1855.* Five-shot, single-action, percussion, rifled with 7 grooves, cal .41. Overall length 13.75 in. Octagonal barrel. Barrel and cylinder usually blued, frame and trigger guard usually bronze; walnut grips. Equipped with a disc primer magazine in front of trigger guard. Self-consuming combustible cartridge. Usually marked on top of frame "BUTTERFIELD'S/ PATENT DEc 11, 1855/PHILADA."

No Butterfield revolvers were purchased by the general government and their use during the Civil War was limited.

● *Colt Army Revolver, Model 1847.* Six-shot, single-action, percussion, rifled with 7 grooves, cal .44. Overall length 15.5 in. Round barrel. Finish varied, but usually barrel, cylinder, and trigger blued, frame case-hardened; hammer and loading lever oil finished; brass trigger guard; walnut grips. Cylinder engraved with an Indian battle scene. Marked on top of barrel "ADDRESS SAMl COLT NEW YORK CITY" and on barrel lug "US/1847." Lug also marked with a unit designation and number, for example: "C COMPANY No 154." Loose powder and round ball, later paper cartridge.

The Colt revolver can readily be distinguished from other American revolvers by its open frame (no strap over the cylinder). It was one of only two makes to have engraved scenes rolled into its cylinders. One thousand of this model were manufactured at the Eli Whitney Armory, Whitneyville, Conn., on government contract.

● *Colt Army Revolver, Model 1848.* Six-shot, single-action, percussion, rifled with 7 grooves, cal .44. Overall length varied 14 in. to 14.75 in. Round barrel. Barrel, cylinder, and trigger blued; frame, hammer, and loading lever case-hardened; brass back-strap and trigger guard; walnut grip. Cylinder engraved with Indian battle scene. Marked on top of barrel "ADDRESS SAMl COLT NEW YORK CITY" and on left of frame "COLT'S/PATENT/U.S." Cylinders frequently engraved to indicate a branch of the service: "U.S.N.," "U.S.M.R.," "U.S.M.I.," and "U.S. DRAGOONS." Paper cartridge with round ball, later various types of waterproof and self-consuming combustible cartridges with pointed ball.

This model, called the "Holster Pistol," was manufactured at Hartford, Conn., until about 1860; possibly as many as 30,000 were produced. Many minor variations were made in cylinders, stocks, sights, etc. A detachable shoulder stock with iron fittings was issued with some, the standing breech being notched for engagement. Normally, a single stock was issued for two revolvers and was marked with the serial numbers of both. These stocks carried a sling ring; they were made solid or with a metal canteen placed in the butt. The canteen's mouth emerged at the comb of the stock and was closed with a chain-fastened screw cap.

● *Colt Navy Revolver, Model 1851.* Six-shot, single-action, percussion, rifled with 7 grooves, cal .36. Overall length 13 in. Octagonal barrel. Barrel, cylinder, and trigger blued; frame, hammer, and loading lever case-hardened; trigger guard and grip frame bronze, silver plated; shellacked walnut grip. Cylinder engraved with naval battle scene. Marked usually on barrel "ADDRESS COL. SAMl COLT NEW-YORK U.S. AMERICA" and on left side of frame "COLTS/PATENT." Used a self-consuming combustible cartridge.

This model was called a "belt pistol." Over 200,000 were manufactured at Hartford between 1851 and 1865. Again there were numerous minor variations, including some in the markings. A few revolvers were cut for and supplied with detachable shoulder stocks, having brass fittings. As in the previous model, shoulder stocks were solid, fitted with a metal canteen, or given a coffee mill.

A shorter model, called the "New Model Pocket Pistol," is believed to have been issued experimentally for naval officers. Its cylinder was "rebated" (given a slightly reduced diameter in the rear) and had a stage coach holdup scene engraved on it; overall length was 9.5 in. Manufactured from about 1860 to 1872, and extensively used as a personal weapon by army officers.

● *Colt Army Revolver, Model 1860.* Six-shot, single-action, percussion, rifled with 7 grooves, cal .44. Overall length 13.5–14 in. Barrel was round and the barrel lug removed. Cylinder rebated and engraved with the same naval battle scene as the previous model. Metal finished as on Model 1851 except trigger guard was brass and back-strap iron. Most were notched for a detachable shoulder stock. Marked as previous model. Used self-consuming combustible cartridges of several types. Some had fluted cylinders.

This powerful, sure revolver, called the "New Model Army," was the principal hand weapon of the Civil War. It was manufactured at Hartford and 107,156 were purchased by the general government alone. A shoulder stock was made for this model and the frame was notched to take it, but this stock saw negligible use in the field.

● *Colt Navy Revolver, Model 1861.* Similar in general to the Army Model 1860 except that the cylinder was not rebated, the overall length was 13 in., and the caliber was .36. Barrel, cylinder, and trigger remained blued; frame, hammer, and loading lever remained case-hardened in mottled colors; but both trigger and back-strap were bronze. Less than 100 were cut for shoulder stocks.

This was called the "New Model Navy" but did not prove to be as popular as the Navy Model 1851 and relatively few were made. The War Department purchased 2,056 in 1862–1863.

● *Colt Police Revolver, Model 1862.* Five-shot, single-action, percussion, rifled with 7 grooves, cal .36. Overall length 12–14 in. Barrel round and without barrel lug. Cylinder was plain, rebated, and half fluted. Finish same as previous model. Marked on barrel "ADDRESS SAMl COLT HARTFORD CT" and on left of frame "COLTS/PATENT."

This revolver was called the "New Model Police Pistol" or the "Officers' Model Pocket Pistol." It was popular with dismounted officers during the Civil War and was manufactured from 1862 until 1872.

● *Freeman Army Revolver, Model 1862.* Six-shot, single-action, percussion, rifled with 6 grooves, cal .44. Overall length 12.5 in. Round barrel. Frame, barrel, and cylinder blued; hammer and loading lever case-hardened; walnut grips. The butt was more upright than on most revolvers and had a comb at the top. Marked on frame "FREEMAN'S PAT. DECr. 9, 1862/HOARD'S ARMORY, WATERTOWN, N.Y." Self-consuming combustible cartridge.

The Freeman revolver was not purchased by the general government. It varied somewhat in details. About 1863 the patent was purchased by Rogers & Spencer of Willowvale, N.Y., who produced the revolver which bore their name until 1864.

● *Joslyn Army Revolver, Model 1858.* Five-shot, single-action, percussion, rifled with 5 grooves, cal .44. Overall length 14.3 in. Octagonal barrel. All parts usually blued, but hammer and loading lever were sometimes case-hardened; cross-checked walnut grips. Self-consuming combustible cartridge. Marked on barrel "B.F. JOSLYN/PATd MAY 4th 1858," or "B.F. JOSLYN/STONINGTON,

CONN.," or "B.F. JOSLYN/WORCESTER Mass."

The Joslyn revolver was manufactured in both Stonington, Conn. and Worcester, Mass. At least 3,000 were made and 1,100 were purchased by the general government. Slight variations in size and details are recorded.

● *Manhattan Navy Revolver.* Construction and design similar in most details to the Colt Navy Model 1851, which it imitated. Marked on barrel "MANHATTAN FIRE ARMS CO. NEWARK N.J. PATENTED MARCH 8, 1864." Cylinder engraved with 5 scenes in medallions. No government purchases recorded.

(Massachusetts Arms Company revolver described above under "Adams.")

● *Metropolitan Navy Revolver.* Construction and design similar in most details to the Colt Navy Model 1851, which it imitated. Marked on barrel "METROPOLITAN ARMS CO. NEW-YORK." Cylinder engraved with Civil War naval scene. No government purchases recorded. Metropolitan also made a smaller sized model in cal .36, which exactly copied the Colt Police Model 1862.

● *Pettengill Army Revolver, Model 1858.* Six-shot, double-action, percussion, hammerless, rifled with 6 grooves, cal .44. Overall length 14 in. Octagonal barrel. All parts usually blued, but frame sometimes browned or loading lever case-hardened; walnut grips. Self-consuming combustible cartridge. Marked on top of frame "PETTENGILLS/PATENT 1856" and "RAYMOND & ROBITAILLE/ PATENTED 1858" and sometimes with additional patent dates.

The Pettengill was manufactured by Rogers & Spencer, in Willowvale, N.Y., and 2,001 were delivered to the general government. It was the only martial revolver made during the Civil War with an internal hammer. The mechanism proved to be too delicate for field use and many had to be discarded. The bulk were used in the Army of the Mississippi. Manufacture was discontinued and Rogers & Spencer began the manufacture of the revolver which bears their name.

(Remington-Beals revolvers are described above under "Beals")

● *Remington Army Revolver, Model 1861.* Six-shot, single-action, percussion, rifled with 5 grooves, cal .44. Overall length 13.75 in. Octagonal barrel. All parts blued except case-hardened hammer and brass trigger guard; walnut grips. Self-consuming combustible cartridge. Marked on barrel "PATENTED DEC. 17, 1861/MANUFACTURED BY REMINGTON'S, ILION, N.Y." About 5,000 manufactured in 1862.

● *Remington Navy Revolver, Model 1861.* Identical in all respects to the Army Model 1861 except the caliber was .36, overall length was 13.125 in., and the frame was correspondingly reduced in size. About 5,000 manufactured in 1862.

● *Remington "New Model" Army Revolver (1863).* In external appearance and details very similar to the Army Model 1861. Distinguished from it by the provision of hammer recesses between the nipples (which permitted it to be carried fully loaded with hammer down), by a larger cylinder pin head, and by its markings, which read: "PATENTED SEPT. 14, 1858 [instead of the 1861 date]/ E. REMINGTON & SONS, ILION NEW YORK, U.S.A./NEW MODEL." Overall length 13.5 in.

The Remington New Model was a dependable military revolver, second only in importance to the Colt, and every bit as important during the last two years of the Civil War. The general government purchased 125,314 Remington revolvers during the conflict; over 140,000 had been manufactured by 1875, when the model was discontinued.

● *Remington "New Model" Navy Revolver (1863).* Identical in all respects to the New Model Army except the caliber was .36, overall length was 13.375 in., and the frame was correspondingly reduced in size.

Remington also produced somewhat smaller "belt models" of this revolver in both single and double action.

● *Rogers & Spencer Army Revolver.* Six-shot, single-action, percussion, rifled with 5 grooves, cal .44. Overall length 13.3 in. Octagonal barrel. Barrel, frame, and cylinder blued; loading lever and hammer case-hardened in mottled colors; trigger bright; walnut grips. Self-consuming combustible cartridge. Marked on top of frame "ROGERS & SPENCER/UTICA N.Y." Government purchases are stamped "RPB" in a rectangle on the left grip.

This was a sturdy and fine-handling revolver, related to the earlier Freeman and Pettengill models. It was produced too late in the Civil War to achieve fame and only 5,000 were purchased by the general government in 1865.

● *Savage-North Navy Revolver, Model 1856.* Six-shot, single-action but fitted with a distinctive figure-8 ring trigger which cocked the hammer and operated the cylinder, percussion, rifled with 5 grooves, cal .36. Overall length 14 in. Octagonal barrel. No true trigger guard. Barrel and cylinder blued, loading lever and hammer case-hardened; bronze or iron frame with spur on the backstrap; walnut grips. Self-consuming combustible cartridge. Marked on barrel "E. SAVAGE MIDDLETOWN CT.   H.S. NORTH PATENTED JUNE 17, 1856."

Production of this revolver was stopped in 1859 and the Savage Revolving Firearms Company was formed to produce the model which follows.

● *Savage Navy Revolver.* Six-shot, single-action but fitted with a distinctive secondary ring trigger which cocked the hammer and operated the cylinder, percussion, rifled with 5 grooves, cal .36. Overall length 14.25 in. Octagonal barrel; large and specially shaped trigger guard. Barrel, frame, and cylinder blued; other metal parts case-hardened. Self-consuming combustible cartridge. Marked on barrel "SAVAGE R.F.A. CO. MIDDLETOWN Ct./H.S. NORTH PATENTED JUNE 17 1856/JANUARY 18 1859. MAY 15 1860."

The Savage revolver saw its principal use early in the Civil War; 11,284 were purchased by the general government.

● *Smith & Wesson Revolver, Model No. 2.* Six-shot, single-action, rim-fire metallic cartridge, rifled with 5 grooves, cal .32. Overall length 10.75 in. Octagonal barrel. Barrel, frame, and cylinder blued or in nickel finish; rosewood grips. No trigger guard. Marked on barrel "SMITH & WESSON, SPRINGFIELD, MASS" and on cylinder "PATENTED APRIL 3, 1855, JULY 5, 1859 and DEC. 18, 1860."

Between 1861 and 1874 some 76,500 of these revolvers were manufactured in Springfield. None were purchased by the general government but they were popular with Union officers as a personal or pocket weapon.

● *Smith & Wesson Army Revolver, Model 1869.* Six-shot, single-action, center-fire metallic cartridge, rifled with 5 grooves, cal .44. Overall length 13.5 in.

Fluted barrel. Frame broke open at top. Barrel, frame, and cylinder blued; hammer case-hardened; walnut stock. Marked on barrel "SMITH & WESSON SPRINGFIELD MASS. U.S.A. PAT. JULY 10 60. JAN. 17. FEB. 17. JULY 11. 65 & AUG. 24. 69."

At least 16,000 were manufactured and 1,000 were purchased by the War Department in 1871.

● *Starr Army Revolver, Model 1858.* Six-shot, double-action, percussion, rifled with 6 grooves, cal .44. Overall length 11.6 in. Round barrel. Frame hinged and held by pin beneath hammer. Barrel, frame, and cylinder blued; hammer, loading lever, and trigger case-hardened; solid walnut stock. Self-consuming combustible cartridge. Marked on frame "STARR'S PATENT JAN. 15, 1856" and "STARR ARMS Co. NEW YORK."

About 23,000 were manufactured in the three plants in New York State, following which the double-action feature was given up and the more conventional pattern described below was introduced. The general government purchased 47,952 of these various patterns.

● *Starr Army Revolver, Model 1863.* Similar to above except it was single-action with an overall length of 13.75 in. and a slightly altered hammer. About 31,000 of this pattern were made.

● *Starr Navy Revolver, Model 1860.* Similar to the Starr double-action army model except the caliber was .36, total length was 12 in., and the cylinder was longer. About 1,402 were purchased by the general government and about 3,000 were made.

● *Whitney Navy Revolver.* Six-shot, single-action, percussion, rifled with 7 grooves, cal .36. Overall length 13 in. Octagonal barrel. Barrel, frame, and cylinder blued; loading lever and hammer case-hardened; bronze trigger guard; walnut grips. Self-consuming combustible cartridge. Marked on barrel "E. WHITNEY/N. HAVEN" and on cylinder "WHITNEYVILLE" with a coat of arms and naval scene. About 32,000 were manufactured and over 14,000 were purchased by the general government.

Foreign Revolvers

● *Adams (or Beaumont-Adams) Army Revolver, Model 1857.* Five-shot, double-action, percussion, rifled with 3 grooves, cal .44. Overall length 11.5 in. Octagonal barrel. Metal parts blued; checkered walnut grips. Self-consuming combustible cartridge. Kerr patent compound rammer lay along left side of barrel. Usually marked on right of frame: "PATENT/JUNE 3, 1856," on left, "ADAMS PATENT/MAY 3, 1858," and on rammer "KERR'S PATENT/APRIL 14, 1857." Grips had pronounced spur at top. Made by the London Armoury Co.

The Adams was the first British martial revolver to receive official acceptance. It was purchased for the British army chiefly in cal .44 although manufactured in cal .38 as well. As described in the preceding section, it was manufactured in America under license, usually in cal .36, although possibly in .44 as well.

● *Deane (or Deane-Harding) Army Revolver, Model 1858.* Five-shot, double-action, percussion, rifled with 3 grooves, cal .442. Overall length 12 in. Octagonal barrel. Metal parts blued. Barrel, released by thumb catch, tilted forward to disengage from frame. Marked on right side "DEANE-HARDINGS PATENT" and on top strap "DEANE & SON/LONDON BRIDGE."

The Deane-Harding was made in cals .442 and .32 by J. Deane of London, and there doubtless were other variations. It was not regarded in the British army as a satisfactory weapon but was exported to America in significant numbers.

● *Kerr Army Revolver, Model 1859.* Five-shot, double-action, percussion, rifled with 3 grooves, cal .44. Overall length 10.8 in. Octagonal barrel. Side hammer with frame extended down right side of butt. All parts case-hardened; checkered walnut grips. Ring attached to butt of stock. Self-consuming combustible cartridge. Marked on frame "LONDON ARMOURY CO" and "KERR'S PATENT No. 9224."

The Kerr was made in both cals .44 and .38. When first sold in 1858 it was single-action. It was produced by the London Armoury Co.

● *Lefaucheux Revolver, Model 1855.* Six-shot, single-action, pin-fire, rifled with 4 grooves, cal .45 (12 mm). Overall length 11.5 in. Round barrel; lanyard ring stapled to butt. Tall ball front sight and groove in hammer for sighting. Special pin-fire cartridge. Apparently all metal blued. Loading gate and ejector rod on right. Marked on top of barrel "INVon E. LEFAUCHEUX BRte PARIS." Plain wooden grips.

The Lefaucheux was manufactured in several calibers, with variations in design. The large model described above was the French regulation naval weapon.

● (*LeMat Revolver:* see Chapter 10)

● *Tranter Army Revolver, Model 1853.* Six-shot, double-action, percussion, rifled with 3 grooves, cal .44. Overall length 11.5 in. Octagonal barrel. Loading lever originally separate but later fixed on left side of barrel. Made with a double trigger only until about 1856; thereafter both double- and single-trigger models produced. Grips had pronounced spur at top. Metal parts blued. Self-consuming combustible cartridge and special lubricated bullet. Marked "ADAMS PATENT" on frame and "W. TRANTER'S PATENT" on rammer.

The Tranter was also manufactured in cal .50, cal .38, and in a "pocket size" cal .32. The overall lengths varied to some extent. These revolvers were made by William Tranter in Birmingham, England, and the ones imported to the United States prior to the Civil War bore the names of importers such as T.W. Radcliffe, Columbia, S.C., etc. The cal .50 "Dragoon" model could be supplied with a detachable stock.

Swords

The sword in this period continued to fill its dual function as a mark of rank and as a weapon for the mounted man. For the dismounted NCO on formal occasions and for all officers on virtually all occasions, it served as a badge. Although foot officers did occasionally use the sword as a weapon, this could hardly be called its primary function.

Among dismounted enlisted men, only higher ranking sergeants and musicians were authorized swords, and even they did not too commonly wear them in the field. For the staff and general officer the sword was entirely a badge of office and, apparently, a burdensome one to some. Like the sergeant, the dismounted general tended to restrict his sword to formal occasions, although he usually wore it when mounted.

The saber of the cavalryman was, as has been said, essentially a weapon. The extent to which he was called upon to train with it or employ it in combat depended heavily on his commanding officer. Throughout all our period echoed the dispute about the correct arm for the cavalryman, some officers going so far as to recommend abandoning the saber—the *arme blanche*—in favor of the firearm.

To the light artilleryman the saber—a shorter weapon than that carried by the cavalryman—tended to become a nuisance and was often discarded or left strapped to the limbers. Here again its use depended heavily upon the doctrines of each unit commander.

Almost all regulation swords and sabers in this period were patterned after French official weapons. Only one model of sword was manufactured in a government arsenal. The foremost producer of enlisted men's swords was the Ames Manufacturing Company of Chicopee Falls, Mass. Officers' swords, on the other hand, tended to be manufactured in Europe. The majority of blades and a large number of entire swords were made in France, Belgium, Great Britain, and especially Germany, and imported by one or another of the military outfitting firms in this country. As a result, minor variations in design, size, and decoration among officers' swords and sabers were legion.

There is no question but what earlier models of sword than are described below were worn by officers of state forces and even the regular establishment in the first decade of our period and probably well into the Civil War. For these, in their great variety, the reader is referred to Harold L. Peterson's *The American Sword, 1775–1945*. Where a specific pattern of sword can be associated with a state or with a command, it will be mentioned there.

About presentation swords, given by governments and groups of citizens to officers who had distinguished themselves, we can say nothing here. Most examples were highly ornate and impractical even as a badge of office. Most were richly plated and many were bejewelled. The better ones were individually designed and all were distinctively etched or inscribed with laudatory messages. Collections exist in the U.S. National Museum, West Point Museum, and elsewhere. Those interested are referred to Peterson, *op.cit.*, pp. 189–210, 268.

Swords carried by dismounted men and officers usually had leather scabbards because of their lighter weight. Those that belonged to mounted men had metal scabbards, which could better take the banging against a horse's flanks.

In 1860 a new type of "telescopic" scabbard was introduced into this country from Paris by Major H.S. Lansing, who presented a sword with this device to Colonel Ellsworth of the Chicago Zouaves, then touring the East, and another to Captain Shaler of the 7th Regiment, N.Y.S.M. Ellsworth was carrying the sword when killed in Alexandria, Va., and it is now in Albany.

The scabbard was divided in the center and when the sword was withdrawn it contracted to half its usual length. The obvious advantage of avoiding a "long dangling nuisance" led New York State to approve its use by both officers and mounted men of its militia, but the idea did not catch on. Only a few examples of the "telescopic" scabbard appear to have survived.

Enlisted Men's Swords

● *Heavy Cavalry (Dragoon) Saber, Model 1840.* Curved blade, pommel of Phrygian helmet pattern, half-basket guard, both of brass. Grips of wood covered with leather, wound with twisted brass wire. Overall length 41.5 in.; blade 1.25 in. wide at hilt. Iron scabbard with 2 rings and a drag. Marked at top of blade "N.P. AMES/CABOTVILLE" over year, "AMES MFg. Co./CABOTVILLE" over year, "P.S. JUSTICE/PHILADA," etc. Also, on other side of blade, "US" over initials of inspector, if a general government contract weapon. *See U.S. Dragoons*

This model, based on a French pattern, was regulation until about 1858, after which it was gradually replaced by the model which follows. There were several variations in form of pommel, position of rings on scabbard, etc.

● *Light Cavalry Saber.* Approved in 1856, this saber was first produced by Ames in 1857. It was similar to the Model 1840 except that the blade was lighter and shorter and the grips had a swell in the center. Iron scabbard with 2 rings and a drag. The top of the blade was marked "Made by /AMES MFg. Co./CHICOPEE," etc. Overall length 40.75–41 in., blade 1 in. wide at hilt. General government contract weapons marked as model above. *See 4th U.S. Cav., 1862*

This was the common cavalry saber of the Civil War period. It is often referred to as the "Model 1860" and that terminology will be found in this book. It was manufactured by Ames; Emerson & Silver, Trenton, N.J.; C. Roby & Co., West Chelmsford, Mass.; and others. A version was produced by Tiffany & Co. with an iron rather than brass hilt.

● *Tiffany & Co. Cavalry Saber.* Slightly curved blade, round iron pommel, iron half-basket guard. Grips of wood covered with leather, wound with twisted iron wire. Overall length 40.5 in., width of blade at hilt 1.375 in. Probably iron scabbard with two rings and a drag. Blade marked at top "TC" under a star, and "TIFFANY & CO." Inspectors' initials on other side.

● *Light Artillery Saber, Model 1840.* Curved blade, Phrygian helmet pommel, single branch guard, both of brass. Grips of wood covered with leather, wound with twisted brass wire. Overall length 37–38 in.; blade 1.25 in. wide at hilt. Iron scabbard with 2 rings and a drag. Marked at top of blade "U.S./M.M." and date, and "AMES MFg Co./ CHICOPEE/ MASS." General government contract weapons marked "U.S.," etc. on blade.

See U.S. Light Atry., 1854

This saber, based on a Prussian pattern, was widely carried by regular and state light and field artillery commands until nearly the end of the 19th century.

Plate I

● *Foot Artillery Sword, Model 1833.* Straight blade with 2 broad fullers near the hilt and one below, trilobate brass pommel decorated on both sides with an American eagle, straight cross quillons. Cast brass hilt decorated with scales. Overall length 25.25 in., blade 1.75 in. wide at hilt. Black leather scabbard with brass throat and tip. Stud on throat for frog attachment.

Marked at top of blade with "US" or "UNITED STATES" over inspectors' initials, and "AMES MFG CO/ CHICOPEE / Mass.," or "N.P. AMES/ SPRINGFIELD."

This sword, based on a French pattern, resembled the popular conception of the Roman short sword. It remained regulation until about 1870.

See U.S. Colored Troops; 7th Ohio Vol. Inf.

● *NCO's Sword, Model 1840.* Straight blade, round brass pommel with a capstan rivet, brass single branch guard with a double kidney-shaped counter-guard cast integrally. Cast brass grips ribbed in imitation of wire. Overall length 37.5–38.5 in., blade .875 in. wide at hilt. Black leather on metal scabbard with brass throat and tip with drag; hook for frog attachment on throat. Occasionally iron scabbard, japanned black. Marked at top of blade with "U.S." and inspectors' initials if a general government contract weapon; initials sometimes found on guard. Also marked on blade "Made by /AMES MFg Co./ CHICOPEE/MASS," "C. ROBY/ W. CHELMSFORD, MS.," etc.

Also based on French pattern, this sword was worn by sergeants of the dismounted arms well into the 20th century.

Plate III

Musicians' Sword, Model 1840. Similar to the NCO's sword above except that its blade was 3–4 in. shorter and it lacked the double counter-guard.

● *Militia NCO's Swords.* This class of sword possessed certain general characteristics but examples differed considerably in detail. Blades were straight and double edged; pommels were usually brass and either ball shaped or in the form of a helmet; grips were of wood or more usually of bone, fluted vertically; guards consisted solely of cross quillons. Overall lengths varied from about 31 to 33 in. Blades were often etched with floral and martial designs. Scabbards were usually black leather, brass mounted, with hook for frog attachment.

See 6th Regt., NYSM, 1853

These swords were sold by military outfitters to state commands and were rarely described in dress regulations.

Officers' Swords

Fig. 20

● *Staff and Field Officers' Sword, Model 1850.* Slightly curved blade. Phrygian helmet pommel on the rear of which were floral sprays and a national shield; half-basket guard, the spaces filled with pierced floral designs and the letters "US." Hilt of gilded brass with grips of wood covered with fish skin and wrapped with twisted gilt wire. Overall length 38 in.; blade 1.2 in. wide at hilt. Blade etched with floral and military designs, and with the national eagle on the obverse, and "U.S." on the reverse. Browned or bright iron scabbard with gilded brass throat, middle band, and tip, the last having a drag; two suspension rings. Marking on the blade varied with the source of the sword, among them "W. Clauberg/ Solingen," "Ames Mfg Co,/ Chicopee/ Mass.," etc.

This was the usual staff and field officers' sword of the period although officially replaced by the Model 1860 in that year. Variations in detail were many, especially in decoration. Pommels and knuckle bows were often more elaborate; half-basket guards contained panoplies of flags, oak leaves and acorns, and other devices to the exclusion of the "US." Grips had different shapes; some were leather covered and were wound with both twisted and plain strands of wire. Blade lengths varied from 37 to 42 in.

Scabbards were sometimes of black leather instead of iron, and the gilded brass bands were often decorated with floral sprays.

● *Staff and Field Officers' Sword, Model 1860.* Straight blade; Phrygian helmet pommel decorated with an eagle and a shield; single branch guard with a kidney-shaped counter-guard, both ornamented. One guard was usually hinged, and could be lowered by pressing a button. Hilt of gilded brass with wooden grips covered with black fish skin wound with gilded wire. Overall length 37.5 in.; blade .625 in. wide at hilt. Nickled steel scabbard with gilded brass upper band (with 1 or 2 rings), middle band (with 1 ring), and tip with drag. Blade etched with designs resembling those on the Model 1850 sword.

See U.S. Staff Officers, 1861–1865

Markings on blade reflected the maker or dealer. These included "THE HENDERSON AMES CO. KALAMAZOO, MICH.," "U.S./ Armory/ Springfield/ Mass.," etc.

This purely decorative sword with its frail blade was prescribed for staff and field officers but its use was not made mandatory. Many officers until 1872 continued to carry the sturdier Model 1850. General Francis C. Barlow said he wanted a large saber so that when he hit a straggler the man would feel it.

● *Cavalry Officers' Saber, Model 1840.* Similar to the enlisted men's model of that year in most details. The guard, however, had floral designs at the ends of the branches and the pommel was also modestly decorated. The outer branch of the guard was usually higher, and the blade was etched as in other officers' swords.

This saber was in common use by 1851 and many saw service in the Civil War. It was manufactured by Ames and many other firms.

● *Officers' Light Cavalry Saber.* Similar to the enlisted men's light cavalry model except in its modest use of floral designs on the hilt and the decorative etching on the blade. The scabbard was of bright or blued iron and, if the latter, had gilt bands and tip. Etched on blade with name of seller, as "WH/ HORSTMANN/& SONS/PHILADELPHIA." Lengths varied from 37.5 in. to 41 in.

This was the popular mounted officers' saber of the Civil War. It was manufactured by Ames and others.

● *Light Artillery Officers' Saber, Model 1840.* Similar to the enlisted men's light artillery saber of that year except in its use of ornamental gilt mountings and etched blades. Grips tended to be covered with fish skin instead of leather.

Photographs suggest that while this was worn by field artillery officers in the Civil War, the use of the cavalry officers' saber was about as common. Officers assigned to heavy artillery commonly carried the same swords as infantry officers.

● *Foot Officers' Sword, Model 1850.* Slightly curved blade; Phrygian helmet pommel; single branch guard expanding into an oval counter-guard with a pierced design of branches and scrolls on its obverse. Hilt of brass, and grips of wood covered with fish skin wound with brass wire. The grips are formed to fit the hand. Blade etched with floral and military designs as in other models. Overall length 36–37 in.; blade 1.125 in. wide at hilt. Black leather scabbard with brass throat, middle band, and tip with drag.

See Conn. Vols., 1861–1865

Markings on blade reflected the maker or dealer. These included Horstmann & Sons, Ames Manufacturing Co., etc.

This was the sword of the company officer of infantry and foot artillery. It was based upon a French pattern and was widely worn in the period. Variations include greater ornamentation, addition of a branch to the guard, etc.

● *Schuyler, Hartley & Graham Officer's Sword.* Slightly curved blade, bird's head pommel with back-strap, half-basket hilt with 2 branches on one side and one on the other. Iron hilt with wooden grips covered with fish skin and wound with twisted iron wire. Blade etched with floral and military designs including a ribbon bearing the words "IN HOC SIGNO VINCES." Overall length 37.75 in.; blade 1 in. wide at hilt.

Blade marked at top with a gilded circular stamp bearing a cross and the word "PROVED." Around the stamp is etched "SCHUYLER HARTLEY/ & GRAHAM/NEW YORK." The maker's name "W./CLAUBERG /SOLINGEN" is stamped on the reverse.

This non-regulation sword was the only iron-mounted pattern to enjoy significant use by Northern officers during the Civil War. It was sometimes sold with brass mountings and with minor variations in design.

● *Medical Staff Sword, Model 1840.* Straight blade, pineapple-shaped pommel, no knuckle bow, specially molded grips bearing oak leaf and acorn devices and a national eagle, scrolled quillons with leaf motifs, all gilded brass. Quillons bear two shields, the obverse one carrying "MS" in Old English script letters, the reverse one plain. Blade etched with floral and military designs. Overall length 34–37.5 in.; blade approx. .75 in. wide at hilt. Gilded brass scabbard, heavily decorated, with 2 upper suspension rings and 1 lower. Drag decorated in high relief.

See Surgeon, 22nd Mass. Vol. Inf.

Markings on blade reflected the maker or dealer. These included "THE PET-TIBONE/ MFG. CO/ CINCINNATI. O."

This Medical Staff sword was regulation throughout the period. It was probably worn only on dress occasions and there is some question if all medical officers owned one. Variant styles have been found; see Peterson, *op. cit.,* pp. 140–142.

● *Pay Department Sword, Model 1840.* Similar to the Medical Staff sword of the same year in all details except the letters "PD" in silver are soldered on the obverse shield and "U.S. Pay Department" is etched on the blade. This pattern was worn by paymasters throughout the period.

Knives

The tradition of the knife lies deep in American history. By 1851 certain distinctive forms had come into being which can be categorized roughly as the folding pocket knife, the hunting knife, and the fighting knife. Of course, any sizeable knife could be, and often was, used for all three purposes, but the distinctions remain valid nonetheless.

A pocket or jackknife was the personal possession of the soldier, and he set great store by it. By means of it he prepared his food, mended his clothing and equipment, and performed a hundred other tasks. With it he might, at times, be called upon to defend his life. All soldiers, it is safe to say, carried a knife of some sort. Such knives were commercially made in about the same variety as they are made today, ranging from those with a single strong blade to the farrier's knife with two blades, saw, fleam, punch, gimlet, corkscrew, stone hook, and screw driver. With this last type the horseman could care for his mount's hooves on the march and open a bottle, repair a wagon, or slaughter a pig. Several complex pocket knives offered various combinations of knife, fork, and spoon; and buttonhooks, scissors, files, and bottle openers were included in others.

The hunting knife, usually carried in a sheath, was the companion of the frontiersman, a simple, sturdy affair often constructed by a local blacksmith. Larger than the jackknife, it was employed for hunting and trapping and, if necessary, for personal defense. This has been the rifleman's knife, referred to in official records as the "butcher" or "scalping" knife, and included the one specific pattern established by the U.S. Army during the period. The type, in all its sizes and variations, is in common use today.

The American fighting knife of the mid-19th century was *par excellence* the "bowie knife." The term itself defied definition in those days as it does today, but a rough description would be a large sheath knife, usually with a small cross guard and a clipped point, whose story began in the American Southwest about 1830. By the Civil War the bowie was firmly established as the weapon of the Western gambler and man of violence. It was being extensively manufactured in Europe for importation to America, as well as made locally. Thus, when war came, it was eagerly accepted by the early volunteers on both sides. The Northern soldier soon discarded the big knife, but the Confederate tended to hold on to it, both from tradition and from the fact that his other weapons were not as effective as those of his opponent. Confederate bowie knives will be described under Confederate weapons (Chapter 10); here we will mention briefly the sheath knives carried by the U.S. Army and by men from the Northern states.

In 1848 the U.S. Ordnance Department purchased from the Ames Manufacturing Company, Cabotville, Mass., 1,000 "knives for the Regiment of Mounted Riflemen." The Ames knife had an 11.75 in. spear-point blade, brass guard, and walnut handle curved at the end and pierced for a thong or lanyard. The blade, 1.625 in. wide at the hilt, was stamped "AMES MFG CO./ CABOTVILLE/ 1849." The sheath or scabbard was of black leather with brass tip and throat; a stud for frog attachment was fixed to the throat. This was the only official army knife in the period.

Many Union volunteers of 1861 carried sheath knives, generally of English manufacture. In Massachusetts it was not unusual for entire companies to be presented with knives by the towns from which they were recruited; this distribution will be mentioned in more detail under that state. In other states the acquisition of sheath knives was on a more personal basis.

Lances

Lances were carried by at least two or three state militia commands in the 1850's, but these were entirely for parade. So far as is known, no American cavalry was trained in the combat use of the lance before 1861 and probably even after that no training with the weapon was given which was remotely comparable to that required of lancer regiments in European armies.

Only one Union regiment as such was officially issued the lance: the 6th Pennsylvania Volunteer Cavalry. It carried the lance until 1863 when the weapon was discarded. The lances carried by this and smaller commands in the North are described under the states concerned.

SOURCES

The following books are those found most useful by the authors in the preparation of this chapter. There are scores more, plus a wealth of magazine articles and special studies. And behind these lies a formidable collection of manuscript sources, plus the weapons themselves, which must be investigated by anyone anxious to learn more of the subject.

For help in the preparation of this chapter we are indebted to many individuals. Among those who gave freely of their time and knowledge over the years were Harold L. Peterson, the late Robert L. Miller, Sydney C. Kerksis, Jeremiah J. Reen, Roger Stahel Cohen, Jr., the late Gerald C. Stowe, and H. Michael Madaus. We are also indebted to Lieutenant Colonel Richard A. Johnson, Francis Von Muller, Ralph Steinhauer, William B. Edwards, and the late Colonel James E. Hicks.

The staff of the former Springfield Armory museum was more than helpful in making their impressive collection of small arms easily accessible. Important help was secured from numerous museums and private collections mentioned elsewhere in this book.

Comment should be made on a most important source of information on the small arms issued Union regiments in the Civil War: the "Summary Statements of Ordnance and Ordnance Stores on Hand," in Record Group 156, National Archives, Entries 230–232, a total of thirty-five volumes. These Statements record issues to both Federal and state regiments in great detail. These data, immensely condensed, are recorded in the orders of battle that appear in later chapters. Although the terminology used in the Statements does not always coincide with that found in this chapter, it has been for the most part retained.

Maurice Bottet, *Monographie de l'arme à feu portative des armées françaises de terre et de mer, de 1718 à nos jours*, Paris, (1900 ?).

Robert V. Bruce, *Lincoln and the Tools of War*, Indianapolis, Ind., 1956.

Werner Eckardt and Otto Morawietz, *Die Handwaffen des brandenburgisch-preussisch-deutschen Heeres 1640–1945*, Hamburg, 1957.

William B. Edwards, *Civil War Guns . . .*, Harrisburg, Pa., 1962.

J.N. George, *English Guns and Rifles . . .*, Plantersville, S.C., 1947.

——, *English Pistols and Revolvers . . .*, Onslow County, N.C., 1938.

Arcadi Gluckman, *United States Martial Pistols and Revolvers*, Buffalo, N.Y., 1939.

——, *United States Muskets, Rifles and Carbines*, Buffalo, N.Y., 1948; reprinted, Harrisburg, Pa., 1959.

Charles T. Haven and Frank A. Belden, *A History of the Colt Revolver . . .*, New York, 1940.

James E. Hicks, *Notes on United States Ordnance*, 2 vols., Mt. Vernon, N.Y., 1940; reprinted 1957. With illustrations by Andre Jandot, this is one of the clearest and most useful general coverages of U.S. regulation firearms.

Berkeley R. Lewis, *Small Arms and Ammunition in the United States Service*, Washington, D.C., 1956.

Herschel C. Logan, *Cartridges . . .*, Huntington, W.Va., 1948.

J. Margerand, *Armement et équipement de l'infanterie française du XVIe au XXe siècle*, Paris, 1945.

Alfred Mordecai, *Military Commission to Europe in 1855 and 1856* (Senate Ex. Doc. 60, 36th Cong., 1st Session), Washington, D.C., 1860.

Harold L. Peterson, *The American Sword, 1775–1945*, New Hope, Pa., 1954. The classic work in the field.

——, *American Knives: The First History and Collectors' Guide*, New York, 1958.

Caesar Ruestow, *Die Kriegshandfeuerwaffen*, Berlin, 1857.

James E. Serven, *Colt Firearms, 1836–1954*, Santa Ana, Cal., 1954.

Philip B. Sharpe, *The Rifle in America*, New York, 1938.

Winston O. Smith, *The Sharps Rifle: Its History, Development and Operation*, New York, 1943.

C.M. Wilcox, *Evolutions of the Line, as Practiced by the Austrian Infantry and Adopted in 1853*, New York, 1860.

Alonzo Gray, *Cavalry Tactics as Illustrated by the War of the Rebellion . . .*, Fort Leavenworth, Kan., 1910.

Howard L. Blackmore, *British Military Firearms, 1650–1850*, London, 1961.

Claud Fuller, *The Rifled Musket*, Harrisburg, Pa., 1958.

Robert M. Reilly, *United States Military Small Arms, 1816–1865*, Baton Rouge, La., 1970.

Rodney Hilton Brown, *American Polearms, 1526–1865 . . .*, New Milford. Conn., 1967.

Albert N. Hardin, Jr., *The American Bayonet, 1776–1964*, Philadelphia, Pa., 1964.

C.H. Roads, *The British Soldier's Firearm, 1850–1864*, London, 1964.

(See also checklist of material on Confederate weapons, Chapter 10.)

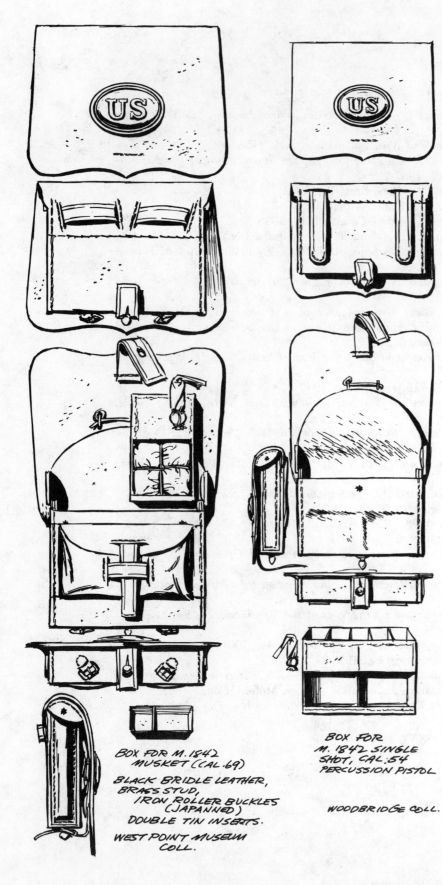

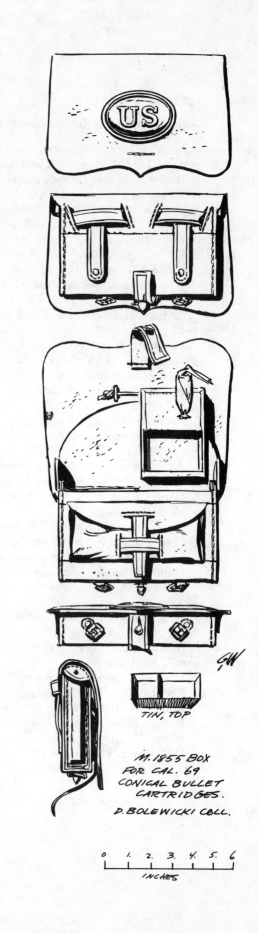

BOX FOR M. 1842
MUSKET (CAL.69)

BLACK BRIDLE LEATHER,
BRASS STUD,
IRON ROLLER BUCKLES
(JAPANNED)
DOUBLE TIN INSERTS.

WEST POINT MUSEUM
COLL.

BOX FOR
M. 1842 SINGLE
SHOT, CAL.54
PERCUSSION PISTOL

WOODBRIDGE COLL.

M.1855 BOX
FOR CAL. 69
CONICAL BULLET
CARTRIDGES.

D. BOLEWICKI COLL.

TIN, TOP

0 1. 2. 3. 4. 5. 6
INCHES

Fig. 48.   U.S. regulation musket and pistol cartridge boxes.

CHAPTER IV

Accouterments

By "accouterments" was meant the equipment habitually carried by a soldier on his person, in distinction to his arms and clothing.* Accouterments included containers and hangers, plus the belts and straps from which they were suspended. By means of these devices the soldier carried weapons, ammunition, water, food, clothing, and other possessions. Another word sometimes used was "personal equipment" and this distinguished accouterments from the category of camp and garrison equipage—items not normally carried on the person and designed for domestic rather than warlike uses.

Accouterments may conveniently be divided into those carried by infantrymen, cavalrymen, and so forth, or they may be classed by type, such as cartridge boxes, knapsacks, belts, and so on. The latter method will be employed here as it seems to be the more useful for the average student. First, however, it would be well to deal with the subject generally before entering into detail.

The American soldier, on the whole, was not fond of his accouterments and wore as few as he could. Part of this attitude stemmed from indiscipline or improvidence, but part, too, came from a very strong desire of the young American male to travel light and to rely upon ingenuity to make up for articles missing at the end of a march. The Confederate infantryman was especially noted for his tendency to lighten the load. After throwing away his knapsack and overcoat, he might give up his percussion cap box and carry the caps in his pocket. Unless his officers were watchful he might throw away his bayonet or his canteen. Some even felt the cartridge box was unnecessary.

Well aware of this trait, American ordnance officers and quartermasters designed and manufactured relatively light accouterments, and commanders on both sides in the Civil War rarely insisted in the field upon uniformity of equipments or upon exactly how they were worn. Parade, of course, was a different matter; where sufficient accouterments were available they were uniformly worn within a regiment.

---

* This is the modern approved spelling. British usage a century ago tended to restrict "accouterments" to the belts which supported arms and pouches; the name for the larger category was "appointments," rarely used in America. "Gear" was a term usually confined to horse furniture.

Within the 1851–1872 period, the accouterments authorized in the regular army for use with weapons—the cartridge box or the bayonet scabbard, for example—were issued by the Ordnance Department and are listed and classified in *Ordnance Regulations,* 1852, pages 42, 49–50. They are also described in great detail in *Ordnance Manuals,* 1850, pages 201–207; and 1862, pages 227–233. Valuable as are these tabulations and descriptions, they omit more than half of the ordnance accouterments in use during the Civil War. Other accouterments, like knapsacks and canteens, were the province of the Quartermaster Department. For these no such useful manuals exist, probably because there was not the same need for precision of manufacture and issue as existed for ordnance items.

The care of accouterments was covered in the *Regulations for the Army of the United States.* In addition to prescribing how they would be marked, the *Regulations* of 1857 stated,

> 98. When belts are given to a soldier, the captain will see that they are properly fitted to the body; and it is forbidden to cut any belt without his sanction.
> 99. Cartridge-boxes and bayonet-scabbards will be polished with blacking; varnish is injurious to the leather, and will not be used.

In the main, the American accouterments at this time were made of black leather or black painted cloth. Notable exceptions to this rule were canteens and a fairly extensive use of russet leather and unpainted cloth in the Confederacy.

Cartridge Boxes and Other Ammunition Containers

The essentials of a military cartridge box were several. It had to be stout enough to stand abuse and to prevent the fragile paper cartridge of the day, when unpackaged, from being smashed. It had to be waterproof enough to shield the ammunition at least from rain and snow. It had to present the cartridges in a fixed position so that the soldier could find one in the excitement of battle with the minimum of fumbling and without having to look around. It had to contain a device whereby the cartridges were held rigidly in place on the march, lest they be broken by the incessant movement of the box riding on the soldier's hip. It had to be adjusted in its gross weight to what the soldier could conveniently carry for a long period. Finally, it had to provide some protection for the soldier should the box "blow" or explode.

The regulation American infantry cartridge box of this period was made of black bridle leather and at first contained two tin inserts. Twenty paper cartridges stood upright in the upper sections of the inserts and were withdrawn by the soldier as needed. When this supply was exhausted the man pulled up the two inserts and removed from their lower sections two packages containing twenty reserve cartridges. These he opened and placed in the upper sections. At the same time he transferred the supply of percussion caps packed with each package of cartridges to his cap pouch. The normal supply in such a box, thus, was forty cartridges (3.5 pounds), half ready on top, half in reserve in the bottom. On occasion troops were ordered to carry an extra twenty rounds (two packages) or more in their pockets.

Earlier in the 19th century cartridge boxes had been fitted not with tin inserts but with a block of wood bored with a series of holes of the proper size. The introduction of an improved quality of powder about 1837, and the advent of the percussion system in 1841 (which did away with the need of priming the pan), permitted a shorter and lighter cartridge than before and enabled the soldier to carry a larger supply on his person. It was also found that tin trays with dividers served as well as bored blocks to keep the paper cartridges in usable condition and were far more economical of space.

The change to caliber .58 in 1855 led to more alterations in cartridge box size and design, while the advent of breechloading weapons brought a host of new and unusual styles. Whereas there were only three patents for cartridge-carrying devices recorded prior to the Civil War, the war itself saw sixteen new patents, and the years 1865–1872 brought forth a total of thirty-seven. One aspect of this last development was the return of the bored wooden block as a necessity for holding the peculiarly shaped and often fragile cartridges invented. When the full, self-contained, metallic cartridge was perfected and in use, the looped cartridge belt became the obvious method of carrying it. Such belts, made of leather and later of canvas, were used as field expedients as early as 1866, but their real development came after our period.

Paper cartridges for regulation weapons were packed ten in a bundle, in two tiers of five each, alternating front to back. In each bundle was placed a package of twelve percussion caps. During 1862–1864 one or more Williams "clean-out" cartridges was put in every bundle of ammunition for the caliber .58 rifle musket, and possibly other models. This cartridge, wrapped in colored paper, was especially designed to remove powder fouling from the bore of a rifle. It did this, but soldiers objected to it and the issue was discontinued late in the Civil War.

Cartridges were normally packed in boxes containing 1,000 each. These boxes were made of white pine boards, dovetailed and nailed together with the lid screwed on. Boxes were clearly marked to indicate the number and caliber of the cartridges contained, and the weapon for which they were intended. Sometimes they were distinctively colored. Bundles of regulation ammunition, on the other hand, were usually not marked, although the variety of cartridges brought into use during the Civil War led to more careful marking of cartridge bundles.

Combustible and skin cartridges required better packaging, and in some cases small blocks or tin inserts were included with the cartridges to permit adjustment of regulation cartridge boxes to unusually sized ammunition. Cartridges for single-shot breechloading carbines and rifles came in bundles or cardboard boxes of different sizes and shapes containing from seven to fifty rounds. This wide and ever changing variation in cartridge making and packaging was reflected in the numerous sizes and styles of cartridge boxes used during the Civil War.

Cartridge boxes were suspended in several ways. The most common was by means of a leather belt over the left shoulder which permitted the box to rest on the rear of the soldier's right hip—the traditional position to which troops had been trained for over a century. Troops were sometimes trained to swing the box to the front of the body in action. A somewhat more convenient method, of almost equal antiquity, was to attach the cartridge box to a waist belt. The box was worn either over the stomach or, by the Civil War era, at the small of the back and was slid around toward the front in action. With it positioned in front, the soldier could more readily reach his cartridges and even see them if necessary.

Despite its antiquity, suspension from a shoulder belt had its disadvantages and its critics. General William B. Hazen in *A Narrative of Military Service* (p. 391) summed it up this way.

> The plan of carrying all the cartridges in a box suspended from the shoulder, and all on one side, had three serious defects. By suspending the weight from a point two feet away from the center of gravity of a person, it created a leverage to be overcome and kept in adjustment; it produced curvature of the person; and by the pressure of the shoulder belt it prevented free evaporation from the surface of the body. The soldier readily overcame the first and third of these evils by throwing away the shoulder-belt altogether, and carrying his cartridge-box on his waist-belt; and the second he overcame, when permitted, by using two boxes, one on each side. This provided the easiest way to carry ammunition.

Such defects led to experiments with other kinds of cartridge boxes, notably by Colonel William Dalton Mann.

The disadvantage of the waist belt method was that a full box uncomfortably weighed down the belt and could produce hernia. It was used, therefore, only when relatively few cartridges had to be carried or when the cartridges were smaller than normal. The regular establishment had not used this model box since the early 19th century, but the introduction in 1841 of the caliber .54 rifle with its lighter weight ammunition (compared with the standard caliber .69) offered an opportunity to return to the waist belt box. When the new line of caliber .58 weapons was issued in 1855 it was decided to equip all cartridge boxes to fit on either shoulder or waist belts. Hardee's *Rifle and Light Infantry Tactics* also appeared in 1855, and this manual prescribed the sliding type of box. Thereafter its use became associated with all types of light infantry.

The seams of better made boxes were designed so that the force of an accidental explosion of their contents would blow outward, away from the body of the soldier. An actual occurrence of this sort in recent years left the man with no bodily injury and only slight damage to his clothing.

Rifle flasks and bullet pouches were not common items in the years after 1851, although they were listed in the *Ordnance Manual* of 1850. They were supposed to be used by riflemen when firing individually at long range; otherwise paper cartridges were drawn from a box as was the practice for infantrymen. No regular regiments carried flasks and pouches in this period, their use being confined to a few militia rifle units and then only for target firing. Flasks, too, had an uncomfortable habit of exploding on occasion.

A third method of suspension, employed for carbine boxes, was on the carbine sling. It does not seem that this was common, judging from the very few boxes fitted with loops large enough to admit the standard 2.5-inch sling. When so slung, the box rode on the small of a man's back and was prevented from sliding down to the hook by the brass buckle.

Paper pistol cartridges were habitually carried by officers in their saddle holsters. Five or six tin tubes were attached to each holster under its flap, until the belt holster came into use. Even after this date—in fact, throughout the Civil War—saddle holsters continued to be used on the finer, non-regulation saddles ridden by general officers and their staffs.

About 1842 a special box for pistol ammunition was prescribed for dragoons. When the Whitneyville-Walker model Colt revolver was adopted in 1847, a brass flask of the rifle type came with it, together with a bullet mold and a combination tool. By 1851, however, the use of separate powder and ball had almost entirely given way to the paper cartridge as far as military use in the field was concerned. While the flask is listed as a component part of the Colt revolver well into the 1850's, it and the bullet mold were probably retained in quarters or barracks where cartridges could be made by hand as necessary. Paper cartridges for use with the Colt were being manufactured commercially as early as 1851, when the Army purchased 393,304.

Use of the belt holster by officers and mounted soldiers led to the adoption of special cartridge boxes for the paper and, later, combustible and metallic cartridges required. As the manufacture of revolver cartridges developed during the late 1850's, considerable thought was given to methods of packaging in order to protect these fragile items from the inevitable jostling they received. By the Civil War the most satisfactory method was a block of wood bored with holes, wrapped in paper and varnished to keep out moisture. Each package contained one full load for the cylinder of the model revolver the cartridges were made for. In 1859 Colonel Samuel Colt patented a rip-string system for rapidly opening the several kinds of cartridge packages then in common use.

Safe packaging in a block of wood removed the necessity for providing special protection in the cartridge box itself. Furthermore, with the revolver it was usually more convenient to load all chambers of a cylinder at one time. Thus about 1861 a group of small leather pouches were developed for pistol ammunition which consisted merely of a pocket holding two packages, between double layers of leather. These pouches were worn in the main by officers when they were worn at all. Experience showed that packaged pistol ammunition was about as safe in a man's pocket as on his belt and less in the way, and this would account for the scarcity of pictures showing these boxes in use.

Percussion caps were commonly carried throughout the period in a small leather pouch attached to the right front of the waist belt. There is no evidence that a pouch was ever fixed to a shoulder belt, as was often the practice in Europe. On the other hand, uniforms manufactured after 1842, when percussion lock weapons were first issued by the army, often had small pockets cut in their breast, usually on the left, to hold caps. With the wide use of the leather cap pouch after 1850 this practice generally ceased, only to be revived in the Confederacy during the Civil War.

As has been mentioned, caps were packed with cartridges for use by the soldier equipped with a cartridge box. Otherwise, they were packed in small round "pill boxes" which could readily be carried by officers in their pockets.

The principal kinds of cartridge containers used by the U.S. Army in the period 1851–1872 included U.S. regulation boxes for muskets and rifles, U.S. regulation boxes for carbines and pistols, commercial carbine boxes, Mann's patent boxes, foreign and unidentified boxes, and percussion cap pouches.

There were, of course, many other types of cartridge box used in the U.S. during these years. Navy boxes are described in Chapter 13, and boxes of Confederate manufacture or importation in Chapter 10. While U.S. regulation boxes were widely, almost universally, worn by state troops during the Civil War, some states did contract for these accouterments with consequent variations in manufacture. There was also a considerable variety of boxes with patent leather outer flaps. In the main these were dress boxes provided in peacetime by military outfitting firms for the wealthier state corps or, perhaps, for a state as a whole. Where these have been identified they are described under the proper state. Most sizes and varieties were furnished to New York regiments and a general survey of such dress boxes is included in a subsequent volume. Patent leather, of course, could be found on some regulation and field service boxes.

All dimensions are *inside* and are of the box proper. They are given in this order: length (right to left), width (or thickness), and depth (top to bottom). In connection with these measurements it should be kept in mind that leather often shrinks with age and that cartridge boxes—like other accouterments— could be and were often handmade in small saddlery shops, with consequent variation in dimensions.

The kind of ammunition a box was designed to hold can usually be determined by the type and dimensions of its insert. What makes identification difficult today is that inserts are often missing. Furthermore, inserts were easily changed and older boxes thus adapted for newer weapons. Indeed, this seems to have been a common practice.

Many boxes display stampings that resemble asterisks. These are "vice-marks" produced by the tool with which the leather worker gripped the leather, and have no significance.

U.S. Regulation Boxes for Muskets and Rifles

Fig. 48

● *Cartridge Box for M1842 Musket.* Black bridle leather, double flaps, implement pocket. Inside dimensions 7.2 x 1.6 x 5.8 in. Two tin inserts; oval brass "US" plate, 3.5 x 2.2 in., with two eyes. Two horizontal loops on rear and 2 buckles on bottom to engage shoulder belt; after 1855 made with both horizontal and vertical loops. This box held 40 rounds of cal .69 spherical ball or buck and ball paper cartridges—10 loose in the 2 upper compartments of each insert, and two packages of 10 each in the lower compartments. This was the common box of the Mexican War and was widely used by state troops during the early Civil War. It was sometimes adapted for carrying cal..58 cartridges by removing the dividers in the top sections of the inserts and fitting a wooden block bored for 7 cartridges. Made by H.A. Dingee, etc.

● *Cartridge Box for M1841 Rifle.* Black bridle leather, double flaps, no implement pocket. Inside dimensions 7.2 x 1.6 x 5 in. Single tin insert divided into 2 lower and 5 upper compartments; oval brass "US" plate, 2.8 x 1.6 in., with two eyes. Two vertical loops on rear to fit a waist belt. Held 40 rounds of cal .54 paper cartridges. This box was also used with the cavalry, artillery, and sappers M1847 musketoons, and Hall-North carbine M1843. Made by R. Dingee, C.S. Storms, etc. *Fig. 54*

● *Cartridge Box M1855 (for cal..58 Rifle Musket).* Black bridle leather, double flaps, implement pocket. Inside dimensions 6.8 x 1.4 x 5.2 in. Two tin inserts of same design as M1842 musket box; oval brass "US" plate, 3.5 x 2.2 in. Both horizontal and vertical loops on rear, with 2 buckles on bottom, to fit either shoulder or waist belt. Held 40 rounds of cal .58 Minie ball paper cartridges. Sometimes made with horizontal loops only. *Fig. 49*

● *Cartridge Box M1855 (for cal..69 Rifle Musket).* Same as above except inside dimensions are 7.8 x 1.6 x 4.7 in. *Fig. 48*

● *Cartridge Box M1864.* This was the same as the M1855 box but instead of a brass plate on the flap the "US" within an oval was embossed into the leather. Made for both cal .58 and cal .69 rifle musket. Made by H.G. Haedrich, R. Nece, Watertown Arsenal, etc. There are instances where a brass plate has been fastened over the embossing. *Fig. 49*

● *Cartridge Box for M1866 Rifle (Allin Alteration).* Black bridle leather, single flap, implement pocket. Wooden insert bored for twenty .50-70 government center-fire metallic cartridges. Inside dimensions 6.8 x 1.5 x 3.5 in. Two horizontal and 2 vertical loops, 2 buckles on bottom. Stamped on rear: "U.S. ARMORY/SPRINGFIELD/MASS/1867." One example, used at U.S.M.A., has a wooden insert bored both top and bottom for lightness, with holes alternating 1.2 in. and 1.4 in. in depth; able to carry blank cartridges only. This model may have been used only at West Point.

● *Experimental Cartridge Box for M1866 Rifle (Allin Alteration) (and U.S. M1868 Rifle?).* Black bridle leather, rounded shape, single flap, no implement pocket. Inside dimensions 7.1 x 1.6 x 2 in. Tin insert with holes in top and bottom for nineteen .50-70 government center-fire metallic cartridges. Two vertical loops on rear. Stamped on flap: "U.S/WATERVLIET/ARSENAL." Special brass fastening device; sheepskin sewed under flap to fit over cartridges. Examples also exist with wooden inserts holding 20 cartridges. *Fig. 49*

U.S. Regulation Boxes for Carbines and Pistols

● *Cartridge Box for Pistol M1842.* Black bridle leather, double flaps, no implement pocket. Inside dimensions 6.2 x 1.3 x 3.5 in. Single tin insert divided into *Fig. 48*

192

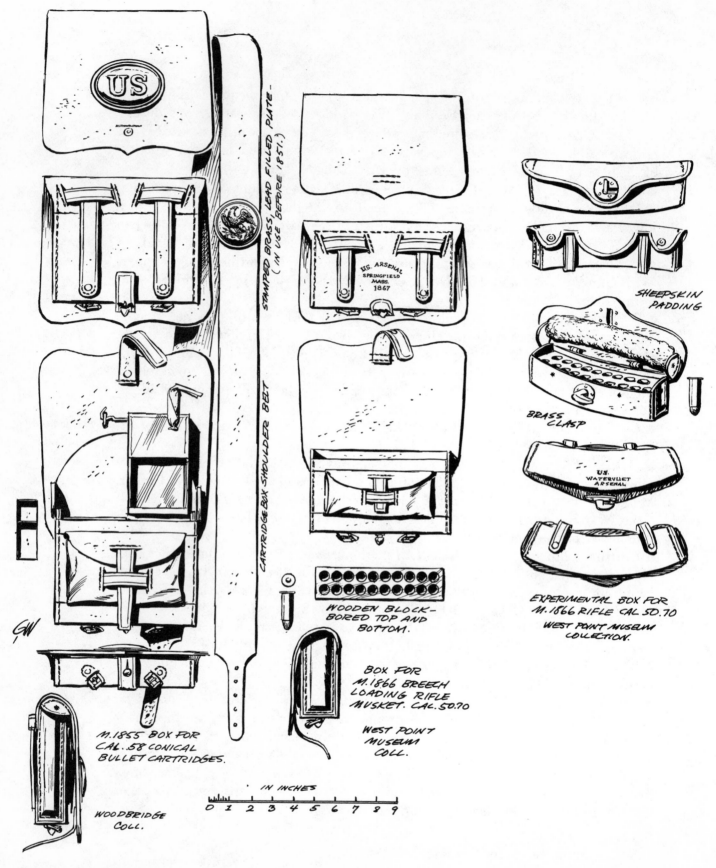

STAMPED BRASS, LEAD FILLED PLATE -
(IN USE BEFORE 1851.)

CARTRIDGE BOX SHOULDER BELT

U.S. ARSENAL
SPRINGFIELD
MASS.
1867

M.1855 BOX FOR
CAL..58 CONICAL
BULLET CARTRIDGES.

WOODBRIDGE
COLL.

WOODEN BLOCK-
BORED TOP AND
BOTTOM.

BOX FOR
M.1866 BREECH
LOADING RIFLE
MUSKET. CAL.50.70

WEST POINT
MUSEUM
COLL.

IN INCHES
0 1 2 3 4 5 6 7 8 9

SHEEPSKIN
PADDING

BRASS
CLASP

U.S.
WATERVLIET
ARSENAL

EXPERIMENTAL BOX FOR
M.1866 RIFLE CAL.50.70
WEST POINT MUSEUM
COLLECTION.

Fig. 49. U.S. regulation rifle and musket cartridge boxes.

2 lower and 5 upper compartments. Two vertical loops. Oval brass "US" plate, 2.8 x 1.6 in. Contained forty cal .54 paper pistol cartridges. This box was often adapted to hold other kinds of cartridge, and examples with altered insert or a wood block are known.

● *Cartridge Box for M1855 Carbine and Pistol-Carbine.* Black bridle leather, double flaps, implement pocket. Inside dimensions 6.1 x 1.5 x 3.6 in. Contained two tin inserts similar except for size to M1855 box. Vertical loops on rear. No examples found with plate. Held 40 cartridges cal .58, a little under 2 in. length. *Fig. 50*

● *Cartridge Pouch for Revolver (various models).* Black bridle leather, no insert, single flap. Single compartment without insert about .75 in. wide, protected by 2 layers of leather. Carried three packages of six revolver cartridges *Fig. 50* each. Two vertical loops on the rear. Inside dimensions varied from 5.5 x .8 x 3.6 in. to 4.9 x .75 x 3 in. Made by E. Gaylord, J.E. Condict, J.T. Pittman, etc.

Commercial Carbine Boxes

● *Burnside Carbine Box.* Russet or black bridle leather with wooden insert bored for 20 Burnside brass case cal .54 cartridges (holes .5 in. diameter). Had implement pocket, double flaps. One horizontal and 2 vertical loops; 2 buckles *Fig. 51* on bottom. Inside dimensions 7 x 1.5 x 2.5 in. Some boxes fitted with small size oval brass "US" plate. (With minor variations in size and insert this type of box served to hold other varieties of carbine ammunition.)

● *Merrill Carbine Box.* Black bridle leather, double flaps, implement pocket on inner flap. Dimensions 5.75 x 1.8 x 4.75 in. Specially designed wooden insert divided into 4 layers, each bored for 7 Merrill combustible cartridges cal .56. *Fig. 51* Two vertical loops on rear. Stencilled inside outer flap: "MERRILL THOMAS & CO/BALTIMORE/Patent Appld For." No plate.

● *Breechloading Carbine Box.* Black bridle leather, single tin insert without compartments. Implement pocket, single or double flap. Two vertical loops on rear. Inside dimensions 6 x 1.5 x 3.5 in. Held 20 Sharps paper or linen cartridges, *Fig. 51* packaged or loose, also other makes of carbine cartridge of comparable size such as the Merrill, Union, and Starr. Made by C.S. Storms, etc.

● *Breechloading Carbine Box.* Black bridle leather, implement pocket, double flaps. Inside dimensions about 6.1 x 1.3 x 4 in. Two tin inserts with lower compartments 2.75 in. high and upper fitted with 10 tin tubes, .57 in. diameter, *Fig. 51* soldered in. Two vertical and 1 horizontal loops on rear, 2 buckles on bottom. Made to carry paper or linen cartridges such as cal .52 Sharps, cal .54 Starr, cal .56 Merrill, etc.

● *Henry Repeating Rifle Box.* Black bridle leather, implement pocket, double flaps; 2 narrow straps riveted to rear which pass under box and engage studs on front of outer flap. Inside dimensions 6.5 x 1.6 x 5 in. Four wooden inserts, *Fig. 51* each bored for thirty-five cal .44 rim-fire Henry cartridges. Open bottom with brass spring on each side which engaged channels in the blocks. Example stamped "R. NECE/PHILAD.," with embossed "US" on flap.

● *Spencer (or Joslyn) Rifle   Carbine Box.* Black bridle leather, single tin insert divided in center and scalloped in front; implement pocket, double flaps. Inside dimensions 4.2 x 1.9 x 3.7 in. (4 in. capacity in height). Two vertical loops on rear. Held full carton (6 packs) of 42 Spencer .56-52 metallic cartridges. A version was fitted with buckles and a horizontal loop for shoulder belt suspension.

Fig. 52

● *Spencer (or Joslyn) .56-52 Rifle or Carbine Box.* Black bridle leather, wide implement pocket, with wooden insert bored for twenty-four .56 in. wide metallic cartridges. Double flaps; one horizontal and 2 vertical loops, 2 buckles on bottom. Inside dimensions vary from 7 x 1.5 x 2.4 in. to 8.5 x 1.5 x 2 in. Made by E. Gaylord, J.T. Pittman, Dingee & Lorrigan, J. Davey & Co., Hoover, Calhoun & Co., J. Cummings, etc. A number of minor variations in size and fittings exist in this type.

Fig. 52

● *Blakeslee Patent Spencer Carbine Box, 6-tube Model.* Rectangular block of wood encased in black bridle leather and containing 6 tinned iron tubes, each sized to hold seven .56-52 or .56-50 Spencer metallic cartridges. Leather pocket with flap held by buckle or button for tools or patches; 2 loops with D-rings riveted to box, to which an adjustable leather carrying strap was attached; vertical loop riveted and sewn on rear for attachment to waist belt; leather cover with leather or brass pin hinge. Inside dimensions 10.5 x 2.75 x 2 in.

Fig. 52

● *Blakeslee Patent Spencer Carbine Box, 10-tube Model.* Same general construction as above but hexagonal in shape; held 10 tubes; had no leather pocket. Inside dimensions 12 x 3.5 x 2.25 in. Stamped on leather cover: "BLAKESLEE'S CARTRIDGE BOX /U.S./PATd. DEC 20, 1864/REISSUED FEB. 7, 1865/W.H. WILKINSON/MAKER/SPRINGFIELD, MASS./U.S." and on fastening strap, in script, "T.I. Shepard."

Mann's Patent Boxes

Fig. 53

William Dalton (or D'Alton) Mann was a resident of Detroit, Mich., when he secured a commission as captain in the 1st Michigan Cavalry in August 1861. He rose rapidly in rank, becoming colonel of the 7th Michigan Cavalry in December 1862. His military record is difficult to gauge, but about his abilities as an inventor and promoter there is ample evidence. Early in the Civil War he turned his versatile mind to the matter of suspension equipments and by the end of 1863 was so involved in their design and manufacture that he went on leave and ended his active military career by resignation in March 1864. During the previous December he had been granted a patent on his accouterments and he wasted no time in securing testimonials which he included in a promotional booklet published in 1864. Mann's actions now commence to resemble those of a confidence man. Through contact with high ranking officers he sought nothing less than to have his cartridge boxes and other gear adopted as regulation for the Union Army. In this he did not succeed, and he went on to other and shadier projects, including mining and petroleum. He was arrested for fraud in 1865, amid much scandal, but the case was dismissed. His subsequent career,

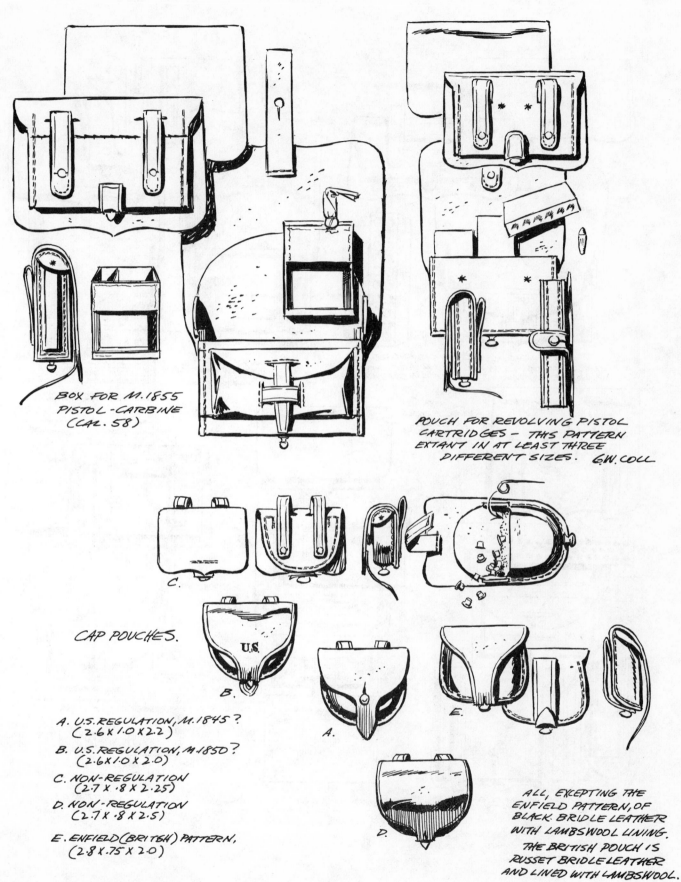

BOX FOR M.1855
PISTOL-CARBINE
(CAL. 58)

POUCH FOR REVOLVING PISTOL
CARTRIDGES — THIS PATTERN
EXTANT IN AT LEAST THREE
DIFFERENT SIZES. G.W. COLL

CAP POUCHES.

U.S.

A. U.S. REGULATION, M.1845?
(2.6 X 1.0 X 2.2)

B. U.S. REGULATION, M.1850?
(2.6 X 1.0 X 2.0)

C. NON-REGULATION
(2.7 X .8 X 2.25)

D. NON-REGULATION
(2.7 X .8 X 2.5)

E. ENFIELD (BRITISH) PATTERN,
(2.8 X .75 X 2.0)

ALL, EXCEPTING THE
ENFIELD PATTERN, OF
BLACK BRIDLE LEATHER
WITH LAMBSWOOL LINING.

THE BRITISH POUCH IS
RUSSET BRIDLE LEATHER
AND LINED WITH LAMBSWOOL.

Fig. 50. Boxes for pistol cartridges; cap pouches.

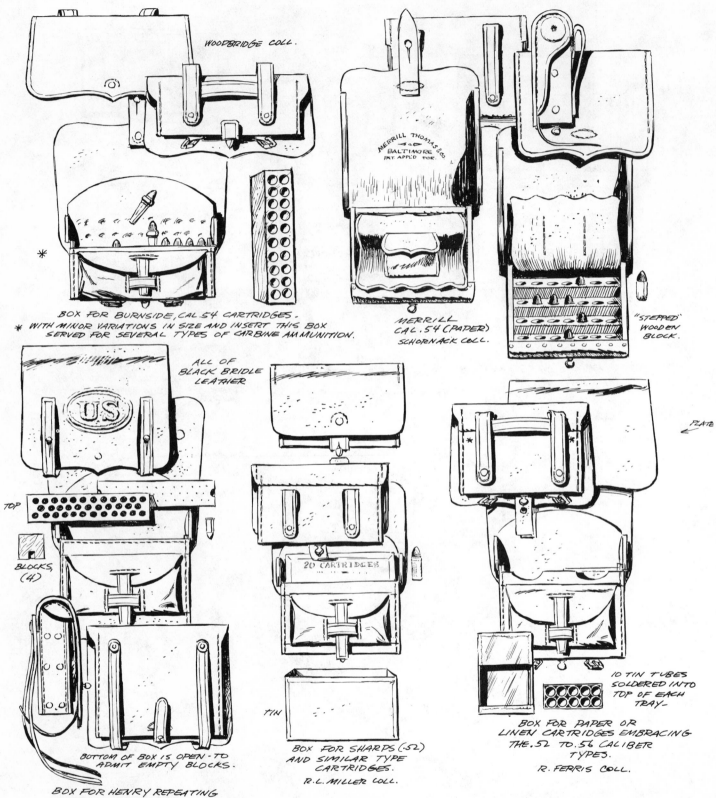

WOODBRIDGE COLL.

MERRILL THOMAS & CO.
BALTIMORE
PAT. APPL'D FOR.

BOX FOR BURNSIDE, CAL. 54 CARTRIDGES.
* WITH MINOR VARIATIONS IN SIZE AND INSERT THIS BOX
SERVED FOR SEVERAL TYPES OF CARBINE AMMUNITION.

MERRILL
CAL. 54 (PAPER)
SCHORNACK COLL.

"STEPPED"
WOODEN
BLOCK.

ALL OF
BLACK BRIDLE
LEATHER

US

TOP

BLOCKS,
(4)

PLATE

20 CARTRIDGES

TIN

BOTTOM OF BOX IS OPEN - TO
ADMIT EMPTY BLOCKS.

BOX FOR HENRY REPEATING
RIFLE CARTRIDGES (44 RIMFIRE)
A. KRAUSE COLL.

BOX FOR SHARPS (.52)
AND SIMILAR TYPE
CARTRIDGES.
R. L. MILLER COLL.

10 TIN TUBES
SOLDERED INTO
TOP OF EACH
TRAY—

BOX FOR PAPER OR
LINEN CARTRIDGES EMBRACING
THE .52 TO .56 CALIBER
TYPES.
R. FERRIS COLL.

Fig. 51.   Cartridge boxes for breechloading weapons.

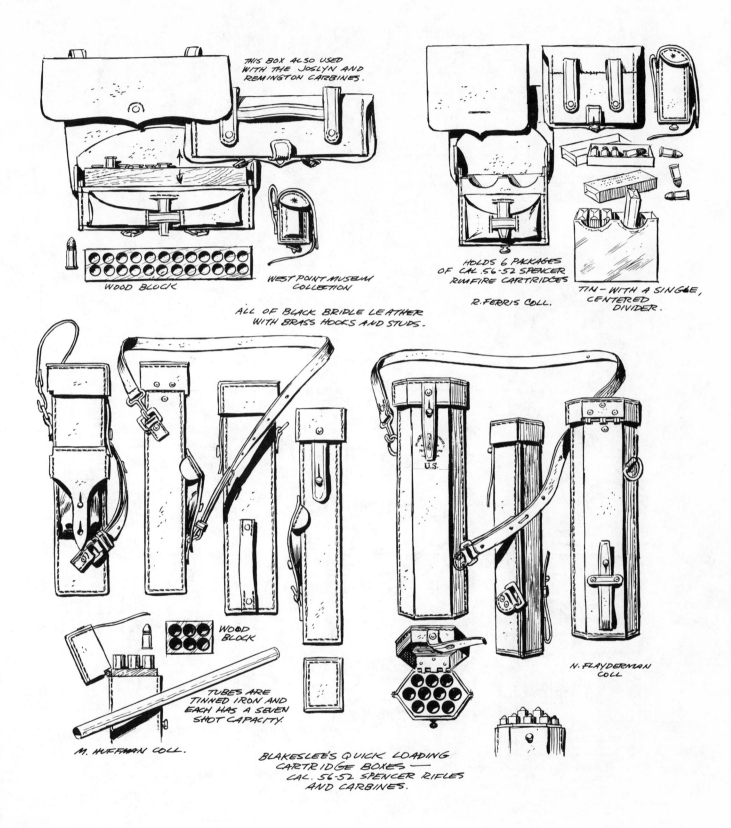

THIS BOX ALSO USED WITH THE JOSLYN AND REMINGTON CARBINES.

WOOD BLOCK

WEST POINT MUSEUM COLLECTION

ALL OF BLACK BRIDLE LEATHER WITH BRASS HOOKS AND STUDS.

HOLDS 6 PACKAGES OF CAL .56-52 SPENCER RIMFIRE CARTRIDGES

R. FERRIS COLL.

TIN - WITH A SINGLE, CENTERED DIVIDER.

WOOD BLOCK

TUBES ARE TINNED IRON AND EACH HAS A SEVEN SHOT CAPACITY.

M. HUFFMAN COLL.

N. FLAYDERMAN COLL

BLAKESLEE'S QUICK LOADING CARTRIDGE BOXES — CAL. 56-52 SPENCER RIFLES AND CARBINES.

Fig. 52. Cartridge boxes for Spencer rifles and carbines.

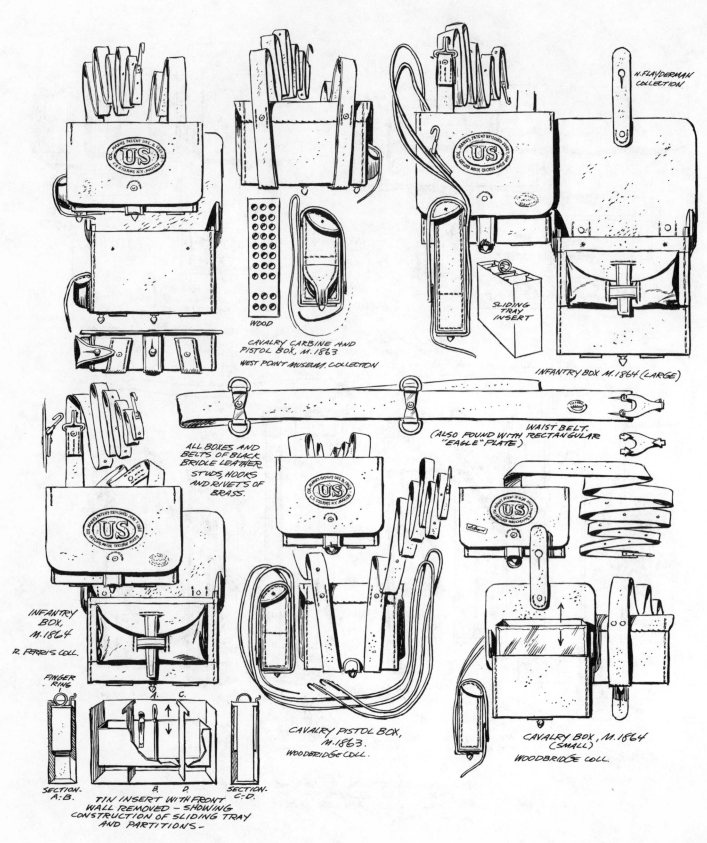

CAVALRY CARBINE AND
PISTOL BOX, M. 1863

WEST POINT MUSEUM. COLLECTION

N. FLAYDERMAN
COLLECTION

SLIDING
TRAY
INSERT

INFANTRY BOX M.1864 (LARGE)

WAIST BELT.
(ALSO FOUND WITH RECTANGULAR
"EAGLE" PLATE)

ALL BOXES AND
BELTS OF BLACK
BRIDLE LEATHER.
STUDS, HOOKS
AND RIVETS OF
BRASS.

INFANTRY
BOX,
M. 1864

R. FERRIS COLL.

FINGER
RING

SECTION.
A.-B.

SECTION.
C.-D.

TIN INSERT WITH FRONT
WALL REMOVED - SHOWING
CONSTRUCTION OF SLIDING TRAY
AND PARTITIONS -

CAVALRY PISTOL BOX,
M. 1863.
WOODBRIDGE COLL.

CAVALRY BOX, M. 1864
(SMALL)
WOODBRIDGE COLL.

Fig. 53. Mann's patent boxes.

which does not concern us here, amply justifies the term "notorious" which has been applied to him.

The Mann cartridge boxes were first manufactured by C.S. Storms of New York City and later by Emerson Gaylord of Chicopee, Mass. At what moment the change occurred, or even if Gaylord was merely an additional maker, is uncertain. Colonel Mann secured a re-issue of his patent in June 1864—the only significant change being added detail on fastening a knapsack—and this may have some bearing on the shift in makers. There seem to have been four principal models, although several minor variations occur. All of the boxes were issued in black leather; the russet appearance of many surviving examples is probably due to poor dying.

Despite promotional literature devised by their inventor suggesting large numbers of Mann boxes in use, the actual number sold was probably very small. It is evident that Mann arranged to have sizeable lots used in the field without charge for purposes of experiment and advertising. The types of cartridge box identified are:

● *Mann's Cavalry Carbine and Pistol Box, M1863.* Black bridle leather, inside dimensions 6.25 x 1.75 x 4.2 in. Had a percussion cap pouch fastened to side; 2 tapering shoulder slings with brass hooks on the ends, sewn and riveted to rear; single flap, no implement pocket. An irregular shaped wooden block rested on leather shoulders, leaving an open space in the bottom of box; block was bored with 30 holes; 24 for cal .46 metallic cartridges, 1.25 in. deep, and 6 for pistol cartridges of same caliber, .75 in. deep. Stamped on flap in double oval: "COL. MANN'S PATENT DEC. 8th 1863/ C.S.STORMS. NY. MAKER" and large "US".

● *Mann's Cavalry Pistol Box, M1863.* Black bridle leather, inside dimensions 4.5 x 1.5 x 4 in. No percussion cap pouch, single flap; 2 tapering shoulder slings as above; no implement pocket. Contained a plain tin insert without dividers. Same stamping as above.

● *Mann's Infantry Box, Model M1864.* Black bridle leather, inside dimensions 6.25 x 1.5 x 4.25 in. No cap pouch; implement pocket about 5.8 x 3.25 in. Single flap; 2 tapering shoulder slings riveted and sewn to box, 36.5 in. long, with brass hook fitted to each sling in front for knapsack attachment. Contained Mann's improved tin magazine, divided into 3 compartments; an inner section pulled up and latched. A 1.6 in. leather waist belt was sold with this box; it had 2 brass attachments with D-rings above and below, and a brass hook for fastening. Stamped on flap in double oval: "COL. MANN'S PATENT REISSUED JUNE 7th 1864/E. GAYLORD MAKER CHICOPEE, MASS." and large "US." Also on flap and waist belt, in a smaller oval: "A.D. LAIDLEY/U.S. ORD DEPt/ SUB INSPECTOR."

● *Mann's Infantry Box, Large Size, M1864.* Similar in all respects to the 1864 infantry box, above, except that its height was 7 in. rather than 4.5. The 2.75 in. space below the tin magazine insert was empty but fitted with a tin floor; it held two 10-round packages of ammunition. Some examples lack the inspector's stamp.

● *Mann's Cavalry Box, Large Size, M1864.* Black bridle leather; no implement pocket or cap pouch. Single tapering sling with brass hook on end, riveted to rear of box and forming a single loop there. Single flap. Inside dimensions about 6 x 1.1 x 3.5 in. Plain tin insert without dividers. Same markings as above.

● *Mann's Cavalry Box, Small Size, M1864.* Similar to above except for inside dimensions which were about 5.25 x 1.5 x 2.5 in. Some examples carry inspector's stamp in a rectangle: "T.I. Shepard."

Foreign and Unidentified Boxes

See C.S.A. accouterments

● *Enfield (British) Rifle Musket Box.* Black harness leather; double flaps, the inner one having deep side pieces; outer flap attached to brass stud on bottom by a white buff leather strap. Inside dimensions 6.9 x 3 x 3.1 in. Single tin insert divided into 5 equal compartments, each holding eight cal .577 paper cartridges. Two broad horizontal loops on rear and 2 buckles on bottom. Many stamped inside outer flap: "S. ISAAC CAMPBELL & Co/. . . JERMIN ST/LONDON." Others were marked "A. ROSS & CO/C&M 1861." Suspended on a 2-in. black leather belt.

● *Unidentified cal .58 (?) Box.* Black bridle leather, double flaps, 7.2-in. implement pocket. Wooden insert bored for twenty metallic cartridges; holes 1.2 in. deep, approx. .65 in. diameter. Two vertical and one horizontal loop on rear, 2 buckles on bottom. Inside dimensions 7.7 x 1.5 x 1.8 in. Stamped in oval on inner flap: "J.E. CONDICT/ NEW YORK."

● *Unidentified cal .58 (?) Box.* Black bridle leather, double flaps, 7.2-in. wide implement pocket. Inside dimensions 7.4 x 1.6 x 2.5 in. Wooden insert bored for twenty metallic cartridges; holes 1.1 in. deep, approx. .65 in. diameter. One horizontal and two vertical loops on rear; 2 buckles on bottom. Stamped on inner flap in oval: "DINGEE & LORIGAN/MAKERS/NEW YORK"; no plate or stamp on outer flap. Remade from older box.

Percussion Cap Pouches

Fig. 50

Cap pouches were manufactured at government arsenals and by contractors, and several variations in size and style existed. The more common are listed below. Navy pouches and those identified as Confederate are mentioned in the appropriate chapters.

● *U.S. Regulation Cap Pouch, M1845 (?).* Black bridle leather, double flaps, 2.6 x 1 x 2.2 in. inside dimensions. Lined inside with sheepskin and fitted with a cone pick on left side; 2 vertical loops on rear. Outer flap had rounded corners and engaged a brass stud on the front of the pouch. Occasionally stamped "US" on outer flap in .3-in. letters.

● *U.S. Regulation Cap Pouch, M1850 (?).* Same as above except the outer flap was longer and the brass stud was attached to the bottom of the pouch. Inside dimensions 2.6 x 1 x 2 in.

Non-Regulation Cap Pouch. Similar to M1850 except its outer flap was rectangular in shape. Size 2.7 x .8 x 2.25 in.

● *Non-Regulation Cap Pouch.* Similar to M1850 except its outer flap was very long, almost covering the pouch. Size 2.7 x .8 x 2.5 in. Made by Nece.

● *Enfield (British) Cap Pouch.* Russet leather, double flaps, inside dimensions 2.8 x .75 x 2 in. Not lined and no cone pick. Short, narrow flap engaged brass stud on bottom. Single broad vertical loop, either riveted or tied at top. Body of the pouch was slightly wider at bottom than at top.

CARTRIDGE BOX
FOR MODEL 1841 RIFLE.

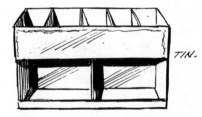

TIN.

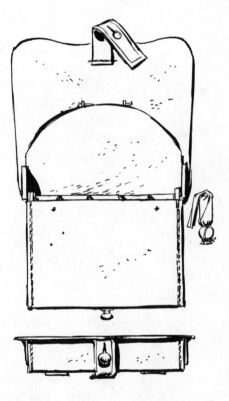

Fig. 54. Cartridge box for Model 1841 rifle.

Knapsacks, Haversacks, Canteens, and Mess Equipment

Knapsacks fall generally into two classes, the rigid and the non-rigid. The first was the formal parade knapsack of the period whose size remained constant whether filled or empty and hence gave a pleasing uniformity within a regiment. The second was essentially the field knapsack, lighter in weight and pliable enough to serve as a pillow in bivouac.

During the Mexican War the regular infantry had worn a rigid knapsack whose outer flap or "cover" was coated with India rubber. In 1853 a new non-rigid model was adopted which continued in use with minor modifications until after 1872. State troops, however, continued as a rule to carry the rigid type on all occasions.

The majority of American knapsacks were made of cotton cloth painted black or coated with some preparation of this color which rendered them waterproof. Canvas was used for the better knapsacks and oil cloth, sometimes called "enamelled canvas," was also employed. The outer flap of a knapsack was often made of a heavier material than its sides.

Black leather knapsacks were sometimes used, both in the rigid style by militia outfits and in the non-rigid by officers in the field. Yet the skin knapsack covered with its hair, so common in Europe for so long, was rarely worn. Only in the Marine Corps, the U.S. Sharpshooters, and a few regiments could it be found.

Knapsacks were also made of cloth covered with India rubber and gutta percha, and since these materials were adapted for other kinds of accouterments it might be well to consolidate their story in one place. India rubber was an article of commerce long before our period begins; during the 1840's considerable experimentation had been carried out by the War Department with knapsacks, haversacks, and canteens made of it. These had not been successful and in 1851 the Quartermaster General arranged for the sale of all items made of this product. Thereafter we hear relatively little about India rubber.

Gutta percha, which was introduced to the United States somewhat later, was quite a different product. Patents for its use for accouterments were taken out by John Rider and John Murphy in 1852–1854, and in 1855 the Quartermaster General ordered a substantial quantity of experimental knapsacks, haversacks, and canteens, plus a number of other items, covered with this substance. Field trials proved disappointing and all gutta percha equipment was disposed of by 1859 except the talma.

Despite this setback the manufacturers of gutta percha continued operations and in the press of the Civil War marketed a number of articles waterproofed by this method. A gutta percha knapsack is described below.

In its simplest form, the rigid knapsack consisted of an almost square wooden frame, about 4 inches wide, usually made of white pine. The sides and front were covered with a medium weight waterproof cloth or canvas, glued and tacked to this frame; the rear was secured by two inner flaps and one outer one. It was simply a box, about 14 x 14 inches, without divisions or pockets.

This model knapsack had two small straps on top to secure a rolled blanket, two larger (1 in.) straps passing down the rear and buckling underneath to contain the outer flap and hold extra articles outside in an emergency, and the carrying straps. These last consisted of three parts: (1) two shoulder straps, about 15 in. long, riveted to the wooden frame; (2) two armpit straps attached to the ends of the shoulder straps by brass studs, the right one buckling to the bottom of the knapsack, while the left hooked into a ring there to allow the knapsack to be easily unslung; and (3) the breast straps. These last, attached to the same brass studs that united the other straps, buckled together over the chest and kept the knapsack firmly on the man's shoulders. In one way or another, all of these straps were adjustable to size. In 1855 the breast straps of the regulation knapsack were fitted to attach to the waist belt and so better distribute the load.

From this simple box type evolved more complex models. The attachment of a bag with gussets to the inside of the rear flap afforded some of the advantages of the non-rigid style. By being left unfilled on parade, the bag did not destroy the uniformity of knapsacks. Another variation lay in constructing the frame large enough—and rounding it off on top—to permit a blanket being carried *inside* the knapsack and thus kept dry.

One rigid type found in New York State was made to open in the front (lying against the soldier's back) rather than the rear (outside), possibly offering better protection to its contents in heavy rain. Many styles used leather or patent leather flaps, or were made entirely of these materials.

Finally, one type contained a removable wooden frame which allowed it to be used as either a rigid or non-rigid knapsack.

Non-rigid knapsacks had been used long before the rigid styles were evolved, and some of the older kinds were still in use during the Civil War. The simplest form was an ordinary bag, without gussets, of waterproofed cloth, equipped with a pair of carrying straps and a flap. But the type in general use in the 1850's and 1860's was what we have called the "double-bag," two more or less complicated bags or envelopes attached at their tops and folded with their less protected sides inward. The attachment was often achieved by a strip of stiff leather on which blanket roll straps and other fixtures could be fastened.

Army Regulations of 1857 specified that all knapsacks were to be painted black:

. . . Those for the artillery will be marked in the centre of the cover with the number of the regiment only, in figures of one inch and a half in length, of the character called full face, with yellow paint. Those for the infantry will be marked in the same way, in white paint. Those for the ordnance will be marked with two cannon, crossing; the cannon to be seven and a half inches in length, in yellow paint, to resemble those on the cap. The knapsack straps will be black.

106. . . The knapsacks will also be marked upon the inner side with the letter of the company and the number of the soldier, on such parts as may be readily observed at inspections.

107. . . Haversacks will be marked upon the flap with the number and name of the regiment, the letter of the company, and number of the soldier,

in black letters and figures. And each soldier must, at all times, be provided with a haversack and canteen, and will exhibit them at all inspections. It will be worn on the left side on marches, guard, and when paraded for detached service—the canteen outside the haversack.

Knapsacks were issued to all infantrymen and other soldiers who habitually served on foot. In the field artillery the cannoneers received knapsacks which they generally strapped to the spare wheel or some other part of the caisson, but the drivers and other mounted men were issued the valise, described under horse furniture.

In certain regiments, or more accurately under certain commanding officers, infantrymen were permitted to dispense with their knapsacks and carry their belongings in blanket rolls slung over either the right or left shoulder. It is difficult to assess the extent of this practice; it was probably more common in Western armies than Eastern, but certainly was never formally authorized for regulars or, for that matter, for Federal regiments of any sort. The knapsack was issued and used throughout the war.

The reason for a change to the blanket roll lay, of course, in its relative lightness and greater comfort. A soldier on field service was supposed to pack in or on his knapsack a double wool blanket, half a shelter tent, a rubber blanket, an extra pair of shoes, mess equipment, toilet articles, and spare clothing. The inexperienced soldier might add stationery, a book or two, photographs and letters, extra clothing, and any number of other things that would bring the weight of the knapsack to well over twenty pounds. Naturally it could become an unendurable burden on a long march under a hot sun, and Northern soldiers soon found they could carry the really essential items in a blanket roll.

Knapsacks, being relatively easy to manufacture, were produced in many places and in wide variety. A few of the more common or characteristic types are described below, others whose use is believed to be confined to a specific state will be described thereunder. Three patterns believed to have been issued by the Confederate Ordnance Department are described in Chapter 10.

Rigid Knapsacks

Fig. 55

● *Militia Box Knapsack.* Frame of white pine, upper corners braced; covered with black painted canvas tacked on. Outside dimensions: 15 in. wide, 4 in. deep, 13.5 in. high. Closed in rear by two horizontal flaps which tie in the center, and by the outer flap. Outer flap double thickness, retained by two vertical straps rivited to the top and buckled on the bottom. Two blanket straps on top and two carrying straps riveted to the upper front. No pockets.

This was the simplest of several patterns worn by New York State troops throughout the entire period of this study. Minor variations were common. Most examples inspected bore a number painted in white on the outer rear flap.

● *Militia Box Knapsack.* Frame of white pine, as in model above, covered with high grade painted canvas, tacked on. Outside dimensions: 15 in. wide, 4 in. deep, 12.8 in. high. This model *closed in front* (side touching the man's back)

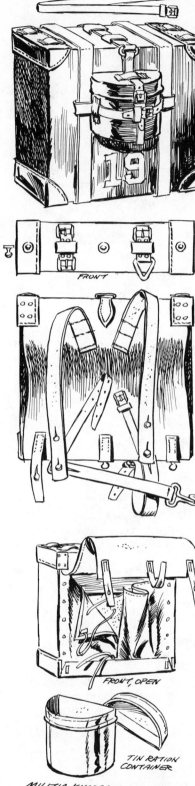

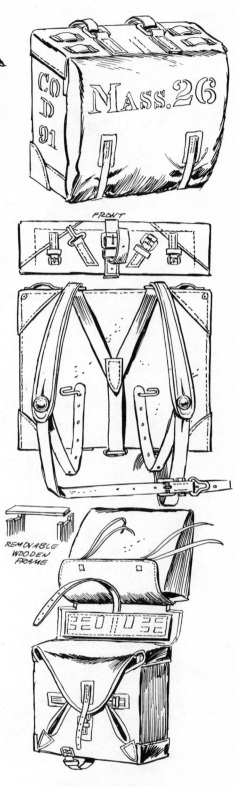

CO
D
91

MASS.26

FRONT

FRONT

FRONT

REMOVABLE
WOODEN
FRAME

FRONT, OPEN

TIN RATION
CONTAINER

MILITIA KNAPSACK BLACK
PAINTED CANVAS, IRON BUCKLES,
BRASS HOOKS AND STUDS.

WASHINGTON'S H.Q. NEWBURGH,
N.Y.

SAID TO HAVE BEEN WORN BY
A CONNECTICUT SOLDIER DURING
THE WAR.

LITCHFIELD HISTORICAL
SOCIETY.

MILITIA TYPE
SIMILAR IN CONSTRUCTION AND
MATERIAL COMPOSITION TO
THE SPECIMEN AT LEFT.

R.L. MILLER COLLECTION.

Fig. 55. Rigid knapsacks.

with two horizontal flaps, held by two small buckles, and an outer flap of the same height and width as the box. Two blanket straps. Three straps on the bottom of this flap fastened on to buttons on the box bottom. Two double buckles on bottom holding vertical back straps and carrying straps.

This was another New York State pattern; the example inspected was worn by the 13th Regt, NYSNG.

● *Militia Box Knapsack.* Same general type as above but cover and outer flap made of black leather. Outside dimensions 16 x 3.5 x 13 in. All straps are of white buff leather; large size 1.25 in., small size .75 in. Three blanket straps plus an additional small strap on rear to hold a semi-circular mess can. The example inspected had white "19" painted on rear and was carried by the 19th Regt, NYSM prior to the Civil War.

● *Expanding Box Knapsack.* Frame of white pine, covered with black enamelled canvas, no division inside; envelope with gussets sewn inside rear flap. Box portion closed by four triangular flaps, buckling across. Outside dimensions 14 x 3.5 x 12 in. Rear flap held by three straps, two sets of blanket straps, and usual carrying straps. Example inspected was worn by Sgt. Alvord, 5th Conn. Vol. Inf., but the pattern is not known to have been confined to that state.

● *Adjustable Box Knapsack.* Frame of white pine, with interlocking corners, which can be removed, converting this into a double-bag, non-rigid type. Made of high grade black enamelled cloth. Rigid front section, 15 x 4 x 12 in.; rear section forming flap 14.5 x 13.5 in. Sections are connected by a 5-in. cloth strip reinforced with leather; front section buckled into a container by four cross-over flaps; rear section is an envelope with 6.5-in. flap and gussets 3.5 in. at top decreasing to zero. Two blanket roll straps on top held by four loops; rear flap fastened by two straps. Carrying straps in form of a "Y," the stem buckled to bottom and running up front, branching out and passing through two D-rings on top, thence over shoulders; thereafter resembles U.S. regulation model in attachments and breast straps. Example inspected was carried by the 26th Massachusetts Volunteer Infantry Regiment.

● *Pasteboard Frame Box Knapsack.* Frame of pasteboard covered with water proofed canvas sewn together at the seams. Outside dimensions 13.25 x 4.5 x 14 in. Box enclosed by horizontal flaps, held by two straps and buckles plus five brass-edged eyelets on each flap for tying together. Inside these flaps were two vertical triangular flaps closed by one strap and buckle. Flap covered pockets on both sides, running full length and width of sides, fastening with straps and buckles. Outside flap just covered face of box; inside this flap was a large pocket made of pillow ticking, closed by two straps and brass buttons. Box lined with pillow ticking. Two sets of two loops for blanket straps, and conventional carrying straps.

Fig. 56 ● (*S. Isaacs, Campbell Single-Bag Knapsack*: see Chapter 10).

Non-Rigid Knapsacks

Fig. 56 ● *U.S. Army Regulation Double-Bag Knapsack.* Two bags, attached by a 5-in.

U.S. REGULATION
KNAPSACK.
BLACK RUBBERIZED CANVAS.
RUSSET LEATHER STRAPS.
THE INNER TIES ARE OF
RAWHIDE. IRON (JAPANNED)
BUCKLES, BRASS HOOKS

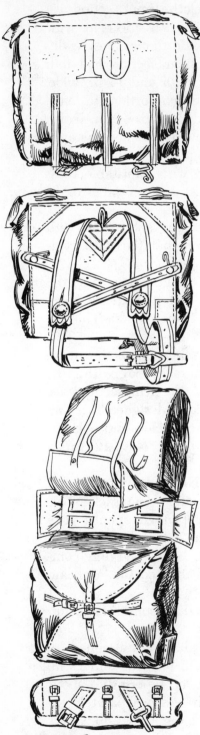

WOODBRIDGE COLLECTION.

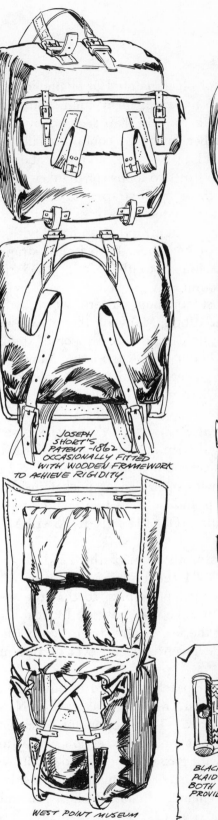

JOSEPH
SHORT'S
PATENT -1862
OCCASIONALLY FITTED
WITH WODDEN FRAMEWORK
TO ACHIEVE RIGIDITY.

WEST POINT MUSEUM

FRONT

WEST POINT MUSEUM.

BLACK RUBBERIZED
CANVAS WITH LEATHER CORNER
REINFORCING. MADE BY
S. ISAACS CAMPBELL, LONDON.

SOLDIER'S "HOUSEWIFE". MADE OF
BLACK OILCLOTH (OUTSIDE), BLACK MUSLIN (INSIDE)
PLAID COTTON POCKETS. THE THIMBLE IS OPEN AT
BOTH ENDS AND FITS INTO THE SOCKET
PROVIDED FOR IT IN THE PADDED CYLINDER.

W. M. DANIELS COLLECTION.

Fig. 56. Semi-rigid knapsacks.

flexible strip at top, of black painted or enamelled cotton cloth. Front section was partial envelope 13.5 in. wide, 14 in. high, with gussets on each side 6 in. wide at top, decreasing to zero; 8 in. flap secured by two rawhide thongs. Inside this envelope was a leather fitting to contain small objects. Rear section had four triangular flaps, buckling together, and was about 11 in. high and 14 in. wide. Top strip had two sets of two loops for blanket straps. The two portions fastened at the bottom with three small straps and buckles. Shoulder straps (2 in. wide) sewed to back and terminated with brass studs, to which were attached the armpit and breast straps. Right armpit strap fitted with a triangular ring for fastening to hook on bottom of knapsack. Both breast straps fitted with adjustable brass hooks to allow attachment to the Model 1855 rifle waist belt or later to be hooked under the common waist belt.

This was the most common pattern worn by U.S. troops and came with numerous minor variations. Many of these knapsacks were painted with regimental designations and carried U.S. inspectors' stamps.

● *Officer's Model, Double-Bag Knapsack.* Same general design and size as the U.S. regulation, but gussets of rear section only 4 in. wide at top. Made of black enamelled canvas. There was a leather pocket inside the front section. This example was carried by a New York officer.

● *Joseph Short Patent Knapsack.* Two-piece type of black enamelled canvas, attached by 4 in. rigid strip at top. Front section was open-faced bag with cross straps to contain objects; dimensions about 14 x 2.25 x 15 in. Rear section was only the outer flap with open canvas pocket inside. Specially designed carrying straps buckled at top and bottom; two containing straps encircled entire knapsack. Stencilled inside "JOSEPH SHORT/SALEM MASS/ Pat. Nov. 12, 1861/ Jan. 28, 1862."

Fig. 56

George W. Wingate, historian of the 22nd Regiment, NGSNY, writes as follows: "In October 1864 the regiment adopted 'Short's patent knapsack.' This was made upon scientific principles, so that the weight depended upon a yoke on the shoulders. It was kept in position by two short arms on each side of the waist, thus avoiding the use of any straps across the chest. It was the only comfortable knapsack the Twenty-second ever carried, until it adopted the 'Merriam pack' in 1895."

The Short-patent knapsack is known to have been carried by some Massachusetts and New Hampshire regiments as well as New York.

● *Double-Bag Knapsack.* Two sections of black enamelled canvas attached by 4 in. stiff leather strip at top. Front section was a full bag 15 in. wide and 12 in. high, open on top, with gussets on each side, 4 in. wide at top tapering to about .2 in. Rear section consisted of a plain flap, inside which was a separately attached small bag of enamelled cloth, 14 in. wide and 7 in. high. Two .5-in. straps inside top to hold a coat (?). Three blanket roll straps on top, and three for fastening flap, all riveted. Shoulder straps, 1.25 in., riveted to top, attached by brass studs to straps riveted to back; ample slots for adjustment in both. Same studs held breast straps which buckled in front. Knapsack could be slid off shoulders by unbuckling the breast strap. One example carried by 24th Ohio

Fig. 57

Volunteer Infantry Regiment.

● *Double-Bag Knapsack.* Two sections of black enamelled canvas attached by 3.5-in. strip of reinforced canvas. Front section was a bag, 15 in. wide at top, 11.5 in. high, 3.5 in. gussets, closed at top by two flaps with cloth ties. Rear section formed into a container by two vertical flaps, each 9 x 20 in., tied together. Two 1-in. straps encircled knapsack, being riveted on top and bottom and buckling near bottom. Two blanket roll straps attached to top by same rivets. Carrying straps similar to U.S. regulation model.

Fig. 57

(See also the "Illinois" and "Missouri" double-bag types described in Chapters 27 and 39 respectively.)

● *Mann's Improved (?) Knapsack.* Double-bag style of black enamelled canvas, both sections having 4 in. edges or sides of russet leather supported on a rectangular iron frame. The two frames are connected and so join the sections. Front section is concave without cover or pockets; rear section buckled into a container by four cross flaps. Two loops on top for blanket roll straps. Tapering carrying straps sewed at both ends to front and adjustable by buckles; no breast straps. The two sections of this knapsack are buckled together by two straps on each side and on the bottom. Size when closed about 14.5 x 5 x 12 in.

Colonel Mann did not patent a knapsack as such and there is some question that this is the model he designed. Robert L. Miller, however, procured a specimen from Bannerman & Son on the basis of the identification of this type in their 1907 catalog as "Knapsack, Mann's patent, with iron frame. . ." The knapsack seems to be unusually cumbersome and expensive, offering little carrying space. It was probably difficult to remove from the shoulders.

● *Rhode Island Combination Knapsack-Canteen.* A knapsack having a canteen attached to its bottom was issued to some Rhode Island troops in the fall of 1861. The canteen was fitted with a tube and filter mouthpiece, which passed under the left arm. No example has been found. In one company, at least, these were condemned in January 1862. (See Chapter 50.)

● *Gutta Percha Knapsack.* Single-bag style made of two layers of natural colored canvas enclosing a layer of black gutta percha. Overall size: 15 in. wide, 3 in. deep, 13 in. high; flap 17 in. high, held by three straps buckled to bottom. Flap bound with blue tape. Bag closed by two vertical flaps riveted to body and closed by rawhide thongs. Two blanket straps on top and conventional carrying straps. Example painted on outside flap; "D. Heydon/Co. E./149th Regt./N.Y. Vols," in black letters.

● *Gutta Percha Tent Knapsack.* In 1859 Captain William B. Johns, 3rd Infantry, patented a combination tent and knapsack made of cloth covered with gutta percha which he persuaded the Secretary of War to place on trial. It was manufactured by John Rider of New York City. One thousand of the knapsacks, together with three hundred gutta percha waterbags, were purchased in 1859 and issued for trial. (The article is described and illustrated in William Gilham, *Manual of Instruction for the Volunteers and Militia of the United States*, Philadelphia, 1861, pp. 641–642 and fig. 174.)

● *Baxter's Knapsack Supporter.* Patented 7 January 1863 by Colonel de Witt

RUSSET LEATHER STRAPS.

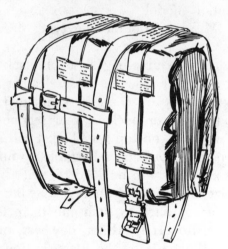

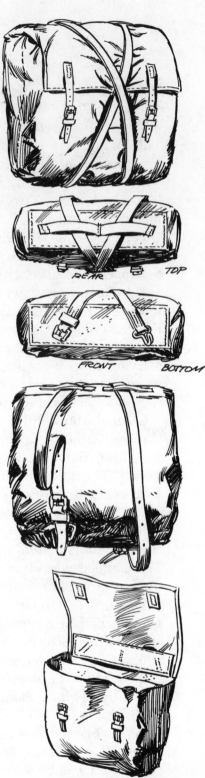

REAR   TOP

FRONT   BOTTOM

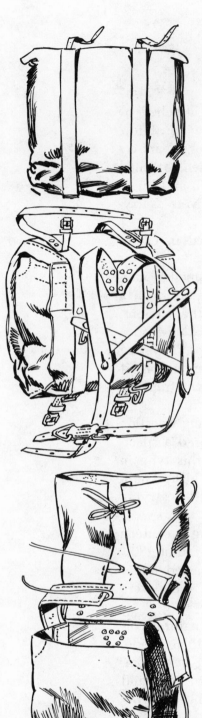

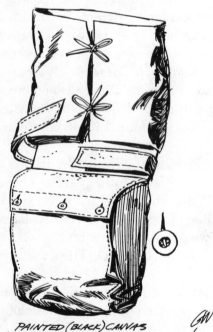

BLACK WATERPROOFED
CANVAS WITH RUSSET
LEATHER - BRASS RIVETS

R.L.MILLER COLL.

PAINTED (BLACK) CANVAS
KNAPSACK OF SIMPLE
CONSTRUCTION USED
IN THE WEST

R.L.MILLER COLL.

SINGLE BAG KNAPSACK OF
(BLACK) TREATED CANVAS.
REINFORCING STRIPS ON TOP
AND BOTTOM (INSIDE).

WEST POINT MUSEUM.

Fig. 57. Non-rigid knapsacks.

C. Baxter, 72nd Pennsylvania Volunteers, it was designed to distribute the weight of the knapsack evenly over the body. The supporter consisted of two wooden strips extending from the shoulders to the hip, and horizontal strips of leather, to which were attached straps for securing the knapsack. Baxter outfitted his regiment with them, and 25,000 were later recommended for issue to the army, but the war ended before this could be done. They were sold commercially by Burr & Scholfield of Philadelphia. Experimental field tests with Baxter's knapsack supporter were conducted by the army in 1868.

Haversacks and Other Food Containers

Every soldier on field service was issued a haversack, or "bread bag," in which he carried his rations and eating utensils on the march. It was worn over the right shoulder and rested on the left hip, with a tin cup usually buckled to the strap. In its regulation form it was a medium weight cotton cloth bag painted black on the outside, suspended by a broad black cloth or canvas strap, and containing a removable, unpainted inner bag. Field or "marching" rations—hard bread, salt pork or fresh meat, sugar, coffee, and salt, issued unpackaged and loose—quickly soiled this inner bag, but it could readily be removed and washed when water was available. In addition, some soldiers contrived their own little bags and containers for segregating the items of a marching ration and so kept their haversacks comparatively clean. Most men, however, allowed their haversacks to become grimy and well soaked with grease.

Fig. 58

Dismounted officers carried haversacks or some equivalent food container if they could not depend upon the wagon train or pack mules to arrive with their food for the noonday or evening meal. All officers owned at least a food container of sorts, together with a mess kit, and these tended to be commercially made bags not unlike the modern woman's handbag. Mounted men, as a rule, carried their food in one of their saddle bags although it was not unheard of for some to use haversacks.

Fancy patent leather haversacks with two or three compartments sometimes came into the hands of enlisted men during the early months of their service in the Civil War, either by gift or purchase. Usually these were ordered replaced by the regulation painted cloth pattern. At the other extreme was the simple bag of unpainted cotton, often homemade, carried by poorly equipped units.

The black painted haversack of the Civil War was the result of a series of experiments which began prior to 1851. In that year a trial lot of cloth haversacks treated with India rubber was sold as unsatisfactory. Painted or "varnished" ones were ordered and in 1855 experiments began with haversacks of duck covered with gutta percha. These also proved unsatisfactory and by 1859 the War Department had resolved upon Russia sheeting painted black. So far as can be told, the form and size of the haversack remained essentially the same throughout the entire period 1851–1872.

Other issue food containers included the tin ration box, which was strapped on the rear of a rigid knapsack, and various combination knapsack-haversacks and canteen-ration boxes of either home or commercial manufacture. The patterns used most commonly are listed below.

● *Unpainted Cloth Haversack (Mexican War Pattern)*. Simple unpainted cotton cloth envelope without insert; 13 in. wide, 12 in. high. Flap had three points and was held by three plain pewter buttons. Non-adjustable cotton carrying strap sewed to the bag, 1.8 in. wide, 30 in. long.

● *Massachusetts Cloth Haversack*. Unpainted cotton canvas drill envelope with removable inside bag held by two buttons. Slight flare at bottom; 10 in. maximum width, 9.5 in. high. Flap 4.5 in. long held by two bone buttons. Non-adjustable cotton carrying strap sewed to bag, 1.5 in. wide. Stamped inside flap: "STATE OF MASS/INSPECTED/ACCEPTED." A version of this pattern was slightly larger and had the flap, rear, and carrying strap covered with painted cloth.

● *U.S. Army Regulation Cloth Haversack*. Bag of black painted cotton cloth with 5-in. rounded or pointed flap, buckled by a single strap. Dimensions 12.5 x 3.5 (at bottom) x 13 in. Removable unpainted cotton bag held by three buttons. Cloth carrying strap, 1.8 in. wide, non-adjustable.

A variation of this pattern was made of black enamelled cotton; it had no gussets but was cornered at the bottom; about 13 x 13 in. and slightly rounded. The carrying strap was 2 in. wide.

Another variation was 12 x 11 in. in size, with a 3-in. gusset at the bottom and a 1.5-in. carrying strap.

● *Officer's Leather and Canvas Haversack*. Shield-shaped two-piece bag of rubberized canvas with maximum dimensions 13 in. wide, 12 in. high. Inner half was a bag or envelope with buckled flap and 3-in. gusset all around; inside was a removable unpainted canvas food bag. Two extra pockets for eating equipment on the front side. The outer half consisted of a tooled black leather flap, inside which was sewn a simple bag with a shallow flap, tied by strings. One-inch leather carrying strap, adjustable and fitted with spring hooks to fit into rings on the top.

● *Officer's Leather Haversack*. One-piece valise design of black grained leather, with metal frames fastened at top by two catches and a lock. Outer flap fell 8 in. and was buckled by a strap; underneath was an open pocket for eating equipment. Dimensions 13 x 4 (max.) x 10 in. Leather carrying strap .8 in. completely encircled bag as well as fastening to two rings on the top.

● *Officer's Leather Haversack*. One-piece valise design of black grained leather, as above, but with no outer flap and fastened only by the lock. Carrying straps, .5 in., snaphooked into two rings on top. Dimensions 11 x 3 x 9 in. Extra bag on outside with 4-in. flap.

● *Ration Box*. Tin, semi-circular with close fitting tin cover. No divisions inside. Dimensions 5 in. high, 6.25 in. across back. Covered with black painted canvas. Loops on sides and bottom allow 1-in. straps to fasten the box to the rear of a rigid knapsack. Four laces were provided to tie across the top. This box was used

3 BONE
BUTTONS SEWN
TO INSIDE OF
HAVERSACK FOR
FASTENING
INNER BAG.

(REDUCED)

U.S. HAVERSACK
PAINTED (BLACK) CANVAS WITH
REMOVABLE INNER BAG OF UNPAINTED CANVAS.
APP. 12½ X 14"
R. MILLER COLL.

U.S. HAVERSACK C. 1848
PLAIN WHITE CANVAS
13 X 12"
PEWTER BUTTONS.

DRINKING
CUPS OF TIN OR
SHEET IRON,
TINNED.

OFFICER'S
LEATHER
HAVERSACK
WITH REMOVABLE
UNPAINTED CANVAS
BAG WITHIN LOWER
COMPARTMENT.
ABOUT 12 X 13"

Comp'y A
Conn. Volunteers

PATENT
APRIL 22, 1861

NON-REGULATION COMBINATION
LIQUID/RATION CANTEEN.
TOP SECTION IS DIVIDED INTO
TWO COMPARTMENTS.
PAINTED MEDIUM BLUE.
W. LEWIS COLLECTION

U.S. HAVERSACK, BLACK
PAINTED CANVAS WITH REMOVABLE
BAG.
10¾ X 14"   WOODBRIDGE COLL.

EATING
UTENSILS.
N. FLAYDERMAN COLL.

FOLDING
CONTOURED HANDLES
MESS TIN.
D. BOLEWICKI COLL.

SIX-PIECE MESS/COOKING KIT OF
TINNED IRON
W. M. DANIELS COLL.

HARDTACK
AND GROUND COFFEE
WITH SUGAR IN BAG.

Fig. 58. Haversacks and food containers.

with parade accouterments and held, at the most, one ration. Extensively carried by New York militia regiments.

● *"Connecticut" Combination Canteen-Ration Box.* Tin, circular, and divided into three compartments. Diameter 8 in., thickness 2.8 in. Divided in the center and hinged; held closed by a simple hook. Lower section held rations while the upper was divided into two liquid compartments, each with an off-center spout and cap. Tin loops for a strap. Caps marked "PATENT APRIL 22, 1861." Painted medium blue with lettering on one side: ". . . Conn. Volunteers." Issued 1st Connecticut Volunteer Infantry Regiment in 1861 and possibly other corps.

Canteens

Fig. 59

The canteen or water bottle was the vessel in which the soldier on active service carried his drinking water or some other refreshing liquid.* Canteens were made of several materials, but wood and tin were by far the most usual in this period.

A canteen had to be durable, light in its own weight, and sized to contain the weight of liquid a man could readily carry on the march. This was considered to be between 2.5 and 3 pints. Furthermore, it was important that the material of which the canteen was made should not contain any substance that would affect its liquid contents. Metal canteens were frequently covered outside with cloth to reduce the noise of their contact with hard objects and to provide an envelope that could be wet and thus, by evaporation, keep the liquid inside cool.

In England, in the 1850's and 1860's, the regulation army canteen was either cylindrical or barrel-shaped and made of wood, in France it was flask-shaped and made of tin, and in the Prussian service it was made of wood in the shape of a bottle. Elsewhere in Europe could be found other shapes and other materials.

In the U.S. Army, from its establishment to about the Mexican War, the regulation canteen had been a flat, cylindrical wooden container. This was the "barrel rim" type listed below: relatively simple to construct, sturdy, and possessed of the ability to keep water cool and sweet. This canteen enjoyed occasional use throughout our period, being most common in the Confederate service.

During the Mexican War and throughout the 1850's experiments were conducted with other kinds of canteen. By 1851 canteens made of wood, sewn leather, tin covered with cloth, and India rubber were on trial in the field. In 1855 gutta percha was added to the list of materials. In December 1858 the Quartermaster General wrote, "I coincide fully . . . in his opinion of the worthlessness of India Rubber and Gutta Percha canteens, and have sold all that we had at Philadelphia; none but tin canteens covered with cloth will be issued

---

* The name was also given to a small trunk or chest that carried cooking and drinking utensils and supplies for the use of officers; and to the sutler's establishment in a garrison where troops could buy food and drink.

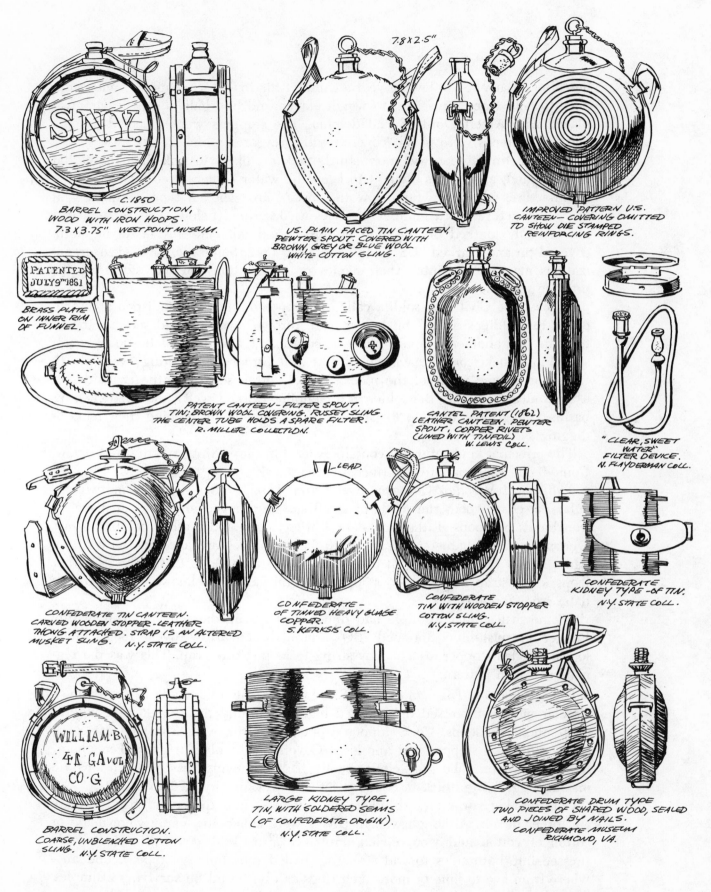

C.1850
BARREL CONSTRUCTION,
WOOD WITH IRON HOOPS.
7.3 X 3.75" WEST POINT MUSEUM.

7.8 X 2.5"

U.S. PLAIN FACED TIN CANTEEN,
PEWTER SPOUT. COVERED WITH
BROWN, GREY OR BLUE WOOL
WHITE COTTON SLING.

IMPROVED PATTERN U.S.
CANTEEN— COVERING OMITTED
TO SHOW DIE STAMPED
REINFORCING RINGS.

PATENTED JULY 9TH 1861

BRASS PLATE
ON INNER RIM
OF FUNNEL.

PATENT CANTEEN— FILTER SPOUT.
TIN; BROWN WOOL COVERING. RUSSET SLING.
THE CENTER TUBE HOLDS A SPARE FILTER.
R. MILLER COLLECTION.

CANTEL PATENT (1862)
LEATHER CANTEEN. PEWTER
SPOUT. COPPER RIVETS
(LINED WITH TINFOIL)
W. LEWIS COLL.

"CLEAR, SWEET
WATER"
FILTER DEVICE.
N. FLAYDERMAN COLL.

LEAD.

CONFEDERATE TIN CANTEEN.
CARVED WOODEN STOPPER - LEATHER
THONG ATTACHED. STRAP IS AN ALTERED
MUSKET SLING. N.Y. STATE COLL.

CONFEDERATE—
OF TINNED HEAVY GUAGE
COPPER.
S. KERKSIS COLL.

CONFEDERATE
TIN WITH WOODEN STOPPER
COTTON SLING.
N.Y. STATE COLL.

CONFEDERATE
KIDNEY TYPE -OF TIN.
N.Y. STATE COLL.

WILLIAM·B
4TH GA VOL
CO·G

BARREL CONSTRUCTION.
COARSE, UNBLEACHED COTTON
SLING. N.Y. STATE COLL.

LARGE KIDNEY TYPE.
TIN, WITH SOLDERED SEAMS
(OF CONFEDERATE ORIGIN).
N.Y. STATE COLL.

CONFEDERATE DRUM TYPE
TWO PIECES OF SHAPED WOOD, SEALED
AND JOINED BY NAILS.
CONFEDERATE MUSEUM
RICHMOND, VA.

Fig. 59. Canteens.

hereafter." Early the following year a contract for 15,000 "tin canteens with stoppers, to hold three pints, and to weigh eleven and one half ounces, each," was placed with Albert Dorff of Philadelphia. The stoppers were specified as cork and the canteens were to be "covered with grey or sky-blue kersey."

This new tin canteen was more sturdy and less likely to leak than the earlier wooden kind, and it was thought to keep the water cooler. It cost 17.5 cents to manufacture, which was far below the cost of any wooden type. Ultimately, it was manufactured in a number of styles as described below. The canteen was not officially marked on the side in this period; all canteens made of cloth-covered tin and marked "US" date from after 1872. Some men and even organizations may have painted their names or designations on one side, but the practice was uncommon.

At least one Civil War soldier called his canteen "the most indispensable article in the soldier's outfit," but many were thrown away in field service. It was to some just another flapping piece of equipment and a small bottle of water stored in a pocket or the haversack did as well. Streams and springs were plentiful enough along many of the roads. Soldiers often separated the two sides of a tin canteen (melting the solder in a campfire worked well) and used them as basins, frying pans, or soup dishes; or even as shovels in ditching their tents or digging shelter trenches.

The principal kinds of water containers used in the U.S. Army are listed below. Confederate canteens are described in Chapter 10.

● *Cylindrical Wooden Canteen, Barrel-Rim Type.* Sides made from two circular pieces of wood, rim made of small staves, grooved and held in place by iron bands or hoops. Either metal or leather loops and leather or cloth strap. Dimensions 7 in. diameter, 2.8 in. width. Painted black or dark gray, with 1.5 in. white letters "S.N.Y." and (on the other side) stamped "E. ARENTS." Leather loops; cloth strap and wooden stopper. Several variations known: This example dates from about 1810.

(Somewhat similar example had dimensions 7.3 in. diameter, 3.75 in. width. Painted greenish-blue. Stamped "BO" around broad arrow, over "1854." Metal loops, wooden stopper attached by string to loop; cloth strap. This was the regulation British pattern.)

● *U.S. Regulation Tin Canteen, M1858.* Oblate spheroid made of two convex circular pieces of pressed tin soldered together around the rim. Pewter mouthpiece and 3 tin loops. Cork stopper capped with tin, with iron ring attached; chain connected stopper and one loop. Covered with blue or gray "Petersham" fabric, sewed on. The gray cloth usually had a brownish cast. Dimensions 7.8 in. diameter; 2.5 in. thick in center. Cloth strap. Capacity 2.75 to 3 pints.

Considerable variation existed in the thickness and quality of the tin plate and other details. Although woolen covers were called for, many were made of cotton or cotton and wool mixed. Probably after 1861 concentric rings were pressed into both sides to add strength (called the "bullseye type"), and anywhere from five to nine or more such rings can be found on surviving examples. In many instances the maker's name is stamped on the stopper or neck.

● *Leather Canteen, Cantel Patent, 1862.* Consisted of two pieces of leather fastened with copper rivets and lined inside with tinfoil adherred to the leather. Height, including neck, 9 in.; maximum width 6.7 in. thickness, circa 1.75 in. Stamped on side, in a circle around "L.C.," the words "PATENT/OCT. 14 1862." (Under U.S. Patent No. 36641, Lazare Cantel of New York, N.Y., offered this "improved canteen" for sale. The essential feature of the patent was the lining inside of tinfoil or other metal.)

● *Bartholomae Patent Tin Filter Canteen, 1861.* Curved tin flask of the "kidney" type with filter and drinking spouts plus a tube for storing an extra filter. Dimensions about 6 in. high, 6.5 in. wide, and 2.3 in. thick in center. The filter spout was a funnel capped by a cork; the other two capped by pewter screw tops, all caps chained to the flask. Brown wool cover, sewed on; cloth strap. Brass plate on inner rim of funnel: "PATENTED JULY 9th 1861." Water was poured into the filter spout and in theory purified. This canteen was sold by Schuyler, Hartley & Graham and other outfitters.

● *Russell Patent Water Filter.* Not a container but a device designed to produce "clear, sweet water" from a muddy or stagnant source. Comprised a rubber tube about 2 feet long with a wooden mouthpiece on one end and a round pewter box containing a felt filter on the other. Extra filters were provided. These devices were sold in 1861–1862 but soon abandoned as useless.

(Oil canteens carried by signalmen are described in Chapter 6.)

Mess Equipment

In the period of our study enlisted soldiers were expected to prepare and cook their own rations. It was also expected that they would supply the equipment for so doing except for two items: camp kettles and mess pans. Iron pots were furnished in place of camp kettles to troops in garrison. The men, therefore, owned a variety of mess gear that, except on occasions, was neither regulated nor even standardized. *Fig. 58*

Officers in garrison normally ate meals at home, and in the field formed an officers' mess. Pooling their allowances, they hired cooks and waiters or employed soldiers. The mess equipment used in these messes was essentially domestic in kind and will not be covered here. On the other hand, most officers on field service possessed some sort of eating gear and those of higher rank often extended this to beautifully cased sets of the finest silver, glass, and china ware.

Many compact sets of mess gear were for sale in the North and these were purchased by enlisted soldiers as well. Among the more popular was the combination knife, fork, and spoon made in jackknife form.

In the field a soldier might elect or be forced to cook his own food, but usually cooking was done in small groups or messes with the cook's job rotated or some other division of labor worked out informally. In more permanent camps company messes were formed with an experienced cook permanently detailed, and this was always true in garrison. In all instances the mess equipment used was civilian in kind and quite heterogeneous. Beside camp kettles and mess pans, there might be coffee pots, frying pans, skillets, and so forth, plus tin plates and cups, knives, forks, and spoons. No generalizations are possible as to what kinds of utensils were the most common and the examples below are selected almost at random.

- *U.S. Army Camp Kettle.* Heavy sheet iron vessel of cylindrical form, usually without lid, 13–15 in. high and 7–12 in. diameter. Fitted with a heavy wire bail or handle. The Quartermaster General reported in July 1859 that the same pattern of camp kettle "had been used for years."
- *U.S. Army Mess Pan.* Open vessel of sheet iron with sloping sides, about 6 in. high and 12 in. diameter at the top. Like the camp kettle, the pattern had been used for years prior to 1859 and continued in use throughout our period.
- *U.S. Army Iron Pot.* Heavy iron rounded vessel with iron bail and 3 legs. Size about 12 in. high and 10 in. diameter at top. As above, the pattern did not vary materially during our period.
- *Combination Knife-Fork-Spoon Sets.* Made on the jackknife principle with a knife blade and 2-pronged fork at one end and a short-handled spoon at the other. Sold commercially, doubtless in several varieties.
- *Iron Coffee Pots.* One example, used by a Connecticut soldier, was made of sheet iron painted black, and was cylindrical with a convex, unhinged lid, 4.75 in. high and 4.5 in. diameter. It was fitted with an iron bail or handle for hanging over a fire; no interior fittings.

Coffee pots became practically obsolete after the first 6 months, being found only in the organized messes. Soldiers found that a fruit can with its top removed and a wire bail added made an adequate substitute. Coffee mills also became rare; most men ground their beans by pounding them with a rock or gun butt.

- *Tin Cups.* Several kinds and sizes were in common use. Cups were both straight sided and bowl shaped; made of tin or iron. As mentioned above, cups were not issue items in this period and never bore a "US" marking.
- *Flasks.* Sold in sizes from a pint to a pint and a half. These were made of a high grade metal and were often leather covered. The "Britannia Dram Flask" advertised by Schuyler, Hartley & Graham is an example.

Belts, Frogs, Holsters, and Slings

This category of accouterments experienced, within the period 1851–1872, numerous minor changes but no radical alterations of type. For convenience the types will be arranged in order of those worn by dismounted enlisted men, mounted enlisted men, and officers. As before, the main discussion will be confined to models used by troops of the general government or procured by its agents. Almost all of the items mentioned in this section were the province of the Ordnance Department and many were specified in the *Ordnance Manuals* of 1860 and 1861. Models exclusively procured for and used by state troops will be mentioned under the state concerned.

It is probable that white buff leather belts of the different models were worn by some regular regiments for a few years after 1851, but these will not be considered. The same belt was easily blackened and the *Ordnance Regulations* of 1852 calls for all belts to be black.

Infantry and Rifle Belts

Infantrymen in 1851 wore a black buff leather waist belt, 1.5 in. wide and 38.5 in. long, with a leather loop at the left end. To the right end was attached an oval brass plate, 2.8 x 1.6 in., stamped with "US" (described under Insignia) and having on its rear an arrowhead-like stud and a hook. The brass plate was pushed through the loop and hooked directly into the belt.

Fig. 60

On this waist belt the soldier carried his percussion cap pouch, invariably just to the right of his belt plate, and his bayonet scabbard, invariably on his left hip. The use of a waist belt rather than a shoulder belt to suspend the bayonet or sword was an advance in accouterment design made a decade or more before our period, and was aimed at relieving the constriction on the soldier's chest caused by cross belts. The rifleman's waist belt, as will be seen, went even further by eliminating both shoulder belts.

Despite the general acceptance of these improvements by most armies of the world, many state regiments clung to the cross belts (and even cross belts of white buff leather) for parade, at least until the early days of the Civil War.

The cartridge box for the musket and rifle musket was suspended from a shoulder belt of black buff (later bridle) leather, 2.25 in. wide and 55.5 in. long, having a billet* at each end. These billets fastened to buckles on the bottom of the box. The regulation U.S. Army cartridge box belt had a circular brass "eagle" plate attached (so as to be centered on the soldier's breast) by two eyes of iron wire; it served no function other than decoration. Other shoulder belt (or "breast") plates, it should be recalled, were functional, serving either to hold two cross belts centered or to vary the length of one of them.

No change was made in the specifications for this belt as long as the musket cartridge box was worn, but numerous minor variations can be found in surviving examples, due to local manufacture. Frequently the brass plate was omitted and the use of black shoe (or upper) leather was possible.

The scabbard for the triangular socket bayonet then in use (Model 1840) was made of black bridle leather, overall length 19.5 in., with a brass ferrule and tip. A frog of black buff leather (which slid on the waist belt) was sewn to a socket of black bridle leather which fastened to the top of the scabbard. Scabbards for bayonets Model 1822, 18 in. long, were still authorized.

---

* Billet: Here, a strap that passes through a buckle. The term also may mean a loop that receives the end of a buckled belt.

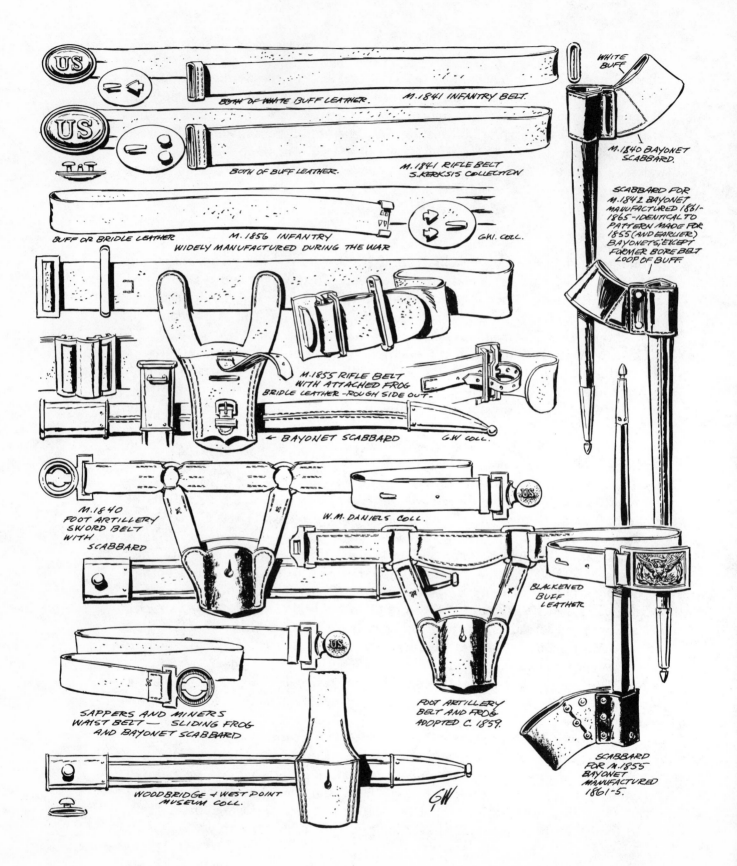

Fig. 60.   Belts, frogs and scabbards.

This scabbard continued in use throughout the period. The socket was riveted as well as sewn to the frog in later models, and frogs of upper leather were used. In August 1862 a patent was granted to J.E. Emerson for an all-steel bayonet scabbard. This came in the same size as the leather scabbard which it began to replace. The steel was blued and there was no tip as found on the older styles.

A swivel frog was patented in May 1860 and some apparently saw use in the Civil War.

A waist belt was required by men armed with the Model 1841 rifle, for its cartridge box had only vertical loops. The belt was black buff leather, 2 in. wide, with the same large (3.5 x 2.2 in.) oval "US" buckle as used on the infantry cartridge box, but having two studs and a hook on the rear. Since at first no bayonet was provided with this rifle, only the cap pouch, cartridge box and Ames knife rode on the belt. This belt was worn in the regular service after 1851 only by the Regiment of Mounted Riflemen. It was a favorite, however, of numerous state rifle companies, who often added other embellishments to the belt.

About 1856, with the adoption of a new line of weapons, certain changes were made in these belts. The waist belt for use with the Model 1855 rifle musket (for the normal infantryman, that is) increased to 1.9 in. wide, with the larger size oval brass buckle (3.5 x 2.2 in.). This had two studs and a hook on the rear and was fastened to the right end of the belt by means of the studs. The hook fastened directly into holes in the left side of the belt, and the excess length of belt was kept trim with the main part by means of brass jaws permanently pinned on the left end. This remained the common infantry belt throughout the Civil War, later ones being made of dressed leather.

State issue infantry waist belts often varied from this U.S. model. A common form used a rectangular plate with a loop on one side of its rear and a broad clasp on the other. The right end of the belt was doubled through this loop and held fast by a loose loop, while the left end was sewn or riveted to a third loop into which the clasp fitted.

Infantry armed with the Model 1855 rifle and men trained under the Hardee manual carried their cartridge boxes on waist belts of one sort or another. The box normally rested in the middle of the soldier's back until he required ammunition, when he slid it around to his right side.

Since a heavy sword bayonet had to be carried with the Model 1855 rifle, the rifle belt was considerably strengthened. It was made of shoe leather, black on the outside and dressed russet on the inside, and was 2.2 to 2.4 in. wide. The prescribed length was 42.5 in.; examples today vary somewhat one way or the other. The belt had a strap or billet sewn on the inside at each end to secure in place two rectangular brass clasps. The belt ends, passing through these clasps, were held in place by two brass loops with eyes at the top through which the brass hooks on the knapsack breast straps could be hooked to distribute the weight of the knapsack. A black leather frog for the sword bayonet, having a billet and buckle to hold the scabbard in place, was sewn to the waist belt by means of a V-shaped sling. The scabbard itself was of black bridle leather with brass throat and tip. Its overall length was 23 in.

The Model 1855 sword bayonet belt was most distinctive and a considerable departure from all other accouterments used. It was a close copy of the belt issued to the *chasseurs a pied* of the French army in 1838, which remained one of the distinguishing features of the dress of that celebrated corps until about 1867. In the American service it was first issued to the 9th and 10th Infantry Regiments, which were raised in 1855 as rifle corps.

The first frog used on these belts required that the scabbard be fitted with a brass loop at the throat through which the billet could pass, which had been the French system for many years. Later scabbards were made independent of the belt and (for reasons not clear) had buttons instead of loops. Some surviving frogs show evidence of having been forced to accommodate the buttons. Other scabbards carried their own billets, thus eliminating the need for a billet on the frog.

In the infantry and foot artillery all sergeants and all musicians were authorized to wear a straight sword having a scabbard designed to hang from a frog. These swords in 1851 were suspended from a shoulder belt of black buff leather which passed over the right shoulder and joined by the left hip in a permanently attached frog. The belt was 2.1 to 2.3 in. wide and made in two branches, 16–17 in. and 40 in. long; the branches were connected over the breast by a round brass eagle plate, similar to the one worn on the cartridge box belt but having three hooks on its rear instead of eyes. These hooks permitted change in the length of the belt and a leather loop sewed to the long branch kept the loose end in place. Other company sergeants of infantry—and this was especially true in certain state regiments—wore their sword and bayonet in a double-frogged shoulder belt, similar to the belt described above except for an extra frog attached to the bottom of the long branch. This belt is listed in *Ordnance Regulations* of 1852.*

With this shoulder sword belt the NCO and musician always wore a waist belt. At first this was the ordinary infantry belt with oval buckle, but about 1852 a new belt was introduced. It was of black buff leather, 1.9 in. wide and from 36 to 40 in. in length. The new belt was given the Model 1851 rectangular brass plate, 3.5 x 2.2 in., bearing the national coat of arms encircled by a wreath of German silver—the belt plate specified for the entire army in 1851 but never widely worn. A brass loop was fixed to the left end of the belt, which engaged a narrow hook on the rear of the plate; a brass hook on the right end served to hook the belt after passing through a slot on the right side of the plate, and a leather loop held this fold together.

The waist belt served to hold the shoulder belt firmly to the body. Since all company sergeants carried muskets in addition to swords, this waist belt was used by some to support their bayonet scabbards and possibly (in the 9th and 10th Infantry Regiments) their cartridge boxes as well.

* The illustrations in the Horstmann edition of the dress regulations of 1851 are very faulty in their NCO and musician swords and sword belts.

During the Civil War, and perhaps before and afterwards, many sergeants and musicians hung their swords from their waist belts, thus eliminating the shoulder sword belt entirely. To do so they used a simple black leather frog with a loop which slid on the belt. These frogs exist today in a variety of styles and sizes, many of which—made double—served also to carry a bayonet. Some types resembled the Model 1855 rifle frog in having two arms and loops, but were independent of the belt.

Belts for Foot Artillerymen and Engineers

Ten out of the twelve companies in each of the four regular artillery regiments served as foot or heavy artillery in the years from 1821 to 1861. For infantry drill in 1851 they carried the artillery musketoon without bayonet. In *Fig. 60* place of the bayonet, privates and corporals were issued a distinctive sword— the Model 1833 "Roman" pattern—which required a special belt. This belt was made of white buff leather, 1.7 in. wide, and came in three sections united by two brass rings. From each of these rings hung slings 1.3 in. wide and 3.5 in. long, which were sewn to a frog for the scabbard. The belt had a two-piece brass buckle carrying the raised letters "U.S." The scabbard was of light bridle leather, jacked, blackened, and varnished, with a brass ferrule and tip; overall length 20 in.

About 1859 the foot artillery companies were issued the Model 1855 rifle musket and bayonet, and ordinary infantry accouterments. However, the foot artillery belt was still prescribed in the *Ordnance Manual* of 1861; by then it was a little wider (1.9 in.), of black leather, and fitted with the universal rectangular brass plate. It seems to have been worn by some sergeants throughout the Civil War.

Engineer soldiers of the Company of Sappers, Miners, and Pontoniers, armed in 1851 with the musketoon Model 1847 and its special sword bayonet, were authorized a special belt. It was of black buff leather, 2 in. wide and 36–40 in. long, fitted with the same two-piece brass plate as the foot artillery. A leather frog slid on the belt. The bayonet scabbard was made of black bridle leather, jacked and varnished, with a brass ferrule and tip. It was straight and 21.8 in. overall. It carried a brass button on the ferrule for attachment to the frog. With this the sappers wore an infantry cartridge box, belt, plate, and cap pouch.

After about 1856 the engineers were rearmed with the rifle. Whether they were given regulation rifleman's accouterments, together with the sword bayonet, has not yet been determined.

Belts for Mounted Men

Until about 1856 the two regiments of dragoons used much the same type of accouterments they had worn in the Mexican War. This comprised a white and later black buff leather waist belt, 2 in. wide and 36–40 in. long, fitted with a *Fig. 61* shoulder strap and two saber slings, both 1.2 in. wide, also of buff leather. These

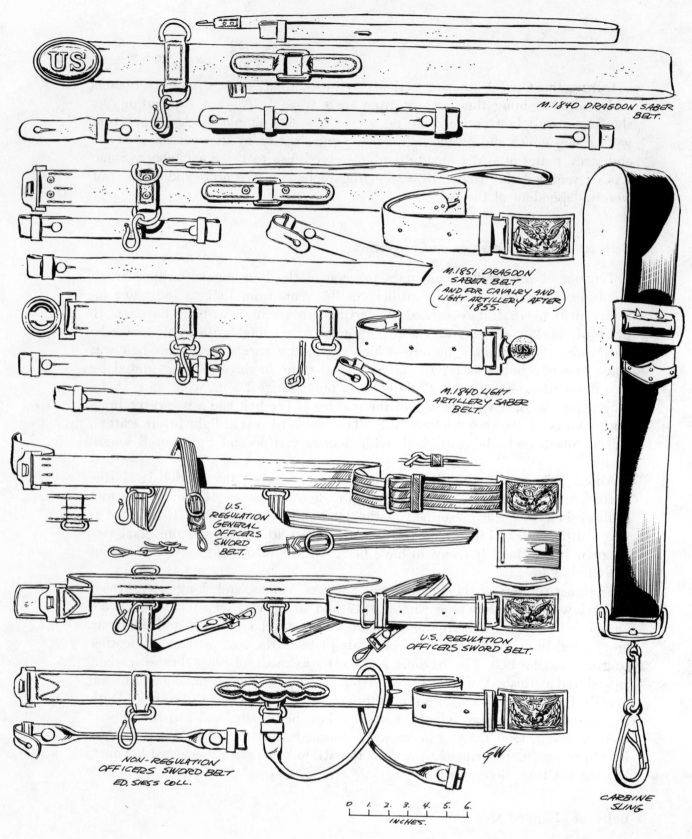

M.1840 DRAGOON SABER BELT.

M.1851 DRAGOON SABER BELT (AND FOR CAVALRY AND LIGHT ARTILLERY AFTER 1855.

M.1840 LIGHT ARTILLERY SABER BELT.

U.S. REGULATION GENERAL OFFICERS SWORD BELT.

U.S. REGULATION OFFICERS SWORD BELT.

NON-REGULATION OFFICERS SWORD BELT ED. SIESS COLL.

0 1 2 3 4 5 6
INCHES.

CARBINE SLING

GW

Fig. 61. Belts and slings.

straps were attached by means of two special fixtures sewn onto the belt: a leather loop with two brass D-rings and a saber hook forward, and two loops with a brass square ring to the rear. Both ends of the slings were closed by means of brass studs. The belt had an oval brass "US" plate similar to the large infantry cartridge box plate (3.5 x 2 2 in.) but having two studs and a hook on the rear.

About 1856, with the introduction of the Model 1855 pistol-carbine, these belts were made slightly narrower and the belt plate was changed to the Model 1851 rectangular model already mentioned. Rivets often supplemented stitching on belt fixtures. This remained the dragoon, and later the general cavalry belt, throughout the period. The same belt appears to have been worn by the two cavalry regiments from 1855 to 1861.

The use of a shoulder strap was necessitated by the weight of the dragoon saber. When the weight was reduced somewhat by the light cavalry saber, and when supporting pads had been added to the rear of the uniform jacket, the need for the shoulder strap was partially removed. Judging from photographs, many a cavalryman left off his strap in field service.

In August 1859 a board of cavalry officers recommended the adoption of a new method for attaching the saber to the waist belt devised by 1st Lieutenant J.E.B. Stuart, 1st Cavalry. This was a brass device which fastened to only one position on the belt, from which it could be readily detached. The principal advantage lay in the celerity with which a trooper could remove his saber in order to fight on foot. A patent was granted to Stuart on October 4. Before the end of the month the War Department paid Stuart $5,000 for all rights to the attachment, and the patent was transferred to the Department. In November 1859 Frankford Arsenal was directed to make 500 attachments for issue when required. The attachment was also commercially available from Knorr, Nece & Co. of Philadelphia. It saw no service in the Confederate cavalry, and only a small quantity was issued for use with the standard issue cavalry waist belt in the Union service during the Civil War. In 1864 the Frankford Arsenal was ordered to arrange for the manufacture of 10,000 "Stewart" attachments, 2,000 of which were to be sent to Emerson Gaylord, Chicopee, Mass., to be used in the manufacture of Mann's patent cavalry accouterments. Quite a number of Stuart attachments were issued from 1865 to 1871.

The waist belt of the Regiment of Mounted Riflemen has already been described under the infantry section. The men were not issued sabers. Whether they wore the Model 1855 rifle belt is still open to question; the strong probability is that they did not, since they almost certainly did not use the sword bayonet.

Mounted artillerymen in 1851 wore a simplified version of the cavalry saber belt. It was of buff leather (white at first and black later), 1.7 in. wide, 36 to 40 in. long, with two brass oval rings suspended from leather loops, sewed to the belt. Saber slings and a hook, similar to the cavalry type, hung from these rings. The buckle was a brass two-piece "US" type, permanently fixed on the left and adjustable on the right by means of a brass hook and leather loop.

About 1856 some light artillery may have been given the general cavalry belt mentioned above, but the light artillery belt just described was manufactured in limited quantities even after the Civil War.

Slings

Figs. 61 and 62

The regiments of dragoons and cavalry, when armed with weapons fitted with sling rings (the musketoon, rifled carbine, and almost all of the patented breech-loading carbines) attached them to a sling that was worn over the left shoulder with its buckle to the back. This carbine sling was made of black buff leather and was 56 in. long and 2.5 in. wide. It was adjusted in its length by means of a brass buckle, had a brass tip, and was fitted onto a bright iron chain and swivel terminating in a hook that snapped into the carbine ring.

By 1861 some carbine slings were being made of black harness leather dressed only on the outside. In one or another style they continued in use after 1872. There is some evidence that a cartridge box was occasionally worn on this sling, but the practice was uncommon. The cavalryman wore his sling both mounted and dismounted.

The pistol-carbine Model 1855, which had its own sling, came apart, and could easily be transported in a saddle holster, required no carbine sling. Neither the Model 1841 nor the Model 1855 rifles, with which the Regiment of Mounted Riflemen was armed, were fitted with sling rings. Apparently the Rifles carried these weapons strapped to their saddles or across their backs.

Holsters

Fig. 62

With the mounted services consideration must be given to the subject of pistol holsters. Saddle holsters were a normal attachment for all military saddles until the middle 1850's, and they continued to be used by mounted officers, particularly generals and staff officers, throughout the Civil War. Saddle holsters, however, will be treated under Horse Furniture; here only the belt holster will be discussed.

When and by whom the belt holster was developed is a matter of some question, but it is clear that it came as a direct result of the Colt revolver. There are instances of single-shot pistols being carried in belt holsters long before the 1850's, but not in the American military service. The five or six shots in a revolver made it practical to confine one's armament to a single pistol and hence more conveniently to carry it on the person.

As early as 1851 a Colt agent was selling "Patent leather belts with holsters, thongs & pouch," and belt holsters exist which were clearly made for the Whitneyville-Walker revolver. In 1855 the War Department made its first purchase of the Colt Model 1851 Navy (caliber .36) revolver, 1,100 being accepted that year. The Colt *Manual* was adopted as official (GO 8, 25 June 1855). This weapon was considered to be a "belt pistol" and there is considerable evidence that belt holsters (called "pistol-cases") were first purchased at the same time.

227

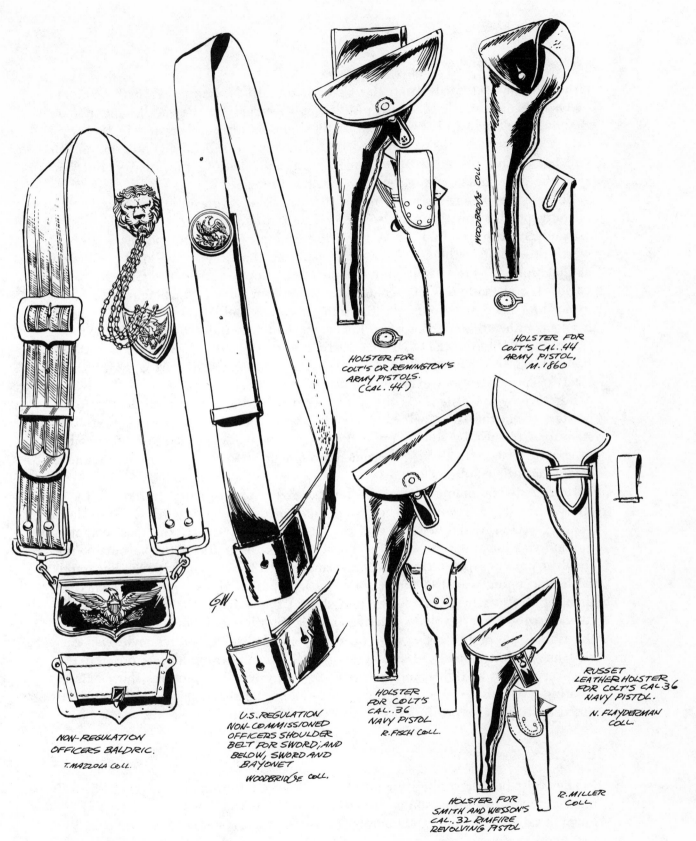

HOLSTER FOR
COLT'S OR REMINGTON'S
ARMY PISTOLS.
(CAL. 44)

WOODBRIDGE COLL.

HOLSTER FOR
COLT'S CAL. 44
ARMY PISTOL,
M. 1860

NON-REGULATION
OFFICERS BALDRIC.

T. MAZZOLA COLL.

U.S. REGULATION
NON-COMMISSIONED
OFFICERS SHOULDER
BELT FOR SWORD; AND
BELOW, SWORD AND
BAYONET

WOODBRIDGE COLL.

HOLSTER
FOR COLT'S
CAL. 36
NAVY PISTOL

R. FISCH COLL.

RUSSET
LEATHER HOLSTER
FOR COLT'S CAL. 36
NAVY PISTOL.

N. FLAYDERMAN
COLL

HOLSTER FOR
SMITH AND WESSON'S
CAL. 32 RIMFIRE
REVOLVING PISTOL

R. MILLER
COLL

Fig. 62. Belts, baldrics and holsters.

although not necessarily from the Colt factory. In November 1856 the Colonel of Ordnance wrote: ". . . horse pistols being carried on the saddle and not on the waist belt . . . Colt's revolvers of the light pattern are carried in the army in a pouch, or half-holster attached by a loop to the sabre belt—but this pouch will not receive the horse-pistol, unless enlarged." During the fiscal year 1855–1856 the government purchased 3,381 belt holsters.

These holsters were normally made of leather; however, an experimental order of gutta percha holsters was also secured and issued to a squadron each of the 1st and 2nd Cavalry in 1855. A surviving example of a gutta percha holster is worth describing, although there is no evidence that it was the kind purchased at that time. It was a righthanded type (see below) and fit the Colt Navy revolver. It was made of cloth, coated inside and out with gutta percha of a black finish, and lined with red felt; the flap strap was held fast by fitting under a flat loop rather than over a stud. Inside the flap was painted the maker's mark, reading: "VULCANIZED GUTTA PERCHA/MADE BY . . . NORTH AMERICAN/GUTTA PERCHA/CO . . ./RIDERS & MURPHYS/1852 & 1854/ PATENT." The holster, however, was not a success.

For three years after 1855 the War Department continued to order "pairs of holsters" from the Colt factory. After 1858 the orders specifically mention "holsters for Colt pistols." Based upon this and other evidence, it seems reasonable to assume that in 1859 the government commenced to equip all of its mounted troops with belt holsters.

Holsters were manufactured in several sizes, often being fashioned for a specific model of revolver. They were also made in "righthanded" and "lefthanded" styles. At the beginning of the Civil War, apparently the most common method was for a man to wear the holster on his right side with the butt of the revolver pointing to the front; he drew and fired the weapon with his left hand. Both officers and cavalrymen in combat carried their drawn sabers attached to their right wrists by sword knots, and shifted the reins to their sword-hand before drawing their revolvers. Occasionally a righthanded holster was worn on the right side, permitting a straight draw, or a holster of either style was carried on the left side. By 1864, at least, U.S. Cavalry Regulations ordered the revolver used as a "right-hand" weapon. Several Civil War pictures show officers wearing two holsters, one on either side. Finally, horsemanship permitting, men did drop their reins on the horse's neck and fight with both hands.

Belts for Officers

The waist belt prescribed for all officers between 1851 and 1872 was 1.5 to 2 in. wide, with two saber slings (about 1 in. wide; perhaps 9-12 in. and 22-27 in. long), a saber hook, and a rectangular brass plate. Except for general officers, the belt and slings were made of plain black leather. Generals wore one of red Russia leather with three stripes of gold embroidery or gilt tooling running lengthwise on both belt and slings; the slings were embroidered on both sides. The rectangular sword belt plate was the universal model for all ranks and branches; it

Fig. 60

is described under Insignia (Chapter 2).

On officers' belts the right end passed through the fixed slot in the right side of the plate and fastened back on itself by a buckle and two slides, rather than by the hook of the cavalry model. The left end of the belt on most models was designed to lay behind the plate, a separate leather fixture holding the brass loop that engaged the hook on the rear of the plate.

Officers could purchase belts of several designs. On some the rings or loops for the saber slings were permanently fixed to the belt. On others, one or both rings were attached to loops which slid on the belt. It was also possible to buy leather shoulder straps which could be attached to the belt to take the weight of the saber. Occasionally one finds a picture showing double shoulder belts in use.

The baldric was another form of sling or belt not specified in regulations but occasionally carried by adjutants and regimental staff officers for full dress. Invariably worn over the left shoulder, it comprised a belt about 2.5 in. wide, a *Figs. 21 and 62* small leather box (often designed to hold revolver cartridges), a small metal lion's head or other device, and a small metal shield. In America, both the shield and the box tended to be decorated with the national eagle. The belt was adjusted in length by a buckle, and attached by loops and rings to each side of the box; the lion's head and shield (fixed on the front of the belt) were connected by three small brass chains. The whole was patent leather or elaborately laced, and usually had brass or gilt fittings. The three chains originally held prickers for pistol touchholes, but by the Civil War they were entirely ornamental.

A baldric of a different type, it should be noted, was worn by drum majors. This too was a non-regulation item, quite ornamental. Its distinctive feature was a shield with two miniature drum sticks, often connected by chains to a lion's *Fig. 2* head or eagle placed above it on the baldric.

SOURCES

U.S. Ordnance Dept., *The Ordnance Manual for the Use of the Officers of the United States Army,* 2nd ed., Gideon & Co., Washington, D.C., 1850. Also: 3rd ed., J.B. Lippincott & Co., Philadelphia, 1862.

U.S. Ordnance Dept., *Instructions for Making Quarterly Returns of Ordnance and Ordnance Stores* [Ordnance Memorandum No. 1], Washington, D.C., 1863. Also a rev. ed., 1865. Useful because it lists the various arms, accouterments, and ordnance stores issued during the Civil War.

U.S. Ordnance Dept., *Regulation for the Government of the Ordnance Department,* Gideon & Co., Washington, D.C., 1852. Commonly referred to as *Ordnance Regulations,* 1852.

Berkeley R. Lewis, *Small Arms and Ammunition in the United States Service,* Smithsonian Institution, Washington, D.C., 1956.

William Dalton Mann, *Colonel Mann's Infantry and Cavalry Accoutrements, Patented December 8, 1863 . . .,* New York, 1864.

J. Margerand, *Armement et équipement de l'infanterie française du XVIe au XXe siècle,* Paris, 1945.

Charles T. Haven and Frank A. Belden, *A History of the Colt Revolver . . .,* New York, 1940.

James E. Serven, *Colt Firearms: 1836–1954,* Santa Ana, Cal., 1954.

The Medical and Surgical History of the War of the Rebellion, part 3, vol. I, "Medical History," pp. 869–874.

"A Late Captain of Infantry," *Hints Bearing on the United States Army* . . ., Philadelphia, 1858.

The greater part of the information in this chapter is based upon tangible evidence secured from museums and private collections. Foremost among the latter were the collections of the late Robert L. Miller, Sydney C. Kerksis, James S. Hutchins, Norm Flayderman, William S. Cornwell, and Richard N. Ferris. All of these men, and many more, gave liberally of their time and knowledge.

CHAPTER V

Horse Furniture

Saddles

Military saddles can be divided into four broad categories: 1) regulation cavalry or dragoon patterns; 2) regulation artillery drivers' and off-horse patterns; 3) officers' and essentially civilian riding saddles; and 4) pack saddles and aparejos.

The requirements for a military riding saddle were many and in some respects conflicting. It had to be sturdy enough to carry strapped to it a considerable weight of accouterments and clothing and yet be as light as possible to save the horse in long marches. It had to fit both horse and rider comfortably and permit both to function freely. It had to be reasonably standardized as to size and design, yet suited to the wide variations in weight and configuration found in both men and horses of a single regiment. Finally, its construction had to be simple enough for repair in the field.

The failure of a saddle to measure up to one or more of these requirements could result in a disabled and useless horse or an exhausted rider, and many such cases could end the effectiveness of a mounted command. Equally as dangerous was ignorance on the part of soldiers concerning how to adjust their saddles, and American cavalrymen were at times far from being well trained horsemen. Cavalry and artillery commanders came to fear the evil results of defective and maladjusted saddlery as much as they feared an enterprising enemy.

There is little wonder, then, that officers were continually seeking to improve the design and construction of saddles and that the 1850's and 1860's witnessed the introduction of numerous new types, despite the fact that this relatively simple apparatus had by then been in constant use throughout the world for over two thousand years.

The heart and soul of a saddle was its frame or "tree." If the tree was defective, it mattered little how many good points the saddle might possess; it was on its tree that the style and reputation of a saddle rested. The military saddle tree commonly used in America in this period had two side bars of wood shaped to fit a horse's back, joined by relatively high end pieces which formed the pommel and cantle. When assembled, the tree was covered with leather. The rider sat astride the side bars rather than on a seat fixed over them, and the saddle could be placed directly on a horse's back although a blanket or pad was commonly used.

Leather was, with few exceptions, black. All military saddles had several rings and staples to which accouterments could be attached. In addition, pommels and cantles were often mortised to permit passage of additional straps. Cruppers were often used but breast straps rarely.

Girths were of leather or some fabric like cotton, fishcord, mohair, manila, horsehair, or canvas. If made up of other than leather, girths were either woven or worked into separate cord strands and held in place by a cross bar of the same material. Fabric girths were, in the West, called "cinchas" or "cinches" although the Army used the American term "girth" for all types. A broad fabric belt called the "surcingle" was sometimes buckled entirely around the saddle and the horse's belly better to hold the saddle in place. Leather girths were always fastened by buckling, but those of fabric were sometimes fitted on the near side with a long leather cinch strap which circled several times between the girth rings and was held in place by pressure on itself.

The Grimsley Saddle

Fig. 63;
Plate XVIII

The dragoon saddle in general use by the regular army in 1851 was the Grimsley, or "St. Louis pattern." Originally designed and submitted to the War Department in 1846 by Colonel Stephen Watts Kearny, improvements and patent by Thornton Grimsley of St. Louis, Mo., and subsequent production in his saddlery house, caused it to be given his name (although in other cases the name of the inventor was frequently used). Its adoption had been formally recommended by a board of officers in 1847 and it replaced the earlier Ringgold saddle.

The Grimsley saddle tree was fully described by its inventor in his patent specifications (Patent No. 5396, 11 Dec. 1847), and is illustrated in the Horstmann edition of the 1851 dress regulations. It resembled "the French hussar (or old dragoon regulation) saddle tree" but its high, gracefully sloping pommel and cantle were attached to the side bars by screws or perhaps pegs, over which was applied a laced rawhide cover, rather than by metallic fastenings. The "winding" side bars were specially designed to fit a horse's back comfortably without padding. Both of these devices were borrowed from the Mexican saddle of that era.

The Grimsley saddle tree could be distinguished from other models by the pronounced shoulder that projected downward at the forward end of each side bar, to which—on the dragoon model—the fronts of the stirrup bars were riveted. Its pommel and cantle were high (so high as to cause complaint from short-legged troopers), somewhat pointed and sloping, edged with brass, and each pierced with a morticed hole at the top. The cantle had a distinctive "duck tail" appearance. The tree was covered over completely with dressed black leather and fitted with a dressed leather seat, quilted or padded by means of parallel rows of stitching.

On both sides of the saddle fell long, rounded skirts of heavy harness leather which projected forward at the bottom. Both girth and surcingle were made of blue woollen webbing. The stirrups were straight-sided and of brass—the same pattern furnished the 1st Dragoons in 1834. The issue saddle had two rings and one staple in front, and two rings and four staples in the rear. By means of these the Grimsley carried as normal equipment for enlisted men a pair of black leather saddle holsters without brass tips, a valise of dark blue cloth over strong canvas, stiffened with plates of leather, a shoe pouch attached below the cantle on the near side, a crupper and a breast strap (the last passing along the holster tubes on each side), and a carbine boot suspended on the off side from a long double strap. All leather was black. The enlisted man's valise bore a brass disk at each end on which the company letter was applied; an officer's valise had his regimental number in brass fixed to each end. Officers' saddle holsters ordinarily had brass tips.

The Grimsley dragoon saddle was used by the Regiment of Mounted Riflemen as well as the two dragoon regiments. It remained regulation from 1847 to 1859 and was in use for a decade or more after that. Grimsley also made artillery saddles, pack saddles, and all sorts of horse furniture for officers and, of course, private citizens.

Experimental Saddles, 1855–1859

The year 1855 saw several significant developments in the area of American military horse furniture. On 21 May (GO 5) the responsibility for "all horse equipments for the troops" was transferred from the Quartermaster General to the Chief of Ordnance. This change ushered in a five-year period of experimentation during which the Ordnance Department purchased in some quantity four new patterns of saddles, the Grimsley remaining the regulation all the while despite a mounting volume of criticism of it. The new saddles were the Campbell, the Hope (or Texas), the Jones, and the McClellan.

Another development that year was the establishment of the 1st and 2nd Cavalry Regiments and the decision by the Secretary of War, Jefferson Davis, to use them as a means of experimentation in mounted arms and accouterments. As a part of his program, Mr. Davis appointed the field officers of these regiments to a Cavalry Equipment Board and ordered it to convene in Washington in July 1855. Within a month this Board had submitted its report and on 15 August the essential features were published in General Orders 13. As far as saddles were concerned, one squadron of each regiment was ordered to be equipped provisionally with the Campbell saddle after it had undergone certain modification.

Daniel Campbell seems to have been a resident of Washington, D.C. and presumably was a harness maker. His ideas on saddles were well known to American cavalry officers although his two patents were not granted until after the Board had convened. No example of a Campbell saddle is known to have survived and it is chiefly through these patents that we have any idea what his improvements were. Campbell was granted a patent 10 July 1855 (No. 13,213)

Figs. 63 and 64

234

on a saddle tree whose side bars were united to the pommel and cantle by stiff springs that allowed the tree to adjust itself comfortably to the back of the horse. His second patent, granted 4 December of the same year (No. 13,864), introduced specially designed holsters and a valise which could be used with his new saddle, or with any other saddle for that matter.

The Campbell tree as patented was shaped much like the Grimsley dragoon tree, but its girth straps (quarter straps) curved around the pommel and cantle arcs to meet on either side in a common girth ring. This style was not original with Campbell but it was new to the American service; together with one or two other features it foreshadowed the McClellan saddle yet to come. Before issue, upon recommendation of the Cavalry Equipment Board, Campbell's cantle was rounded off and lowered to facilitate mounting and dismounting.

The Campbell saddle was brass mounted, had wooden stirrups, and all its buckles were the brass mounted barrel type. To the pommel was attached a combination holster and shoe pouch; the former was quite distinctive in that its hood was attached to the bottom edge of the holster proper by an iron rivet which allowed the hood to pivot off and downward. The valise, attached to the cantle, was actually two leather receptacles, each with its cover held down by a buckled strap. At first the saddle was placed on a saddle pad ("moss rug") rather than a blanket.

The Campbell, like all the other patterns, received its share of praise and condemnation. The defect that developed in the end lay in the springs, which weakened in time. It seems to have been withdrawn from service in 1857.

The 1st and 2nd Cavalry were riding both the Grimsley and Campbell saddles on the Kansas and Texas frontiers respectively in the winter of 1855–1856. Here the officers (who, it must be recalled, purchased their own saddles) became impressed with the Hope or Texas model, widely used by frontiersmen. Lieutenant Colonel Joseph E. Johnston, commanding the 1st Cavalry, wrote in 1856 that all the officers who could obtain a Hope saddle used it, "except that they have the California tree instead of Hope's." Who Hope was, where he worked, and exactly what his saddle looked like remains a mystery, but it is quite apparent that it was a modification of the Mexican saddle of the period.

Fig. 65 To attempt to discuss here the Mexican saddle, the "California style" which grew out of it, and the numerous frontier modifications of both, would exceed the scope of this work. Suffice it to say that the Hope saddle had permanently attached skirts, fairly long and with rounded bottoms—long enough, in fact, to preclude the need for sweat leathers. Its seat was broad and of smooth dressed leather, its cantle very low, and its pommel capped by a small, flat horn. It probably had a Mexican woven cinch, drawn up and secured with a latigo or cincha strap, and bent wood stirrups, fitted out with leather hoods (*tapaderos*) with trailing ends. Long leather thongs hung down from points near the pommel and cantle. Typically, it used no iron in its construction, which made for lightness and comparative ease of repair in the field, features of considerable importance to cavalrymen scattered widely across the Indian frontier.

The Chief of Ordnance reported in 1857 that his department ·had caused to

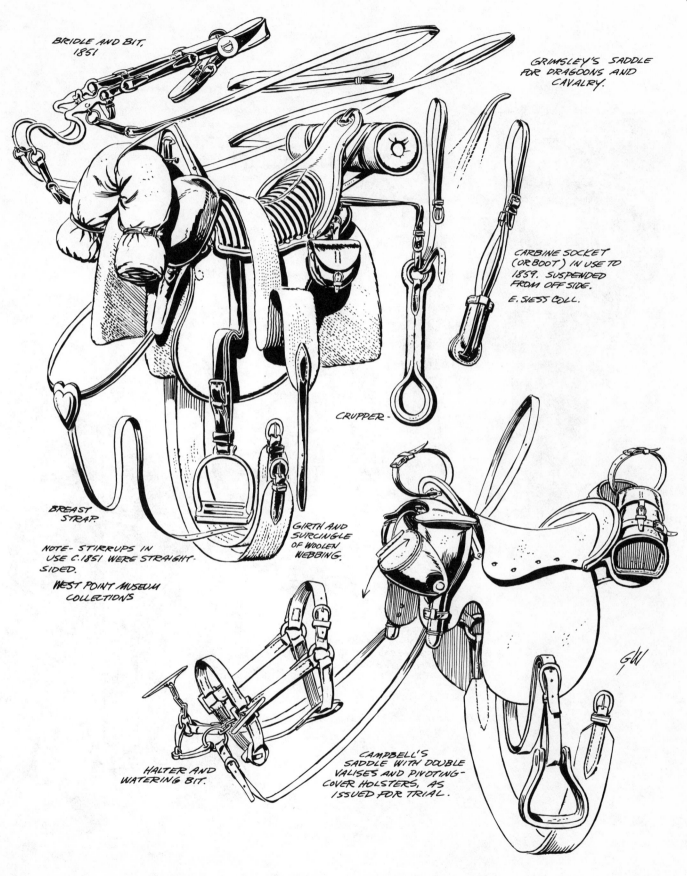

BRIDLE AND BIT, 1851

GRIMSLEY'S SADDLE FOR DRAGOONS AND CAVALRY.

CARBINE SOCKET (OR BOOT) IN USE TO 1859. SUSPENDED FROM OFF SIDE. E. SIESS COLL.

CRUPPER.

BREAST STRAP

NOTE- STIRRUPS IN USE C.1851 WERE STRAIGHT- SIDED.

WEST POINT MUSEUM COLLECTIONS

GIRTH AND SURCINGLE OF WOOLEN WEBBING.

HALTER AND WATERING BIT.

CAMPBELL'S SADDLE WITH DOUBLE VALISES AND PIVOTING- COVER HOLSTERS, AS ISSUED FOR TRIAL.

Fig. 63. Grimsley and Campbell saddles.

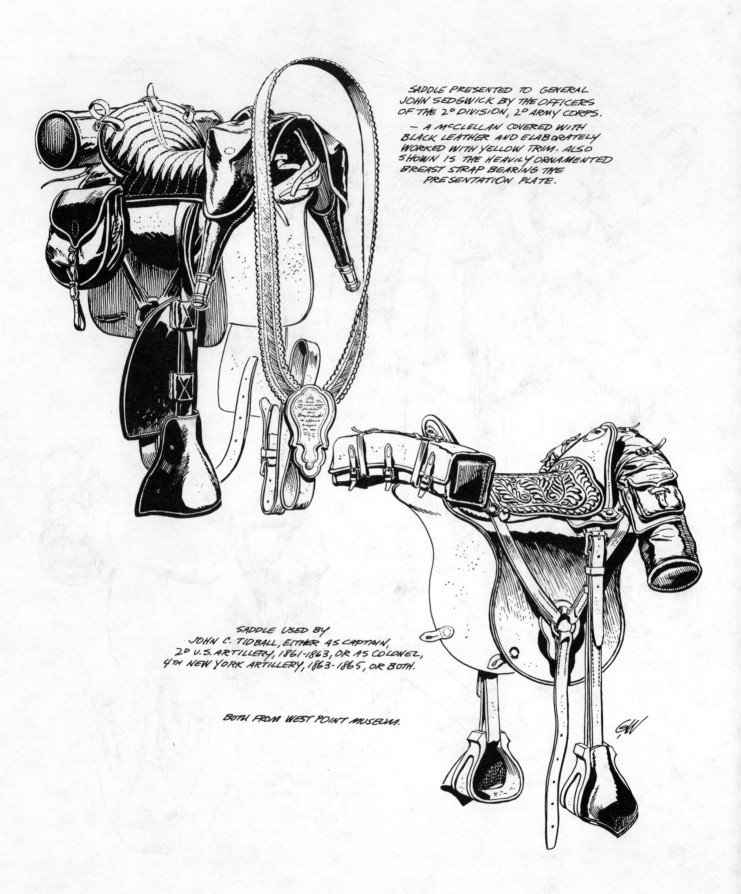

SADDLE PRESENTED TO GENERAL JOHN SEDGWICK BY THE OFFICERS OF THE 2º DIVISION, 2º ARMY CORPS.

— A McCLELLAN COVERED WITH BLACK LEATHER AND ELABORATELY WORKED WITH YELLOW TRIM. ALSO SHOWN IS THE HEAVILY ORNAMENTED BREAST STRAP BEARING THE PRESENTATION PLATE.

SADDLE USED BY JOHN C. TIDBALL, EITHER AS CAPTAIN, 2º U.S. ARTILLERY, 1861-1863, OR AS COLONEL, 4TH NEW YORK ARTILLERY, 1863-1865, OR BOTH.

BOTH FROM WEST POINT MUSEUM.

Fig. 64. Variant Civil War saddles.

be manufactured and put into service several hundred sets "of the pattern known as Hope's saddle and much used in Texas . . . The use of these [that is, the Campbell, Hope, and Jones models] and the Grimsley equipment in actual service will afford the means of comparing their actual merits." So far as is known, the Hope saw service only in two companies of the 2nd Cavalry. It was procured from Rice & Childress, San Antonio, Texas.

Reports of ordnance items issued Union cavalry regiments in California and some other parts of the West often include "Ranger saddles." These are believed to have been California style saddles, locally procured and probably not governed by government specifications. Almost certainly they had low cantles and flat horns on their pommels, woven cinches, and bent wood stirrups covered by *tapaderos*. It is possible that some or all were fitted with saddle covers (*mochilas*) to which leather pouches or saddle bags were attached.

William E. Jones was a 1st lieutenant in the Regiment of Mounted Riflemen. In 1854, having developed a new model of saddle tree (patented 13 June 1854, No. 11,068), he presented one for the inspection of the Secretary of War and offered to furnish twenty-four of the same kind for experiment. In August of the same year the Quartermaster General asked Jones to call on him about the offer. What Jones had developed was a pair of specially fashioned spring steel plates hinged together at both ends and also connected by an adjustable steel bar. The plates in effect formed a saddle tree capable of being made wider or narrower to fit the back of any horse. Jones also claimed it was more durable and lighter than the ordinary tree.

Perhaps as a result of his talks with the Quartermaster General, Jones took out on 17 April 1855 an Additional Improvement (No. 121) on his original patent. Further negotiations followed, of which we know little, until sometime in 1857 or early 1858 about 300 of his saddles were purchased and issued. Exactly what the Jones saddle as a whole looked like, and how it differed from the Grimsley in details other than the steel tree, can only be guessed at. In all probability it bore a close resemblance to the regulation model.

The Jones saddle was given quite a bit of informal trial from 1855 on and received much praise. Unfortunately, the mechanical resources of the day were inadequate to meet the tests of hard usage and too many broke down in the service.

It was at this time also that the McClellan saddle was introduced experimentally and the Campbell saddle withdrawn, leaving four patterns in service by the middle of 1858 about which, as the Chief of Ordnance reported, ". . . the reports, as yet received, have not warranted the preference of either to the exclusion of the others." Yet Colonel Craig, the Chief, realized that a single pattern ought to be selected and felt this should be handled "by a board of officers of rank and experience representing each of the five mounted regiments." His recommendation led to the appointment of the 1859 Cavalry Board and to the adoption of the McClellan saddle.

The McClellan Saddle, Model 1859

Figs. 64 and 65

The McClellan, with some modification and more discussion, remained the regulation U.S. cavalry saddle from 1859 until the era of the troop horse ended in World War II. It was also widely used during this time by mounted men of other sorts—officers, artillerymen, teamsters, and the like. It is clearly the most important article of horse furniture to be considered.

This saddle, as is well known, was the development of George B. McClellan, later to become commander-in-chief of the Army. Attempts have been made to minimize the credit due him, but the fact that different features of the saddle were based upon ideas he had gained in his travels on the frontier, in Mexico, and in Europe makes his adaptions of them all the more creditable. McClellan never patented his saddle and probably never profited from its manufacture. He advanced his ideas in October 1856 and was authorized by the Secretary of War to have a model saddle fabricated. This he offered the army for trial. The Ordnance Department bought 170 of his saddles at the same time it procured the Jones pattern and issued these on an experimental basis. They were favorably received and brought to the attention of the 1859 Cavalry Board. This Board considered the merits of all the saddles given a trial in the field and, after recommending certain alterations, selected the McClellan as regulation. It is described in detail in the *Ordnance Manual* for 1862.

McClellan himself wrote that his basic model was the "Prussian Cavalry Equipment," the tree of which was known as the "Hungarian." However, he suggested removal of unnecessary iron, reduction of the height of the cantle, use of only one utensil pouch, adoption of saddle bags as used by the French Chasseurs d'Afrique, and several other changes. Furthermore, Secretary of War Davis added advice about using a hair or woolen yarn girth, and avoiding steel stirrups. When the model saddle was made it so closely resembled the Campbell saddle that its inventor complained about patent infringement. There can be little doubt that McClellan was well aware of the good features of the Campbell saddle and adopted them, but he did not use any of the features specifically mentioned in Campbell's patents. All in all, the McClellan was a government saddle created out of the ideas of many men and considerable experimentation.

The McClellan's side bars were joined to moderately high and gently sloping pommel and cantle by glue, rivets, and two iron "arcs." The whole was first painted with a coat of white lead then covered with rawhide, put on wet and sewed with thongs of the same. The space between the side bars was left open. The rawhide, when dry, produced a smooth surface and served to strengthen the tree.

There were three mortised holes for straps in the cantle and one at the top of the pommel. Around this latter was a shield of sheet brass that listed the size of the saddle and, later, its maker's name and date of manufacture. There were two staples and two rings fixed on the front and four staples, two rings, and a saddle bag stud on the rear. Girth straps passed over and were stapled to the pommel and cantle arcs, and met in a common D-ring on both sides. From

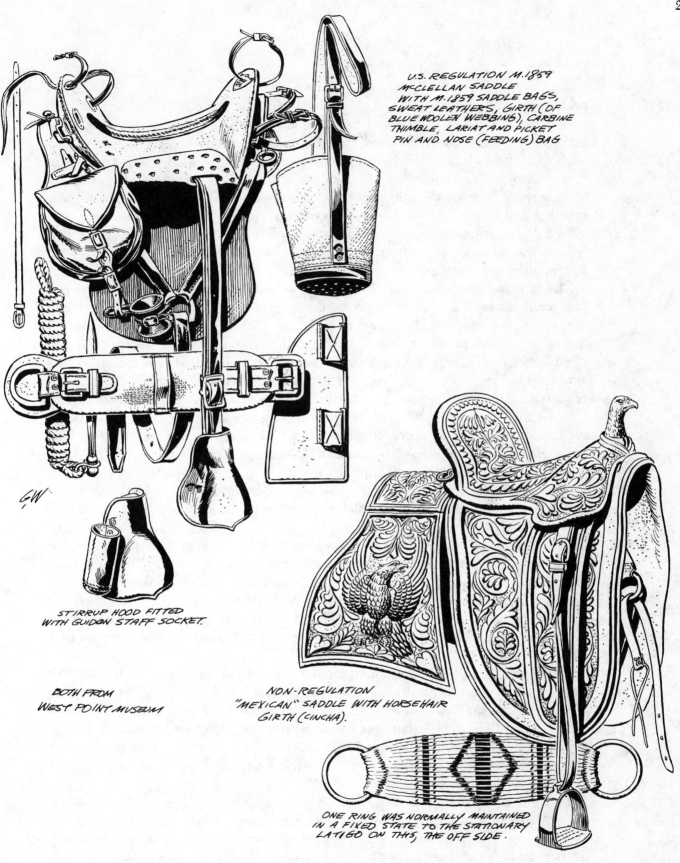

239

U.S. REGULATION M.1859
McCLELLAN SADDLE
WITH M.1859 SADDLE BAGS,
SWEAT LEATHERS, GIRTH (OF
BLUE WOOLEN WEBBING), CARBINE
THIMBLE, LARIAT AND PICKET
PIN AND NOSE (FEEDING) BAG

STIRRUP HOOD FITTED
WITH GUIDON STAFF SOCKET.

BOTH FROM
WEST POINT MUSEUM

NON-REGULATION
"MEXICAN" SADDLE WITH HORSEHAIR
GIRTH (CINCHA).

ONE RING WAS NORMALLY MAINTAINED
IN A FIXED STATE TO THE STATIONARY
LATIGO ON THIS, THE OFF SIDE.

Fig. 65. McClellan and Mexican saddles.

each ring hung a girth billet. The girth or cinch, 4.5 inches wide and of blue woolen webbing, was buckled to the off girth billet. The near girth billet, considerably longer, was first passed through the ring on the girth, then doubled back over the D-ring itself, then drawn up tight and buckled fast to the girth.

A skirt of thick harness leather was fastened to each side of the saddle by brass screws; it was as a rule about 15 inches wide and the same high, slightly rounded and shaped. It lay under the girth straps and a slit on either side permitted the stirrup loops to pass through. Unlike the Grimsley, the McClellan saddle was not issued with the small inner skirts which lay under the girth straps, although these are often found on officers' models.

The stirrups provided with the McClellan saddle were one of its more distinctive features. They were made from one piece of hickory or oak, bent into shape and covered with hoods of thick harness leather. These hoods protected the rider's feet from mud, rain, and vegetation but they soon became the object of criticism. The principal objections were that the hood was too short and was set too close to the stirrup. While the Ordnance Department did nothing about this defect during our period, the soldiers often did. One method was to connect the hood to the front of the stirrup by a strip of bent metal, thus pushing it out in front and preventing the rider's toe from becoming wedged. The same end was accomplished by inserting a leather strip to block the toe. Another trick was to cut holes through the hoods in front, and still another was to remove the hoods altogether.

The regulation McClellan saddle, then, was issued with its seat open and covered solely with rawhide, and with no brass molding on the pommel or cantle. "Fenders"—triangular shaped sweat-guards—were provided for attachment to the stirrup leathers since U.S. cavalrymen, wearing their trousers over their boots, needed protection from the horses' lather. There were six straps provided for attaching coats or blankets to pommel and cantle, while a specially designed pair of leather saddle bags took the place of the valise. These were kept in place by a stud behind the cantle and by being buckled to the rear edge of the skirts.

Part of the McClellan's equipment included a carbine thimble, merely a leather ring with a strap and buckle that allowed it to be fastened to the D-ring on the off side of the saddle; a blue wool webbing surcingle; and a crupper (but no breast strap). The McClellan was issued in three sizes, called Nos. 1, 2, and 3, governed by the length of the seat. Considerable variation from these standard dimensions, however, could be found in saddles produced under contract during the Civil War.

There is some reason to believe that the McClellan saddles first purchased for experiment were entirely covered with fair tanned leather over the rawhide. The Cavalry Equipment Board of 1859 recommended that they be "of russet leather throughout" but the War Department, probably for reasons of economy, decided to use rawhide alone on the seat. The results of this decision are well known: often the rawhide split and the seat then became most uncomfortable. One Civil War veteran noted that, after a hard day's ride, the saddle was not only covered with rawhide but filled with it as well.

One of the most common alterations made in the regulation saddle was to cover the rawhide with dressed leather, sometimes completely but more commonly in the early years only the pommel and cantle. This was a comparatively easy task that could be performed by any saddler. At times all the saddles of a troop or even regiment were so covered and those purchased by officers usually came this way. Following the Civil War the Ordnance Department gradually adopted the practice of covering the saddle with dressed leather. Another way to overcome the discomfort was to use a leather seat cover, often padded and quilted, like the seat of the Grimsley saddle. This, of course, covered the opening in the seat. Officers' saddles usually had brass moldings on pommels and cantles.

The McClellan was not issued with pistol holsters since, by 1859, the soldier was carrying his revolver on his person.

Artillery Saddles

The artilleryman in this period used a markedly different saddle from the cavalryman. It came in two types: the driver's saddle, used on the left or "near" horse of a team, and the valise saddle, on the other (the "off") horse of the team. The latter was intended to carry the driver's valise, but could be ridden in an emergency. Outriders such as sergeants and musicians were authorized to draw cavalry equipments, complete—six per battery in 1854. This practice continued throughout our period.

See R.I. Light Arty., 1861

The driver's saddle in use in 1851 had a very low pommel and cantle, bound with brass. To each side was attached an almost rectangular skirt, about 15 inches wide and 24.5 inches long. Underneath this were quilted pads stuffed with hair and lined with linen, rendering a saddle blanket unnecessary. The girth was leather and the stirrups were iron. The saddle was fitted with six iron loops: three on the pommel (one to engage a strap attaching the collar and two for holsters) and three on the cantle (one for the crupper and two for cloak straps).

The valise saddle of this pattern was a considerably reduced version of the driver's, being only 9 inches from pommel to cantle. It had no stirrups, but was fitted with four iron loops and a hook on the pommel for the rein. The valise, made of black bridle leather, was 18.5 inches long and 7.25 inches in diameter, and was held on by two straps.

About 1861 new patterns of artillery driver's and valise saddles were adopted. The former was given a modified Grimsley tree with high pommel and cantle, although it did not have as pronounced shoulders as its dragoon ancestor and its cantle lacked the ducktail curl at the top. It had no padding (thus requiring a blanket), but retained the brass binding on pommel and cantle. Its leather skirts were long and somewhat concave on the sides; its girth was leather. Most important, it was given a quilted leather seat. The model can easily be distinguished by its two brass escutcheons, one inside the pommel indicating the size and the other, morticed, inside the cantle, marked with "USA" entwined. It appears to have been a more comfortable saddle than the McClellan.

The valise saddle resembled the driver's model except that it was smaller and had a brass hook on the front to hold the off-horse's reins, and straps front and back permitting attachment to the draft harness. There were two staples on the front and three on the rear. The girth was narrow—not quite 1.75 inches—but the other attachments held the saddle in place. The valise was not altered.

One of the peculiarities of the valise saddle is the rarity today of an actual valise despite the existence of numerous saddles. This has been attributed to their sale after the war as workmen's kit bags, much as gas mask carriers were sold to school boys after World War I.

Officers' Saddles

Since the officer could and did purchase his own saddle, and since the whims and theories among horsemen on the subject of gear were manifold, the variety of saddles used were limitless. Grimsley also made private saddles for officers and in attempting to satisfy the individual whims of his customers was forced into hybrid combinations without end. In some cases the divergence from regulation might lie only in an ornamental stitching on the seat, in others it might take the form of ordering a militarized stock saddle with a horn on the pommel. Officers evidently preferred the artillery driver's saddle to the McClellan and used it when they could.

As mentioned earlier, officers' McClellans were usually covered, in part at least, with dressed leather and carried brass moldings. Many officers preferred the valise to the saddle bags and its use on a McClellan required removing the stud behind the cantle. To the collector of saddles such changes from issue models will be obvious although it is well to remember that they could have been made long after the military life of a saddle had ceased.

It will be enough here to describe one deluxe model presentation saddle as an illustration of what can be expected in this category. In the West Point Museum are the saddle and accessories presented to Major General John Sedg-*Fig. 64* wick by the officers of the 2nd Division, 2nd Corps. The saddle is a McClellan, leather covered and brass bound. The blue cloth shabraque, with its gold lace and embroidered eagle, is regulation. Most of the leather is black trimmed with yellow cord or intricately worked leather of the same color. There are both saddle bags and a valise, each of special design; a heavily ornamented bridle, reins, and breast strap, the last bearing a brass presentation plate in place of the usual heart-shaped ornament. Finally, there is a pair of pistol holsters with brass tips and leather covers that match the other furniture.

Speaking of the McClellan saddle, Roemer wrote in 1863,

A saddle so extensively used could not fail to engage the attention of inventors, who, designing further improvements, have devised various changes and modifications, which have not always bettered the original. Most of these intended improvements are nothing but old contrivances revived, and in no instance have we seen or heard of any invention involving a new principle, except, perhaps, one recently brought out by Messrs. Peck Brothers, saddlers in New York; and even in this case, we are by no means sure that a careful research will not discover its prototype among the saddles of the middle ages, or even of later times. The plan consists in the application of two spring-steel guards, slightly padded and covered with leather, and so placed as to brace the thighs of the rider, and thus, as it is claimed, prevent him from being thrown forward by any motion of the horse, however violent; . . . . There has not yet been time to thoroughly test the merit of this arrangement . . . .

Pack Saddles

Pack saddles used in the military service seem to have been of two general types: the pattern adopted by the Ordnance Department for the transport of the 12-pounder mountain howitzer Model 1841 and its ammunition, and the types used by the Quartermaster Department to transport general supplies in country too difficult for wagons.

The mountain artillery pack saddle and its harness are described in *Ordnance Manual* 1862, pages 151–154. Briefly, it consisted of two wooden arcs connected by two wooden "transoms" and a pad of webbing and leather. Both arcs and transoms were notched to hold the gun tube and its trunnions, which was placed lengthwise on the animal. The rig was fitted with billets for lashing straps and for the three girths used. The trail rode in the same fashion as the tube while the wheels and ammunition boxes were lashed to the sides of the saddle. All animals wore breeching and breast strap, and the bridle was fitted with winkers.*

The cargo pack saddle was based upon the single-rigged "sawbuck" type used widely in the West. It is illustrated in the Horstmann edition of the 1851 dress regulations (plate 24). It was shaped something like a riding saddle with high, straight pommel and cantle, sometimes covered with rawhide and sometimes of plain wood. It sat on a broad stuffed leather pad and was fastened with a single, wide hair girth and cinch strap. This saddle used a leather breast-strap, breeching, and lash-strap. Since the supplies carried on the saddle were of all sizes, shapes, and weights, real skill was required in arranging the items and lashing them to the saddle.

Fig. 66

The government pack saddle was made by Thornton Grimsley of St. Louis. Opinions about it varied widely. Captain Randolph B. Marcy, who wrote *The Prairie Traveler,* regarded it as the best saddle he had ever seen. Harvey Riley, Superintendent of the Government Corral at Washington, D.C. during the Civil War, thought it "a worthless thing." He greatly preferred the Mexican pack saddle which was haphazardly made of leather without a tree, stuffed with hay, and was very large, covering almost entirely the animal's back.

Riley's opinion eventually won out and the cargo saddle generally used toward the end of our period was the *aparejo,* an improved version of the Mexican type. Actually it was a rather complicated device, comprising six parts. First to go on

---

* Also termed "blinders" or "blinkers."

the pack mule was a canvas lined, three-ply blanket called the "corona." Next came a standard army blanket, folded to fit exactly over the corona; it was the same blanket used by the packers at night. On top of this came the leather *aparejo*, carefully stuffed with hay. To facings on each of its sides was laced a wide leather crupper to keep the load from sliding forward. Finally, on top of all was placed the "hammer cloth" (the Mexican *sobre jalma*), made of canvas and fitted with a 20-inch long stock on each side to which the load was lashed. A single cinch with latigo strap held the saddle together and on the animal.

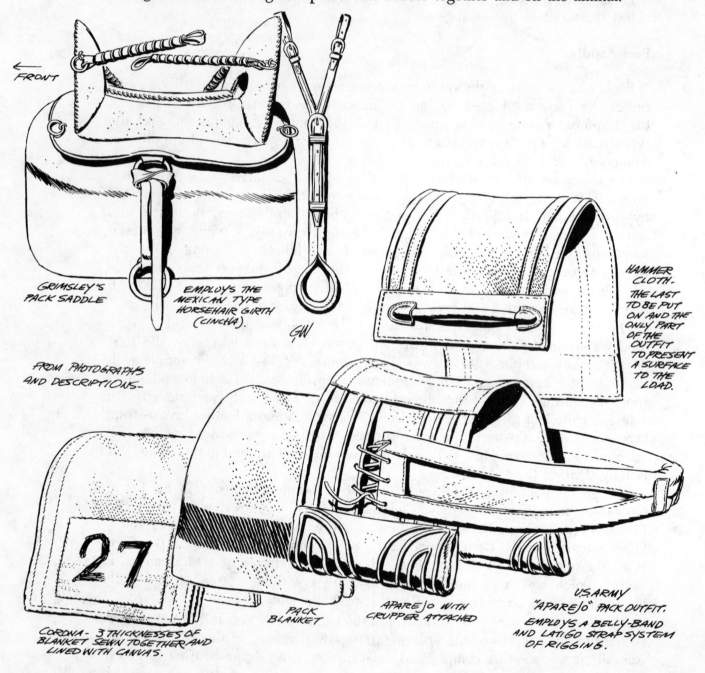

← FRONT

GRIMSLEY'S PACK SADDLE

EMPLOYS THE MEXICAN TYPE HORSEHAIR GIRTH (CINCHA).

FROM PHOTOGRAPHS AND DESCRIPTIONS—

HAMMER CLOTH. THE LAST TO BE PUT ON AND THE ONLY PART OF THE OUTFIT TO PRESENT A SURFACE TO THE LOAD.

27

CORONA — 3 THICKNESSES OF BLANKET SEWN TOGETHER AND LINED WITH CANVAS.

PACK BLANKET

APAREJO WITH CRUPPER ATTACHED

U.S. ARMY "APAREJO" PACK OUTFIT. EMPLOYS A BELLY-BAND AND LATIGO STRAP SYSTEM OF RIGGING.

Fig. 66. Pack saddles.

Bits and Bridles

The variety of bits, even when confined to the few years of this study, seems to be endless. As with saddles, styles advertised as having this or that newly discovered advantage were continuously coming on the market, often to enjoy a few years of popularity, then to disappear. Then there were the different bits designed for riding and driving, for training horses, for hard and soft mouths, for mounts of one sort or another, and so forth. The subject of bits presents no great problem if it can be confined to regulation U.S. Army models, but, as in all forms of accouterments, this would omit many kinds that were in fairly common military use at the time.

Fig. 67

The terminology of the bit, bridle, and related harness is treated briefly in Plate 67. Since horsemanship is a rare accomplishment today, it may be well to add a few explanatory remarks on these accouterments. The bit and reins, of course, are the rider's or driver's principal means of controlling both the speed and direction of his horse. All bits have some form of mouth piece which rests on the "bars" of the horse's mouth, that is, the right and left portions of his jaw, lying between his incisors and his two rows of molars, that are devoid of teeth. The horse's tongue lies in a groove between the bars and hence underneath the mouth piece of the bit. Under his chin, just above his lower lip, lies a depression called the "chin groove" or "curb groove." It is on the bars, the tongue, or the chin groove, or all, that more or less severe pressure is exerted by the bit.

Bits can be arranged under three general classes:

● 1. *Bar bits,* or those with a solid mouth piece that exert no lever action; these exert a minimum pressure on the bars and a maximum on the tongue, and are the lightest form of bit, used for driving rather than saddle horses.

● 2. *Snaffle bits* are those with jointed mouth pieces and no cheek pieces through which a lever action can be obtained. Here the pressure is on the tongue and bars alike, and the power applied to the reins is conveyed unaltered to the horse's mouth. The snaffle is the oldest and most common form of bit, especially for riding, and is nearly as light on the horse's mouth as the bar bit.

● 3. *Curb bits,* by which a lever action is secured by means of cheek pieces and a curb chain or strap. This leverage increases the amount of pressure that can be brought to bear on the bars of the mouth. Curb bits were made in various forms, some being designed to produce pain on the roof of the mouth as well as on the bars. The upper branch of the cheek piece is always straight, but the lower branch can be straight or curved.

Some of the specialized styles of bit in use in the 1850's and 1860's are explained in the glossary. One important form was the "bit and bridoon" which meant a snaffle and a curb bit used in combination which required, of course, two reins. This was thought to be the most humane and effective bitting for all classes of riding that called for cross-country work and sudden changes of gait. It also required a relatively great degree of skill and training on the part of the rider and rarely found favor in the American service.

Since a soldier was required to ride with his reins in only one hand, his horse was trained to change direction in response to pressure of the reins on one or another side of his neck and of the legs upon his flanks. A horse so trained was said to be "bridle-wise." In driving, on the contrary, the horse's head was pulled by the reins toward the direction desired.

We have only an imperfect idea of the regulation cavalry bit in use prior to the adoption of the Grimsley saddle in 1847; indeed, we cannot be certain if a new model bit was introduced that year. But it seems reasonable that the "Pattern 1841" horse equipment was in use and that it comprised both curb and snaffle bits which could be worn separately or together. The former was made of burnished iron and its only brass members were the escutcheons bearing the national coat of arms, riveted to the branches to cover the points where the branches join the mouthpiece. The lower parts of the branches formed an elaborate "S" curve, while the upper parts were almost triangular in shape. The lower branches were round except in the upper portion of the "S" where they flattened out considerably. This bit was carried on a simple bridle of black leather without nose band. The curb bit came in three sizes and with three varieties of port.

The Pattern 1841 snaffle bit, when used, was attached to the squares of a halter and was made of burnished iron. Both bridle and halter had to be used when the curb and snaffle bits were put on simultaneously.

The Pattern 1841 cavalry accouterments are described in detail in the *Ordnance Manual* of 1841. They are included in this study since they probably saw some use in the Civil War.

In 1847 or earlier, Brevet Lieutenant Colonel Charles Augustus May submitted a new dragoon bit, and it was adopted by the Cavalry Board of that year. This bit is illustrated in the Horstmann edition of the 1851 dress regulations (plate 24). It was fitted with two sets of rein rings and so eliminated the snaffle bit. It was made of iron, but brass plated on the outside, away from the horse's mouth. It was fixed to the same curb bridle as used earlier, and the halter, when worn, was used solely for tying the horse.

The branches of this dragoon bit were flattened and it had a strengthening cross bar connecting the branches at the bottom. This was the article referred to in Civil War times and later as the "Grimsley bit" or "Old Dragoon bit." It was also the bit prescribed on 15 August 1855 (GO 13) for the two new regiments of cavalry.

The halter adopted in 1847 was the same pattern furnished the 1st Dragoons in 1839 and it continued in service almost without change into the 20th century.

A new cavalry bridle was adopted in 1859 which was intended for use with a halter. The headstall was fitted with a single-rein curb bit of blued iron or tin alloy, whose S-shaped lower branches swept straight back from the junction of the mouthpiece. A second or watering bit was provided for attachment to the halter; this was a snaffle bit with its own reins. According to specifications, the curb bit had "2 bosses (cast iron) bearing the number and letter of the regiment and the letter of the company, riveted to the branches with 4 rivets."

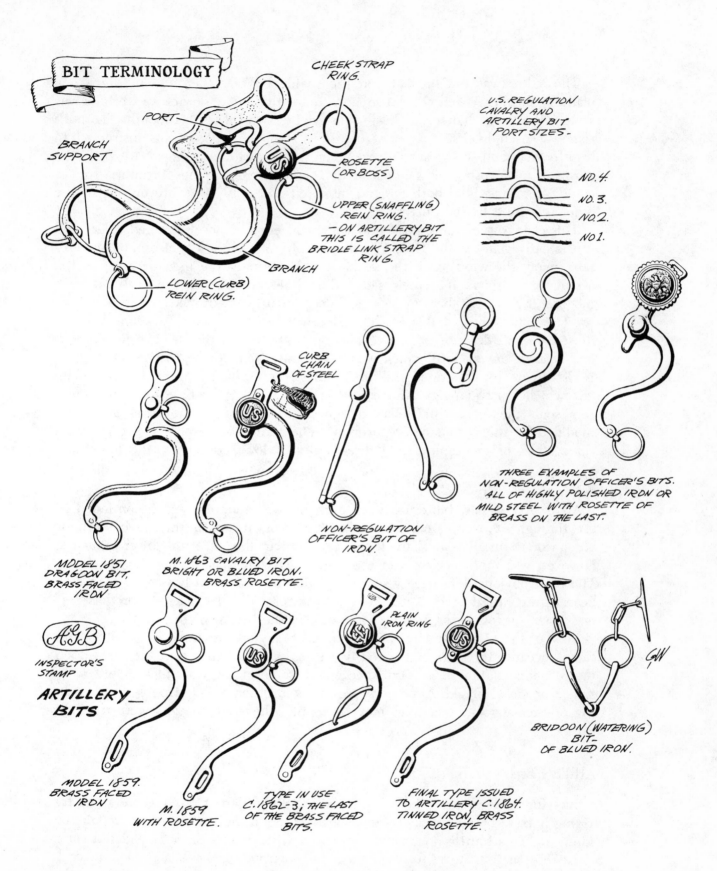

BIT TERMINOLOGY

PORT

CHEEK STRAP RING.

BRANCH SUPPORT

ROSETTE (OR BOSS)

UPPER (SNAFFLING) REIN RING.
— ON ARTILLERY BIT THIS IS CALLED THE BRIDLE LINK STRAP RING.

BRANCH

LOWER (CURB) REIN RING.

U.S. REGULATION CAVALRY AND ARTILLERY BIT PORT SIZES.

NO. 4.
NO. 3.
NO. 2.
NO. 1.

CURB CHAIN OF STEEL

THREE EXAMPLES OF NON-REGULATION OFFICER'S BITS. ALL OF HIGHLY POLISHED IRON OR MILD STEEL WITH ROSETTE OF BRASS ON THE LAST.

NON-REGULATION OFFICER'S BIT OF IRON.

MODEL 1851 DRAGOON BIT, BRASS FACED IRON

M. 1863 CAVALRY BIT BRIGHT OR BLUED IRON, BRASS ROSETTE.

INSPECTOR'S STAMP

ARTILLERY BITS

MODEL 1859. BRASS FACED IRON

M. 1859 WITH ROSETTE.

TYPE IN USE C. 1862-3; THE LAST OF THE BRASS FACED BITS.

PLAIN IRON RING

FINAL TYPE ISSUED TO ARTILLERY C. 1864. TINNED IRON, BRASS ROSETTE.

BRIDOON (WATERING) BIT- OF BLUED IRON.

Fig. 67. Bits.

The halter was put on first and the snaffle bit was then added to make a watering bridle. When the horse was to be ridden in service the bridle was attached over the halter, the horse thus having two bits in his mouth. The curb rein was used by itself on most occasions, but the trooper was instructed to transfer his hand to the snaffle rein when practical to ease the mouth from the curb bit, when using his saber in action, and when jumping. A trained soldier could, of course, hold both reins in his hand and apply pressure on one or the other rein by a twist of his wrist.

This changing of reins was bothersome to new and poorly trained riders and in the early years of the Civil War the cavalryman tended to use only his curb rein, many throwing away the snaffle bit. Eventually the men became, as the saying was, "shook into their saddles" and learned to use the curb bit with moderation, but not before many a horse's mouth was ruined.

(The appearance of this Model 1859 curb bit is open to question. A bit is illustrated and described (plate 6 and pp. 149–152) in McClellan's *Regulations and Instructions* of 1861 which would certainly seem to be the one, but there is also a curb bit illustrated and described in the *Ordnance Manual,* 1862 (plate 22) which has equal rights for consideration. It seems possible that the former represents the bit as McClellan designed or adapted it, the latter as it was modified by the Ordnance Department. The former seems to have come with three styles of mouthpiece and three styles of lower branches; the latter had four styles of mouthpiece, with two heights of upper branches and "all alike below the mouthpiece.")

About 1863 a new pattern cavalry curb bit was adopted, which continued in use throughout our period. Like its predecessor, it was a single-rein curb of blued iron or tin alloy. In shape it was very similar; the "S" of the lower branches, however, was more perfect and the rein rings were placed more to the front. The most obvious difference was the addition of cast brass bosses on each side bearing the raised block letter "US" in a circle. The bit, like its predecessor, was issued in four sizes, varying primarily in the height of the port.

Most of the M1859 and M1863 bits found today appear to be bright steel, but this is because their original blued finish has worn off in use. After 1868, upon the recommendation of an Ordnance board, some of the war stock of bits were tinned or nickel plated. Apparently the issue curb chain gave trouble by stretching or breaking and examples may be found where curb straps were put into use.

Artillery Bits

Bits for artillery draft horses were markedly different from those used for riding horses. There appear to have been in use in our period three regulation kinds, unless a fourth, developed during the Civil War, can be considered such.

In 1851 the bit in use for the near horse was probably still a single-rein curb with straight branches, each having an eye at the top of the cheek strap of the headstall, an eye at the mouthpiece, and a third eye at the bottom. Although only one rein was used, it could be attached to either of the two lower eyes. The bit was iron, left bright, and came in three sizes.

The off horse was given a snaffle bit. Both bits were fastened to black leather bridles without nose bands, and could be removed for attachment to a halter, also provided. The off-horse bridle was fitted with a coupling strap that passed through both rings of the snaffle and formed, in effect, a curb strap. These bridles are described in *Ordnance Manual,* 1841.

The next edition of the *Manual* (1850) describes a new bit which was worn by both horses of a team. It was a single rein curb with straight branches, but with an eye or ring at the mouthpiece. It was made of iron which was tinned. It came in three sizes with different degrees of severity of the port.

A third and quite different artillery bit was made regulation about 1859. Its lower branches had an S-shaped curve and it was brass-plated on the outside. At the top were slits to receive the check straps and a hole for the curb chain. At the mouthpiece were attached rings, while near the bottom were slits; both were designed to hold reins although, as before, only one rein was employed. There was a cross bar at the extreme bottom between the lower branches. This bit had no bosses on its sides although the ends of the mouthpiece, passing through the branches, were rounded and plain. This bit is described in the *Ordnance Manual* of 1862.

At some time (still uncertain) during the early Civil War two changes were made in this pattern of bit. The hole for the curb chain was enlarged into a slit for a curb strap and the raised letters "US," or "USA" intertwined, were added to the rounded ends of the mouthpiece. "USA" types made under contract by Frazee & Co. and Barclay, both of Newark, are common and indicate war manufacture. This new type is also interesting as indicating the use of leather curb straps by the artillery before their adoption by cavalry.

A pattern of artillery bit often found is very similar in shape to the kind just described but is heavily tinned and has brass bosses on its sides bearing the raised block letters "US" in a circle—similar to the M1863 cavalry bit. There is also a slot for a curb strap. Some were made at Watervliet Arsenal. It is believed that this is a post-Civil War pattern, possibly experimental.

Officers Bits

There was, of course, no distinctive bit prescribed for officers anymore than there was a distinctive saddle. One often hears artillery bits described as "officer's bits," possibly due to labelling in Bannerman's catalogs, although they were never called such at the time. Actually, to judge from Civil War photographs, mounted officers used every style of bit imaginable, from regulation to civilian styles, from very plain to very fancy. Except to say that the more antique and foreign kinds were rare and that new types like the Shoemaker had not yet come into use, we must let the matter rest.

Bridles and other gear were equally variant. Although most were simple types resembling regulation patterns, one can find nose bands, martingales, breast straps, crossed diagonal cords over the face, and Western braided rawhide rigs in contemporary photographs. It is on officers' bridles that one occasionally finds colored or metallic brow bands and rosettes, although these were not always confined to commissioned personnel.

Officers, as has been said, bought their own horse furniture and were given great leeway in its selection. Under some conditions officers could purchase regulation horse equipments and in 1863 (GO 277, 8 Aug) officers who were required to be mounted temporarily were allowed to draw such equipments from Quartermaster stores on a hand receipt.

Saddle Blankets, Pads, and Housings

See U.S. Staff Officers, 1861–1865

It is always necessary to place some yielding substance between the saddle bars and the horse's back. This may be accomplished by padding the under surface of the bars or by using some form of removable pad or blanket. Padding, common on civilian saddles, is found in the military harness of our period only on certain models of artillery saddle. All other military saddles required a pad or blanket.

Removable pads made of felt or hair were used with some officers' saddles and for a time with the experimental Campbell model, but the saddle blanket was the most common form of protection for the horses of officers and men alike. In its regulation form it was made of closely woven wool, 75 x 65 inches in size, and in 1851 was of plain dark blue color. This blanket was folded over twice and placed on the horse so that its last fold was foremost. It could also be used, opened up, to cover the horse in bad weather or to soften the trooper's bed in the field.

In 1859 the dragoon blanket was given an orange colored border, 3 inches wide, 3 inches from the edge, on two sides, and the letters "U.S." in orange, 6 inches high, in the center. At the same time, a scarlet blanket was adopted for artillery having dark blue borders and letters. A plain gray woolen blanket was also provided for general use.

Saddle pads, worn under saddles, were made of wool, felt, or hair. They were usually edged with leather but otherwise plain, of dark blue color, with the front corners slightly rounded. The average dimensions were about 2 x 4 feet. There is evidence also that volunteer officers sometimes used pads that were somewhat larger, with pointed rear corners like the shabraque about to be described. Presumably such pads carried gold lace borders, devices, and regimental numbers as given below.

After 1851 and until 1855 all mounted officers were authorized to wear a saddle housing or "shabraque" over their saddles made of dark blue cloth, lined with strong canvas or oilcloth. A portion of the cloth covered the seat of the saddle but contained no padding. Enlisted men were not authorized saddle cloths and most officers abandoned them in field service as bothersome and unnecessary.

Shabraques were usually pierced on the top with two slits through which passed the pommel and cantle of the saddle, and by slits on each side through which the stirrup leathers passed. Most were edged with leather and had leather reinforcements front and back of the saddle and below the stirrup leather openings. They also were edged on the outside with strips of gold lace or cloth, and carried insignia in their rear corners, as follows.

General officers.   Two rows of gold lace, the outer one 1⅝ inch and the inner one 2.25 inches wide; gold embroidered eagle with three stars over his head for the Major General Commanding the Army, two for other major generals, and one for brigadier generals. (During the era of the Grimsley saddle it was customary to cut the shabraques of generals and staff officers fuller in front and let them completely cover the saddle holsters.)

General Staff officers except ordnance.   One row of gold lace, one inch wide, no device.

Dragoon field and staff officers.   Edged with patent leather and with one row of gold lace, 1.5 inches wide; gold embroidered regimental number, two inches high.

Dragoon company officers.   The same except the lace and number were made of orange cloth and orange colored silk, respectively.

Mounted Riflemen officers.   The same as dragoons except that for company officers the lace and number (in this case a "1") were made of emerald green cloth and silk.

Light Artillery officers.   The same as dragoon company officers except the lace and regimental number were of scarlet cloth and silk.

Foot Artillery field and staff officers.   A smaller cloth with a row of gold lace, ⅝ inch wide and a scarlet edging; regimental number in gold embroidery.

Infantry field and staff officers.   The same except the edging of the cloth was light blue.

Ordnance officers.   The same except the edging of the cloth was dark blue.

Regimental numbers 1.5 inches high were also placed on the ends of the valise and on the breast strap by officers of dragoons, mounted riflemen, artillery, and infantry.

Although the shabraque was generally discontinued in 1855 it remained in use by general officers throughout the rest of the period, at least for ceremonial occasions. It changed in no essential during that time. All letters and numbers on horse equipments were given up in January 1854 (GO 1).

Other Furniture

Girths

Girths have been mentioned in connection with the various saddles but can be summarized here. Cavalry saddles, as a rule, employed a girth made of woolen webbing, whereas artillery saddles had leather girths. The latter and some of the former were fastened around the barrel of the horse by buckling. Another method involved the use of a long leather strap, or latigo, which was passed back and forth between the quarter strap and cinch rings on the near side, then tightened and tucked under.

The surcingle, also made of woolen webbing, was used to keep a loose blanket on a horse while it was cooling off. But it could supplement the girth by being fastened over the saddle and under the horse's belly. The surcingle was apparently quite commonly employed with the Grimsley saddle.

Stirrups

The McClellan hooded stirrup has already been fully described. One of its early ancestors, the Ringgold dragoon stirrup of the 1840's, was made of wrought iron, japanned black. Its sides were slightly curved and its bar, or tread, was roughed on the upper side.

In 1847 the dragoon was given cast brass stirrups with sides a little wider at the top than the bottom. The treads were almost rectangular in shape and divided into three sections. Their overall height was 6.25 inches. About the same time artillery drivers received somewhat similar brass stirrups. These were shorter (almost 5.5 inches overall) and had a solid, almost rectangular tread, roughed on top, but their shape was that of the dragoon model. In the West Point Museum is a pattern brass stirrup engraved on the bottom: "US Model 1863. 1 pt zinc, 2 pts copper. 1¼ lbs." It closely resembles the earlier model except that the ends of the treads are slightly larger and more rounded.

Stirrups could be equipped with guidon rests or cups on the off side as required. These were made of leather and either strapped to metal stirrups or rivetted to leather hoods.

Picket Pins and Ropes

These were made of iron, painted black, and were 14 inches long with a pronounced swell about a third of the way from the point. Pointed at one end, they had a figure-8-shaped ring on the other to which the lariat was fastened. Several more advanced models of picket pin were developed after the Civil War which should not be confused with this type. The rope (or "lariat") was made of hemp and was thirty feet long.

A picket pin was used when no picket line could be set up and no corral was available. The historian of the 9th New York Cavalry, however, wrote that the troopers of his regiment discarded their pins and ropes as useless.

Saddle Bags and Valises

As mentioned earlier, the cloth and leather valise was a regulation accessory of the Grimsley dragoon saddle and continued as such until 1859. Yet saddle bags were in use long before that. In April of 1851 the Quartermaster General authorized the issue of eighty-five of them to Company K, 1st Dragoons, at Fort Leavenworth. He wrote Brevet Major J.H. Carleton, the company commander, that he was sending these, adding:

> I agree with you in opinion as to the relative merits of saddle bags and valises for campaigning but Dragoon Officers, it seems, think otherwise, and have preferred the valise, establishing it as the regulation equipment.

Since this supply was found in stock at the Clothing Establishment in Philadelphia, there is reason to believe that saddle bags may have seen even earlier service in the army.

No indication is found of further issue of saddle bags for several years, although the Quartermaster General instructed that the stock on hand in Philadelphia be retained "as they are sometimes required in Texas and New Mexico."

The Model 1859 McClellan saddle bags comprised two pouches of black leather sewed to a "seat." Each pouch was about 9 inches wide at its maximum dimension, and 10 inches high. It had gussets on the sides, two compartments inside with the larger compartment closed by covers laced with thongs. There was a single flap held by a strap and buckle. Straps on top of the bags fitted into staples behind the cantle; straps on their bottom buckled to the skirts.

Saddle bags supplied to officers by commercial houses differed from the above in both size and design. Some of the larger models had leather handles sewn on top of each pouch to facilitate carrying dismounted.

Forage Bags

These were not commonly issued in the American service. In this connection the Quartermaster General wrote on 20 May 1854:

> Forage bags are provided out of the appropriations for the Quartermasters Department. They are used by Cavalry, on scouting parties, for transporting two or three days supply of grain, and have usually been procured from New Orleans or Saint Louis. Their particular capacity and make I am unable to give you, and wish you therefore to consult in regard to them with some experienced Cavalry Officer, if there are any such in or near Philadelphia . . . Forage bags should hold about two bushels of corn or oats.

Nose Bags

All mounted men were supplied with a strong, white linen or cotton duck nose bag with a leather bottom and headstrap. It was unmarked and was carried when not in use tied somewhere convenient on the saddle.

Carbine Boots and Thimbles

The boot in use in 1851, and described in the dress regulations of that year, probably dated from 1847. It consisted of a small leather cup, or "boot," attached to a double strap; a brass ring on this strap fitted to a staple on the off side of the saddle near the pommel. The soldier placed the muzzle of his musketoon into the boot, then lashed the butt by means of another strap or let it hang from his shoulder sling. This device took care of the Model 1847 musketoon and appears to have remained in service until 1859. It was, of course, removed when the trooper carried his weapon slung on his back or in a saddle holster.

With the coming of the Sharps carbine a simpler device was issued as part of the McClellan saddle. This was a leather "thimble," about 2.5 inches high and large enough to accept the carbine barrel. It was buckled to the D-ring on the off side of the saddle by means of a single strap.

The larger carbine "sockets" and full "boots" came after our period and saw no use in the Civil War.

Draft Harness

Field carriages for artillery up to the 12-pounder gun and 32-pounder howitzer were normally drawn by three 2-horse teams. Because of their use and construction, such carriages required a harness different in several respects from that of common wagons. The principal differences lay in the fact that a driver was supplied for each team and that the wheel horses (those next to the limbers) supported the pole directly, while the traces of leading horses were attached to those of the horses in rear instead of to leading bars (whiffle trees).

The principal parts of artillery draft (spelled "draught" a century ago) harness in 1851 were the leather collar and iron hames, traces with their chains and supporting straps, and the breeching. To these parts must be added the two types of saddle and the bridles, already mentioned. The details of all of these parts are given in the *Ordnance Manuals* and need not be repeated except to point out the few changes and when they occurred.

The 1841 *Manual* shows the old rope traces that passed through leather side pipes. These had been replaced by leather traces before the Mexican War, although doubtless some remained in store for years afterward. The Mordecai plates of 1849 and the 1850 *Manual* show the artillery harness used about 1849–1859. These illustrate the leather traces, now connected to the collar and other traces by iron trace chains and toggles. At all periods only the wheel teams were fitted with breeching to permit backing and slowing and to prevent the team from being overrun by the carriage.

The Model 1859 artillery harness differed from the earlier model principally in the saddle and bridle, already described; the draft harness remained essentially the same.

The draft harness used for supply wagons, ambulances, and other vehicles was of the type in common civilian use at the time.

SOURCES

U.S., Ordnance Dept., *The Ordnance Manual for the Use of the Officers of the United States Army*, 1st ed., 1841; 2nd ed., 1850; 3rd ed., 1862. Contain detailed descriptions of regulation saddlery and harness; however, only artillery harness is covered in the 2nd edition since dragoon harness was at the time the responsibility of the QMG.

William H. Carter, *Horses, Saddles and Bridles*, Baltimore, 2nd ed., 1902. A clear and readable text book by an American cavalry officer.

George B. McClellan, *Regulations and Instructions for the Field Service of the U.S. Cavalry in Time of War*, Philadelphia, 1861.

Main & Winchester's Illustrated Catalogue No. 7, San Francisco, 1887.

J. Roemer, *Cavalry: Its History, Management and Use in War*, New York, 1863.

Edward Davis, "Cavalry Equipment—Past and Present," in *U.S. Cavalry Journal*, XXVI (1915–16), 218–235.

Jno. J. Boniface, *The Cavalry Horse and His Pack*, . . ., Kansas City, Mo., 1903.

Harvey Riley, *The Mule* . . ., Philadelphia, 1869.

Randolph B. Marcy, *The Prairie Traveler* . . ., New York, 1859.

Nick Eggenhofer, *Wagons, Mules and Men* . . ., New York, 1961.

James S. Hutchins, *The United States Cavalry Saddle, McClellan Pattern, Model 1857, in Tojhusmuseet, Copenhagen*, Copenhagen, 1970.

The basis of this chapter was an unpublished MS prepared by James S. Hutchins, especially for our use, wherein he discussed in great detail his personal collection of saddlery and his extensive research into military horse furniture. For his immense help we are greatly indebted.

The late Colonel Harry C. Larter also prepared a series of notes for our use, but did not live to review this chapter, as he had promised to do. We are also grateful to Stanley J. Olsen, whose collection of horse furniture forms an important part of the holdings of the West Point Museum. He has been of great assistance in preparing this chapter.

Plate I

Private, Foot Company, — Artillery Regiment, 1853—4

Plate II

Maj. Gen. G.A.Custer, 1864–5

Plate III

Bandsman, U.S. Marine Corps, 1859 (with Contrabass B Flat Saxhorn)

Plate IV

Corporal, Co. 'A', 10th Veteran Reserve Corps—1864

AMERICAN MILITARY EQUIPAGE

1851 · 1872

VOLUME II

AMERICAN MILITARY EQUIPAGE

1 8 5 1 • 1 8 7 2

*A description by word and picture of what the American
soldier, sailor and marine of these years wore and carried,
with emphasis on the American Civil War.*

VOLUME II

PART ONE
THE UNITED STATES ARMY
(continued)

TABLE OF CONTENTS

MILITARY EQUIPAGE
AMERICAN
1851·1872

VOLUME I

VOLUME II

PART ONE (continued)
THE UNITED STATES ARMY

TABLE OF CONTENTS (continued)

Abbreviations

Abbreviations used in the body of the narrative and in the descriptions of equipage are those in common use and require no explanation. Extensive use, however, is made of specialized abbreviations in the orders of battle, and these are explained below.

AC	Army Corps	HQ	Headquarters
a.d.	African Descent		
AG	Adjutant General		
AGO	Adjutant General's Office	in	inch or inches
		inf	infantry
ANV	Army of Northern Virginia		
A of P	Army of the Potomac	M	Model
arty	artillery	Mil Div	Military Division
		mos	months
bn	battalion		
brig	brigade	organ	organized or organization
btry, btrys	battery, batteries		
		QMG	Quartermaster General
c.	circa, about		
cal	caliber		
cav	cavalry	redesig	redesignated
Cir	Circular	reg	regulation
comp, comps	company, companies	regt	regiment
consol	consolidated, consolidation	reorgan	reorganized, reorganization
CS	Confederate States		
CSA	Confederate States of America	serv	service
		Smith.	Smithsonian Institution
dept	department		
disb	disband, disbanded	US	United States
div	division	USA	United States of America
D of Ark	Department of Arkansas	U.S.C.T.	United States Colored Troops
D of Cum	Department of the Cumberland		
D of Ohio	Department of Ohio		
D of WVa	Department of West Virginia	vol	volunteer
		WDGO	War Department General Orders
EM	enlisted man or men	WDSC	War Department Signal Corps
Fed	Federal	WPM	West Point Museum
		yrs	years
GHQ	General Headquarters		
GO	General Orders		

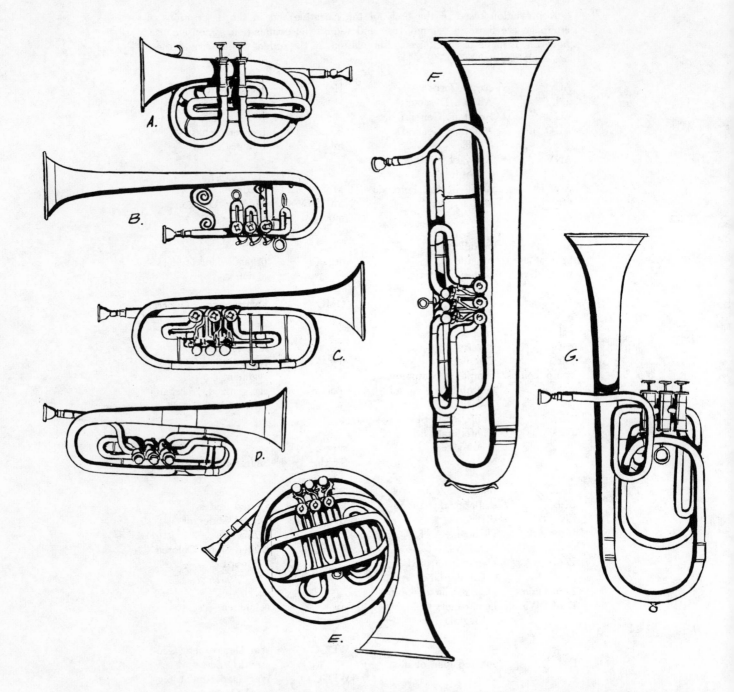

Fig. 68. Some wind instruments of a wind band of the mid-19th century: A, two valve cornet; B, saxhorn, B flat soprano; C, trumpet, B flat; D, flugelhorn; E, French horn; F, tuba:, in F; G, saxhorn, B flat tenor. The instruments are not drawn to scale. B is an over-the-shoulder pattern. B,C, and G are from the Metropolitan Museum of Art collections, New York; the remainder are illustrated in Anthony Baines,ed., *Musical Instruments Through the Ages,*London, 1961.

CHAPTER VI

MUSICAL INSTRUMENTS AND SPECIALIZED EQUIPMENT

Musical Instruments

It must be pointed out at the start that this section was not written for musicians. Rather, it was prepared in the hope that it would assist the unmusical in the identification of the several kinds of instruments used by military bands during the period 1851-1872. The musical characteristics of these instruments are well described in the texts cited.

Musical instruments in the period served two military purposes. By far the oldest was that of communicating orders and commands, both in camp and in battle. This was accomplished primarily by the drum and the trumpet or bugle. One or the other of these instruments sounded the camp calls from "the reveille" to "lights out," the combat commands from "the charge" to "retreat." The trumpet or bugle was used for this purpose in mounted commands, while the bugle was commencing to replace the drum to this end in dismounted units. Before the Civil War, in the regular army, trumpets were issued to the mounted riflemen and cavalry regiments. Dragoons and light artillery received the bugle. During, and especially after the war, trumpets tended to be given to foot troops whereas mounted troops received bugles.

American bugle and trumpet "sounds," as well as the "beats of the drum" with accompanying fife parts, were given in the various manuals of infantry and cavalry tactics. Most of these calls were derived from the French, although relics of British calls were interspersed. More or less distinctive calls were prescribed for mounted and dismounted commands. The result was confusing, and in 1867 steps were taken to revise and assimilate the calls into a single system in conjunction with General Emory Upton's revision of the combat arms tactics during the postwar era. This task was assigned to General Truman Seymour.

The second purpose was fulfilled by the marching band, and this was a relatively new thing in the Western world since it dated back only to the late 17th century. Such an organized body of musicians really served two functions: that of enlivening hearts and stirring souls, and of enabling soldiers to march on parade in cadence.

The drummers and buglers of an infantry regiment often performed, or tried to perform, all these functions through their organization into drum corps, or, as these were sometimes called, field music. This they did in conjunction with a regimental band, if one existed, or alone if it did not. Drum corps were common in the volunteer militia. In 1854, for example, New York State prescribed that each infantry company have three musicians and, in addition, regiments could organize "bands of musicians" if they could support them. In 1858 it permitted companies to enlist boys as musicians. Two side drums and a trumpet per company was a common allotment of instruments although these were not specifically prescribed.

Some regiments used only side drums for their field music, still others harkened back to older times and added fifers and a bass drum. Drum corps were presided over by one or two "chief" or "principal musicians," non-commissioned officers commonly called "drum" and "fife majors" or, in mounted corps, "trumpet majors." If a regiment had both a drum corps and a band, each was commanded by one of the principal musicians, the one in charge of the band being called its "leader." In state military bands the leader could be a civilian or even a commissioned officer.

Wealthier corps of the volunteer militia and most regular regiments had bands. In the regular army these bands, of from sixteen to twenty-four enlisted musicians plus two principal musicians (not including two musicians per company), were raised and paid as such. Yet there was no allowance made by Congress for band instruments, and regimental officers commonly contributed to a fund to provide them, together with distinctive uniforms, and the means by which the group could be converted as needed from a marching band to a dance or concert orchestra. In 1861 regimental bands of twenty-four musicians were also authorized for volunteer infantry regiments, and of sixteen musicians for cavalry (GO 15, 4 May 1861). Many such bands were organized, but the scarcity of trained musicians and the cost of musical equipment prevented a general enlistment of bands.

State military corps either made long term contracts with professional bands or hired them as they were needed for parades. Such bands sometimes adopted a regimental designation and uniform, but as a rule their hired bandsmen remained civilians.

In the beginning of our period, American military bands were numerous but often poor, even for those days. Small in size, composed frequently of amateur musicians of limited skill, playing instruments that could not blend, and with limited repertoires, most bands of the 1850's were credits neither as soldiers nor musicians.

In the larger centers one did find notable exceptions to this mediocrity. Far above all others was Dodworth's Cornet Band in New York City, the first brass band in the nation. Others of note were Gilmore's Band; the Boston Brigade Band, one of the oldest in the country; the Boston Brass Band; Beck's Band, of Philadelphia; Chandler's Band, of Portland, Maine; Green's American Band, of Providence R.I. (which accompanied the 1st Regiment Rhode Island Detached Militia and took part in the first Battle of Bull Run); Jones' Band, of Troy, N.Y.; and Smith's Armory Band, Richmond, Va., organized about 1848, which became the First Virginia Regiment Band in 1860. Good or bad, many were the civilian bands who marched out with state regiments in 1861 and played their part as musicians and stretcher bearers during the first year of the Civil War.

Almost all of the volunteer regiments raised in 1861 had a brass band and some of these bands numbered as high as fifty pieces. This meant that there were three or four bands to each brigade, while a single army corps, often camped in a small area, might have as many as forty bands of varying sizes and skill. Not only did this excess of bands lead to musical confusion, but it proved to be needlessly expensive and wasteful of manpower. The result was an Act of Congress approved 17 July 1862 which abolished all regiment bands and all extra pay for musicians. There was a provision, however, that entitled each brigade to keep a band of its own at headquarters.

The abolishment of regimental bands came at a time when most of them had seen hard service on the Peninsula or elsewhere, and the musicians accepted their discharges and went home, almost to a man. The enthusiasm of the drummers and fifers who remained subsided and instrumental practice just about ceased. The army, in consequence, was left almost without music.

The soldiers keenly felt the want of music and some regiments raised funds to support small bands at their own expense. Gradually new brigade bands or at least fife and drum corps, were raised and trained, and Civil War letters tell of the delight of the men at the arrival and excellent music of the new bands. Yet even these required the liberal support of the officers of the brigade.

With the end of the Civil War came a gradual return of regimental bands and by 1872 they were once again a commonplace, especially in the larger cities of the North.

Below are descriptions of the principal musical instruments found in drum corps and military bands of 1851-1872.

Instruments: Field Music

● *Side Drum.* This was the common or "snare" drum, issued to infantry and foot artillery. It usually had a wooden shell, although brass shells are sometimes found in this period. The size varied somewhat; in head diameter from 16 to 17 inches, and in shell depth from 13.5 inches to the regulation 16 inches. The short drums found today are usually the result of their being cut down in later years for boys' drum corps.

See U.S. Inf. Musician, 1866

The "batter" (top) and "snare" (bottom) heads were rope-tensioned, that is, connected by a continuous rope or cord strung through holes in the wooden hoops which could be tightened by forcing down sliding leather "braces" (also called "ears" or "lugs"). Rod-tensioned drums, whose heads could be separately tensioned, were in use but probably confined to orchestras. Some rope-tensioned drums were fitted after about 1855 with metal hooks on the hoops around which the rope passed. The snares, which give the side drum its peculiar dry and rattling quality of tone, consisted of a group of eight or ten cords of gut stretched across the lower head.

For marching, side drums were hung on a canvas or leather sling passing around the neck or over the right shoulder; infrequently, they were suspended from a waist belt. When not being played they could be slung over the drummer's back by a fabric strap, or by a braided rope ("dragrope") which was actually a continuation of the rope by which the drum was strung. Sticks came in pairs and were all wood. When not in use they were stuck into the tubes of a drum stick "carriage," a rectangular brass plate with clipped corners fixed to the front of the drum sling. If no carriage was worn, the sticks could be slipped under the rope on the side of the drum.

Drums made under U.S. government contract were painted according to regulations. "The front of the drums will be painted with the arms of the United States, on a blue field for the infantry, and on a red field for the artillery. The letter of the company and number of the regiment, under the arms, in a scroll" (*Regulations*, 1857, par. 108; etc.). In contract drums of the Civil War period the unit designation is almost always omitted. Markings on state drums will be noted hereafter; occasionally drums were presented as awards, in which case they bore non-regulation design. One example, in the West Point Museum, carries an unusual national eagle, painted in gold, with the legend: "PRESENTED TO ISAAC BIRDSLEY FROM Co. A. U.S. ENGs."

Instrument makers customarily placed their labels inside the shell so that it would be visible through an air hole in the side.

● *Kettle Drum.* There is some evidence that the kettle drum was used in American cavalry bands before and during the Civil War. However, we have seen neither a description nor a picture of one.

(Bass and tenor drums are covered under "Instruments: Bands," hereafter.)

● *Field or Natural Trumpet.* This was a copper or brass instrument played with a cupped mouthpiece, having neither slide nor valves. It was characterized by a long, narrow tube, largely cylindrical and curved for convenience into a single or double loop. This length of cylindrical tubing produced the trumpet's characteristic brilliancy of tone, in contrast to the comparatively mellow notes of the bugle. Regulation trumpets were brass and were pitched in F.

Most valveless trumpets could not be altered in pitch and hence were unsuited for use in a band. A few were provided with extra lengthening pieces called "shanks" or "crooks" which could be added to change the key. Even then, however, they produced only the natural overtones (harmonics) of that key.

American trumpets had an overall length of from 14 to 19 inches, the shorter size for use by foot troops. This refers to the length of the instrument and not, of course, to the "sounding length" of the tube. They were fitted with worsted cords ten feet long, with a tassel at each end, to permit slinging on a man's back. These cords were provided in branch colors; yellow or green.

● *Field Bugle.* The bugle was a brass or copper valveless instrument which differed from the trumpet in having a wide conical tube, giving it a more mellow tone. Most bugles were pitched in C, although they did appear in other keys such as B flat. Regulation bugle calls required only five different notes, and the bugle (or rather, the bugler) was capable of producing only two or three more than these.

The regulation bugle of the 1850's and 1860's was wreathed upon itself in one flattened loop. Overall instrument length was approximately 15-18 inches. Bugles only about 9 inches overall, having three loops, were used in some commands. Bugles, like trumpets, were fitted with worsted cords in branch colors: sky blue, orange, scarlet, and possibly more. They were first issued in the regular army to dismounted corps, dragoons, and light artillery. Later they were used principally by mounted troops.

● *Fife.* A small, cylindrical wind instrument of the flute family which was held at right angles to the body while being played with its open end toward the right side of the player. Fifes were made of wood — cocoa, boxwood, rosewood, plum, and cherry being common. It had six fingerholes; sometimes one key was used (D sharp) but rarely more. The fife emitted a high, shrill note, audible above the noise of battle, but its chief claims to popularity lay in its simplicity, its low cost, and the fact that it was relatively easy to learn to play. The U.S. Army regulation fife came in two sizes, 14.5 and 16.5 inches long, and had a brass ferrule on each end.

Instruments: Bands

In 1851, the normal American military band was a brass band of from fifteen to twenty-five musicians. This represented a change from two decades earlier when marching bands tended to use both reed and brass instruments, along with fifes and drums. In great part the change was due to Antoine Joseph (Adolphe) Sax, who, in 1842 in France, had entered the field of brass wind instruments and thereby revolutionized military music. He developed and gave his name to a family of horns called "saxhorns" which, when played together, gave a new uniformity and homogeneity of tone to the music. Sax also, in 1846, invented the saxophone, a brass instrument played with a single reed.

See U.S. Mil. Acad. Band 1860

The brass band continued in popularity throughout our period, but the limited compass of the cornet or saxhorn family was gradually recognized as leading to monotony. Allen Dodworth was among the first to re-introduce such reed instruments as the flute, clarinet, oboe, and bassoon to his band, and other bands gradually followed suit. Toward the end of our period the proportion of reed to brass instruments in leading foreign bands of from sixty to eighty-five players varied from thirty-five to fifty-six percent, plus from four to six percussion instruments. But these were not strictly marching bands, or in any event they were organizations far beyond the size and skill found in American regimental bands of the same period.

One of the most important instrument manufacturers and music publishers of the period was Henry Distin of London. He played a significant part in introducing the saxhorn to America and in standardizing military band instruments. Other makers or suppliers of instruments to American military bands were:

Stratton & Foote, New York	Boardman & Gray, Albany, N.Y.
E.G. Wright & Co., Boston	Charles H. Parsons, New York
G.H.W. Bates & Co., Boston	Schreiber Cornet Mfg. Co., New York

The instruments commonly found in American military bands of this period are listed below. Since woodwinds were relatively rare, and not materially different from the kinds played today, they will not all be treated in detail. In this broad category were the flute and piccolo, single-reed instruments like the clarinet, and double-reed ones like the oboe and bassoon. Of these, the clarinet was by all means the most commonly found.

● *Bombardon:* see *Tuba.*

● *Cornet (cornet à pistons).* A copper or brass instrument with a conical tube of narrow diameter and distinctive mouthpiece that gave it a different tone quality from other wind instruments, described as "gay and homely." It had three valves and was commonly made in B flat and E flat. The cornet was anywhere from 13 to 18 inches in instrument length. Introduced about 1830, it largely replaced the key bugle in military bands during the 1850's.

The cornet's mouthpiece was deeper than that of a trumpet, and its cup more gently shouldered into the throat. Its appearance differed considerably, especially in its crooks and arrangement of tubing. Its valves in this period were either piston or rotary. Cornets were often silverplated.

● *Clarinet.* A woodwind instrument played with a single beating-reed and by 1851 supplied with from six to fourteen keys. It came in different sizes and tonalities, although an overall length of 25 or 26 inches and the key of B flat were the most usual. During the period of ascendency of the brass band, the clarinet saw relatively little use in American marching bands.

● *Flugelhorn.* A valved brass instrument pitched in F, E flat, B flat or C, which resembled the cornet in appearance. It differed from the cornet in having a wider bore, larger bell (about 6-inch diameter), and a deeper mouthpiece. Its tone was mellower and more like the bugle. In reality, it was a valved bugle.

● *French Horn.* This instrument, usually made of brass, had originated centuries before as a hunting horn, being adapted as a band instrument in the early 18th century. Its slender tube of great length (from 7 to 18 feet), with widely flared bell, was always curved into one or more circles. In the band version it became known as a "hand horn," and to accommodate crooks the space inside the circular tubing was often filled with tubing of other shapes. Valves were also applied to the French horn about 1818 and as a valved, chromatic instrument it saw some service in American bands of our period.

The simple hunting horn in the 18th and early 19th centuries had been the signalling instrument of light infantry corps in Europe and America, but in the United States it had been replaced by the bugle well before the Civil War.

● *Key (or Kent) Bugle.* A copper or brass instrument with cupped mouthpiece that belonged to the same family as the serpent, klappenhorn, ophicleide, and several others having either finger holes or "clapper keys." All of these were being superseded during the 1840's and 1850's by rotary and piston valve instruments, and hence were relatively rare in the Civil War. The key bugle had from six to eleven openings covered by keys; it was cylindrical for one-third of its length and conical for two-thirds, with an overall instrument length of about 14 to 18 inches. It was made in several keys and during its period of popularity, from about 1815 to 1855, it furnished the leading brass soprano voice of a band. Some silver bugles were made, others were silver plated.

● *Oboe.* A conically bored woodwind of considerable antiquity and variety, having in our period fifteen or more note-holes, ten or so covered with keys, and a double-reed, mounted clear of the instrument on a metal tube or staple, covered with cork. The oboe had a slight bell mouth and was almost always straight in shape. It had a high pitch and a compass of about 2.5 octaves.

● *Ophicleide.* The largest of the key bugle family, a brass instrument (sometimes silver plated) with conical bore throughout and from nine to twelve keys. It was made in different sizes and keys, but usually furnished the bass voice of the band. It was introduced into European bands about 1821 and in a decade or so had largely replaced the serpent. It was in turn replaced by valve instruments in the 1850's, notably the bombardon or tuba. The ophicleide consisted of a main tube with keys, folded in a close U, to the smaller end of which was fitted a circular or oblong crook terminating in the mouthpiece. Although the sounding lenth for the contra-bass was as much as 13 feet 9 inches, the instrument length was usually about 72 inches.

● *Sarrusophone.* A family of brass instruments of conical bore, played with a double reed. They were designed in 1856 by Sarrus, a bandmaster in the French army, with an eye to replacing oboes and bassoons in military bands. The sarrusophone, which resembled the saxophone in keywork and fingering, failed to gain important acceptance, even in France. Only an occasional instrument of this sort found its way into American military bands.

● *Saxhorns.* A family of usually seven brass instruments, generally similar in design and construction but differing in size, and in features like mouthpieces, in order to produce a gradually increasing breadth of tone. They were invented and first manufactured by Adolphe Sax. All had more or less conical tubes and three valves, and in this period were designed as "bell-over-the-shoulder" instruments. The seven members were:

Plate III;
See also 10th Regt.
Vet. Res. Corps,
and 11th N.Y.
Vol. Cav.

E flat sopranino	B flat baritone
B flat soprano	B flat bass
E flat alto	E flat bass
BB flat bass	

The saxhorns were introduced about 1843, and two years later Sax brought out another group called saxotrombas. These closely resembled the earlier instruments but had bores of smaller scale with the idea of providing a tone-color more like that of the trumpet. The saxotrombas, indeed, appear to have been designed primarily for French cavalry bands and were given tall upright shapes that could be managed readily with a single hand. It is doubtful if many saxotrombas reached the United States.

In shape and appearance the members of the saxhorn family were much alike. Their tubing was folded in a form resembling a large trumpet. In overall size they varied from about 1 to 4.5 feet. The instruments were first introduced into French military bands in 1845 and ten years later the family was complete. By then they had virtually eliminated other instruments from brass bands and had themselves been subjected to numerous minor variations. A decade later the family began to break up, individual instruments being retained or discarded on their own merits.

● *Saxophone.* A brass instrument with a single-reed mouthpiece, invented by Adolphe Sax and patented in 1846. Originally designed as a family of instruments for orchestras and military bands, the saxophone did not at once gain acceptance in America. Its real popularity lies after our period.

● *Slide Trombone.* This brass, cupped-mouthpiece instrument was related to the trumpet, to which, in its several varieties, it formed the natural alto, tenor, and bass. It was cylindrical in two-thirds, and conical in one-third of its length. The tubing was of narrow diameter and its harmonics were those of the open tube. It was operated by manipulation of a slide which gave it, in the hands of a skilled musician, the ability to produce more accurately the notes in its chromatic range than was possible by any other wind instrument. The slide trombone was somewhat eclipsed during our period by valved instruments, and during the popularity of the "bell-over-the-shoulder" horns was sometimes given this design.

● *Trumpet.* The trumpet used in bands was fitted with three valves. In common with the field or natural trumpet, it had a long, narrow, and largely cylindrical tube which produced a distinctively brilliant tone. It was a brass instrument, usually 20-25 inches overall, with its tube arranged in a variety of designs and with valves in the center. Trumpets came in different keys.

● *Tuba.* A general class of wide-bore, deep-toned, valved, brass instruments used as double bass to the rest of the brass. Included in the group were such instruments as the euphonium and bombardon. The tuba made its appearance about 1840, when it began to replace the ophicleide. The deeper members of the saxhorn family were tubas, although not usually called such. In our period the instruments of the family varied considerably in size and design.

● *Bass Drum.* This was a 3- or 4-fold enlargement of the side drum, but with proportionately lower sides. Heads were about 32 inches in diameter while depth of the shell was about 18 inches. It was carried strapped to the drummer's chest, in an upright position with the heads vertical. The instrument was drummed with a single stick having a padded head about the size of a tennis ball. The sides of a bass drum were of wood and it was tensioned by cross-roping, tightened by leather "braces" or "lugs," as used on the side drum.

Some drum corps from New England included in their line of drums an old fashioned bass drum sometimes called the "Eli Brown," after a master drum craftsman in Connecticut. In shape, it was much deeper and narrower than described above. In playing it the musician was not content merely with punctuating the rhythms of the side drums. Using two large wooden beaters, he played what the other drummers played.

● *Tenor Drum.* In its simplest form, this was a side drum without snares, capable of giving off a peculiar dull sound. It was usually played with felt-headed sticks smaller than those used for a bass drum. The true tenor drum had a head diameter of from 17 to 18 inches and was as deep as the largest side drum, which in other respects it resembled.

Specialized Equipment

Under this heading falls that equipment which has not been covered thus far and which was worn or carried in the field by officers, artillerymen, and enlisted men of the staff departments.

Like musical instruments, the items of specialized equipment were often identical with comparable items used in civilian life. The kit carried by an army surgeon, for example, contained instruments in no wise different from those used by a civilian surgeon, only their casing possibly differing. For this reason it will not be practical, in many instances, in a book on military gear to pursue these accouterments very far. Another limiting factor is the inclusion only of equipments worn or carried by a soldier or his horse. Many specialized implements were normally transported on vehicles or were part of the furnishing of structures. Only if they were transported to a substantial degree on a man's person are they included here.

Artillery Implements

See U.S. Light Arty, 1854

This category of objects (as distinct from the accouterments carried by an artilleryman on his person under arms) is described in the *Ordnance Manuals* as follows: 1841, pages 69-81, 227-236; 1850, pages 103-119, 299-341; 1862, pages 128-141, 332-373. It is also covered in great detail in Mordecai's work, cited below, and in Gibbon's *Artillerist's Manual*, also cited, pages 324-384. These implements were carried on field carriages or kept near heavier pieces of ordnance when the cannon were not in action. The implements used with a 6-pounder field gun are illustrated in Chapter 8. Those described below represent the regulation patterns for the more usual pieces of artillery.

• *Gunner's Haversack*. Made of russet bag leather, the bag 13x13 in. or slightly less, with 5 in. gussets on ends and bottom. Implement pocket (sometimes omitted) inside, 7.5x7.5 in. Pointed flap 8x14 in. fastened by strap and buckle. Russet leather carrying strap, 1.5 in. wide with buckle and loop. Usually not marked but many were made at Watervliet Arsenal and some may bear this name. Used for passing ammunition from the chest to the piece. When not in use the haversack was carried in the limber chest.

• *Port-Fire Case*. Made of sole leather to hold twelve port-fires. Length 15.6 in.; interior diameter 2.75 in. Cover 5.8 in. high, with two belt loops attached; two loops for the port-fire stock, one on cover and other on the case. Carrying strap, 1 in. wide with buckle and loop. There was a small pocket for port-fire cutters.

The port-fire case is not listed in the 1862 edition of the *Ordnance Manual* since the use of the port-fire (a long paper tube, filled with a highly inflammable but slow-burning composition, which fitted into a wooden stock) had by then been officially superseded by the friction tube (or "primer") in communicating fire through the vent of the gun to the cartridge.

• *Tube Pouch (Primer Box)*. Russet bridle leather, double flaps, no insert. Box narrows toward bottom; 3.75-4.75 in. high, 6.75-7 in. wide, sides 1.75-2 in. wide at top and .9 in. wide at bottom, all inside measurements. Pointed outer flap, 8-8.5 in. wide, fastened to brass button on bottom of box. Two vertical loops on rear, extending above top of box. This pouch held the friction tubes, thumb stall, and lanyard used in priming and firing the cannon. It varied somewhat in size and design. Sometimes stamped on outer flap "US" in .25-in. letters or "US" in .4-in. letters under "WATERTOWN/ARSENAL/1864", or other year of manufacture. Sometimes stamped on inner flap "WATERTOWN/ARSENAL" over year of manufacture.

This pouch was worn on a separate russet leather belt, 1.4 in. wide, having an iron buckle and a loop. A vent pick (or "priming wire") was stuck into the loops of the pouch. When not in use the pouch and belt were carried in the limber ammunition chest.

• *Priming Horn*. Basically a cow's horn, capable of holding at least one pound of powder, about 13 in. long, 3 in. diameter at bottom and 1 in. at neck. The bottom was blocked off by a wooden insert, having a .75-in. hole at its center fitted with a screw plug. The neck was closed either by a wooden stopper or a brass mouth piece and valve, closed by a spring device. A 1-in. leather strap allowed the horn to be carried over the artilleryman's shoulder; it was fastened to the neck of the screw plug and to a ring on the brass mouthpiece or around the neck of the horn. In essence, a large powder horn.

The priming horn is not listed in the 1862 edition of the *Ordnance Manual* since priming with loose powder had by then been superseded by use of the friction tube.

• *Thumb Stall*. Padded leather guard for a gunner's thumb, usually with two thongs for attachment to hand. The best ones were made of thick buff leather although other kinds of leather were used. The pad was stuffed with hair. Worn by a gunner to close the vent while his gun was being loaded.

● *Lanyard.* Hemp cord with wooden toggle or handle on one end and an iron S-hook on the other. Length of cord varied with the size of the cannon, but 12 to 15 feet was average. Used to pull friction tubes inserted into the vent and so ignite the cartridge.

● *Breech Sight.* Brass bar graded in degrees, having a vertical slot down the center along which ran a slide for sighting. The lower portion was curved at its bottom to fit the base ring of the gun for which it was designed. Of different lengths. Used primarily on larger guns to determine the correct elevation of the piece.

● *Tangent Scale.* Sheet brass plate shaped on its bottom to fit the base ring of the piece and cut in steps on one side. Each step was marked at a quarter of a degree and notched for sighting. Used to determine the correct elevation of the piece, this device had been largely superseded by the breech sight and pendulum hausse.

● *Pendulum Hausse.* Brass bar, graded to five degrees and open in its center for a sliding sight, ending in a heavy brass pendulum head. Overall length 8.75 in. Inscribed with national eagle at top and with "U.S./WATERVLIET/ARSENAL" over year of manufacture and the type of cannon designed for. Russet leather case, 9.25 in. overall, with .6 in. shoulder strap riveted on. Used as a corrective in sighting the piece when the trunnions were not horizontal.

The pendulum hausse came in different sizes for the 6-pounder gun, 12-pounder howitzer, 12-pounder gun-howitzer, 3-inch ordnance rifle, and possibly others. The leather cases also varied in design and size, the figures above being for the 3-inch rifle. Some cases were marked "U.S./ST. LOUIS/ARSENAL."

● *Gunner's Perpendicular.* Sheet brass device having two legs terminating in short iron rods. Fitted on rear with a spirit level and a pointed iron slide for positioning on top of gun tube. Inscribed on front with national eagle over "U.S./WATERVLIET/ARSENAL" over year of manufacture. Width across legs 6.4 in. Used on siege guns and mortars when their platforms were not level.

● *Gunner's Calipers.* Two-part sheet brass device hinged so as to gauge the diameter of ammunition and the caliber of cannon. Also marked for use as a 12-inch rule in measuring lengths of fuzes and for other purposes. Length of each arm 7 in. Marked "U.S." on one arm.

● *Gunner's Quadrant.* Wooden bar, flat on one side, with a quarter circle attached at one end, the disk graded in degrees. A round lead weight on a string was stored in a hole at the other end, covered by a brass door. Length of bar 23.5 in. Used on mortars and long artillery pieces as a sighting device.

The quadrant was also made of brass and one type, 29.5 in. overall, was inscribed on the bar "Wm. Wuerdemann, Washington, D.C."

Medical Field Equipment

Fig. 69   The best summary of what the surgeon liked to call *materia chirurgica* is given in the *Medical and Surgical History* cited below.

285

EARLY PATTERN (1861)
HOSPITAL KNAPSACK - OF WICKER, COVERED
WITH BLACK ENAMELLED CLOTH.
15" X 7½" X 18"
WEIGHT WHEN FILLED : 18 POUNDS.

NEW REGULATION
HOSPITAL KNAPSACK (1862)
IMPROVED FOR DURABILITY AND EASY ACCESS.
12½" X 6" X 16"

WEIGHT WHEN FILLED : APP. 20 POUNDS.

CARRIED BY A HOSPITAL ORDERLY, WHO ACCOMPANIED
THE REGIMENTAL SURGEON INTO ACTION.

SURGEON'S FIELD COMPANION -1863.
OF LEATHER , 13" X 6" X 7½" WITH SHOULDER
AND WAIST STRAPS.   THIS PIECE OF EQUIPMENT
WAS NORMALLY CARRIED BY A HOSPITAL ORDERLY
BUT WAS DESIGNED AND SUPPLIED FOR THE PERSONAL
USE OF A SURGEON.

THE HOSPITAL MEDICINE CHEST, MESS CHEST
AND BULKY HOSPITAL SUPPLIES WERE TRANSPORTED
BY WAGONS OF THE SUPPLY TRAIN.

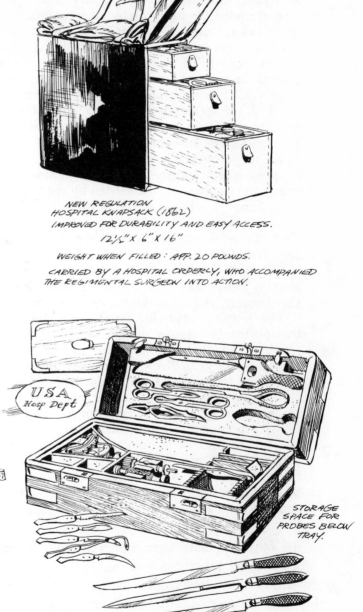

USA
Hosp Dept

STORAGE
SPACE FOR
PROBES BELOW
TRAY.

SURGEON'S INSTRUMENT CASE OF BRASS-BOUND
WALNUT. APP. 15"LONG.   PURPLE VELVET LINING
THE LONG KNIVES ARE HANDLED WITH EBONY,
THE SMALL, BLADED INSTRUMENTS WITH IVORY.
WEST POINT MUSEUM COLLECTIONS.

Fig. 69. Medical equipment

At the beginning of the war each regimental Surgeon was furnished with a suitable equipment for his regiment for field service, consisting of medicines, stores, instruments, and dressings, in quantities regulated by the Standard Supply Table. In action he was accompanied by a hospital orderly, who carried a knapsack containing a limited supply of anaesthetics, styptics, stimulants, and anodynes, and material for primary dressings. This hospital knapsack had been recommended for adoption by an army board in 1859; it was made of light wood, 18 inches in height, 15 inches wide, and 7½ inches deep, but subsequently wickerwork, covered with canvas or enamelled cloth, was substituted for the wood, its weight when filled was 18 pounds. This knapsack was in general use in the first year of the war and served an excellent purpose.

In 1862 it was changed for what was known as the new regulation knapsack, in which the arrangement and character of the supplies were modified. The new pattern was 16 inches high, 12½ inches wide, and 6 inches deep; the contents were packed in drawers, which were more accessible than in the old style and less liable to become disarranged or broken. The weight when packed was nearly 20 pounds. Notwithstanding its convenience and general adaptability it was too heavy and cumbrous to be carried by the Surgeon himself, and, when entrusted to other hands, was liable, in the vicissitudes of battle, to be lost.

In the early part of 1863 Medical Inspector R.H. Coolidge, U.S.A., arranged a field case or companion to take the place of the knapsack. It was something after the plan of the one used in the British service, and was intended to be carried by the Surgeon himself, if necessary. The "companion" is a leather case 13 inches long, 6 inches wide, and 7½ inches deep; it is supported by a strap passing over the shoulder, and is provided with a waist strap to steady it when carried.

The hospital medicine chest, mess-chart, and bulky hospital supplies were transported in wagons of the supply train and were often inaccessible when required. To obviate this inconvenience panniers were provided containing the most necessary medicines, dressings, and appliances; they were designed to be carried on the backs of pack-animals, but were found to be inconveniently heavy to be transported in this manner, and were more generally carried in one of the ambulance wagons and filled from the medicine chest as required. [The illustrations] represent the pannier arranged for army use by Dr. Squibb, of Brooklyn, N.Y.; it consists of a wooden box strongly bound with iron, 21-1/8 inches in length, 11-5/8 inches in breadth, and 11-3/8 inches in depth; it weighs, when filled, 88 pounds. The medicines are well packed in japanned tin bottles and boxes, and room is left for an adequate supply of dressing material. The pannier had two compartments.

All footnotes have been removed from the above quotation. These describe the medicines and other items carried in the several knapsacks and chests. The *History* continues with descriptions and illustrations of medicine wagons, hospital tents, litters, ambulance wagons, hospital cars, and ships.

Nowhere are surgical operating sets mentioned since they were the types used in civilian surgery. A fair number of these sets survive today but it has not been possible to form them into useful categories. A set obviously designed for general military surgical needs is in the West Point Museum. It is housed in a brass-bound mahogany box, 15.75 x 6 x 3.5 in. in size, which bears on its cover, roughly inscribed on a brass cartouche, the words "U.S.A./Hosp. Dept." This was not an official designation, which may mean the set dates from some years before the Civil War. Its surviving contents are:

2 scissor forceps	Scapel
Tweezer type forceps	3 surgical knives
Forceps	4 scapels
Surgical saw	2 probes
Radial saw	Trepanning saw and handle

Tourniquet

Speaking of a surgeon's field equipment, Dr. S.D. Gross had this to say in his *Manual of Military Surgery*, widely used by both sides in the Civil War.

> The surgical *armamentarium* should also be as simple as possible. It should embrace a small pocket case, with a screw catheter; a full amputating case, with at least three tourniquets, two saws of different sizes, and several large bone-nippers; and, lastly, a trephining case. Several silver catheters of different sizes, a stomach pump, small and large syringes, feeding-cups and bed-pans should also be put up.
>
> Under the head of *apparatus* may be included bandages, lint, linen, adhesive plaster, splints, cushions, wadding, and oiled silk.

The C.S. Army *Regulations for the Medical Department*, under "Supply Table for Field Service" (page 24), lists five sets (amputating, pocket, assorted splints, teeth extracting, and trepanning), plus twenty other instruments required for field surgery, from ball forceps and catheters to needles and trusses. The contents of several surgical cases are listed in Lord's *Collector's Encyclopedia*, cited below, pages 166-168.

Smaller hospital knapsacks than those described in the *History*, above, existed. One example inspected was 10.5 in. high, 5 in. wide, and 2.5 in. thick. It comprised two tin trays fitted into a wooden frame, in a black painted canvas case which formed a sizable pocket below the frame. Two leather carrying straps with buckles were sewn on. This pattern has not been identified. The McEvoy Hospital Knapsack, patented in 1862, is described in Lord, page 163. A "Regulation Field Medicine Case" is also illustrated on page 162.

The hospital knapsack of the Confederate Medical Department is described in its *Regulations* (p. 25).

> According to pattern, of the same dimensions with ordinary knapsacks, of light material, and to be covered with canvas. It is to be carried on a march or in battle, by a hospital orderly, who is habitually to follow the medical officer. The purpose of this knapsack is to carry such instruments, dressings, and medicines, as may be needed in an emergency on the march or in the field.

What went into the hospital knapsack was left, apparently, to the medical officer concerned, although the instruments, dressings, and medicines are listed in the field service supply table.

Signalling Equipment

Regulation signalling equipment for the U.S. Army, much of it developed by Colonel Albert J. Myer, the Chief Signal Officer, is described and illustrated in the *Manual of Signals*, 1866 edition, cited below. The pertinent sections are quoted below, omitting only the references to illustrations.

Fig. 70

U.S. ARMY
SIGNAL PISTOL,
BRASS FRAME.

LOCKING
LEVER

SIGNAL CARTRIDGES
(COMPOSITION FIRES)
WITH PERCUSSION CAPS
PRE-FIXED.

W.P.M.

US. ARMY SIGNAL 1862 PISTOL A.J.M.

MARKINGS ON BUTT
STRAP.

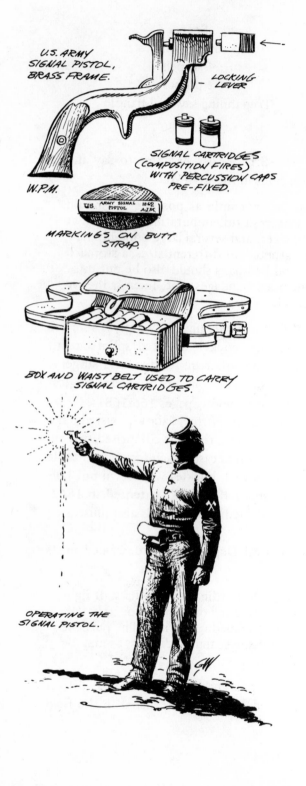

BOX AND WAIST BELT USED TO CARRY
SIGNAL CARTRIDGES.

OPERATING THE
SIGNAL PISTOL.

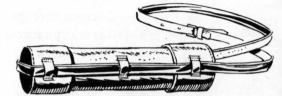

U.S. ARMY SIGNAL CORPS TELESCOPE,
OF BRASS, WITH LEATHER SAFETY
CASE.

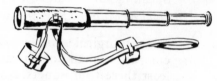

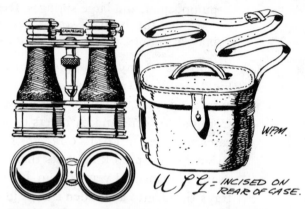

W.P.M.

U P L = INCISED ON
REAR OF CASE.

FIELD GLASSES (OF FRENCH MANUFACTURE)
USED BY GENERAL U.S. GRANT DURING THE WAR.
THREE SEPARATE LENS SETTINGS CAN BE
OBTAINED BY MEANS OF THE SMALL THUMBSCREW
ON THE RIGHT TUBE; THE SETTINGS ARE MARKED ON
THE FLATS OF THE SCREW SLEEVE: THEATRE,
CAMPAGNE AND MARINE.

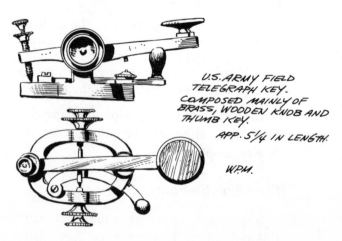

U.S. ARMY FIELD
TELEGRAPH KEY.
COMPOSED MAINLY OF
BRASS, WOODEN KNOB AND
THUMB KEY.

APP. 5 1/4 IN LENGTH.

W.P.M.

Fig. 70. Signal equipment

A Regulation Set of Signal Equipments, when packed complete, is comprised in three pieces:

The Kit — or canvas signal-case, containing the signal-staff, flags, torch-case, and torches. These all compactly rolled together and bound by straps.

The Canteen — made of copper, with one seam, and soldered — capable of containing one half-gallon of turpentine or other burning-fluid.

The Haversack — in which are packed wicking, matches, shears and pliers for trimming torch, a small funnel for filling the torch, and the two flame-shades, etc.

The Kit Case, Canteen, and Haversack are fitted with shoulder-slings or straps, by which they may be easily carried.

The Service Can — is a strong copper can, with rolled seams hard-soldered. The nozzle is fitted with a screw-cap, to prevent leakage. It is capable of containing five gallons of burning-fluid.

The Kit Case contains:

1st. The signal-staff — a staff of hickory, made in four joints or pieces, each 4 ft. long, and tapering as a whole from 1¼ in. at the butt to ½ in. at the tip.

The joints are feruled at the ends with brass, and fitted to be jointed together as some fishing-rods are jointed. The third joint is guarded with brass for six inches at its upper extremity, to protect it from the flames of the torch, which is always attached to this joint.

The tip or fourth joint is that to which the flag is attached for day-signals.

2d. The Signal Flags — made of muslin, linen, or some other very light and close fabric. The flags are seven in number:

1. The six-foot white — six feet square, white, having at its centre a block or square of red, two feet square.

2. The six foot black — six feet square, black, having at its centre a block or square of white, two feet square.

3. The four-foot white — four feet square, white, having at its centre a block, red, sixteen inches square.

4. The four-foot black — four feet square, black, having at centre a block, white, sixteen inches square.

5. The four-foot red — four feet square, red, having at centre a block, white, sixteen inches square.

6. The two-foot white — two feet square, white, having at centre a block of red, eight inches square.

7. The two-foot red — two feet square, red, having at its centre a block of white, eight inches square.

All of these flags are fitted with tapes or ties, by which to tie them to the staff. This is found the most simple and the best mode of attaching. Two tapes, six inches long, and sewed together at the tie-edge of the flag, make a tie. The ties are one foot apart.

3d. Torch Case and Torches.

The Torch Case is a piece of rubber cloth about three feet long by two feet six inches broad, fitted on one side with pouches, in which the torches are inserted.

At the opposite edge are ties. The torches are packed by being placed in the pouches, with the case then rolled around them so as to envelop them in two or three folds of cloth. The ties retain the package in this form.

The Flying Torch — is a copper cylinder, eighteen inches long and one and one-half inch in diameter; it is closed at one end, with the exception of a nozzle, through which it can be filled, and which closes with a screw-cap; it is open at the wick end, and on its sides, at this end, are four fenestra or openings, one inch long, half an inch broad, which open into the wick, so providing that however the flame may be driven by the wind, it will find a portion of the wick exposed.

The Foot Torch — is a copper cylinder, eighteen inches long and two inches in diameter. It is similar in its structure to the flying torch.

The torches are trimmed by fitting into the mouth a wick of cotton wicking six inches long. This must fit closely. The body of the torch is then filled with turpentine or other burning-fluid, as petroleum, etc. The flying light attaches to the staff "third-joint" by clamp-rings and screws.

Flame Shades — Each torch is fitted when in use, with a flame-shade — a ring of thin copper, two inches wide, and fitting by a socket upon the torch in such a way that the ring projects on all sides. This is placed about one inch below the fenestra or openings. The use of this shade is to prevent the flame from travelling down the side of the torch and thus over-heating it. The flame-shade is always detached when the torch is packed.

A shade, called a Wind Shade, is sometimes used in high winds. It consists of fine strips of copper attached to a socket, and is adjusted upon the torch in the same way as the flame-shade.

The Funnel, Pliers, and Shears are used for filling and trimming the torch.

A screw is placed in the torch-case to be used when the wick may, by accident, be drawn so far into the tube of the torch that it cannot be seized by the pliers.

SIGNAL DISKS

Single Signal-Disks are made of white canvas or other strong cloth, stretched upon light rings or hoops of wire or tough wood, and having attached handles, by which they may be conveniently grasped and moved.

The disks are about a foot or eighteen inches in diameter. They bear at the centre a round black or red spot, of a diameter equal to about one-fourth of that of the disk.

The handles are from a foot to eighteen inches in length. They may be fitted with sockets, so as to permit the disk to be attached to longer rods or handles when there is the occasion.

Signal-disks may be attached to long and light canes, or to the end of a musket, or to the arms of a semaphore, to add to their utility.

Double Signal-Disks consist of two signal disks, one attached at each extremity of a staff about six feet long. The disks are about eighteen inches in diameter. They may be of the same color , or of different colors, as one red and one white.

The dependence in signalling should be on the position and not on the colors of the disks. They are often not distinguishable. Disks are sometimes colored red on one side and white on the other. This device is useful, permitting the color of the disk to be suited to the background. Disks, intended for constant use, as to permanent stations, are sometimes woven of basket or wicker work.

Two types of signalman's canteen have been identified:

(*With spout*): Round copper flask with flat faces and curved edges, 9.75 in. diameter, 3 in. thick. Four 3 in. copper loops, 2 in. spout and hole on top with screw top. Leather strap, 1.7 in. wide. Circular indentation on both faces; ridge around sides.

(*Without spout*): Round copper flask with concave faces, 9.75 in. diameter, 4.5 in. thick in center. Four 2.2 in. copper loops. Hole on top with screw top. Leather (?) strap. Circular indentation on both faces; soldered seam around sides.

The signalman's haversack had these dimensions:

Plain unpainted cotton, 12 in. wide, 11 in. high, 4 in. gusset at bottom. Rounded flap buckles by single leather strap. Carrying strap 2 in. wide, of same material, 29 in. long.

These were the normal items of signal equipment; there were others that saw only experimental usage. Flash lanterns using slides of colored glass, and "magic lanterns" (then commonplace for civilian entertainment) with flash-slide attachment, were listed as auxiliary equipment, especially for use on shipboard. There were several pyrotechnic devices, among them the candle bomb which was fired from a signal mortar, exploding high in the air with a shower of brilliant stars. These bombs could also be charged with smoke or noise-producing explosives. Puffs of smoke and flashes of light were explored as signalling devices, as were various forms of signal rockets. These rockets consisted of pasteboard cylinders filled with powder and were fired from a frame. Under proper conditions they were visible up to eight miles.

Signal lights were fired in specially designed caplock pistols, two types being used. Signal cartridges burned with great intensity of light and color and came in as many as ten colors. However, red, white, and green were found to be the most suitable for field use.

● *Army Caplock Signal Pistol (Myer Pattern).* Brass barrel and frame, walnut grips. Nipple set on rear of barrel; center-hung iron hammer. Iron lever extended below barrel and along front of the frame. Dimensions: barrel caliber at muzzle .69 in.; top of barrel to end of butt, 8 in. Example inspected stamped on butt strap "U.S. ARMY SIGNAL/-PISTOL/1862/AJM". The initials are those of the Signal Officer, Albert J. Myer. This is the pistol illustrated in the 1879 *Manual.*

● *Navy Caplock Signal Pistol (1861 Pattern).* Brass barrel, frame, and grips, formed of two pieces joined longitudinally and held by two screws. Nipple set on top of barrel with iron hammer far forward on frame. Iron lever attached underneath barrel. Overall length 9.5 in.; barrel caliber at muzzle .69 in. Examples inspected stamped on left side of frame "U.S.O.Y.W/W.N.J./1864."

The heliograph is also described in the 1879 *Manual* which, of even more importance, contains a detailed discussion of electrical signalling. The telegraph instruments and other devices used in the field during the Civil War are described and many are illustrated. Since they were similar to the instruments employed in civilian telegraphy they will not be covered here. A telegraph key is illustrated in Figure 70.

Engineering Instruments and Pioneering Tools

The instruments employed by Engineer and Topographic Engineer officers for map making, surveying, and construction were in no way different from those in civilian use. They included azimuth instruments, theodolites, stadia, map measurers, telemeter whistles, slide rules, camera lucidas, sextants, drafting equipment, and, of course, compasses and telescopes. Of these only one, the military stadia, is known to have been arsenal-manufactured especially for army use. This was a flat brass device with a sliding sight and chain, used for roughly measuring distances. The example seen was stamped "FRANKFORD ARSENAL." Stadia are illustrated in Lord's *Collector's Encyclopedia,* page 264.

Figs. 71a and 71b

The organization and equipment of the pioneer parties of the Army of the Potomac were formalized by General Orders No. 15, 5 April 1864. The unit of organization was by brigade and there was one pioneer selected and equipped as such for every fifty men. Pioneer parties marched at the head of each brigade infantry column.

292

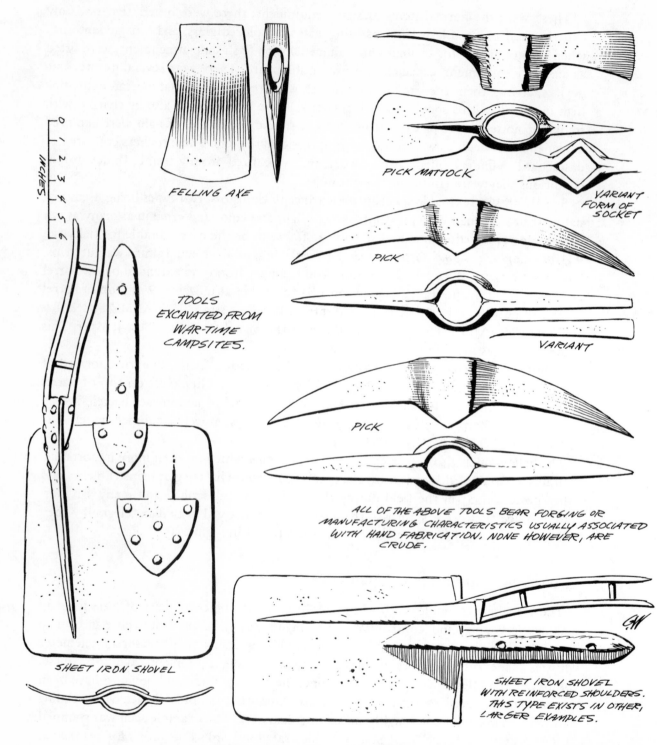

FELLING AXE

PICK MATTOCK

VARIANT FORM OF SOCKET

INCHES

TOOLS EXCAVATED FROM WAR-TIME CAMPSITES.

PICK

VARIANT

PICK

ALL OF THE ABOVE TOOLS BEAR FORGING OR MANUFACTURING CHARACTERISTICS USUALLY ASSOCIATED WITH HAND FABRICATION. NONE HOWEVER, ARE CRUDE.

SHEET IRON SHOVEL

SHEET IRON SHOVEL WITH REINFORCED SHOULDERS. THIS TYPE EXISTS IN OTHER, LARGER EXAMPLES.

ALL FROM BEVERLY M. DUBOSE COLLECTION

Fig. 71a. Pioneer Implements

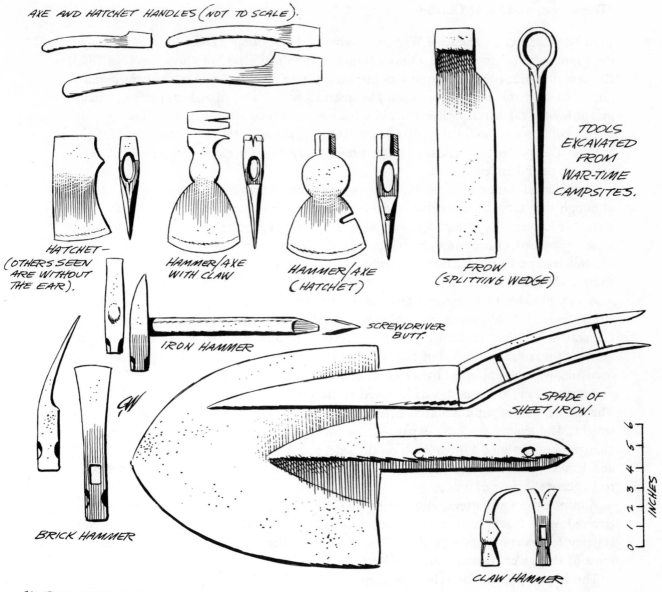

AXE AND HATCHET HANDLES (NOT TO SCALE).

TOOLS EXCAVATED FROM WAR-TIME CAMPSITES.

HATCHET— (OTHERS SEEN ARE WITHOUT THE EAR).

HAMMER/AXE WITH CLAW

HAMMER/AXE (HATCHET)

FROW (SPLITTING WEDGE)

IRON HAMMER

SCREWDRIVER BUTT.

BRICK HAMMER

SPADE OF SHEET IRON.

INCHES

CLAW HAMMER

ALL FROM BEVERLY M. DUBOSE COLLECTION

Fig. 71b. Pioneer implements

Tools were furnished the pioneers in these proportions: 5/10 axes, 3/10 shovels, 2/10 picks. They were usually carried in panniers on pack mules during a march, one mule carrying the tools for forty pioneers. The men themselves retained their arms. Although some axe slings are known to have been used, there were usually no special accouterments worn for carrying tools.

Telescopes and Field Glasses

Fig. 70

Fifty years before the Civil War all viewing of distant objects was done by means of the monocular telescope with jointed frame — the "spy glass" of those days. In 1823 the portable binocular telescope was invented (or re-invented) and it was considerably improved over the next thirty years. The instruments developed and sold commercially in 1861 were far handier than the old telescope, and they afforded a depth perception not possible with monocular glasses, but they remained little more than double telescopes. The prism field glasses of the present day did not come into use until years after our period ended.

The pair of binoculars of the 1860's was what we today call an "opera glass," although that term in those days meant an instrument weaker than the field glass. The term "field glass," furthermore, was also used to describe the monocular telescope, which remained in use throughout the period, especially by signalmen and others who did not require too portable an instrument. They were usually mounted on tripods or some other fixed base.

A fair number of telescopes and binoculars used in the Civil War have survived. A sturdy pair of field glasses, with a velvet lined case of black leather, was carried by General G.K. Warren. It was made of brass, partially covered with leather. Fully closed, it was 4.5 in. long, but full focus added .8 in. It was fitted with sun shades and focussing was accomplished by a wheel between the glasses.

Another pair, also cased, was believed to have been carried by General U.S. Grant. The frame was of an aluminum silver alloy, hence the pair was remarkably light in weight. The length was 5 in., expansible by focussing to 6.3 in. The eye lenses could be changed by revolving a brass knob on the side, stamped with the serial number "3349" and a bee. The lens bar was marked "THEATRE," CAMPAGNE", and "MARINE" to indicate the type of lens in use.

A quite different pattern, also carried by Grant, was 10.5 in. long with a brass frame, covered with black leather. Two other sizes are illustrated full scale in Schuyler, Hartley & Graham's 1864 catalog. Clearly all binoculars were commercially made and most of them were manufactured in Europe.

The largest monocular telescope inspected was 38.5 in. closed and 57.5 in. when opened to its fullest. Although too long and heavy to be used without a rest, it carried no fittings for attachment to a tripod. Its frame was brass, partially covered by black leather. Earlier telescopes were achromatic (providing an image free of color) but this example was chromatic, an essential feature in a signalman's instrument. Inside the frame was the inscription "B. Pike's Son, Optician/518 Broadway/New-York."

Naval telescopes were often about 16 in. closed and 36 in. open; field telescopes 10 and 22 in.; and the smallest seen was 2.25 and 6.25 in.

SOURCES: MUSICAL INSTRUMENTS

Arthur A. Clappe, *The Wind-Band and its Instruments*, New York, 1911. Clappe once taught music at the U.S. Military Academy.

William C. White, *A History of Military Music in America*, New York, 1944.

H.W. Schwartz, *Bands of America*, New York, 1957.

H.W. Schwartz, *The Story of Musical Instruments from Shepherd's Pipe to Symphony*, Garden City, N.Y., 1943.

Henry G. Farmer, *The Rise & Development of Military Music*, London, 1912.

Eric Blom, ed., *Grove's Dictionary of Music and Musicians*, 5th ed., 9 vols., New York, 1955.

Frank Rauscher, *Music on the March, 1862-'65...*, Philadelphia, 1892.

Lyndesay G. Langwill, *An Index of Musical Wind-Instrument Makers*, 2nd ed., Edinburgh, Scotland, 1962.

Harry H. Hall, *A Johny Reb Band from Salem: The Pride of Tarheelia*, Raleigh, N.C., 1963.

Frederick Fennell, "The Civil War: Fort Sumter to Gettysburg," vol. I, and "Gettysburg to Appomatox," vol. II, notes for Mercury Records LPS 2-901, 1961, and LPS 2-902, 1963.

Marshall M. Brice, *The Stonewall Band*, Verona, Va., 1967.

This section was read in manuscript by Harold L. Peterson, P.A. Munier (President, Military Association of Drum Majors), and Specialist Norman Schweikert (U.S. Military Academy Band). We have profited greatly by their comments and criticisms.

SOURCES: SPECIALIZED EQUIPMENT

C.S., War Dept., *Regulation for the Medical Department of the C.S. Army*, Richmond, Va., 1862.

S.D. Gross, *A Manual of Military Surgery...*, Richmond, Va., 1862. Widely used by surgeons of both armies in the Civil War; first published in 1861 in Philadelphia.

U.S., Ordnance Dept., *Ordnance Manual for the Use of Officers of the United States Army*, Washington, D.C., 1841; 2nd ed., 1850; 3rd ed., 1862.

Alfred Mordecai, *Artillery for the United States Land Service*, 2 vols., Washington, D.C., 1849. The first volume of text and the second (folio) volume of plates represent the most detailed and exhaustive compilation of American artillery equipment in print.

John Gibbon, *The Artillerist's Manual, Compiled from Various Sources, and Adapted to the Service of the United States*, New York, 1860.

Surgeon General, U.S. Army, *The Medical and Surgical History of the War of the Rebellion*, Washington, D.C., vol. II (Surgical History), part III, pp. 899-986.

Albert J. Myer, *A Manual of Signals: For the Use of Signal Officers in Field...*, New York, 1866. Revised and enlarged editions in 1868, 1877, and 1879.

Francis A. Lord, *Civil War Collector's Encyclopedia: Arms, Uniforms, and Equipment of the Union and Confederacy*, Harrisburg, Pa., 1963.

Frank Russell, "Early U.S. Martial Signal Pistols," in *The Gun Report*, August, 1970.

Fig. 72. "Return of the Flags, 1865," by Thomas Waterman Wood, painted in 1869. This romantic painting shows the arrival of a Union regiment in New York harbor. in the distance is Castle William while relatives wave from the approaching pilot launch. A little Negro boy, probably a regimental mascot, peers out at the new world. There is nothing to indicate the regiment but it is believed to be the 69th Volunteer Infantry of the Irish Brigade which returned to New York City in July 1865. The veterans wear overcoats. (West Point Museum)

CHAPTER VII

COLORS AND FLAGS

The attention showered by students of the national flag — the "Stars and Stripes" — has from early days obscured that due other kinds of military banners. This neglect cannot be laid to lack of evidence, since a wealth of examples survive today.

The largest collection of the older military colors and flags belonging to the general government, and available to the public, rests in the West Point Museum. In past years some of these flags have been transferred to other museums, notably those of the Artillery and Guided Missile Center at Fort Sill and the Engineer School at Fort Belvoir. Another important flag collection once reposed in the Chapel of St. Cornelius the Centurian, Governors Island, New York, although its present status is uncertain. The Military Order of the Loyal Legion, Philadelphia (referred to hereafter as MOLLUS) and the Chicago Historical Society both own sizeable groups of Civil War flags. In virtually every state capital are collections (often of impressive size) of colors and flags carried by the troops of that state, and many more can be found in local museums and historical societies.

The military flags of the period 1851-1872 fall into four principal classes: regimental colors and standards, guidons and other small flags, flags used to distinguish commands higher than a regiment, and garrison flags. Flags of the third category were almost entirely a product of the Civil War. Flags of the fourth category merge with numerous sorts of national flags, semi-civilian in nature. To these can be added signal and hospital flags, while naval flags comprise an entire class in themselves and are covered in Chapter 13.

Regimental Colors and Standards

Of all the flags mentioned, by far the most significant to this study were the regimental colors, the term "color" normally meaning at this period a large flag carried by foot-soldiers while "standard" referred to a smaller one carried by a mounted unit. The regiment was then the highest permanent organization of an army, and its color reflected this permanence.

Colors still played an important tactical role: they established the position of the line of battle and furnished a rallying point in time of need. Their display was steeped in tradition to the point where the color, in a sense, was the regiment. A regiment was officially credited with advancing in battle to the point its color reached, not necessarily where the bulk of its men penetrated.

Traditionally and by regulation, a United States regiment of infantry had two colors: a national color which was after 1841 the stars and stripes, and a regimental color

Fig. 73

(sometimes called the "banner"), which bore the arms of the United States or some other device. These two constituted its "stand" of colors although this word was also used to mean a single flag. On campaign, regiments normally carried only one color, usually the national. Oddly, when two colors were carried the national frequently was placed on the left of the regimental — a position not ruled out until as late as 1923, when it was determined that the national color would be positioned on its own right.

The variety of colors and methods of their display among state regiments was very pronounced. Although the stars and stripes was often carried, the militia corps used state or local, rather than U.S. devices, as did most of the volunteers. More often than not, colors were privately purchased by civilian groups for presentation, or were sewn by wives and sweethearts, and it was not uncommon in early 1861 to find regiments in which every company carried its own color. In a short time, however, state regiments trimmed down to one or, at most, two colors, both as a practical matter and by order of higher command.

Infantry colors were carried by specially selected sergeants called "color bearers" and were escorted by a color guard of six or more corporals detailed from different companies. This color party was attached to the right center company of the line, called the "color company." Color bearers were the prime target for enemy rifles and stories of their bravery in combat and high rate of casualties are legion. The color of the 44th New York Volunteers is said to have had twelve bearers killed and eighteen wounded while carrying it.

Cavalry regiments usually carried a single standard (described later); at the same time each of their companies or sometimes squadrons had a guidon. Sergeant W.A. Ferris of the 1st New York Dragoons recalled:

> At Suffolk I was detailed as one of the color guard [while the regiment was still infantry]. When the regiment was transferred to cavalry, the guard was reduced to three, . . . [Two of the guard were wounded at Todd's Tavern and] from then to the close, in all the campaigns and battles of the regiment, I carried the colors, the other guards being frequently changed. In the Valley I was advanced to sergeant, and received my warrant as "Color Bearer."

It would seem, then, that the regiment carried only one standard, despite the sergeant's reference to "colors." Three colors of this regiment survive. One, a large infantry color dating from the regiment's first year, was probably not carried by Sergeant Ferris. The other two are cavalry standards, one is medium sized and the other unusually small.

Colors, over 6 by 6 feet square, were heavy and cumbersome to carry. By the Civil War the use of color slings or "belts" had become a regular item of issue but they were not always worn, some bearers preferring to hold and wave a flag with both hands. This was especially true with the smaller Confederate battle flags. On the march the color was carried furled (and even cased) across a bearer's shoulder. The large size of these flags was due to the necessity of having them visible to an entire regiment in line amidst the battle smoke.

Colors and standards were usually made of silk and had yellow fringes. Colors bore cords and tassels as a rule; standards of mounted units rarely did. Most colors and standards were fitted with sleeves through which their staff passed. Rarely was any other method of attachment used in the Regular service except for some semi-official battle flags. Staffs for colors were called "pikes"; for standards and other mounted flags they were known usually as "lances." The pike, by regulation, was 9 feet 10 inches long. Both pikes and lances were tipped by "spears." The spears on regular army colors were heart-shaped or partially so, although occasionally one finds pointed spearheads with a cross bar, called the "spontoon" head. State units, on the other hand, frequently used eagles, halberds, crosses, and other devices on top of the color pikes.

Fig. 74

A color could last a regiment for years or it could be ripped to pieces in action in a few months. Many of the flags brought home by Union regiments after the Civil War were in shreds and all the more proudly carried because of the fact.

● *Battle Honors.* With no apparent sanction, prior to the Civil War certain regiments began to paint on the regimental colors the names of battles in which they had participated. Possibly these honors were placed on the actual flags carried in the battles listed, but more likely this took place on new flags procured after a campaign. A color of the 6th Infantry at West Point, dating prior to the Mexican War, bears the word "OKECHOBEE" painted below the eagle. On a later regimental color of this regiment the names of no less than ten Mexican War battles were painted. At what period these names were added and how far the practice extended is not known, but it is clear that even before the Civil War the display of battle honors was in actual use.

Fig. 73. "The Halt of the Line of Battle," an etching by Edwin Forbes in his *Life Studies of the Great Army* (1876), based on sketches and notes made in the field. The single color bearer here stands in the front rank center of the color company, his usual position.

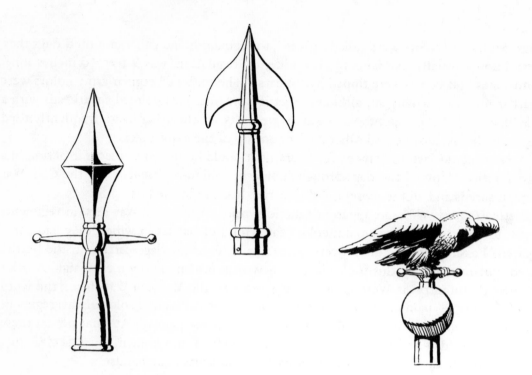

Fig. 74. Spearheads for pikes and lances. At left is a type sometimes called the "spontoon" head; in the center is one shaped partially like a heart — a common Regular Army pattern; at right is one of several eagle types carried on the colors of state regiments. (West Point Museum)

One of the earliest battles of the Civil War was that fought at Wilson's Creek near Springfield, Missouri, on 10 August 1861. The Federal pluck shown there somewhat overcame the disgrace of Bull Run and in recognition Congress gave every unit participating the right to embroider in gold "SPRINGFIELD" on its national color. War Department General Orders No. 111 publishing the right is dated 30 December 1861, and is the first instance of formal recognition of battle honors.

Colors so inscribed came to be called "battle-flags," as much for their inscription as for the fact they were carried in battle. Early in 1862 the growing demand for the recognition of honors was met, appropriately, on Washington's Birthday, by the following order of General McClellan:

General Orders   Headquarters of the Army
No. 19   Adjutant General's Office
Washington, February 22, 1862

The following order has been received from the War Department: It is ordered that there shall be inscribed upon the colors or guidons of all regiments and batteries in the service of the United States the names of the battles in which they have borne a meritorious part. These names will also be placed on the Army Register at the head of the list of the officers of each regiment.

It is expected that the troops so distinguished will regard their colors as representing the honor of their corps — to be lost only with their lives; and that those not yet entitled to such a distinction will not rest satisfied until they have won it by their discipline and courage. The general commanding the Army will, under the instruction of this Department, take the necessary steps to carry out this order.

Regular army regiments, troops, and batteries lost no time in marking their colors. Since the first order listing approved battle credits was not published until March 1865, it seems clear that each regiment selected and inscribed the honors it desired to show including, in some instances, battles prior to the Civil War.

Billings (*Hardtack and Coffee*) believed only the regulars were intended to display battle honors, but such was hardly the case. Long before any honors were authorized, the state volunteer regiments began adding the honors they felt they were entitled to or those that some lenient corps commander authorized. Billings felt there were some flags with "inscriptions of battles which the troops were hardly in hearing of," and some regiments were prone to include minor skirmishes along with genuine battles; all of which led in time to the formal authorization of credits. Honors were placed on both the national and the regimental color, though more usually on the former since it was the one commonly carried in battle.

The first order authorizing battle honors in any number, for inscription on colors and guidons, was General Orders No. 10, Army of the Potomac (A of P), published 7 March 1865. Its twenty-six pages included state volunteers, U.S. Sharpshooters, and the regular artillery. For some reason it omitted mention of the regular infantry and cavalry. The honors had been arrived at by "boards convened to examine into the services rendered by the troops concerned." Subsequently, more complete lists of battle honors were published in regular and volunteer army registers.

Confederate regiments, as will be mentioned later, also displayed battle honors and in much the same manner as Union regiments. Judging from a regimental color of the 36th Virginia, which bears the name of four questionable and relatively unimportant engagements, Confederate soldiers were sometimes just as prone to exaggerate their triumphs as their opponents.

Regiments that lost their colors through cowardice or misconduct were severely reprimanded and not permitted to carry other colors until they had "fully retrieved their tarnished honor." (GO 37, A of P, 23 Sept. 1864) Colors were also taken from regiments that had misbehaved and not returned until they had proven themselves worthy to bear them. On the whole, a regiment's colors were treated as its most important symbols.

Colors of Regiments of Foot

● *Colors of the Regular Infantry.* Since 1841 infantry regiments had carried the stars and stripes as a national color. It was a silken flag 6 feet 6 inches fly, and 6 feet on the pike. The regimental designation was painted or embroidered in silver on the center red stripe. The union was narrow and contained a small, silver, five-pointed star for each state, arranged usually in rows. Its fringe was yellow and its cords and tassels were blue and white silk, intermixed.

Figs. 75 and 76

This model of the national color continued in use until about 1872 with a few changes. After silver ceased to designate infantry in 1851 it was customary to paint the stars and sometimes the regimental name in gold. Battle honors were added officially in 1862 and about that time it became popular to arrange the stars in an oval. In general, it can be said that the number and arrangement of stars is a poor guide to the age of a

Fig. 75. National color, 2nd Battalion, 18th U.S. Infantry, carrying battle honors earned chiefly with the 14th Corps, Army of the Cumberland. The honors are most of those listed in the 1866 Army Register, although certain place names differ. These same honors were carried by the 1st Battalion and often by two companies of the Third. Clearly a post-Civil War "battle flag." (West Point Museum; before restoration)

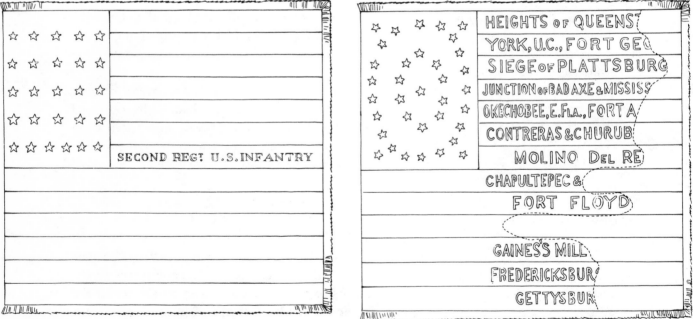

Fig. 76. Infantry national colors: (left) 2nd U.S. Infantry, issued about the time of the Mexican War. The stars were silver. (Based on a photograph in Davis.) (right) 6th U.S. Infantry, issued after 1862, with battle honors dating back to the War of 1812. The affair on the Bad Axe occurred in the Black Hawk War, and Fort Andrews was an engagement in Florida, in 1839. The name following Chapultepec was "City of Mexico," while the missing honor below Fort Floyd may be either "Yorktown" or "Mechanicsville." The regiment was so occupied listing its honors that it omitted its designation. The stars are golden. (West Point Museum)

color, although on infantry national colors some attempt was made to add new stars when new states were admitted to the Union.

Figs. 77 and 78

The infantry regimental color was a silken flag of the same size as the national, with the same fringe, cords, and tassels. Its field was a medium blue on which was embroidered or painted the "arms of the United States" with "the name of the regiment in a scroll [ribbon], underneath the eagle." Regulations called for embroidery, but in 1857 the Quartermaster General decided to save money by having the colors painted. The eagle, depicted in natural colors, held in his beak a red scroll with the motto "E Pluribus Unum" in gold letters. On his breast was a gold edged shield having thirteen stripes and a perfectly plain blue chief. Above the eagle were two arcs of five-pointed golden stars roughly corresponding to the number of states. The scroll beneath was red with gold edging and letters, usually arranged in this fashion: "EIGHTH REGt. U.S. INFANTRY".

This model regimental color dated back to at least 1841. Earlier models, which had been carried as national colors in the infantry, had differed in several respects, especially in lacking a motto in the eagle's beak and showing a "US" on the shield.

The eagle was "volant" (in flight). On the obverse of the color he flies to sinister (left) and looks to dexter (right), on its reverse he flies to dexter and looks to sinister, for the paintings on the two sides of a single piece of silk had to cover each other. The lettering on the reverse, however, was placed correctly for reading.

About 1863 (no authority for this has been found), the design of infantry regimental colors was noticeably altered. The facings of the eagle on both sides were reversed and he was made smaller, the arcs of stars were made more compact, and all gold ornaments on the scroll beneath the eagle were omitted. The scroll itself was rearranged. Regimental designations now took a variety of forms, from the simple "4th U.S. INFANTRY" to more explicit ones like "THIRD REGULAR U.S. INFANTRY". On the color bearing this latter legend, in the upper left, is a Maltese cross with the words "FIRST BRIGADE" above it and "2nd. DIVISION, 5th CORPS" below, indicating that assignment to a higher command was at times marked on regimental flags. This color was carried by the Third in 1863-1865.

At West Point is an infantry national color inscribed on the center stripe in gold letters "2nd BATTALION, 18th. U.S. INFANTRY". Another, a regimental color — probably a presentation battle flag — has on its scroll: "1st BATTALION, 11th INFANTRY". These and similar examples suggest that the large, three-battalion regular infantry regiments, 11th through 19th, were issued separate stands of colors for their 1st and 2nd Battalion which normally were employed separately. Their 3rd Battalions, intended to serve as depots, remained unorganized in five of the regiments and were only partially organized in the others. It is doubtful if colors were furnished them.

Fig. 79

Fig. 80

● *Colors of the Regular Artillery.* The national color resembled that of the infantry except its stars and regimental designation were embroidered or painted in gold, and its cords and tassels were red and yellow silk, intermixed. The regimental color was a yellow flag of the same size, with the same fringe, cords, and tassels. It bore in the center two golden crossed cannon with a red scroll above bearing the letters "U.S." and another below bearing the regimental designation. Edging, lettering, and ornamentations on these were gold. Typical lettering read "FIFTH REGT, ARTILLERY".

About 1863, the regimental color was slightly changed by lengthening out the ribbons and somewhat altering the shape of the crossed cannon. Nowhere is this change specified and we cannot be sure, therefore, whether or not this was merely a variation introduced by some colonel or contractor.

The colors mentioned above were, of course, carried by the regiments only when serving as foot or fortress artillery or as infantry. Since all but five of the companies of the five regular regiments served separately as field artillery batteries during 1861-1865, it is apparent that artillery regimental colors were displayed rarely if at all in those years. The flags actually carried by the regular artillery in the Civil War were guidons and special battle-flags which are described later.

Fig. 81

● *U.S. Engineer Battalion.* In 1851 there was only one company of engineer soldiers; in 1861 three additional companies were raised but no legal battalion organization existed until 1866 (although the companies were so organized in orders), and no colors were authorized. In 1866 (WDGO 93), two colors were authorized the Engineer Battalion. In the same year it was granted a long list of battle honors commencing with "VERA CRUZ, MEXICO, MARCH 9 and 28, 1847" and ending with "SIEGE OF PETERSBURG, JUNE, 1864 to APRIL, 1865." The national color was like that of the infantry and two flags of this sort are at West Point. One, which lists only ten Civil War battles through June 1863 and has thirty-six stars, is believed to be the first national color carried. Indeed, this color could well have been informally issued as early as 1863. Its honors are embroidered with gold bullion.

The battalion color introduced in 1866 (now on Governors Island) was of an entirely new design: "of scarlet, of the same dimensions as [the national color], bearing in the center a castle with the letters "U.S." above and the word "ENGINEERS" below in silver; fringe white." Cords and tassels were red and white silk intermixed on both colors.

● *1st and 2nd Regiments, U.S. Sharpshooters.* Both regiments were issued regulation infantry colors. No designations or battle honors are inscribed on the one national color which has survived, but a Model 1863 regimental color of the 1st Regiment is covered with the names of battles, painted on with unusual artistry. The name on the scroll reads "1st REGT./U.S. SHARP/SHOOTERS". Strangely, the scroll in the eagle's mouth is gray, not red, and the honors are painted in white letters.

Fig. 77. Infantry regimental colors: (left) A color believed to have been carried in the Mexican War and of the pattern in use circa 1841-1863. (right) One of the 1863 pattern colors, to which three new stars have been added. (Both based on photographs in Davis.)

Fig. 78. Infantry regimental colors: (left) This color was probably carried by the 6th Infantry in the 1850's while serving in the West. (right) An 1863 pattern color which makes it entirely clear that the Army's oldest Regular regiment was indeed Regular and serving with Sykes' celebrated Division of Regulars. According to museum records, its pike was shot in two at Gettysburg. (West Point Museum)

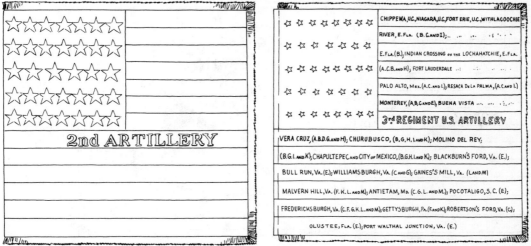

Fig. 79. Artillery national colors: (left) Color reported as having been carried during the Civil War. The stars and lettering are gold (West Point Museum). (right) Post-Civil War "battle flag" detailing services, generally as authorized by the 1866 *Army Register,* by companies rather than the regiment as a whole (present location unknown).

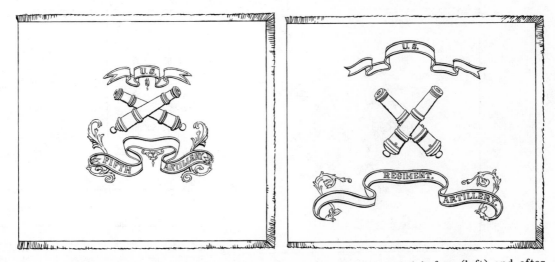

Fig. 80. Artillery regimental colors illustrating patterns carried before (left) and after (right) 1863 (West Point Museum and Governors Island).

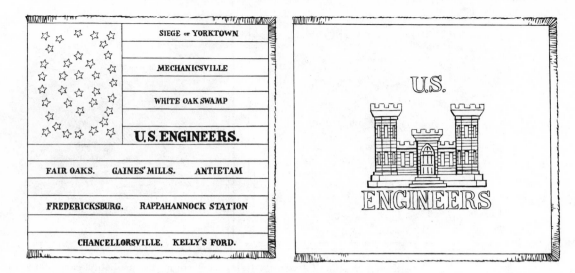

SIEGE OF YORKTOWN

MECHANICSVILLE

WHITE OAK SWAMP

U.S. ENGINEERS.

FAIR OAKS.   GAINES' MILLS.   ANTIETAM

FREDERICKSBURG.   RAPPAHANNOCK STATION

CHANCELLORSVILLE.   KELLY'S FORD.

U.S.
ENGINEERS

Fig. 81. U.S. Engineer Battalion colors: (left) Believed to be the first Engineer national color issued, presumably in 1866; honors embroidered with gold bullion (West Point Museum). (right) Battalion color of scarlet silk with letters and castle embroidered in silver, also believed to date from 1866. (Based on a painting in Davis).

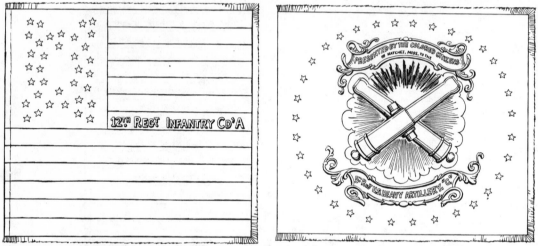

12TH REGT INFANTRY CD'A

PRESENTED BY THE COLORED CITIZENS OF MATCHEZ, MISS. TO THE

5 REGT US HEAVY ARTILLERY "C"

Fig. 82. U.S. Colored Troops colors: (left) National color, 12th Infantry Regiment, Corps d'Afrique, raised in 1863 in Louisiana. (right) Regimental color, 5th Heavy Artillery Regiment, U.S. C. T., raised in 1863 and stationed at Natchez and Vicksburg until discharged in 1866 (West Point Museum).

E PLURIBUS UNUM

1ST REGT   U.S.A.
VET.RES.CORPS

1ST REGT Q.M. FORCES
JOHNSONVILLE TENN
NOV. 4. 1864.
NASHVILLE TENN
DEC. 15 & 16. 1864

Fig. 83. Regimental color, Veteran Reserve Corps and (right) national color, Quartermaster Forces, Department of the Cumberland.

• *U.S. Colored Troops.* Enlistment of Negro troops by several Northern states began Fig. 82
in 1863 but eventually, with the exception of three Massachusetts regiments and one
from Connecticut, all Negro regiments were mustered directly into the Federal service.
Some earlier regimental designations carried the letters "a.d." at the end, for "African
Descent". The first general name assigned them was "Corps d'Afrique", but this was
changed in April 1864 to "U.S. Colored Troops." The corps, at its maximum,
contained some 148 regiments of infantry, cavalry, and heavy artillery, and ten
companies of light artillery.

The colors of these Negro regiments were as varied as their background. In general,
after 1864 at least, they were issued regulation infantry or artillery colors, both national
and regimental. A national color of the 12th Regiment (organized in Louisiana) has
painted on the center stripe "12th REGt. INFANTRY C d'A". A second national color
displays "37th REGt. 1st BRIG. 3d. DIVn. 24th. CORPS" and the battle honor "NEW
MARKET HEIGHTS". This is another example of a regiment's assignment being
inscribed on its color, in this case, it would seem, incorrectly. The 37th Regiment was
raised early in 1864 as the 3rd Regiment, North Carolina Volunteers, and redesignated
as above in February. It served until 1867. In June 1864 it was assigned to the 1st
Brigade, 3d Division of W.F. Smith's 18th Corps. When this Corps was broken up in
December it went, with all the other Negro regiments in the Army of the James, to the
25th Corps and not to the 24th. The regiment is officially credited with participation
in the Battle of New Market Heights, Virginia, September 1864.

One interesting regimental color has survived to illustrate the enthusiasm shown
toward the corps by the Negro population in general. It is a handsome yellow silk
artillery regimental color bearing on the obverse above its crossed cannon the designation "PRESENTED BY THE COLORED CITIZENS OF NATCHEZ, MISS. TO
THE" and below: "5th REGt. U.S. HEAVY ARTILLERY "C"." This regiment was
organized at Vicksburg, Mississippi in 1863, and was first designated the 9th Regiment,
Louisiana Volunteers, a.d. It became the 1st Regiment, Mississippi Heavy Artillery,
a.d., in September 1863, and the 5th U.S. Colored Heavy Artillery in April 1864.

The reverse of the color (now covered by canvas restoration) probably was a repetition of the obverse.

• *Veteran Reserve Corps.* The twenty-four regiments and 188 separate companies of Fig. 83
this corps (until March 1864 called the Invalid Corps), when under arms at all, served
solely as infantry. The regiments were issued regulation infantry national and regimental colors of the 1863 model, the former unmarked and the latter painted on the
scroll "1st REGt. VET. RES. CORPS U.S.A." Sometimes "U.S.A." was omitted. It is
possible that the earlier regimental colors carried "INVALID" in place of "VET. RES."
and were repainted after March 1864, but no flags so marked have survived. In view of
the duties of these regiments, none of their colors carry battle honors.

• *Other Federal Organizations.* No information has been found on the colors of the
six regiments (1st-6th) of the U.S. Volunteer Infantry raised in 1864 and 1865 from
Confederate prisoners of war to serve in the West against Indians. None of these regiments were granted battle honors and it is possible that they were not issued colors.

At West Point there are both national and regimental colors for the 1st through 8th Fig. 83
Regiments, Quartermaster Forces, Department of the Cumberland. Organization of

these regiments — ultimately nine in all, formed into three brigades — began 17 May 1864 at Nashville, Tennessee, for the defense of the Union depots in that city from Confederate raiders. This temporary force consisted of civilian employees of the Quartermaster Department, U.S. Military Railroads, and others, both white and colored, and totalled over 7,000 men with supporting cavalry and artillery. The men drilled several times a week, had arms and colors but, apparently, were not completely uniformed. The force took part in the battle of Nashville in December 1864 and probably continued into 1865.

The colors of the Nashville Quartermaster Forces are of regulation infantry size. The national colors are painted with elaborate legends in arcs with gold letters giving designation and battle honors; the regimental are dark blue with the eagle like the 1863 infantry colors. Below, on simplified red scrolls, are regimental designations in varying styles, as "1st REGt. Q.M.F." or "2nd REGT. Q.M. FORCES". Fringes, cords, and tassels were the same as on infantry colors.

Regiments of Quartermaster Volunteers were raised on a provisional basis at other locations and probably had similar colors, but only one has survived. This is a color (at West Point) of the 3rd Regiment, Quartermaster Volunteers, organized at Alexandria, Virginia, in July 1864. It closely resembles those carried at Nashville in size and design. A regimental color of the U.S. Treasury Guards has also survived and is displayed in Ford's Theatre, Washington, D.C., where it hung on the night President Lincoln was assassinated. It differs in no marked respect from the others already described.

Standards of Dragoons, Mounted Riflemen, and Cavalry

See 2nd. Mass. Vol. Cav.

For obvious reasons, mounted organizations carried much smaller flags than those serving on foot. Not only would a 6 by 6 foot flag have been impossible to carry on a horse at a canter, but there was not the need for cavalry or artillery units identifying themselves on the battlefield to the extent infantry had to do.

Fig. 84

Under the regulations in force between 1834 and 1895, mounted regiments were authorized only one standard, to be of silk, 2 feet 5 inches fly, and 2 feet 3 inches on the lance. The standards carried by the 1st and 2nd Dragoons from their organizaton to 1861 were blue and small editions of the Model 1841 Infantry regimental color. The designation of the latter read "SECOND REGT U.S. DRAGOONS". It had a somewhat longer fringe but did not — nor did many other such standards, so far as can be told — carry cords and tassels. When all the mounted regiments were converted to cavalry in 1861, this same model of standard was issued with new designations on the scroll and the gold stars above the eagle reduced to thirteen. The eagle may or may not have been reversed.

The Regiment of Mounted Riflemen was issued the same standard but on a light emerald green ground. A surviving example shows only minor variations in design from the dragoon standards. On its scroll the designation reads "1st REGIMENT OF MOUNTED RIFLEMEN". A new standard was issued the riflemen in 1852 which followed this same design and color.

The standards issued the two cavalry regiments raised in 1855 were in all respects like those of the dragoons, so far as can be told. Unfortunately, none have survived. It might be added here that the standards of U.S. mounted regiments did not use the Stars and Stripes until 1895.

Prior to and after the Civil War, and to a certain extent during the conflict, more than two or three companies of the regular mounted regiments seldom served together. There was, therefore, little opportunity to parade a regimental standard and these flags must have spent most of their days cased in a corner of the headquarters. No example of their being inscribed with battle honors is known. Like the light artillery, the mounted arm relied more on its guidons than on its standards.

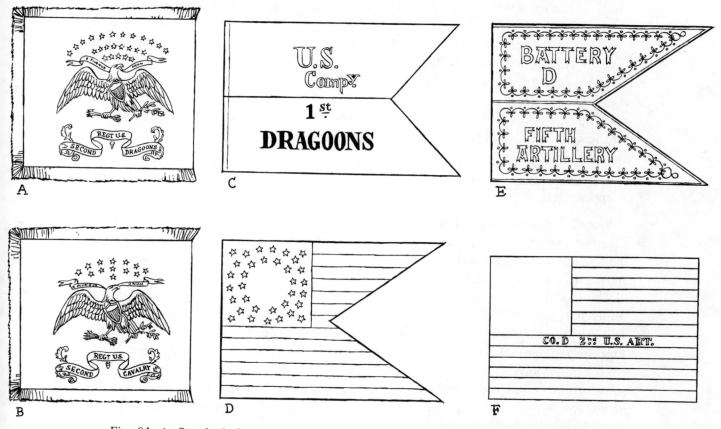

Fig. 84. A, Standard, 2nd Dragoon Regiment, before 1861; the reverse side is shown (based on a photograph in Davis). B, Standard, 2nd Cavalry Regiment, after 1861; also reverse (West Point Museum). C, Dragoon guidon, before 1862. D, Cavalry guidon, 1862-1885 (Governors Island). E, Non-regulation guidon, Griffin's Battery D, 5th Artillery Regiment, 1861 (West Point Museum). F, Flag, Battery D (Horse Artillery), 2nd Artillery Regiment, cir. 1861-1865; the stars are missing from the union (West Point Museum).

Guidons and Other Small Flags

It has been mentioned above that the component companies of the mounted regiments rarely served together before and after the Civil War. As a result, each company (or "troop," as they were beginning to be called) carried its own small, forked flag called a "guidon." Since 1835 the guidon in the regular service had been:

. . . swallow-tailed, three feet five inches from the lance to the end of the swallow-tail; fifteen inches to the fork of the swallow-tail; and two feet three inches on the lance. To be half red and half white, dividing at the fork, the red above — on the red the letters U.S. in white, and on the white the letter of the company in red. The lance of the . . . guidons to be nine feet long, including spear and ferrule.

These specifications are repeated in the *Regulations* of 1841, 1857, and 1861 with only minor changes in wording. Lanceheads were brass and no cords and tassels were carried. Apparently some latitude was allowed in the inscriptions, for the only dragoon guidon in the West Point Museum dating from the 1850's has "U.S./Compy" in white on the red half, and "1st Dragoons" in red on the white. This one is made of cotton cloth with a finer weave than bunting; the painted letters show through backwards on the reverse.

War Department General Orders No. 4, 18 January 1862, brought an entirely new type of guidon, a swallow-tailed stars and stripes. There can be little doubt that this style resulted from the need to more clearly identify separate troops of cavalry in combat. The idea was conceived by Lieutenant A.B. Chapman, 1st Dragoons, before his resignation to join the Confederacy in May 1861, but no serious action was taken on the idea until late in the year. The resulting order read:

Under instructions from the Secretary of War, dated January 7, 1862, guidons and camp colors for the army will be made like the United States flag, with stars and stripes.

The size of these new guidons was the same as the earlier ones. They were made of silk; the stars in the union were golden, arranged in circles; and the union itself was a light shade of blue. Sevaral surviving examples bear a troop letter within the circle of stars. This was the model of guidon carried until 1885.

The Model 1862 cavalry guidon was also issued to volunteer cavalry regiments and some of those which survive today are heavily painted with battle honors. There is a curious note, however, in the history of the 9th New York Volunteer Cavalry which suggests that guidons may not have been carried as generally as we suppose. After considerable delay this regiment, then on the Peninsula, was finally mounted. "Each squadron carried a bright new guidon and the regiment looked quite gay when in line or on the march. After a few weeks' service the guidons became worn and were discarded as a useless incumbrance. . . ."

● *Battery Guidons and Flags.* There is no clear record of the type of guidon or flag carried by companies of light or field artillery (after 1861 commonly called "batteries") from 1851 to 1861 if, indeed, they carried any. But in the early years of the Civil War they used the same red and white style as the cavalry. When Griffin's West Point Battery was assigned to the newly created 5th Artillery in July 1861, it carried an elaborate red and white swallow-tailed guidon, resembling the regulation pattern except for its extra decorations. A woodcut of an unidentified Union "Battery E" on the Peninsula in mid-1862 shows (for what it is worth) a red and white guidon with "U.S." above, "E" below, and crossed cannon in between. The guidon appears to be fringed.

The remains of a red and white flag at West Point is said to have been carried by Battery I, 1st Artillery, in various battles from Bull Run to Bristol Station in October 1863. It is larger than the normal guidon and may have been rectangular. The white stripe is uppermost.

After 1862 most field batteries carried either stars and stripes guidons similar to those of the cavalry, or sometimes small rectangular national colors bearing the battery designation, or special "battle flags." An example of the second type at West Point is about 2 by 3 feet, made of silk, and has "CO. D. 2nd U.S. ART." painted in gold on the white stripe just below the center red one.

No example has been discovered of battle honors being painted on a regular army stars and stripes guidon, although there are cases of this among volunteer batteries (the 11th New York Independent Battery, for example). The vehicle for honors among the regular artillerists was the "battle flag" or "commemorative guidon," an entirely non-regulation flag, roughly half way in size between a standard and a color.

The typical artillery battle flag was rectangular, averaging 3 by 4 feet, made of scarlet silk with gold bullion fringe, on which was embroidered in yellow thread two crossed cannon, battery designation, and numerous battle honors. In some cases the battles date back to the Mexican War, in others they are from the Civil War only. At least eleven specimens survive today, representing batteries in all the regular regiments. All vary somewhat in design and fabrication.

Fig. 85

Such battle flags were carried in combat during the Civil War and for some years thereafter, though for how long it is difficult to say. A few of the surviving examples have their original lances which are tipped with espontoon type spears, fitted with gold cords and tassels, and sometimes ringed with silver bands. The flags have cotton headings with grommets instead of sleeves, and were fastened either by rings to a steel bar

Fig. 85. Artillery "battle flag," Battery A, 5th Artillery Regiment. There is reason to believe that this flag was procured during the Civil War and honors added as they were earned.

Fig. 86. "Skirmish at Lee's Mills before Yorktown, April 16, 1862"; contemporary drawing by Winslow Homer. A regimental left general guide, with his marker, is visible in the center. (Courtesy of the Cooper-Hewitt Museum of Design, New York City)

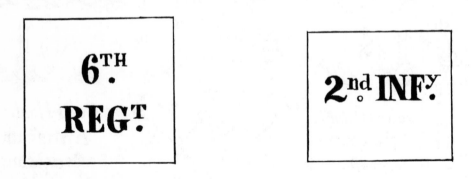

Fig. 87. Camp colors (or markers) carried by U.S. infantry regiments during the period 1851-1872.

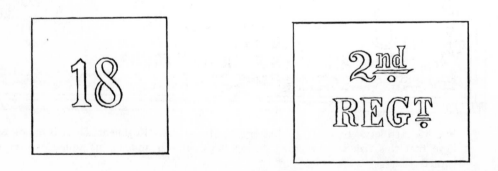

attached to the lance or by ribbons. All of these devices indicate the unofficial character of the artillery battle flag.

● *Infantry Small Flags.* Infantry regiments were not authorized company guidons until many years after the Civil War, but they did carry small bunting flags called "camp colors." The 1836 *Regulations* stated:

> The camp-colors to be of bunting, eighteen inches square; white for infantry, and red for artillery, with the number of the regiment on them. The pole eight feet long.

Camp colors, also called "field colors" or "markers," were employed to mark the right and left of a regimental line on parade or when forming camp. They were sometimes used in battle; today they still are employed for marking formal parade grounds. In the period of the Civil War there were normally only two to a regiment or separate battalion and they were carried by sergeants called the right and left general guides. Sometimes these small flags had their own poles with brass spearheads, and sometimes they were fixed on short poles which could be fitted into the barrels of the sergeants' muskets.

Fig. 86

In the regular army the former system applied. Designations painted in red on the infantry camp colors varied: "2nd Infy.", "6th REGT.", "10th REGT.", or merely "18". Artillery camp colors were inscribed with white paint on red bunting. In all cases the lettering read correctly on the obverse and backwards on the reverse since the paint came through the fabric.

Fig. 87

Camp colors of state units often assumed more elaborate forms, depending on the whims of commanding officers. Silken camp colors, with gold lace and fringes, were not uncommon. The 55th New York started off its field service with two small French tricolors as markers.

General Orders No. 4, 18 January 1862, specified that "camp colors . . . will be made like the United States flag, with stars and stripes." How far this order was put into effect during the Civil War is difficult to say, but the stars and stripes camp color was regulation in the 1870's. The two camp colors of the 128th New York were the U.S. flag with thirty-five stars. They were 18 x 22 inches in size, made of bunting with the colors stencilled on, and each had the number "128", on a dark blue cloth base, sewn on. These colors also bore a U.S. Inspector's stamp.

Garrison Flags

The garrison flag was the stars and stripes. It was made of wool bunting and was the only flag of all those considered thus far which was not carried on a lance or pike. Being made to fly from a flag pole, it was, instead, given a canvas heading with a grommet top and bottom. The red and white stripes were sewn together, and usually cut-out, white, 5-pointed stars of various kinds of cloth were sewn to the union. Variations in the arrangement of the stars were as common as in all other national flags of this period.

In size, the garrison flag (by U.S. *Army Regulations* of 1857) was 20 feet hoist (on the pole) and 36 feet fly. Flags of this large size were flown in good weather on holidays and important occasions. A smaller size, called a "storm flag," was 10 by 20 feet and was flown on all other days. A still smaller "recruiting flag," 52 by 127 inches, was issued for display over small buildings.

There was little to distinguish these garrison flags from thousands of other national flags used by public and private groups and they need not be discussed further. Preble, Harrison, and others go at length into their several variations of design and into the romantic stories that surrounded many of them.

Hospital Flags

A flag was prescribed for hospitals in the Army of the Potomac on 24 March 1862 (GO 102, A of P). It was yellow and of uncertain size. Apparently yellow was generally, if informally, used thereafter to designate hospitals although red and green flags were sometimes employed. The matter was formalized on 4 January 1864 when General Orders No. 9 specified a yellow bunting flag, 5 by 9 feet with a 24-inch green bunting letter "H" in the center, for general hospitals. For post and field hospitals, the flag was the same except in dimensions, 4 by 6 feet. Yellow bunting flags, 14 by 28 inches with one-inch green borders, designated ambulances and marked the route to field hospitals. These are illustrated in *OR* atlas, cited below under "Sources."

Headquarters or Corps Flags

Fig. 88

The use of distinctive flags to designate military headquarters, from brigades to armies, began in the American service during the opening stages of the Peninsular Campaign. At this period — March 1862 — the practice was confined to the Army of the Potomac.

The purpose of these flags was to mark the location of commanders or their headquarters for the benefit of staff officers and couriers. Headquarters flags were posted in front of the tents of commanders when they were in residence, or carried behind them when they were in the saddle. The scheme was undoubtedly borrowed from Europe where various armies had used it during the 1850's. Sometimes the system of designating flags was carried down to the level of the regiment, so that a commander or staff officer could, by glancing at a line of battle, tell just what regiments were included.

From this entirely functional beginning in 1862, the use of headquarters flags expanded the following year into an institution of considerably greater significance. The 1862 flags had been designed to be little more than tactical signals; the 1863 flags came to represent specific commands. Their unique devices often became symbols of commanders who created them and, in time, of their own men. The devices were adopted as badges, widely worn (in the East at least) during the last two years of the war, and thereafter by hosts of loyal veterans. They were, thus, the direct ancestors of the corps and divisional insignia of the 20th century.

The history of these headquarters flags (or "corps flags" as they were commonly called) is confused and often legendary. The wearing of corps badges and the display of corps flags by veteran societies led to embellishment or standardization of the original devices and to the fabrication of a vast store of legend about their adoption and display. It is even difficult now to say which came first, the corps flag or the corps badge.

In General Orders No. 102, Army of the Potomac, 24 March 1862, from his camp *Fig. 89* near Alexandria, Virginia, General McClellan established an elaborate system of head-quarters flags.* His own was the national flag; each of his four army corps had the same but with a "small square" flag flying beneath it, of these colors:

1st Army Corps — red
2nd Army Corps — blue
3rd Army Corps — red and blue vertical stripes
4th Army Corps — red and blue horizontal stripes

The system of division, brigade, and regimental flags was the same for all corps. Division flags were 5 feet on the staff and 6 on the fly, colored as follows.

1st Division — red
2nd Division — blue
3rd Division — red and blue vertical stripes
4th Division — red and blue horizontal stripes

Brigade flags were more complicated, since it was desirable to be able to identify a brigade independently of its division. All were the same size as division flags and colored:

1st Brigade, 1st Division — red and white   vertical stripes
2nd   ''   ''   '' — white, red, white   ''   ''
3rd   ''   ''   '' — red, white, red   ''   ''
1st   ''   2nd   ''   — blue and white   ''   ''
2nd   ''   ''   '' — white, blue, white ''   ''
3rd   ''   ''   '' — blue, white, blue   ''   ''
1st   ''   3rd   ''   — red, white, blue   ''   ''
2nd   ''   ''   '' — red, blue, white   ''   ''
3rd   ''   ''   '' — white, red, blue   ''   ''
1st   ''   4th   ''   — red, white, blue   horizontal stripes
2nd   ''   ''   '' — red, blue, white   ''   ''
3rd   ''   ''   '' — white, red, blue   ''   ''

Within each brigade the infantry regiments were designated by numbers 1, 2, 3, or 4, and each carried, in addition to its normal colors, the same flag as its brigade plus the designating number on one of the bars. Flags were also prescribed for artillery, cavalry, and engineers, being variant forms of the flag of the division to which the unit was assigned, although it is difficult to believe they were ever carried.

The Regular Brigade was first given a red flag with a white star, but this was changed on 30 April to a blue flag with a white star. This is illustrated in *HQ Flags*, cited under "Sources," which shows a silver fringe and a silver wreath around the star. Probably this was a ceremonial version since it seems to be made of silk and is much smaller than regulation. The original hung in the Chapel on Governors Island. Hospitals were to be distinguished by yellow flags, and subsistence depots by green ones. The yellow hospital flag has been mentioned above; there is no record the green flag ever saw service.

The 1st and 2nd Brigades, Cavalry Reserve, received yellow flags with one and two blue stars respectively. The Artillery Reserve received a red flag with a white star. All

*This was slightly amended by GO 110, 26 March and GO 119, 30 April, same year.

Fig. 88. Woodcut after a drawing by A.R. Waud. This somewhat contrived scene shows Major General Meade conferring with corps commanders of the Army of the Potomac, probably on the eve of the Mine Run Campaign. Clearly visible are the flags of the 3rd,

5th and probably 6th Army Corps, plus Meade's own headquarters flag. The Maltese Cross and the diamond are on divisional flags. The flags of the 1st and 2nd Army Corps are not present, but in one regimental history the print was doctored to include the latter.

of these flags, as has been said, were 5 by 6 feet and rectangular. General Irvin McDowell's original 1st Corps, Army of the Potomac, was reorganized on 4 April 1862 into the Department of the Rappahannock. On 19 June this Department adopted a system very similar to McClellan's; only the Department Headquarters flag — a national flag — differed.

The weaknesses of the McClellan system are obvious. By including regiments it tried to cover too much ground, and by relying entirely on arbitrary combinations of three colors it put too much strain on memory. It did not utilize numbers save in the regimental flags and, above all, it did not capitalize on distinctive symbols that could readily be identified and recalled. It is probable that these flags, hanging partially limp as was usually the case, served very little purpose.

General Philip Kearny, as was mentioned in the chapter on Insignia (pp. 93-94), designed an identifying square cloth patch for his 3rd Division, 3rd Corps, and on 28 June 1862, during the Seven Days' Battles on the Peninsula, ordered it worn on his officers' caps. There is no evidence that this or any other device was placed on a flag that year in the Army of the Potomac. However, there was an early instance of something like it in General Burnside's Department of North Carolina. There, in November 1862, the 3rd Brigade, 1st Division dubbed itself the "Red Star Brigade" and adopted a red flag with white canton in which was a red, 5-pointed star. It seems to have been used for a few months and is illustrated in *HQ Flags*.

When General Joseph Hooker became commander of the Army of the Potomac on 26 Janaury 1863 he sought for ways to improve its morale. Doubtless he remembered the Kearny Patch, for he had commanded the 2nd Division, 3rd Corps when it was adopted. In his Chief of Staff, General Daniel Butterfield, he found the man to carry out a plan to give comparable devices to all the higher commands of the Army.

Hooker's first step was to order, on 7 February 1863 (GO 10, A of P), that each of his army corps be designated by a blue swallow-tailed flag bearing a white "Maltese cross" in its center, with the corps' number in red on the cross. No size was prescribed, but 3 by 5 feet were the dimensions generally adopted. Hooker at that time had the 1st, 2nd, 3rd, 5th, 6th, 9th, 11th, and 12th Corps under his command.

There is no indication, however, that the Maltese cross was ever used on corps headquarters flags (except, later, by the 5th Corps, which had this kind of cross as its distinctive badge). For a reason not now clear, these flags were issued with a version of what is called the "cross botonny (or "botonée"), a cross having trefoils or triple buds issuing from each limb. The reason may lie in General Butterfield's interpretation of the word "Maltese cross." As early as 25 November 1862 he had recommended a designating flag for the 5th Corps, sending an illustration of a cross botonny but calling it a "Greek Cross." This device, furthermore, appears to have been grossly misinterpreted, particularly in *Battle Flags* and the plates of the official atlas wherein it is depicted as a "cross pommé," i.e., a cross in which the limbs terminate in a single ball. But the order did establish, once and for all, the blue swallow-tailed flag, about 3 by 6 feet, with a white device of some kind in its center, bearing the corps number in red, as the flag of a corps headquarters. The first ones procured were made of silk. After the Gettysburg campaign they were replaced by similar flags made of bunting. In the spring of 1864 it appears that the white devices used throughout 1863 were replaced by the corps

Note on illustrations of Headquarters Flags: Descriptions read from top to bottom, left to right. Drawings based upon actual flags or contemporary pictures have full shading; those based upon descriptions or pictorial reconstructions are in simple line. Sizes are approximate.

Fig. 89. *Flags prescribed by GO 102, A of P, 1862:* All except A are based on originals in the West Point Museum and New York State Military Collection and are cir. 5.5 x 6.5 ft. in size. From top left to bottom right: 1st Regiment, 3rd Brigade, 1st Division; 1st Regiment, 1st Brigade, 1st Division; 2nd Regiment, 2nd Brigade, 1st Division; 3rd Regiment, 2nd Brigade, 2nd Division; 4th Regiment, 1st Brigade, 3rd Division; 1st Brigade, 2nd Division; 1st Brigade, 4th Division. The Regular Brigade flag (A, at Governors Island) is cir. 1.5 x 3 ft., blue with white star inside a silver wreath.

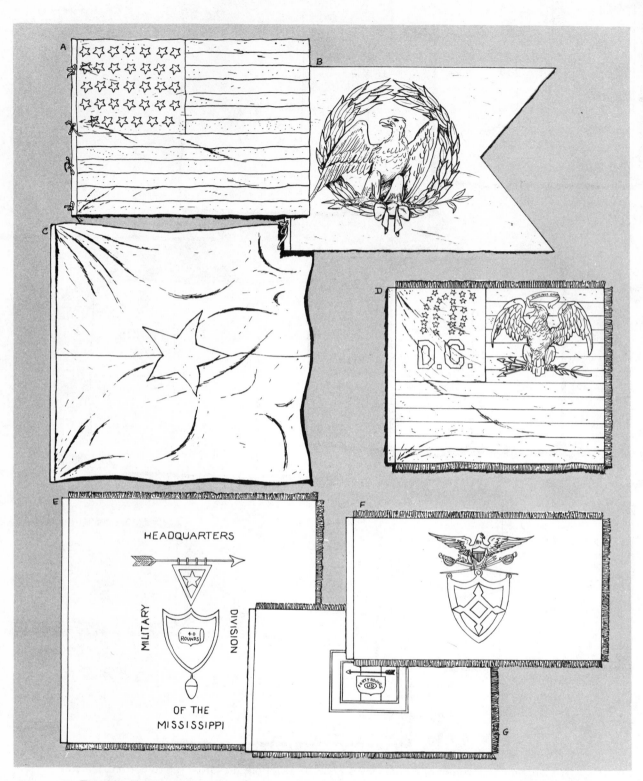

Fig. 90. *Headquarters of Armies:* A, Army of the Potomac, 1863, 4 x 5.5 ft. (Military Order of the Loyal Legion of the U.S. [MOLLUS] museum, Philadelphia). B, Army of the Potomac, 1864, 4 x 6 ft. (same source). C, Army of the James, 1864, 6 x 6 ft., red over blue, white star (Smithsonian Institution and Waud drawing). D, Department of the Cumberland, 1864, cir. 4 x 4.5 ft. (West Point Museum). E, Military Division of the Mississippi, 1865, cir. 5.5 x 5.5 ft. *(HQ Flags).* F, Army of North Carolina (formerly Ohio), 1865, 3.5 x 5 ft., gold and silver on blue with corps devices in color *(HQ Flags).* G, Army of the Tennessee, 1865, cir. 3.5 x 5 ft., blue with corps devices in color *(HQ Flags).*

badge on the headquarters flags for the four corps then forming the Army of the Potomac: the 2nd, 5th, 6th, and Cavalry Corps.

A circular issued by the Army of the Potomac on 21 March 1863 established the badges of all its corps. The 4th Corps had been broken up in September 1862 and the 9th had been transferred to the Department of Ohio two days before, hence these were not included. The 1st Division of the 4th Corps had previously adopted its own cap badge but there is no evidence of it being used on a flag.

The next step was taken on 12 May 1863, when General Orders No. 53 (A of P) established the form and colors of the flags of divisions and brigades. In every instance the newly established corps badges were used. The flags of divisions were to be rectangular (about 4.5 by 6 feet) — white with red badge for the 1st, blue with white badge for the 2nd, white with blue badge for the 3rd, and white with green badge for the Light Division of the 6th Corps.

Brigade flags were ordered to be triangular (about 4.5 by 6 feet) and to have the same color system as the division of which they were a part. The 1st brigade of a division had merely a triangular verison of the division flag, the 2nd brigade added a 6-inch stripe next to the lance, and the 3rd brigade added a 4.5-inch border on all sides. In any 1st division the stripe and border on brigade flags were blue; in any 2nd or 3rd division, they were red. (Later, provision was made for a 4th brigade flag by filling in its three corners with pie-shaped pieces of these same colors.)

General Orders No. 53 (A of P) also prescribed designating flags for the Cavalry Corps and the Artillery Reserve. Only the latter survives in a photograph of General Robert O. Tyler, copied in *Battle Flags*: a large swallow-tailed red flag with white crossed cannon.

It must be remembered that all the flags mentioned thus far were for the Army of the Potomac. Other armies followed suit as the advantages of these designating flags became apparent. The Army of the Cumberland, for example, adopted its first system on 19 December 1862 (GO 41, D of Cum). It proved unsuccessful and a new series was substituted on 25 April 1863 (GO 91, D of Cum). Neither of them incorporated corps badges, for these were not introduced in the West until 1864. A third system followed in April 1864, again not using badges except for the 20th Corps, and a fourth, which finally incorporated them.

Some Union Army commands never wore a badge or carried a designating flag. Others did so, but record of what they were has been lost. What follows below is a summary of information on those commands where such exists, together with suggestions where pictures of the flags can be found, since it is impractical to attempt to illustrate all the myriad styles here. We have reproduced the flags that exist today, and those of which there are photographs or reliable contemporary drawings, in shaded lines — the flags recreated solely from secondary source references are shown in outline

In addition to designating the headquarters of armies, army corps, divisions, brigades, and sometimes regiments by these flags, it was common to use them for the artillery brigade of an army corps, and for its Chief Quartermaster, at least in the eastern armies. By the final year of the war, these flags had become standardized and are illustrated in *HQ Flags*.

GHQ, Armies, and Departments

Fig. 90

● *GHQ, Army of the Potomac* (25 July 1861-28 June 1865). The first flag, prescribed 24 March 1862 (GO 102, A of P), was the national flag, which was flown during the commands of Generals McClellan, Burnside, Hooker, and Meade. The one used by Meade was 4x5 feet. In May 1864 he adopted a forked flag of "solferino" color, about 4x6 feet, bearing a golden eagle inside a wreath of silver leaves. A.R. Waud, the war artist, recalled General Grant commenting when he first saw this showy standard, "What's this! — Is Imperial Caesar anywhere about here?" All are illustrated in *HQ Flags*.

● *GHQ, Army of the James* (28 April 1864-31 January 1865). On 3 May 1864, the same date that corps headquarters and division flags were described for the 10th and 18th Corps of this force, a 6 foot square flag was also adopted, divided horizontally into red and blue bars and bearing in the center of this field a large, white, five-pointed star.

● *GHQ, Department and Army of the Cumberland* (24 Oct. 1862-c. Nov. 1864).* General W.S. Rosecrans established a system of battle flags for the Army of the Cumberland on 25 April 1863 (GO 91, D of Cum), the one for Army Headquarters being described as the national flag, 5x6 feet, "with a golden eagle below the stars, two feet from tip to tip."

In his orders of 26 April 1864 (GO 62, D of Cum) General G.H. Thomas prescribed a somewhat similar flag, 5x5 feet, which is illustrated in *HQ Flags*. However, the flag that has survived, and is also illustrated in *HQ Flags*, is a national color bearing a gold "D.C." in the canton and a gold eagle on the bars. Both obverse and reverse bear this same painted device but its placement varies somewhat.

● *GHQ, Military Division of the Mississippi* (16 Oct. 1863-27 June 1865). A yellow flag with the "40 Rounds" insignia of the 15th Corps and other corps' badges is shown in *HQ Flags*. It is said therein to have been used from the Chattanooga Campaign until the end of the war. This is manifestly impossible since some of the devices were not adopted until early 1865. It is probable that a plain yellow flag (5 feet square) was used at first and the devices painted on later. Sherman's Headquarters also flew a national color which is illustrated in the same source.

● *GHQ, Army of the Ohio* (1862-1865). A flag is illustrated in *HQ Flags* which shows the devices of the 10th and 23rd Corps, suspended from sabers surmounted by an eagle. The field of the flag is blue, its size is shown as 3.5x5 feet, and its fringe, cords, and tassels are blue and gold. It would seem to be more likely that this was the designating flag of the Department of North Carolina (27 March-1 Aug. 1865), which was held by these two corps.

● *GHQ, Army of the Shenandoah (Middle Military Division)* (August 1864-June 1865). It is probable that during Major General Philip Sheridan's command (to Feb. 1865) his personal forked red and white guidon, with two stars, was the Army Headquarters flag. This is illustrated in *HQ Flags*. There hangs in the Chapel on Governors Island an interesting version of this, called the "Five Forks Flag." It resembles the original in all respects save that both of the stars are formed out of forks.

*See also 14th Army Corps, for the earliest GHQ flag.

Several flags are attributed to cavalry commands of the Army of the Shenandoah and these will be mentioned later. None bore devices peculiar to the Army.

● *GHQ, Department and Army of the Tennessee* (Oct. 1862-Aug. 1865). The flag illustrated in *HQ Flags* is blue with a gold fringe, and bears in the center the devices of the 15th and 17th Corps on a vertical red-white-blue background. It could not have been adopted until March 1865. Because it is similar to that of the Army of the Ohio (North Carolina), the two may have been adopted after those two armies joined under Sherman in North Carolina in 1865.

● *GHQ, Department and Army of West Virginia* (28 June 1863-June 1865). A system of flags was adopted 3 January 1865 (GO 2, D of WVa), including one for the Department Headquarters: divided vertically into blue and red with a flying eagle in gold. Illustrated somewhat inaccurately in *HQ Flags* (see also "Army of West Virginia," *post*).

● *GHQ, Department of North Carolina* (27 March-1 Aug. 1865). See GHQ, Army of the Ohio, above.

Army Corps, Divisions, and Brigades, 1863-1866

● *1st Army Corps, Army of the Potomac* (3 March-4 April 1862). McDowell's corps used the 1862-type flags even after it became the Departmant of the Rappahannock.

● *1st Army Corps, Army of the Potomac* (12 Sept. 1862-24 March 1864). Badge, a disk or circle, prescribed 21 March 1863 (Cir A of P). When broken up its troops formed the 2nd and 4th Divisions, 5th Corps, and were permitted to keep their flags. The first forked HQ flag had a white cross botonny, bearing the red figure "1" on a blue field. This is illustrated as "General Reynold's Flag" in *HQ Flags* and a fragment is in the MOLLUS museum, Philadelphia. *HQ Flags* also shows a white circle device, and *Battle Flags* shows crossed-cannon mouths; the former may have been carried in early 1864. *Fig. 91*

● *1st Army Corps, Veteran Volunteers* (28 Nov. 1864-11 July 1866). A septagon badge was authorized in June 1865 for some elements, and there is evidence that at least two flags were manufactured. A set for one division is illustrated in *HQ Flags*.

● *1st Army Corps, Army of Virginia* (26 June-12 Sept. 1862). No information.

● *2nd Army Corps, Army of the Potomac* (3 March 1862-28 June 1865). Badge, a trefoil (three-leaf clover), prescribed 21 March 1863 (Cir A of P). Various specimens exist today. The first forked corps HQ flag had a white cross botonny, bearing the red figure "2" on a blue field. *Battle Flags* shows a cross pommé device carried in July 1863. In the spring of 1864, General W.S. Hancock received the regulation pattern shown in *HQ Flags* (which has a trefoil), which accompanied the Corps throughout the rest of the war. *Fig. 92*

● *2nd Army Corps, Army of Virginia* (26 June-12 Sept. 1862). No information.

● *3rd Army Corps, Army of the Potomac* (3 March 1862-24 March 1864). Kearny's division of this corps was the first to adopt a badge: the red flannel square. The very similar lozenge or diamond device was adopted 21 March 1863 (Cir A of P). When broken up in 1864, its 1st and 2nd Divisions were permitted to continue carrying their old flags. Various specimens exist today including markers for regiments (99th Pennsylvania, for example, in MOLLUS, Philadelphia). The first HQ flag had the white cross botonny with red "3" found in other Army of the Potomac corps. It may have been changed to the regulation diamond device depicted in *HQ Flags* early in 1864, *Fig. 92* if changed at all.

● *3rd Army Corps, Army of Virginia* (26 June-12 Sept. 1862). This was the original 1st Corps, Army of the Potomac, which later, as the Department of the Rappahannock, adopted a set of 1862-type flags by Circular 19 June 1862.

● *4th Army Corps, Army of the Potomac* (3 March 1862-26 Sept. 1862). In May 1862, one of the divisions of this corps was detached to form the 6th Army Corps. In September 1862, a second division was also detached to that corps while the remaining division was transferred to the Suffolk District of Virginia. The 1862 flags probably remained in use.

● *4th Army Corps, Department of Virginia* (4 May 1863-1 Aug. 1863). Two divisions were redesignated from 7th Corps troops in the Suffolk area after Longstreet's siege. This new 4th Corps and the 7th Corps, were merged into the 18th Corps. Flags bearing the equilateral triangle and following the Army of Potomac system are depicted in *HQ Flags*, but it is extremely unlikely that such flags were ever used by the eastern corps bearing these numbers.

Fig. 93 ● *4th Army Corps, Army of the Cumberland* (28 Sept. 1863-1 April 1865). This Western 4th Corps was a consolidation of the 20th and 21st Corps, and bore no relationship to the earlier command of the same number in the East. It was authorized an equilateral triangle as its badge on 26 April 1864 (GO 62, D of Cum), but it is possible that this device was used informally earlier. The same orders prescribed a system of designating flags which made no use of the triangle badge. These flags were red with blue cantons. White bars in the cantons designated the divisions and white stars below the cantons designated the brigades. The Corps HQ flag had a golden eagle in the canton. The system is illustrated in *HQ Flags*.

● *5th Army Corps, Army of the Potomac* (3 March-4 April 1862. This was Banks' corps which transferred to the Department of the Shenandoah. No record of any flags carried.

Fig. 94 ● *5th Army Corps, Army of the Potomac* (18 May 1862-28 June 1865). Badge, a Maltese cross, prescribed 21 March 1863 (Cir A of P). Various specimens exist today. The first forked HQ flag had a white cross botonny with a red "5". A new pattern with the Maltese cross was received in the spring and formally adopted in August 1864 and carried through the rest of the war. The shape of the Maltese cross sometimes varied on these flags. The brigade and division flags are illustrated in *HQ Flags*.

Fig. 95 ● *6th Army Corps, Army of the Potomac: Army of the Shenandoah* (18 May 1862-28 June 1865). Badge, a Greek cross, prescribed 21 March 1863 (Cir A of P). Later, early in 1864, this was changed to a St. Andrew's cross (that is, the Greek cross lying in an "x" position). The first forked flag bore the white cross botonny with red "6". *Battle Flags* shows an unusual cross pommé device with a red "6" on the HQ flag carried at Gettysburg. In early 1864 the device was changed to a St. Andrew's cross. The 3rd Division flag carried the Greek cross; all others existing today have the St. Andrew's pattern. The 2nd Brigade, 2nd Division had the letters "VERMONT BRIGADE" painted on its designating flag.

● *7th Army Corps, Department of Virginia* (22 July 1862-1 Aug. 1863, when broken up and merged into 18th Corps). No information on flags carried, if any.

Fig. 96 ● *7th Army Corps, Department of Arkansas* (6 Jan. 1864-1 Aug. 1865). Badge, an inverted crescent with star, adopted 1 June 1865(Cir D of Ark). Apparently a full set of flags was made up but their use was limited since the corps was deactivated shortly after their adoption. Two exist in the West Point Museum.

● *8th Army Corps, Middle Department* (22 July 1862-1 Aug. 1865). Although no authority is known for its adoption, the corps badge is said to have been a 6-pointed star. *HQ Flags* shows a full set of flags.

● *9th Army Corps, Army of the Potomac; Department of the Ohio; Department of Washington* (22 July 1862 - 1 August 1865). Corps badge, a shield with foul anchor crossed with a cannon, adopted 10 April 1864 (GO 6, 9th AC) when the corps returned to the East and Burnside was about to resume command. The first corps HQ flag was the familiar blue forked model with the white cross botonny and the red number "9". This was presented by the "Ladies of Lexington, Ky.," where the corps was enjoying pleasant occupation duty. It was carried through the Vicksburg and Knoxville campaigns until the corps returned to the East.

Fig. 97

Burnside, upon taking command in April 1864, adopted a national flag with the new corps badge in its union, surrounded by an oval of stars. This was carried until the corps was again assigned to the Army of the Potomac in May 1864. The next flag, adopted then or (according to *OR* atlas) on 1 August, was the blue regulation model bearing the corps badge in white. All three flags are illustrated in *HQ Flags.*

A system of flags for the divisions and brigades of the 9th Corps was adopted about May 1864. These flags are not illustrated in *HQ Flags*, but various photographs substantiate their use, and one example is in the West Point Museum. In this system the divisional flags had a field of the color of the division with a border and a corps device of the usual contrasting color. The brigade flags, on the other hand, showed three vertical stripes whose color arrangement is not entirely clear. Each had the corps device and the brigade number on separate stripes.

The next system, which is illustrated in *HQ Flags*, was approved on 1 August 1864.

● *10th Army Corps, Department of the South* (3 Sept. 1862-17 April 1864). No known flags, although it is probable that when the 1st Division, 11th Corps was assigned to the 10th Corps on 3 September 1863 it retained its old flags bearing the crescent badge.

● *10th Army Corps, Army of the James* (28 April-3 Dec. 1864). On 3 May 1864, shortly after this corps was first created, a series of flags was adopted (see *OR* atlas). All were large blue flags, the one for corps HQ bearing a white "10" while the three division flags had one, two, and three white stars, respectively. When Major General D.B. Birney took command he adopted the square bastioned fort badge (GO 18, 10th AC, 25 July 1864) and a set of flags bearing this device was made. He was, however, photographed with the older "10" flag which, indeed, he may have continued to carry.

Fig. 98

● *10th Army Corps, Department of North Carolina* (27 March-1 August 1865). When this corps was recreated, Major General Alfred H. Terry was made its commander. He had earlier commanded the 10th Corps in Birney's absence in the Army of the James and was then photographed with the second headquarters flag of the corps, a blue forked flag bearing the white cross botonny with red "10". He may have continued to use this flag in North Carolina prior to adopting a similar blue forked flag bearing a red bastioned square and having a white stripe along the staff edge. Since Terry readopted

Fig. 98

the old 10th Corps badge (GO 2, 10th A.C., 6 April 1865), it is probable that the flags following the system of the Army of the Potomac continued its use in North Carolina.

Fig. 99

● *11th Army Corps, Army of the Potomac; Department of the Cumberland* (12 Sept. 1862-14 April 1864). Badge, a crescent, prescribed 21 March 1863 (Cir A of P). The first forked HQ flag had a white cross botonny with a red "11", and this was probably used through 1863 at least. A set of divisional and brigade flags was in use by the Battle of Gettysburg. When the 1st Division was transferred to the Department of the South and assigned to the 10th Corps (3 September 1863) it apparently kept its old flags.

● *12th Army Corps, Army of the Potomac; Army of the Cumberland* (12 Sept. 1862-4 April 1864). Badge, a 5-pointed star, prescribed 21 March 1863 (Cir A of P). There were only two divisions in this corps and they were commonly called the "Red Star" (i.e., 1st, using a white flag) and "White Star" (2nd, on a blue flag) divisions. The blue star flag shown in *OR* atlas was never used in this corps. Apparently corps HQ displayed the white cross botonny, or white crossed-cannon mouths, with a red "12". These flags were continued by the 20th Corps, *q.v.*

Fig. 99

● *13th Army Corps, Army of the Tennessee; Department of the Gulf* (24 Oct. 1862-11 June 1864). On 16 August 1863 the Department of the Gulf instructed its Chief Quartermaster to supply the 13th Corps with a set of flags down through brigades. This was similar to the set adopted by the 19th Corps in February 1863 but with differences in coloring and position of the numbers on corps and division flags, and in the vertical striping on the brigade flags. No such flags survive, nor do any pictures of them; it is possible they were never issued.

● *13th Army Corps, Army of the Gulf* (18 Feb.-20 July 1865). The survival of a brigade flag from this corps strongly suggests that a system may have been employed based on the Army of the Cumberland flags of 1864.

● *14th Army Corps, Army of the Cumberland; Army of Georgia* (24 Oct. 1862-1 Aug. 1865). This corps used at least four different sets of flags. The earliest system was prescribed 19 December 1862 (GO 41, D of Cum), when this Corps represented the entire Army of the Cumberland. All of the flags described were to "be attached to a portable staff, fourteen feet long, made in two joints, and will be habitually displayed in front of the tent, or from some prominent part of the house or vessel occupied by the Officer, whose Head-Quarters they are intended to designate; and, on the march, will be carried near his person."

General Headquarters was to be indicated by the "national flag, six feet by five, with a golden eagle below the stars, two feet from tip to tip." This continued to be the flag of General Headquarters, Army of the Cumberland after April 1863.

The three "wings" of the corps (army) were designated by flags 6 feet *on the staff* and 4 feet fly: "plain light crimson" for the Right Wing, "plain light blue" for the Centre, and "plain pink" for the Left Wing. To these basic designs were added stars and numbers to indicate the divisions and brigades of each wing, on flags 5 feet *on the staff* and 3 feet fly. All 1st Divisions, for example, had "one white star, eighteen inches in diameter, the inner point one inch from the staff"; all 1st Brigades had a figure "1" 8 inches long, in the center of each star of the division flag. Special flags were prescribed for the Artillery Reserve, Cavalry Reserve, and Engineer Corps, and for Hospital, Subsistence, and Quartermaster depots. So far as can be discovered, no flags

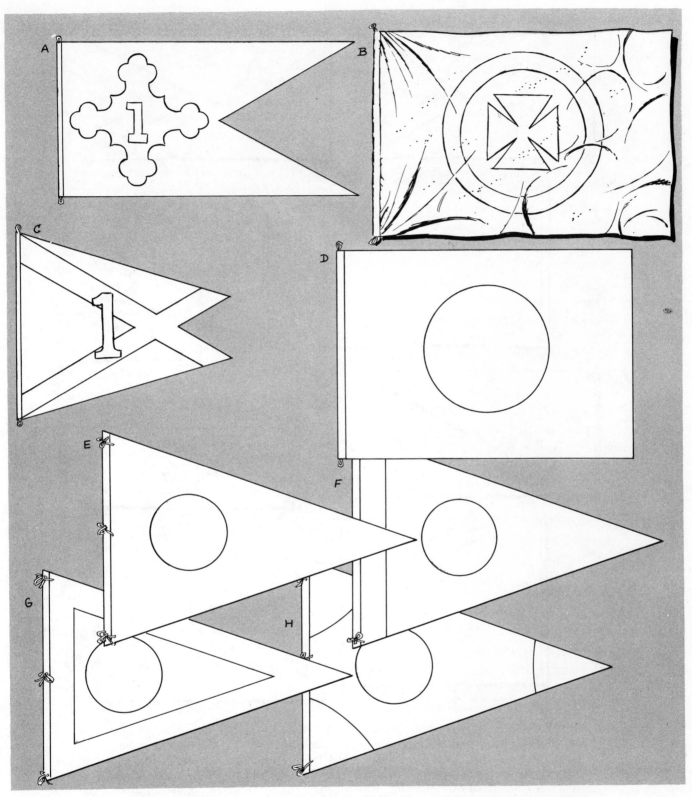

Fig. 91. *1st Army Corps:* A, Headquarters, 1863, 3x6 ft. (*HQ Flags* and surviving fragments). B, 3rd [old 2nd] Division, 5th Army Corps (the 1st Corps was discontinued in 1864; its men became the 2nd and 4th Divisions of the 5th Corps), 1865, 4.5x6 ft., blue circle and cross on white (drawing accompanying Special Field Order 320 in National Archives). C, Chief Quartermaster, 1863, 4x5 ft., white cross on blue, red "1" (*HQ Flags*). D, 2nd Division, 1863, 4.5x6 ft., red disc on white (1875 reproduction, West Point Museum, and *HQ Flags*). E-H, brigade flags, 1st Division (*HQ Flags*).

328

Fig. 92. *2nd Army Corps:* A, Headquarters, 1863-1864, 3x5.5 ft., white cross on blue, red "2" (West Point Museum). B, Headquarters, 1864-1865, 3x6 ft., white clover on blue, red "2" (same source). C, 1st Division, 1864, 4.5x6 ft., red clover on white (1875 reproduction in West Point Museum). D, Chief Quartermaster, 1864, 4x5 ft., red clover and cross on white (MOLLUS Museum, Philadelphia). *3rd Army Corps:* E, Headquarters, 1863, 3x6 ft., white cross on blue, red "3" (contemporary photo). F, Chief Quartermaster, 1863, cir. 4x5.5 ft., probably red with white diamond enclosing blue one (contemporary photo). G, 2nd Division, 1863, 4.5x6 ft., white diamond on blue (flag collections in Massachusetts and New Jersey state capitols). H, 3rd Division, 2nd Army Corps, 1865, 4.5x6 ft., white flag with red diamond enclosing white one, enclosing blue clover (flag collection New Jersey state capitol). (When 3rd Corps was deactivated, its men became the 3rd and 4th divisions of the 2nd Corps.)

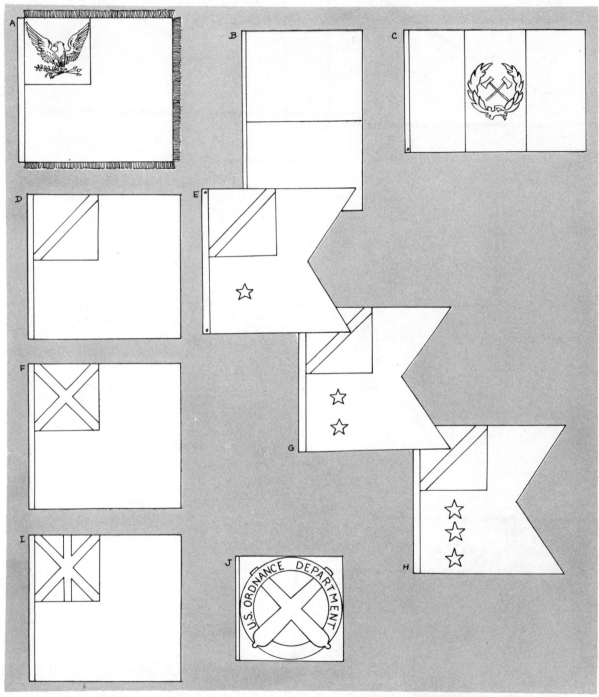

Fig. 93. *4th Army Corps, Army of the Cumberland.* All flags from *HQ Flags* and Corps orders, and are dated 1864-1865: A, Headquarters. 5x5 ft., red with blue canton and golden eagle. D,F, and I, divisions, 5x5 ft., red with blue canton and white bars. E, G and H, brigades, same size and colors with white stars. B, Engineer Brigade, blue over white, 6x4 ft. C, Pioneer Brigade, blue-white-blue with blue device, 4x6 ft. J, Division Ordnance officer, 3x3 ft., white devices on bright green, black letters. The Corps Ordnance officer flew this flag beneath a 4-foot long crimson streamer marked "Chief of Ordnance."

Fig. 94. *5th Army Corps:* Headquarters, 1863 (?), 3x5 ft., white cross on blue, red "5" (West Point Museum). B, Headquarters, 1863-1864, 3x6 ft., same colors MOLLUS Museum, Phildelphia). C, Headquarters, 1864-1865, 3x6 ft., same colors (West Point Museum and contemporary photo). D, 1st Division, 1864-1865, 4.5x6 ft., red cross on white (contemporary photo). E, originally 2nd Division,1st Army Corps, 1863-1864, when made 2nd Division, 5th Army Corps, 4.5x6 ft., white disc on blue; blue cross added after September 1864 as 3rd Division (William Penn Museum and contemporary photo). F, 2nd Division, 1863, 6x6 ft., white cross on blue (West Point Museum).

Fig. 95. *6th Army Corps:* A, Headquarters, 1863-1864, 3x6 ft., white cross on blue, red "6" (Gettysburg National Museum and Flags in Vermont capitol). B, Headquarters, 1864-1865, 3x6 ft., same colors (contemporary photo). C, 2nd Division, 1864-1865, 4.5x6 ft., white cross on blue (1875 reproduction in West Point Museum and contemporary photo). D, 3rd Division, 1863, 6x6 ft., blue cross on white (West Point Museum). E, Quartermaster, 2nd Division, 1864, 4x5 ft., blue cross on red, white numbers (West Point Museum). F, 2nd (Vermont) Brigade, 2nd Division, 1864-1865, 4.5x5.5 ft., white cross (edged in black) on blue with red bar (flags in Vermont capitol).

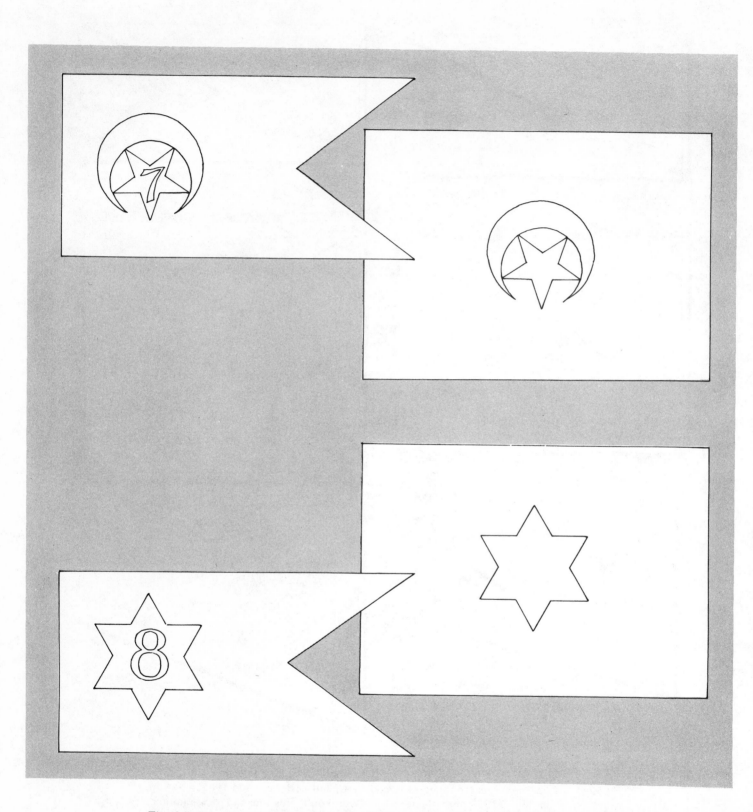

Fig. 96. *7th Army Corps of Arkanasa:* Headquarters, 1865, 3x6 ft., white crescent and star on blue, red "7"; division flags, 4.5x6 ft.,(1875 reproductions, West Point Museum and *HQ Flags). 8th Army Corps, Middle Department:* Headquarters, 3x6 ft., white star on blue, red "8"; division flags 4.5x6 ft. *(HQ Flags).*

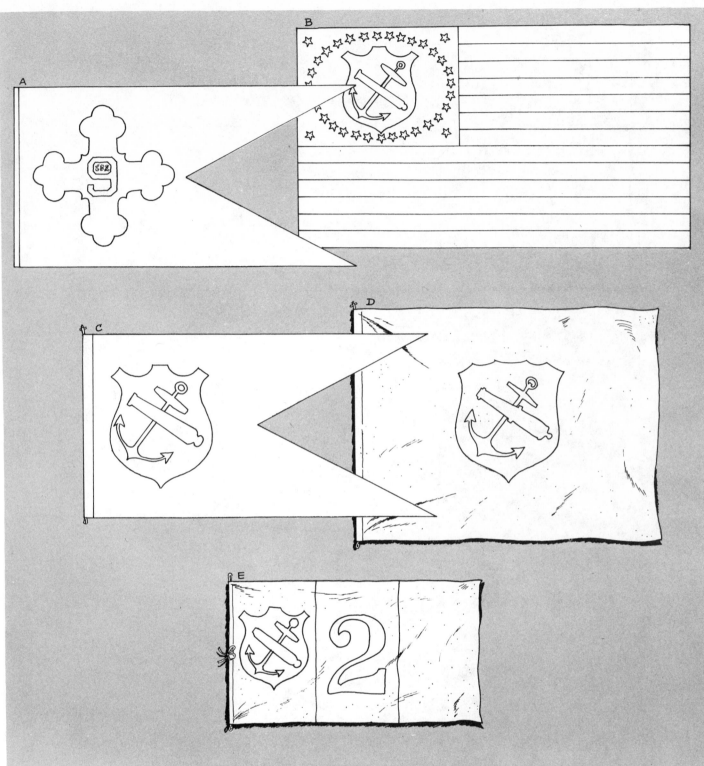

Fig. 97. *9th Army Corps:* A, Headquarters, 1863-1864, 3x6 ft., white cross on blue, red "9" with "LGN" on reverse in upper loop of number, *(HQ Flags).* B, Headquarters, 1864, 4.5x6 ft., national flag with white shield in canton bearing red anchor and gold cannon, white stars, *(HQ Flags).* C, Headquarters, 1864-1865, 3x6 ft., white shield on blue, blue anchor and red cannon, *(HQ Flags).* D, 1st Division, 1864, 4.5x6 ft., red shield on white, white anchor and blue cannon (flags in Michigan capitol). E, 2nd Brigade, 4th Division, 1864, 2.5x4 ft., green-blue-red stripes with red "2" and white shield, blue anchor and red cannon (West Point Museum).

Fig. 98. *10th Army Corps, Army of the James:* A. Headquarters, 1864, cir. 6x6 ft., white "10" on blue (contemporary photo and *OR* atlas). B, C and D, division flags, 1864, 6x6 ft., white stars on blue (*OR* atlas and Corps orders of May 1864). *10th Army Corps, Department of North Carolina:* E, Headquarters, 1865, cir. 2.5x5.5 ft., red fort on blue with white bar (*HQ Flags* and drawing in the National Archives). F, 2nd Division, 1864-1865, 4.5x6 ft., white fort on blue (contemporary photo and *HQ Flags*). G, Headquarters flag used in late 1864 in Army of the James and probably early 1865 in Department of North Carolina, 3x6 ft., white cross on blue with a red "10" (contemporary photo).

335

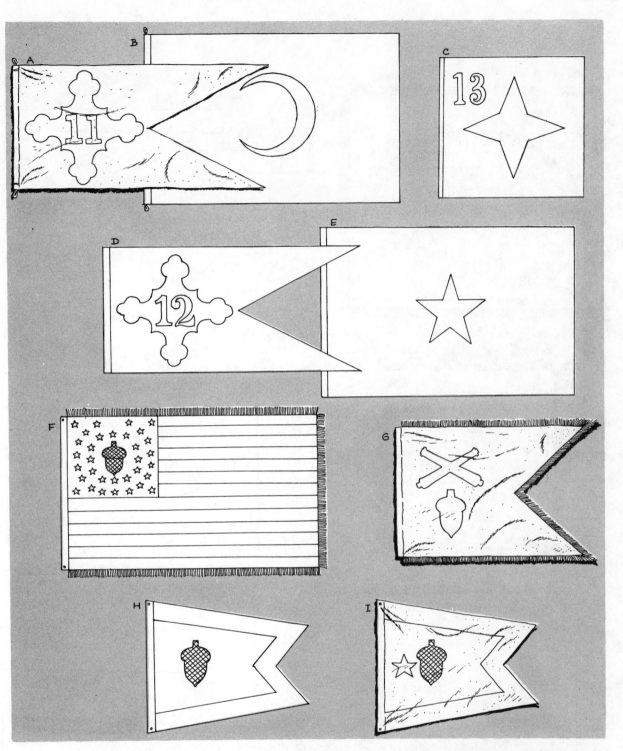

Fig. 99. *11th Army Corps:* A, Headquarters, 1863, 3x6 ft., white cross on blue with red "11" (Smithsonian). B, 1st Division, 1863, 4.5x6 ft., red crescent on white (*HQ Flags* and 1875 reproduction in West Point Museum). *13th Army Corps, Department of the Gulf:* C, Headquarters, 1863-1864(?), 4x4 ft., blue star on white with red "13" (Dept. letter dated 16 August 1863). *12th Army Corps:* D, Headquarters, 1863, 3x6 ft., white cross on blue with red "12" (*HQ Flags*). E, 1st Division, 1863, 4.5x6 ft., red star on white (*HQ Flags*). *14th Army Corps, Army of the Cumberland:* F, Headquarters, 1865-1865, 4.5x6 ft., national flag with brown acorn in canton (*HQ Flags*). G, Artillery Brigade, 1864-1865, cir. 4x5 ft., red cannon with white acorn on blue (West Point Museum). H, 1st Division, 1864-1865 4x4.5 ft., red acorn on blue, red border (*HQ Flags*). I, 1st Brigade, 1st Division, 4x4.5 ft., same colors with white star (West Point Museum).

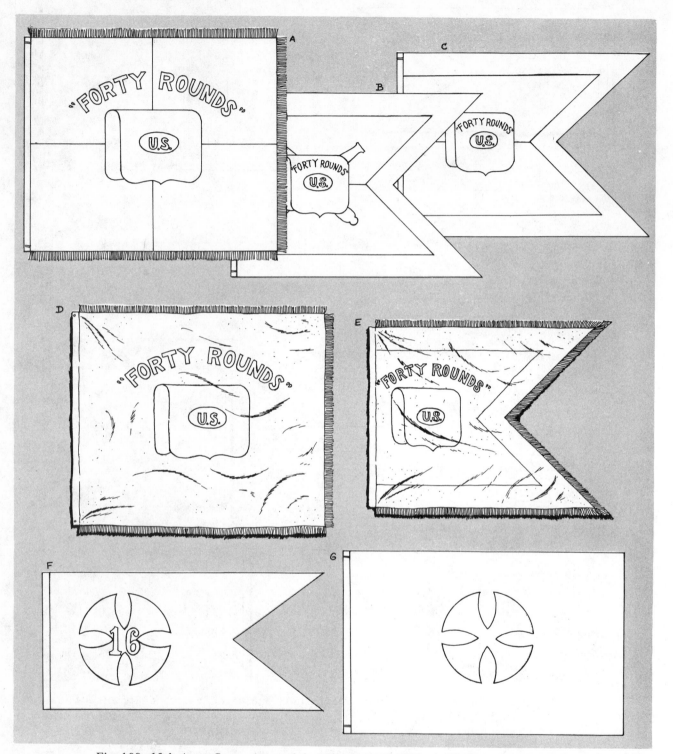

Fig. 100. *15th Army Corps, Army of the Tennessee,* all 1865: A, Headquarters, 5x5.5 ft., corps device on red over white, blue border *(HQ Flags)*. C, Chief Quartermaster, 4.5x 5.5 ft., corps device on white over blue, red border *(HQ Flags)*. D, 1st Division, 5x5.5 ft., corps device on red (West Point Museum) E, 1st Brigade, 1st Division, 4x5 ft., corps device on red, white border (West Point Museum). *16th Army Corps, Army of the Tennes-see*: F, Headquarters, 1865 (?), 3x6 ft., white device on blue, red "16" *(HQ Flags)*. G, 1st Division, 1865 (?), 4.5x6 ft., red device on white *(HQ Flags)*.

prescribed by this order have survived.

These first flags were found to be "not sufficiently marked to be readily distinguished from each other," and a new system was prescribed by the Army of the Cumberland for the 14th, 20th and 21st Corps on 25 April 1863 (GO 91, D of Cum), these corps having replaced the wings. Under this the 14th Corps was given "a bright blue flag, six feet by four, fringed, with black eagle in center, two feet from tip to tip, with the number '14' in black on shield, which shall be white." Divisions received an unfringed flag of the same size and color but omitting the eagle and adding from one to five black stars, placed near the staff, indicating the division number. Each brigade used the flag of its division with its own number in white on the stars. The system was quite complex and extended down to such lower elements as batteries of artillery. The staff department flags bore little relationship in color or design to those carried by the combat elements.

When the new flags described above arrived in July, they were found to be made of dark rather than "bright" blue. The black stars had to be changed to white, and the brigade numbers thereon to black (GO 177, D of Cum, 1 Aug. 1863).

On 26 April 1864 (GO 62, D of Cum) the system was again changed, this time to a blue flag with a red canton for all elements. An eagle in the canton designated corps HQ; a single white bar, 1st Division; two bars, 2nd Division, and three, the 3rd. Brigade flags were smaller, forked, and used white stars to indicate the brigade number.

The same order that introduced these blue flags also prescribed the corps badge, an acorn. The idea of capitalizing on this symbol was not long arriving and on a date yet to be determined, the last flag system was authorized. Corps HQ used the national flag *Fig. 99* with an acorn among the stars in the union. All the other flags were forked and bore an acorn: 1st Division, blue edged red; 2nd, red edged white; 3rd, red edged blue. Again the brigades were indicated by the number of stars. Both the third and fourth systems are illustrated in *HQ Flags*.

● *15th Army Corps, Army of the Tennessee* (18 Dec. 1862-1 Aug. 1865). Badge, a cartridge box, adopted 14 February 1865 (GO 10, 15th AC). On 9 April (GO 21, 15th *Fig. 100* AC) a system of designating flags was adopted, all embracing this badge. The HQ and division flags were 5x5.5 feet; 1st Division, red; 2nd, white; 3rd, blue; 4th, yellow; corps HQ, quartered, bearing these four colors. Brigade flags were forked, 4.5x5 feet, and employed the division color plus colored borders. The badge is painted on in all surviving examples: a cartridge box with brass "US" plate, above which — in an arc and in quotes — are the words "FORTY ROUNDS". The flags were adopted too late in the war to see service in combat. All are illustrated, not quite correctly, in *HQ Flags*.

● *16th Army Corps, Army of the Tennessee; Army of the Gulf* (18 Dec. 1862-20 July *Fig. 100* 1865). The flags carried by this corps have not been clearly established. It is apparent that at an unknown date a corps badge was adopted, a circle with four minie balls pointed at the center which produced a sort of Maltese cross. Some flags were made bearing this design, *HQ Flags* pictures a full set and several examples survive. *OR* atlas shows no flags for this corps.

● *17th Army Corps, Army of the Tennessee; Army of the Gulf* (18 Dec. 1862-1 Aug. *Fig. 101* 1865). Badge, an arrow, adopted 25 March 1865 (GO 1, 17th AC). On 25 and 28 April (GO's 2 and 4, 17th AC), a system of designating flags was worked out using this badge. It is illustrated in *HQ Flags* and *OR* atlas, but these sources differ utterly on the colors. Red division and brigade flags accord with the later order issued, but surviving examples are blue, in accord with the earlier order.

Fig. 101

● *18th Army Corps, Department of North Carolina; Army of the James* (24 Dec. 1862-3 Dec. 1864). Badge, a cross botonny, adopted 7 June 1864 (Cir 18th AC). However, prior to this on 3 May 1864 the corps (like the 10th Corps) adopted a simple designating flag system for its HQ and three divisions. The former was indicated by 6x6 foot flag of red bearing the white numeral "18", the latter by flags of the same size and color with one, two, and three white stars. Probably in July a new series was adopted using the cross botonny badge. It is illustrated in *HQ Flags*.

Fig. 102

● *19th Army Corps, Army of the Gulf; Army of the Shenandoah* (14 Dec. 1862-20 March 1865). An unusual system of designating flags, in part utilizing a 4-pointed star device, was adopted 18 February 1863 (GO 17, 19th AC). It is illustrated in *HQ Flags*. Also illustrated there, but incorrectly, is the corps second system, prescribed 17 November 1864 (GO 11, 19th AC), which included the corps badge, a form of Maltese cross, prescribed in the same order. Three of the flags survive and show that the system as illustrated in the *OR* atlas is correct but not complete.

Fig. 102

● *20th Army Corps, Army of the Cumberland* (9 Jan.-28 Sept. 1863). This first short-lived corps, under Major General Alexander M. McCook, was authorized a series of designating flags on 25 April 1863 (GO 91, D of Cum). The HQ flag, 4x6 feet, was red with a gold fringe and bore a black eagle on which was placed a white shield with the black number "20". This flag, still surviving, is made of red silk and the device is painted. Each division carried a flag of the same size and color, omitting the eagle and adding from one to three black stars, as in the 14th Corps. Brigades had the same flag as divisions but with their numbers on the stars. Following the Chickamauga Campaign the corps was merged into the new 4th Corps.

● *20th Army Corps, Army of the Cumberland* (4 April 1864-1 June 1865). The second 20th Corps was formed by combining the 12th Corps, composed of two veteran divisions, with the two divisions of the 11th Corps that accompanied them west, adding more regiments, and reorganizing the whole into three divisions. A fourth division served elsewhere. On 26 April 1864 (GO 62, D of Cum) it was given its badge, "a star, as heretofore worn by the 12th Corps." The same orders prescribed its flags: HQ got a blue swallow-tailed type with a white "Tunic cross" and red numeral "20"; divisions got the old 12th Corps flags, 6 feet square, adding a blue star on a white flag for the 3rd Division, and green star on a red flag for the 4th. Brigades received triangular flags, each side being 6 feet, with device and color used by their division and differentiated by stripes and borders as in the Army of the Potomac. Several of these flags survive today, and the system is illustrated in *HQ Flags*. However, this source illustrates a second series for the same corps, containing four brigades, which cannot be substantiated.

Fig. 103

● *21st Army Corps, Army of the Cumberland* (9 Jan.-28 Sept. 1863). A system of flags was prescribed on 25 April 1863 (GO 91, D of Cum) to include brigades. It was described as "A bright red, white and blue flag (horizontal)." The corps HQ was designated by an eagle on the center white stripe bearing a shield on its breast containing the number "21". Divisions had from one to three black stars there, and brigades used the same flags as divisions, but with white numbers on the stars. This system is illustrated in *HQ Flags* and *OR* atlas, except the dimensions are incorrect in both. These were 6 feet hoist and 4 feet fly rather than the reverse, as shown. Following the Chickamauga Campaign the corps was merged into the new 4th Corps.

- *22nd Army Corps, Department of Washington* (2 Feb. 1863-11 June 1866). No information has been found as to when the corps badge, a pentagonal cross, was adopted. *HQ Flags* shows the full system of flags utilizing this badge, but when and by what commands these flags were used is impossible to say in view of the abnormal composition of the Department. *Fig. 103*

- *23rd Army Corps, Army of the Ohio; Department of North Carolina* (27 April 1863-1 Aug. 1865). The corps badge, a shield divided into three parts, was adopted 25 September 1864 (SFO 121, D of Ohio); at the same time a flag system was pre-scribed, extending to brigades. It is illustrated incorrectly in *HQ Flags*. Corps HQ also used a national color, in whose union the thrity-six stars were arranged in the form of the shield device, and on whose red stripes were painted the principal battle honors (Knoxville, Atlanta, Franklin, Nashville, and Wilmington). *Fig. 104*

- *24th Army Corps, Army of the James* (3 Dec. 1864-1 Aug. 1865). The corps badge, a heart, was adopted 18 March 1865 (GO 32, 24th AC). A complete flag system was adopted soon afterwards using the Army of the Potomac method of designation in the main. It is illustrated in *HQ Flags*. *Fig. 104*

- *25th Army Corps, Army of the James; Army of Occupation in Texas* (3 Dec. 1864-8 Jan. 1866). The corps badge, a square, was adopted 20 February 1865 (Orders, 25th AC). A complete flag system was adopted soon afterwards using the Army of the Potomac method of designation but adding a few new features and making the divisional flags more elongated than usual (2 feet 7 inches hoist, 5 feet 9 inches fly). Illustrated in *HQ Flags*. *Fig. 105*

- *Army of West Virginia* (28 June 1863-27 June 1865). This command resembled an army corps in having divisions and brigades. An eagle was adopted as the army badge on 3 January 1865 (GO 2, D of WVa) and a system of flags adopted at the same time. It is illustrated in *HQ Flags*. This source also shows an entirely different pattern of flag for the 3rd Division (red, white, and blue slanting stripes with three blue stars on the white stripe), which was adopted 23 March 1864 (GO 7, 3rd Div, D of WVa?). This 3rd Division was General George Crook's command and had been General E.P. Scammon's division until his capture. Crook's 3rd Division was redesignated 2nd Division in April 1864, only a few days after the system of flags is supposed to have been adopted. *Fig. 106*

- *Reserve Corps, Army of the Cumberland (formerly called Army of Kentucky)* (Feb.-9 Oct. 1863). A system of flags was prescribed for this corps of three divisions on 1 August 1863 (GO 177, D of Cum). Corps HQ had a 6 x 4 foot fringed flag of red, white, and blue diagonal stripes, red uppermost, with a light blue circle in its center. In the center was a 5-pointed golden star, and on the star was an eagle perched upon a national shield. In the upper right and lower left were the letters "RC" in gold and red. *Fig. 106*

The other flags were 3 x 4.5 feet in size, apparently triangular, divided horizontally red and blue, and bore one, two, or three white crescents in their centers by which the commands were designated. The crescent was not, however, considered a corps badge.

● *Terry's Provisional Corps, Department of North Carolina* (6 Jan.-27 March 1865). No known flags. This corps was merged into the reorganized 10th Corps, *q.v.*

Cavalry and Artillery Corps, Divisions, and Brigades, 1863-1866

Fig. 107

● *Cavalry Corps, Army of the Potomac* (Feb. 1863-May 1865). Cavalry organizations from regiments up had been furnished distinguishing flags in 1862. The actual style used seems to have been the one prescribed on 30 April 1862 (GO 119, A of P) for the Cavalry Reserve: yellow flag (size not given) with a blue St. Andrew's cross for HQ; with a single blue star for 1st Brigade; and two blue stars for 2nd Brigade. None of these flags are known to have survived.

The Cavalry Corps was not given a badge in March 1863 when the other corps received theirs, but a flag was prescribed for its HQ on 12 May 1863 (GO 53, A of P). It was the same size and shape as those furnished the infantry corps, but yellow with white crossed sabers. This, the accepted cavalry symbol, was treated as the badge of all cavalry corps in the several armies.

For over a year after May 1863 the cavalry divisions and brigades seem to have decided upon their own flags. One popular type was a forked flag about 2.5 feet on the staff, divided horizontally into red and white, with white on the bottom and the number of the division on each stripe. This style is known to have been carried by General Gregg in mid-1863 and General Torbert the next year, while General Custer carried a very similar 3rd Division flag in 1865. General Judson Kilpatrick, who commanded the 3rd Division from June 1863 to April 1864, had the unusual "Tuebor" flag, illustrated in *HQ Flags*. The word "Tuebor," taken from the state seal of Michigan, means "I will defend."

Another popular design in the Cavalry Corps, Army of the Potomac was a forked flag, usually 3 feet on the staff and 4 on the fly, divided into three triangles — from top to bottom, blue, white, red. Crossed sabers, painted or applied, decorated the white triangle, and a golden star often appeared in the other two. These seem to have been used late in the war.

With such variety in mind it is hard to believe the full set of flags, approved 1 August 1864 by the Army of the Potomac and illustrated both in *HQ Flags* and *OR atlas*, was widely used. Yet the corps HQ flag of this set — a forked blue guidon, 3x6 feet, with white crossed sabers surmounted by a red "C", is shown in a group photograph of General Sheridan and his subordinates. And a pennant of the 2nd Brigade, 2nd Division — blue with a red stripe along the staff — still exists today.

Fig. 108

● *Cavalry Command, Army of the Cumberland* (9 Jan. 1863-29 Oct. 1864). A flag system was prescribed 26 April 1864 (GO 62, D of Cum) for the four divisions of this corps with their brigades. Corps HQ used a 4x6 foot fringed flag having three equal vertical stripes — blue, white, red — surmounted by golden crossed sabers. The division and brigade flags followed generally the Army of the Potomac system. The system is illustrated in *HQ Flags* and *OR atlas*.

Fig. 108

● *Cavalry Corps, Military Division of the Mississippi* (29 Oct. 1864-26 June 1865). A flag system was prescribed 24 November 1864 (GO 3, HQ Cav Corps Mil Div Miss) for the seven divisions of the Corps, with their brigades, and is partially illustrated in

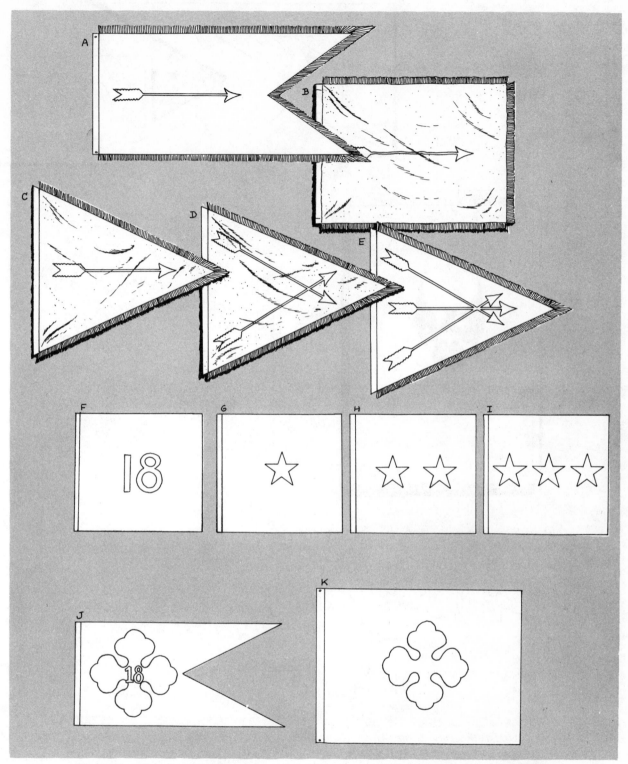

Fig. 101. *17th Army Corps, Army of the Tennessee*, all 1865: A, Headquarters, 3x6 ft., white arrow on blue (*HQ Flags*). B, 1st Division, 3.5x4.5 ft., red arrow on blue (West Point Museum). C and D, 1st and 2nd Brigades, 1st Division, 4x4 ft., same colors (West Point Museum). E, 3rd Brigade, 1st Division, 4x4 ft., same colors (*HQ Flags*). *18th Army Corps, Army of the James:* F, Headquarters, 1864, 6x6 ft., white "18" on red (*OR* atlas and Corps orders 3 May 1864). G, H and I: 1st, 2nd and 3rd Divisions, 1864, 6x6 ft., white stars on red (same sources). J, Headquarters, late 1864, 3x6 ft., white cross on blue, red "18" (*HQ Flags*). K, 1st Division, late 1864, 4.5x6 ft., red cross on white (1875 reproduction in West Point Museum).

Fig. 102. *19th Army Corps, Army of the Gulf, Army of the Shenandoah:* A, Headquarters, 1863-1864, 4x4 ft., white star on blue, red "19" (*HQ Flags*). B, Headquarters, 1864-1865, 3x6 ft., white cross on blue (West Point Museum). C, Chief Quartermaster, 1864-1865, 2.5x3.5 ft., red cross on white disc, on blue (West Point Museum). D, 2nd Division, 1864-1865, 3.5x6 ft., white cross on blue (1875 reproduction in West Point Museum). E, Artillery Brigade, 1864-1865, 3x5 ft., blue cannon on white with red border (drawings with corps orders of 17 November 1864, in National Archives). *20th Army Corps, Army of the Cumberland:* F, Headquarters, 1863, 6x4 ft., black "20" on white shield, on black eagle on red (Ohio Historical Society). G, Headquarters, 1864, 3x6 ft., white cross on blue with red "20" (*HQ Flags*). H, 1st Division, 1864, 6x6 ft., red star on white (*HQ Flags* and 1875 reproduction in West Point Museum).

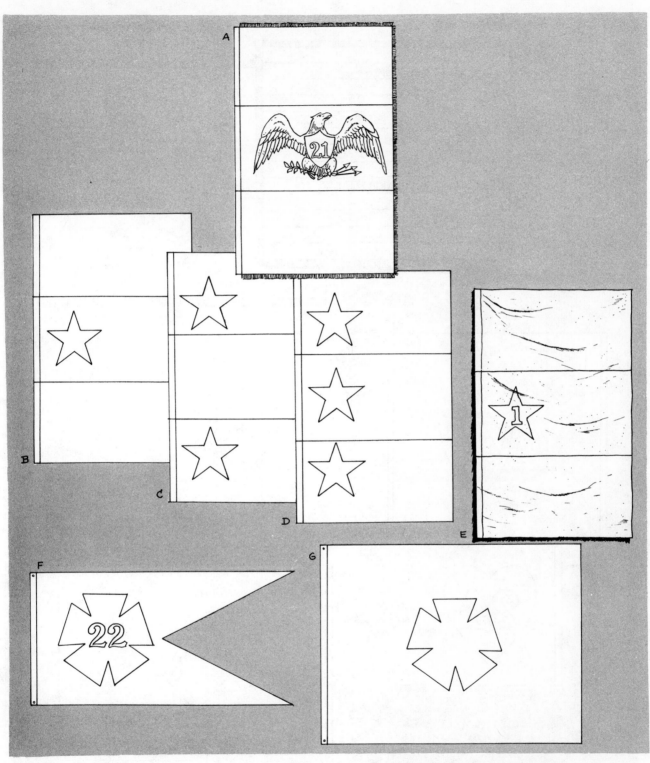

Fig. 103. *21st Army Corps, Army of the Cumberland,* all 1863: A, Headquarters, 6x4 ft., black eagle with white shield bearing black "21," on red, over white, over blue flag (departmental orders, 25 April 1863). B, C, and D: 1st, 2nd, and 3rd Divisions, 6x4 ft., black stars on same flag (same source). E, 1st Brigade, 1st Division, 6x4 ft., black star with white "1" on same flag (West Point Museum). *22nd Army Corps, Department of Washington:* F, Headquarters, 1864 (?), 3x6 ft., white cross on blue with red "22" (*HQ Flags*). G, 1st Division, 1864 (?), 4.5x6 ft., red cross on white (*HQ Flags* and 1875 reproduction in West Point Museum).

Fig. 104. *23rd Army Corps, Army of the Ohio, Department of North Carolina:* A, Headquarters, 1865, 4.5x5 ft., national flag with gold painted stars and letters (West Point Museum). B, 1st Division, 1864-1865, 6x6.5 ft., red shield with gold border on blue (departmental orders 25 September 1864 and fragments formerly in West Point Museum). C and D: brigade flags, same size and colors (same sources). *24th Army Corps, Army of the James:* E, Headquarters, 1865, 3x6 ft., white heart on blue with red "24" (*HQ Flags*). F, 1st Division, 1865, 4.5x6 ft., red heart on white (*HQ Flags*).

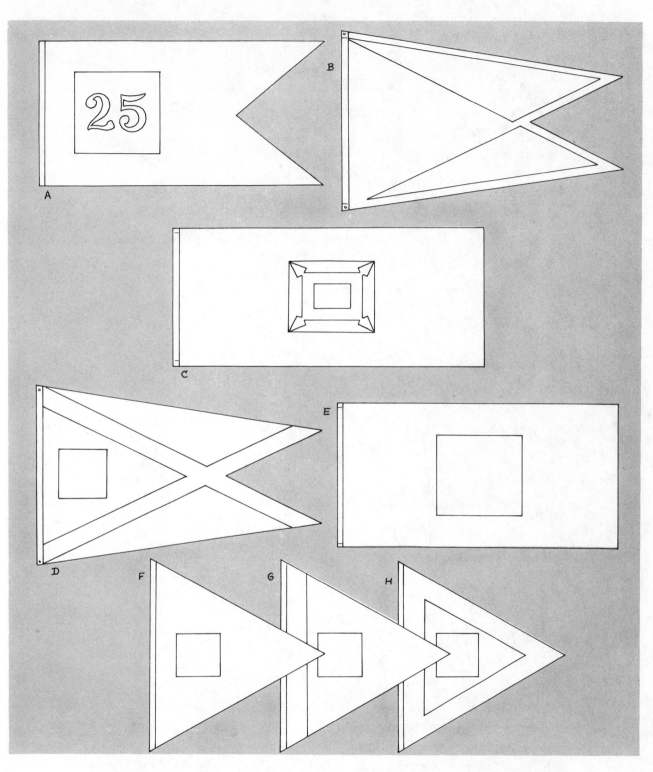

Fig. 105. *25th Army Corps, Army of the James,* all 1865 and all based on *HQ Flags*: A, Headquarters, 2.5x5.75 ft., white square on blue with red "25." B, Chief Quartermaster, 3x5.75 ft., red triangle above blue triangle on white. C, Artillery Brigade, 2.5x 5.75 ft., blue rectangle inside white one, inside red one, on white. D, Quartermaster, 1st Division, 3x5.75 ft., blue cross and red square on white. E, 1st Division, 2.5x5.75 ft., red square on white. F, G and H: 1st, 2nd and 3rd Brigades, 1st Division, 5x5 ft., (?), red squares and blue bar or border, on white.

Fig. 106. *Army of West Virginia,* all based on *HQ Flags:* A, Headquarters, 1865, 4.5x 6 ft., golden eagle on blue-red flag. B, 1st Division, 1865, 4x5.5 ft., white eagle on red. C, Artillery Brigade, 1865, 4x4.5 ft., white eagle on red over blue. D, E, F, and G: patterns of Brigade flags, 4x4.5 ft. H, 3rd Division, 1865, 5x6 ft., red, over white, over blue, with blue stars. I, 1st Brigade, 3rd Division, same size and colors with white "1's." *Reserve Corps, Army of the Cumberland:* J, Headquarters, 1863, 6x4 ft., red over white over blue, with light blue circle bearing golden star and natural colored eagle and national shield, with red and gold letters. K, 1st Brigade, 1st Division, 1863, 3x4.5 ft., red over blue, white crescent and "1" (J and K based upon departmental order, 1 August 1863).

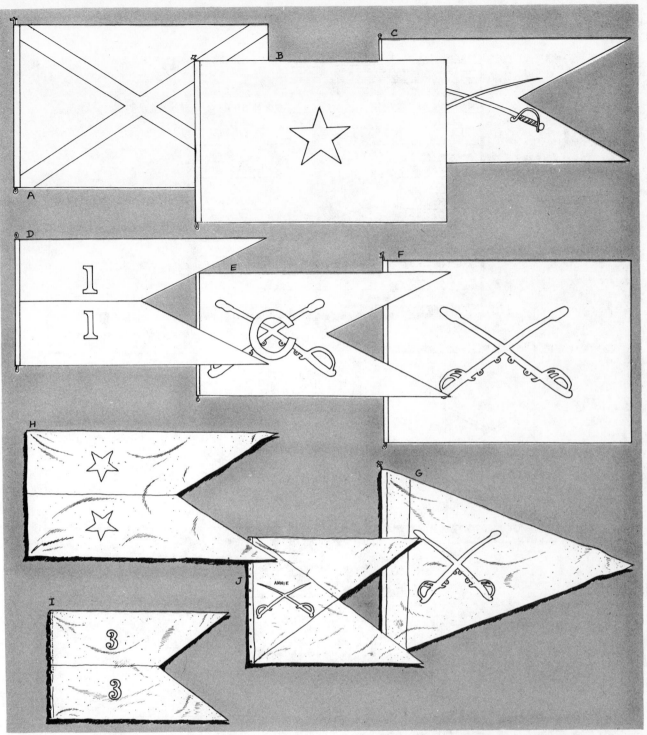

Fig. 107. *Cavalry Corps, Army of the Potomac:* A, Headquarters , Cavalry Reserve, 1862, 5x6 ft. (?), blue cross on yellow (A of P orders 30 April 1862). B, 1st Brigade, Cavalry Reserve, 1862, 5x6 ft. (?), blue star on yellow (same source). C, Headquarters, 1863, 3x6 ft., white crossed-sabers on yellow (A of P orders 12 May 1863). D, 1st Division, 1864, 3x6 ft., red over white with white and red numbers (contemporary photo). E, Headquarters, 1864-1865, 3x6 ft., red "C" on white crossed-sabers, on blue (contemporary photo). F, 1st Division, 1865, 4.5x6 ft., red crossed-sabers on white (*HQ Flags*). G, 2nd Brigade, 2nd Division, 1865, 4.5x6 ft., white crossed-sabers on blue with red bar (West Point Museum). H, Sheridan's personal flag, 1865, 3x6 ft. (?), red over white with white and red stars (Daughters of the American Confederacy Museum, Dallas). I, 3rd Division, 1864-1865, 2.5x4 ft., white over red with red and white numbers (Vermont Historical Society). J, Cavalry Reserve Brigade, 1st Division, 1864-1865, 3x4 ft., colors from top, blue-white-red with yellow crossed-sabers (West Point Museum).

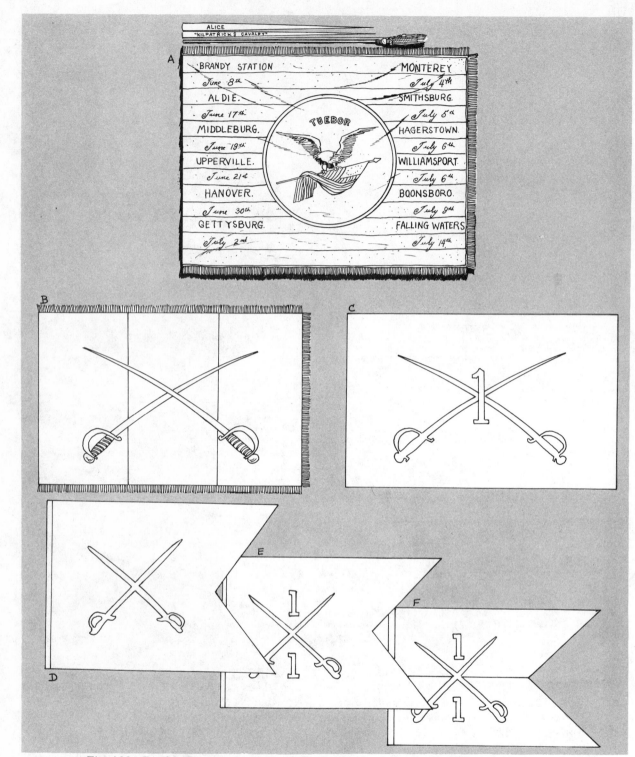

Fig. 108. *Cavalry Command, Army of the Cumberland*: A, General Kilpatrick's personal flag, 1864, 3x4 ft., red and white stripes with white disc showing eagle and flag in natural colors (contemporary photo). B, Headquarters, 1864, 4x6 ft., golden crossed-sabers on blue-white-red (*HQ Flags*). C, 1st Division, 1864, 4x6 ft., red sabers and blue "1" on white (*HQ Flags*). *Cavalry Corps, Military Division of the Mississippi*, 1864-1865: D, Headquarters, 4x6 ft., yellow sabers on red (Corps orders 24 November 1864). E, 1st Division, 3.5x5 ft., blue sabers and red numbers on white (Corps orders and 6th Division flag in West Point Museum). F, 2nd Brigade, 1st Division, 3x4.5 ft., red over blue with blue and red numbers and white sabers (Corps orders and 2nd Brigade, 6th Division flag in Michigan Historical Commission Museum, Lansing).

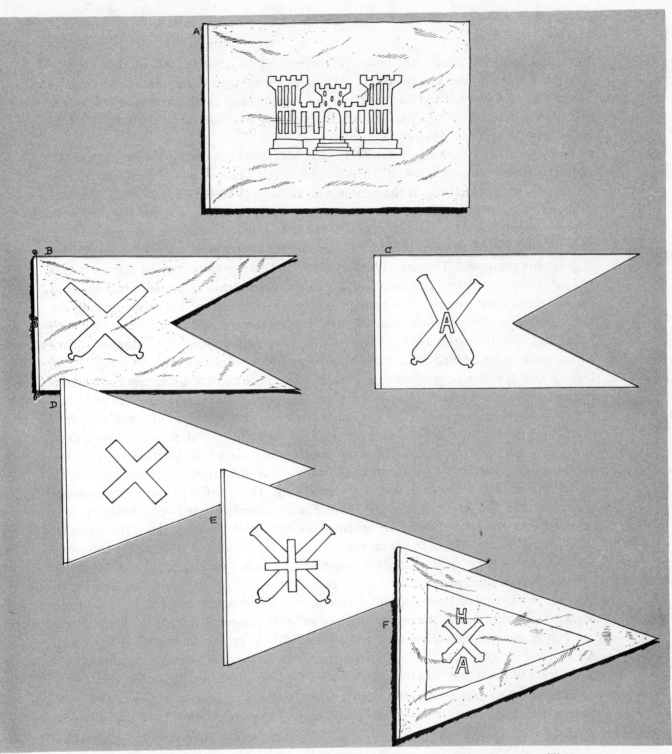

Fig. 109. A, *Chief of Engineers, Army of the Potomac*, 4.5x6 ft., red castle on blue (West Point Museum). *Artillery, Army of the Potomac:* B, Artillery Reserve, 1863, 3x6 ft., white cannon on red (A of P orders 12 May 1863 and contemporary photo). C, Chief of Artillery, 1864-1865, 3x6 ft., white cannon on blue, red "A" (*HQ Flags*). D, Artillery Brigade, 6th Army Corps, 1863-1864, 4.25x5.5 ft., white cross on red (description in National Archives and *HQ Flags*). E, Artillery Brigade, 6th Army Corps, 1864-1865, 4.5x6 ft., white cannon and blue cross on red (description in National Archives). F, Horse Artillery Brigade, Army of the Potomac, 1864, 4.5x6 ft., red cannon and letters on white, blue border (Smithsonian).

HQ Flags and *OR* atlas with, however, differences in coloring. All of these forked flags have crossed sabers; corps HQ is red and 4x6 feet while the divisions and brigades are smaller (3.5x5 feet) and differentiated by numbers and combinations of red, white, and blue. A surviving example of the 6th Division flag has blue sabers with red numbers suggesting the *OR* atlas coloring is correct.

Fig. 109

● *Artillery, Army of the Potomac* (Oct. 1861-May 1865). A distinguishing flag for HQ Artillery Reserve was prescribed 30 April 1862 (GO 119, A of P): rectangular, 5x6 feet, red with a white star in the center. On 12 May 1863 (GO 53, A of P), this was changed to a swallow-tailed flag of the same shape and size as a corps flag, red with white crossed cannon, and is illustrated in *Battle Flags*. Sometime during 1864 it appears that Brigadier General Henry J. Hunt, Chief of Artillery, adopted a designating flag for his command. This was a forked blue flag bearing white crossed cannon with a red "A" over its center. The commanders of the corps artillery brigades had received flags earlier. These were simple triangular brigade flags having red fields bearing the corps badge in white. A new issue of this design was approved for manufacture with other flags on 1 August 1864, but on 13 October new designs were adopted substituting gold crossed cannon bearing a blue corps badge in place of the previous device. During October, the Horse Artillery brigade also requisitioned a distinctive flag, a blue-bordered white triangular field bearing red crossed cannon and the letters "H" and "A".

● *Chief Quartermaster and other staff flags, Army of the Potomac.* Many of the army corps, independently of orders, adopted flags for the artillery and quartermaster chiefs, and many of these have been illustrated with the ordered designating flags of the various corps. Only in the Army of the Potomac was any attempt toward uniformity made, and at first even in this army it was lacking. The 3rd Corps had its own special Quartermaster flag in November of 1863. Early in the following year, however, it is believed that the pattern and color scheme was made uniform throughout the Army of the Potomac. Red, white, and blue combinations predominated in coloring the fields and devices on these flags, but the arrangement of colors varied from corps to corps. The flags were swallow-tailed or forked pennants, 4 feet on the staff but tapering to 1.5 feet at the tips of the tails, and 5 feet on the fly. A saltire crossed this field from corner to corner, and in the center of the field was the corps numeral. These devices contrasted in color to one another and to the field. They are illustrated in *HQ Flags*. An unusual variation for the 2nd Division, 6th Army Corps survives having a small "2" in the loop of the white "6"; the remainder of the flag is red, bearing a blue saltire.

Fig. 109

Flags of other staff commands, such as the Chief of Engineers who flew a dark blue bunting flag 3.5x6 feet (bearing a red castle on its rectangular field), have also survived.

SOURCES

Gherardi Davis, *The Colors of the United States Army, 1789-1912*, privately printed, New York, 1912. The one and only serious study of army colors, based on long research. Beautifully illustrated in color and very scarce.

U.S. Army, Quartermaster General, *Flags of the Army of the United States Carried During the War of the Rebellion, 1861-1865, to Designate the Headquarters of the Different Armies, Army Corps, Divisions and Brigades*, Washington, D.C., 1887. Illustrates flags carried late in the war. Contains no text and no record whatever of sources. Clearly incorrect in some places, probably in many more, but extremely comprehensive in coverage of headquarters flags, containing many colored plates. Cited as *HQ Flags*. This book was printed by Burk and McFetridge of Philadelphia. Correspondence exists in the National Archives concerning its preparation and certain errors discovered after publication. It is evident that the great majority of the flags illustrated were based on actual specimens, but they have not been available for use in this study. *HQ Flags* is quite rare today, but copies do exist in some of the larger libraries.

James Beale, *The Battle Flags of the Army of the Potomac at Gettysburg, Penna., July 1st, 2d & 3d, 1863*, Philadelphia, 1885. This work is more limited and shows earlier versions of headquarters flags than the 1887 QMG book, above. There is a strong family resemblance between the two, suggesting that Beale may also have been the compiler of the QMG book. Cited hereafter as *Battle Flags*. This book was probably the source for the designating flags shown in John D. Billings, *Hardtack and Coffee*. In general it should be used with caution.

Official Records, op. cit., atlas, plate CLXXV. An abbreviated coverage, containing only flags of corps and divisions. Differs materially from the two sources above. Cited as *OR* atlas.

U.S. Army, *General Regulations for the Army of the United States...*, Washington, D.C., 1847, pars. 848-854; also ed. of 1857, pars. 1368-1372; ed. of 1861, pars. 1436-1441; ed. of 1861, with appendix containing changes to 25 June 1863, pars. 1464-1469 and Appendix B, pars. 8, 11.

George Henry Preble, *Origin and History of the American Flag...*, new ed., 2 vols. Philadelphia, 1917.

Peleg D. Harrison, *The Stars and Stripes and Other American Flags*, 5th ed., Boston, 1914.

George B. Keester, "Battle Flags of Mounted Batteries, U.S. Artillery, 1862-1865," in *Military Collector & Historian*, XIII (1961), 9-13.

H. Michael Madaus, "McClellan's System of Designating Flags, Spring-Fall, 1862," in *Military Collector & Historian*, XVII (1965), 1-14; "The Personal and Designating Flags of General George A. Custer, 1863-1865," in *ibid.*, XX (1968), 1-14; "Battleflags of Mounted Batteries, U.S. Artillery, 1864-1865," in *ibid.*, XXI, 25, 26.

Milo M. Quaife, *et al., The History of the United States Flag...*, New York, 1961.

Whitney Smith, *The Flag Book of the United States*, New York, 1970.

Once again we must acknowledge the help given on headquarters flags by H. Michael Madaus.

Fig. 110. Brevet Brigadier General Albert Sidney Johnston, commanding the Utah Expedition of 1857-1858. Still in his uniform as Colonel, 2nd U.S. Cavalry, he wears a dark blue double breasted frock coat, crimson net sash, buff gauntlets, dark blue forage cap, sky blue trousers with yellow welt. His saddle, a Grimsley, is covered by a dark blue saddle cloth edged with 1½ inch gold lace and decorated with a gold embroidered "2." An overcoat might have been attached to the pommel. (Based on *Harper's Weekly*, 30 January 1858 and dress regulations).

CHAPTER VIII

COMMAND AND STAFF; REGIMENTS AND CORPS

The commands whose equipage is covered in this chapter include the regular army and the various temporary corps raised and maintained by the general government during and immediately after the American Civil War. In addition, some attention will be paid to other temporary commands raised by or in the states and later turned over to the general government, notably some of the regiments of U.S. Colored Troops. Not included here are the numerous regiments, battalions, and other commands raised and maintained (but not necessarily uniformed, armed, accoutered or paid) by the several states and territories, North and South. These form the contents of the final volumes of this work.

*　　　　　　*　　　　　　*

The dress regulations of 12 June 1851, as has been said, form the starting point of this study of the uniforms of the general government. But to assume that the army began at once to wear this clothing would be a serious error. The Quartermaster General summed up the situation in a letter written to Lt. Col. Philip St. George Cooke, 2nd Dragoons, on 28 April 1855 (nearly four years later), explaining why that regiment was still required to wear the older pattern uniform.

I have received your letter dated the 11th instant, on the subject of Clothing for your command. When a former Secy of War, on the recommendation of a few Officers of the Army, ordered a change of the Uniform, there was a large War Stock on hand of the old pattern sufficient for several years supply of the reduced Peace establishment. The change was most injudicious at the time and under the circumstances, in which it was made. The great extension of our territories had quadrupled the expenditures of the Military Establishment; Congress alarmed at these expenditures, was reducing the most necessary appropriations. The question came up whether the large stock on hand was to be sacrificed, and appropriations asked to supply the deficiency or whether it should be issued and worn until exhausted — to have adopted the former course would have involved a loss of from four to five hundred thousand dollars for the supply of which an appropriation would have been necessary. As I did not mean that any of the responsibility of a measure which had originated in so much folly should rest on me, I meant should I be required to present an Estimate to cover the loss of so large a stock to state all the facts so as to bring the matter fully before Congress; but in place of an order to present an estimate, I was instructed to issue the old pattern uniform while any of it remained on hand. The stock having been so far reduced as not to be sufficient for a years supply to the whole Army, the present Secretary

354

of War directed that certain companies should be designated to receive and use such of the old pattern as remained.

The requirement that articles of old patterns had to be exhausted before the new could be issued applied to the entire period under study and to all items of clothing, but it applied, of course, only to depots where older stocks *did* remain. The widespread, scattered condition of the army and the difficulties of transportation rendered the balance of these stocks extremely uneven, with the result that companies of one branch or even regiment might be issued a new pattern years before other companies got it. Some attempt was made to shift stocks around among depots, and to confine new or old issues to specific companies or regiments, but variety of dress was, nonetheless, the common condition. (See, for example, the detailed allocations prescribed 21 May 1853 (GO 13).)

In this 1851-1872 period, there were several significant overall developments in clothing that can be summarized here. The details must be sought in the orders themselves, in pictures, and in actual uniforms.

12 June 1851 (GO 31): Established the Model 1851 dark blue frock coat in an officer's and an enlisted man's length; sky blue pants (with a 1/8-inch welt for all ranks save general officers); dark blue cloth dress cap, with pompon and a variety of insignia; oil cloth cap cover; branch colored plastron for all musicians (replacing the former use of red coats). Prescribed worsted epaulets for dismounted troops, brass scales for mounted. Did not prescribe any fatigue or cotton clothing. Definitely ordered that no new pattern clothing would be issued until the supply of the old on hand was exhausted.

6 November 1851 (MS QMG letter): Authorized issue of new pattern cap with old pattern dress uniform.

29 June 1852 (GO 24): Ordered sky blue fatigue jackets (still being worn) trimmed with lace of branch color.

26 August 1852 (MS QMG letter): Ended issue of the cotton shirt.

12 September 1853 (MS QMG letter): Fixed the weight of dark blue uniform cloth at 12 ounces per yard.

20 January 1854 (GO 1): Replaced all enlisted men's epaulets with brass shoulder scales; removed their colored cap band, cuffs, and collar, leaving only a welt of branch color; introduced the Model 1854 uniform jacket for mounted troops; did away with colored welts on all pants. Probably the musicians' plastron was changed to strips of branch-colored lace at this time.

26 March 1855 (GO 4): Altered the pattern of the frock coat and pants to the "French chasseurs-à-pied" model.

(?) 1855 (MS QMG letter, 25 May): Ended the general issue of cotton fatigue clothing.

15 August 1855 (GO 13): Introduced the Model 1855 cavalry hat and the gutta percha talma for issue only to cavalry.

(?) July 1857 (MS QMG letter): Adopted the forage cap for engineer soldiers.

28 November 1857 (MS QMG letter): Adopted the flannel sack coat (blouse) for all mounted corps.

24 March 1858 (GO 3): Introduced the Model 1858 felt hat; altered the color of all pants to dark blue; and established a new system of pants stripes and welts (1/8-inch gold cord for staff officers, 1/8-inch welt of branch color for other officers, 1.5-inch stripe for sergeants, half-inch for corporals, nothing for privates); restored the Model 1847 cocked hat for general and field officers; extended issue of the sack coat to all corps; eliminated the "French chasseurs-à-pied" tailoring of coat and pants; eliminated the regimental number from coat collars of enlisted men.

8 May 1858 (MS AG letter): Ordered hat cords to be of branch color and with tassel ends.

29 November 1858 (MS QMG letter): Authorized Model 1858 forage cap (with branch colored welts, plain for recruits). On 11 April 1859 the conversion of Model 1851 cloth dress cap into a forage cap was authorized.

25 January 1859 (MS QMG letter): Authorized issue of Model 1851 dress cap with horsehair plume for light artillery companies.

12 February 1859 (MS QMG letter): Authorized scarlet cords and tassels for the same.

24 September 1859 (MS QMG letter): Chin straps authorized for cavalry hats.

6 August 1860 (GO 20): Introduced the light artillery officer's jacket; authorized issue to light artillerymen of sky blue pants; and confirmed their use of a distinctive dress cap.

26 February 1861 (GO 4): Ordered all Model 1858 forage caps made with dark blue welt as for recruits; gutta percha talma made article of issue for dragoons and mounted riflemen.

13 March 1861 (GO 6): Summarized and clarified existing dress regulations and generally determined the uniform of the Civil War.

25 November 1861 (GO 102): Authorized wear of enlisted man's mounted overcoat by all officers "in time of actual field service."

16 December 1861 (GO 108): Reintroduced sky blue pants for all regimental officers and enlisted men, with infantry NCO's given dark blue stripes.

Before discussing the uniforms worn by the different branches, several general features of the 1851-1872 U.S. Army dress can be summarized.

● *Officers.* Officers commonly wore the frock coat, even when their men were otherwise dressed. For fatigue and field service they replaced the epaulets with shoulder straps, or wore shell (stable) jackets and, after 1861, sack coats. The sword was worn on all occasions of duty and the sash at all such times except stable and fatigue duty.

In combat during the Civil War, regimental officers usually carried one holster pistol on the right side of their sword belt, but this was rarely worn at other times. Ankle boots were authorized and commonly worn by mounted officers under trousers; other styles of boot were privately purchased and worn outside. Spurs were universally worn by mounted officers.

Officers rarely wore knapsacks or carried the issue haversack or canteen. However, specially designed (and privately purchased) haversacks were common and some company officers carried rolled or folded overcoats on their backs.

● *Non-Commissioned Staff.* All NCO's above the rank of sergeant (including Principal or Chief Musicians) wore a red worsted sash and the appropriate chevrons. If in foot troops, they also wore, for ceremonies, a special sword, as did the sergeants. In artillery regiments and heavy artillery companies this was usually the Model 1833 Foot Artillery Sword; in other corps it was the Model 1840 NCO's sword. Normally, regimental NCO's carried the sword alone while company sergeants had a musket in addition. Regimental NCO's, like officers, usually were not required to carry knapsacks and other field equipment. It was not uncommon for the higher ranking NCO's of a regiment — and especially a volunteer regiment — to wear officers' swords of various patterns.

• *Bands.* According to regulations, a band wore the uniform of the corps to which it belonged. However, commanding officers were allowed to "make such additions in ornaments" as they desired if the cost was borne by the corps. Most often the officers stood the cost of such embellishments. Regimental bands were abolished in 1862 and thereafter the cost of outfitting the bands of brigades and higher commands was apportioned somehow among a larger group of officers. Brigade bands and drum corps were often composed of men detailed from different regiments; the fifes and drums of the 1st Brigade, 2nd Division, 15th Army Corps contained musicians from six regiments, drawn from three states.

Command and Staff

Fig. 29

• *General Officers.* The dress regulation of 1851 authorized for generals (and required them to wear by 4 July 1852) a double-breasted dark blue frock coat, plain dark blue pants, and a blue cloth cap with a band of dark blue velvet. On the cap front was a gold embroidered wreath encircling the silver letters "U.S." in Old English characters. The pompon was a gold embroidered net acorn rising above the regulation "eagle." The buttons of the coat were arranged in three sets of three for a major general, four sets of two for a brigadier general; its collar and straight cuffs were dark blue velvet.

The cocked hat (chapeau bras) of long memory was eliminated. On duty, a general officer wore gold bullion epaulets; "when not on duty and on certain duties off parade" he substituted gold bordered shoulder straps. These were either sewn or tied to the shoulders or fastened by one of several patented devices. These straps were slightly larger than the kind worn later, and often were bordered by three rows of gold bullion. The field was black velvet, the stars silver.

With the frock coat a general wore a Russian (red) leather belt with three stripes of gold embroidery on all straps plus the usual rectangular plate. His sash was of buff silk net, tied on the left hip after twice encircling the waist. The sword authorized was straight, with "gilt hilt, silver grip, brass or steel scabbard." In practice it could be the General and Staff Officers' Model 1832, the Staff and Field Officers' Model 1850, or, later, the Staff and Field Officers' Model 1860 (see Peterson, *Sword, op. cit.*, pp. 126-136).

Generals, in common with all officers, wore as an overcoat the "cloak coat," with five braids of black silk arranged in a knot on each sleeve. Gauntlets of buff or white leather were growing popular and largely replaced gloves by 1861.

A general off duty could wear a more informal plain dark blue civilian "body coat" with roll collar. This bore no insignia except regulation buttons. Buff, white, and dark blue vests were also authorized for wear off duty. All officers, in fact, were authorized to wear the body coat and the vest.

With the undress uniform it was usual to wear a dark blue, wide-crowned forage cap with the same branch insignia as on the dress cap. Oil cloth covers were provided for both this and the dress cap for use in rainy weather. In fitting this on the dress cap, the pompon was removed.

With a few changes, this remained the general officer's uniform during the entire period under study. In 1858 the black felt hat replaced the cloth cap for dress and a little later that year the new pattern forage cap was introduced. The trimmings of the hat comprised a gold cord with acorn-shaped ends, a brass or embroidered "eagle" that looped the brim up on the right side, three black ostrich feathers, and the same device on front as before. The formal cocked hat with three black ostrich feathers was authorized in 1858 for optional wear with full dress. Also, in 1858 a 1/8-inch gold cord was added to the dark blue trousers.

During the Civil War, epaulets, dress hats, and sashes were rarely worn in the field and many general officers omitted even their swords and sword belts. General Grant himself habitually left his coat unbuttoned to show a dark blue vest, white shirt, and black cravat, and many generals followed his lead. The almost universal headdress was a black felt hat of civilian origin decorated only with a gold cord. Now and then after 1863 a commander wore the device of his corps or division pinned on the front of the hat. Gauntlets and high leather knee boots were commonly worn when mounted, although neither were prescribed by regulations. The boots had to be large enough at the top to accept the full trousers of the day.

Fig. 111

The Civil War added to a general's wardrobe the blouse, sometimes a long, full, double-breasted garment and at others the regulation flannel blouse of the soldier. The blouse was widely worn in camp, usually fitted with shoulder straps but sometimes conspicuously plain. Occasionally, a general officer might wear a double-breasted shell jacket, but this was rare.

Fig. 112

The rank of lieutenant general was created in 1864 but the button arrangement remained the same as for major generals. In 1866, however, when the rank of general was established, a coat was introduced having two rows of twelve buttons each, placed by fours. General Grant was the first officer to wear this coat; the only other one in our period was Sherman.

Uniforms *à la fantaisie*, although rare, were not unknown among general officers. General Winfield Scott set the style. As late as 1856 (when he was painted by Robert W. Weir) he was still wearing the dress (tail) coat of the 1847 and earlier uniform regulations, with high buff collar, cuffs, and facings that matched his buff sash. By 1861 he had changed to a dark blue frock coat of his own design, with a broad turn-over collar embroidered with gold oak leaves, as were his cuffs. His waist belt bore the same gold oak leaves and had a round gilt buckle with the raised letters "US" and a fluted border. His pants were regulation dark blue. Scott always wore a chapeau bras with his dress uniforms despite the absence of this item from the dress regulations until 1858.

The two general officers most renowned for gaudy dress were Custer and Torbert, both cavalrymen. The former, who hardly needs introduction to American readers, was a brigadier general and an outstanding cavalry leader at the age of 23. He had eleven

Fig. 111. Brigadier General Rufus Ingalls, Chief Quartermaster, Army of the Potomac, April 1864. His equipage shows an interesting combination of full dress and field service. The buff sash, red Russia leather waist belt supporting a Model 1860 Staff and Field Officer's sword, and dark blue saddle housing, were all regulation for general officers. But the modified black felt hat, the high riding boots, gauntlets, and several items of horse furniture (like the bearskin holster covers, open wooden stirrups, and decorative bridle rein) were matters of personal choice. (Photograph from Library of Congress.

horses killed under him and was certainly the ideal *beau sabreur*. Theodore Lyman, in his *Meade's Headquarters*, said he "looks like a circus rider gone mad! He wears a huzzar jacket and tight trousers of faded black velvet trimmed with tarnished gold lace . . . the General's coiffure [consists of] short, dry flaxen ringlets." Among Custer' uniforms — for, like Marshal Murat, he sported several unusual styles — was one comprising a dark blue double-breasted jacket, said to be made of velvet, piped in gold and with gold lace loops in the French manner on both sleeves. A wide blue shirt collar was allowed to fall from his neck. With this went dark blue full trousers with two half-inch gold stripes, high boots, and a wide-brimmed black felt hat. His best remembered symbol, however, was a scarlet kerchief or necktie. At the close of the war the men of his 3rd Cavalry Division adopted this necktie as their division badge.

Plate II

Alfred Thomas Archimedes Torbert, a West Pointer who began his Civil War career as a colonel of the 1st New Jersey Infantry, did not hold a command in the Cavalry Corps, Army of the Potomac, until April 1864. Thereafter he is pictured in a dark blue jacket with a wide turn-over collar like Custer's, and two rows of buttons. The jacket was actually single-breasted, having a wide black velvet band covering the hooks and eyes and extending around the bottom edge. His black felt hat was creased in the center. had a single star in a wreath on the front, and crossed sabers pinned on the right side.

Not all uniforms *à la fantaisie* were confined to cavalry generals. The historian of the 6th New York Cavalry, describing the Battle of Savage Station (29 June 1862), mentions Thomas Francis Meagher, commanding the Irish Brigade, "dressed in a suit of dark green velvet, trimmed with gold lace, a broad-brimmed straw hat surmounted with a heavy plume."

General Staff and Staff Corps

In this category, which is the terminology used in the dress regulations, fell the officers of the several staff corps and departments: adjutants-general, inspectors-general, quartermasters, commissaries of subsistence, surgeons, paymasters, officers of engineers and topographical engineers, officers of ordnance, and judge advocates. To these must be added the aides-de-camp, detailed from line regiments, who formed a general officer's personal staff. In 1851 there was but one Judge Advocate; only after July 1862 were sufficient officers assigned to legal duties to constitute a department. It was established as the Bureau of Military Justice in June 1864 and continued to be so called throughout our period.

Provost marshals, although found in all major commands, were not prescribed distinctive uniforms or insignia. Like the aides-de-camp, they were detailed from the line.

After 1851, staff officers wore the normal dark blue frock coat with a distinctive   *Fig. 20* style of gilt button (officers of engineers, topographical engineers, and ordnance wore the buttons of their corps and devices of their corps on their caps), dark blue trousers with a 1/8-inch buff welt (after 1858, gold cord), blue cloth cap with a band of the same color and with the same insignia as general officers save for the three corps above. On this cap were distinctively colored pompons, reminiscent of the varicolored plumes that had adorned the hats of staff officers in earlier years. The colors are described under "Insignia of Branch and Unit," page 80-92.

Staff officers wore black leather belts and crimson silk net sashes, except officers of the Medical Department whose sashes were emerald green. The epaulets of the Medical, Pay, and Ordnance Departments and the two Engineer Corps had distinctive insignia; the others were plain within the crescent, as were those of aides-de-camp. All staff shoulder straps had a dark blue base.

Staff officers were authorized a new saber in 1850 — the same given field officers of infantry, artillery, and riflemen — which was worn by all except the Medical and Pay Departments until 1860 and by many until 1872. Medical officers and Paymasters were given special swords, described in Chapter 3.

Fig. 112. Brigadier General Alfred Pleasonton, Commanding 1st Division, Cavalry Corps, Army of the Potomac, about April 1863. His austere field equipage contrasts strongly with that of General Ingalls: sack coat, soft leather top boots, officer's cavalry saber suspended from a waist belt beneath the coat, regulation McClellan saddle on a dark blue saddle blanket, and single curb rein. (Photograph from Library of Congress.)

Fig. 113. Representative U.S. Army Staff Officers, 1861-1865. The officer at lower left holds a Model 1860, Staff and Field Officers' Sword. It will be noted that the sword knots shown (all with gold lace straps and gold bullion tassels) were of the sort that were permanently attached to the sword.

The dress of staff officers after 1851 underwent the same changes as that of generals. Doubtless many wore the dark blue jacket with shoulder straps — single- or double-breasted according to rank — authorized for mounted officers before 1861. After that date, the variation of clothing seen among staffs was unlimited. A glance at Civil War photographs of such groups shows frock coats, blouses, and jackets of all styles and qualities. Some generals expected uniformity, others cared little how their assistants dressed. The staff officers of General Burnside, for example, wore high crown felt hats with brims turned down like the one their chief-affected, while the staff of Major General David B. Birney (in one picture at least) was carefully clothed in frock coats as if at inspection. Obviously, however, the officers on the staffs of Generals Warren, Griffin, Bartlett, and many others wore, while being photographed, whatever they pleased.

Fig. 113

Observers of the Civil War scene often commented on the appearance of staff officers:

> . . . those dashing young aides who rode with the army of the Potomac in gold laced French forage caps, natty jackets with Russian shoulder knots, corduroy breeches bleached gray-white after many washings, high boots and Mexican spurs, and whose swords were always lashed under the skirts of their saddles.

General staff officers and aides-de-camp, called upon to spend much of their time on horseback, tended usually toward high boots and the clothing of the mounted arms. Required to carry maps and papers, they often used dispatch cases.

Fig. 114

Regular Cavalry

1st and 2nd Dragoons. The enlisted men of the two dragoon regiments in 1851 had as a dress uniform essentially the one worn throughout the 1840's: a double-breasted tail coat of dark blue cloth with yellow collar, pointed cuffs, and facings; brass shoulder scales; sky blue reinforced trousers with ¾-inch yellow stripes (two such on each side for sergeants). The dress cap was made of felt reinforced with leather and of a distinctive design, more pointed toward the top than the dismounted style. It had a drooping white horse-hair plume and yellow cords and tassels, besides the distinctive star and eagle cap plate. Musicians wore a scarlet tail coat with yellow collar, cuffs, and facings. Company officers had the same uniform as the sergeants but with yellow metal epaulets and gold lace. Field officers wore dark blue pants and all officers wore silk net sashes of a deep orange color. The non-commissioned staff and the first sergeants had yellow sashes. The non-commissioned staff also wore yellow worsted aiguilettes and all NCO's had yellow chevrons.

Fig. 115

The fatigue dress of enlisted men comprised a dark blue woolen shell jacket trimmed with yellow lace on collar, cuffs, and shoulder straps; the same pants as for dress; and a dark blue cloth, wide-crowned M1839 forage cap (with a yellow band for the 2nd Regiment) carrying the company letter. There probably were no distinctions in color or in lace for musicians in this uniform. As in the dress uniform, the NCO's wore yellow chevrons. White cotton jackets were often worn in hot weather.

Dragoon officers for fatigue and field service wore a dark blue frock coat with a distinctive pattern of half-epaulet, or they could use a shell jacket resembling that worn by the men, except trimmed with gold lace. Their forage cap was a dark blue with a 6-pointed gold star.

The Model 1851 dress uniform authorized the dragoons was of the same pattern as given the rest of the army — dark blue frock coat, sky blue pants, and a dark blue cloth dress cap, all trimmed with orange, the distinctive branch color decided upon for dragoons. Another distinction allowed was brass scales, made in two or three patterns depending upon the rank of the wearer, instead of the worsted epaulets of the dismounted corps. All sashes were red and in this uniform the non-commissioned staff did not wear aiguilettes.

It does not appear that this dress uniform was worn to any significant extent. For some reason the stock of old pattern dragoon dress uniforms was unusually large and as late as the spring of 1855 they were still being issued. The Model 1851 dress was authorized for the permanent party at the Dragoon Recruiting Depot at Carlisle Barracks in December 1851, the Military Academy Detachment of Dragoons in August 1852, and thereafter for a few selected companies and recruiting rendezvous. But the two regiments as a whole did not receive new pattern clothing until about 1856, by which time the style had been considerably altered. The only important exception here was in caps; a sizeable supply of Model 1851 Dragoon caps did go out in March 1854 and their issue continued thereafter.

The dress uniform of the 1st and 2nd Dragoons from 1856 into 1858 consisted of the Model 1854 "uniform" jacket of dark blue laced with orange, and with brass scales; sky blue, *chasseur à pied* pattern, reinforced pants without stripes; dark blue cloth caps with an orange welt and pompon; cap cover; and a sky blue, mounted pattern greatcoat. Officers wore the frock coat, sky blue pants with 1/8-inch orange welts, and the cloth dress cap without the welt.

For fatigue and the rougher field service, dragoon enlisted men were given old pattern jackets of several kinds, resulting in complaints about the uneven appearance of the soldiers, especially in parties of recruits. For a time in 1854 and 1855, some companies were given sky blue kersey jackets and for a while thereafter old pattern

Fig. 114. Captain George A. Custer, additional aide-de-camp, Cavalry Corps, Army of the Potomac about 1863. This celebrated *beau sabreur*, shortly before his promotion to brigadier general, wears equipage of a simple and serviceable, if unusual sort. His upper garment appears to be a dark blue jacket, open at the top to expose a flowing kerchief. Sky blue trousers are stuffed into riding boots, and a revolver holster is attached to his waist belt. The saddle has not been identified. See also Plate II. (Photograph from Library of Congress.)

OFFICER, SERVICE DRESS 1852

FATIGUE DRESS, CAMPAIGN, 1851

1855

1858-1861

Fig. 115. 1st and 2nd Regiments, U.S. Dragoons, 1851-1859. The corporal in the left foreground, wearing buckskin leggings with Indian beadwork, carries a Model 1840 Heavy Cavalry Saber and a Model 1847 Cavalry Musketoon; his jacket is an early model based on an example in the Fort Snelling Museum. The sergeant of the 2nd Dragoons, on the right, has a Model 1855 Sharps breechloading carbine. Above, a dragoon of 1855 wears a pre-1851 dress uniform with Model 1854 dress cap. At upper left a trooper in flannel shirt worn outside rides on a Grimsley saddle. The officer still wears his pre-1851 forage cap.

dress coats were cut down for fatigue wear. To this medley the dragoons added non-regulation features of their own, notably flannel shirts and wide-brimmed hats. The adoption of one such hat in 1853 by the 2nd Dragoons has been mentioned in Chapter 1. Percival G. Lowe, a corporal of B Company, 1st Dragoons, in Texas in 1851 and later, told of the men using garments like "blue shirts worn in the field in place of the regulation uniform," "drab hats," and "a very large red and yellow silk hand-kerchief, a luxury I have always indulged in on the plains." He tied the last item "around my hat and brought it around so as to cover my neck and most of my face to keep off the sun and the pestiferous gnats."

Fig. 115

By regulation, the dragoon was permitted to wear mustaches and some wore rings in their ears. While the 1st Dragoons is credited with being relatively dignified and properly dressed, the 2nd Dragoons appears to have perpetuated its Mexican War reputation as rough and colorful right up to the Civil War. So far as we know, they continued to wear yellow bands on their forage caps into the middle 1850's.

The year 1858 brought certain changes in the dragoon uniform: the Model 1858 black felt hat was substituted for the cloth dress cap; dark blue trousers, with orange stripes for NCO's, took the place of sky blue ones; and the flannel blouse was issued for fatigue wear. Not all companies received the new clothing promptly, of course. In 1859 dragoons were issued new pattern forage caps, at first trimmed with an orange colored welt.

Just before commencement of our period, the enlisted dragoon had been armed with a Model 1840 cavalry saber made by the Ames Manufacturing Company, one Model 1843 percussion pistol, and a Model 1847, caliber .69 Cavalry Musketoon, fitted with a sling ring. The latter had no bayonet. In 1851 its ramrod attachment was slightly modified. The dragoon attached this weapon to a sling, worn over his left shoulder except on long marches; on such occasions, when no fighting was expected, he lashed the musketoon to the saddle pommel.

It is apparent that even the dragoon armament was not standardized. Modifications were made to meet the character of the country being policed and the enemy expected, both factors conditioning the decision whether to fight on horse or on foot. There were also, of course, the personal preferences of company and regimental commanders. Major Albert G. Brackett, 1st Cavalry, later wrote, "The sabre in Indian fighting is simply a nuisance; they jingle abominably, and are of no earthly use." But on numerous occasions dragoon parties did attack Indians with the saber, and successfully.

In July 1858, Colonel H.K. Craig, Ordnance Office, wrote a useful review of the armament of the mounted regiments which bears out its changing and experimental character. In December 1849, the Model 1848, caliber .44 Colt revolver was first supplied the regular dragoons, and this arm gradually superseded the percussion pistol. It was carried in one of the saddle holsters and some men carried the old-style pistol in the opposite one. Saber, percussion cap pouch, and a Model 1841 rifle cartridge box were suspended from a waist belt of black buff leather. This constituted a heavy load when the full forty rounds were in the box, but the belt was supported by a strap over the soldier's right shoulder.

The need was felt for more accurate and powerful firearms for use on foot, and this led to arming some men of a company, or even an entire company, as sharpshooters. In

February 1853 some Sharps carbines were issued the dragoons as experimental arms and subsequently these arms were supplied both regiments in substantial numbers. We hear of Captain Henry W. Stanton, 1st Dragoons, using his Sharps with great effect in a fight with Mescalero Apaches in 1855, at the time of his death.

Another development was the adoption, about 1856, of the Model 1855 pistol-carbine, caliber .58, in place of the musketoon. This was a muzzle loading, singleshot, rifled pistol which could be attached to a walnut stock and transformed into a light, 28-inch shoulder weapon. The pistol-carbine was easily transported, powerful, and, for a carbine, accurate. Used primarily as a carbine, it found favor with the dragoons but did not at once replace the musketoon, which remained in use as late as 1858.

A few Burnside breechloading carbines were tried out after 1856, and about 1858 five companies of the 2nd Dragoons were issued Colt Army Revolvers with detachable stocks on requisition of Brevet Colonel Charles A. May; these presumably replaced their pistol-carbines.

This diversification of armament led to corresponding changes in accouterments. So long as the musketoon was employed, the dragoon wore his sling. But the pistol-carbine was designed to be carried in a saddle holster and was fitted for an infantry-type sling; hence the larger Dragoon sling was momentarily set aside. The revolver, after about 1856, was carried in a belt holster. Some combination saddle holsters were made to carry a pistol-carbine plus its stock on one side, and a dragoon revolver on the other. Finally, the saddle holsters were eliminated entirely and the sling brought back into use for the Sharps carbine.

Regiment of Mounted Riflemen. The year 1851 found the Rifles in the midst of reorganization at Jefferson Barracks, Missouri, having turned over most of its men and horses to the 1st Dragoons in the Pacific Northwest. Recruits were plentiful and by December the regiment, less two companies, was transferred to Texas. There, and in New Mexico and Arizona, it served until the beginning of the Civil War.

The Rifles had never been authorized a dress uniform and it so happened that the supply of its old pattern fatigues — jackets of dark blue with yellow lace and dark blue pants with distinctive stripes — had become exhausted. Thus, in September 1851, the Quartermaster General authorized a full issue of new pattern clothing — dark blue frock coats trimmed with "medium or emerald green cloth," sky blue pants, cloth caps trimmed with emerald green and with pompons of the same color. The dress regulations appear to have considered the regiment as a dismounted command and ordered the men to wear green worsted epaulets instead of brass scales; probably these were worn for the first year or two, although by 1853 it would seem that scales had been substituted.

Fig. 119

Officers wore the frock coat and on their caps was an emerald green pompon and a "trumpet, perpendicular, embroidered in gold," possibly later with the number "1" in silver within the bend. Enlisted riflemen wore only company letters on their caps until 1858. Trumpeters and bandsmen had full green plastrons over their chests. For fatigue, enlisted soldiers wore cotton jackets and reinforced cotton overalls with dragoon forage caps until about 1855, when the Model 1854 uniform jacket was introduced and replaced the frock coat. This jacket was trimmed with emerald green lace and had brass scales. Thereafter, the regimental uniform underwent the same changes as that of the dragoons.

In 1851, the regiment carried the Model 1841 rifle, caliber .54, without bayonet, one Colt's army revolver, but no saber except for officers and possibly NCO's. Some may still have worn the rifleman's knife, manufactured by the Ames Manufacturing Company and issued the regiment in 1849. In service, the rifle was worn slung across the back. As described in Chapter 4, riflemen wore only a waist belt of black buff leather, 2 inches wide, with the large-size brass oval "US" buckle, on which a regulation rifle cartridge box was hung.

After 1856, the mounted rifleman may have carried the improved Model 1841 rifle, continuing to support his cartridge box on his waist belt. He probably received the Model 1855 rifle around 1858, as well as the Colt army revolver fitted to accept a shoulder stock. The rifleman is believed to have been issued two revolvers and one stock, which he carried in his saddle holsters, but the extent to which this weapon was carried is not clear. It was probably an experimental issue to a few companies; 942 were purchased from Colt in 1858, but a large number went to the dragoons. Almost none were bought thereafter.

Fig. 116. Private, 1st U.S. Cavalry in 1857, wearing the black felt hat adopted in 1855 and an early pattern of the dark blue uniform jacket, trimmed with yellow braid. His reinforced trousers are sky-blue. This arrangement of the yellow hat cord is shown in Robert Weir's edition of the 1851 dress regulations. The trooper carries a U.S. pistol-carbine, M1855, issued to two of the companies, and the heavy caliber saber, M1840. Since the carbine was carried in his saddle holsters he needed no sling. Not visible is an M1855 cartridge box on the rear of his belt. (By Michael J. McAfee after photographs, drawings and descriptions.)

1st and 2nd Cavalry (1855-1861). The initial dress uniform issued the two regiments in May was the same authorized (but not fully supplied) the regiments of dragoons, but with yellow instead of orange lace; uniform jacket, sky blue reinforced or "saddled" trousers, cloth dress cap with cover and yellow pompon. In fact, there is some reason to think the Clothing Establishment did not trouble to remove the orange lace from the jackets.

On 9 July 1855, the field officers of the two cavalry regiments, then organizing at Fort Leavenworth and Jefferson Barracks, were appointed to a Cavalry Equipment Board convened at Washington. Its report and recommendations were approved and published in General Orders No. 13, 15 August. In the area of clothing the Board introduced two items: the black felt hat and the gutta percha talma or raincoat. Both have been described earlier, but it should be noted that the cavalry hat was not exactly similar to the one later issued to all the army. As sent out in 1855, it was looped up on the right side and had three black feathers on the left for field officer, two for company officers, and one for enlisted men. It was trimmed with a gold cord for officers and one of yellow worsted for the men. It also had a chinstrap.

The uniform was worn, subject to army-wide modifications, through 1861. As late as October 1858, the "Cavalry hat" is specified in clothing estimates as distinct from the dress hat issued other troops. The cavalry probably first received a sky blue woolen jacket, trimmed with yellow, for fatigue; then in 1858 came the flannel sack coat. The same year saw the introduction of dark blue pants, and the following year brought in the new forage cap and authorized the cavalry to continue to wear chinstraps in their hats.

The initial armament of the two cavalry regiments reflects the experimental character of the corps. Four weapons were selected for trial.

1st Cavalry

6 companies — Rifled carbine M 1855, caliber .58
2 companies — Pistol-carbine M 1855, caliber .58
2 companies — Merrill, Latrobe and Thomas breechloading carbine, caliber .58

2nd Cavalry

6 companies — Rifled carbine M 1855, caliber .58
2 companies — Pistol-carbine M 1855, caliber .58
2 companies — Perry breechloading carbine, caliber .54

All of the men were supplied with the Model 1840 cavalry saber plus one Colt navy revolver, caliber .36, carried in a belt holster. Apparently, all men received the Model 1855 cartridge box, which was also worn on the waist belt. Two companies of each regiment were ordered to use saber scabbards, "pistol cases" (belt holsters), and cartridge boxes, all of gutta percha, as an experiment.

It is clear that neither of these two breechloading carbines was too successful, for the government purchased only 170 Merrill's and 200 Perry's in 1855. According to Colonel Gluckman (*U.S. Martial Pistols and Revolvers*, p. 87), the pistol-carbine also was never liked by the cavalry. The point of strike differed when this weapon was fired as a pistol from when fired as a carbine, which gave the men small confidence in the arm. The rifled carbine (only 1,020 of which were manufactured in 1855-1856), was the favored cavalry weapon until the Sharps breechloader could be procured. The Burnside breechloading carbine was given a limited trial in the late 1850's and in 1858 the cavalry armament was as follows.

1st Cavalry

8 companies — Sharps breechloading carbine, caliber .52
2 companies — Burnside breechloading carbine, caliber .54

2nd Cavalry

8 companies — Rifled carbine M 1855, caliber .58
2 companies — Sharps breechloading carbine, caliber .52

Except for the Perry and the Model 1855 pistol-carbine, all the cavalry carbines could be attached to a shoulder sling, which was used. The reason for issuing caliber .36 navy revolvers was a mystery to Major Brackett, historian of the U.S. Cavalry, but

Fig. 117A. Private, 4th U.S. Cavalry 1862. Two companies (A and E) of this regiment acted as personal escort to General McClellan for much of the year while the remainder served in the West. The trooper here is armed with a Sharps carbine, Colt army revolver, and light cavalry saber. For the carbine he wears a cartridge box on his belt in rear; he might also have worn a smaller box for revolver cartridges. His clothing is regulation but carelessly worn. On escort duty such would not have been the case, for McClellan was a stickler for neatness; brass scales and white gloves were then the rule. (By F.P. Todd, after a drawing by Winslow Homer.)

it must have been due to a desire to lighten the load carried on the soldier's waist belt, a not inconsiderable factor.

It was the disturbingly experimental character of the mounted man's equipage in 1858 that led to Colonel Craig's letter, mentioned above. In it he wrote:

> . . . there is now no regularly prescribed fire-arm for the Dragoons and Cavalry but the Revolver pistol. I may add that there is no regularly prescribed pattern for Cavalry or Dragoon horse-equipments — the various patterns in use, viz; Grimsley's, McClelland [sic], Jones and Hopes' being all experimental.

● *Cavalry (1861-1872).* With outbreak of the Civil War and the conversion of the six regular mounted commands into regiments of cavalry, their armament tended to become more standardized. It is given in some detail in the order of battle that follows. The patterns of small arms listed there are condensed from "Summary Statements of Ordnance and Ordnance Stores on Hand in Cavalry Regiments," a record kept intermittently from 1862 to 1871 and now in Record Group 156 (Entry 237), in the National Archives. Only patterns issued in substantial numbers are listed in our conden-

Fig. 117B. Private Henry I. John, G Company, 1st U. S. Cavalry, at winter quarters near Culpeper, Va., on Christmas Day, 1863. John then 15 years old, had just received the gauntlets and boots (together with a turkey and other edibles) in a Christmas box from his mother. His dark blue flannel blouse and forage cap without insignia suggest the informal life of winter quarters; he had not yet transferred his spurs to his new boots. (By F.P. Todd, after photograph)

sation, and a pattern that remained in use is usually not repeated after its initial listing.

All regiments were armed with the carbine, saber, and revolver. The carbine in the early war years was the Sharps. This was replaced in some regiments by other makes, more probably because of procurement problems than any thought of improvement. Not until the end of the war did the Spencer repeating carbine reach the regular cavalry, despite their desire for it. Major Brackett, in his history of the U.S. Cavalry, written during the last year of the war, commented:

> Within the last eighteen months there has been a decided improvement in the carbines and accoutrements which have been issued to the cavalry. It is now conceded that the Spencer carbine, or rifle, is, by all odds, the best shooting weapon ever issued to mounted men; and the cartridge-box invented by Colonel Erastus Blakeslee, late of the 1st Regiment of Connecticut Cavalry, leaves but little to be desired. This cartridge-box is carried by a belt over the right shoulder, thus relieving the strain on the abdomen. With it seven cartridges are loaded as quickly as one by the ordinary method, and it is more easily carried than any box in use.

The Blakeslee cartridge box was the only major change in accouterments introduced for the cavalry during the war, although minor variations in other models of box were common.

The light cavalry saber was introduced a few years before the war and gradually came into general use. Its blade was lighter but in most respects it resembled the earlier pattern, which continued to be made and issued. The revolver issued was usually the Colt or Remington army model, both caliber .44, six-shot, single-action weapons. Both fired a self-consuming, combustible cartridge (which were interchangeable), or could be loaded with loose powder and ball. Some caliber .36 navy models of these makes were issued and carried by troopers, but these lighter revolvers tended to be officers' side arms.

Determination of the relative use made by American cavalry of the saber, revolver, and carbine is difficult. The sword or saber had been from time immemorial the weapon *par excellence* of the cavalry, and its defense as such was to many cavalry officers an act of faith. Cavalry regimental histories often devote chapters to infrequent but glamorous actions fought with the saber and say nothing about the day-in, day-out work with the carbine. Most alarming to the *beau sabreur* was the fact that the revolver appeared to have taken precedence in the *mêlée* over the saber, and that some Confederate mounted commands of admitted excellence had actually given up the latter arm. How far traditionalists among the officer corps may have gone to uphold the reputation of the saber is difficult to assess.

The light cavalry saber (referred to below as the "Model 1860") and the caliber .44 cap-and-ball revolver remained regulation arms of the U.S. cavalry until after 1872, despite the growing use of metallic cartridge pistol ammunition. For five years after the Civil War, the regular cavalry continued to carry the repeating carbine, but in 1868 about 300 single-shot Springfield cut-down rifle muskets were altered to breechloaders by the Allin system and later issued for trial along with some other carbines to the mounted service. For reasons of economy (the repeating carbine was considerably more expensive than an arsenal manufactured single-shot weapon, and was believed to lead to great wastage of ammunition), durability, weight of the ammunition required, and perhaps other reasons, the army returned to the single-shot breechloader. In 1871 the issue of the U.S. carbine Model 1870 was begun, and with this our period ends.

Fig. 118. Trooper, 9th U.S. Cavalry, 1871, in overcoat. He carries a light cavalry saber and one of the Remington breechloading carbines issued to the cavalry regiments that year for trial. His forage cap is the "Artillery and Cavalry" pattern being sold in 1871 by military outfitters. In a year or so it would be replaced by the chasseur pattern.

ORDER OF BATTLE: CAVALRY

- 1st Dragoon Regt — to 1861
  1st Cav Regt — 1861 on
  1861-1862: Smith and Sharps carbines; Colt army and navy revolvers; M1840 and M1860 sabers. *1863-1865:* chiefly Sharps carbine, Colt army revolver, M1860 saber. *1866-1867:* some Maynard carbines and Remington army revolvers. *1870:* issued Spencer carbines, cal .50; some M1868 breechloading rifles, cal .50. *1871:* chiefly Spencer carbine, some improved Sharps carbines and US carbine M1870; Colt and Remington army revolvers, some Smith & Wesson revolvers.

- 2nd Dragoon Regt — to 1861
  2nd Cav Regt — 1861 on
  1861-1863: Sharps carbine; Colt army revolver; M1840 and M1860 sabers. *1864-1865:* M1860 saber only. *1866:* Spencer carbine; some Starr carbines and Remington army revolvers. Comp I issued Stuart saber attachment. *1867:* Spencer carbine, cals .50 and .52. *1870-1871:* improved Sharps carbine chiefly; some US carbines M1870 and Remington carbines, cal .50; some Smith & Wesson revolvers. Comps L and M also issued Stuart attachment; Comp C issued 20 "Howlets patent cartridge box."

- Regt of Mounted Riflemen — to 1861
  3rd Cav Regt — 1861 on
  1861-1863: Sharps carbine; Colt army and navy revolvers; M1860 saber; some Burnside carbines. *1864-1865:* Sharps and Smith carbines; some Starr carbines; some M1840 sabers. *1866:* some Remington army revolvers. *1867:* Sharps carbine; some Spencer carbines, cal .50. *1870-1871:* improved Sharps carbine; some Spencer carbines, cal. 50 and Smith & Wesson revolvers; some M1868 rifles.

- 1st Cav Regt — 1855-1861
  4th Cav Regt — 1861 on
  1861-1862: Sharps carbine; 4 comps issued Colt revolving rifle; Colt army and navy revolvers, Remington army revolver; M1840 and M1860 sabers. *1863:* Colt rifle replaced by Burnside and Smith carbines. *1864:* Spencer carbine cal .52 issued; Comp G issued 13 Stuart saber attachments. *1866-1867:* Spencer carbines cals .50 and .52, entirely; Colt and Remington army revolver; M1860 saber entirely. *1870-1871:* Spencer carbine cal .50, only; 4 comps had Stuart attachment; some Smith & Wesson (nickel plated) revolvers.

- 2nd Cav Regt — 1855-1861
  5th Cav Regt — 1861 on
  1861-1864: Sharps carbine; Colt army revolver; M1840 and M1860 sabers. *1865-1867:* some Remington army revolvers. *1870-1871:* some M1868 rifles and Smith & Wesson revolvers issued.

- 3rd Cav Regt — 1861 (May-Aug)
  6th Cav Regt — 1861 on
  1861-1862: Sharps carbine; Colt army and navy revolvers; M1840 and M1860 sabers. *1863-1864:* some Whitney and Remington army revolvers. *1866-1867:* Sharps and Spencer (cals .50 and .52) carbines; Colt and Remington army revolvers. *1870-1871:* some M1868 rifles; generally M1860 sabers; 4 comps had Stuart saber attachment. Some US M1870 and Sharps M1870 carbines issued for experiment late in 1871.

- 7th Cav Regt — 1866 on
  1866-1870: Spencer carbine cals .50 and .52; Remington army revolver; M1860. *1871:* some US M1870, Remington M1870, Sharps M1870 carbines issued for experiment.

- 8th Cav Regt — 1866 on
  1866-1870: Spencer carbine cal .50; Colt army revolver; M1860 saber; some Remington army revolvers. *1871:* issued same experimental weapons as 7th Cav Regt.

- 9th Cav Regt — 1866 on
  1866-1870: Spencer carbine cal .50; Remington army revolver; M1860 saber. *1871:* issued same experimental weapons as 7th Cav Regt.

- 10th Cav Regt — 1866 on
  1867-1870: Spencer cal .50 and Sharps carbines; Colt and Remington army revolvers, Colt army and navy revolver; M1840 and M1860 sabers. *1871:* some M1866 rifles issued.

Fig. 119. U.S. Mounted Rifleman, cir. 1855. He wears the newly-issued dark blue uniform jacket with high, two-hook collar - an early pattern based on a specimen in the Smithsonian Institution; it has emerald green lace. His dark blue cap has green piping and a green pompon. The reinforced trousers are sky blue. His weapon is the Model 1841 rifle. (By F.P. Todd, after regulations)

Regular Artillery

Each of the four regular artillery regiments contained twelve companies, and prior to 1861 two of these companies normally were equipped and trained as "field" or "light" artillery. The other ten garrisoned coastal forts where they drilled with heavy cannon and were designated "heavy" or "foot" companies. In keeping with an American military practice of long standing, they were also trained to serve as infantry and, with minor modification, were armed and equipped as such.

The two kinds of artillerymen dressed differently — the light companies in a mounted uniform which resembled that of the dragoons, the foot companies in a dismounted uniform such as worn by the infantry. Whenever a light company was temporarily dismounted for reasons of economy — and this happened to several of them and for two or three years at a time — it was usually reuniformed and reequipped as heavy artillery. This distinction lasted until 1861 when all but five regular artillery companies were given field guns and horses, and about fourteen were converted to "horse" artillery, in which all the gunners were mounted. Following the Civil War the regiments returned to their dual role.

● *Heavy Companies.* Since the new heavy artillery uniform resembled that worn by the infantry in all respects save the color of facing and piping (which was scarlet), it need not be separately described at any length. The existing dress uniform in 1851 for enlisted men was a single- or double-breasted tail coat of dark blue cloth with

Fig. 120. Companies of Light Artillery, 1854. We see a company at drill and inspection, the men wearing dark blue shell jackets trimmed with scarlet lace, sky blue pants, and dark blue forage caps with red bands. The figure in the foreground is a driver, his right leg encased in a leather guard to prevent it being crushed against the off horse.

yellow worsted epaulets, scarlet skirt lining and turnbacks, and yellow lace and buttons; sky blue pants; dress cap of the infantry model with crossed cannon instead of bugle and a scarlet plume or pompon; and yellow metal. Musicians wore scarlet tail coats with white lining and turnbacks, yellow lace, and white plumes. Issue of new cloth caps of the Model of 1851 began late that year; otherwise the old uniform was worn until the fall of 1852 when issue of the new pattern commenced.

Plate I

For fatigue and field service, the heavy artilleryman wore at first the same uniform he had used in the Mexican War: a sky blue woolen fatigue jacket and pants trimmed with yellow lace on collar and shoulder straps, and a dark blue M1839 forage cap. Officers and sergeants were authorized 1.5-inch scarlet trouser stripes; there were no distinctions for musicians. In the fall of 1852 these jackets were issued trimmed with scarlet lace instead of yellow, and were so worn until 1855. White cotton jackets and pants were supplied regiments that requisitioned them through 1854.

Issue of the Model 1851 dress uniform, comprising a dark blue frock coat with

Fig. 121. Sergeant of Griffin's West Point Battery, about May 1861. This light battery, armed with four 12-pounder Napoleons and made up of men transferred from the dragoon and artillery attachments at the U.S. Military Academy, was somewhat a law unto itself as regards clothing and other matters. The sergeant wears a well-tailored, dark blue uniform jacket and reinforced trousers of the same color, both trimmed with scarlet. His dress hat has been modified but still carries a plume and scarlet cord. In July the command became Battery D of the newly formed 5th Artillery Regiment. (By F.P. Todd after a drawing by Thomas Nast)

scarlet epaulets, sky blue pants, and dark blue cloth cap, all trimmed with scarlet and yellow metal, began about August 1852 and by mid-1853 most if not all the heavy artillery companies were so supplied. Thereafter, this uniform succumbed to the same modifications as will be described for infantry: replacement of the cap band by a colored welt and later of the cap itself by a hat; change from worsted epaulets to brass scales; adoption of dark blue pants, etc.

When the supply of sky blue fatigue jackets was exhausted in 1855, it became necessary for the men to perform fatigue duties in their shirts or cut their old frock coats into jackets. This condition lasted until 1858 when the sack coat appeared. The supply of the old model wide-crowned forage caps also ended in 1855, and until 1859 artillerymen wore dress caps or hats on fatigue. The Model 1858 forage cap (the familiar Civil War pattern) was first issued in early 1859 with scarlet welts and was so decorated until the Civil War.

Fig. 6

The regular artillerymen in the Civil War, as has been said, generally wore light artillery clothing, but there were numerous heavy artillery regiments raised by the War Department and by the states that used the infantry-style uniform. Being stationed in coastal forts or in the fortifications of larger cities, they had ample time for parade, and it is these regiments in the main that displayed the full dress uniform in all its parts during the years 1861-1865.

When our period opens in 1851, the heavy artilleryman carried the Artillery Musketoon Model 1847, caliber .69. Apparently, at that time he was not issued a bayonet. In its place he received the distinctive and almost useless Model 1833 Foot Artillery Sword which required a special belt. This belt, described in detail earlier, was of black buff leather and had a frog of the same suspended from rings. Its buckle was a two-piece brass circular pattern bearing the raised letters "US". Otherwise he was accoutered as an infantryman.

At some point before the Civil War — the date is uncertain but it may have been 1859 when fabrication of the musketoon ceased — the men were given the Model 1855 rifle musket with bayonet and ordinary infantry accouterments. Apparently, some sergeants wore the Model 1840 NCO's sword and belt while others, even into the Civil War period, carried the artillery sword and special belt. For what it is worth, the post-war official photographs show a sergeant major with an NCO sword, while a quarter-master sergeant and sergeant wear the artillery pattern. Musicians were accoutered as in the infantry.

● *Light Companies.* In 1851, the dress uniform of enlisted men in the eight light companies was a tail coat like that worn by the heavy companies but with a scarlet collar and scarlet *pointed* cuffs (the dragoon style, that is), edged with yellow lace. Pantaloons were sky blue with a .75-inch scarlet stripe for all men and two such for sergeants. These pants were, of course, reinforced, for all mounted personnel. Caps were of the dragoon pattern with scarlet horsehair plumes and scarlet cords and tassels, but with the eagle, crossed cannon, and the other insignia of the heavy companies. They were called "Ringgold caps." Rank of NCO's was indicated by chevrons, as in the dragoons, instead of by loops on the cuffs, and all men wore brass shoulder scales in place of epaulets. Musicians wore scarlet coats with white collar, facings, and pointed cuffs, trimmed with yellow lace.

For fatigue, the light companies apparently wore dark blue shell jackets trimmed with scarlet worsted lace, dark blue wide-crowned forage caps, probably with red bands, and sky blue pants. The drivers and NCO's, and perhaps all the men, wore ankle boots. There was no distinction for musicians in the fatigue uniform.

Fig. 120

The Model 1851 dress uniform for the light companies differed from that authorized other artillerymen only in allowing them "brass shoulder knots [scales] (as for Dragoons)" in place of worsted epaulets. It is well to say at once that most light companies viewed the frock coat with distaste and did what they could to avoid accepting it. Fortunately General Jesup, the Quartermaster General, considered the light artillery "as a child of my own" and, as shall be seen, favored the companies in every way he could.

The first new pattern item to be issued beginning in the summer of 1852 was the Model 1851 cloth dress cap with scarlet pompon. Soon afterward, the old pattern dress coats were exhausted and the light companies received Model 1851 frock coats in 1853. Under General Orders No. 1, 20 January 1854, however, they were authorized a "uniform jacket" in place of the coat, and as soon as they could most companies disposed of the longer garment. Strangely, some companies specifically requisitioned coats. As late as March 1859 Captain T.W. Sherman's battery — E of the 3rd Artillery — did this, and a picture in *Harper's Weekly* of 8 June 1861 shows them in frock coats and Hardee hats. Clearly, there was much difference in dress among the light companies. Their elite and almost independent status in the army, General Jesup's favoritism, and the confused condition of Quartermaster supply allowed them much leeway in clothing.

The old pattern fatigue jackets soon ran out but Jesup directed the Clothing Bureau to provide instead "dark blue jackets of the Ordnance or Engineer pattern, with the material necessary to alter them." White cotton jackets were worn as long as they were available. When, by late 1854, the companies were being provided with both a fatigue and a uniform jacket, it was decided to drop the former except for issue to recruits. In its place the light artillerymen wore old uniform jackets or shirts until the flannel sack coat began to appear in 1858.

The uniform jacket, Model 1854, became the characteristic garment of the light artilleryman, rivalled only by his dress cap whose development is described below. The lace was scarlet and for trumpeters it covered the breast in the herring-bone form prescribed by regulations. Brass scales were worn in two models (there was no non-commissioned staff). Officers wore frock coats, with either epaulets or shoulder straps. In 1857 they were authorized a plain dark blue cloth jacket for stable duty, and in 1860 a special "round jacket . . . of dark blue cloth, trimmed with scarlet, with the Russian shoulder knot" for undress.

Fig. 127

Fig. 121

When the trousers of the army were altered to dark blue in 1858, the light companies struggled, usually successfully, to avoid accepting the new pattern. In 1860 they were formally given permission (GO 20) to retain their sky blue pants. It is in their headdress, however, that they achieved the most distinctive note.

When the supply of "Ringgold caps" ran out in 1852, the light companies were issued the Model 1851 dress cap of dark blue cloth with wide scarlet band and scarlet pompon, company letter, new eagle, and waterproof cover. The scarlet band disap-

378

Fig. 122. Farrier (or "artificer" as he was called in the Artillery) of a field battery, 1863. He wears a cotton shirt and regulation sky blue trousers, over which hangs a farrier's leather apron. His non-regulation hat was black felt. (By F.P. Todd after photograph)

Fig. 123. 2nd Lieut. C.L. Best, Jr., 1st U.S. Artillery, cir. 1870. His cap lacks the leather reinforcing bands worn by enlisted men and continues to have the embroidered 1851 eagle pattern rather than a spread eagle. Dark blue cap with scarlet plume, dark blue frock coat and sky blue pants. The bewildering maze of gold cords formed by his cap cords and the non-regulation aiguilettes of an aide-de-camp, worn incorrectly. (By Michael J. McAfee, after photographs)

peared after 1854, replaced by a scarlet welt. By 1858 some of the companies were requisitioning scarlet horse-hair plumes. None were in stock in Philadelphia, but the obliging General Jesup found some old dragoon plumes and had them dyed and sent out. At the same time he authorized those light companies that so desired to continue to wear their Model 1851 caps instead of changing to the newer Hardee hat. In fact, he called in all available caps and horse-hair plumes from the field to effect a supply.

Nothing short of the return of the pre-1851 "Ringgold cap," with its traditions of the Mexican War, would satisfy light artillery commanders. In February 1859, authority was given to issue them scarlet cap cords and tassels and to place crossed cannon and regimental numerals on the front. When there was difficulty getting the flimsy cloth caps to bear the added weight of plumes and cords, the Clothing Bureau was instructed to reissue the Ringgold cap with large spread eagle, formal authority for this being given in August 1860 (GO 20). The cap that developed, and was worn after the Civil War, *Figs. 15 and 123* was made of cloth-covered cardboard reinforced with leather, somewhat lower than the 1840's model and with a smaller visor. It was, in short, the old Ringgold cap in a more modern style. The officers' version worn in the late 1860's lacked the leather bands.

The basic, and usually the only personal weapon of the light artilleryman was his saber. The model was adopted in 1840 and was regulation throughout this entire period. It was a principle among artillerists that a cannoneer should look on his piece as his most effective weapon, and that when he was concerned with defending himself with a a personal arm his work at the gun suffered. Drivers, however, sometimes carried revolvers — at least after 1861 — as did musicians, guidon bearers, sergeants, and officers.

Even sabers were left off by cannoneers, probably with the encouragement of their battery officers, since they actually were only a nuisance in the standing gun drill. At first they were kept strapped to limber chests, but later they gravitated to the wagons, from which they eventually disappeared. Because of the inconsistency of their armament, the small arms carried by light companies are not mentioned in the order of battle that follows.

Light artillerymen, as a result, were lightly accoutered, and most of their gear was carried on the horses or the limbers. The saber belt provided for them was of a distinctive pattern: 1.7 (later 1.9) inches wide, of black buff leather, with two chapes sewn on the outside to hold the brass rings to which the saber slings were attached. The brass plate was circular and two-piece, with the raised letters "US" on it. No shoulder sling was provided as on the cavalry belt. Sometime in the late 1850's the plate was changed to the standard rectangular model.

Artillery drivers were provided with a leather whip about 30 inches long. Made of raw hide, covered with India rubber cloth, covered in turn with leather, it had a hand loop. They also were given a leather guard, reinforced with an iron plate .1-inch thick, for the right legs. It had four straps buckling around the leg and one around the foot.

Fig. 120

ORDER OF BATTLE: ARTILLERY

- 1st Regt   entire period
  (*Light Comps:* I and K until 1861; all comps, 1861-1865; I and K, 1865-1869; K after 1869. Comps E/G, H/I and K equipped as Horse Arty, 1861-1865) *1862-1863:* Enfield rifle. *1865-1867:* M1863 rifled musket. *1871:* M1868 breechloading musket cal .50.

- 2nd Regt   entire period
  (*Light Comps:* A and M until 1861; all comps except H, I and K, 1861-1865; A and M, 1865-1869; A after 1869. Comps A, B/L, D, G and M equipped as Horse Arty, 1861-1865) *1862-1867:* Springfield rifled musket. *1871:* M1868 breechloading musket cal .50; and experimental arms (about 60 of each): M1870 Springfield breechloading musket cal .50; M1870 Sharps rifled musket cal .50; M1870 Remington breechloading rifled musket cal .50.

- 3rd Regt   entire period
  (*Light Comps:* C and E until 1861; all comps except B and D, 1861-1865; C and E, 1865-1869; C after 1869. Comps C, F and K equipped as Horse Arty, 1861-1865) *1862-1867:* Springfield rifled muskets. *1871:* M1868 breechloading musket cal .50; and experimental arms (about 60 of each): M1870 Springfield breechloading musket cal .50; M1870 Sharps rifled musket cal .50; M1870 Remington breechloading rifled musket cal .50.

- 4th Regt   entire period
  (*Light Comps:* B and G until 1861; all comps, 1861-1865; B and G, 1865-1869; B after 1869. Comp G served as cav 1855-1856; thereafter dismounted until 1861. Comp A and C/E equipped as Horse Arty, 1861-1865) *1862-1867:* Springfield rifled musket. *1871:* M1868 breechloading musket cal .50.

- 5th Regt   1861 on
  (*Light Comps:* all comps, 1861-1865; F and G, 1865-1869; F after 1869) *1867:* Springfield rifled musket. *1871:* M1868 breechloading musket cal .50.

Regular Infantry

Fig. 124

The infantryman of 1851 wore for dress a dark blue cloth tail coat, single- or double-breasted depending on rank, with white lace, lining, and worsted epaulets. His pants were sky blue, his dress cap was a rigid beaver or felt model with white pompon, eagle, and bugle-horn device. All metal was white and all officer's lace was silver. Musicians wore scarlet coats with white lining, lace, and plume. Officers and high ranking NCO's wore white plumes. This was the "old pattern" dress uniform.

The fatigue uniform consisted of a sky blue kersey jacket and pants, laced with white, with a dark blue cloth forage cap. Officers and sergeants wore 1.5-inch white pants stripes with both uniforms. There were no distinctions for musicians in the fatigue uniform.

The Model 1851 "new pattern" uniform for enlisted men consisted of a dark blue cloth frock coat, sky blue pants, and dark blue cloth cap. The collar, cuffs, chevrons, worsted epaulets, pompon, and cap band were of "light or Saxony blue," a somewhat different color than the pants. The pants stripe was 1/8-inch for all ranks, of dark blue cord.

Musicians were distinguished by a wide Saxony blue plastron, while officers wore a severely plain frock coat, longer than that of the enlisted men, double-breasted for field officers and single-breasted for those of company grade. The officer's cap had a gold embroidered bugle-horn on its front and no colored band. The enlisted man wore a one-inch brass company letter (or regimental number for the non-commissioned staff) instead.

Shoes were black, and the leather stock was still being worn by enlisted men. Officers wore a crimson net sash, and NCO's above the rank of sergeant wore one of red worsted. Both were tied on the left hip. The overcoat for an enlisted man was single-breasted with five large buttons, a stand-up collar, and was made of heavy blue-grey cloth. It had, permanently attached, a cape of the same material reaching to the elbows. It was fastened by six small brass buttons. Officers wore a dark blue cloak coat.

The supply of old pattern dress caps being exhausted late in 1851, Model 1851 caps were authorized for issue. The Quartermaster General concluded, "they are not incongruous with the old uniforms." A few full uniforms of the new pattern were given to recruiting parties, but the infantry regiments as a whole had to wait until late in 1854 before getting frock coats and other new pattern items. Some companies were still being issued old pattern tail coats in April 1855.

In the meanwhile, in January 1854, and thus before the bulk of the infantry could have received them, the light blue epaulets were abolished, replaced by brass scales, and the light blue cuffs and collar were exchanged for colored welts. The colored cap band went at the same time as probably did the musician's full colored plastron, to be replaced by the laced button-hole pattern.

Fatigue clothing was not mentioned in the dress regulations of 1851, but the stock on hand was large and the sky blue kersey jackets and pants, with the dark blue forage cap, were issued until 1857. In 1852 their lace was changed from white to dark blue. Cotton fatigue clothing was issued to regiments requesting it until the supply ran out in early 1855.

Fig. 124. Lieutenant, 10th U.S. Infantry, cir. 1858. His dress uniform is regulation except for his use of gauntlets, probably buff in color. The embroidered golden eagle and bugle, and silver "10," are clearly shown. His frock coat does not appear to be pleated around the waist, a style which ended about this time. (Photograph from the collection of Herb Peck, Jr.)

Fig. 125. Corporal, 9th Infantry, 1857 or 1858. He wears the chasseurs-a-pied pattern frock coat and the rifle belt, both introduced in 1855, and holds a Model 1855 rifle with its saber bayonet. The bayonet scabbard is supported by a frog sewn to the belt. Note the two "half chevrons" on his lower sleeve, indicating 10 years service. His rifle is fitted with a Maynard primer, thus eliminating the need for a cap pouch.

All regiments at first carried the caliber .69 musket, Model 1842, with socket bayonet. For accouterments the men wore the regulation cartridge box holding forty rounds, with its buff leather shoulder belt placed over the left shoulder. On a buff leather waist belt was a percussion cap pouch and a bayonet scabbard. These belts had been white prior to 1851 or 1852, but they seem to have been blackened about that time. These accouterments and the others carried are described in detail in Chapter 4.

"The Government have in view the organisation of a Corps of Foot Riflemen," wrote the Quartermaster General to the Count de Sartiges, Envoy of France in June 1854. He went on to request that a complete outfit of a private soldier of the *Chasseurs à pied* be provided by the French government. "By complete outfit I mean the cap, coat, trousers, knapsack, haversack, cartridge box and belts." A comparable request was made by the Chief of Ordnance. The results of this importation were the uniform and accouterments of the 9th and 10th Regiments of Infantry, established by General Orders No. 4, 26 March 1855. To a lesser degree the entire army was affected.

The chasseur pattern of coat and pants has already been described; it was in use for about three years. The two new regiments wore it but in so doing they differed in no wise from the rest of the infantry.* Where they did differ was in their use after 1857, of the Model 1855 rifle with its saber bayonet; in the chasseur waist belt with connecting knapsack straps and Model 1855, caliber .58, cartridge box suspended from it; and in employing buglers instead of drummers. Their uniforms had light blue trimmings, not green.

Commencing about 1857, the eight old regiments exchanged their caliber .69 weapons for the new caliber .58 rifle musket. With it came the smaller Model 1855 *Fig. 126* cartridge box and a somewhat larger waist belt with the familiar 3.5 x 2.25-inch oval brass buckle. Thereafter, the changes in uniform, arms, and accouterments were those prescribed for the army as a whole: adoption of the black felt hat, dark blue pants and sack coat, and return to plainer tailoring in 1858; issue of new pattern blouses and forage caps, and return to the sky blue pants. In 1867, breechloading rifles began to appear as described below.

Regular infantry regiments during the Civil War tended to dress more formally than the volunteers, but the differences — from what little can be discovered — were matters of degree. After the War there was no alteration in the issue clothing for enlisted men. Officers, however, adopted a new form of the felt dress hat, already described. Experiments with breechloading arms after 1866 led to some changes in cartridge boxes, but it is difficult to gauge the extent to which the various new patterns were worn.

Infantry musicians (drummers and fifers) and bandsmen carried no other weapon *Fig. 127* than the sword. This was the Musicians' Sword Model 1840, a straight model with brass hilt and black leather scabbard, closely resembling the NCO's sword adopted at the same time. In the 1850's, so far as can be learned, the usual practice was to suspend this sword from a black leather shoulder belt (see Chapter 4) and to wear a waist belt in addition, fastened by the common rectangular belt plate. This was the regulation

*The "Foot Rifleman" illustrated in the Horstmann edition of the 1851 dress regulations and the checkers-playing "Foot-Rifles" in H.A. Ogden's plate XXI, refer to the Regiment of Mounted Riflemen.

Fig. 126. Enlisted men, 5th U.S. Infantry, dressed for the Utah Expedition of 1857-1858. The men wear dark blue model 1839 forage caps and uniform jackets, the latter normally given only to mounted troops. These items had been specifically issued for the campaign. The lace on the jackets was probably of several colors or it could have been omitted entirely. In all probability, the men got heavy boots, mittens and mufflers. The man on the right wears an infantry overcoat. Both carry the Model 1855 rifle musket. (By F.P. Todd after woodcuts in *Harper's Weekly*, 30 January 1858 and dress regulations.)

way, but after 1861 by far the most common method was to suspend the sword on the left side from a sliding leather frog on the waist belt. Actually, in the field the Musicians' Sword was rarely worn except, perhaps, by principal musicians. Drum slings were commonly made of white canvas or webbing and worn around the neck, although the style of sling that passed over the right shoulder was plentiful enough. Cases for fifes, extra bugles, and other paraphernalia of the musicians of European armies were virtually unknown.

Fig. 127. U.S. Infantry Musician, 1866. His sword is not of the correct pattern, but the photograph clearly shows the Infantry bugle and side drum, and a brass drum stick carriage. (U.S. Army official photograph in Smithsonian Institution; the series is described on page 21.)

ORDER OF BATTLE: INFANTRY

- 1st Regt (absorbed 43rd Inf Regt 1869)   entire period
  1862-1867: Springfield rifled muskets. *1870:* M1866 breechloading rifle cal .50. *1871:* M1868 breechloading rifle cal .50.

- 2nd Regt (absorbed 16th Inf Regt 1869)   entire period
  1862-1867: Springfield rifled muskets. *1870:* M1866 breechloading rifle cal .50. *1871:* M1868 breechloading rifle cal .50.

- 3rd Regt (absorbed part of 37th Inf Regt 1869)   entire period
  1862-1867: Springfield rifled muskets. *1867:* Spencer rifle. *1870:* M1866 breechloading rifle cal .50. *1871:* M1868 breechloading rifle cal .50 (56 nickel plated). (In 1871 this and 15 other regts were issued about 60 experimental arms: M1870 Springfield breechloading rifle cal .50; M1870 Sharps rifled musket cal .50; M1870 Remington breechloading rifled musket cal .50. Hereafter this will be indicated by "experimental arms.")

- 4th Regt (absorbed 30th Inf Regt 1869)   entire period
  1862-1866: Springfield rifled muskets. *1867-1870:* M1866 breechloading rifle cal .50. *1871:* M1868 breech-loading rifle cal .50; and experimental arms.

- 5th Regt (absorbed part of 37th Inf Regt 1869)   entire period
  1862-1867: Springfield rifled muskets. *1870-1871:* M1868 breechloading rifle cal .50 and experimental arms.

- 6th Regt (absorbed 42nd Inf Regt 1869)   entire period
  1862-1867: Springfield rifled muskets. *1870:* M1866 breechloading rifle cal .50. *1871:* M1868 breechloading rifle cal .50; and experimental arms.

- 7th Regt (absorbed 36th Inf Regt 1869)   entire period
  1862-1867: Springfield rifled muskets; 242 Colt revolving rifles 1864. *1870-1871:* M1866 and M1868 breechloading rifles cal .50.

- 8th Regt (absorbed 33rd Inf Regt 1869)   entire period
  1862-1867: Springfield rifled muskets. *1870:* M1866 breechloading rifle cal .50. *1871:* M1868 breechloading rifle cal .50.

- 9th Regt (absorbed 27th Inf Regt 1869)   1855 on
  1857-1862: M1855 rifle. *1862-1867:* Springfield rifled muskets. *1870-1871:* M1868 breechloading rifle cal .50; and experimental arms.

- 10th Regt (absorbed 26th Inf Regt 1869)   1855 on
  1857-1862: M1855 rifle. *1862-1867:* Springfield rifled muskets. *1870:* M1866 breechloading rifle cal. 50. *1871:* M1868 breechloading rifle cal .50; and experimental arms.

- 1st Bn, 11th Regt   1861-1866
  11th Regt (absorbed 34th Inf Regt)   1866-1869
  16th Regt   1869 on
  1862-1867: Springfield rifled muskets. *1871:* M1868 breechloading rifle cal .50; and experimental arms.

- 2nd Bn, 11th Regt   1861-1866
  20th Regt   1866 on
  1867: M1863 rifled musket. *1870:* M1866 breechloading rifle cal .50. *1871:* M1868 breechloading rifle cal .50.

- 3rd Bn, 11th Regt   1861-1866
  29th Regt (consol with 24th to form 11th Inf Regt)   1866-1869
  1867: M1863 rifled musket.

- 1st Bn, 12th Regt   1861-1866
  12th Regt   1866 on
  1862-1866: Springfield rifled muskets. *1867:* Springfield breechloading rifle (Allin's alteration), cal .58. *1870:* M1866 breechloading rifle cal .50. *1871:* M1868 breechloading rifle cal .50; and experimental arms.

- 2nd Bn, 12th Regt   1861-1866
  21st Regt (absorbed 32nd Inf Regt 1869)   1866 on
  1867: M1863 rifled musket; some with Allin's alteration. *1870:* M1866 breechloading rifle cal .50. *1871:* M1868 breechloading rifle cal .50.

ORDER OF BATTLE: INFANTRY (continued)

- 3rd Bn, 12th Regt — (not organ until 1866)
  30th Regt (merged into 4th Inf Regt) — 1866-1869
    1867: M1866 breechloading rifle cal .50.

- 1st Bn, 13th Regt — 1861-1866
  13th Regt — 1866 on
    1863-1867: Springfield rifled muskets. *1870*: M1866 breechloading rifle cal .50. *1871*: M1868 breechloading rifle cal .50; and experimental arms.

- 2nd Bn, 13th Regt — 1861-1866
  22nd Regt (absorbed 31st Inf Regt 1869) — 1866 on
    1867: M1863 rifled musket and M1866 breechloading rifle cal .50. *1871*: M1868 breechloading rifle cal .50.

- 3rd Bn, 13th Regt — (not organ until 1866)
  31st Regt (merged into 22nd Inf Regt) — 1866-1869
    1867: M1863 rifled musket.

- 1st Bn, 14th Regt — 1861-1866
  14th Regt (absorbed 45th Inf Regt 1869) — 1866 on
    1862-1867: Springfield rifled muskets. *1870*: M1866 breechloading rifle cal .50. *1871*: M1868 breechloading rifle cal .50; and experimental arms.

- 2nd Bn, 14th Regt — 1861-1866
  23rd Regt — 1866 on
    1867: M1863 rifled musket. *1870*: M1866 breechloading rifle cal .50. *1871*: M1868 breechloading rifle cal .50; and experimental arms.

- 3rd Bn, 14th Regt — (not organ until 1866)
  32nd Regt (merged into 21st Inf Regt) — 1866-1869
    1867: M1863 rifled musket.

- 1st Bn, 15th Regt — 1861-1866
  15th Regt (absorbed 35th Inf Regt 1869) — 1866 on
    1862-1867: Springfield rifled muskets. *1870*: M1866 breechloading rifle cal .50. *1871*: M1868 breechloading rifle cal .50; and experimental arms.

- 2nd Bn, 15th Regt — 1861-1866
  24th Regt (consol with 29th Inf Regt) — 1866-1869
  11th Regt — 1869 on
    1867: M1863 rifled musket. *1870*: M1866 breechloading rifle cal .50. *1871*: M1868 breechloading rifle cal .50; and experimental arms.

- 3rd Bn, 15th Regt — 1861-1866
  33rd Regt (merged into 8th Inf Regt) — 1866-1869
    1867: M1863 rifled musket.

- 1st Bn, 16th Regt — 1861-1866
  16th Regt (merged into 2nd Inf Regt) — 1866-1869
    1862-1867: Springfield rifled muskets. *1870*: breechloading rifle cal .50.

- 2nd Bn, 16th Regt — 1861-1866
  25th Regt (merged into 18th Inf Regt) — 1866-1869
    1867: M1863 rifled musket.

- 3rd Bn, 16th Regt — 1861-1866
  34th Regt (consol with 11th to form 16th Inf Regt) — 1866-1869
    1867: M1863 rifled musket.

- 1st Bn, 17th Regt — 1861-1866
  17th Regt (absorbed 44th Inf Regt 1869) — 1866 on
    1862-1867: Springfield rifled muskets. *1870*: M1866 breechloading rifle cal .50. *1871*: M1868 breechloading rifle cal .50.

ORDER OF BATTLE: INFANTRY (continued)

- 2nd Bn, 17th Regt — 1861-1866
  26th Regt (merged into 10th Inf Regt) — 1866-1869
    1867: M1863 rifled musket.

- 3rd Bn, 17th Regt — (not organ until 1866)
  35th Regt (merged into 15th Inf Regt) — 1866-1869
    1867: M1863 rifled musket.

- 1st Bn, 18th Regt — 1861-1866
  18th Regt (absorbed 25th Inf Regt 1869) — 1866 on
    1862-1867: Springfield rifled muskets. *1870:* M1866 breechloading rifle cal .50. *1871:* M1868 breechloading rifle cal .50; and experimental arms.

- 2nd Bn, 18th Regt — 1861-1866
  27th Regt (merged into 9th Inf Regt) — 1866-1869
    1866: M1866 breechloading rifle.

- 3rd Bn, 18th Regt — 1861-1866
  36th Regt (merged into 7th Inf Regt) — 1866-1869
    1867: M1863 rifled musket; M1866 breechloading rifle cal .50.

- 1st Bn, 19th Regt — 1861-1866
  19th Regt (absorbed 28th Inf Regt 1869) — 1866 on
    1862-1867: M1863 rifled musket. *1870:* M1866 breechloading rifle cal .50. *1871:* M1868 breechloading rifle cal .50.

- 2nd Bn, 19th Regt — 1861-1866
  28th Regt (merged into 19th Inf Regt) — 1866-1869
    1867: M1863 rifled musket.

- 3rd Bn, 19th Regt — (not organ until 1866)
  37th Regt (merged into 3rd and 5th Inf Regts) — 1866-1869
    1867: Sharps rifle.

- (20th-37th Regts, 1866-1869, see above)

- 38th Regt (colored) (consol with 41st Inf Regt) — 1866-1869
  24th Regt (colored) — 1869 on
    1867-1870: M1866 breechloading rifle cal .50. *1871:* M1868 breechloading rifle cal .50, and experimental arms.

- 39th Regt (colored) (consol with 40th Inf Regt) — 1866-1869
  25th Regt (colored) — 1869 on
    1867: M1863 rifled musket. *1870:* M1866 breechloading rifle cal .50. *1871:* M1868 breechloading rifle cal .50; and experimental arms.

- 40th Regt (colored) (consol with 39th Inf Regt) — 1866-1869
    1867: M1863 rifled musket.

- 41st Regt (colored) (consol with 38th Inf Regt) — 1866-1869
    1867: M1863 rifled musket.

- 42nd Regt (merged into 6th Inf Regt) — 1866-1869
    1867: M1863 rifled musket.

- 43rd Regt (merged into 1st Inf Regt) — 1866-1869
    1867: M1863 rifled musket.

- 44th Regt (merged into 17th Inf Regt) — 1866-1869
    1867: M1863 rifled musket.

- 45th Regt (merged into 14th Inf Regt) — 1866-1869
    1867: M1863 rifled musket.

Fig. 128. Enlisted soldiers of the 3rd U.S. Infantry, 1870. The standing private wears a dark blue blouse, sky blue trousers and, for field service, a battered felt hat, blanket roll wrapped in an oil-cloth cover, and M1864 cartridge box on his waist belt. He holds an M1866, caliber .50, breechloading rifle, received in 1870.

The seated company quartermaster sergeant (with half chevrons showing 20 years service) is in dress uniform, with dark blue frock coat, sky blue trousers with dark blue stripe, and a red worsted sash. His black felt hat is dented in the then fashionable style, but carries its full quota of insignia. Not being on the regimental non-commissioned staff, his brass scales are of the sergeant's pattern. He has removed his brass NCO sword from its black leather frog. (By Michael J. McAfee, from photographs and descriptions.)

Regular Engineer Troops

The Company of Engineer Soldiers stationed at West Point was wearing the uniform given it in 1846 when our period commences, and it continued to do so until 1854. This comprised a dark blue, single-breasted tail coat with black velvet collar and cuffs, but otherwise like the coat worn by foot artillery; sky blue pants with black stripes for sergeants or welts for others; and a beaver or felt cap with the "turretted castle" device, a black upright hackle for sergeants, and a black pompon for other men. Musicians (who were buglers) wore red coats with the same collar and cuffs but lined with white. All metal and lace were yellow, belts were of white buff leather, and insignia was distinctive.

Officers of the Corps of Engineers (by whom the Company was commanded) did not continue to wear the old pattern uniform after 1851, but changed to the pattern authorized that year. This uniform and side arms have already been described above.

The uniform prescribed for engineer soldiers in 1851 apparently was never sent them, for the modifications of January 1854 were in force when, in March of that year, they were authorized to wear the new pattern clothing. This consisted of a dark blue frock coat with collar and cuffs of the same color but edged with yellow cord, brass scales, sky blue pants without stripe or cord, and a cloth dress cap piped with yellow. A brass castle was worn on the cap and both sides of the collar. Subject to the army-wide changes, this remained the dress uniform of the Company and later Battalion of Engineers throughout out period. Apparently the wearing of castles on the collar ceased after 1858.

When the Company found it could not procure the new pattern dress uniform in 1851 it requested and was sent enough 1/8-inch yellow cord to convert its dress pants to the new regulations of that year.

The fatigue uniform of engineer soldiers presented some unusual features. In 1851 it comprised a dark blue shell jacket with a black velvet collar piped with yellow; sky blue pants with a black welt; and a distinctive dark blue forage cap with a band of black velvet and a brass castle on the front. Like men of other branches, the engineers also wore a white cotton shell jacket and pants in summer. Being school troops, the Company was well supplied with this clothing and required to keep it in good condition. The white fatigue was worn until about 1855, the blue until sack coats were issued in 1858. For some reason not clear, the Company wore fatigue jackets in 1861 while guarding public property in Washington, D.C.

Fig. 129

Alone of all the army, the engineers were supplied with white cotton canvas "overalls." These are described as being "one garment to cover the whole of the body below the waist, the breast, the shoulders and the arms; sleeves loose, to allow a free play of the arms, with narrow wristband buttoning with one button; overalls to fasten at the neck behind with two buttons, and at the waist behind with buckle and tongue."

The engineers were the first troops to receive the new-pattern forage cap, being specially authorized to adopt it by the Secretary of War in July 1857.

During the Civil War and until 1872 the Engineer Battalion wore for parade the regulation dress uniform piped with yellow. In the field the men were as unpredictable in their fatigue dress as the rest of the army, but no matter what type of hat they had on,

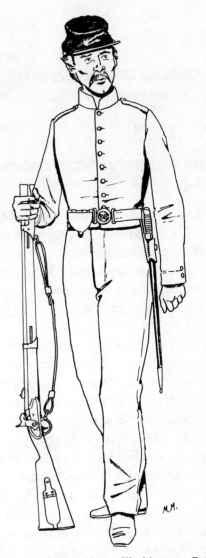

Fig. 129. U.S. Engineer soldier in fatigue dress, Washington, D.C., April 1861. His shell jacket is a light shade — either sky blue or grey — and his trousers are dark blue, in common with most of the army. His forage cap, here with an oil cloth cover, bore a brass turreted castle insigne. The man carries a U.S. rifle M1841, altered to caliber .58, with saber bayonet. His belt is the Sappers and Miners pattern with two-piece buckle; on it rides a frog holding the bayonet scabbard, an M1855 rifle cartridge box in the rear, and a cap pouch. (By Michael J. McAfee, after woodcut in *Frank Leslie's Illustrated Newspaper.*)

it invariably carried the turretted castle.

The arms and accouterments of the engineer soldiers were somewhat distinctive. The weapon in 1851 was the caliber .69 Sapper's Musketoon Model 1847 with its long sword bayonet. The latter was worn on a special model waist belt of black buff leather, 2 inches wide, fitted with the same two-piece brass plate as worn by the foot artillery. A black buff leather frog held the bayonet scabbard, and it seems probable that the Model 1841 rifle cartridge box also was slid on the belt. This musketoon and bayonet were withdrawn in 1855 and replaced by the U.S. Rifle Model 1841, altered to caliber .58 in 1855. With that, the engineers used a saber bayonet. From 1862 to the end of our period the battalion was armed with Model 1861 or Model 1863 rifle muskets.

The engineer soldiers, of course, frequently carried tools of various sorts but there is almost no evidence that they were supplied with portable tools having specially designed cases. Tools were carried in wagons or on pack animals on the march.

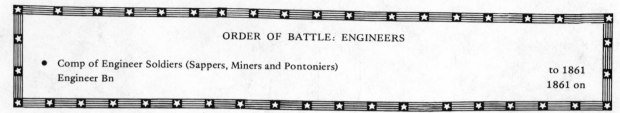

- Comp of Engineer Soldiers (Sappers, Miners and Pontoniers)   to 1861
  Engineer Bn   1861 on

Ordnance Sergeants and Men

The Ordnance Department consisted of officers (who comprised the Ordnance Corps), a limited number of enlisted men including the Ordnance Sergeants, who served as caretakers of Ordnance and other stores at army installations, and civilian employees of the various Federal armories and arsenals. The uniforms and accouterments of the officers of the Corps have been described earlier under Staff. The Ordnance enlisted men wore the distinctive uniform, described below. Most of the civilians were not uniformed.

The dress prescribed for an Ordnance Sergeant by the Regulations of 1847 was a dark blue, double-breasted tail coat with collar edged with red, four loops and buttons on the slashed cuff flaps, similar to those worn by a sergeant major of heavy artillery, and yellow worsted epaulets. His trousers were sky blue with a 1.5-inch dark blue stripe, and on his artillery dress cap he wore an upright red hackle, 12 inches long. Privates of Ordnance wore the same but with red "shoulder-straps" (worsted half epaulets) and only two loops and buttons on the cuffs. Their pants had no stripes.

The fatigue uniform of ordnance men was quite distinctive: dark blue shell jacket and pants, the jacket collar and trousers seams piped with scarlet, and a dark blue, wide-crowned forage cap. With these uniforms was worn a white (later black) buff leather waist belt with the two-piece brass buckle bearing the raised letters "US" similar to that of the heavy artillery. Ordnance Sergeants wore red worsted sashes and carried the NCO's sword Model 1840. Ordnance men were armed and equipped as infantry.

The old pattern ordnance dress clothing appears to have been issued until about May 1854, when new pattern 1851 uniforms began to go out to the scattered ordnance detachments. This was the same uniform as worn by engineer soldiers except that its collar and cuffs were piped with crimson (the branch color now authorized for ordnance), a yellow metal shell and flame was fastened to each side of the collar and on the cap, and the half-inch trouser stripes and pompon were crimson. For a time the men wore crimson worsted epaulets (of the sergeant major's and private's patterns), but soon after 1854 these were changed to brass scales.

The dark blue ordnance fatigue clothing was worn for some years longer and was probably supplemented by cutting off the tails of old dress frock coats. Otherwise the changes were those that applied to the army as a whole.

Military Storekeepers. Military Storekeepers were civilian employees of the Ordnance and Quartermaster Departments who were given the "rank, pay and emoluments" of a captain or major of cavalry. In 1861, according to H. L. Scott's *Military Dictionary*, there were fifteen in the former department and seven in the latter. They were responsible for stores in an arsenal or depot and could serve as paymasters.

The dress regulations of 1851 prescribed a uniform for them, which applied throughout our period:

A citizen's frockcoat of blue cloth, with buttons of the departments to which they are attacned; round black hat; pantaloons and vest, plain, white or dark blue; cravat or stock, black.

Medical Department and Related Services

Prior to the Civil War, the personnel of the Medical Department comprised the surgeons and assistant surgeons who formed the "Medical Staff" of the army, civilian physicians hired on contract, and hospital stewards. These last were male nurses with some knowledge of practical pharmacy and were first authorized in 1856. Before that date, stewards had been soldiers detailed to hospital service from the line. A regiment serving together would have a surgeon, an assistant surgeon, and a hospital orderly, but it was more common in the 1850's to find surgeons assigned to posts. Laundresses (or "matrons") were often employed in hospitals.

To these were added, during the Civil War, medical cadets (medical students appointed for a year who acted as dressers and hospital assistants) and female nurses (who were volunteers or civilian employees of the Quartermaster Department), both authorized by law in 1861. Later, the civilian staffs of general hospitals were increased by hiring cooks and male nurses who, in 1862, were incorporated into the Hospital Corps of the U.S. Army. Medical Storekeepers (trained apothecaries or druggists) were also added in 1862 and in the following year an Ambulance Corps was organized in the Army of the Potomac. An army-wide Ambulance Corps was established in 1864. None of these wartime additions were continued in the post-war establishment.

Fig. 130

● *Medical Staff.* The uniform of army surgeons and assistant surgeons (including those of volunteers, veteran reserve corps, and other elements of the Union Army, Medical Inspectors, and Medical Purveyors), who were staff officers, has been briefly described earlier. After 1851 it consisted of a dark blue cloth frock coat with gilt epaulets bearing the silver letters "M.S." inside a gold wreath, both embroidered, or shoulder straps with a dark blue base; dark blue cloth trousers with 1/8-inch buff welts; dark blue cloth cap without piping, having a green and buff pompon and a silver "U.S." within a gold wreath in the front. The most distinctive features of the dress were an emerald green sash and a straight sword of special pattern.

This Medical Staff sword had been adopted in 1840 and remained regulation until 1902, undergoing only minor changes (Peterson No. 124). Its hilt was of gilded brass, without knuckle-bow but with gracefully scrolled quillons and two shields, one bearing the letters "MS" above a group of stars. Its scabbard was gilded brass and quite decorative. At least one variant form of this sword is known (Peterson No. 125) which has a knuckle-bow. Probably most surgeons owned a Medical staff sword but it seems to have been worn only on ceremonial occasions, and rarely if ever while engaged in professional duties.

The Medical Staff uniform underwent the usual army-wide changes. During the Civil War, surgeons wore frock coats or blouses of dark blue, pants of the same color with a 1/8-inch gold cord, either hats or caps, and very often dark blue vests. Sword belts and sashes were commonly omitted. In this dress the surgeon made his rounds and performed his operations, for this was before the days of even antiseptic surgery. There

Fig. 130. Medical and ambulance personnel, Army of the Potomac, 1864. Shown is a hospital steward recording litter cases and, behind him, a surgeon. The litter bearer on the right is a detailed soldier, on the left a private of the Ambulance corps with green cap band and green half chevrons. A teamster of the Quartermaster Department holds the horses. The ambulance is the "Rucker" type, adopted late in the war, having a capacity for four litter patients.

were no white gowns, rubber gloves, or operating masks in use in the hospitals of the Civil War.

• *Hospital Stewards.* Soldiers detailed to the hospital service were first authorized a distinctive insignia in 1851 (GO 53), a half chevron of green piped with yellow bearing a caduceus device (see Chapter 2). This was the initial use of this celebrated insignia in the army. It replaced other sleeve insignia, although the Hospital Steward was authorized sergeant's epaulets (of his actual branch) and later sergeant's brass scales. A uniform was established for him in 1857 (GO 2), after the grade had been made permanent. It was the same as worn by Ordnance Sergeants but with a green and buff pompon and a silver "U.S." in a brass wreath on the cloth cap. He continued to wear the green half chevron as his only sleeve device. His worsted sash was scarlet and his sword of the NCO model.

When the felt hat was adopted, the Hospital Steward wore his looped up on the left side with a cord of buff and green mixed and the same "US" device as before. On hospital duty, however, his usual dress was an officer's pattern chasseur cap or black campaign hat, blouse or frock coat open to show a dark blue vest, dark or sky blue pants with a 1.5-inch crimson stripe or quite plain, and neither belt nor sash. The *Hospital Steward's Manual* stressed that the steward "should always wear his undress uniform in the hospital, except on those occasions, such as musters and inspections, on which it is necessary for him to appear in full dress." The half chevron was also worn on the blouse.

In 1867 (GO 40) a new insignia was authorized for a Regimental Hospital Steward: "Three bars and an oval, with a 'caduceus' embroidered in dark blue silk in the center of the oval."

Contract Surgeons. No uniform was prescribed for contract surgeons, but practical considerations led most to adopt some form of officer's dress, omitting the insignia of rank. Long, dark blue blouses with General Staff buttons and black felt campaign hats were among the clothing worn on active service.

A photograph exists showing what is thought to be a contract surgeon with a shield-shaped cloth patch sewn to his upper left sleeve. Embroidered thereon is a caduceus. The colors are not known nor has the insignia been identified.

Medical Cadets. The uniform of a Medical Cadet was that of the Medical Staff, except the welts on his trousers were of buff rather than gold, and instead of the usual shoulder straps he wore straps of green cloth 3.75 inches long and 1.25 inches wide on which were placed strips of gold lace, one-half by 3 inches in size. The headdress authorized was a forage cap of officer's pattern, but without doubt campaign hats were also worn. His sword and sword belt were those of a non-commissioned officer.

Female Nurses. Nurses were either volunteers or hired civilians and, as such, had no authorized uniform. They served almost entirely in general or permanent hospitals in the larger cities where there was no need for field clothing. Dorothea Dix, Superintendent of Female Nurses, required in the way of dress for nurses that it be "plain almost to repulsion" and forbade "colored dresses, hoops, curls, jewelry, and flowers on their bonnets." These restrictions were sometimes evaded, especially in the Western hospitals and toward the end of the war.

Fig. 131

Roman Catholic Sisters also served as nurses, first in the West where they replaced regular female nurses in the large general hospital at Mound City, Illinois, in 1862. Before the end of the war, a considerable number of good-sized institutions were being staffed by them. Soldiers referred to them all as "Sisters of Charity" but actually three other orders participated: the Sisters of Mercy, Sisters of St. Joseph, and Sisters of the Holy Cross. All, of course, wore the clothing prescribed for their orders.

Hospital Corps. Under regulations issued 5 June 1862 by the Surgeon General (SGO Cir. 4), the men of the Hospital Corps were authorized to wear "the undress uniform of a private soldier, with a green half chevron on the left fore-arm." It will be recalled that these men were civilians and the extent to which they were so dressed is not clear. Possibly the regulations cited applied only to hospitals in the vicinity of Washington. No pictures or examples of the "green half chevron" have been found, though it probably resembled the insignia of a Hospital Steward without the caduceus and yellow edging.

Abulance Corps. During the first days of the Civil War, most regiments formed their own provisional ambulance detachment or "corps." Its officers, drivers, and attendants wore the regimental uniform without distinctions, just as the ambulances were often marked with regimental designations. By early 1862, it had become the practice to consolidate these detachments, still provisionally, under brigade or even higher control so that regimental ambulance corps could be made to serve more than their own regiments. But the system remained haphazard and inadequate. Control had to be concentrated at even higher levels of command and a more permanent organization effected.

In August 1862 (SO 147, A of P), an Ambulance Corps was established in the Army of the Potomac. Its personnel, although still detailed, wore distinctive insignia which was prescribed as follows:

> The uniform of this corps is — for privates, a green band, two inches broad, around the cap, a green half-chevron, two inches broad, on each arm above the elbow, and to be armed with revolvers; non-commissioned officers to wear the same band around the cap as the privates, chevrons two inches broad, and green, with the point toward the shoulder, on each arm above the elbow.

A year later, in August 1863, the Army of the Potomac issued revised regulations for the insignia of the Corps (GO 85, A of P):

> The corps will be designated for sergeants by a green band, one and a quarter inches broad, around the cap, and chevrons of the same material, with the point toward the shoulder, on each arm above the elbow. For privates, by a band, the same as for sergeants, around the cap, and a half chevron of the same material on each arm above the elbow.

Ambulance corps were formed in other armies and some were provided with distinctive insignia. The ambulance personnel of the 18th Army Corps in the Department of North Carolina were, on 30 December 1862 (GO 85, 18th AC), directed to wear a broad red band around the cap with its knot upon the right side. In January 1864, the Army of the Cumberland (GO 2, A of C) adopted for its ambulance personnel the same green devices as were being worn in the Army of the Potomac.

It should be pointed out that in some instances ambulance drivers were civilians, employed by the Quartermaster Department. Whether they wore the prescribed insignia is not certain.

Fig. 131. Inside a military hospital, 1864. Two Sisters of Mercy work with patients while a hospital steward carries a tray of medicines. The wounded man from the 5th Army Corps has been awarded the Medal of Honor.

On 11 March 1864, Congress created an Ambulance Corps for the entire army, very much along the lines of the one existing in the Army of the Potomac. This law provided that "the officers, non-commissioned officers, and privates of the Ambulance Corps shall be designated by such uniform or in such manner as the Secretary of War shall deem proper." The action taken on this by the Secretary, if any, has not been discovered. It is presumed that in the field armies were allowed to continue their distinctive Ambulance Corps insignia.

The personnel of an ambulance corps were attendants, drivers, blacksmiths, saddlers, and the like. They were not litter bearers or field hospital orderlies. This work was performed, especially in the first two years of the war, by regimental bandsmen augmented by details from the companies, perhaps twenty-five men in all from a full size regiment. These litter-bearers wore no insignia as such, but they were sometimes provided with first aid equipment. In addition to litters, they had to carry forward to the "primary station," set up just outside musketry range, at least one hospital knapsack for the use of the assistant surgeon. These accouterments have been described in Chapter 6.

• *U.S. Sanitary Commission.* This Commission was created by approval of the President in June 1861, essentially as a volunteer civilian organization with broad powers of investigation and advice on medical and sanitary conditions in the Union Army. Before long the Commission was involved in furnishing medical and hospital supplies and in operating activities from hospital ships to feeding stations. Its personnel were entirely civilian and there is no indication that uniform clothing was prescribed for them. Photographs do suggest, however, that some agents in the field may have worn garments of a military sort, including hat insignia.

A U.S. Sanitary Commission button is described and illustrated by Albert (FD 71, p. 284), although the time and extent of its use are not known. The same applies to an interesting badge owned by Company of Military Historians Fellow Michael J. Winey: an oval band with the Commission's name, enclosing a Greek cross. Since the Red Cross symbol was not adopted until about 1863 in Geneva, this badge could represent one of its earliest uses.

Chaplains

There was no organized corps of chaplains during the period 1851-1872, and no uniform was prescribed for these officers until late in 1861. Prior to that the chaplain was supposed to wear his usual clerical garb.

Fig. 132

On 25 November 1861 (GO 102), chaplains were ordered to wear a plain black frock coat with standing collar and one row of nine black buttons, plain black pants, and a "black felt hat, or army forage cap, without ornament." If he wished, a chaplain could wear "a plain chapeau de bras" on occasions of ceremony.

This order was modified on 25 August 1864 (GO 247) by adding a "herring bone of black braid around the buttons and button holes" of the coat, and a gold-embroidered wreath on a black velvet ground encircling the letters "U.S." in silver, Old English characters, to the cap or hat. So far as the cap insignia is concerned, this order probably confirmed a practice by then well established. In addition, many chaplains

Fig. 132. Chaplain S.A. Bliss, 51st New York Veteran Volunteer Infantry, 1864 or 1865. His uniform is black and unadorned save for the crosses on his collar. (By Michael J. McAfee, after photograph.)

were, by 1864, wearing gold officers' hat cords and corps badges. From the beginning, most seem to have worn black vests and kept their frock coats open, and some wore crosses on their collars.

Signal Corps

There were no provisions for field signalling in the U.S. Army (save at short range by drum or bugle) until 27 June 1860 when Albert J. Myer was gazetted Major and Signal Officer. Thereafter for three years, signal communications were handled, somewhat experimentally, by acting signal officers — subalterns of volunteer regiments specially detailed for the purpose. The Act of 3 March 1863 created the Signal Corps and authorized officers for it ranging in rank from lieutenant to colonel and enlisted men in the grades of private and sergeant. Signal officers and men sometimes were mounted.

The Signal Corps was continued in the military peace establishment by the Act of 28 July 1866, with an allowance of six officers and 100 enlisted men detailed from the Battalion of Engineers. Throughout the Civil War, signalmen served in small bodies attached to the higher headquarters and sometimes the fleet. They operated primarily

Fig. 133. Signal Corps men and Equipment, 1864. In the foreground enlisted signalmen pour turpentine into a torch, while on the unrolled case at their feet lie the pliers and shears used to trim its wick. The right figure wears a haversack to carry those objects associated with night signalling. At right center stands a Signal sergeant with a kit case containing signal flags, and an officer with a telescope case slung around his neck.

with flags and torches; the military electric telegraph remaining in large measure the province of another branch, the Military Telegraph Service.

Uniforms. The uniform of a Signal Officer (Major Myer himself) was ordered to be "that of a Major of the General Staff" on 15 June 1861, but the acting signal officers detailed to him wore the dress of their original corps. Not until 1864 were the men and officers of the Signal Corps given a distinctive device, the familiar crossed flags, to be worn by the men on their sleeves and the officers on their hats and caps.

Signal Corps orders on 22 August 1864 (GO 36, HQSC) specified:

Description of Badge for Officers.

Hat and Cap: Same as for other officers, with the following ornament: a gold embroidered wreath in front, on black velvet ground, encircling crossed signal flags, with lighted torch, and supported by the letters "U.S." in silver in old English characters. *Color of flags:* one red, with white centre; the other white, with red centre. *Size of flag:* three-eighths of an inch square; size of centre, one-eighth of an inch square; length of staff, one and one-sixteenth inches.

Description of Badge for Enlisted Men

Device on Arm: Crossed signal flags, red and white, on dark blue cloth. *Size of flags:* three-fourths of an inch square; centre, one-quarter of an inch square; length of staff, three inches. Sergeants will wear the designation of the corps placed in the angle of the chevron upon the left sleeve. Privates will wear the designation of the corps in the same position on the left sleeve as the chevron of sergeants.

Requisition can be made upon this Bureau by Signal Officers in charge of detachments or sub-detachments of the corps for such number as may be required for their commands.

These badges will be furnished by the manufacturer at the following prices: badges for officers, fifteen (15) dollars per dozen; badges for enlisted men, three (3) dollars per dozen.

Signal Corps officers wore Staff Corps trousers — dark blue with an 1/8-inch gold cord — after March 1863 and to some extent even before. Otherwise their uniform and accouterments were that of the line. Cavalry boots and telescopes in black leather cases were common equipment.

Signalmen do not seem to have been distinctively dressed until late in the Civil War and probably not all then. However, a photograph of the Central Signal Station in Washington, April 1865, shows an enlisted group all in short dark jackets with ten buttons and dark trousers. Only the sergeant wears the crossed flags on his arms. Other photographs suggest that the cavalry jacket, sometimes without lace, was the commonly accepted dress of the Corps during the war. A man who joined the service in December 1862 remembered, "For arms we had Colt's revolvers . . . For uniform, cavalry jackets . . . and cavalry trousers, with reinforced seats." He was supposed to have a horse but never received one.

Fig. 133

The first regulations governing the dress of enlisted signalmen appeared 22 October 1868 (GO 88). The order specified that they would be uniformed as cavalry and wear on their coat, "above the elbow on each arm, the crossed flags after the pattern in the office of the Chief Signal Officer of the Army." These crossed flags were to be worn by the non-commissioned officers above the chevron.

Signal enlisted men were, as a rule, armed as infantry, and in common with signal officers, often carried the specialized accouterments of their trade: telescope, a canteen of lantern oil, case of signalling flags, torches, and the signalman's bag. These accouterments have been described in detail in Chapter 6.

The fertile mind of the Signal Officer devised, in early 1862, a method of rewarding an officer who skillfully and bravely carried his signal flag in action (GO 24 HQ SC, 19 Mar 1862). The officer was awarded a star instead of the square that occupied the center of the flag, with the name of the battle inscribed in black letters on the upper point of the star. Subsequent actions in which the officer distinguished himself were marked on other points. The flag so decorated was carried on all occasions of ceremony. It was first planned to allow these flags of honor to become the personal property of the officer; later they were ordered deposited at Headquarters, Signal Corps, for return at the end of the Civil War. Such a flag is pictured in the atlas to the *Official Records*, plate CLXXV, and is called a "badge." There is no record, however, that the Signal Corps insignia itself ever showed a flag with a star.

Military Telegraph Service (or Corps)

The Military Telegraph Service was organized in November 1861 to operate all electrical communication for the Union Army and was not part of the Signal Corps. Its personnel were in the main civilian and comprised skilled telegraphers and construction crews, nominally employees of the Quartermaster Department but in reality under the direct control of the Superintendent of the Military Telegraph Service or the Secretary of War himself. This organization, with the related War Department Telegraph Office, was broken up by 1866.

No uniform was prescribed by the War Department for military telegraph personnel. Indeed, it was a matter of Stanton's policy to stress the fact that operators were civilians and not subject to the orders of field commanders. This independence was bitterly resented and led several commanders, including Grant, into conflict with the Department over control of the Service. It also worked a hardship on operators and crews who, on their own, often took to wearing parts of the army uniform as protection and identification.

Since the field telegraph lines frequently approached enemy territory and were subject to raids, operators and repairmen in civilian clothing ran grave danger when captured. This was especially serious in the valleys of the Cumberland and of the Tennessee where very long lines were required. Probably as a result, the operators in the Department of the Tennessee were, on 5 July 1864 (GO 14, A of Tenn), "authorized to wear an undress uniform" described as follows:

BLOUSE: Light blue
TROWSERS: Light blue cloth, with silver cord, one-eighth of an inch in diameter, along the outer seam.
VEST: Buff: white or blue
FORAGE CAP: Like that worn by commissioned officers, but without any distinctive mark or ornament, except a small silver cord around the band.
BUTTONS: Like those worn by officers of the General Staff

No other case of a prescribed telegrapher's uniform has been found.

U.S. Military Academy

The Military Academy at West Point was administered by the Corps of Engineers until 1866 when its supervision was taken over by the War Department, and its Superintendents thereafter were selected from any arm of the service. It was always (and still is) a law unto itself as regards the regulation and procurement of cadet clothing. Whereas some uniforms and most weapons and accouterments were provided from army stocks, many items were, likely as not, specially fabricated for West Point. Cadet dress regulations may have been approved by the Chief of Engineers and the Secretary of War, but there was little hesitation on the part of the Superintendent of the Military Academy to alter these in a hundred minor ways. Such changes occurred frequently and are only partially recorded in the archives at West Point. Thus, a belt plate or method of wearing the overcoat which was correct for one year could change a dozen times in as many years, with little or no record made of the changes.

● *Battalion of Cadets.* In 1851, the cadet of the Military Academy wore for parade and many other activities a tail coat of "cadet gray" cloth, single-breasted with three rows of eight brass bullet buttons. These were connected by narrow black silk cord which terminated in crow's-feet and formed (despite regulations) a straight rather than herring-bone pattern. Three bullet buttons, with cords ending in crow's-feet and arranged in a herring-bone pattern, decorated each cuff and skirt. One button with cord was placed on each side of the collar, and six buttons lined the plaits of the skirts. The cuffs were of double thickness, indented at the front, slashed on the side, and held by three hooks. Cadet rank was indicated by a system of gold lace chevrons. Except for the double cuff, the coat closely resembled the pattern worn today.

Fig. 134

Trousers, for winter wear, were made of the same cloth with a one-inch black stripe; for summer they were of white duck. The headdress was the regulation Engineer Corps beaver or felt cap bearing an eagle, turreted castle, and shell and flame pompon holder, all of brass, and a black leather chinstrap. Cadet officers wore a black cock's feather plume while ordinary cadets had an 8-inch black worsted pompon.

For drill and parade, the cadet wore a 2.5-inch white canvas belt over his left shoulder from which hung a Model 1842 cartridge box. A similar belt, with a square brass plate, went around the waist and held a cap pouch and white leather frog with the bayonet scabbard. Cadet officers wore a 2.5-inch white canvas sword belt, with a plain rectangular brass plate in front, over the right shoulder, and a crimson silk net sash, tying on the left side. All cadets wore white cotton gloves on parade.

The collar of the cadet dress coat stood about 2.5 inches high, was trimmed with black silk lace, and hooked straight up the front. The soft white collar of the cadet's shirt was allowed to fall down over the top of the collar. In 1852 a more comfortable collar was introduced, opening wide in front to show the black bombasine stock. A strip of white cloth, giving the appearance of the shirt collar, was fastened to its top.

The cadet wore two patterns of fatigue clothing. One was a simple gray cloth shell jacket with black lace and two buttons on its collar and a single row of eight flat gilt "CADET" buttons, worn with gray or white reinforced pants with instep straps. This was the riding dress, and with it he wore a black leather waist belt, fastened with a two-piece buckle bearing the raised letters "US", and buckskin gauntlets. Later, this uniform was adapted for general winter fatigue use. Chevrons were worn with it.

The cadet's other fatigue clothing was of brown linen — a shell jacket and pants. With both of these suits the cadet wore a dark blue cloth forage cap of a distinctive pattern: 5 to 6 inches high, non-rigid, slightly larger in the crown than in the band, with sharply sloping visor and no insignia. A black velvet band, however, was sometimes added, possibly when going on furlough. It carried in gold embroidery the letters "USMA", encircled by a laurel wreath and palm fronds. His overcoat was double breasted, of gray cloth, with a 16.5-inch cape and flat gilt "CADET/USMA" buttons. The lining was the same as the body. India rubber capes had been issued in 1849 but seem to have enjoyed only limited use.

Fig. 30

Fig. 135

Cadets were authorized to wear a plain blue officer's frock coat while on leave. This coat probably had the same buttons as the overcoat but no insignia of rank. With it were worn pants of white drilling, or dark blue cloth with a one-inch stripe of black velvet, and a "furlough cap," closely resembling, if not the same style and color as, the forage cap.

The gray dress coat was the common article of war, being used without belts in the classroom and on social occasions and with belts for drill and parade. Off duty it could be worn partially open, at least in the beginning of the period. A few cadets of high academic standing were appointed Cadet Assistant Professors and distinguished by the addition on their dress coats of extra rows of buttons and cord, making fifteen rows in all. In our period no insignia was worn to distinguish one class from another.

Vests, of gray trimmed with black braid or of white linen, were still worn off duty, but this practice ceased about the time of the Civil War.

During the period 1851-1872, cadet dress underwent several other minor changes. In the summer of 1853, Superintendent Robert E. Lee succeeded in introducing a more modern dress cap, smaller in the crown and sloping slightly forward. The eagle, castle, shell and flame pompon holder, and plume remained as before, but the pompon was reduced in height to 3 inches. In 1861, the cadet received an officer's pattern chasseur cap with straight visor for ordinary wear. For some years it appears to have been without insignia, but in 1867 a device was added: an embroidered eagle in flight beneath the letters "USMA".

At some point in the early 1860's the extra thickness was removed from the cuffs. A new dress cap, lower than the previous one, was adopted in 1866. For about three years it bore a small Engineer Corps castle and a brush-like pompon. Then, in 1869, a brass sunburst plate (with a shield in the center embossed with the insignia of Engineers, Artillery, Cavalry, and Infantry) was adopted and worn until 1878. The 3-inch black worsted pompon was brought back in 1869. Brown linen fatigue clothing was replaced by white linen in 1870. A regulation dressing gown (forerunner of many similar garments) was introduced the same year and all civilian models were forbidden in the cadet barracks.

Throughout all the years 1851-1872, the cadet was armed with a special musket or rifle, essentially a lighter and smaller version of the service arm of its period. The first of these was the Cadet Musket Model 1841, a caliber .57 smoothbore, about 55 inches overall. In 1857 a number of this model were rifled and sighted. The Cadet Rifle Model 1858, a caliber .58 weapon closely resembling the Model 1855 rifle musket but lighter

GREY KERSEY OVERCOAT, CHASSEUR CAP, 1863

FULL DRESS (SUMMER) 1851

UNDRESS, 1859 SHOWING WATERPROOF CAP COVER OVER OLD PATTERN FATIGUE CAP.

RIDING JACKET, 1860

G.WOODBRIDGE

CADET CAPTAIN, FULL DRESS, 1863

EMBROIDERED INSIGNIA FOR FORAGE CAP C. 1870

1 INCH.

Fig. 134. Cadets of the U.S. Military Academy, 1851-1872.

and taking a smaller charge arrived about 1859. This was carried during the Civil War and until the fall of 1867.

The first of the converted breechloaders arrived that year and at least three models or versions were sent to West Point before 1872. These have been identified as the Cadet Rifle Models 1866, 1868, and 1869. All were caliber .50, had the hinged action devised by Mr. Allin, and were shorter versions of corresponding service arms, with correspondingly reduced parts. It is possible that two or more of these models were in use simultaneously, and certainly the latest was used up to the time the cadets were issued the Cadet Rifle Model 1873.

All of the muskets and rifles listed carried socket bayonets. The first cartridge box of our period was, almost certainly, the Model 1842. This was used until about 1859 when the Battalion of Cadets received the Model 1855 rifle musket box for caliber .58 ammunition. Following the Civil War, a special cartridge box was manufactured for the Battalion at Springfield Armory to hold the short, caliber .50 metallic cartridges. It was issued about 1867 and was carried until the caliber of ammunition changed in 1873.

There is some evidence that the cadet was issued a knapsack and other field service accouterments. If so, they were worn only during the summer encampments and were probably the regulation issues.

Fig. 135. Cadet, U.S. Military Academy in "furlough uniform," cir. 1851. His frock coat is dark blue and without insignia; his forage cap has a black velvet band with gold embroidery (See Howell and Kloster, p. 45). He appears to be wearing general service buttons although one would expect the "CADET" pattern.(Daguerreotype - not retouched - from the collection of Herb Peck,Jr.)

The cadet officer carried a distinctive pattern straight sword with a blued iron scabbard and all-brass hilt. It had straight cross quillons, urn-shaped pommel, and langets in the form of shields bearing an eagle and thirteen stars. This sword had been introduced abut 1839 and was worn until 1872, when it was replaced by a similar, but somewhat more decorative model. All cadets engaged in riding exercises wore the Model 1840 cavalry saber and, after about 1855, the Colt army belt pistol with holster. All other accouterments worn for specialized training were similar to those issued regular troops at the time.

● *West Point Band.* Whereas the school troops stationed at the U.S. Military Academy wore regulation dress and accouterments in the main, the West Point Band was distinctively dressed. Its uniform in 1851 comprised a dark blue frock coat with red tabs on the front of the collar and red pointed cuffs, sky blue pants with two .75-inch red stripes, red worsted epaulets, stiff beaver or felt cap of the artillery pattern with red plume and cords, and black leather waist belt with a regulation rectangular plate. For fatigue wear, the bandsmen used a dark blue cloth jacket trimmed with red lace, and a dark blue forage cap.

This unusual uniform, flavoring strongly of the artillery, had been introduced about 1850 but did not last long. In March 1852, the Secretary of War directed that the band wear the uniform prescribed for engineer musicians under the 1851 dress regulations, and a few months later it received forty new pattern cloth caps with castles and yellow pompons, fifteen new engineer musician coats, and a supply of yellow worsted epaulets. With these went enough yellow cloth for fashioning plastrons, and enough yellow binding and cord to replace all red on coats, fatigue jackets, and pants.

Before long, further embellishments appeared. A photograph of the band about 1859 shows some of the changes that had taken place. The blue frock coat by then had three rows of nine buttons, the outer rows edging the yellow plastron; dark blue collars piped with yellow, over which white shirt collars are folded; deep pointed yellow cuffs; and brass scales. Trousers were still sky blue, and the felt dress hat (first issued in 1858) carried a new, distinctive insignia of a lyre, authorized in early 1857. Such was the parade uniform.

Fig. 136

Another photograph taken about the same time shows the band's service dress: regulation dark blue frock coats and pants, and hats with the lyre device. It is probable that this uniform replaced the parade dress described above about 1861 and was the one worn during the war years and until 1867.

The drum major of the West Point Band was given a dark blue frock coat, sky blue pants, and a tall bearskin hat with a towering feather plume. He also wore gold epaulets, gilt aiguilettes on his left arm and chest, a red sash, and a baldric decorated with an immense grenade and the traditional miniature drum sticks.

The need for an entirely new uniform was felt after the Civil War, and in 1867 it was introduced. It consisted of a white tail coat and pants, elaborately trimmed with red, and a Model 1866 Cadet cap with red horsehair plume. Collar, round cuffs, shoulder knots, aiguilettes, double trouser stripes, Austrian knots on the pants, and lace on the front edging of the coat were all scarlet. The drum major and field music wore scarlet coats with white trimmings, and the former's bearskin cap was topped by immense feathers, two scarlet and one white. This was the final uniform worn during the

Fig. 136. U.S. Military Academy Band, cir. 1859-1861. One of several uniforms worn during our period, this comprised a dark blue coat with yellow plastron, sky blue pants, and dress hat with plume. The hat device was a gilt lyre. Much of the same uniform, but without the plastron and with dark blue pants, was worn during the Civil War.

period covered.

● *Teaching Staff.* Professors and others who were officers wore their regulation uniforms without change. Others not in the line of the army, including the Sword and Riding Masters, wore "a citizen's blue cloth dress-coat, with buttons of the Corps of Engineers, round black hat," white or dark blue vest and pants, and a black cravat. The Chaplain wore "the dress usually worn by the clergy."

One U.S. Military Academy cap device remains unidentified. It appears on a carte de visite photograph of about 1870 and shows "USMA" over a castle, within a large wreath.

The Cavalry School

A depot and school for the mounted service was constituted at Carlisle Barracks, Pennsylvania in 1833 and continued in operation there save for a period around 1855, and for a time in the summer of 1863 when its buildings were destroyed by Confederate raiders under General J.E.B. Stuart.

The school troops at Carlisle, as mentioned earlier, were supplied with the most up-to-date clothing and accouterments, but these were regulation as far as can be told. The school also maintained a mounted band, but nothing unusual has been discovered concerning its dress.

The Artillery School

The Artillery School was re-established at Fort Monroe, Virginia on 18 May 1858 (GO 5), four artillery companies being transferred there as school troops. It was closed at the outbreak of the Civil War and not re-opened until about 1868.

The school troops were uniformly dressed and equipped according to regulation, and in addition were supplied with white duck trousers and a round straw hat for summer wear. Officers, too, were allowed similar hats with white linen coats. In the general order establishing it, the school was given distinctive flags: a color "similar to the artillery color, with the words ARTILLERY SCHOOL on a scroll above the cannon, and camp colors like those of artillery, substituting the letter A for the number."

United States Sharpshooters

The uniforms, arms, and accouterments of these two regiments were largely determined by Colonel Hiram Berdan who was authorized in the summer of 1861 to establish his own specifications. President Lincoln himself persuaded Governor Morgan of New York to equip a company in the outfit Berdan desired, and the other states followed suit.

Plate V

Both regiments wore essentially the same uniform, but there is some question as to just what this uniform was. The frock coat was dark green, and a surviving example in the collection of the Company of Military Historians shows it to have been an officer's pattern of satinette. It has round cuffs with three buttons on each, six buttons and false pocket flaps on the rear of the skirts, and no lace or piping. There is no indication, however, that this was ever worn by an officer. On the other hand, in the Smithsonian Institution is another example which resembles in all ways the regulation infantryman's frock coat, except that its color is dark green piped with light green. This style is partially borne out by a contemporary sketch.

At first (according to the *New York Tribune* of 5 September 1861), the trousers were of "Austrian blue gray" cloth (possibly flannel) but these were exchanged by 1862 for others of dark green satinette, although some light colored pants were in use as late as July of that year. Presumably chevrons and pants stripes were of regulation pattern but of emerald green color.

The 1st Regiment, when organized, and probably the 2nd, were issued two kinds of headdress. One was described as "a gray, round hat with wide, black visor," called a "havelock," made of felt with a leather visor, flap to cover the neck, and holes for ventilation. The other was a forage cap of normal pattern but fashioned out of dark green cloth. A single black ostrich feather was attached on its right side and curved around its front and left. The felt hat was abandoned because of its color in the spring of 1862, as was the black plume on the cap.

Berdan had been persuaded to accept a seamless overcoat of the pattern studied by the army in 1859. It was made of gray felt and some or all were trimmed with light green. It was a superior garment except for one defect: when wet it became "as stiff as a board," as a man who wore one reported. In 1862 this overcoat was exchanged for the regulation sky blue kersey dismounted pattern. Another unusual article of dress was high leggings of russet leather, but these were given up in about a year. A dark green fatigue blouse of regulation cut was issued and worn from the start.

Except as noted, this uniform was worn by officers and men alike. The musicians of the regiments were all buglers; no drums were carried. There is no proof that these musicians were distinctively dressed.

Some of the enlisted men brought their personally owned target rifles into the army with them, but after a series of tests Berdan decided upon the breechloading Sharps caliber .52 rifle for both regiments. He could not get delivery until May and June of 1862, and meanwhile the men were issued Colt's repeating rifles except for those of two companies who got heavy target rifles (weighing up to 34 pounds) with telescopic sights. All companies took over the Sharps in mid-1862. Both socket and saber bayonets were used with the Sharps.

For accouterments, the men preferred wearing only a waist belt to which the cap pouch and cartridge box were attached. Their knapsack was said to be of a Prussian army model, having an outer flap of hair-covered calfskin. To this a cooking kit was attached which the men found "compact and useful."

Photographs of Colonel Berdan and other officers of the 1st U.S.S.S. show an unusual insignia on their forage caps: within a wreath is a pair of crossed rifles, above them is "US", while below, "SS". The parts were apparently embroidered on a black velvet base. Enlisted men at some point seem to have worn a brass insigne on their caps with "USSS", interpreted by wags as meaning "unfortunate soldier sadly sold." One photograph appears to show this same device with a "2" beneath it, while another shows it pinned to a soldier's coat front. We still have much to learn about the insignia of the sharpshooters.

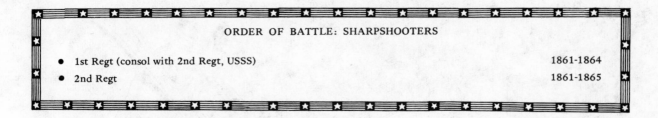

- 1st Regt (consol with 2nd Regt, USSS)   1861-1864
- 2nd Regt   1861-1865

Veteran Reserve Corps (Formerly Invalid Corps)

The Invalid Corps was constituted in April 1863 and recruited in the main from partially disabled soldiers in general hospitals and convalescent camps in the various states. It represented an attempt to keep reasonably effective men in the service and to provide a system for guarding and staffing army hospitals. Its designers found ample precedents for such an organization in European armies.

The initial organization of the Corps was by separate numbered companies, 240 of which were regimented between 10 October 1863 and 24 February 1864 into the 1st through 24th Regiments, Invalid Corps. About 188 independent companies remained unassigned to regiments.

The name and composition of the Corps proved unpopular ("I.C." was jokingly translated as "inspected and condemned"), and in March 1864 it was redesignated Veteran Reserve Corps. A large number of physically sound soldiers who did not wish to reenlist for combat service were enrolled, and the power to appoint officers was placed in the hands of the Provost Marshal General, who commanded the Corps. A VRC regiment normally comprised ten infantry companies, six in its 1st Battalion and four in the 2nd. Men who could handle a musket and make light marches were placed in a 1st Battalion company and used for guard duty on railways, bridges, and government property, and guarding drafted men and prisoners of war. Others less physically able served in the 2nd Battalion of a regiment as clerks in offices or cooks and even nurses in hospitals. In emergencies, as it turned out, 2nd Battalion companies sometimes performed more strenuous duties. The last VRC company was mustered out of service in October 1866.

A uniform was prescribed for the Invalid Corps on 15 May 1863 (GO 124). It comprised a polka-skirted jacket ("cut like the jacket for United States cavalry") of sky blue kersey, with dark blue lace edging collar, shoulder straps, pointed cuffs, and the jacket itself; regulation sky blue pants; and dark blue forage cap. Two weeks later an order (GO 158 and Notice, 11 June) authorized officers to wear a sky blue cloth frock coat with dark blue velvet collar and cuffs, otherwise of the same pattern as prescribed for infantry officers; sky blue pants with a double stripe of dark blue cloth, each 1/2-inch wide with 3/8-inch space between; dark blue velvet shoulder straps of normal pattern; and a regulation officer's pattern forage cap.

Plate IV

Companies of the 1st Battalion were issued 3rd class infantry small arms. Returns were not made by regiment in 1863, but the "Summary Statements of Ordnance and Ordnance Stores" for that year show such issues to the Invalid Corps as "Smoothbore muskets altered to percussion, calibre .69," "Rifled muskets Austrian, Prussian and Saxony, calibre .69 to .72," and "Smooth bored muskets English cal .69 and .70."

Fig. 137. Bandsman, 10th Veteran Reserve Corps, 1864. This entirely non-regulation uniform, whose colors we can only guess at, led street parades and gave concerts in Washington during the later months of the Civil War. Other V.R.C. bands must have performed similar functions elsewhere, and in uniforms equally bizarre. The musician holds a B flat baritone saxhorn. (After a photograph in the Library of Congress.)

Fig. 137

The Corps was also issued a great many revolvers, chiefly for its 2nd Battalions, including the Starr, Lefaucheux, and Savage patterns. The regimental issues made in 1864 are listed in the order of battle that follows.

The Corps also received infantry accouterments, knapsacks and haversacks being issued as required. Some companies, by 1865, had been given regulation dark blue blouses and, in these, resembled infantry except in small details. For insignia the men wore the brass infantry bugles on top of their caps while officers used the embroidered infantry bugle on the cap front.

Men of the 2nd Battalion companies were issued swords, (probably Model 1840 NCO), but how much these side arms were worn is not clear. One of the complaints heard from members of the early Invalid Corps was about wearing "toy swords" around. Officers, too, objected to the sky blue frock coat which caused them to stand out in great contrast to the line. By 1865, many were wearing regulation dark blue frock coats while others had adopted sky blue shell jackets (probably by cutting down the frock coats) left open to show sky blue waistcoats.

One of the missions taken over by the V.R.C. was to supply music for hospitals, parades, and other occasions. By 1865 the 9th and 10th Regiments, stationed in Washington, had both bands and drum corps, and these were given resplendent uniforms, entirely non-regulation. It is probable that this was the case in other cities.

The regiments of the Corps are listed below, together with their more important areas of activity in 1864.

ORDER OF BATTLE: VETERAN RESERVE CORPS

- 1st Regt (Elmira, N.Y.)   1863-1865
  1864: M1842 smoothbore musket.

- 2nd Regt (Detroit, Mich.)   1863-1865
  1864: M1842 smoothbore musket; three comps armed with Starr revolvers, and one comp with Enfield rifle.

- 3rd Regt (Washington, D.C., etc.)   1863-1865
  1864: M1842 smoothbore musket; Austrian, Prussian, and French smoothbore muskets.

- 4th Regt (Illinois)   1863-1866
  1864: M1842 smoothbore musket; Austrian, Prussian, and French smoothbore muskets.

- 5th Regt (Indiana, etc.)   1863-1865
  1864: M1842 smoothbore musket; Austrian, Prussian, and French smoothbore muskets.

- 6th Regt (Ohio)   1863-1865
  1864: Springfield rifled muskets.

- 7th Regt (Washington, D.C.)   1863-1865
  1864: M1842 smoothbore musket.

- 8th Regt (Illinois)   1863-1865
  1864: Enfield rifle.

- 9th Regt (Washington, D.C.)   1863-1865
  1864: Springfield rifled muskets; some M1842 smoothbore muskets.

- 10th Regt (Washington, D.C.)   1863-1865
  1864: M1842 smoothbore musket.

- 11th Regt (Maryland, etc.)   1863-1865
  1864: M1842 smoothbore musket; some Austrian rifled muskets cals .54 or .55.

- 12th Regt (Alexandria, Va.)   1863-1865
  1864: M1842 smoothbore musket.

- 13th Regt (New England)   1863-1865
  1864: Springfield rifled muskets; M1842 smoothbore musket.

- 14th Regt (Washington, D.C., etc.)   1863-1865
  1864: Springfield rifled muskets.

- 15th Regt (Chicago, Ill.)   1863-1865
  1864: Springfield rifled muskets.

- 16th Regt (Pennsylvania)   1863-1865
  1864: Springfield rifled muskets.

- 17th Regt (Indianapolis, Ind.)   1864-1865
  1864: Springfield rifled muskets.

- 18th Regt (Washington, D.C.)   1864-1865
  1864: M1842 smoothbore musket.

- 19th Regt (Elmira, N.Y.)   1864-1865
  1864: Springfield rifled muskets.

- 20th Regt (Baltimore, Md.)   1864-1865
  1864: M1842 smoothbore musket.

- 21st Regt (New Jersey, Pennsylvania, etc.)   1864-1865
  1864: Austrian, Prussian, and French smoothbore muskets.

- 22nd Regt (Indiana, Illinois, etc.)   1864-1865
  1864: Springfield rifled muskets.

- 23rd Regt (Wisconsin, Minnesota, Iowa, etc.)   1864-1865
  1864: M1842 smoothbore musket; Austrian, Prussian and French smoothbore muskets.

- 24th Regt (Washington, D.C.)   1864-1865
  1864: Springfield rifled muskets.

- Independent 1st Bn Comps, VRC   1863-1866
  1864: Springfield rifled muskets; Enfield rifle; M1842 smoothbore musket; Austrian, Prussian, and French smoothbore muskets.

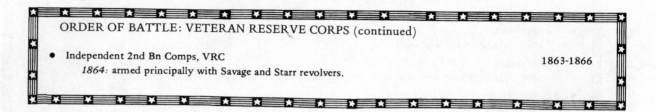

ORDER OF BATTLE: VETERAN RESERVE CORPS (continued)

● Independent 2nd Bn Comps, VRC   1863-1866
     1864: armed principally with Savage and Starr revolvers.

U.S. Colored Troops

Negroes were employed in the Union Army as servants, teamsters, and laborers from the first days of the Civil War. Many of these men were given pieces of military clothing but they were neither employed as military corps nor were they uniformed. In 1862, a number of Negro military units were formed provisionally in South Carolina, Louisiana, and Kansas, but the official and large-scale acceptance of Negro troops did not commence until 1863. All of the early regiments bore state designations, often followed by the letters "a.d." for "African descent."

In mid-1863, some Negro regiments in the Department of the Gulf were formed into the Corps d'Afrique, which contained at its maximum one regiment of cavalry, one of heavy artillery, five of engineers and twenty-five of infantry. In 1864, it was decided to incorporate Negro commands into a single organization and about April all the regiments (except four from Connecticut and Massachusetts) were redesignated as U.S. Colored Troops. About sixty Negro regiments were employed in combat and a good many saw service as occupation troops following the Civil War. The last U.S.C.T. regiments were disbanded in December 1867.

While some of the earlier Negro regiments were provided with distinctive clothing, from 1864 on all were issued U.S. regulation uniforms. Negro troops as a rule took more readily to dress uniforms than did whites and it is probable that they closely followed the prescribed dress. The only suggestion of special uniforms lies in a letter from the Army Clothing & Equipage Office to the Quartermaster General, 3 March 1864, reporting the issue of undersize "French zouave clothing" to the "Musicians and Bands of Colored Regiments."

Colored troops received 1st and 2nd class small arms in about the same ratio as white regiments. There is no reason to believe their accouterments differed in any marked respect.

Some of the first colored regiments were formed by various northern states and their men, wherever actually recruited, credited to the states' quotas. From early 1863, however, the Federal government began organizing regiments of United States Colored Volunteers — a title later changed to United States Colored Troops (U.S.C.T.) — which had no official ties to any specific state. Subsequently, most of the state units were transferred to the U.S.C.T.

At its maximum, the U.S.C.T. embraced the 1st-6th Regiments of Cavalry; 1st, 3rd-6th, 8-14th Regiments of Heavy Artillery; 2nd Regiment of Light Artillery; and 1st-93rd, 95th-104th, 106th-125th, 127th, 128th, 135th-138th Regiments of Infantry.

In this book, for convenience, all colored regiments are included in the orders of battle for the states in which they were raised, whether they had any real association with that state or not. A later volume will contain a complete order of battle of the

U.S.C.T. In the meanwhile, detailed listings can be found in the *Official Army Register of the Volunteer Force . . .*, part VIII, published by The Adjutant General and in Dyer's *Compendium.*

U.S. Veteran Volunteers

In order to "increase the armies now in the field," the War Department on 25 June 1863 (GO 91) established a category of enlisted men called "Veteran Volunteers." These were soldiers already in the ranks of a state volunteer command who re-enlisted for three years or the war. They were, as reward, given a furlough and a bounty, and authorized service chevrons "as a badge of honorable distinction" (see page 104).

Volunteer regiments whose term of service had expired but half of whose men at least had re-enlisted and become Veteran Volunteers, were continued in service and allowed to add the term "Veteran" to their designations. Many regiments were able thus to stay in existence after their original muster-out date had passed. Veteran volunteers, as individuals, were allowed to remain with their old regiments or enter others in the field.

Here we are concerned with ten regiments, having no state connection, which were raised in the final year of the Civil War and called "U.S. Veteran Volunteers." The first of these was a Veteran Volunteer Engineer Regiment, formed in the Department of the Cumberland from the Pioneer Brigade of that Department in July 1864. It was mustered out in 1865.

Fig. 138. First Sergeant, 4th Regiment, U.S. Colored Troops, cir. 1864. The senior sergeants of this regiment, serving in the Defenses of Washington, apparently were permitted to wear the dark blue shell jacket allowed officers. This man wears sergeants' shoulder scales and a red woolen sash; his M1840 N.C.O. Sword is held at the position of parade rest. Since he wears a cap box, we can assume that he also carried a musket in other formations. For some reason he does not wear the prescribed 1 1/2-in. dark blue stripes on his sky blue trousers. (By Michael J. McAfee after photograph in the Library of Congress.)

On 28 November 1864 (GO 287), the War Department reconstituted the 1st Army Corps and gave its command to Major General Winfield Scott Hancock. Its nine Veteran Volunteer infantry regiments were composed of veterans re-enlisted in 1864 and 1865 for from one to three years. The war ended before the regiments were ready for combat, and all were mustered out by August 1866.

Uniforms and accouterments were U.S. regulation in all respects. However, in January 1865 it was announced in the *Army and Navy Journal* that "the corps will be armed with new breech-loading rifles, and will wear a new style of equipment; and . . . each man will have his own name marked on his gun, and will retain it as his own on expiration of his term of service." On 18 June 1865, a distinctive badge was prescribed for the Corps, a 7-pointed star or "septagon." It was worn on top of the cap or front of the hat by both enlisted men and officers. When straw hats were worn, the badge was placed in front with the number of the regiment in white metal in the center of the badge and this was often the case with badges on top of the cap.

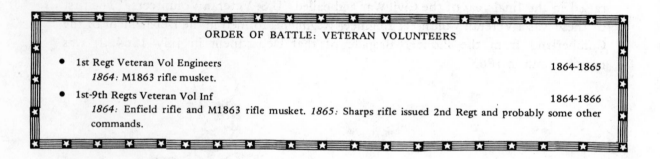

ORDER OF BATTLE: VETERAN VOLUNTEERS

- 1st Regt Veteran Vol Engineers   1864-1865
  1864: M1863 rifle musket.
- 1st-9th Regts Veteran Vol Inf   1864-1866
  1864: Enfield rifle and M1863 rifle musket. *1865:* Sharps rifle issued 2nd Regt and probably some other commands.

U.S. Indian Home Guards

When the Confederate government undertook to bring the civilized Indian tribes of the Indian Territory in on their side, and to raise Indian regiments among them (see Chapter 12), those native families with Unionist sympathy were driven north into Kansas. These families, principally of Cherokee, Creek, Wichita, and Seminole tribes, under the leadership of Opothleyola, spent the severe winter of 1861-1862 near Le Roy, Kansas. Despite all that could be done for them, the several thousand Indians suffered intensely from lack of clothing, food, and shelter. Yet the majority survived, and in the spring and summer of 1862 the Federal authorities raised three mounted regiments from among them. The commands were called "home guards" and their purpose was to assist the War Department in returning the Indian refugees to their former homes and to counteract Confederate influence in the Territory.

The Indian regiments were issued uniform clothing but it seems only to have accentuated their bizarre appearance. In the beginning they wore their native costume. Wiley Britton has described a command of Indian scouts starting out on a march "decorated in war paint and feathers." A novel feature was "the war whoop commencing at the head of the column and running back to the rear, to be repeated several times."

New clothing, sent in by wagon train from Fort Scott, reached the Union forces at Fort Gibson in May 1864. When issued there was a:

marked difference in appearance between the Indian and white soldiers . . . What was known at the time as the "Hancock Hat" was issued to the Indian soldiers, while the white soldiers generally wore the regulation cap. The Indian mounts were nearly all ponies. Care was not taken to see to it that the clothing . . . fitted them properly. The pants legs were frequently too short or too long, and the coat rarely ever fitted as a white soldier would have insisted that it should, giving the Indian soldiers a comical appearance . . . with their long black hair falling over their shoulders, and legs astride their mounts coming down near to the ground.

Arms for the Indian regiments were of a unique sort. Wiley Britton has written that most companies "were soon armed with a long barrel rifle known as [the] Indian Rifle, that used a round bullet that was quite effective at close range. The Government had on hand at Fort Leavenworth enough of these rifles to arm part of the organized Indians and issued them to the new regiments. Indeed, the Indians generally preferred them to the army musket then in use, and when fighting in the timbers where they could get a rest for their rifles, they were not to be despised on account of being antiquated; they used a percussion cap instead of flint and powder pan, which was passing out of use." This "Indian Rifle" was probably a converted U.S. rifle of the Model 1817. Its issue in any numbers, however, is not borne out by Ordnance records.

ORDER OF BATTLE: INDIAN HOME GUARDS

(All wore native clothing at first and at times applied war paint and ceremonial trappings. Issued at times US reg inf and cav clothing, including the dress hat; general appearance described above.)

- 1st Mounted Regt   1862-1865
  1863-1864: M1841 rifle; M1842 smoothbore musket; Austrian, Prussian, and French smoothbore muskets; Belgian or Vincennes rifles with saber bayonets in 1864.

- 2nd Mounted Regt   1862-1865
  1862-1864: Springfield rifles musket; US M1841 and M1845 rifles; M1842 smoothbore musket; Austrian, Prussian, and French smoothbore muskets; Belgian or Vincennes rifles with saber bayonets in 1864.

- 3rd Mounted Regt   1862-1865
  1862-1864: Austrian, Prussian, and French smoothbore muskets; US M1841 rifle; Austrian rifles musket, cal .58, with block and leaf sight; "Dresden" and "Suhl" rifled muskets in 1864.

- 4th and 5th Regts: failed to complete organ

U.S. Volunteer Infantry

These six regiments were recruited in 1864 and 1865 from Confederate prisoners of war for service on the Indian frontier and specifically not against the Confederacy. All were mustered out by November 1866.

So far as is known, all the regiments wore U.S. regulation uniforms, arms and accouterments.

```
ORDER OF BATTLE: U.S. VOLUNTEER INFANTRY

● 1st-6th Regts Vol Inf                                           1864-1866
```

There were still other types of troops raised by the general government, all for special service of one kind or another. These will be covered elsewhere or are omitted because they present no unusual features. Various part-time commands, composed of civilian employees of the War or other Departments, were formed in Washington and elsewhere; the U.S. Quartermaster Forces and the Treasury Guards are examples. When in uniform, all of these commands wore regulation clothing, insignia, and accouterments.

SOURCES

Theo. F. Rodenbough and William L. Haskin, eds., *The Army of the United States...*, New York, 1896. Compilation of historical sketches previously published in the *Journal* of the Military Services Institution of the U.S.

Raphael P. Thian, *Legislative History of the General Staff of the Army of the U.S....from 1775 to 1901*, Washington, D.C., 1901.

H.A. Ogden, artist, *Uniforms of the Army of the United States*, U.S. Army, Quartermaster General: Washington, D.C. (ca. 1890).

U.S. Army dress regulations, especially the illustrated edition of the June 1851 regulations published by William H. Horstmann & Sons, Philadelphia, 1851.

Edgar M. Howell and Donald E. Kloster, *United States Army Headgear to 1854,...*, vol. 1, Washington: Smithsonian Institution, 1969.

Albert G. Brackett, *History of the United States Cavalry...*, New York, 1865.

U.S. Army, Office of the Chief of Military History, *Army Lineage Series, Infantry, Part I: Regular Army*, Washington, D.C., 1972, and *Armor-Cavalry, Part I: Regular Army and Army Reserve*, Washington, D.C., 1969.

Charles D. Rhodes, *History of the Cavalry of the Army of the Potomac...*, Kansas City, Mo., 1900.

William E. Birkhimer, *Historical Sketch of the Organization, Administration, Materiel and Tactics of the Artillery, U.S. Army*, Washington, D.C., 1884.

George W. Adams, *Doctors in Blue: The Medical History of the Union Army in the Civil War*, New York, 1952.

Joseph J. Woodward, M.D., *The Hospital Steward's Manual...*, Philadelphia, 1863.

Jonathan Letterman, M.D., *Medical Recollections of the Army of the Potomac*, New York, 1866.

Albert J. Myer, *Manual of Signals...*, Washington, 1866.

Frederick P. Todd, *Cadet Gray: A Pictorial History of Life at West Point as Seen through Its Uniforms*, New York, 1955.

Randy Steffen, *United States Military Saddles, 1812-1943*, Norman, Oklahoma, 1973.

Robert M. Utley, *Frontiersmen in Blue: The United States Army and the Indian, 1848-1865*, New York, 1967.

Wiley Britton, *The Civil War on the Border...*, 2 vols., New York, 1890.

————, *The Union Indian Brigade in the Civil War*, Kansas City, Mo., 1922.

U.S. Army, Adjutant General's Office, *Official Army Register of the Volunteer Force*, Part VIII, Washington, D.C., 1867.

The reader is also referred to titles listed in the Preface, notably Dyer's *Compendium*, Dornbusch's *Military Bibliography*, and the *Photographic History of the Civil War*.

PART TWO

THE CONFEDERATE STATES ARMY

SERGEANT   PRIVATE   MUSICIAN

INFANTRY

LITH. DRAWING BY E. CREHEN, RICHMOND   APPROVED BY WAR DEPARTMENT   LITH PRINTING BY VALORY PETERSBURG VA

Fig. 139. Uncolored page from Blanton Duncan's edition of the Confederate dress regulations of 6 June 1861. According to a "Memorandum" appended to the regulations, the basic "cadet gray" coats shown on these infantrymen were to have light blue collars, cuffs, "edging to tunic," and chevrons. The trousers were to be sky blue and those worn by the sergeant had 1¼-inch dark blue stripes. The caps at first appear to have been grey with a light blue band; on 24 January 1862 the regulations were altered to make the caps light blue with a dark blue band. The sergeant was prescribed a red worsted sash. (Reproduced from the Riling-Halter facsimile of 1952.)

CHAPTER IX

CONFEDERATE CLOTHING AND INSIGNIA

The preceding chapters have described the general patterns of clothing, small arms, accouterments, and other equipage in use in the United States during the years 1851-1872. Later chapters will cover the adoption and employment of this equipage by the several states that comprised the Confederacy. There were, however, items prescribed and issued by the Confederate government itself, and worn or carried by Confederate commands not credited to a specific state, during the period 1861-1865, and these shall be considered here.

Procurement of Clothing in the Confederate Army

In almost every respect the procurement and issue of clothing in the Confederate service differed from that carried out in the Union. In the first place, the process of development was more gradual. Volunteer companies were being raised and uniformed in the South as early as the summer of 1860. Until the fall of 1861 there was no centralized Confederate quartermaster agency, and even after one got started it was never able to assume responsibilities comparable to those of its Northern counterpart. There was a wide difference between the tailoring industries of the North and the South, as has been noted earlier. Different procurement methods were demanded, wholesale fabrication was far more difficult in the South, and in short order importation of cloth and uniforms from Europe became uncertain at best. Scarcity of clothing was the rule, not the exception, throughout the war. Finally, there were almost as many reasons for not using the United States Army uniform as a model as there were for so doing. The sum total of all these conditions cannot be said to have produced either uniformity or variety in Confederate military dress. Instead there grew up a sort of homogeneous informality and often raggedness among which it was possible to distinguish only the men of one state from those of another, and not always to do this.

It should be stressed at the outset that the Southern soldier did not think in terms of "uniforms" as much as of "clothing." He was not accustomed to the idea of putting a large body of men into a standardized and regulated dress, both because of the industrial difficulty of so doing and his familiarity with diversity.

A Confederate regiment drawn up in line in early 1861 would have presented a bizarre appearance by today's standards — each company with its own uniform and flag, its field and staff probably in regular army blue, its band, likely as not, a civilian organization with its own trappings, and its field music made up of company drummers and fifers in various hues and styles. Yet this variety was perfectly natural to the contemporary observer, accustomed to volunteer parades and drills of earlier years. It demonstrated the rugged individuality of the independent volunteer company which, like the local newspaper and the local business house of that day, was a far cry from the chains and combines of later generations.

This variety within a single regiment is why, most probably, so little data on Confederate uniforms has come down to us. In 1861, when newspapers in the North were describing the dress of regiment after regiment as they formed in or passed through a city, comparable journals in the South were silent on the subject. Either the medley of uniforms was too confusing or the men didn't wear any. In practice one simply could not, in most cases, identify a regiment by its clothing. Indeed, in 1861 one could not have identified many regiments as Confederate, and thus much thought was given during the early months to standardized devices like arm bands and "wings," although they were rarely worn. By the time standardization had set in, shortages of supply had also arrived and the variety continued for other reasons.

In its earliest legislation on the subject, approved 6 March 1861, the Confederate government decided that "volunteers shall furnish their own clothes" and "shall be entitled, when called into actual service, in money to a sum equal to the cost of clothing a non-commissioned officer or private in the Regular Army of the Confederate States of America."

Under the commutation system, the value of a soldier's clothing was fixed at $21 (later $25) for six months. This money was paid to the captains of companies (or, in some cases, to regimental commanders) upon rendering vouchers to the Quartermaster Department that their men had been furnished with clothing according to regulations for the time specified. The men who provided their clothing received their full commutation. When the state or some local agency had furnished the clothing directly to the regiment, the commutation money was paid by the regiment to the state or agency, or the account was settled at a higher level. When the clothing, in whole or in part, came from a Confederate quartermaster, the commutation money was withheld in due proportion.

Meanwhile, as early as 19 April 1861 the War Department had authorized the issue of clothing in kind to recruits for the Regular Army of the Confederacy. This comprised a dark blue smock "worn as a blouse," steel gray pants, forage cap (color not specified), and white or red flannel undershirt. These garments represented the first clothing given out by the general government as contrasted with the states.

The fallacy of the commutation system was soon apparent. Regiments presented themselves for muster into the Confederate service without uniforms or, at best, with a hopeless melange of clothing which clearly could not survive the first campaign. Neither the states from which they came nor the men themselves could give assurance of an adequate, to say nothing of a uniform, supply of clothing. The result was that the Confederate government had to act itself, despite legislation. On 24 July the Confederate Secretary of War announced to President Davis that his Quartermaster's Department "has been directed to provide clothing for the Army," and in the month following the law was changed accordingly.

The War Department was thereafter "authorized and required to provide, as far as possible, clothing for the entire forces of the Confederate States" (act approved 30 August 1861). At the same time it was manifestly impossible to do so, and thus the law also provided that any state that supplied clothing would be reimbursed its money value. The Department went even further than this. Secretary Walker appealed to the state governors that they make up without delay, and charge to the Confederacy, enough woolen clothing to supply the needs of the army. The old commutation arrangement was continued in force to compensate the small suppliers until 8 October 1862, when it was abandoned entirely and the Secretary of War was ordered to "provide in kind to the soldiers, respectively, the uniform clothing prescribed by the Regulations of the Army . . ." Even then, should a soldier not receive all his authorized clothing in any period, he was supposed to be paid the difference in cash.

By early 1862, a considerable stock of clothing had been gathered by the Confederate Quartermaster General but his problems in this direction had certainly not ended. Quality and quantity could not be controlled and this led to repeated arguments with the states, which were the big suppliers. The states, on the other hand, complained of difficulties in collecting commutation money, of competition between state and Confederate contracting officers, and of the general government's refusal to clothe certain of their troops. Finally, as in the North, transportation rather than manufacture became the chief source of delay in clothing the men. As the war wore on these difficulties tended to increase, yet it must be borne in mind that the Confederate War Department did play an important role in clothing the entire army and in putting it into a more or less standardized garb.

The Nature of Confederate Military Clothing

Two regulations governing the uniform and dress of the Confederate Army appeared in print. The first, issued in late May 1861, seems to have been released unofficially. The second was published officially on 6 June 1861. These regulations were designed primarily if not entirely for the regular army, established by the act of 6 March 1861, which scarcely existed. How much they might have been considered as a guide for the provisional army being formed can only be guessed at. The celebrated illustrated edition of the June regulations published by Blanton Duncan was not available until some time in the fall of the year.

In a number of Southern newspapers on 25 May 1861 and later appeared brief articles which announced that "Army regulations had been issued for the uniform adopted by the War Department of the Confederate States." They then proceeded to summarize the regulations, which differed in several respects from those issued the following June. Among these differences were the blue uniforms prescribed for general and staff officers, and the wearing of officers' insignia of rank on the collar only. The account given in the *New Orleans Bee* attributed the information to "Mr. E. Cain, the military tailor of Commercial Alley," who had just returned from Montgomery "where his suggestions were adopted by the War Department." According to this account, Cain had been "authorized to furnish the materials for the making up of the necessary number" of uniforms. It seems clear that Cain had been summoned to Montgomery by the Confederate Quartermaster General and had played a part in selecting the Confederate uniform. Either he returned to New Orleans with a mistaken notion about the blue uniform and other details, which he turned over to the newspapers, or the details were reconsidered and changed by the authorities. One Quartermaster official wrote Cain on 1 July and sent him a copy of the June 1861 dress regulations, adding: "I cannot conceive where you got the idea of 'Dark Blue' for Generals and Staff."

It should be recalled that at the time of the first article the Confederate executive offices were still in Montgomery. There is a story favored in Alabama that this initial gray uniform was designed by Nicola Marschall, a German artist who had come to America in 1849 and settled in that state. He studied abroad later and, while passing through Verona, Italy about 1859, noticed troops of an Austrian *feldjaeger* battalion — in double-breasted gray frock coats trimmed with green collar, cuffs, and piping. This practical yet striking uniform made a deep impression on Marschall and when, in early 1861, he was asked to design a uniform for the Confederate army, he used the Austrian *jaegers* as a model, changing their high feathered hat to a cap and their green facings to the American system of branch colors. Marschall's sketches, made apparently in February 1861, have not survived nor is there documentary evidence that they were seriously considered. Yet there is a remarkable similarity between these Austrian uniforms and the ones later drawn for Blanton Duncan's book.

Fig. 139   The June 1861 regulations called for double-breasted frock coats (or "tunics") of "cadet gray" with facings of branch color on collar and cuffs; rather full sky blue trousers for enlisted men and regimental officers, and dark blue ones for the Staff and higher ranks; gray forage caps "similar in form to that known as the French kepi" with cap bands of branch color; cadet gray overcoats cut like those of the United States Army; and a rather novel method of officer's rank insignia. All ranks were authorized to wear for fatigue purposes "a light gray blouse, double breasted, with two rows of small buttons, seven in each row," and a small turn-over collar. Early in 1862 the colors of the forage caps were altered so that the cap itself was of branch color, with a dark blue band in every case (A & IG, CSA, GO 4, 24 Jan 1862). Gold braid rank insignia was added to the caps of officers at the same time.

In the meantime, the cut and color of Confederate clothing were being determined, first by the companies as they formed individually, next by the several Southern states as they took over the burden of clothing procurement for their own regiments, and finally by the Confederate War Department. The tardiness of publication, the expensive character of the uniforms prescribed, and the fact that the general government could not take over any serious issue of clothing until late in 1861 makes it difficult to believe that many Southern enlisted men wore this official uniform. Few if any double-breasted coats of the sort ordered are known to exist today, but there are some photographs which show enlisted men so clothed.

On the other hand, the regulations did accomplish several things. They established branch colors, insignia of rank, and the patterns of buttons. They set the style of the uniform of the Confederate officer and, above all, they made gray the official color of the upper garment in contrast with the dark blue being specified about the same time in the North.

The color gray appears to have been adopted naturally by most Southern companies as they outfitted themselves for active service. Among twenty-five South Carolina companies organized in 1860-1861 for which we have some record of clothing, twenty-three adopted a shade of gray for coat or jacket. All save one of the companies of the 1st Virginia Volunteers had, by April 1860, exchanged their older uniforms for ones of gray, and a year later the entire regiment wore that color. The reasons for the selection are the same as given earlier for Union outfits: gray cloth was easier to procure since it was a commoner civilian color than blue, and gray was a traditional dress of the volunteer militia — distinct both from the common militia and the regulars, and sanctified by use in such well-known regiments as the 7th New York. Cain and Marschall may well have pointed the way to gray in their designs for the Confederate uniform but others were thinking along the same lines.

An account of the clothing of the LaFayette Volunteers from Walker County, Georgia gives some idea of the problems met with and how they were solved:

> The next important thing to be considered was a uniform for the company. That was really a matter for serious consideration . . . an outfit complete for a whole company. But our noble and whole-souled friends . . . came forward and offered material, which was in texture just what was needed for service . . . but the goods were white . . .

How to dye so large a quantity of heavy goods was no light matter, but it was decided to immerse the cloth in a vat of tan ooze.

> . . . After lying for some days in the vat, the goods absorbed the tan color, which all the vicissitudes of wind and weather failed to change. Mr. Rogers, our tailor, had the not enviable job of measuring the soldiers and cutting out the suits. There were but two sewing machines in town [and] the ladies volunteered to make the uniforms.

This turned out to be more difficult than they had imagined since the goods were heavy and hard to manage. Not having any rules to go by, the coats were made swallow tail or claw hammer and given black velvet braiding on the chest. But they served for the initial uniform.

Professor Wiley, from his extensive study of contemporary letters and memoirs, believes gray was also the usual color for trousers in the Confederate service. Yet there is evidence that sky blue was about as common and, for what it is worth, this was the regulation color. Captured Union stocks furnished many a Southern soldier with his sky blue trousers; it was the one Yankee outer garment he could wear without hesitation. As the war drew on and as the blockade tightened, the South was forced more and more to resort to emergency measures. One such was the increasing use of a dye made of copperas and walnut hulls, producing a color called "butternut." With this was stained much of the woolen and cotton clothing worn by Confederates, until the men themselves came to be called "butternuts." In some units the wearing of butternut jackets and sky blue trousers became accepted as the standard uniform.

We must return for a moment to the officer's uniform. Until 1865 this was always

426

privately purchased and usually tailor-made, and here the Confederate dress regulations were customarily the guide. Although jackets, blouses, and other kinds of coat exist in collections and can be seen in photographs of Southern officers, the vast majority wore gray frock coats (called "tunics" in the dress regulations) tailored like the officer's coat in the North. As called for by regulations, these coats were usually double-breasted with seven equally spaced buttons in each row for colonels and below. General officers wore buttons in groupings of two's as a rule, although major generals and higher could and did group them in three's. Usually the rows were straight, 4 inches apart at the top and 3 at the waist, but coats with rows as much as 6 or 7 inches apart at the top are known, and some officers had their coat fronts cut to allow curving lines of buttons, 10 inches or more wide in the center. There seems to have been no reason for these variations save personal whim.

Single-breasted gray frock coats were sometimes worn by lower ranking officers, but here again the reason was personal. All coats had pointed cuffs, either of solid branch color or piped that way, and most were "edged throughout with the facings designated." Color was often found on collars and piping on the false pockets of skirts. The use of gold braid cuff loops was very general, and of regulation collar insignia almost universal. Only in the early part of the war does one find Confederate officers with epaulets or shoulder straps. When officers wore jackets, these carried the same collar insignia as the frock coat but often omitted the gold braid loops on the sleeves.

The character and quality of the clothing issued enlisted men of the provisional army by the Confederate Quartermaster General are far from clear. By 23 May he had determined upon the dress uniform of the regular establishment and there is some indication that he looked upon this uniform as suitable for the provisional force should it ever reach the dress uniform stage. The only reference to fatigue clothing, then and later, was mention of a double-breasted blouse of "light gray cloth" in late May. This garment was soon abandoned in favor of the more familiar jacket. If fatigue clothing in general was omitted from Confederate dress regulations we should not be surprised — there was no mention of fatigue clothing in the U.S. Army dress regulations of 1851 either.

By 3 June 1861, the Quartermaster's Department was well aware of two facts: the "mean description of cloth that the Volunteers have been provided with" by their states and home towns, which would render them destitute of most articles of clothing in a few weeks, and the relative convenience of ordering the shell jacket — which every tailor knew how to make and which required the least amount of cloth — over the double-breasted blouse. On the 3rd, Colonel A.C. Myers, the Acting Quartermaster General, ordered 5,865 "grey jackets . . . grey pants, or [of] any color you can get at once" sent to Virginia. Two days later he wrote Captain J.M. Galt, his representative in New Orleans, to discontinue making up clothing for regular army recruits and to have "clothing of every description — jackets, pants, shoes, drawers, shirts, flannel socks, made up as rapidly as possible, of proper material." All this happened before the Confederate Army dress regulations were formally issued, and months before the law authorized the War Department to issue clothing directly.

Fig. 140   Thus was the shell jacket empirically established as the standard upper garment of the Confederate enlisted man. As issued thereafter, it remained of indifferent uniformity and color. It was made initially of wool but before long the most likely cloth was

PRESIDENT'S
GUARD.

INFANTRYMAN

INFANTRYMAN.

ENGINEER SOLDIER.

Fig. 140. Confederate States Infantry and Engineers, 1861-1865.

mixed wool and cotton. An act of the Confederate Congress, approved 8 October 1862 and designed to encourage the manufacture of clothing for the army, called for garments "of such kind, as to color and quality, as it may be practicable to obtain, any law to the contrary notwithstanding."

The footwear worn by the Confederate soldier included all the patterns already described in Chapter 1 plus a few types he was forced to wear by circumstances. The clothing accounts of the 7th Louisiana Infantry, kept during 1862-1863, list "English shoes," "Confederate shoes," "Canvas shoes," and "wood sole shoes." The first of these, of course, were imports and usually displayed excellent workmanship and fine leather. They came in different patterns, but what was considered as the military shoe had fairly high quarters, at least three holes for lacing on each side, and pegged soles with hobnails.

The second were products of shoe factories established by the Quartermaster's Department throughout the South. The "army shoe" was defined by the Department in July 1861 as "an unbound, sewed brogan, low heel and wide bottoms, sizes six to ten," for which it was willing to pay $2.25 per pair. So were the third type, which also reflected the shortage of upper leather which had developed by 1863. Canvas was used as a substitute, but it failed to withstand the rigors of winter and heavy marching.

"Wood sole shoes" were the result of the perennial shortage of sole leather. Large stocks of wooden soles discovered in Atlanta after its capture made it clear that a substantial number of cavalrymen and even foot soldiers were obliged to wear this most unfomfortable article. Further, to add to the rigidity of the wooden sole it was often faced with thin iron plates on sole and heel, or with semi-circular iron strips like horseshoes nailed on.

The full clothing allowance for enlisted men, formally established in December 1862 (A & IG, CSA, GO 100), contained the following items for a three year enlistment:

4 caps, complete	12 pairs of socks
3 cap covers	1 leather stock
7 pairs of trousers	1 great coat
4 jackets	1 stable frock (for mounted men)
9 shirts	3 pairs of fatigue overalls (for engineers and ordnance only)
12 pairs of shoes	
7 pairs of drawers	2 blankets

Details on all these items are lacking. The list, of course, is based generally on U.S. Army allowances, but certain items like cap covers, stocks, and stable frocks must have had a most limited issue.

It is interesting to compare this theoretical list with the same or equivalent items as actually issued during 1862 by the Chief of the Clothing Bureau of the Trans-Mississippi Department (*Official Records*, 1, XXII, part 2, 1136):

Caps and hats	19,732	Pairs of drawers	48,704
(cap covers)	none	Pairs of socks	5,356
Pairs of pants	41,157	(Leather stocks)	none
Jackets	22,557	Overcoats	637
Overshirts	2,210	(Stable frocks)	none
Shirts	54,585	(Fatigue overalls)	none
Boots and shoes (pairs)	40,860	Blankets and quilts	22,236

There were, at the time of the report, roughly 22,000 men in the Department present for duty.

Headdress

Earlier, on page 64, we mentioned that the Confederate soldier on campaign wore black and brown felt hats, straws, and virtually every style of headdress known to the haberdasher. True as this statement is, we have no real idea what percentage of these civilian hats were issued by Confederate quartermasters, by the states, or were personally procured. But it can be said that the forage cap was the regular item of issue and was worn as frequently as the hat by all branches and ranks, and that the current image of the Confederate soldier in a battered felt or straw hat is only partially correct.

In the first few months of the war the ladies of the South succumbed to the romantic notion of sewing havelocks as generally as those of the North. Stonewall Jackson, among others, protested against the waste of time, yet the havelock was formally prescribed for wear in hot weather on 24 January 1862 (GO 4), as was an oilskin cover "with an apron to fall over the coat collar" for wear "in winter in bad weather."

Overcoats

The Confederate overcoat prescribed for enlisted men was the Union Army model except as to the color, which was "cadet gray." For some reason, no overcoat was prescribed for officers. In some areas the overcoat soon became an object of great rarity in the Confederate service. Carleton McCarthy wrote:

> The men came to the conclusion that the trouble of carrying them on hot days outweighed the comfort of having them when the cold day arrived. Besides they found that life in the open air hardened them to such an extent that changes in the temperature were not felt to any degree. Some clung to their overcoats to the last, but the majority got tired lugging them around, and either discarded them altogether, or trusted to capturing one about the time it would be needed. Nearly every overcoat in the [Confederate] army in the latter years of the war was one of Uncle Sam's captured from his boys.

Despite this statement, the Confederate Quartermaster General continued trying to secure overcoats. In October 1863 he listed "material for overcoats" with blankets and shoes as the three "articles most needed." In this endeavor he was partially successful. Frank Rauscher, the band leader of Collis' Pennsylvania Zouaves (*Music on the March*, p. 134), commented on some Confederates he saw in December 1863:

> The prisoners here taken were better clothed than any we had before seen; all were provided with overcoats and jackets of much better material than our own. They were of English manufacture, a much darker blue than the U.S. [sky blue overcoat] and they furnished conclusive evidence of successful blockade running.

Some soldiers found that the cape of the overcoat sufficed for much of the bad weather encountered. A soldier of the 11th Mississippi asked his mother to make him a "cape for my coat. All the boys," he wrote, "have them and they are a great advantage ."

Fitted with buttons, he felt it would "answer for a dress coat and overcoat too."

To furnish clothing (as well as other supplies) to the troops mustered into Confederate service, the Quartermaster's Department established depots throughout the South where supplies could be collected and distributed. At first it counted heavily, as the states were doing, on the putting-out system whereby bulk cloth plus patterns were turned over to groups of women volunteers and female relatives of soldiers to be sewn up. Where possible it purchased cloth or made-up clothing from abroad. Finally, beginning in the fall of 1861, it opened garment shops in centers where the conditions were suitable. Large shops were established east of the Mississippi in Richmond, Augusta, Atlanta, and Columbus. Shoe factories were organized in Atlanta, Columbus, and elsewhere.

By the end of 1862, the Clothing Bureau of the Trans-Mississippi Department had established similar garment and hat shops, shoe factories, woolen and cotton mills, and other sources of clothing and equipage throughout Arkansas, Louisiana, and Texas.

A large share of the uniform cloth made for Confederate uniforms came from the Eagle Manufacturing Co., more commonly called the Eagle Mills, of Columbus, Georgia. Other important suppliers of uniform cloth were Barnett, Micon & Co., Tallassee, Alabama; B.C. Flannagan & Co., Charlottesville, Virginia; Richmond Manufacturing Co., Rockingham, North Carolina; Jamestown Woolen Mill, Old Jamestown, North Carolina; Scottsville Manufacturing Co., Scottsville, Virginia; and the Crenshaw Woolen Co. of Richmond. Private uniform manufacturers included James G. Gibbes of Columbia, South Carolina, whose plant had a capacity of 1,000 suits a day and turned out boots, shoes, saddles, and felt hats. Another supplier was S. Rothchild of Columbus, Georgia.

Blankets

In no area of supply could there have been as much diversity of color and quality, and even of size, as in the Confederate soldier's blanket. A large percentage must have been homemade, while quilts were carried by many soldiers and were actually an item of issue. The Federal blanket of gray wool with its "U.S." stitched in black outline, 7x5.5 feet in size, must have been about as common as any other kind. A Confederate blanket in the collection of Wendell Lang is made of roughly spun wool with a herringbone weave. Its color is a soft light brown, or dark buff, and it has a 5 inch stripe of darker brown around all sides, about 4 inches from the edges. It is almost square, about 5x5 feet.

Throughout the war some states continued to clothe their own men, albeit irregularly. From the very start the Confederacy had agreed that clothing furnished by a state need not be uniform in order to be accepted. The Southern soldier always looked to home for help in clothing himself and often received it. All collections of soldier letters contain correspondence about garments made by wives and mothers.

The reasons for what we have called the "homogeneous informality and often raggedness" of the Confederate soldier should by now be apparent. But one more source of the condition should be stressed and this one is important in visualizing what he looked like in the field. The Confederate soldier, and especially the cavalryman who was in a better position to raid Northern depots, counted heavily on supplying himself with Union uniforms, arms, and accouterments, usually by stripping the dead on the battlefield. Edward A. Moore, an artilleryman, wrote:

> To give an idea of the ready access we had to the enemy's stores, I had been the possessor of nine gum-blankets within the past three weeks, and no such article as a gum-blanket was ever manufactured in the South. Any soldier carrying a Confederate canteen was at once recognized as a new recruit, as it required but a short time to secure one of superior quality from a dead foeman on a battlefield.

Sky blue pants were frequently appropriated and the practice of reshoeing at the expense of prisoners of war and the dead, as Professor Wiley points out, was so common that the remark became trite among troops: "All a Yankee is worth is his shoes."

Even blue coats and overcoats were worn, at times over half the men of a Confederate regiment might be so clothed. General orders repeatedly condemned the practice but it apparently continued, at least in the lulls between battles.

The enlisted man's and officer's clothing, as described above, will be called "CS clothing" in the descriptions which follow.

Insignia

Military insignia was relatively rare in the Confederate service, and many a Southern enlisted man marched and fought without identification of any sort. Others wore state insignia and apparently not a few fashioned devices for themselves. Other than the dress regulations already mentioned, very few orders or specifications governing insignia have been found.

General Service Insignia: Belt Plates

Almost all the evidence about Confederate belt plates is circumstantial. The only direct reference in dress regulations is to a type apparently never worn, and the prescriptions in ordnance regulations cannot be taken too seriously. Were it not for the studies of advanced collectors (such as the works of William C. Gavin and Sydney C. Kerksis, cited below) we would have scant idea of the possible origins or the relative usage of the different types of belt plate known to exist.

Confederate belt plates (as distinct from those bearing some state device) fall into three broad categories: 1) two-piece types usually bearing "CS" but sometimes "CSA", believed to have been worn both by officers and enlisted men; 2) rectangular types bearing "C.S.A." as a rule, but occasionally "CS", also worn by both officers and enlisted men; and 3) oval types marked "CS" and worn by enlisted men of infantry, both as belt and cartridge box plates. The reader, of course, should bear in mind that an unadorned, open-frame belt buckle was more common by far than these types with insignia, and probably even more common still were the Union Army belts and plates worn without change.

1) Two-piece buckles were worn on sword belts and were of cast brass. Most seem to have been locally manufactured in small quantities in the South with many minor

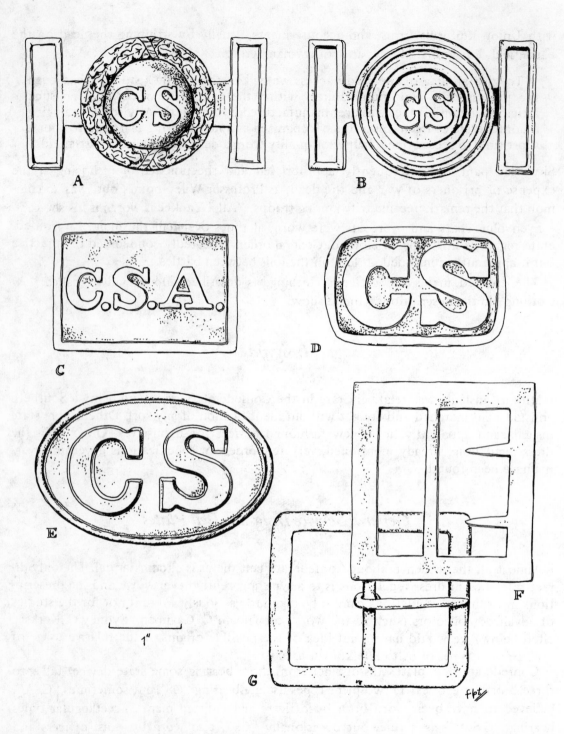

Fig. 141. Confederate waist belt plates and buckles: A, Cast brass, two piece type, overall diameter 1.9 in. B, Same, illustrating variations in lettering and frame, with overall diameter 2.1 in. C, Cast brass rectangular type, 1.9x2.75 in., the kind most commonly found. D, Another fairly common variation of the rectangular plate, 1.8x2.9 in. E, Oval, die-stamped brass type, 2.1x3.4 in., bearing three hooks on the rear. F, One-piece frame buckle of cast copper, 2.5x2.8 in. overall, one of several styles worn; the great majority had two teeth. G, Two-piece frame buckle of brass, copper or iron. (By F.P. Todd, after

variations in the design as the result. In construction and dimensions the majority follow the U.S. foot artillery plate specified in ordnance regulations of 1841. Most bear the letters "CS" but some have been found with "CSA" and one example believed made in England bears a Confederate battle flag.

2) The 1861 dress regulations specified that the sword belt plate for all officers and enlisted men would be "gilt, rectangular; two inches wide, with a raised bright rim; a silver wreath of laurel encircling the 'arms of the Confederate States'." This paraphrase of the U.S. regulations was never followed (no arms were adopted until April 1863) but there is some reason to believe it led to the official adoption of the rectangular plate bearing a simple "C.S.A.". This pattern, about 1.9 x 2.75 inches, made of cast brass, is the one most commonly found and is known to have been fabricated in the Confederate Arsenal at Atlanta, Georgia and possibly in other ordnance installations. It was widely worn in the Army of Tennessee, but also seems to have seen some use in the East. Several variations of this buckle have been found. There are larger sizes, some bear merely "CS", while some were made from other metals than brass. One type with rounded corners and a large "CS" was fairly common and is believed to have been worn in the western Confederate armies.

3) Oval plates, based upon the common "US" waist belt plate, are relatively rare and of great variety. Most found were made of stamped brass, sometimes backed with solder, and all seem locally produced. These oval plates were probably made in conjunction with sets of accouterments early in the war and also came in the form of cartridge box plates. In one variety or another, this type of plate was worn in all Confederate armies, although more commonly in the western ones.

The Confederate War Department produced no shoulder belt plates and almost no hat insignia of any sort. Furthermore, cartridge box plates were quite rare and their issue must have ended in 1862 or soon thereafter. Most students of this subject feel that a simple, cast, one-piece square frame buckle was the common device issued for fastening the soldier's waist belt.

Wings and Armbands

Lack of standardization on both sides in the color of uniforms during the early months of the war, with the consequent danger of firing on friendly troops, led Confederate commanders to adopt distinctive devices as expedients. On the eve of First Bull Run, General Beauregard devised a system of "wing badges," arm and cap bands for wear in combat. At almost the last moment it was discovered that some Union commands had resorted to the same devices and the plan was hastily dropped except for certain corps, probably those wearing blue coats. The men of the Washington Artillery battalion, who were so clothed, wore red flannel stripes on their left arms, above the elbow.

General Magruder, operating in the Peninsula later that year, for a time adopted white hat bands and required his scouts to carry a white sash "from shoulder to hip." Even earlier, the troops in the Valley of Virginia under Generals Loring and Jackson had begun to wear "a short strip of white cotton cloth, about an inch wide and six long," around the top of their caps when they expected to meet the enemy. This practice continued from August through December 1861, and possibly longer.

Insignia of Branch or Unit

Except for buttons, no devices distinctive of a soldier's branch or organization were authorized. Yet some were worn. Many 1861 photographs show Confederates wearing U.S. branch insignia carried over from pre-war state uniforms, and this use may well have continued after 1861. An interesting insignia once worn on a dark blue forage cap by Colonel T.M.R. Talcott, 1st Regiment Engineer Troops, Provisional Army, is in The Museum of the Confederacy. It consists of a white metal "E" in German text, similar to the "E" prescribed in the June 1861 dress regulations for the Engineer button, mounted on a square black velvet background which has a very narrow gold cord border. The entire insignia is about 1.5 in. square.

Some Confederate army chaplains designed non-regulation devices for themselves and apparently wore them. These will be found in Chapter 12, where several other examples of non-regulation branch insignia are mentioned.

The June 1861 dress regulations did establish branch colors which were: buff for general officers and for the Adjutant General's, Quartermaster General's and Commissary General's Departments, and for Engineers; black for the Medical Department; yellow for Cavalry; red for Artillery; and light blue for Infantry. These colors were widely worn during the war, especially by officers. Sashes, of four colors, also indicated branch as well as rank; they are described below.

Insignia of Rank, Function, and Long Service

The story of Confederate officer rank insignia during the first months of the war is understandably confusing. Most officers wore state uniforms and rank devices or those of the U.S., which were usually the same.

Some months after First Bull Run there appeared a widely circulated photograph of "Stonewall Jackson" bearing the name of "Brady-New York." In it, Jackson wore a double-breasted frock coat with evenly spaced buttons and a fairly high collar. On this collar appeared a shield-shaped device flanked by stars and, even more remarkable, up each of his shoulders ran a wide strap, edged with a double row of lace and containing a star (see *Photo. History*, X, 97). It is now thought that the original of this photograph was a daguerreotype made in 1851, later retouched in the Brady studio — for one thing, Jackson had grown a beard by the time he was appointed brigadier general.

This singular insignia is certainly not U.S. regulation. It could be dismissed as fanciful except for the fact it appears in portraits of several other Confederate generals of the early period (Buckner, *Battles and Leaders*, I, 408; Marshall, *ibid*, 396; Crittenden, *ibid*, 383; Branch, *ibid*, 648; etc.). To dispel any remaining doubts, General Buckner's actual uniform bearing these devices is in the Kentucky Room, The Museum of the Confederacy, Richmond. The collar, shoulder straps, and cuffs are black velvet and the devices on the first two are made in silver embroidery, the collar shield having a narrow

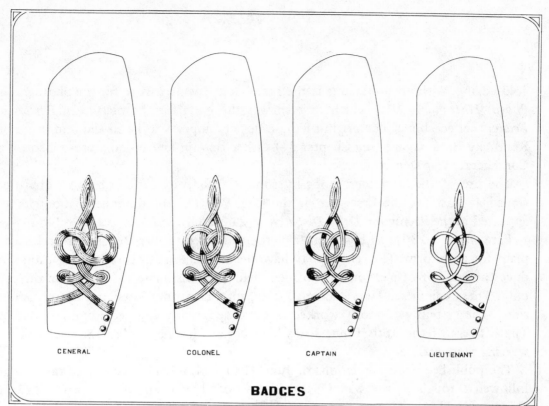

LITH. DRAWING BY E. CREHEN, RICHMOND   APPROVED BY WAR DEPARTMENT   LITH. PRINTING BY VALORY, PETERSBURG. VA.

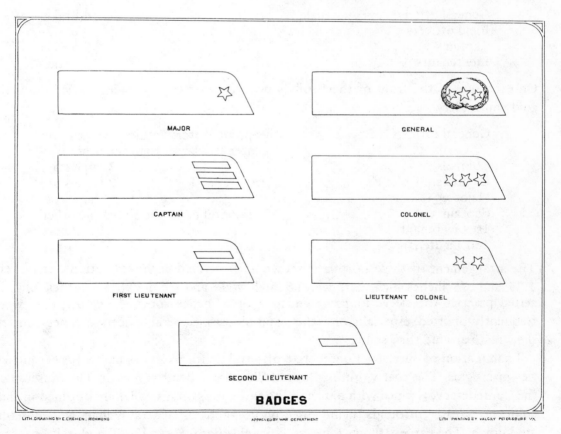

LITH. DRAWING BY E. CREHEN, RICHMOND   APPROVED BY WAR DEPARTMENT   LITH. PRINTING BY VALORY, PETERSBURG. VA.

Fig. 142. Officers' insignia of rank, from Blanton Duncan's edition of the Confederate dress regulations of 6 June 1861. All lace and embroidery was gold. In actual practice, the sleeve loops varied considerably in form and were often omitted altogether. (Reproduced from the Riling-Halter facsimile of 1952.)

gold edging. Without doubt this is the same coat Buckner wore for the photograph in *Photo. History*, I, 191, which in turn was the basis for the picture in *Battles and Leaders*, cited above. The origin of these devices appears to lie in the uniform of the Kentucky State Guard (see Chapter 31) rather than in any insignia prescribed by the Confederate War Department.

The use of U.S. shoulder straps by some Confederate officers seems to have continued at least for the first year of the Civil War for an admonition about its wear appeared in the Richmond *Daily Dispatch* of 21 March 1862.

Late in May 1861, as has been said, the Confederate War Department released its plans for a uniform. The release may have been premature or garbled, but it did introduce the wear of officers' insignia (called "badges of distinguished rank") on the collar only. These comprised large and small stars, and "horizontal bars" in various combinations. The system was poorly worked out and apparently enjoyed a limited following. The officers of the 16th Tennessee, which began forming in May 1861, are pictured wearing these early devices.

The published dress regulations of June 1861 laid down the system of rank insignia followed throughout the war. On the sleeves of their coats officers wore .125 inch stripes of gold braid looped in a specified pattern, extending to the bend of the elbow:

General officers . . . . 4 braids
Field officers . . . . 3 braids
Captains . . . . 2 braids
Lieutenants . . . . 1 braid

On each side of the front of their collars officers wore the following devices, done in gold embroidery:

General officers . . . . 3 five-pointed stars within a wreath, the
center star larger than the other two
Colonels . . . . 3 large stars
Lieutenant Colonels . . . . 2 large stars
Major . . . . 1 large star
Captain . . . . 3 horizontal bars, one above the other
1st Lieutenant . . . . 2 bars
2nd Lieutenant . . . . 1 bar

Fig. 142 The arrangement of these insignia is shown as prescribed in the regulations. Stars were 1.25 and .75 inches high, bars were .5 inch wide and from 3 to 3.5 inches long. In actual practice the sleeve loops extended 2 or 3 inches above the elbow; they were frequently omitted, especially on jackets and blouses. General officers at times omitted the wreath around their stars.

Examination of surviving Confederate officers' uniforms shows numerous eccentricities in insignia. The coat worn by General W. Dorsey Pender, now in The Museum of the Confederacy, is piped with blue and the three stars on his collar are outlined in that color; no wreath surrounds them. Three photographs of General William N. Pendleton are known. The earliest shows him as a colonel (*Photo. Hist.*, V, 59) and in it he wears a single-breasted coat with three stars. The collar is probably red and the coat the same as he wore when captain of the Rockbridge Artillery. Another appears in Wise's *The Long Arm of Lee* (I, 64). Pendleton was by then a brigadier general, but his coat is still

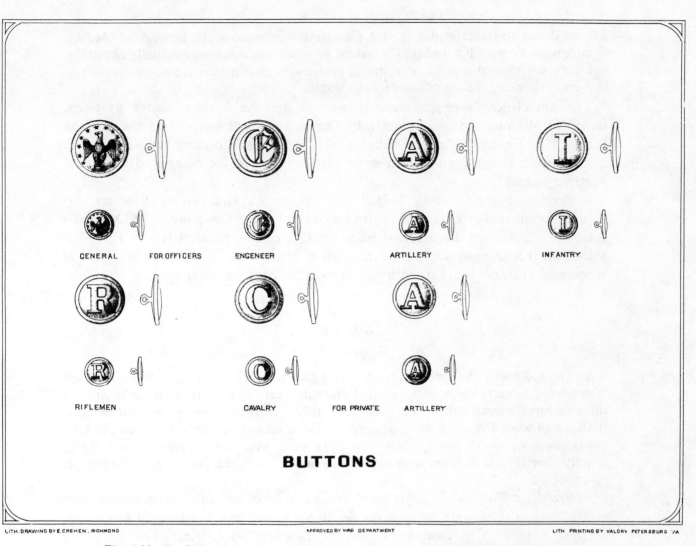

GENERAL   FOR OFFICERS   ENGENEER   ARTILLERY   INFANTRY

RIFLEMEN   CAVALRY   FOR PRIVATE   ARTILLERY

BUTTONS

LITH. DRAWING BY E. CREHEN, RICHMOND   APPROVED BY WAR DEPARTMENT   LITH PRINTING BY VALORY PETERSBURG VA

Fig. 143. Confederate buttons as illustrated in the dress regulations of 6 June 1861. Variations from these designs and relative sizes were numerous, the small enlisted man's size was never produced.

single-breasted. He has added a wreath around the collar stars but has on U.S. shoulder straps. The third photograph (Freeman, *Lee's Lieutenants*, II, xxxv) shows him late in the war. He seems to be wearing the same coat that is preserved in The Museum of the Confederacy. It is double-breasted, piped with scarlet, with buttons set in two's. The collar is gray with the stars sewn on red cloth. Despite regulations, Pendleton remained the artilleryman.

Insignia of Enlisted Men

Non-commissioned rank was indicated by chevrons patterned directly upon those of the U.S. Army. However, only the six primary grades were specified; the Confederacy had no insignia for a hospital steward, pioneer, signalman, or company QM sergeant,

Fig. 29

and no device to indicate long service. Chevrons were made of silk or worsted binding, .5 inch wide, of branch coloring. The extent to which chevrons were actually issued has not been determined, and there is strong probability that most were home-made or at best issued in non-regulation forms by the states.

The Ambulance Corps (comprising unarmed stretcher bearers assisted by Negro slaves) of McLaws Division, Longstreet's Corps, wore "red badges" on their hats in June 1863. Similar "infirmary detachments" wore distinguishing badges and it is quite possible that a red badge of some sort came to be the recognized insignia of stretcher bearers.

A curious "Sharp Shooter's Badge" exists in the Maryland Historical Society. According to museum records it was worn by Henry A. Wise, Company B, 2nd Maryland Infantry, C.S.A., and was received from the Confederate Soldiers Home, Pikesville, Maryland. It is an eight-sided, 1½-inch patch of black cloth on which is sewn a sort of cross made of scarlet felt. No confirmation of its use has been discovered.

Buttons

Fig. 143

An enlisted man's uniform fabricated in or issued by a Southern state during the Civil War tended to carry the buttons of that state if it carried uniform buttons at all. One manufactured abroad carried buttons made there, more than likely without detailed patterns to work from. As the war wore on and brass buttons became scarcer, civilian types made of wood, bone, horn, and even glass were pressed into service. Thus, strictly Confederate buttons were not as common on enlisted men's clothing as might be expected.

Officers' buttons, on the other hand, tended to be of one of the Confederate patterns. Some of these were made in the South by a small group of firms in Richmond, Virginia, of which E.M. Lewis & Co. was the most important. Others were imported, usually from England.

Beginning probably as early as the 1880's, button manufacturers like the Waterbury Button Co. and Steele & Johnson commenced to make reproductions of "CSA" buttons for veteran groups in the South. These can readily be distinguished from the earlier ones by the makers' names on the back.

The dress regulations of June 1861 specified eight patterns of buttons; the six officer patterns were to be in two sizes, the two enlisted man patterns in only one size. All were gilt, rounded at the edge, and slightly convex, Sanders-type buttons, with raised designs. One pattern was never manufactured.

● *General and General Staff Officers.* Eagle, head to right, standing on a pedestal, no shield on its breast, "with stars surrounding it." Regulations called for two sizes: 1 inch and .5 inch. While no buttons exactly fitting these descriptions were made, there were many that were close to it. The eagle may look left or right; there were normally eleven stars, but buttons with twelve, thirteen, or fourteen stars are known, sometimes 5-pointed and sometimes 6. On some, the eagle bears a shield on its breast with the letters "CSA" or "CS". Sizes varied from almost 1 inch to .55 inch (Albert, CS 1-44).

● *Corps of Engineers.* "Raised E in German text," otherwise plain; same sizes as above. At least the large size was manufactured, although not exactly as illustrated. The "E" is usually in what is called "Old English" text, but a version exists with an odd manuscript "E". One style, made in England, bears a turretted castle and "CONFEDERATE STATES ENGINEERS" (Albert, CS 151-166).

● *Artillery.* Roman letter "A", otherwise plain. Officers wore two sizes: .875 inch and .5 inch; enlisted men .75 inch only. All of these sizes were produced, and versions of the larger officers' button exist with an Old English "A" and a cursive manuscript form of the letter (Albert, CS 101-102).

● *Cavalry.* Roman letter "C", otherwise plain. This and the two buttons that follow were prescribed in the June 1861 regulations only for officers, in sizes .875 inch and .5 inch. By a decision made in May the letters "C" and "I" were authorized for enlisted men's buttons. Several types and sizes were produced, including variations with an Old English "C" and a cursive manuscript "C" (Albert, CS 126-144).

● *Infantry.* Roman letter "I", otherwise plain. Same sizes and variations as described for cavalry (Albert, CS 171-189).

● *Riflemen.* Roman letter "R", otherwise plain. Same sizes as prescribed for cavalry, but only the larger size is known today. A version having a German text letter "R" also exists. The organizations for which this button was designed are not known and probably only a limited number were manufactured, all abroad (Albert, CS 201-221).

● *Regimental type.* One pattern prescribed in June 1861 called for a plain button, .75 inch in size, bearing "the number of the regiment, in large figures." This was to be worn by enlisted men of cavalry, infantry, and riflemen. On 24 May 1861, the Quartermaster's Department announced: "For the present let the buttons be made for infantry and a few for cavalry, with I and C instead of numbers." This rule was never changed.

This completes the buttons prescribed in June 1861. For the patterns that follow we have found no specifications or mention of any sort in orders:

● *General Service, "C.S.A." type.* Roman letters "C.S.A." (sometimes without periods) otherwise plain. Usually found in two sizes: .875 inch and .5 inch. Manufactured by S. Buckley & Co., Birmingham, England, and possibly other English firms (Albert, CS 81-93). This pattern was extensively reproduced after the Civil War and is being produced commercially today. Apparently some of the original buttons were cast and others made of white metal.

● *General Service, Star types.* Buttons, not fully identified, bearing 5-pointed stars and other devices, have been found in some number and appear to have been manufactured for general wear. One type (Johnson 1001) has an outlined star surrounded by the words "SOUTHERN CONFEDERACY." Another cast type (Johnson 1031) bears the letters "CS" inside the star, while the star alone may well have been used. Albert attributes all of these types to Texas.

● *"A.G.D." type.* An unusual button, made by "G & Cie" in Paris in two sizes, about .55 and .875 inch, bearing the Confederate battle flag, above which is "CONFEDERATE ARMY" and below, "A.G.D.". It is hard to accept the fact that the Confederate Adjutant and Inspector General would have authorized and ordered a button so marked, or, indeed, a distinctive button at all, but no other explanation has so far been advanced (Albert CS50).

Sashes

In its 1861 regulations for sashes, the Confederacy differed substantially from the Union. These are given in full:

41 . . . For General Officers — buff silk net, with silk bullion fringe ends; sash to go twice around the waist, and to tie behind the left hip; pendent part not to extend more than eighteen inches below the tie.

42 . . . For officers of the General Staff and Engineers, and of the Artillery and Infantry — red silk net. For officers of the Cavalry — yellow silk net. For medical officers — green silk net. All with silk bullion fringe ends; to go around the waist, and to tie as for General Officers.

43 . . . For Sergeants — of worsted, with worsted bullion fringe ends: red for Artillery and Infantry, and yellow for Cavalry. To go twice around the waist, and to tie as above specified.

General Lee's sash is described in Chapter 12. It is of buff (really yellow) silk net, and other examples of the use of silk exist. Yet many officers' sashes, like the ones illustrated, must have been made of wool or possibly other material. Colors of the red sashes varied from scarlet, through crimson, to magenta. Finally, there is some question as to the extent sashes were actually worn by officers and sergeants on active service. Photographs are not overly helpful in this connection.

Medals and Decorations

Despite the fact that the Confederate Congress authorized the President to bestow "medals with proper devices" and "badges of distinction" as rewards for valor and good conduct, only one such is known to have been issued. This was a small silver medal inscribed on one side: "Sabine Pass/ Sept 8th/ 1863," and on the other, "DG" with a Maltese cross. About forty-two were presented by President Davis to the Davis Guards, an element of the 1st Texas Heavy Artillery Regiment, for its gallant and vigorous defense of the fortifications at Sabine Pass, Texas.

During the Civil War, medallions were struck in France for members of the Stonewall Brigade. These did not reach this country until after Appomatox, according to one account, while another maintains they were run into Wilmington, North Carolina but had to be hidden in Savannah to escape capture by Sherman's army. Apparently they were offered for sale for the benefit of C.S.A. veterans sometime after 1895. Being medallions, they were not meant to be worn.

All other Confederate decorations were established a generation or more after the Civil War.

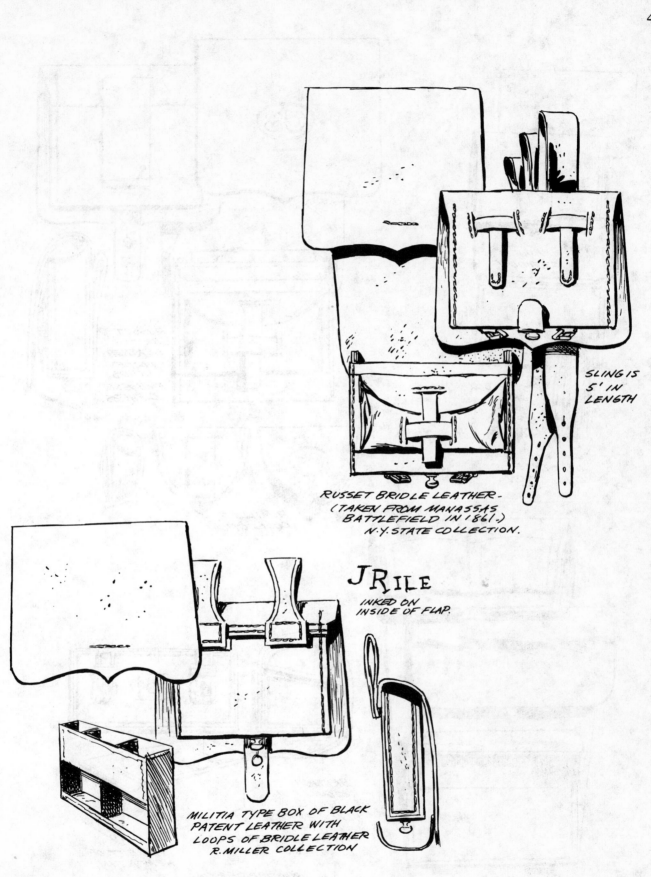

RUSSET BRIDLE LEATHER-
(TAKEN FROM MANASSAS
BATTLEFIELD IN 1861.)
N.Y. STATE COLLECTION.

SLING IS
5' IN
LENGTH

J RILE
INKED ON
INSIDE OF FLAP.

MILITIA TYPE BOX OF BLACK
PATENT LEATHER WITH
LOOPS OF BRIDLE LEATHER
R. MILLER COLLECTION

Fig. 144a. Confederate cartridge boxes.

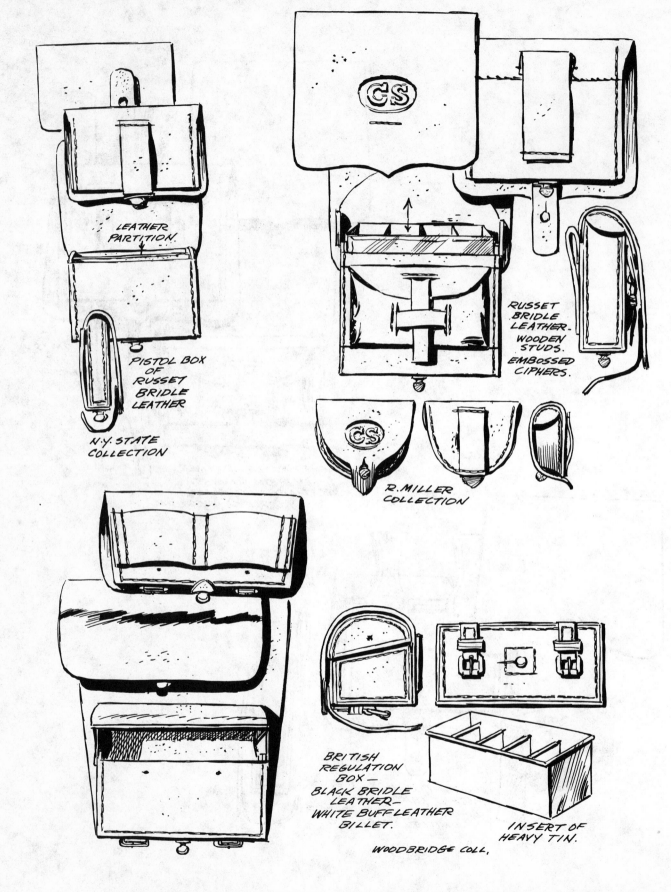

LEATHER
PARTITION.

PISTOL BOX
OF
RUSSET
BRIDLE
LEATHER

N.Y. STATE
COLLECTION

CS

RUSSET
BRIDLE
LEATHER.
WOODEN
STUDS.
EMBOSSED
CIPHERS.

CS

R. MILLER
COLLECTION

BRITISH
REGULATION
BOX —
BLACK BRIDLE
LEATHER —
WHITE BUFF LEATHER
BILLET.

INSERT OF
HEAVY TIN.

WOODBRIDGE COLL.

Fig. 144b. Confederate cartridge boxes. The British Enfield box is described on page 200.

SOURCES

Confederate States of America, Adjutant and Inspector General (Blanton Duncan, publisher), *Uniform and Dress of the Army of the Confederate States*, Richmond, Va., 1861; 2nd ed. (with colored plates), 1861. Reprinted 1952 in facsimile by Ray Riling and Robert Halter; reprinted 1960 in a revised edition with colored plates and introduction by Richard Harwell. This introduction gives the story of the publication.

————— , ————— , *Regulations for the Army of the Confederate States*, Richmond, Va., 1861, 1862, 1863, 1864.

Bell Irvin Wiley, *The Life of Johnny Reb: The Common Soldier of the Confederacy*, New York, 1943.

Carlton McCarthy, *Detailed Minutiae of Soldier Life in the Army of Northern Virginia, 1861-1865*, Richmond, Va., 1882.

Edward A. Moore, *The Story of a Cannoneer Under Stonewall Jackson*, New York, 1907.

William G. Gavin, *Accoutrement Plates, North and South, 1861-1865*, Philadelphia, Pa., 1963.

Alphaeus H. Albert, *Record of American Uniform and Historical Buttons*, Hightstown, N.J., 1969.

David F. Johnson, *Uniform Buttons: American Armed Forces, 1784-1948*, 2 vols., Watkins Glen, N.Y., 1948.

John Wike, "Individual Decorations of the Confederacy," in *Military Collector & Historian*, VI (1954), 93-94.

Sydney C. Kerksis, "Confederate State Buttons," in *ibid.*, XII (1960), 103-106.

————— , *Plates and Buckles of the American Military, 1795-1874*, Kennesaw, Ga., 1974.

James L. Nichols, "Confederate Quartermaster Operations in the Trans-Mississippi Department," MS master's thesis in the University of Texas Library, 1947.

Bauman L. Belden, *War Medals of the Confederacy*, Glendale, N.Y., 1970.

MS, "War Department Collection of Confederate Records" (Record Group 109), in National Archives.

MS, "Letters and Telegrams Sent, 1861, C.S. Quartermaster Department" (Record Group 109), in National Archives.

William A. Albaugh, III, *Confederate Faces: A Pictorial Review of the Individuals in the Confederate Armed Forces*, Solana Beach, California, 1970.

————— , *More Confederate Faces*, published by the author, 1972.

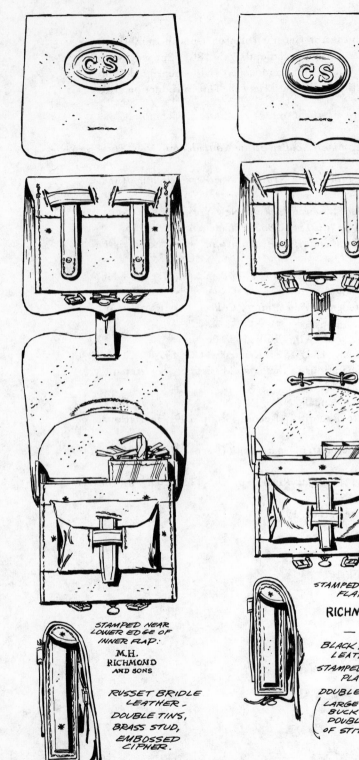
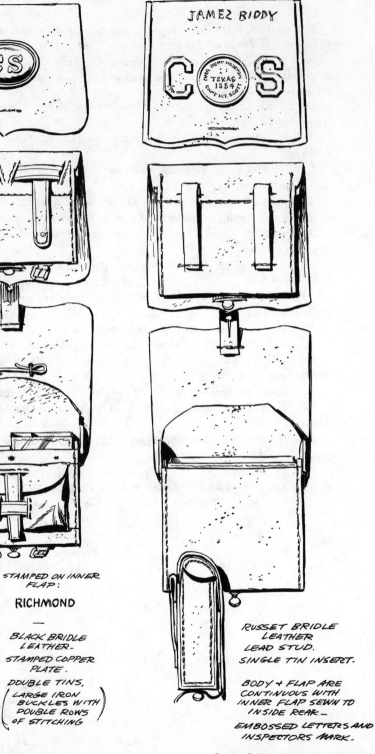

STAMPED NEAR
LOWER EDGE OF
INNER FLAP:

M.H.
RICHMOND
AND SONS

RUSSET BRIDLE
LEATHER.
DOUBLE TINS,
BRASS STUD,
EMBOSSED
CIPHER.

BEVERLY M. DUBOSE JR. COLL.
ATLANTA. GA.

STAMPED ON INNER
FLAP:

RICHMOND
—
BLACK BRIDLE
LEATHER.
STAMPED COPPER
PLATE.
DOUBLE TINS,
(LARGE IRON
BUCKLES WITH
DOUBLE ROWS
OF STITCHING)

JAMES BIDDY

RUSSET BRIDLE
LEATHER
LEAD STUD.
SINGLE TIN INSERT.

BODY + FLAP ARE
CONTINUOUS WITH
INNER FLAP SEWN TO
INSIDE REAR.
EMBOSSED LETTERS AND
INSPECTORS MARK.

RUSS A. PRITCHARD COLL.
M.C.&H. FALL 1962

Fig. 145. Confederate cartridge boxes.

CHAPTER X

SMALL ARMS AND ACCOUTERMENTS

In contrast with its policy on clothing, the Confederate War Department assumed responsibility from the very start for the procurement and issue of arms and accouterments to its Provisional Army. In February 1861, President Davis urged Congress to place all "arms and munitions . . . under the control of the General Government," and this it voted to do. On 1 March, the Secretary of War wrote the Southern governors requesting them "to communicate to this Department without delay the quantity and character of arms and munitions of war which have been acquired from the United States . . . and all other arms and munitions which your State may desire to turn over and make chargeable to this Government."

Whereas the states tended to welcome this acceptance of responsibility, the extent to which they proved willing to turn over their munitions of war differed considerably, then and later. The War Department was unwilling and usually unable to arm any but regiments mustered into the Confederate service. This left it up to the states to arm and equip their militia, home guards, and other local troops, and thus led to a series of controversies which were to persist throughout the Civil War. Procurement and issue of arms at the general government and state levels continued on a competitive basis in the South as it did in the North, but usually with far less harmony. State procurement will be outlined in later chapters and only the operation of the general government will be mentioned here.

The Confederate Ordnance Department (or "Bureau"), under the able direction of Major Josiah Gorgas, was responsible for an even wider variety of materiel than its Northern counterpart. In addition to arsenals, armories, and all public buildings as well as artillery and ammunition of all kinds, the Department handled "small-arms . . . pistols and holsters . . . sabers, swords, carbines, and pistols . . . cavalry equipments . . . sets of cavalry accouterments . . . sets [of] infantry accouterments, knapsacks, haversacks and canteens." The dearth of these items and the appalling lack of manufacturing in the South has been stressed too often to need repetition here. The Confederate armories and mills at first were inadequate to the enormous demands made upon them, but more were created from improvised and captured equipment and managed to function. Foreign purchase was resorted to with considerable success, and a systematic use of captured materiel was developed. By 1863, Gorgas had his Ordnance Department operating efficiently and the Confederate soldier tolerably well armed. By then the soldier himself had learned to do without many of the accouterments usually considered essential.

Some idea of the relative importance of the three methods of procurement may be gained from a report by Colonel Gorgas for the year ending 30 September 1864: small arms imported — 30,000; manufactured — 20,000; and captured — 45,000.

The problems of standardization followed close upon those of procurement. Forced to accept an assortment of captured, foreign, and locally made small arms ranging in caliber from .54 to .79, the Ordnance Department could accomplish little in the first year of the war. In 1862, however, it published a *Field Manual* for ordnance officers which established certain standard infantry weapons and described others in common use. Wherever possible, weapons manufactured in Southern armories followed standard U.S. or European patterns, although a few distinctive types were developed. A uniform caliber of .577 was adopted for all rifles and rifle muskets, and ammunition designed that would fit both U.S. and British arms. The standard rifled muzzleloading shoulder weapons of the Civil War varied slightly from near caliber .577 to .58 in the bore. The U.S. weapons were bored caliber .58 and called for a bullet diameter of .577. Such bullets, pressed from worn molds, could cause difficulty in loading the .577 Enfield, so the Confederate ordnance regulations called for balls of .562 diameter to guarantee easy loading of both classes of weapons.

When possible, existing weapons like the caliber .54 Mississippi rifle were altered to .577. Special ammunition had to be manufactured for the other small arms and a continuous effort was made thereafter to reduce this burden.

Confederate regulation small arms will be described in the same order as used in Chapter 3: muskets and rifles, carbines and musketoons, pistols and revolvers, swords and other edged weapons, and specialized types. Where a model has been described before it will merely be listed. Weapons of Confederate manufacture will be placed after models upon which they were based, if such was the case.

The bayonets manufactured for and used with the long arms listed below can only be guessed at in many instances. Variations are numerous and confusing, and very little study has been given to this topic. In general, the Confederate Ordnance Department followed its Northern counterpart by issuing socket bayonets with muskets and rifle muskets, and saber bayonets with the shorter rifles. Among the former it became the practice to contract for one-third to fit the U.S. Model 1842 musket and two-thirds for the U.S. Model 1855, Enfield, and Richmond rifle muskets.

Shortages of steel led to the adoption of a socket bayonet of iron tipped with steel. Orders were issued on 14 January 1864 (GO 6) to end the manufacture of all saber bayonets, which had come to be considered too awkward and heavy, and to use the socket pattern in their place. Already the variety among saber bayonets had caused trouble and led to the design of a patented "bayonet adapter" by Boyle, Gamble & *Fig. 147* MacFee of Richmond by which most rifles or muskets could be made to carry a saber bayonet. A unique and rare feature among Confederate bayonets was the bowie bayonet made by the same firm, a finely made brass-hilted weapon with a 15-inch blade, encased in a tooled leather scabbard.

A word should be said about the Confederate arms imported from Europe. Certainly these represented an impressive share of the total used, and one authority has expressed the belief that more than half of the shoulder arms in the hands of

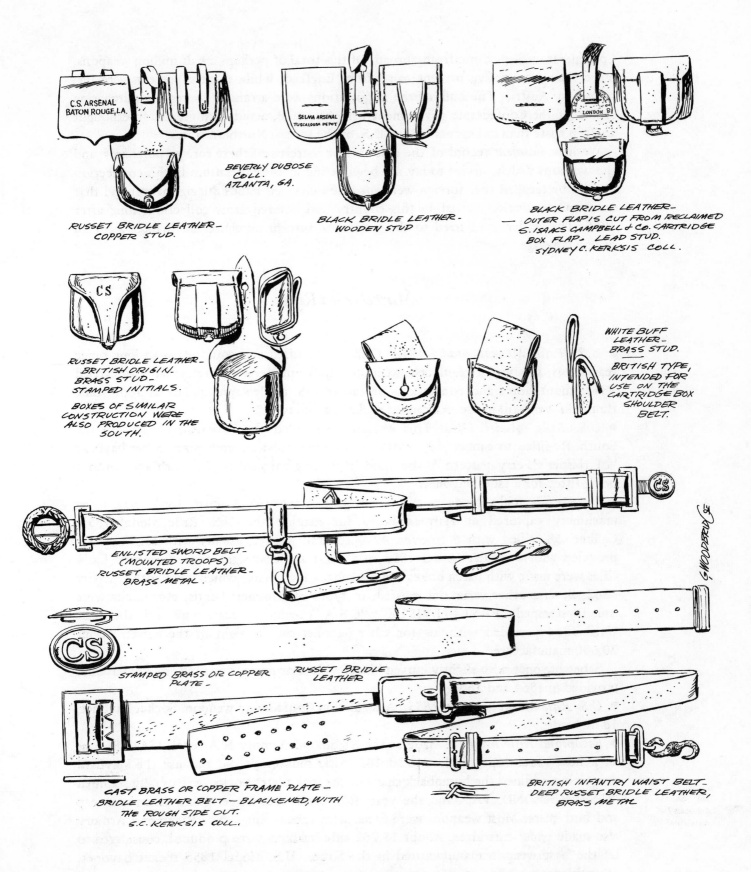

C.S. ARSENAL
BATON ROUGE, L.A.

RUSSET BRIDLE LEATHER -
COPPER STUD.

BEVERLY DuBOSE
COLL.
ATLANTA, GA.

SELMA ARSENAL
TUSCALOOSA DEPOT

BLACK BRIDLE LEATHER -
WOODEN STUD.

ZIG ZAG
LONDON

BLACK BRIDLE LEATHER -
— OUTER FLAP IS CUT FROM RECLAIMED
S. ISAACS CAMPBELL & CO. CARTRIDGE
BOX FLAP. LEAD STUD.
SYDNEY C. KERKSIS COLL.

CS

RUSSET BRIDLE LEATHER -
BRITISH ORIGIN.
BRASS STUD -
STAMPED INITIALS.

BOXES OF SIMILAR
CONSTRUCTION WERE
ALSO PRODUCED IN THE
SOUTH.

WHITE BUFF
LEATHER -
BRASS STUD.

BRITISH TYPE,
INTENDED FOR
USE ON THE
CARTRIDGE BOX
SHOULDER
BELT.

ENLISTED SWORD BELT -
(MOUNTED TROOPS)
RUSSET BRIDLE LEATHER -
BRASS METAL.

CS

STAMPED BRASS OR COPPER
PLATE -

RUSSET BRIDLE
LEATHER

CAST BRASS OR COPPER "FRAME" PLATE -
BRIDLE LEATHER BELT - BLACKENED, WITH
THE ROUGH SIDE OUT.
S.C. KERKSIS COLL.

BRITISH INFANTRY WAIST BELT -
DEEP RUSSET BRIDLE LEATHER,
BRASS METAL

G.WOODBRUF 92

Fig. 146. Confederate States cap pouches and enlisted men's waist belts, 1861-1865.

Confederate troops came from abroad. Of this total of perhaps a half million weapons, more than seventy-five percent came from England, while twenty percent were furnished by Austria. The bulk of the importations were arranged by regular purchasing agents of the Confederate government who, as a rule, acted with greater forethought and less haste than did agents for the U.S. or the several Northern states.

We have no clear record of the amounts or patterns of these foreign purchases, and the weapons which survive today are bewildering in their variation. In this connection it must be recalled that foreign weapons often changed hands during the war and that numerous examples arrived in this country and entered arms collections long after 1865. The reader is referred to the section on foreign purchases in Chapter 3 for an overall coverage.

Muskets and Rifles

● *U.S. (Rifle) Musket, Model 1842.* Caliber .69, rifled and equipped with long range rear sights; this was a regulation weapon. The Confederate infantryman also carried 1842 smoothbores and conversions of earlier U.S. models, and as late as 1862 some flintlocks were still in use. All carried socket bayonets.

● *U.S. Rifle, Model 1841.* This weapon was called the "Mississippi rifle" in the South. Re-rifled to caliber .58, it was one of the regulation small arms. Saber bayonet "of Harper's Ferry pattern." Also used in its original caliber .54. with and without being fitted for a saber bayonet.

● *Fayetteville Rifle.* Made at the Fayetteville Armory & Arsenal, 1862-1865, using machinery captured at Harpers Ferry for making the U.S. Rifle Model 1855. Caliber .58, rifled with 6 grooves, 49 in. overall. Barrel, usually with bright finish, provided with a regular Model 1855 rifle front and rear sight, brass furniture. Early rifles were made with patch boxes and humpback lock plates which were not used after 1862. Several other variations existed; in types of hammer, bands, etc. Locks were usually stamped "FAYETTEVILLE", "C.S.A." under an eagle, and with the year. Until 1864 provided with lug for saber bayonet on the right of the barrel: About 20,000 manufactured.

Saber bayonet with slightly curved blade, wide near point, brass hilt; socket bayonet provided in 1864 and 1865.

● *U.S. Rifle Musket, Model 1855.* A regulation Confederate weapon. Socket bayonet, 18 in. blade.

● *Richmond Rifle Musket.* Made at the Richmond Armory & Arsenal, 1862-1865, as an almost exact copy of the Model 1855 rifle musket. It did not use the Maynard primer but retained the humpback shape of the lock plate. Locks were usually stamped "C.S./RICHMOND, VA." and the year. Iron bands and trigger guard, brass nose cap and butt plate. Most weapons were fitted with canvas slings. The Richmond Armory also made paper cartridges. About 11,762 rifle muskets were produced, considered to be the best weapon manufactured in the South. U.S. Model 1855 socket bayonet, 18 in. blade.

See 37th Arkansas Inf. Also, Plate VII

- *U.S. Rifle, Model 1855.* A regulation Confederate weapon. Saber bayonet, 21.5-21.75 in. blade.
- *Enfield Rifled Musket, Pattern 1853.* A regulation Confederate weapon, probably the most widely used of all. Socket bayonet. All Enfields were caliber .577. *Fig. 33*
- *Enfield short rifles Patterns 1856, 1858, and 1860.* While not listed separately as regulation weapons, large numbers were used by Confederate infantry and the patterns were considered regulation. Saber bayonet, 22.75-in. yataghan blade. *Fig. 34*
- *Tyler, Texas, Enfield Rifle.* Made at the Tyler, Texas, Armory when operating under the Confederate Ordance Department, 1864-1865. Used old barrels of the short Enfield patterns with caliber .577, 5-groove rifling, lug for saber bayonet, and 2-leafed rear sight. Brass furniture, butt shaped like U.S. regulation rifle, overall length 48.5 in. Variations from the above probably were common, such as iron bands, shorter length, etc. Various markings on lock plate but usually "TEXAS RIFLE/TYLER", with "C.S." or "Enfield RIFLE". Not known how many were produced. Saber bayonet. *Fig. 147*

The Tyler Armory also produced an "Austrian Rifle," caliber .54, based on a caliber .54 Austrian barrel; it is doubtful that many were produced.
- *Cook Infantry Rifle.* Made by Cook & Brother, Athens, Ga. under contract with the Confederate Ordnance Department, 1863-1864. Patterned after the short Enfield with caliber .577, 5-groove rifling. Brass furniture, overall length 49 in. Sling swivels on forward band and butt stock. Lock plate marked "COOK & BROTHER ATHENS, GA.", with date and serial number, and a Confederate flag to the rear of the hammer. Probably more than 20,000 produced. Saber bayonet with curved blade and brass hilt; later socket bayonet.

Sharpshooters' Rifles

Small bore caliber .45 rifles produced in England were exported to the Confederacy as arms for sharpshooters. They could only have formed a tiny portion of the South's stock of firearms, and their importance has probably been exaggerated in recent years, much as that of the Pennsylvania rifle in the American Revolution. These rifles were relatively expensive and were produced in considerable variety. The more common types are listed below.
- *Enfield type Sharpshooter's Rifle.* Percussion muzzleloader, caliber .45, rifled with 5 grooves. Overall length 49.2 in. No provision for bayonet; heavily checkered stock. In general appearance similar to the Enfield Short Rifle Pattern 1858. Metal either case-hardened or browned. Rings for sling swivels on upper band, trigger guard, and underside of butt. Rear sight graduated to 1000 yards. Marked on lock plate: "BIRMINGHAM/SMALL ARMS TRADE" (no crown), on top of barrel "TURNER'S PATENT".

Another type was similar to above in most respects; overall length 52 in., sight graduated to 1200 yards. Caliber .45, rifled with 7 grooves on the system later used in the Martini-Henry rifle. Marked on top of barrel: "HENRY'S PATENT RIFLING"; lock plate marking uncertain.
- *Whitworth Rifle.* This was a special sharpshooter's rifle made by the Whitworth Rifle Co., Manchester, England, in several different models. Hexagonal bore with slightly rounded corners, caliber .45; used an elongated bullet weighing 530 grains.

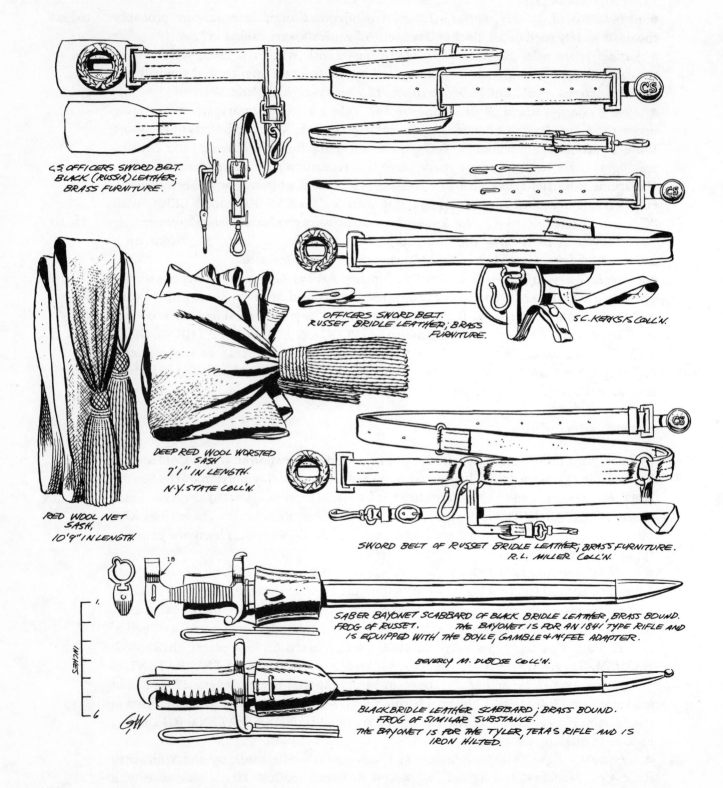

CS OFFICERS SWORD BELT.
BLACK (RUSSIA) LEATHER;
BRASS FURNITURE.

OFFICERS SWORD BELT.
RUSSET BRIDLE LEATHER; BRASS
FURNITURE.

S.C. KERKSIS COLL'N.

DEEP RED WOOL WORSTED
SASH
7'1" IN LENGTH.
N.Y. STATE COLL'N.

RED WOOL NET
SASH,
10'9" IN LENGTH.

SWORD BELT OF RUSSET BRIDLE LEATHER; BRASS FURNITURE.
R.L. MILLER COLL'N.

SABER BAYONET SCABBARD OF BLACK BRIDLE LEATHER, BRASS BOUND.
FROG OF RUSSET.   THE BAYONET IS FOR AN 1841 TYPE RIFLE AND
IS EQUIPPED WITH THE BOYLE, GAMBLE & McFEE ADAPTER.

BEVERLY M. DUBOSE COLL'N.

BLACK BRIDLE LEATHER SCABBARD; BRASS BOUND.
FROG OF SIMILAR SUBSTANCE.
THE BAYONET IS FOR THE TYLER, TEXAS RIFLE AND IS
IRON HILTED.

INCHES

Fig. 147. Confederate States belts, sashes, frogs and scabbards, 1861-1865.

Overall length 49 in., iron mounted and usually provided with an attachment for a telescopic sight. Lock plate marked "WHITWORTH RIFLE CO., MANCHESTER".

The Whitworth was considered the most accurate weapon of its period. It was exceptionally well made, with all the characteristics and the high cost of a fine sporting rifle. Some were imported and issued to special sharpshooter units.

See 4th Georgia Inf.

● *Kerr Sharpshooter's Rifle.* Another imported sharpshooter rifle was made by the London Armoury Co. Caliber .45, with rifling in 6 grooves, ratchett form, without angles. Same bullet as the Whitworth. Overall length c. 53 in. Lock plate marked with crown over "V.R." and "L.A. Co." under a year, while the breech was stamped or engraved "KERR'S PATENT", etc. The Kerr resembled the Pattern 1858 Enfield and was sometimes referred to as the "Enfield .45." Its barrel was shortened in front to bring the muzzle 1.2 in. from the nose cap; there was no provision for a bayonet. In some examples all mountings were iron; in others the trigger guard, butt plate, and nose cap were brass. Floral designs were engraved on lock plate, hammer, butt plate and other parts.

Other Rifles

Some 100,000 Lorenz Model 1854 rifles of different sizes, but all caliber .54, were imported from Austria. They functioned well with the caliber .54 ammunition used with the U.S. Model 1841 rifle, of which there was a considerable supply.

Other infantry shoulder arms recognized by the Confederate Ordnance Department but not considered regulation were the British infantry muskets of Patterns 1839 and 1842, the Brunswick rifle, and various Liège-made rifles, all described under U.S. small arms in Chapter 3. Infantry weapons made in small lots under state contracts will be described under the state involved.

A final general statement should be made about Confederate rifles and muskets. Whereas all U.S. models were fitted with leather slings, issue of this piece of equipment had to be stopped due to the shortage of leather. Its place was taken by a cotton cloth sling until the Ordnance Department in 1864 was able to furnish "gunslings made of good leather." Yet the supply hardly kept up with the demand. In a list of items issued from the Richmond Arsenal during three and a half years of war there appear 323,231 infantry arms but only 115,087 gun and carbine slings.

Carbines and Musketoons

The Ordnance *Field Manual* of 1862 commented that "no model has yet been adopted for a carbine for the cavalry service; several different patterns are now in the hands of the troops." Nor was any single carbine ever adopted as regulation throughout the war unless we except the Tallassee model, which was manufactured too late to see service. The only breechloading carbine made in any number — the Richmond Sharps — was the subject of considerable criticism.

At first the Confederate cavalry companies were supplied with whatever arms they could find themselves. Double-barrel shotguns were common; sabers were often available, and here and there a few companies were supplied with pistols or revolvers, or with miscellaneous carbines calling for different ammunition. The Secretary of War wrote in February 1862 that he would accept lancers and provide the lances if necessary. The Confederate Ordnance Department at that time had no pistols to issue, and few of anything else.

As the war progressed the Confederate cavalryman learned to pick up Federal arms and equipment and in time nearly every regiment was well supplied. But this practice had its drawbacks since the carbines captured or recovered were of a dozen different varieties, most requiring special ammunition that the Confederates were in no position to provide. In the end the soldier's practice of exchanging his own weapon for a better one on the battlefield had to be officially forbidden because of its disastrous effect on the ammunition supply. Despite a continuous call from the field for breechloaders, the Confederate Ordnance Department had, in the end, to settle for muzzleloaders, as much because of the ammunition problem as any other.

The principal carbines and musketoons issued by the Confederate Ordnance Department were as follows.

- *Enfield Cavalry Carbine, Pattern 1858.* Probably imported in considerable numbers, particularly late in the war. Some fitted with sling swivels, others with bars and sling rings. Carbine "scabbards" sometimes furnished.
- *Richmond Carbine.* Made at the Richmond Armory & Arsenal, 1862-1865, from parts of the Richmond Rifle Musket which it resembled except in length. Caliber .577; overall length 40.5 in.; bright barrel; iron furniture but bronze butt plate and nose cap. High front sight and leaf rear sight; two bands with sling swivel on front band, trigger guard, and butt stock. Lock plate stamped "C.S. RICHMOND, VA" and the year. At least 2,700 of these carbines were produced by October 1863.
- *Tallassee Carbine.* Made at the Tallassee, Ala., Armory in 1865, under Confederate Ordnance Department control. Caliber .58; overall length 40.5 in. Bright barrel, Enfield type lock marked "CS Tallassee Ala." and date, brass furniture, sling swivels on upper band and in rear of lock plate. Swivel ramrod similar to that on U.S. musketoons; no sling bar or ring. This carbine was the only model officially designed and adopted for the Confederate service. A board of officers of General J.E.B. Stuart's command determined upon it in August 1863. About 500 were made but it would appear that none were issued in time to see service.
- *Cook Artillery Musketoon (or Carbine).* Made by Cook & Brother, Athens, Ga. Resembled the Cook infantry rifle except for length, which was 40 in. overall. Caliber .577, 5-groove rifling. All brass furniture; sling swivels on upper band and butt stock. Lock plate marked "COOK & BROTHER, ATHENS, GA." with date and serial number, and Confederate flag. No bayonet provided. At least 2,379 made. Like the rifle, often called "Cook's Enfield."

See 11th Georgia Cav.

- *Cook Cavalry Carbine.* Made as above and generally resembling the artillery carbine except in length, which was 36.5 in. overall. Swivel ramrod attached by very short swivel bars. Enfield type nipple protector furnished with some. No bayonet provided and no sling rod or ring. The 11th Georgia Cavalry found it to be "easily broken."
- *U.S. Carbine Models 1840, 1842, and 1843 (Hall-North).* Some of these percussion caliber .52 carbines were in Confederate service.
- *Burnside Carbine.* Listed as in use; caliber .54.

- *Maynard Carbine.* Listed in use in two calibers, .52 and .37, both fitted with the Maynard primer.
- *Sharps Carbine.* Model 1859 listed as in use; caliber .52 with vertical breechblock.
- *Confederate (or Richmond) Sharps Carbine.* Made at S.C. Robinson Arms Manufactory, Richmond, Va., 1862-1863. This arm was a copy of the Model 1859, above, but without the Lawrence primer device. Brass butt plate and band. About 3,000 produced; despite defects these appear to have been continued in service. Lock plate marked "S.C. ROBINSON/ARMS MANUFACTORY/RICHMOND VA", and date until early 1863; thereafter merely "RICHMOND VA" on barrel.

Conversion of Shotguns and Sporting Rifles

In addition to the carbines and musketoons listed above (plus other patterns personally acquired or provided by states), the Confederate soldier — the cavalryman especially — carried privately owned shotguns and sporting (or "country") rifles. To repair and alter these weapons for use in the field, the Confederate Ordnance Department established shops throughout the South. The Sutherland shops at Richmond were one of the largest establishments, and the weapons they altered were generally so marked. Other important shops were located at Nashville, Pulaski, Memphis, and Murfreesboro, Tennessee.

Alteration of these civilian weapons, naturally, took many forms, but as far as possible they were cut to a uniform length and their barrels bored out and sometimes rifled to the regulation caliber .577. Infantry weapons were fitted with bayonets, and cavalry arms given sling swivels or rings. Flintlocks were converted to percussion arms. Shotguns, if percussion, were usually left pretty much as is, since the opinion of one cavalry officer "that the double-barrel shotgun is the best gun [with] which cavalry can be armed" was widely shared, at least in the early days of the war.

Pistols and Revolvers

The Ordnance *Field Manual* of 1862 stipulated that "a repeating pistol is issued to the cavalry." Unfortunately, this was not entirely possible, even by 1862. As late as February of that year the Secretary of War had written "we have no pistols," and it was to be many months before the Confederate Ordnance Department could issue revolvers in any number to Confederate enlisted men.

This does not mean, of course, that the Confederate officer or cavalryman could not have carried a pistol or even a revolver of current make. In fact, many did. The supply of Colts, Smith & Wessons, and other makes was fairly ample in 1861 in the various Southern military outfitting stores, and it appears that they were able to procure some replenishment of their stocks even as late as 1863. Many early regiments of infantry and artillery went to war with their men carrying personally owned revolvers stuck in their belts — often gifts of families or friends — which quickly used up the stock. But in time the Ordance Department caught up with them. After March 1862, the infantryman carried only his musket as a weapon, and the artilleryman came to rely solely on his field gun, for in that month he was by order not "permitted to carry other side-arms than those issued by the Government, or such as are appropriate to their arm of service" (A&IG CSA GO 17). The pistols and revolvers (and other arms) turned in were purchased by the general government, reconditioned, sorted, and reissued to mounted commands.

The *Field Manual* had this to say about the revolver: "Colt's pistol is used in our service, and is constructed on the revolving principle, with a cylinder containing six chambers and a rifled barrel." It mentioned both the army and navy models but it is clear from other sources that the caliber .36 navy Colt was adopted as the regulation revolver for issue. All Ordnance Department contracts were made for this caliber and all but one for this model; the numerous other revolvers used in the Confederacy were in the main purchased by officers. There was, of course, no regulation governing the sidearms officers could carry.

The principal makes of revolver issued by the Confederate Ordnance Department were:
- *Colt Navy Percussion Revolver, Model 1851.* This caliber .36, six-shot, single-action revolver was, as has been said, adopted as standard. Four copies of it were made in the South under an act of the Confederate Congress to encourage home production, approved 19 April 1862.
- *Leech & Rigdon Revolver.* Made under contract in 1863 in Greensboro, Ga. Marked on top of barrel "LEECH & RIGDON CSA". Trigger guard, handle strap, and front sight of brass. It is believed that this firm made about 350 similar revolvers in Columbus, Miss. prior to the contract.
- *Rigdon, Ansley & Co. Revolver.* Made in 1864 in Augusta, Ga. by successors to the firm above under the same contract. This revolver is similar to the Leech & Rigdon except it was given twelve cylinder stops as a safety device. Marked on top of barrel "AUGUSTA, GA. C.S.A." Including revolvers made by Leech & Rigdon prior to its contract, it has been estimated that at least 2,330 were produced by these two firms.
- *Haiman (or Columbus Fire Arms Manufacturing Co.) Revolver.* Made under contract in Columbus, Ga., 1863-1864, closely resembling the Leech & Rigdon model but of inferior workmanship. Marked on top of barrel: "COLUMBUS FIRE ARMS MANUF. CO., COLUMBUS" and on trigger guard plate: "C.S." Not known how many were produced, but probably less than 100. The plant was taken over by the Ordnance Department but no revolvers appear to have been produced thereafter.
- *Griswold & Gunnison Revolver.* Made under contract at Griswoldville, near Macon, Ga., 1862-1864. Distinguished from others of this type by having a brass frame and no marking except serial numbers and small unexplained letters. Estimated total of about 3,500 made. Change made from a round to a part octagonal barrel housing about half way through production.

The Colt copies produced in Texas by Tucker & Sherrod and Dance Bros. & Park were for private sale.
- *Whitney Navy Percussion Revolver.* This caliber .36, six-shot, single-action revolver was manufactured at the Whitneyville Armory, near New Haven, Conn. Probably considered regulation since it could take the same ammunition as the navy Colt. It served as a pattern for one Confederate-made revolver.
- *Spiller & Burr Revolver.* Made in Atlanta, Ga. under contract, 1863-1864, and thereafter by the Ordnance Department in Macon, Ga. Octagonal barrel, six-shot, caliber .36, rifled with 7 grooves, brass frame. Contract arms marked on top of barrel

"SPILLER & BURR" and sometimes on left side of frame "C.S."; later arms unmarked except for "C.S." and serial number. At least 1,400 made.

One other model of revolver must be considered regulation since it was mentioned in the *Field Manual* and definite contracts were made by the Confederate War and Navy Departments for its manufacture. This was the Le Mat "grapeshot" revolver, the invention of a New Orleans physician, manufactured in France. During its period of manufacture for the Confederacy, the design underwent several changes. Even so, the revolver retained certain marked defects, not the least being its caliber .42 which required special ammunition. Some 2,500 were manufactured and a large share of these reached the South during the war.

● *Le Mat "Grapeshot" Revolver.* Made 1862-1865 (and later) by C. Girard & Co., Paris, France. Upper and under barrel with revolving cylinder containing 9 shots, caliber .42, firing through the upper rifled barrel. Under barrel smoothbore of caliber .60, or about 20 gauge, which served as the axle on which the cylinder revolved. The nose of the hammer could be adjusted to fire either barrel. Made in three general models; the serial number range for these models is believed to be: 1st Model, 1-450; Transition Model, 451-950; 2nd Model, 951-2500. Marking on top of barrel differed considerably with the models, two common ones being "Col. Le Mat's Patent" and "Systeme Le Mat Bte. s.g.d.g. Paris."

Among the American revolvers known to have been used by Confederate officers with some frequency, beside the ones mentioned above, were the Colt army, Remington army and navy, and the Smith & Wesson "Model No. 2." This last model, using a caliber .32, rim-fire metallic cartridge, was popular with officers in 1861 as a personal or pocket side arm, but had to be discarded because of the difficulty in procuring cartridges. These weapons are listed under U.S. revolvers in Chapter 3.

At least nine foreign percussion and cartridge models were imported during the Civil War and saw varying amounts of service. Some of these will be described under the several states. The best known ones were:

● *Deane-Adams Revolver.* Made in England by Deane, Adams, and Deane, between 1851 and 1857, in three sizes with calibers .50, .44, and .32. All were 5-shot, double-action weapons with checkered walnut grips. Several improvements introduced, notably the Beaumont double-action in 1855. Replaced in 1857 by the Adams pattern, below.

● *Adams (or Beaumont-Adams) Army Revolver, Model 1857.* Made in England by the London Armoury Co. in caliber .44; 5-shot, double-action. The revolver used a self-consuming combustible cartridge, had checkered walnut grips, and all of its metal parts were blued, This model was adopted for the British army.

● *Kerr Army Revolver, Model 1859.* Made in England by the London Armoury Co. in calibers .44 and .38; 5-shot, single- (later double-) action with a side hammer that greatly simplified repair of the weapon. There is some reason to believe that the Confederate purchasing agent in England maintained an exclusive export contract for this revolver during most of the war. Octagonal barrel, checkered walnut grips, lanyard ring on butt.

● *Tranter Revolvers.* Made in Birmingham, England by William Tranter in four principal sizes, all 6-shot, double-action. Calibers were .50, .44, .38, and .32. Both single- and double-trigger actions produced. These revolvers were popular in the South before the Civil War and many were imported by military outfitters there, whose names were stamped on top of the barrel. Probably imported commercially during the war.

- *Lefaucheux Pin-fire Revolver.* Made in France. Calibers 10, 11, and 12 mm.; 6-shot, using a pin-fire metallic cartridge. Cylinder has loading gate on the right side. Plain wooden grips; lanyard ring on butt. Marked on top of barrel "INVon E. LEFAUCHEUX, BRte PARIS".
- *Devisme Revolver.* Made in France. Calibers .36 and .45, 6-shot, octagonal barrel. Loading tool in butt, cocking lever on side. Marked on top of barrel "Devisme à Paris".
- *Raphael Revolver.* Made in France. Caliber .42, 6-shot, double-action, using a center-fire metallic cartridge. Steel trigger guard and walnut grips.
- *Perrin Revolver.* Made in France. Caliber .44, 6-shot, double-action, probably using a center-fire metallic cartridge. Plain wooden grips with lanyard ring on butt. Metal parts bright. Marked on right of frame. "PERRIN/& Cie Bte", and on left: "*/PARIS".
- *Houllier & Blanchard Revolver.* Made in France. Caliber .44, 6-shot (no further data).

Finally, the reader should be reminded that weapons of any sort were none too plentiful in the South during the Civil War, revolvers especially. Many a Confederate soldier carried a single-shot percussion pistol, and not a few for a time had to rely on flintlocks. These pistols reflected all the models produced by U.S. and State armories for twenty or more years before the war, plus homemade contrivances of many sorts. Some effort was made even in Confederate armories during the first year of the war to produce single-shot percussion pistols out of captured parts, but this production was soon abandoned in favor of more profitable work.

Swords and Knives

The first published statement concerning Confederate swords is included in the dress regulations of June 1861: "SWORD AND SCABBARD . . . For all officers — according to patterns to be deposited in the Ordnance Bureau." What these patterns were or, indeed, if any were ever deposited, cannot be determined, but the chances are long that they were the U.S. Army regulations sidearms. The section on swords and sabers in the Confederate *Ordnance Manual* of 1863 is a verbatim copy of the U.S. manual except that "C.S." is substituted for "U.S."

Students of Confederate arms agree with William A. Albaugh, III that edged weapons were made at so many points in the South during the Civil War that it would be an impossibility to record the manufacturers, to say nothing of listing and categorizing all their products. Any blacksmith shop could make a sword or knife and many did. From such virtually homemade weapons the list runs to handsome arms with imported or skillfully fabricated parts. Mr. Albaugh has endeavored with considerable success to record the better known producers of Confederate swords and knives and no attempt will be made here to detail his findings. The account below can only generalize upon the edged weapons believed to have been authorized or issued by the Confederate general government. For broader background the reader is referred to the general treatment of U.S. edged weapons in Chapter 3.

Enlisted Men's Swords and Sabers

- *Cavalry Sabers, U.S. Models 1840 and Light Cavalry.* Copies of these sabers, more or less faithful depending upon facilities, with curved blades 34-36 inches in length, were made by Boyle, Gamble & MacFee; James Conning; E.J. Johnson & Co.; Thomas Griswold & Co.; and others. On 15 November 1863, Colonel Gorgas reported that "the supply of sabers produced under contract is abundant, though the style of workmanship admits of great improvement." A few months before "the sabers issued by the Department" had been called by Lee's Cavalry Brigade "miserably inferior weapons." By then the bulk of the swords of these models in use were captured from U.S. stocks or recovered from the battlefield.

- *"Ames pattern" sabers.* Some of the cavalry sabers produced resembled the U.S. model 1833 dragoon saber produced by N.P. Ames of Springfield, Mass., which in turn was patterned after the British light cavalry saber of 1822. These usually had slightly curved blades of about 34 inches, semi-bird's head pommels, half-basket guards, brass hilts, and steel scabbards. Such swords, representing a type rather than a pattern, were made by Louis Haiman & Bro.; College Hill Arsenal; and others.

- *British Cavalry Saber, Enfield Pattern 1853.* Cut and thrust type; almost straight blade, 34.5 in., with single fuller on either side. Flat iron or brass knuckle bow with 2 branches; flat oval counter-guard with quillon ending in a disk. No pommel, leather grips riveted to the tang with 5 rivets. Iron scabbard with 2 rings. Imported examples were stamped "Isaac & Co" on back of the blade or "MOLE" in the same place and under the guard. Additional stampings included "COURTNEY & TENNANT, CHARLESTON, S.C." (an importer) and "C.S.A."

- *Light Artillery Saber, U.S. Model 1840.* As in the U.S. Army, the use of this weapon was greatly reduced under actual war conditions. Artillerymen preferred other means of defence and their sabers soon found their way into the cavalry. Surviving examples of Confederate-made copies are rare and it is doubtful if any were contracted for by the Ordnance Department or even issued, except in emergencies. Light artillery sabers were, however, made by William J. McElroy & Co. (possibly only for officers); James Conning (under an Alabama contract); and probably others.

- *Foot Artillery Sword, U.S. Model 1833.* There is no evidence that this sword was ever contracted for by the Ordnance Department. A substantial number were on hand in 1861, being worn or in captured stocks, and were probably issued to artillery units during the first year of the war. At least four variants of the model (two marked with "CS") were fabricated in private armories, probably in response to state or local orders. Some were supplied with wooden scabbards. Despite the apparent uselessness of this weapon, it should be remembered it was patterned after a sword that had conquered and held the western world for over five centuries, and a romantic approach to classical history was not dead in the South. In this sense it fulfilled the Confederate soldiers' desire for a side-knife.

- *NCO Sword, U.S. Model 1840.* Again, there is no record of an Ordnance Department issue of this weapon, and certainly the use of swords by Confederate NCO's was limited after the first year of the war. However, there exists an interesting version of this sword, made by W. Walsoneid of Solingen, Germany and bearing the raised letters "CSA" on its turned-down brass counterguard. Crude copies were made locally in the South.

Although the U.S. Army regulation *Musician's Sword* is listed in the Confederate Ordnance Manual, there is no evidence that it was worn to any extent or considered a regulation weapon in the South.

Officers' Swords and Sabers

● *Staff and Field Officers' Sword, U.S. Model 1850.* This model was widely copied by Southern and European swordmakers, with "CS" or "CSA" substituted for the "US" on the original. Considerable variation in size, design, and embellishment can be found from one maker to another, and even within the product of one maker as he strove to satisfy individual whim. Officers, of course, bought their own swords and some carried heirlooms that might date fifty years back in American history.

● *Foot Officers' Sword, U.S. Model 1850.* Copied widely by Southern and European swordmakers; often given added embellishment and the "CS" or "CSA". Considerable variation existed, as mentioned above.

(The U.S. Army regulation *Staff and Field Officers' Sword, Model 1860* is included in the Confederate *Ordnance Manual* of 1863 but does not appear to have been carried to any extent.)

Side Knives

The background of the bowie knife and other knife patterns of the 1850's and 1860's has already been covered in Chapter 3. It is sufficient to repeat that most soldiers in the Civil War carried a knife of some sort, for general use if not for fighting. The use of larger knives, worn normally in a sheath on a belt and designed primarily for fighting, was also fairly general on both sides in 1861, but thereafter the picture changed. The Northern soldier soon discarded the big knife while the Confederate — not so well armed as a rule — tended to hold on to it, in many cases throughout the war.

These larger weapons were officially termed "side knives" although the soldier usually called them all "Bowies." The majority of such knives, it would seem, were homemade from any materials at hand. Many others were produced in Southern factories on a production basis and often of the best English cast steel. Still others were imported. Although one student of the subject has suggested that knives "were issued en masse to Confederate troops" it seems more likely that the knife remained essentially a personally procured weapon. Certainly, small lots of side knives were presented to military companies by local groups, but the idea of a formal issue of them by the Confederate Ordnance Department, or even by the states in any number, is erroneous.

The blades of side knives ranged from 6 to 18 or more inches long; in width, from perhaps 1.5 to 3 inches. They came with both clipped and spear points; guards were of brass or iron, and grips of wood, horn or metal. Some Confederate military knives were fitted with D-shaped knuckle-bows, a feature almost never found before or after the war. Some of the manufactured knives were engraved with "Death to Abolition" and other mottoes.

Lances and Pikes

The lance as a cavalry weapon played as insignificant a role in the South as it did in the North. It had not been carried by any state cavalry commands south of the Potomac as far back as 1851, hence there was no tradition for its use. But as the war entered 1862 and the supply of cavalry weapons dwindled, a few serious and doubtless many romantic voices were raised urging its adoption. General Joseph E. Johnston in early February wrote the Secretary of War recommending additional cavalry be raised as lancers and be given a weapon with a seven- or eight-inch head and a ten-foot shaft, preferably of ash. Apparently his men already had some lances, since he complained that "those furnished to us are — many of them of heavy wood and too short, the heads too thin and unnecessarily broad."

At about the same moment the Confederate Congress instructed its Committee on Military Affairs to inquire into the propriety of arming troops with pikes, lances, spears, or shotguns. According to the memoirs of General Gorgas, some lances had already been manufactured in Confederate arsenals by this time.

A number of Confederate lances and lance pennons have survived. The most common type had an 8-foot ash staff with a flat spear point, 10 inches long and 1.75 inch wide. Wrought-iron straps extended down the staff on two sides, each held by four rivets. The pennon was a forked Stars-and-Bars flag, 17 x 12 inches, crudely sewn, with 11 stars; it was tacked to the staff. A leather wrist loop was attached midway up the staff, and there was an iron ferrule at the bottom.

The spearheads and pennons on other lances differed somewhat in design and there is no record that a standard pattern was ever adopted.

It is probable that one company of the 5th Virginia Cavalry was armed with lances issued by the general government as early as April 1862, and from the memoirs of its colonel, Thomas L. Rosser, it would seem that the regiment carried them in the fight at Catlett's Station that August. If so, it was their last appearance, for Rosser had his men throw away their lances following the battle.

Lances were being carried by Texan cavalrymen even earlier than this, but our knowledge of them is limited. At least one company of the 5th Texas Cavalry of Sibley's Brigade had them at Valverde, 21 February 1862, with blades three inches wide and twelve long, and nine-foot shafts. These will be described further under Texas.

About the only other mention of lances were those carried by a mounted infantry regiment in Colonel Joseph O. Shelby's cavalry brigade in southwest Missouri later in the year. We have no description of them, and it is possible that they were actually pikes rather than lances, although they were given "gay flags." These weapons also were abandoned in short order, and with them the lance disappeared from the Confederacy.

If Confederate lances and information about them are scarce, Confederate pikes and related literature are more than plentiful. They were made in virtually every Southern state during the Civil War. While their use in actual battle was so slight as to be almost unrecorded and certainly unimportant, they did form the armament of state troops from time to time. If pikes were actually manufactured and issued by the Confederate

Ordnance Department, there is no clear record to this effect and we certainly have no indication of any specific pattern that could be called a standard item. For this reason pikes will be treated under those states which are known to have contracted for their manufacture, notably Georgia.

Accouterments

The *Richmond Enquirer* of 1 April 1865, the last number to be published under Confederate rule, carried an official statement of the principal equipments issued by the Richmond Arsenal during the three and a half years prior to 1 January 1865. It included these figures on accouterments:

    375,510 sets of infantry and cavalry accouterments
    180,181 knapsacks
    328,977 canteens and straps
     69,418 cavalry saddles
     85,139 cavalry bridles
     75,611 cavalry halters
     35,464 saddle blankets
      6,852 sets of artillery harness

Since Richmond was only one of several issuing arsenals, some idea can be gained of the work of the Ordnance Department in this area. The clearest picture of the problems faced comes from General Gorgas himself, writing after the Civil War for *The Confederate Soldier in the Civil War* (1897; p. 326).

In equipping the armies first sent into the field the supply of these accessories was amazingly scant; and these deficiencies were felt more keenly, perhaps, than the more important want of arms. We had arms, such as they were, for over one hundred thousand men; but we had no accouterments nor equipments; and these had to be extemporized in a great measure. In time, knapsacks were little thought of by the troops, and we at last contented ourselves with supplying haversacks, which the women (Heaven reward their labors) could make, and for which we could get cotton cloth. But cartridge boxes we *must* have; and as leather was also needed for artillery harness and cavalry saddles, we had to divide the stock of leather the country could produce among these much needed articles. But soldiers' shoes were even more needed than some of these; so that as all could not be fully provided, a scale of preference was established. Shoes and cartridge boxes were most needed, and then saddles and bridles. The President, whose practical sagacity was rarely at fault, early reduced these interests to logical sequence. He said, "For the infantry, men must first be fed, next armed, and even clothing must follow these; for if they are fed and have arms and ammunition they can fight. Thus the Subsistence Department had, in a general way, a preference for its requisitions on the Treasury; my department came next, and the Quartermaster's followed. Of course the Medical Department had in some things the lead of all, for its duties referred to the men themselves, and it was necessary first of all to keep the hospitals empty and the ranks full.

To economize leather, the cartridge boxes and waist belts were made of prepared cotton cloth, stitched in three or four thicknesses. Bridle reins were also so made, and even cartridge-boxes covered with it, except the flap. Saddle skirts, to, were sometimes made in this way, heavily stitched. An ardent admirer of the South came over from Washington to offer his patent for making soldiers' shoes with no leather except the soles. The shoes were approved by all except those who wore them. The soldiers exchanged them with the first prostrate enemy who no longer needed his leathern articles. To get leather each department bargained for its own hides — made contracts with the tanner — procured hands for him by exemption from the army — got transportation over the railroads for the hides and for supplies, and, finally, assisted the tanner to procure food for his hands and other supplies for his tannery. One can readily see from this instance how the labors of the heads of the departments became extended. Nothing but thorough organization could accomplish these multiplied and varied duties. We even established a fishery on the Cape Fear River to get oil for mechanical purposes, getting from the sturgeon *beef* at the same time for our workmen.

Cartridge Boxes and Pouches

Figs. 144 and 145

In his report of 15 November 1863, Colonel Gorgas noted the following about cartridge boxes produced and issued by the armories, arsenals and workshops under his control:

Repaired	2,123
Purchased	126,733
Fabricated	34,666
Issued to the Army	171,251

The "purchased" boxes represented, of course, those secured from Southern firms as well as those imported. The variation among these boxes — among all classes of accouterments, for that matter — in design, size, and quality was very great. Yet it is probably possible to isolate the more common types which were considered as regulation.

The Confederate infantryman preferred to carry his cartridge box on his waist belt rather than on one over his shoulder. For this purpose vertical loops were added to the back of boxes not so equipped. To ease the load around the waist he sometimes put packaged cartridges elsewhere on his person. Yet boxes on shoulder belts were worn and it is a mistake to consider vertical loops a mark of identification for Confederate boxes. The musket and rifle boxes probably treated as regulation were these:

● *U.S. Regulation Boxes Model 1855 (for calibers .58 and .69).* Issued after removal of the brass "US" plate or the substitution of a "CS" plate. However, the relatively small number of boxes "repaired" suggests that such adaption took place chiefly on campaign.

● *C.S. Box for caliber .577 Rifle Musket.* Black bridle leather, double flaps, the inner one stamped "C.S. ARSENAL/BATON ROUGE, LA" in .25-in. letters. Implement pocket; 2 vertical loops on rear. Inside dimensions 6.7 x 1.5 x 4 in. Two tin inserts resembling U.S. regulation except in size. Will accept 40 rounds caliber .577 paper cartridges.

● *Enfield Rifle Musket Box.* This box was imported in considerable numbers.

● *C.S. Box for caliber .577 Rifle Musket.* Russet bridle leather; implement pocket of soft leather, single flap. Inside dimensions 6.2 x 1.3 x 4.5 in. Small vertical and horizontal loops on rear and 2 buckles on bottom. Probably single tin insert with 3 compartments above and 2 below. No markings.

• *C.S. Box for caliber .577 Musket.* Russet bridle leather; implement pocket of soft leather, double flaps. Inside dimensions about 6.5 x 1.6 x 5.8 in. Single tin insert with 4 compartments above and 2 below. Single wide vertical loop on rear. Outside flap embossed with "CS" inside oval.

• *C.S. Box for caliber .577 Rifle Musket.* Russet bridle leather; implement pocket of soft leather, double flaps. Inside dimensions 6.6 x 1.4 x 6 in. Double tin insert, each with 2 compartments above and 1 below. Two horizontal and 2 vertical loops on rear; 2 buckles on bottom. Outside flap embossed with "CS" (letters 1.1 in. high) inside oval; inner flap stamped "M.H./RICHMOND/AND SONS".

• *C.S. Box for caliber .577 Rifle Musket.* Black bridle leather; implement pocket of soft leather, double flaps. Inside dimensions 6.75 x 1.4 x 5 in. Two tin inserts (like U.S. Model 1855 box), each with 2 compartments above and 1 below. Two horizontal and 2 vertical loops on rear; 2 buckles on bottom. Stamped copper oval plate, c. 2.25 x 3.5 in., with "CS" fixed to outer flap; inner flap stamped "RICHMOND".

(Numerous unmarked boxes of about this size, identified with the Confederacy, exist today. They are of both russet and black leather, with horizontal or vertical loops, or both, single and double flaps.)

• *British Revolver Pouch.* Russet leather, semi-circular shape, single flap fastening to brass stud in front. Inside dimensions 6 x .5 x 4.2 in. in center. No insert; leather cap pocket inside, plus round pocket for combination tool and oiler. Single wide vertical loop fastening to stud on bottom. Stamped inside flap: "S. ISAACS CAMPBELL & Co/ . . . JERMIN ST/LONDON".

• *C.S. Revolver Pouch.* Black leather, single flap, no implement pocket. Inside dimensions about 4 x .75 x 2.25 in. Single tin insert without division. Single vertical loop riveted to back of box. No markings.

• *C.S. Revolver Pouch.* Russet leather, single flap, no implement pocket. Inside dimensions 5.2 x .5 x 3 in. No insert. Single vertical loop on rear. No markings.

• *Possible C.S. Pistol Pouch.* Black bridle leather, single flap, no implement pocket. No insert. Inside dimensions 5.5 x 1.2 x 2 in. Single vertical loop on rear, 1.5 in. wide. No markings.

Fig. 146   **Percussion Cap Pouches**

Cap pouches positively or tentatively identified as Confederate issue exist in considerable variety, many in the splendid collection of Beverly M. DuBose, Jr., of Atlanta. Many are clearly arsenal-made while others, in equal number, were products of some local harness or shoe shop. An interesting example, whose outer flap was cut from a reclaimed S. Isaacs, Campbell & Co. cartridge box, is illustrated.

Many pouches were originally lined inside with sheepskin or some soft fabric and contained a cone pick. Today these are often absent and it is difficult to say now whether or not a pouch was so fitted when issued.

Doubtless all U.S. types were used in the South, and the reader is referred to Chapter 4. Below are patterns believed to have been considered regulation by the Confederate Ordnance Department.

• *C.S. Cap Pouch.* Black bridle leather, double flaps, *outside* measurements 3.25 x

1.25 x 3.25 in. Lined with sheepskin; no cone pick. Single wide vertical loop. Wooden stud on front near bottom. Stamped "CS" in oval on outer flap in .45 in. letters.

- *C.S. Cap Pouch.* Russet bridle leather, double flaps. Inside measurements 2.75 x .63 x 2.63 in. Two vertical loops on rear; brass stud on bottom. Stamped on outer flap "C.S. ARSENAL/BATON ROUGE, LA."
- *C.S. Cap Pouch.* Black bridle leather, double flaps. Inside measurements 2.5 x 1 x 2.5 in. Outer flap, which is stamped "SELMA ARSENAL/TUSCALOOSA DEPOT", covers entire front of pouch. Single loop on rear, wider at top than bottom. Wooden stud on bottom. A very similar pouch was stamped "G.N.WYMAN & Co./ AUGUSTA GA." It had a lead button.
- *C.S. Cap Pouch.* Russet bridle leather, double flaps. Inside measurements 3 x .9 x 2.75 in., the last measurement taken at top. Outer flap covers about half of pouch which narrows in depth toward bottom. Single wide loop on rear; brass stud on front. Unmarked.
- *C.S. Cap Pouch.* Black bridle leather, double flaps. Inside measurements 2.75 x 1 x 2 in.; 3 in. overall height in center. Outer flap covers about two-thirds of pouch. Single wide loop on rear; brass stud on bottom. Unmarked.
- *C.S. Cap Pouch.* Black painted canvas double flaps and rear portion, leather body, loop and strap. Inside measurements 3.2 x .6 x 2.4 in. Outer flap covers entire front. Single wide loop on rear; lead stud on bottom. Unmarked.
- *British-made Cap Pouch.* Russet bridle leather. Inside dimensions about 2.8 x .75 x 2 in. Double flaps; outer flap covers top third of front. Single loop on rear; brass stud on bottom. Embossed on outer flap "CS" in an oval. Slightly wider at bottom than top.
- *British Army Cap Pouch.* White buff leather. Single flap covering half of front held without loop by brass stud. Wide loop on rear set at angle for attachment to a cross belt.

Knapsacks and Haversacks

Fig. 148

Although issue of the knapsack by the Confederate Ordnance Department stopped during the course of the war (say, in 1863), over 180,000 were given out in the early years. The prevalent image of the Confederate infantryman wearing only a blanket roll over his shoulder is only partially valid. Knapsacks were carried in addition to the roll, or with the blanket folded or rolled inside. Incidentally, another method of carrying the blanket — with or without the knapsack — was to arrange it in a short roll and sling it on the middle of the back.

We have no information on the patterns of knapsack actually issued by the Ordnance Department. When the war began all the various patterns of rigid dress knapsack were in use in the militia. The first year brought out novel patented models like the Reith knapsack purchased by the Richmond Zouaves, plus far more numerous homemade single- and double-bag types. What the Confederate authorities settled upon as regulation can only now be guessed at, but three models seem most obvious:

- *Leather Double-Bag Knapsack.* Two sections connected by a 4-in. flexible strip at top; made entirely of black leather. Front section was a semi-rigid box closed by 4 triangular flaps, buckling across; about 11 in. high, by 12.5 in. wide, by 4.5 in. deep. Rear section was an envelope with gussets and a small flap; it buckled to the bottom of the front section by 3 leather straps. Shoulder straps, 2 in. wide, sewn to front and

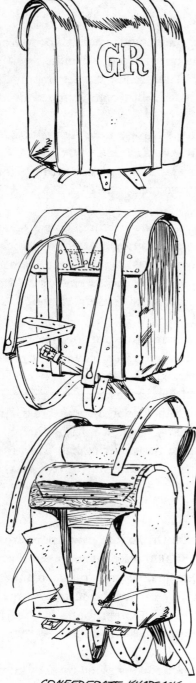

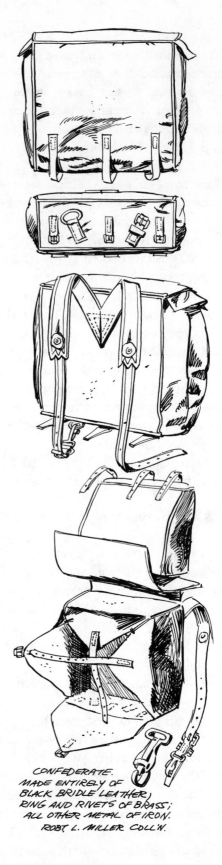

CONFEDERATE KNAPSACK.

WOODEN FRAME WITH CANVAS
FRONT, SIDES AND INNER FLAPS;
A SECTION OF SHEET TIN IS
NAILED TO THE HALF-ROUND TOP
AND A BRIDLE LEATHER FLAP
COVERS THE REAR (OUTER)
FACE. RUSSET LEATHER STRAPS,
IRON BUCKLES.

WORN BY J. CLOARTY, CO "C",
30TH REGT., VA. VOL'S.

N.Y. STATE COLLECTION.

CONFEDERATE.
MADE ENTIRELY OF
BLACK BRIDLE LEATHER,
RING AND RIVETS OF BRASS;
ALL OTHER METAL OF IRON.
ROB'T L. MILLER COLL'N.

Fig. 148. Confederate States knapsacks, 1861-1865.

attached to armpit straps by brass studs; right armpit strap fitted with an iron spring catch that engaged a brass ring on the bottom. No loops for blanket roll straps.

Measurements of this knapsack would have varied considerably. Being made of leather, its production would have ceased by 1862, when it probably was replaced by a painted or rubberized canvas model.

- *Canvas Single-Bag Knapsack.* Non-rigid bag of black painted canvas; approximate size when packed: 15 in. wide, 16 in. high, 3 in. deep. Outer flap was square, 8 in. high, buckled by 2 straps; additional protection on top given by two 3-in. flaps which tied together in center. Two 1-in. straps, riveted and sewn to bottom, completely encircled bag, crossing on the rear, and buckled or hooked again on bottom. By passing under 2 leather loops on top of the knapsack these straps served as carrying straps; a hook and a triangle on one allowed the knapsack to be unslung readily. A piece of ticking inside provided two compartments. No loops for blanket roll straps. (This could as readily have been a Northern militia pattern.)

- *S. Isaacs, Campbell Single-Bag Knapsack.* Semi-rigid box; size fully packed: 14.5 in. high, 15 in. wide, 6 in. deep. Rear enclosed by 3 rectangular flaps buckled by four .75-in. straps, and by outer flap which buckled to bottom by 2 straps. Carrying straps encircled knapsack, being single on the rear and double on the front, attaching to 2 hooks on the bottom. Some stiffening was furnished by leather corner reinforcements and a wooden bar at the top. Stamped inside of flap: "S. ISAACS CAMPBELL/ LONDON". *Fig. 56*

- *Haversacks.* These were of various sizes and styles but followed patterns used in the U.S. Army, or were made like pillow cases with no gussets in the bottom. Unpainted haversacks averaging 12x12 in. with a removable inside bag were the most common.

Canteens

Fig. 59

The remark of a Virginia artilleryman, to the effect that any Southern soldier carrying a Confederate canteen was at once recognized as a new recruit, has already been quoted. Yet the canteen remained a regular article of issue throughout the war, thousands being made in Southern workshops and others imported. It was almost universally worn on campaign by all branches. We have no record of the patterns procured and issued by the Ordnance Department but we can, at least, list four common types used:

- *Cylindrical Tin Types.* "Drum" pattern, round, usually with straight, plain sides. Made of tin and often unpainted, with three tin loops and a tin spout. Diameters from 4.9 to 7.5 in., thickness 1.6 to 2.5 in. Most were fitted with non-adjustable cotton straps and hand carved wooden stoppers. One version, with a single convex face, was 4.9x2.2 (full thickness) and had its top loops set at angles.

- *Convex-sided Tin Types.* Closely allied in design with the types above, were canteens that resembled the U.S. regulation Model 1858. The closest to it, an oblate spheroid of tin, 6.75x2.4 in., was covered with brown wool and fitted with a white cotton sling. Its cork stopper was attached by a chain to one of the loops. A cylindrical type had a narrow flat diameter to which two convex sides were soldered; it was uncovered and unpainted and fitted with a thin russet leather strap. Its size was 8.1x3.75 in. A third version had convex sides pressed with six concentric circles; it was 7.5 x 2.5 in. and painted gray.

• *Cylindrical Wooden, Barrel Rim Type.* This was a very common type, having plain straight sides; many examples have survived. Made of unpainted wood, usually cedar but sometimes cherry, with 2 iron bands, a wooden or tin spout, and 3 tin or iron loops. Diameter usually 7 in., thickness 2.3 in. Cotton strap and wooden stopper, occasionally with ring and chain. The wooden sides consisted of a single round piece and hence were ideal for carving initials and regimental designations.

• *Tin Flask Types.* These probably were imports; they came in various sizes. One pattern was rectangular, of tin, curved to fit the body, and unpainted. It was 5 in. high, 5.5 in. wide, and 2.25 in. thick. It had 4 tin loops. Another had the same general shape but was 7 in. high, 8 in. wide, and 2.3 in. thick. Its spout was placed on the extreme left of the top.

Two additional types, both unusual, should be mentioned. Both were probably produced and issued or sold locally:

• *Wooden Water Cask.* Flattened barrel-like construction of wooden staves and ends, hooped with split willow shoots; unpainted. Brass cover with catch over the spout. Two rings fastened under the hoops for a cotton carrying strap. Dimensions about 12 in. long with 4 in. as the widest diameter at each end.

• *Two-piece Wooden Type.* Consists of 2 round, concave pieces of wood held together by 11 screws; 3 metal loops. Is 7.2 in. in diameter and 3 in. thick. Cotton strap and cork stopper. Probably existed in other sizes.

Federal canteens were sometimes split in half and put to use as cooking vessels or entrenching tools. Some canteens of gutta percha were produced in 1861 but probably not thereafter.

Belts, Frogs, Holsters, and Slings

• *Socket Bayonet Scabbards.* The scabbards manufactured in the South closely resembled the U.S. Army pattern in being made of leather and having a curving leather frog permanently affixed. However, they usually were of inferior materials and workmanship, especially in the use of zinc and lead for tips instead of brass, or by sewing the tip inside the leather. Whereas Union scabbards were sturdily riveted and sewn to frogs, Confederate examples were usually only sewn. Frogs were sometimes made of stiffened fabric instead of leather.

The belts, scabbards and slings specified in the Confederate *Ordnance Manual* of 1863 are all verbatim copies of U.S. patterns. The extent to which these were worn is difficult to say, but at least they were considered regulation and the reader is referred to Chapter 4.

Fig. 146   Four types of enlisted men's waist belt are illustrated to suggest the wide range actually used. Three are of russet leather and that color certainly was more common than black. The cavalry belt shown is of the kind also worn by officers. The infantry belt resembles the U.S. pattern, while the one with the "frame" buckle illustrates what was probably the most common form, fastened with a plain rectangular buckle of one sort or another.

The last type was sometimes called a "snake belt" since its S-shaped buckle sometimes took the form of a snake. In russet and black leather, it was a pattern found in the British army, especially in rifle and colonial corps.

Three officers' sword belts are illustrated in the next plate, all based on surviving examples and all fitted with brass, two-piece "CS" belt plates. Any of these might well have carried the rectangular "C.S.A." plate described above, or one of the several state buckles, or possibly a pattern designed and manufactured abroad. Regulations for sword belts copied those of the Union Army verbatim.

Two examples of saber bayonet scabbards are illustrated; one shows a bayonet with the Boyle, Gamble & MacFee adapter attached.

Horse Furniture

The background of military saddlery has been given in Chapter 5. The Confederate cavalry leaders were familiar with this background as it applied to the U.S. cavalry, but found themselves unable to profit much from it until late in the Civil War.

Fig. 149

Confederate cavalrymen furnished their own saddles and bridles at the beginning of the war. To a considerable extent this practice was continued, and as late as June 1863 we read of mounted regiments being formed in which each recruit had to provide "a good, strong, serviceable horse, saddle, and bridle, the stirrup leather and bridle reins of the best and stoutest material . . . Straps should be provided to buckle on the blankets, clothing, &, to the saddle, for which rings must be securely fastened to it."

Cavalry Saddles

The common saddle in the South prior to 1861 was the "English round tree" model. This was a pleasant and useful saddle for peacetime wear but it was not fitted to carry much equipment, and its use in military service soon led to sore-backed horses. The Ordnance Department, which controlled horse furniture, soon realized it had to provide a military saddle. Its first answer was the Jenifer pattern.

Walter H. Jenifer was a West Pointer from Baltimore who did not graduate. His military service included a year in the 3rd U.S. Dragoons and six years in the 2nd U.S. Cavalry. He resigned in 1861 and throughout the Civil War commanded the 8th Virginia Cavalry. On 26 June 1860 he was granted a patent (No. 28,867) on a new saddle. As pictured in the patent records, it had a flat English seat with a military pommel and cantle capable of carrying equipment but sloping away from the seat gradually — "not rising so abruptly . . . as those in common use," according to its inventor. The saddle called for both girth and surcingle, the latter passing through slots in the flaps.

One distinctive feature of the Jenifer saddle as patented was its curved valise which fitted tightly around and under the cantle and had an opening in the center through which articles could be inserted. But the chief claim to fame of the Jenifer lay in its lightness which, coupled with the English seat, appealed to Southern troopers who liked to ride light. An officer, years after the Civil War, remembered it as "the lightest and pleasantest known for both horse and rider."

The Jenifer saddle worked well for a while then had to be discarded. General Gorgas, writing after the war, summed up the situation as follows:

> In cavalry equipments the main thing was to get a good saddle . . . We adopted Jenifer's tree, which did very well while the horses were in good condition, and was praised by that prince of cavalrymen, General J.E.B. Stuart; but it came down on the horse's backbone and withers as soon as the cushion of fat and muscle dwindled. The McClellan tree did better on the whole, and we finally succeeded in making a pretty good saddle of that kind — comfortable enough, but not as durable as the Federal article.

Colonel J.R. Chambliss Jr., commanding Lee's Cavalry Brigade, wrote in August 1863 the Jenifer saddles were "dreaded, ridiculed, and avoided by officers and men" and recommended copying the McClellan pattern. Even General R.E. Lee echoed the complaint. In reply, Gorgas announced that the McClellan would be used thereafter, "as the general testimony of officers has lately been decidedly in favor of it."

Considering shortages of leather and difficult conditions of manufacture, the Ordnance Department was something less than successful in their production of McClellans, as far as quality was concerned. Apparently the supply was adequate for no mention has been found of shortage.

Artillery Saddles

Fig. 156   Confederate artillery used essentially the same saddlery and draft harness as produced for the U.S. Army. A significant stock of older model artillery harness was captured in 1861; thereafter the Ordnance Department appears to have produced copies of the 1861 U.S. pattern. The saddle was a modified Grimsley type with brass bound pommel and cantle. Both were fitted inside with brass escutcheons stamped "CS"; neither had mortices. Some, and perhaps all, Confederate artillery saddles were given padded underskirts, thus removing the necessity for a blanket. Stirrups were commonly brass.

Valise saddles seem to have resembled their Northern counterpart except that they, too, were padded underneath. They also carried the brass "CS" escutcheons.

Bits and Bridles

U.S. regulation bits were specified as standard for Confederate cavalry and artillery. Various other patterns exist in collections which are believed to have been used by Confederate horsemen, but there is insufficient evidence at hand to enable us to reach any conclusions about Confederate bits as a whole. The same applies to other horse furniture such as pads and housings, stirrups, picket pins and ropes, saddle bags and valises, carbine thimbles, and draft harness. The reader is referred for all to the section on U.S. Army horse furniture in Chapter 5.

The C.S. saddle blanket was of "dark gray color, with a red border 3 inches wide, 3 inches from the edge. The letters C.S., 6 inches high, of orange color, in the center of the blanket." Its dimensions were 75 inches long and 67 inches wide. Of course, any sort of blanket was used, and on most occasions.

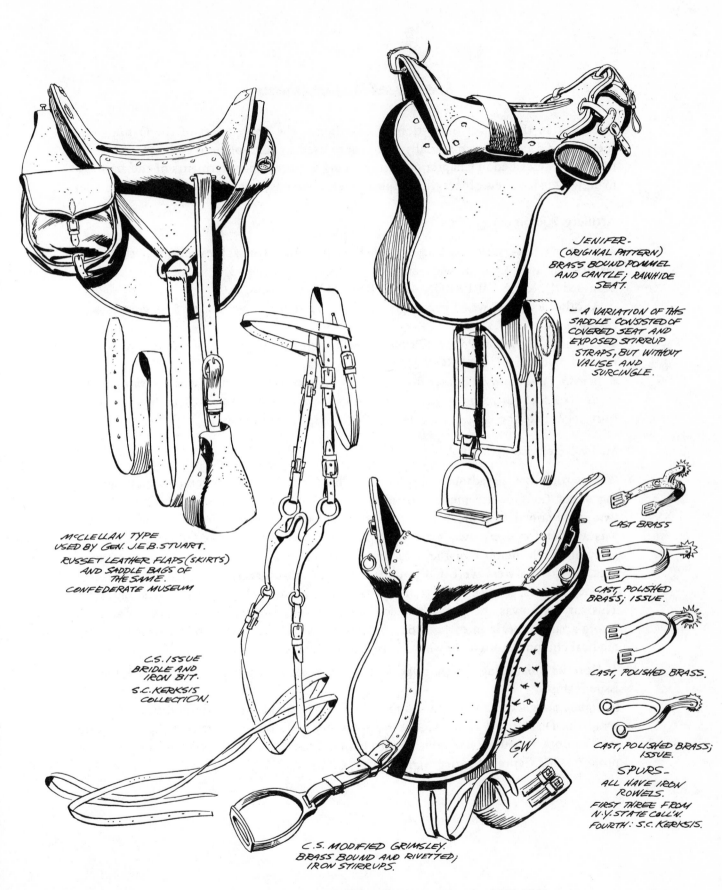

JENIFER-
(ORIGINAL PATTERN)
BRASS BOUND POMMEL
AND CANTLE; RAWHIDE
SEAT.

- A VARIATION OF THIS
SADDLE CONSISTED OF
COVERED SEAT AND
EXPOSED STIRRUP
STRAPS, BUT WITHOUT
VALISE AND
SURCINGLE.

McCLELLAN TYPE
USED BY GEN. J.E.B. STUART.
RUSSET LEATHER FLAPS (SKIRTS)
AND SADDLE BAGS OF
THE SAME.
CONFEDERATE MUSEUM

C.S. ISSUE
BRIDLE AND
IRON BIT.
S.C. KERKSIS
COLLECTION.

CAST BRASS

CAST, POLISHED
BRASS; ISSUE.

CAST, POLISHED BRASS.

CAST, POLISHED BRASS;
ISSUE.

SPURS-
ALL HAVE IRON
ROWELS.
FIRST THREE FROM
N.Y. STATE COLL'N.
FOURTH: S.C. KERKSIS.

C.S. MODIFIED GRIMSLEY.
BRASS BOUND AND RIVETTED;
IRON STIRRUPS.

GW

Fig. 149. Confederate States horse furniture and spurs, 1861-1865.

Specialized Accouterments

Except in the matter of battlefield expedients, the implements of the Confederate specialist did not differ materially from those used by his Northern counterpart, which have been described in Chapter 6. Commencing with the accouterments of the artilleryman, we will list a few objects that appear to have been used only on the Confederate side:

Artillery Equipment

● *Gunner's Haversack.* Resembled the U.S. pattern haversack except that the russet leather bag was 12.5 in. wide and 11 in. high, with only 3 in. gussets on the sides. Stamped "J. & T.S. HEFFRON/MAKERS/ CHARLESTON. S.C."

Another example was 13 in. high and from 13 to 14 in. wide with 5 in. gussets; also russet leather.

● *Confederate Tube Pouch (Primer Box).* Identical to the U.S. issue pouch, but marked on cover "J. DARROW MAKER, Augusta, Ga."

● *British Tube Pouch (Primer Box).* Russet or buff leather pouch with *outside* dimensions 7 x 1.5 x 5 in.; single flap, two vertical loops that fasten to leather studs on bottom. Unlike the U.S. pouch, it was of even depth throughout.

Medical Field Equipment

This topic has already been explored in Chapter 6. "Infirmary detachments" operating under Confederate medical officers in the field were unarmed, except for NCO's who were armed to protect the detachment against "stragglers and marauders." There was a litter for every two men, equipped with two leather shoulder straps for easier carrying. Each member of the detachment was given a canteen, a tin cup, and a haversack. In the last item were 1/8 pound of lint, four bandages, two long and two short wooden splints, sponges and tourniquets, and a pint bottle of "alcoholic stimulant." This, at least, was the prescribed equipment in the Department of South Carolina, Georgia, and Florida in early 1863, and probably did not differ greatly from the field medical equipment used elsewhere in the Confederacy.

More as illustrating the shortage of supplies than an attempt at a standard item of issue is this:

● *Signalman's Canteen.* Round, unpainted, with straight, plain sides; fabricated out of scrap tin. Diameter 9.5 in., thickness 2 in. Three tin loops and cotton strap. Large and small spouts, for filling and pouring into lamps. Used to carry oil. Said to have been the property of a Captain Frazier, Signal Corps, C.S.A.

SOURCES

C.S., Ordnance Dept., *Field Manual for the Use of Officers on Ordnance Duty*, Richmond, Va., 1862.

————, ————, *The Ordnance Manual for the Use of the Officers of the Confederate States Army*, Richmond, Va., 1863. Copied in large measure from the U.S. Ordnance Manual of 1862.

————, ————, *Regulations for the Government of the Ordnance Department of the Confederate States of America*, Richmond, Va., 1862.

Claude E. Fuller and Richard D. Steuart, *Firearms of the Confederacy...*, Huntington, W. Va., 1944.

William A. Albaugh, III, and Edward N. Simmons, *Confederate Arms*, Harrisburg, Pa., 1957.

William A. Albaugh, III, *Confederate Edged Weapons*, New York, 1960.

Harold L. Peterson, *American Knives...*, New York, 1958.

John Lamb, "The Confederate Cavalry," in *Southern Historical Society Papers*, XXVI (1898), 359-365.

Frank E. Vandiver, *Ploughshares Into Swords: Josiah Gorgas and Confederate Ordnance*, Austin, Texas, 1952.

Ben LaBree, ed., *The Confederate Soldier in the Civil War*, Louisville, Ky., 1897.

Francis A. Lord, "Analysis of Photos of Dead Show Equipment of Confederates in '64," in *Civil War Times Illustrated*, April 1966, pp. 18-21.

William A. Albaugh, III, Hugh Benet, Jr., and Edward N. Simmons, *Confederate Hand Guns*, Philadelphia, Pa., 1963.

William B. Edwards, *Civil War Guns...*, Harrisburg, Pa., 1962.

Jac Weller, "Imported Confederate Shoulder Weapons," in *Civil War History*, V, 157-181.

Caleb Huse, *The Supplies for the Confederate Army...Personal Reminiscences and Unpublished History...*, Boston, 1904.

J.N. George, *English Pistols and Revolvers...*, Onslow County, N.C., 1938.

Howard L. Blackmore, *British Military Firearms, 1650-1850*, London, 1961.

J.N. George, *English Guns and Rifles...*, Plantersville, S.C., 1947.

Indispensable to the study of Confederate small arms and accouterments are the collections of artifacts in museums and in private hands. The holdings of The Museum of the Confederacy are, of course, of first rate importance, but those of several smaller museums and historical societies, in the North as well as the South, were found to be highly rewarding.

Private collections, assembled by life-long students of the subject, proved equally valuable, and we owe much to Beverly M. DuBose, Jr., of Atlanta, and to Col. Jeremiah J. Reen, Jr., of Washington.

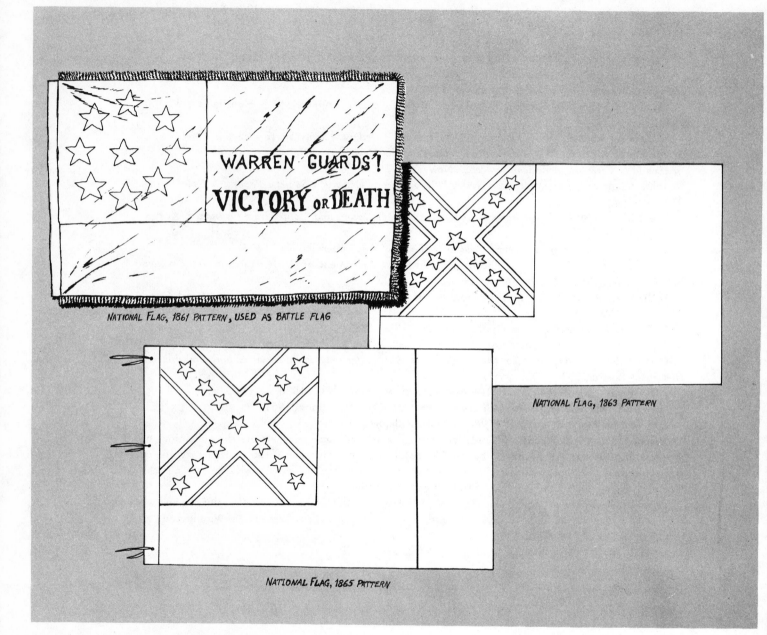

NATIONAL FLAG, 1861 PATTERN, USED AS BATTLE FLAG

NATIONAL FLAG, 1863 PATTERN

NATIONAL FLAG, 1865 PATTERN

Fig. 150. a. Confederate battle flags. (By Michael J. McAfee.)

CHAPTER XI

CONFEDERATE COLORS AND FLAGS

The principal facts and dates in the history of the Confederate flag are generally agreed upon and can be covered briefly. We can then return to the flags used in the military service.

The first national flag was the one adopted 4 March 1861 by a committee of the Confederate Provisional Congress, then sitting in Montgomery, Alabama. It consisted of three horizontal bars of equal width, red-white-red, with a blue union, square in shape, and as wide as two bars, containing seven 5-pointed white stars, arranged in a circle. It was planned to add a star for each state that thereafter joined the Confederacy. In the report of the committee, the red and white areas were called "spaces," but quickly they became known as "bars" and the flag itself as the "Stars and Bars."

Fig. 150. a

In the four months preceding the adoption of this first Confederate flag, numerous banners had been flown throughout the South symbolizing independence, real or intended. Some of them were established state flags, others bore extemporized devices representing states, while still others attempted to honor the Southern states as a whole and thus foreshadowed the Stars and Bars. Among the devices employed to do this, the most widespread was the "lone star." Already the lone star was well established in Texas. The device was simple and the fact that a star represented a state in the U.S. flag led naturally to such symbolism.

When Florida troops raised a flag over the navy yard at Pensacola in January 1861, it bore a single star. When Georgia troops occupied Augusta Arsenal, they raised a white flag with a single red star in its center. And when the Continental Guards of New Orleans constructed their own flag to celebrate Louisiana's secession, it consisted of a single blue star, bearing a yellow pelican device, on a white field, representing "the five States that had set up lone star flags for themselves." Harry McCarthy's line "Hurrah for the Bonnie Blue Flag that bears the single star" certainly had something to do with it.

It was strongly maintained by some that the German artist Nicola Marschall, who was reputed to have suggested the first Confederate army uniform, also designed the Stars and Bars flag. He was then living in Marion, Alabama and was well known to persons of influence in nearby Montgomery. Since the final design was selected out of dozens submitted to the committee, this is entirely possible, but it has never been conclusively proven. Equally strong claims have been made for other persons.

Although the congressional committee had been assured that the new national flag could "be recognized at a great distance," experience in the first major battle of the war, at Bull Run in July 1861, proved otherwise. Furthermore, the Stars and Bars had not met with general approval throughout the South. In short, it too closely resembled the U.S. flag, both visually and symbolically. As a result of the difficulties both sides had at Bull Run in distinguishing U.S. from Confederate colors in action, the Southern commanders there, especially Generals Johnston and Beauregard, determined to adopt a clearly distinctive battle flag. At a meeting in September 1861 they viewed the designs submitted and selected one, the familiar square flag with red field, blue St. Andrew's cross outlined in white, and twelve or thirteen white 5-pointed stars.

This battle flag was never officially adopted by the Confederate government, nor did its armies generally accept it until at least a year later, and even then not by all troops. But it did replace the Stars and Bars as a regimental flag in the Confederate Department of the Potomac by the end of 1862. The old ensign was retained as a post flag and for naval use until 1863.

In April 1863 the question of the national flag was again up for discussion in the Confederate Congress. After considerable debate a white flag having the battle flag as its union was adopted on 1 May. Its dimensions, arrived at somewhat by accident, were prescribed as length double the width, and with the union a square of two-thirds the width.

Finally, on 4 March 1865, Congress once again changed the national flag by placing a broad red bar across its fly end, and by altering its dimensions so that the width was two-thirds the length. This last flag does not appear to have seen much if any military usage during the few months that remained of the life of the Confederacy.

While these changes were taking place, the Confederate armies were experimenting with still other flags and the navy had adopted its own distinctive flag series. Many Confederate regiments continued to carry state or distinctive organizational flags, even during the later years of the war. All in all, the effect was colorful and confusing and a matter of comment by contemporary observers.

Army Flags

The Confederate military flag was not usually called a "color" with good reason. It was smaller than the Union regimental color and in most cases made of bunting or cotton rather than silk. It rarely had a fringe or a sleeve through which a pike could pass; instead it was fastened to a staff — often homemade — by means of three or more ties of rope or ribbon which passed through small holes in the heading of the flag. This was a common method in the South before the Civil War and reflected the necessity of being able to fit a flag on any size of staff, or to run it up on a halyard.

Until 1864, an enlisted man, normally a sergeant, carried a regimental flag. By an act of the Confederate Congress, approved 17 February 1864, the rank of "ensign" was created. This officer had the pay of a first lieutenant and it was his duty "to bear the colors of the regiment."

On the whole, battle flags were items of issue after the first year of the war. Before that they might have been supplied by state or local governments or by civic organizations, or they could have been fabricated by the commands themselves. It is clear, at least, that the Army of Northern Virginia battle flag was an item of issue from the start, and it seems likely that a simple abbreviated regimental designation was painted on each one prior to issue.

Following the adoption of the design, the Chief Quartermaster of the then Confederate Army of the Potomac was directed to have the required flags made. He appears to have thought first of silk which led him quickly to the romantic notion of ladies' dresses. A contract was made with a group of ladies to fabricate the flags and a few dresses were sacrificed to the cause. But his agent was more practical and set forth to buy up all the appropriately colored silk on the market in Richmond. Naturally, the shade used for the fields varied from crimson to pink, but over 100 flags were made this way for both headquarters and regimental use. They carried only twelve stars in deference to Kentucky's neutrality; most were bordered with yellow silk and a few were given fringes. They can be distinguished by their white silken stars.

Soon the supply of silk ran out and the Chief Quartermaster turned to "cotton cloth," issuing a circular letter to the quartermasters of every regiment and brigade in the army to make the flags themselves and to use any blue and red cloth available. The arrival of a shipment of English bunting of fine quality helped considerably and in practice the procurement of these initial battle flags was not as haphazard as this sounds since they were quite formally issued to each regiment. We shall return to these flags in a moment.

National Flag, 1861 Pattern (Stars and Bars)

This flag saw considerable use in the Confederate army. As used in the field, it was about 3x5 feet or 3x4.5 feet in size and almost always made of bunting. It had a linen or canvas heading with three holes, often without grommets. The form was usually as prescribed in 1861, but the number of stars varied; now and then the flag was made with proportions more nearly 4x5.3 feet.

The Stars and Bars flag was often adapted to use as a state flag by placing a device in the union or, in the case of Virginia, by using a single large star around which the letters "VIRGINIA" were encircled. Regimental designations, mottoes, and notices of presentation were commonly painted on the center (white) bar, and at times elsewhere.

In larger sizes the Stars and Bars was used as a post or garrison flag at least through 1863. Its use as a regimental flag probably ended about the time of Antietam in 1862, although examples were captured by Union forces as late as the end of the war.

Army of Northern Virginia (A.N.V.) Battle Flag

This, the most celebrated and widely used regimental flag of all, was, as we have said, prescribed by General Joseph E. Johnston at Fairfax Court House, Virginia, in September 1861, following consultation with General Beauregard and others. It was issued to the regiments of the then "Army of the Potomac" in November-December 1861. Three sizes were established at the time: 4x4 feet for infantry, 3x3 feet for artillery, and 2.5x2.5 feet for cavalry. Examples of the first size are abundant; of the

Fig. 150. b

other sizes, very rare. In actual practice, as we shall see, the infantry size was not always square. All save the first battle flags were made of cotton bunting with white linen or cotton stars, borders, and edgings.

The field in most instances was a bright red, about halfway between crimson and scarlet, upon which was placed a St. Andrew's cross of medium blue extending from corner to corner. On the cross were twelve or usually thirteen white 5-pointed stars. The cross was edged with a white strip from .5 to 1 inch in width. Around the entire flag was a white or yellow border from 1.5 to 2.5 inches wide. The usual method of making the flag was to sew together three pieces of red bunting horizontally, then cut out the areas needed to fit in the blue cross. On many flags the stars were sewn to the obverse only.

The border on the side next to the staff served as a heading and was normally punched with three holes for ropes or ribbons. Regimental designations were often painted in abbreviation on the center of the cross, but they could be and were placed elsewhere on the flag. In some commands it was required that flags be plainly marked with the regiment's number and state so that "in the event of the loss of the colors no misunderstanding may arise as to who lost them."

The display of battle honors on this flag was common, some of them carrying twelve or more. The practice was authorized by the War Department on 23 July 1862 (GO 52) for all battles in which "regiments, battalions, and separate squadrons have been actually engaged." Describing some thirty Confederate flags captured on the third day of Gettysburg, a Union officer called them ". . . these defiant battle flags, some inscribed with 'First Manassas,' the numerous battles of the Peninsula, 'Second Manassas,' 'South Mountain,' 'Sharpsburg' (our Antietam), 'Fredericksburg,' 'Chancellorsville' and many more names." All were not necessarily Confederate victories; "Gettysburg" is on several surviving today.

This display of battle honors appears to have begun in June 1862, shortly after the battle of Seven Pines, and on the initiative of General Longstreet. The two honors authorized were "WILLIAMSBURG" and "SEVEN PINES!" — the exclamation point seems to have been used quite consistently — which were stencilled in black on 4-inch strips of white cotton or canvas. The strips were then sewn to the bunting flags, sometimes at top and bottom, sometimes on the sides, and once at least in dead center. The practice of using cloth strips for displaying battle honors continued, although other Confederate flags have their honors (and unit designations) painted directly onto the flag.

Other A.N.V. Battle Flags

The A.N.V. battle flag was carried by other Confederate commands and there it usually exhibited some variations in size and design. When General Beauregard formed the Army of the Mississippi in March 1862 he ordered sets of A.N.V. battle flags to be made in New Orleans. These seemed to have had 6- rather than 5-pointed stars, and borders of pink rather than white silk. Some of them were unusually rectangular, measuring 3.5 x 6 feet.

Later in 1862, Beauregard was assigned to command at Charleston, S.C. There he again instituted the A.N.V. battle flag which closely resembled the original except it was provided with a bunting sleeve, blue for infantry and red for artillery and cavalry. These flags came in only two sizes, apparently 4 x 4 feet for infantry, heavy artillery, and cavalry, and 3 x 3 feet for light artillery.

In the spring of 1864, General Joseph E. Johnston instituted it in the Army of Tennessee in an attempt to standardize the four or more patterns of battle flag then being used. This version seems to have had no border and was rectangular, usually 3 x 4.25 feet for infantry and cavalry, and 2.5 x 3.3 feet for batteries of artillery.

Finally, the A.N.V. battle flag appears to have been carried in the Army of Mississippi, formed by General Leonidas Polk in May 1864. This version also had no border and was rectangular, approximately 4 x 4.25 feet. For some reason many bore only twelve stars. It came in only one size except for General Nathan Bedford Forrest's Cavalry Corps, which apparently was 3 x 4 feet.

All of these versions of the A.N.V. battle flag, as well as the other patterns of flag described below, could and did carry battle honors. On 17 July 1862 the regiments of the Army of the Mississippi were authorized to inscribe the honor "SHILOH" on their flags. After Murfreesboro, an honor for that battle was authorized. Apparently no uniform method of applying the honors was prescribed and each regiment did the best it could with paint, strips of cloth, or cut-out letters. The same applied to regimental designations although, in abbreviated form, they usually were applied to the upper and lower quadrants of the red field. The battle flags issued the Army of Mississippi in 1864 were somewhat more systematically marked with separately cut-out, white cotton letters sewn to the red field.

There is a reference in John B. Lindsley's *Military Annals of Tennessee* to a curious device on the battle flag of the 4th Tennessee Infantry. At the Battle of Perryville, Kentucky on 8 October 1862, the regiment, he writes, "won the honor of placing the 'inverted cross cannon' on its battle-flag." This device, consisting of two bulbous-breeched cannon tubes, crossed with muzzles down, was authorized on 23 November 1862 by the Army of Tennessee for regiments of General Benjamin F. Cheatham's Division which had overrun and captured Union artillery in battle. The award was expanded a month later to include other regiments of the Army, but thereafter appears to have been restricted to them. The cannon tubes came in both white and black cloth, and were sometimes applied with their muzzles pointing upward.

The A.N.V. battle flag was carried by regiments that had received it to the end of the war, and by order was the only flag permitted to be carried in the Army of Northern Virginia when in action against the enemy. Obviously this could not be the case in the Army of Tennessee and elsewhere, and we can now turn to some of the other patterns of Confederate battle flags.

"Polk Battle Flag"

A distinctive pattern of battle flag was adopted by General Leonidas Polk in early 1862 and possibly even earlier. It was described some years after the war by General Beauregard as having "a blue field with a white St. Andrew's cross, and blue or gold stars," but this description has been questioned and appears to relate to a type of battle flag carried in the Confederate Army of Kentucky, which will be mentioned later.

Fig. 151. a

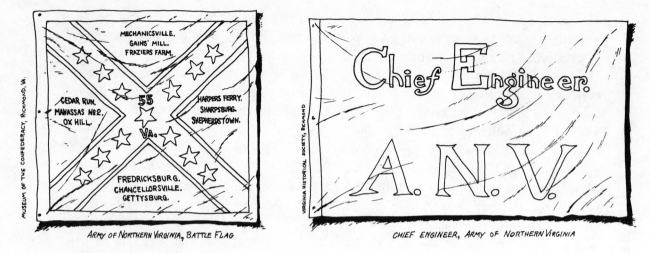

Fig. 150. b. Confederate battle flags. (By Michael J. McAfee.)

The battle flag adopted in March 1862 for the regiments of Polk's Corps, of the newly formed Army of the Mississippi, and made in New Orleans, was something different. It was a dark blue flag, to be sure, but it had a red upright (Greek) cross, edged in white and decorated with eleven white 5-pointed stars. These flags were made of bunting and cotton and measured about 2.25 x 4.25 feet. In a further development, General Jones M. Withers' division of Polk's Corps adopted a version which eliminated the red from the cross as well as the stars, leaving a blue flag with a white Greek cross. Surviving examples of the former type include flags carried by the 10th Mississippi and 1st Tennessee Regiments, while those of Withers' division pattern include flags of the 22nd and 24th Alabama Regiments, plus other units from that state.

"Hardee (or Cleburne) Battle Flag"

Fig. 150. a A better known battle flag was adopted in mid-1861 by General William J. Hardee for his original Arkansas brigade and later for other Western commands. At least seventeen examples survive, carried by Alabama and Arkansas troops, the pattern being used throughout the war. General Beauregard described it as having "a blue field with a full white circle in its centre." The flag by 1863 had a wide (sometimes 4-inch) white border, and a large white ellipse, rather than circle, on which the regimental designation was painted. Battle honors were liberally painted or sewn on whatever space could be found. It was smaller than the A.N.V. pattern and rectangular; the flag of the 1st Arkansas Infantry was 31 x 38 inches including the border. The blue cotton fields were poorly dyed and many faded to a shade of pea-green.

Long after the war, General Simon Bolivar Buckner claimed that he had designed this battle flag at the request of General Albert Sidney Johnston, as one that was perfectly distinctive and could not be mistaken for the national flag of either army. This took place, he said, about September 1861. Mrs. Buckner made one flag for each regiment then stationed at Bowling Green, Kentucky to "be unfurled only in action." It was first used at the siege of Fort Donelson by the regiments of Buckner's division, and later was adopted by Hardee. When General Patrick R. Cleburne took over Hardee's division he was given permission to retain the blue battle flags. Wrote Hardee after the war:

> . . . This was the only division in the Confederate service to carry into action other than the national colors; and friends and foes soon learned to watch the course of the blue flag that marked where Cleburne was in battle.

"Van Dorn Battle Flag" (Trans-Mississippi Department)

Fig. 151. b

By now some idea of the variety of battle flags carried in the Army of the Mississippi and Army of Tennessee will be evident. Another to be recorded is that adopted in the Army of the West on 7 February 1862, some two months before it joined the Army of the Mississippi as Van Dorn's Corps. It had a red field, bordered on three sides in yellow, with thirteen white, 5-pointed stars and a white crescent in the upper, staff corner. It was a relatively large flag, probably about 3.75 x 5 feet.

"Army of Kentucky Battle Flag"

The blue flag with the white St. Andrew's cross described by General Beauregard might well be a pattern used briefly in 1862 in the Confederate Army of Kentucky under General Kirby Smith. Several examples have survived, but too little is known about them to justify definition of a distinctive category. One example is the flag of the 30th Arkansas Infantry which was lost at Murfreesboro, Tennessee in January 1863, when the regiment was in McGown's division of Kirby Smith's corps. It has a blue field with a white St. Andrew's cross, the whole enclosed in a broad white border. There are now no stars, but at one time there may have been. It is 40 x 46 inches in size.

National Flag, 1863 Pattern

As mentioned above, this flag was adopted by the Confederate Congress on 1 May 1863. Its issue as a post flag must have begun shortly thereafter, and it is possible that it had replaced the Stars and Bars before the end of 1863. One example was used by General Jubal A. Early as a corps headquarters flag.

Especially interesting is the use of this pattern as a regimental battle flag, a use possibly more general than heretofore suspected. As early as June 1863, the 32nd North Carolina (of Rodes's Division, Ewell's 2nd Corps, ANV) received a new model flag with "a long white tail on it." The regiment was then in Pennsylvania on the Gettysburg campaign. The pattern was also carried by Florida, Arkansas, Tennessee, and Louisiana commands, and probably others. Examples carried by infantry, light artillery, and cavalry have survived; sizes varied widely, one flag having a fly of six and a half feet.

Guidons, Pennons, and Identifying Flags

Forked guidons were carried by smaller commands of cavalry and light artillery. A North Carolina battery had a red and white guidon of traditional U.S. Army pattern marked with "1st Co. 1st Batl/N.C. ARTILLERY". Mosby's celebrated partisan rangers, according to a contemporary picture, carried a forked version of the ANV battle flag. Its size seems to have been about 1.5 feet on the staff and 2 feet on the fly. And other varieties have survived. Incidentally, the term "guidon" was used to signify the bearer of the flag as well as the flag itself.

More common today are what must once have been lance pennons: forked versions of the 1861 Pattern National Flag. These were about 11 inches on the pike and 16 or 17 inches on the fly. Those which survive differ somewhat in size and design, but unite in being crudely made. A forked pennon, said to have been removed from a "lance staff" of the 5th Virginia Cavalry, is over 2 feet long and 9.25 inches wide. It consists solely of three horizontal stripes, red-white-red. Since a lance pennon must have been made for a lance, the reader is referred to the secton on that subject (Chapter 10).

There is a flag in the Smithsonian Institution said to have been a "battery flag" captured near Nashville in December 1864. It is rectangular, 13 x 20 inches, and is the 1861 Pattern National Flag with its thirteen white embroidered stars arranged in a St. Andrew's cross.

Some Confederate headquarters and tactical commands (brigades, divisions, etc.) carried distinguishing flags, although this usage never approached the permanence and the highly organized systems found in the Union Army. On 19 February 1864 the Army of Tennessee adopted the following system (GO 25):

Army Headquarters: "battle flag of the Virginia army."
Hardee's Corps:
  Corps commander: flag with three horizontal bars, blue-white-blue
  Division commanders: flag with two horizontal bars, white above blue
  Brigadiers: all blue flag
Hindman's Corps: same, with red instead of blue

Fig. 150. b   That other headquarters were sometimes distinguished by flags is indicated by a red bunting flag in Richmond, Virginia marked "Chief Engineer/A.N.V." It is a patently homemade affair, 3 feet, 8.5 inches on the pike and 5 feet, 9 inches on the fly, with 11-inch capital letters of white cloth sewn on. Still another example on record was a blue silk flag bound with white and bearing white stars, said to have been used as a headquarters flag by General Carter L. Stevenson before his surrender at Vicksburg.

Ambulance depots were sometimes indicated by a plain red flag in order to speed the transport of wounded thereto (GO 35, Dept. of SC, Ga and Fla, 5 April 1863).

Much of the information on Confederate military flags is circumstantial and most of this stems from actual flags captured during or at the end of the Civil War. According to Peleg Harrison (p. 259), there were 541 Confederate flags stored in the War Department in Washington following the war, 223 of which could be identified. A War Department order of 7 June 1887 to return these flags, approved by President Cleveland, led to widespread protest from the G.A.R. during which General Lucius Fairchild uttered his celebrated malediction: "May God palsy the hand that wrote that order." As a result, the order was revoked a week later. By the act of Congress, 28 February 1905, the identified flags were returned to the states from which the regiments had come, and by a second act of 29 June 1906, 288 other flags were delivered to the Confederate Memorial Literary Society (Museum of the Confederacy) in Richmond. Some of the returned flags are illustrated in a booklet published by the Cotton Belt Route titled *The Flags of the Confederate Armies: Returned to the Men Who Bore Them by the United States Government*, St. Louis, Mo., 1905.

Not all captured flags, of course, were turned over to the War Department, despite regulations requiring this. A large number have, since 1865, come into the hands of various Northern states or into museums and private collections. One sizeable group in the Chicago Historical Society has recently been studied and recorded by Donald W. Holst.

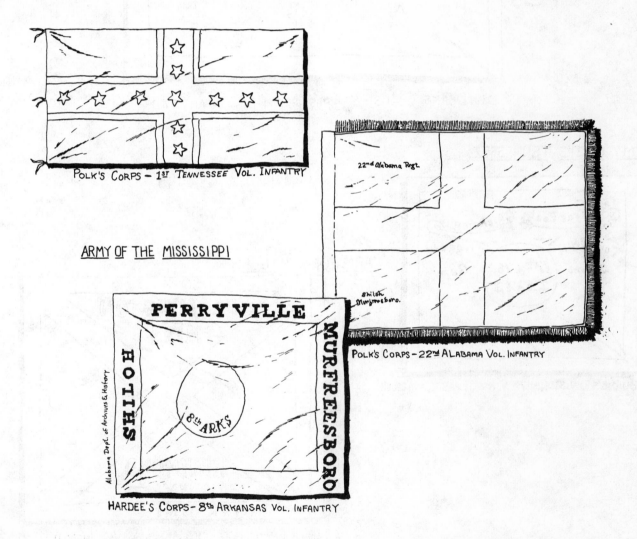

Fig. 151. a. Confederate battle flags. (By Michael J. McAfee.)

482

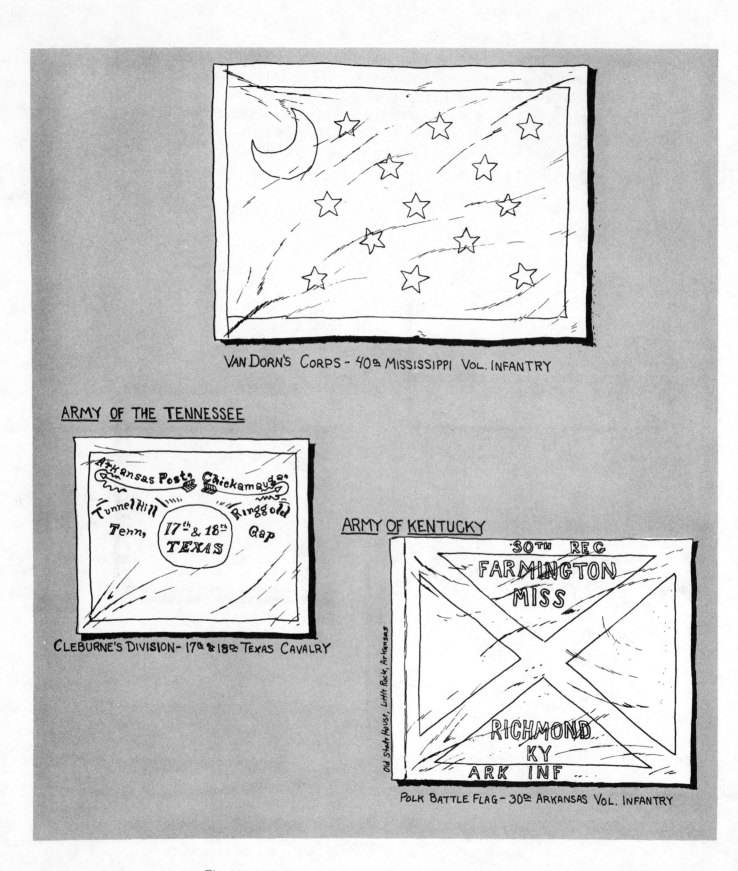

VAN DORN'S CORPS - 40ᵗʰ MISSISSIPPI VOL. INFANTRY

ARMY OF THE TENNESSEE

CLEBURNE'S DIVISION - 17ᵗʰ & 18ᵗʰ TEXAS CAVALRY

ARMY OF KENTUCKY

POLK BATTLE FLAG - 30ᵗʰ ARKANSAS VOL. INFANTRY

Fig. 151. b. Confederate battle flags. (By Michael J. McAfee.)

SOURCES

Forest J. Bowman, "The Unfurled Banners," in *Civil War Times Illustrated*, January 1972.

Peleg D. Harrison, *The Stars and Stripes and Other American Flags...*, 5th ed., Boston, 1914.

H. Michael Madaus, MS research reports: "Silk Issue Battle Flags of the Confederate Army of Northern Virginia, 1861," "Bunting Issue Battle Flags of the Confederate Army of Northern Virginia, 1862-1865," "The Second National Flag as a Regimental Color in the Army of Tennessee, C.S.A.," "Battle Honors on Regimental Colors in the Confederate Army of Northern Virginia, Summer 1862," etc.

Geo. Henry Preble, *Origin and History of the American Flag...*, new [3rd] ed., 2 vols., Philadelphia, Pa., 1917. Admiral Preble's first edition appeared in 1872 when the history of the Confederate flag was still fresh in people's minds. A sizeable section titled "Southern Flags in the Great Rebellion" (pages 494-531) is devoted to this subject.

United Confederate Veterans, *The Flags of the Confederate States of America*, Baltimore, Md., 1907.

United Daughters of the Confederacy, *Flags of the Confederate States of America, 1861-1865* Richmond, Va., n.d.

INFANTRY. UNIFORMS OF REGULAR CONFEDERATE TROOPS. CAVALRY. ARTILLERY.

Fig. 152. Confederate "regular troops" as pictured in *Harper's Weekly*, 17 August 1861. Who the artist was and where he got his information remain unsure, but the other portions of his two-page spread (which show state troops) give evidence of a wide knowledge of Confederate military dress, gained apparently in July in the vicinity of Manassas, Va. Clearly these regular uniforms are not based on dress regulations, which could hardly have been available to the artist and which they do not resemble. Could the artist have sketched them in Richmond?

CHAPTER XII

CONFEDERATE COMMAND AND STAFF; REGIMENTS AND CORPS

The "Army of the Confederate States of America" was established by the act of the Confederate Provisional Congress approved 6 March 1861. This act provided for a Corps of Engineers, a corps of artillery, six regiments of infantry and one of cavalry (later increased to eight and two, respectively, a regiment of zouaves, and a company of sappers and bombardiers). It also included the general staff previously established on 26 February consisting of these departments: Adjutant and Inspector General's, Quartermaster General's, Subsistence (also called "Commissary General's"), and Medical. (The Bureau of Ordnance was created on 8 April 1861 and a Signal Bureau on 29 May 1862.) Finally, the act of 6 March 1861 prescribed the number and rank of general officers, and provided that enlisted men of the army would be issued a yearly allowance of clothing, "the quality and kind . . . to be established by regulations from the War Department."

Except for a few companies, this regular army existed only insofar as it related to the command and staff, departments and bureaus. The actual Confederate Army was the volunteer or Provisional Army established in the acts of 28 February and 6 March 1861, most of whose regiments and battalions in the beginning were raised by and in the states and transferred to the general government.

Fig. 152

Nevertheless, there were a number of distinctive Confederate regiments and battalions, either allotted to no state or made up of companies from several states. In the former category were specialized commands like Engineers, the Invalid Corps, and the Signal Corps; or the regiments and battalions made up of prisoners and deserters, Indians, or Negroes. The recruitment of Indians from the civilized tribes began early in the war and continued with moderate success until near the end; all Indian corps were considered Confederate commands. In March 1865, the Confederate Congress passed a law authorizing the employment of Negroes for military service. Three companies appear to have been raised, chiefly from hospital workers in Richmond, and one of them saw a brief period of service in the city's defenses.

The latter category of Confederate regiments were those which, because of circumstances, were composed of companies from more than one state. Rather than attempt to divide the state allocations, the War Department, from 1862 on, numbered them in a distinctive Confederate series.

Command and Staff

The Uniforms of Robert E. Lee

Robert E. Lee, a Virginian, tendered his resignation as colonel of the 1st Cavalry Regiment, U.S. Army, on 20 April 1861. On the morning of the 22nd, dressed in civilian clothes but with a trunk, he boarded a train at Alexandria, bound for Richmond. His trip was being made at the invitation of the Governor of Virginia, and Lee had good reason to believe he would be offered the command of the military and naval forces of that Commonwealth. There is every likelihood that he carried one or more of his blue uniforms with him, probably in his trunk. Upon arrival, being offered this command with the rank of major general, he accepted. Late in the same evening the Virginia convention unanimously approved the appointment and on 23 April Lee entered upon his duties.

It is safe to assume that Lee knew the prescribed uniform of the Virginia militia at that time to be blue and identical with that of the U.S. Army except for buttons, hat device, and belt plate. There was no reason for him to suspect in April that Virginia would ultimately adopt gray for its military clothing. In whatever way he managed to secure it, it is reasonable to believe that the first uniform he donned was all dark blue — a double-breasted frock coat, trousers with a .125-inch welt of gold, and possibly a blue cloth forage cap or felt dress hat.

Credence is given this hypothesis by a published photograph purporting to show Lee in a Virginia uniform. This widely circulated picture was undoubtedly based upon a daguerrotype taken of Lee about 1851. In the original he wears the "plain dark blue body coat" with brass buttons authorized by U.S. Army regulations and holds in his hand one of the new cloth caps. In the retouched version he has on a field officer's dress coat with epaulets and an unusual turned-over collar. In his hand is the same cloth cap but now it bears "VA" within a wreath with an indistinct eagle device above. Both collar and cuffs are decorated with embroidery — a wide leaf pattern alongside a quarter-inch strip of braid.

Roy Meredith and others have made clear that this uniform was painted onto an older print, but they believe the new details were pure conjecture. Probably we will never know, but the uniform shown does contain several features of interest. Lee was now a major general, but his coat has the button arrangement of a colonel, just what he would have carried down from Arlington. What artist would have imagined the very unusual turned-over collar, the precise pattern of embroidery, the cap insignia? It seems more likely that Lee, while unwilling to sit for a photograph, did permit an artist to sketch the details of his Virginia uniform with an eye to a new picture being published.

Between 1 and 8 June 1861 the forces of Virginia were transferred to the Confederacy and Lee ceased for a time to exercise active command. Also, on 6 June, the Confederate States issued its initial dress regulations, formally establishing gray as the color of all coats. Lee, as a brigadier general of the Confederacy (the highest rank then authorized), would have complied as soon as possible. We can thus establish the middle of June as the latest date he would have worn his blue coat.

Among Lee's well recognized traits were a strong aversion to posing for photog-

Fig. 153. General Robert E. Lee in the later years of the Civil War.

raphers and artists, and an equally strong aversion to the ornate or pretentious in dress. Fortunately for posterity, his fame demanded he stand before a camera on at least five occasions during the Civil War and from these rare shots, plus memoirs, we have some idea of what the great leader wore in camp and field.

Fig. 153

Lee's gray coats were of regulation double-breasted cut with two closely placed lines of buttons, arranged in two's. Invariably he wore his coat collar open with the lapels turned back to expose a white shirt and a short, loosely tied black cravat. Through the year 1863, Lee's uniforms had a low, standing collar, but in the final two war years he seems to have consistently worn coats which were tailored with rolled collars. On these coat collars were three gold embroidered stars, without the wreath specified for general officers. On later uniforms the center star is slightly larger than the others. This was normally Lee's only insignia of rank, for he never wore cuff loops. Indoors, he dispensed with a waist belt and sidearms; his coat was left open, displaying a matching gray waistcoat. In two of the photographs, however, he has buttoned his coat to within four buttons of the neck to permit the addition of a waist belt.

The Vannerson photograph, taken in Richmond probably in early 1864, shows Lee in the closest he ever came to full dress. Here he wears long trousers instead of boots, a belt of Russian leather with three stripes of gold embroidery, and the buff sash of a general officer. His hand rests on the "Maryland sword," described below. Except for the fact that he wore boots, this was essentially the uniform he had on at Appomattox.

Lee's trousers, so far as can be told, always matched the gray of his coats. This color was a "cadet gray" — a shade so tinged with blue in some portraits of Lee that his uniform appears almost Federal in color.

Lee invariably wore a hat of drab colored felt. Its brim was wide, flexible, and slightly curled; its crown was crushed in round at the top and unadorned except by a narrow cloth band. The black felt hats shown in some later portraits of Lee are not corroborated by war time photographs.

His gauntlets were buff colored buckskin and in the field he wore tall, black soft leather boots, usually drawn up above his knees. Those he had on at Appomattox — a shorter style with stiff knee guards — were nearly new and "stitched with red silk," according to one observer. On another pair his nephew General Fitzhugh Lee recalled he wore "handsome spurs."

Lee owned several swords, but we know very little about them. The one he wore at the surrender was his "Maryland sword," now in the Museum of the Confederacy, Richmond. This is an almost straight sword with lion's head pommel, gold-plated and highly ornate basket hilt, ivory grip, and gunmetal scabbard with ornamental brass bands and tip. The sword was made by Devisme of Paris, France, and presented to Lee by "a marylander" in 1863.

His normal accouterments in the field were his field glasses, carried in a case on his right side, an undress sword belt with rectangular buckle, and a revolver in the left saddle holster. It is said that Lee rarely wore a sword or sash although he did put both on for the surrender at Appomattox. This sash is now at the West Point Museum. It is more yellow than the "buff" prescribed for a general officer, of silk net 7 feet 2 inches long plus two tassels, nine inches apiece. Douglas S. Freeman, in one of the rare errors in his monumental life of Lee (IV,118), states that Lee wore a crimson sash at the surrender. This statement has been competently examined and found to be incorrect.

No photographs were made at Appomattox, nor was there an artist present so far as we know. The several reconstructed views of the scene in the McLean house on 9 April 1865 are all based on the memories of those present, more or less carefully examined.

Several, among them Thomas Nast's painting unveiled in 1895, show Lee's coat buttoned to the throat, a most questionable arrangement although based upon Fitzhugh Lee's recorded recollection.

It might be well to comment on some of the more common errors found in the numerous posthumous portraits of the great Southern leader. Most frequent is the grouping of his coat buttons into three groups of three, the regulation arrangement for major generals and higher in the Union Army but one less common in the Confederacy. Another is the black hat, already mentioned. A third, found in Sidney E. Dickinson's portrait at West Point, is the addition of gold lace cuff loops which Lee never wore. Dickinson, for some unaccountable reason, has added a wreath below the stars on Lee's collar.

Stonewall Jackson's Dress

Jackson shared Lee's preference for plain clothes; some descriptions of his appearance make him downright slovenly. Indeed, the first impressions he made on other officers have become an important part of the Jackson legend.

General (then Captain) John D. Imboden, who reported to Jackson at Harpers Ferry in early May 1861, described him and his adjutant as wearing "well-worn, dingy uniforms of professors in the Virginia Military Institute." Dr. J. William Jones, Chaplain of the Army of Northern Virginia, remembered him on 4 July as "dressed in simple Virginia uniform." These men saw Jackson in a dark blue, double-breasted frock coat of U.S. Army model. Apparently he wore this same coat at First Bull Run, with dark blue forage cap and probably dark blue trousers. He may also well have worn the unusual insignia discussed above under Confederate insignia of rank.

It appears that Jackson did not change to a grey uniform until the spring of 1862. Major Jed Hotchkiss, the mapmaker and Jackson's close associate, noted in his journal:

> Monday, May 5th [1862]. The General remained in Staunton where he had his hair cut and laid aside the blue Major's uniform, which he had worn at the V.M.I., and continued to wear up to that time, and put on a full new suit of Confederate grey.

A photograph, said to have been taken at Winchester, Virginia in the fall of 1862 (*Photo. Hist.*, X, 101), shows him in gray with buttons *in threes*; he was then a major general. There is no gold braid on his sleeves and his gray or sky blue trousers have narrow buff stripes down the seams.

General Richard Taylor recalled seeing Jackson in May 1862: ". . . a pair of cavalry boots covering feet of gigantic size, a mangy cap with visor drawn low, a heavy dark beard, and weary eyes . . ." His cap was the "cadet pattern" then much in vogue, whose crown fell far forward over the visor; it was grey in color. This cap saw him through the campaigns of 1862 and until he received from his wife a new one, "greyish-blue" in color and adorned with a band of gold braid. At Fredericksburg in mid-December he finally gave his old cap to Major Hotchkiss, partially as a reward for Hotchkiss having purchased a soft hat for him at Frederick City, Maryland during the Antietam Campaign. The old cap is now in the Virginia Military Institute.

About the same time, General J.E.B. Stuart presented Jackson with a new uniform coat "resplendent with gold lace and marks of rank." It is recorded that his men didn't

SIMON BOLIVAR
BUCKNER,
1861

WILLIAM MAHONE,
1864

J.E.B. STUART, 1862.

GEORGE E. PICKETT, 1863.

Fig. 154. Some Confederate States general officers.

recognize him at first, then word ran down the line, "It is old Jack with new clothes on." In this new coat, which had buttons *in twos*, he was photographed in April 1863 at Hamilton's Crossing, near Fredericksburg (*Photo. Hist.*, II, 115); it proved to be the last picture taken of him, for two weeks later he was mortally wounded.

The cap sent him by Mrs. Jackson proved too gaudy for his taste, and after the Battle of Fredericksburg, in a romantic gesture, he cut off the gilt band and gave it to five-year-old Jannie Corbin, in whose house he had his headquarters. The little girl died a few weeks later and the band found its way into the Museum of the Confederacy.

Jackson's raincoat is also in the museum at V.M.I. It is a plain affair of black rubberized cloth, single-breasted with a roll collar, knee-length, with four buttons. There is no insignia of rank visible. He was wearing this raincoat when he was mortally wounded.

Other General Officers

The overall characteristics of the Confederate general officer's uniform have been described above. The gray frock coat was almost universally worn, its shade varying from a dark bluish-gray to almost a brown. A few cavalry commanders, like J.E.B. Stuart, adopted jackets with yellow linings which could be buttoned back to form colorful facings. Buttons were worn in groups of two or three, although only the first arrangement was actually prescribed. Collars, cuffs, and piping of coats were usually, but not always, buff; it was almost as common to find plain gray collars with perhaps a buff patch for the insignia, and gray cuffs piped with buff. Roll collars, as worn by General Lee, were generally reserved for uniforms worn indoors with accouterments.

Fig. 154

Although dress regulations called for dark blue trousers with two stripes of gold lace for generals, many seem to have worn plain gray or perhaps some serviceable material like corduroy. On campaign, high boots of soft black leather were the most popular; they had to be wide to accommodate the very full trousers of the period. Gauntlets were buff and all leather was usually black.

The use of the dark blue forage cap with four gold braids on four sides (but no other insignia) was about as common as the use of some form of black or drab colored felt hat. Possibly the former was adopted for occasions of ceremony; certainly the "chapeau, or cocked hat" and the "uniform cap" prescribed in 1861 were never worn except, perhaps, by General John B. Magruder. No hat insignia was ever prescribed and most of the hats worn by general officers were severely plain. Yet now and then some sort of decoration was added. Generals A.P. Hill, John B. Gordon, and others, including perhaps Longstreet, wore a U.S. general officer's hat cord, and a photograph of General William Mahone shows a single cloth star holding up the brim on the right side of a wide-brimmed drab colored hat. But the General also wears an unusual jacket with six pleats down its front (reminiscent of the Norfolk jacket) and no sleeve insignia.

Pleated coats were, on occasion, worn by other general officers such as S.B. Buckner and Leonidas Polk. Two of Buckner's coats are in the Kentucky Room, Museum of the Confederacy. One, a frock coat with pleated front, is of brown cloth and has a black turnover collar embroidered with two white stars in a wreath.

Colonel Freemantle, the British observer, called General John B. Magruder the "Confederacy's most elegant general. He was full of foppish mannerisms . . . and had

Fig. 155. Some Confederate States staff officers.

clothes to go with them. Usually he wore red-striped pants, a crimson-lined coat and a black-cocked hat with a huge plume." One of Magruder's caps is in the Museum of the Confederacy; it is a dark blue with much gilt braid. An embroidered "CSA" is on the front. It was made for him in Paris.

General J.E.B. Stuart's gay dress has been commented upon by several contemporaries, and his outfit proves that uniforms *à la fantaisie* were not unknown on the Confederate side. Major Heros von Borcke, who rode with him, wrote that Stuart "had something of Murat's weakness for the vanities of military parade. He betrayed this latter quality in his jaunty uniform which consisted of a small gray jacket, trousers of the same stuff, and over them high military boots, a yellow silk sash, and a grey slouch hat, surrounded by a sweeping black ostrich plume." Many of Stuart's subordinates copied his picturesque dress, including the plumed slouch hat.

Staff Officers

Staff officers were distinguished, if they were distinguished from other officers at all, by their dark blue trousers and caps and the buff color of their collars and cuffs. Major Heros von Borcke described the uniform he purchased in Richmond: "a light grey frock-coat with buff facings, dark blue trousers, and a little black cocked-hat with sweeping ostrich plume . . . which is as picturesque as it is suitable for active service." Von Borcke called this "the regulation dress for staff-officers." Even if we accept this only for the staff officers of J.E.B. Stuart's Cavalry Division, we will not be far from what, at least, the younger staff officers wore.

Fig. 155

Medical officers, alone of all the staff, were authorized black collars and cuffs and green sash. Otherwise their dress was that of the staff except for possibly an "M.S." on cap or hat. A photograph of Dr. Simon Baruch, Assistant Surgeon, 3rd South Carolina Battalion, shows the usual double-breasted frock coat with collar and arm insignia, a sash, but no sword belt. Photographs of other Confederate surgeons show about half wearing black facings and half without colored facings of any sort. Presumably regimental surgeons wore regimental uniforms where such existed. Except for insignia — apparently in most cases a "red badge" — stretcher bearers were not distinctively uniformed, nor were hospital personnel.

Officers and men of the Signal Corps, established 29 May 1862, had no distinctive uniform or insignia. The officers wore the uniform of the general staff of the same rank, while the sergeants were detailed men, wearing the dress of the branch to which they were assigned.

The Invalid Corps, established 17 February 1864, was given no internal organization comparable to the Veteran Reserve Corps in the North. No distinctive uniform or insignia was prescribed for it.

Mention has been made above of the unofficial devices adopted by chaplains. Certainly no distinctive uniforms were authorized for them and few such were worn unofficially. Photographs show ordinary officers' gray clothing. Some chaplains wore insignia of rank on their collars while others had some device suggestive of their calling.

The design of an appropriate insignia was undertaken by the army chaplains themselves. Many words were exchanged on the topic but no general agreement was reached. After much discussion the chaplains of the 2nd and 3rd Corps, Army of Northern Virginia, concluded in June 1863 that their badge would have "the letter C, with a half wreath of olive leaves worked in gold bullion, on a ground of black velvet, the whole about 2½ inches wide." Somewhat later the chaplains of the Army of Tennessee selected a simple Maltese cross, which symbol was later to mark so many graves of Confederate soldiers. Other chaplains chose the Latin cross. The extent to which any of these insignia were actually procured is not known, but several existing coats bear crosses or other devices on the collar.

Finally, we reach the dress of the scouts, guides, and spies. As we can readily imagine, it was varied and imaginative. Captain Thomas Norton Conrad, 3rd Virginia Cavalry, one of J.E.B. Stuart's best secret agents, has recorded his costume for us:

> My wardrobe consisted of three suits — one a chaplain suit, a straight-breasted coat of black cloth; one a scouting suit, a drab-colored English felt jacket and black velvet pants; and a captain's suit of grey with yellow trimmings. The first mentioned I wore on my trips to Washington [posing as a Federal chaplain], the second was my scouting suit within our lines, and the third was used on "dress parade" occasion.

★   ★   ★

In the orders of battle which follow we have listed only those organizations which cannot be associated clearly with a specific Confederate state. They include the tiny regular army, various elements of the Provisional Army, all Confederate Indian regiments and battalions, and the Confederate Negro troops formed late in the war. As in other orders of battle, listing has been confined to units of battalion or regimental size.

ORDER OF BATTLE: CONFEDERATE REGIMENTS AND BATTALIONS

(All commands listed below are assumed to have worn CS clothing unless noted otherwise.)

Regular Army

- Comp A, 1st Cav Regt (consol with 2nd Mississippi Cav Regt)   1861-1865
  US cav dress to 1862; armed with Sharps carbine and US reg accouterments.
- 1st Light Arty Comp   1861-1865
- Detachment of Regular Recruits (also called Inf School of Practice)   1861-1862
  Initially issued "one blue shirt (to be made into a blouse)," steel gray pants, probably gray forage cap.
- Gallimard's Comp of Sappers and Bombardiers   1861-1865

Provisional Army

Cavalry

- 1st Regt (formerly 6th or Claiborne's Regt; also called 12th Regt)   1862-1865
- 1st Bn Trans-Mississippi Cav (also called 1st Bn Arkansas and Louisiana Cav)   1864-1865 (?)
- 3rd Regt (formed from 11th Alabama Cav Bn; also called 11th Regt and 13th Regt)   1862-1865
- 6th Regt (formerly 1st Bn Kentucky Mounted Rangers; reorgan as 1st Cav Regt, *q.v.*)   1862

ORDER OF BATTLE (continued)

- 6th Bn (formerly Jessee's Bn Kentucky Mounted Riflemen) — 1862-1865
- 7th Regt (broken up to form 10th Georgia Cav Regt and 17th North Carolina Cav Bn) — 1862-1864
- 7th Bn (also called Prentice's Bn; organ within Federal lines) — 1863-1865
- 8th Regt (Wade's; also called 2nd Mississippi and Alabama Cav Regt) — 1862-1865
- 8th Regt (Dearing's) — 1864
- 10th Regt (formed by consol of Cav Bn, Hilliard's Alabama Legion and 19th Georgia Cav Bn) — 1863-1865
- 12th Regt: see 1st Regt
- 14th Regt (formed by consol Garland's Mississippi Cav Bn, Cage's Louisiana Cav Bn of Miles' Legion and other elements) — 1863-1865
- 15th Regt (also called 1st Alabama and Florida Cav Regt; formed by consol various elements from Alabama and Florida) — 1863-1865
- 16th Regt: see 12th Mississippi Cav Regt
- 20th Regt (Lay's Regt) — 1864-1865
- Mead's Regt Partisan Rangers — 1864-1865
- Power's Regt — 1863-1864

Artillery

There were no permanent Confederate artillery commands; all batteries, battalions, and regiments of this branch were recognized as belonging to one state or another. However, at least twenty-five provisional battalions of artillery were formed to control and administer the numerous independent batteries in the several Confederate armies. These were called "field organizations," some of which lasted for two years or more. The Stuart Horse Artillery was one of these — a battalion composed of independent batteries from several states serving in the Cavalry Corps, ANV, whose life spanned the years 1862-1865.

Since only a few batteries will be included in the state sections which follow, a general description of Confederate artillery clothing, accouterments, and arms will be added here. Officers as a rule followed the regulation uniform; gray frock coat piped with red, with red collar and cuffs; gray or sky blue pants with red stripe; forage cap with red sides and crown, blue band, and gold lace. Most wore high boots and the U.S. light artillery officer's saber, although any other saber listed above could have been used. Probably many artillery officers wore gray jackets in place of coats, especially in the horse artillery. All carried a revolver in a belt holster.

Enlisted men of artillery wore C.S. standard clothing except for a few relatively distinctive commands, described later. This was usually a simple gray jacket, often with red collar and pointed red cuffs; pants of various colors; felt hat or gray cap with red band. Some wore boots, especially the drivers. Swords and even revolvers were rare and carbines or musketoons virtually unheard of. The Confederate artilleryman dressed lightly and informally; his jacket was usually open and his accouterments confined to those required in the service of the piece or the management of the teams.

Engineers

- 1st Regt — 1864-1865
  (served as field engineers, sappers, and miners; 2 comps equipped as pontoniers. Officers probably wore blue caps with German "E" on front.)
- 1st Bn (Trans-Mississippi Dept; reorgan as 4th Regt) — 1864-1865
  4th Regt — 1865
- 2nd Regt — 1864-1865
- Pressman's Bn (reorgan as 3rd Regt) — 1864-1865
  3rd Regt — 1865
- 4th Regt: see 1st Engineer Bn

Infantry

- 1st Regt (formerly 36th Georgia Inf Regt) — 1862-1865
- 1st Bn (also called Forney's Regt) — 1862-1865
- 1st Foreign Bn (Engineers; also called Tucker's Bn; expanded to form Tucker's Regt) — 1864-1865

ORDER OF BATTLE (continued)

- 2nd Regt (formerly 25th Mississippi Inf Regt; disbanded)   1862
- 2nd Foreign Bn (also called 2nd Foreign Legion; redesig)   1864-1865
  8th Bn   1865
- 3rd Regt (formerly 18th Arkansas Regt and 1st Arkansas Bn; merged into   1862-1865
  1st Consol Arkansas Inf Regt).Carried Hardee battle flag, blue with white border and center, various battle honors. Initially issued flintlock musket. *April 1862*: Enfield rifle musket and accouterments.
- 4th Regt (formerly 1st Alabama, Tennessee and Mississippi Inf Regt; reorgan as 54th   1861-1862
  Alabama Inf Regt)
- 5th (Walker's) Regt (formerly 40th Tennessee Inf Regt)   1862- ?
- 5th (Smith's) Regt: see 9th Confederate Inf Regt
- 8th Bn: see 2nd Foreign Bn
- 9th Regt (formed by consol 2nd [J.K. Walker's] and 21st Tennessee Inf Regts;   1862-1865
  also called 5th Confederate Inf Regt)
- Bradford's Corps of Scouts and Guards (also called Bradford's Bn)   1864-1865
- Brush Bn (organ for Indian frontier service of deserters and skulkers)   1863- ?
- Camp Guard, Virginia Conscripts (Camp Lee, Richmond; 2 comps)   1863-1865 (?)
- Castle Thunder Bn (organ of prisoners)   1864
- Confederate States Barracks (Richmond, also called Soldiers Home;   1863-1865
  garrisoned by Co. H, 1st Invalid Bn; provided lodging, rations, and transportation for soldiers returning to their commands in the field from hospitals, prisons, furloughs, etc.) *1864*: issued caps, jackets, shirts, and pants. Armed with .69 cal. muskets.
- Confederate States Zouaves: see Louisiana Zouave Bn and Dupeire's Louisiana Zouave Bn
- Exchanged Bn (also called Trans-Mississippi Bn and Western Bn; provisional unit formed to   ?
  hold paroled and exchanged prisoners of war)
- Inf School of Practice: see Regular Army, Detachment of Regular Recruits
- President's Guard (Lawson, Huckstep, Dickinson; comp of disabled soldiers detailed to guard 1864-1865
  CS White House) Wore grey cap, jacket, and trousers.
- Tucker's Bn (and Regt): see 1st Foreign Bn
- Ward's Bn (CS prisoners; provisional command formed from prisoners of   1864
  Provost Marshal, Lynchburg, Va.; men pardoned and unit broken up)

Indian Regiments and Battalions

Fig. 157

Not much is known about the dress and arms of these Indian commands. Their ordinary clothing differed both from that of white settlers and the savage Plains Indian, and this must have been worn for the first year at least. They were supplied rifles by the Confederacy early in the war, but the patterns sent have not been identified.

- 1st (Bryan's) Cherokee Cav Bn (expanded)   1863-1865
  Cherokee Regt for Special Service in Indian Territory   (13 May!) 1865
- 1st (Bryan's) Cherokee Partisan Ranger Bn (merged into 2nd Cherokee Mounted Vols Regt)   1862-1863
- 1st (Drew's) Cherokee Mounted Rifles   1861-1862
- 1st (Watie's) Cherokee Mounted Rifles (also called 2nd Regt Cherokee Mounted Rifles)   1861-1865
- 1st (Harris', Reynolds') Chickasaw Cav Bn (reorgan as Shecoe's Chickasaw Bn Mounted Vols)   ? -1864
- 1st Chickasaw Inf Regt (also called Hunter's Regt Indian Vols)   1863- ?
- 1st (Battice's) Choctaw Cav Bn (reorgan)   1862
  1st Choctaw War Regt (also called Mounted Rifles, 2nd Choctaw Cav Regt, etc.)   1862-1864
- 1st (McCurtain's) Choctaw Bn (reorgan)   ? -1864
  3rd Choctaw Regt   1864 (?)
- 1st Choctaw and Chickasaw Mounted Rifles (also called Vols, Cav, etc)   1861-1864 (?)
- 1st (Jumper's) Seminole Cav Bn (expanded)   1861-1864
  1st Seminole Mounted Vol Regt   1864-1865

ORDER OF BATTLE (continued)

- 1st (Chilly McIntosh's) Creek Cav Bn (also called Mounted Vols, Mounted Rifles, etc; expanded)   1861-1862
  2nd Creek Mounted Vols Regt   1862-1863
- 1st (Daniel McIntosh's) Creek Mounted Rifle Regt (also Mounted Vols, etc)   1861-1864
- 2nd (Adair's) Cherokee Mounted Vols Regt (formed from 1st Cherokee Partisan   1863-1864
    Ranger Bn and elements of 1st (Watie's) Cherokee Mounted Rifles; also called Mounted Rifles, etc.)
- 2nd Creek Mounted Vols Regt: see 1st (Chilly McIntosh's) Creek Cav Bn
- 3rd Choctaw Regt: see 1st (McCurtain's) Choctaw Bn
- Cherokee Regt for Special Service: see 1st (Bryan's) Cherokee Cav Bn
- Chickasaw Cav Bn: see Shecoe's Chickasaw Bn Mounted Vols
- Deneale's Bn Choctaw Warriors   1861-   ?
- Drew's Cherokee Mounted Rifles: see 1st (Drew's) Mounted Rifles
- Hunter's Indian Regt: see 1st Chickasaw Inf Regt
- Osage Bn (Broke Arm's)   1862-1865
- Shecoe's Chickasaw Bn Mounted Vols   1864-1865

Negro Troops

Recruits were furnished "when practicable" a gray jacket and pants, blanket, and a pair of shoes. There is evidence that pants, drawers, shirts, shoes, and socks were issued but there is no indication that jackets were supplied.

- Chambliss' Bn (2 comps)   1865
    A parade of bn was reported to have attracted "universal attention and commendation."
- Jackson Bn (organ as local defense troops; included 1 Negro comp)   1865

SOURCES

C.S.A., Adjutant and Inspector General, *Regulations for the Army of the Confederate States*, Richmond, Va., 1861, 1862, 1863, 1864.

Frank Cunningham, *General Stand Watie's Confederate Indians*, San Antonio, Texas, 1961.

Douglas S. Freeman, *R.E. Lee*, 4 vols., New York, 1935.

————, *Lee's Lieutenants: A Study in Command*, 3 vols., New York, 1942-1946.

Roy Meredith, *The Face of Robert E. Lee*, New York, 1947.

Charles F. Pitts, *Chaplains in Gray: The Confederate Chaplains' Story*, Nashville, Tenn., 1957.

Richard P. Weinert, "The Confederate Regular Army," in *Military Affairs*, XXVI (1962), 97-107.

Jennings C. Wise, *The Long Arm of Lee,...*, 2 vols., Lynchburg, Va., 1915.

MS, "War Department Collection of Confederate Records" (Record Group 109) in National Archives.

U.S., War Department, *List of Regiments and Battalions in the Confederate States Army 1861-1865*, Washington, D.C., n.d. Printed by the Adjutant General for internal use, probably in the 1890's, and based upon the "War Department Collection of Confederate Records," cited above. Reprinted subsequently in various forms, one of the latest being William J. Tancig, *Confederate Military Land Units, 1861-1865*, N.Y., 1967.

Fig. 156. Confederate States light artillerymen and horse furniture.

Fig. 157. Confederate States Indian, 1862-1863. Reconstruction based on available contemporary evidence. The figure is not intended to represent any specific Indian tribe or military command.

CONFEDERATE INDIAN

500

Because of the extreme rarity of contemporary Confederate photographs, probably due to supply shortages and a lack of trained personnel, the following pictures from the collection of Herb Peck, Jr., are of special significance. Authentic and unretouched, they clearly illustrate the wide-ranging variety and colorful personal touches utilized by the CSA soldiers in their uniforms and weaponry.

Fig. 158. Captain George Arnold, CSA. This Confederate officer wears the double breasted frock coat prescribed for officers in regulations, with cuffs and collar of branch color, decorated with gold lace to denote his rank. His trousers, however, seem to be of the same color as his coat rather than the regulation sky blue or light blue. Original *carte de visite* photograph in the collection of Herb Peck, Jr.

Fig. 159. Unidentified Confederate Enlisted Man. This Confederate's jacket is clearly home-made with highly-stylized ornamentation and civilian buttons. The D-guard Bowie knife and doublebarreled shotgun would also seem to indicate that the photograph was taken early in the war. Original ambrotype photograph in the collection of Herb Peck, Jr.

Fig. 160. Unidentified Confederate Enlisted Man. This soldier holds a M1841 U.S. Rifle and a civilian top-hammer boot pistol. His accoutrements appear to be federal issue, and he does not hesitate to display a small M1839 belt plate. His uniform, of a very simple cut, is probably gray throughout. Original tintype photograph in the collection of Herb Peck, Jr..

Fig. 161. Unidentified Confederate Enlisted Man. Although turned up and fastened on one side, this soldier's brimmed hat is typical of the slouch hats which became popular during the Civil War. His laced jacket is of a common style worn by pre-war volunteers as well as early Confederate troops. His armament includes a pair of revolvers, knife and a M1816 U.S. musket. Original ambrotype photograph in the collection of Herb Peck, Jr..

Plate V

Private, 1st Regiment, U.S. Sharpshooters, 1862

Plate VI

Confederate States artillery officer, 1862

Plate VII

Confederate States infantryman, 1863—1865

Plate VIII

Rear Admiral John A. Dahlgren, 1864–1865

AMERICAN MILITARY EQUIPAGE

1851 · 1872

VOLUME III

AMERICAN MILITARY EQUIPAGE

1851 • 1872

A description by word and picture of what the American soldier, sailor and marine of these years wore and carried, with emphasis on the American Civil War.

VOLUME III

PART THREE
UNITED STATES NAVY
AND MARINE CORPS

TABLE OF CONTENTS

AMERICAN MILITARY EQUIPAGE
1851·1872

TABLE OF CONTENTS (continued)

VOLUME III

PART THREE
NAVIES AND MARINE CORPS

Abbreviations

Abbreviations used in the body of the narrative and in the descriptions of equipage are those in common use and require no explanation. Extensive use, however, is made of specialized abbreviations in the orders of battle, and these are explained below.

AC	Army Corps
a.d.	African Descent
AG	Adjutant General
AGO	Adjutant General's Office
ANV	Army of Northern Virginia
A of P	Army of the Potomac
arty	artillery
bn	battalion
brig	brigade
btry, btrys	battery, batteries
c.	circa, about
cal	caliber
cav	cavalry
Cir	Circular
comp, comps	company, companies
consol	consolidated, consolidation
CS	Confederate States
CSA	Confederate States of America
dept	department
disb	disband, disbanded
div	division
D of Ark	Department of Arkansas
D of Cum	Department of the Cumberland
D of Ohio	Department of Ohio
D of WVa	Department of West Virginia
EM	enlisted man or men
Fed	Federal
GHQ	General Headquarters
GO	General Orders
HQ	Headquarters
in	inch or inches
inf	infantry
M	Model
Mil Div	Military Division
mos	months
organ	organized or organization
QMG	Quartermaster General
redesig	redesignated
reg	regulation
regt	regiment
reorgan	reorganized, reorganization
serv	service
Smith.	Smithsonian Institution
US	United States
USA	United States of America
U.S.C.T.	United States Colored Troops
vol	volunteer
WDGO	War Department General Orders
WDSC	War Department Signal Corps
WPM	West Point Museum
yrs	years

Fig. 162. Captain in full dress, 1852-1862. Navy blue uniform with gold trim.

Fig. 163. Chief Engineer in full dress, 1858. Navy blue uniform with gold and silver epaulets. His branch is indicated by the wheel-and-anchor collar device and "E" on the epaulet straps.

CHAPTER 13

★ *U.S. NAVY* ★

American naval uniforms differed from those worn by land forces in several marked respects. They were far more restrained in the use of color; dark blue and white were almost the only shades employed. There were no regimental uniforms and relatively little variation in cut or color because of branches or functions. What little there was largely disappeared during our period and distinctions were indicated thereafter almost entirely by insignia only, which led to great complexity of devices. Furthermore, the uniforms worn by officers and those worn by enlisted seamen and other crew members differed far more radically than was the case in the army. Between the senior grades of enlisted men (called "petty officers") and officers existed a third category of "warrant officers," not found in the land service.

There was somewhat more tolerance — even laxity — in the enforcement of naval dress regulations than in the regular service ashore. Much depended on an individual ship commander, especially while at sea. Furthermore, naval uniforms were devised to be worn in greater ranges of temperature and more difficult conditions of weather than were normally expected of army clothing.

Officers' Dress

Our period commences with the dress regulations published 8 March 1852, over nine-tenths of which were devoted to naval officers, with only a meager paragraph left for petty officers and crew. The officers' portion was itself divided, almost evenly, into sections for "sea" or "line" officers and for the non-combatant "civil" or "staff" officers. The former could command at sea, and the latter could not.

The navy had always had civil officers, but their number and kind grew appreciably during this period. The introduction of steam, for example, had brought the engineer, and new developments in the design of ships added the naval constructor to the growing list of civil officers. In 1852 only surgeons and pursers (later called "paymasters") had been given relative rank, but by 1864 this rank had been extended to all types of staff officers, including naval constructors, engineers, secretaries, and professors of mathematics. As these officers were assimilated into the naval hierarchy, their uniforms became more and more like those worn by line officers, until by the end of the Civil War the two could be distinguished only by their insignia.

Naval officers in 1852 had three classes of uniform: full dress, undress and service dress. Each of these in turn had a winter and summer version. In the first this meant merely a change from dark blue cloth pants to others of white drill. In the undress, the officer could wear a light-weight coat and pants in warm weather, or change to white pants and a straw hat. With the service uniform it was possible to wear an entire uniform of white drill in warm climates.

Fig. 162

The full dress for all sea officers, and for surgeons and pursers, was a double-breasted tail coat of "navy-blue" cloth, nine buttons in each row, lined and faced with white silk serge. Navy blue, it should be noted, was a very dark shade of blue used for all naval clothing of that color. Collars and cuffs were the same, and on these were placed the stripes of gold lace or the distinctive embroidery that indicated rank and function, described hereafter. Pants were navy blue with a gold lace stripe or cord of different widths, depending upon rank, and the headdress worn was the "black cocked hat." Gold lace and bullion epaulets, black leather belts, and swords completed the dress.

Fig. 163

Engineers wore this same uniform except their coats were single-breasted, their trousers plain, and for some ranks the cocked hat was not authorized. Professors, secretaries, and clerks wore a single-breasted frock coat for both full dress and undress; it had eight buttons except in the case of clerks, who had seven. The skirts of the naval full dress coat had no turnbacks; the white lining showed only underneath. They did have pointed pocket flaps (laced for captains) over each hip, with four buttons on the center folds.

Chaplains, under the dress regulations of 8 March 1852, continued to wear a single-breasted tail coat of navy blue cloth with nine buttons and plain collar and cuffs of black velvet. New regulations of 3 March 1853 altered the color of the coat to black and ordered the buttons to be cloth-covered. Their frock coat was also black, single-breasted, with the same buttons and the same black velvet trim. With both uniforms they apparently wore a navy blue cloth cap and no insignia of rank.

The full dress uniform was rarely worn and it would appear that some commanders did not even require all their officers to own one. Pictures of Commodore Perry's officers in Japan, where the utmost of ceremony was called for, indicate a surprising absence of dress uniforms; it would seem that only the commodore wore a tail coat and cocked hat. A. T. Mahan, who entered the navy in 1860, speaks of the full dress being reserved "for exceptional occasions, in which, at one festive muster early in the cruise, we all had to appear, to show we had it; but otherwise it was generally done up in camphor."

Fig. 164, 166

"The frock was then the working coat of the navy," Admiral Mahan continues. It served for both undress and service dress and, after 1861, became the full dress coat. It was usually worn rather informally, either open in front or with lapels turned back to expose the shirt. Yet it could be made a very precise uniform, some commanders requiring it to be kept fully buttoned. It was made of navy blue cloth, faced with the same, and lined with black silk serge for all officers except boatswains, gunners, carpenters, and sailmakers. It differed from the army frock coat in having a "rolling" or turned-down

SURGEON, UNDRESS,
1852 - 1856

MIDSHIPMAN,
SERVICE DRESS,
1852 -

CLERK,
SERVICE DRESS,
1859.

LIEUTENANT,
WHITE DRILL OR
LINEN SERVICE
DRESS
(BLUE CAP)
1855.

CAPTAIN,
FOUL WEATHER DRESS
(PILOT-CLOTH OVERCOAT AND
WATER-PROOF CAP COVER),
1859.

G. WOODBRIDGE

Fig. 164. U.S. Navy officers, service and undress, 1852-1859.

collar and a different sort of cuff. Four buttons were placed on the rear folds of the skirts.

The frock coat of all sea officers in 1852 was double-breasted, as was that of surgeons and pursers; other officers wore single-breasted coats. An order of 8 February 1861 gave engineers the double-breasted frock coat, and after 1864 it was worn by all officers except master's mates. Rank insignia were worn on the sleeves; epaulets were worn for undress and shoulder straps for service, in both cases only by those officers entitled to do so. Rank was indicated further by the number of buttons on the front of the coat: nine in each row on the double-breasted pattern, nine on an engineer's or chaplain's single-breasted coat, eight on that of a professor or secretary, and six or seven on a clerk's.

For undress most officers were authorized a cocked hat, but a blue cloth cap with varying embellishment was far more common. Trousers were navy blue, without lace or cord; belts and swords were worn. Service dress for officers — by all means the most common uniform — was the same as undress except that the cap and shoulder straps were worn and swords usually omitted.

Fig. 164 The officer's cap in 1852 bore a larger crown (9-10 inches in diameter) than band and was relatively rigid. Its visor and chinstrap were black patent-leather, and higher sea officers and some others wore gold lace bands of widths depending upon rank. By 1861 the crown was reduced to being only a half inch larger than the band, a difference scarcely noticeable, and by 1864 all gold lace was abolished. A black oilcloth cover was worn in stormy weather. During the Civil War naval officers purchased such an odd assortment of cap styles, favoring those with very low and limp crowns, that the Navy Department was forced to restate the regulation dimensions and require a report from all ships and stations that they were being adhered to.

Naval officers were allowed to wear special uniforms in summer or tropical climates. Frock coats and trousers were made in "dark blue summer-cloth" and had smaller buttons. Jackets of navy blue or white drill could be worn when at sea, and white drill pants could take the place of blue in any uniform. Furthermore, officers could wear white straw hats when aboard ship.

For cold weather officers wore an overcoat of dark blue pilot cloth, double-breasted with rolling collar and skirts falling to three inches below the knees. Shoulder straps were used on this overcoat but otherwise it was plain. In very cold or wet weather, special cloaks of dark blue cloth were allowed, and these were also used in boats or over the full dress uniform on account of its epaulets. In 1864 the overcoat was described as a "caban overcoat and cape, of dark blue beaver or pilot-cloth, lined throughout with dark blue flannel," double-breasted with detachable cape. Insignia of rank were worn on the overcoat collar after 1864; before that, shoulder marks were worn by those entitled to them.

Early in the Civil War the full dress uniform was abolished for reasons of economy and standardization, and the wearing of cocked hats and epaulets was curtailed if not eliminated. All were brought back, however, by 1869 with only slight modification.

Jackets have been mentioned; they formed the service uniform of midshipmen at the Naval Academy and were also authorized for wear by all officers throughout our period. Yet Admiral Mahan recalls that they had merely "informal recognition in the service . . . while here and there some officer would sport one, they could scarcely be called popular." Midshipmen took their jackets to sea to wear them out, but there it usually ended.

Fig. 165. Captain (Commodore) Perry in undress with epaulets. (Lithograph.)

Fig. 166. Lieutenant in undress, 1860. (By Michael J. McAfee after photograph.)

Fig. 167. Midshipman in service dress, 1862; all navy blue.

Fig. 168. Midshipman in full dress, 1852-1869.

Fig. 169. Admiral David G. Farragut in undress, wearing 1862-1864 cuff device.

Fig. 170. Captain in sack coat, 1865. Before 1869 officers could add full insignia to this coat and wear their swords.

Fig. 171. Commander in jacket, 1864-1865. A star on each sleeve now indicates the line officer. (By Michael J. McAfee, after photograph.)

Fig. 172. Master, U.S.N., 1862-1863. Summer service dress.

Fig. 173.
Lieutenant of the Line
in pilot jacket, 1864.

Fig. 174. Admiral Farragut, 1866. (Photograph from Library of Congress.)

Jackets of blue cloth or flannel were also worn by shipped or rated master's mates; these had a rolling collar and were double-breasted with six medium-sized buttons in each row, and three or four small ones on each cuff. By 1864 this jacket was allowed certain higher ranking petty officers, who wore with it a plain blue visored cap and a white cotton or linen shirt (in place of the seaman's frock).

The Civil War introduced the sack coat to the naval officer, with whom it was often known as a "pilot jacket." It was not officially authorized until 1865 and, as a result, took on many styles before then, being both single- and double-breasted. In 1869 it was specified as a blue flannel single-breasted blouse, with five medium-sized buttons and neither shoulder straps nor cuff lace. Rank and function were indicated by devices on the collar, although sleeve lace and shoulder straps were optional, 1865-1866.

Fig. 170,173,176

Warrant Officers' Dress

Boatswains, gunners, carpenters, and sailmakers were warrant officers and, in 1852, on all occasions wore a double-breasted frock coat with turned-down collar and eight large buttons in each row. Three large buttons were placed under each pocket flap on the skirts. Three medium-sized buttons went around each cuff with two small ones at the openings. A loop of gold lace four inches long, with a small button at its point, lay on each side of the collar; the shoulders were bare. Pants were blue or white, without lace. A plain blue cloth undress cap, without lace or insignia, completed the dress in 1852, although a gold lace and blue cap band was introduced the next year. This was their universal uniform; Admiral Mahan recalled the carpenter of the *Congress* "wearing always a frock-coat, buttoned up as high as any one then buttoned . . ."

Fig. 175

Petty Officers' and Seamen's Dress

Petty officers comprised a group of enlisted specialists corresponding roughly to the non-commissioned staff of the army. The master-at-arms was the chief petty officer of his ship and the others were divided into two classes: petty officers of the line, and of the staff. The first class included such men as boatswain's mates, quartermasters, captains of the main-top, and quarter-gunners; the second contained, among others, yeomen, paymaster's stewards, masters of the band, armorers, coopers, and ship's cooks.

With the exception of some higher ratings, petty officers wore the seamen's clothing described below. The coat and cap worn by first-class petty officers in later years were not authorized in this period; instead, as early as 1862, certain higher ratings were allowed jackets, the ratings changing from regulation to regulation. In 1869, at least, seamen gunners, machinists, masters-at-arms, yeomen, apothecaries (formerly called surgeon's stewards), and paymaster's writers (formerly called paymaster's stewards) were ordered to wear a navy blue jacket with white cotton or linen shirt, vest with six small-sized navy buttons, and a plain blue cloth visored cap.

This petty officer's jacket should not be confused with the seaman's jacket mentioned below, although the two types were quite similar; the former had fewer buttons and was

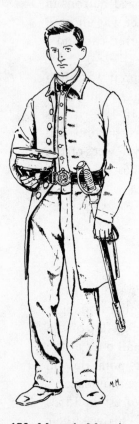

Fig. 175. Master's Mate in undress, 1862-1864. His cap device is a gold anchor without a wreath; in this case it is placed horizontally. (By Michael J. McAfee, after photograph.)

Fig. 176. Shipped or rated Master's Mate of a monitor wearing a pilot jacket. (By Michael J. McAfee.)

Fig. 177. Boatswain's Mate, 1852. This boatswain's mate wears a sennit hat with black ribbon, white frock with blue collar and bib, and blue woolen trousers. (By Michael J. McAfee, after contemporary woodcuts and drawings.)

at times worn buttoned. It could not have differed greatly from a midshipman's jacket.

The clothing worn by firemen, coal-heavers, seamen, ordinary seamen, and other enlisted crew members was only generally prescribed in the 1852 dress regulations. There was still some variation to be found in the patterns worn aboard different ships. While the Navy Department purchased clothing for enlisted men on contract, some seamen made their own clothes according to time-honored practice. By 1869 the amount of attention given to enlisted men's clothing had measurably increased and even more attention was accorded to the devices by then authorized for wear. By and large, however, the cut and color of the seaman's dress saw little change over the period 1851-1872. His principal outer garments were:

●*Blue cloth jacket.* This was a loose, double-breasted broadcloth shell jacket with two rows of medium-sized navy buttons; at least nine buttons were in each row in 1852, spaced less than an inch apart, with less than two inches between the rows. The number of buttons was reduced to six in 1869. The jacket had wide, long lapels. It could be worn unbuttoned, held together by a loop and two buttons at the base of the lapels. It had slashed sleeves, fastened by three or four small-sized buttons. This was the dress garment of the petty officer and crew. *Fig. 180*

●*Blue woolen frock.* This characteristic outer garment for service wear consisted of a loose navy blue shirt without buttons in front, open at the neck, having a wide "sailor's" collar, 6.5 inches deep, hanging down the back. The frock was made during the period with at least three patterns of yoke. There was a small pocket high on the left breast, and its full sleeves were gathered tightly at the wrist into a cuff secured by two buttons. These cuffs and the collar were of white duck from 1852 to 1859. After that they were of the same material as the frock, and at first were issued plain. In 1866 an order directed that a varying number of rows of white tape be worn around the collar and a like number on the cuffs, according to the rating. Three years later all collars were given two rows of white tape, .125 inch apart, and from one to four strips of white tape were placed on the cuffs as rating marks. *Fig. 179,184* *Fig. 181*

The frock, and especially the white frock mentioned next, was not often left as unadorned as it was when issued. Respect for individual taste was something of a characteristic of the navy in pre-Civil War days and seamen handy with a needle were permitted, if not encouraged, to embroider the front of their frocks with designs in various colors. Indeed, some seamen made a specialty of such sewing and for a price would embellish the frocks of less skillful shipmates. It was the recognition of this desire for adornment that led a uniform board after the Civil War to add white embroidery and tape as a regulation part of the dress.

The blue frock was habitually tucked into the top of the trousers.

●*White linen or duck frock.* Designed for wear in warm weather, this garment closely resembled the blue frock in style. Its collar and cuffs could be white or covered with blue dungaree or nankeen, and were at first plain. In 1866 white tape was added, corresponding to the designs on the blue frock. It, too, was habitually tucked into the trousers. *Fig. 177*

●*Blue woolen and white duck trousers.* With the two frocks above, seamen wore these two types of trousers in any combination. Both had wide bottoms — the navy did not use

A

B

Fig. 178, A through D. Petty officers of the USS *Pensacola* in different uniforms, c. 1860. The signal flags are numerical indicators and are believed here to indicate the uniform to be worn aboard ship. (From oil paintings on tin plates in the collection of Alan Sussel.)

C

D

E   F

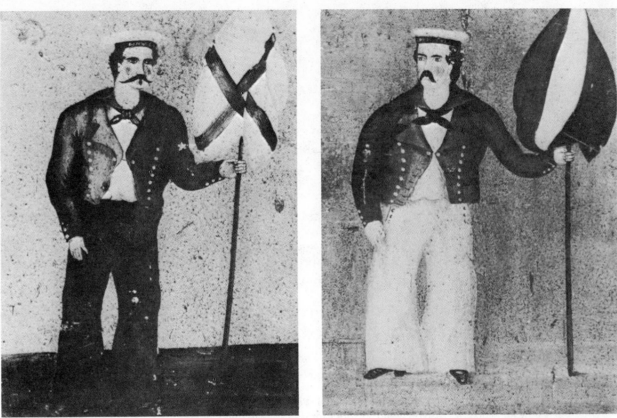

Fig. 178, E through H. The use of a star without an eagle as insignia of rank, and the unusual pointed cuffs on the white blouses, remain unexplained except to suggest that the *Pensacola's* captain gave extraordinary attention to the dress of his crew. (From the collection of Alan Sussel.)

G   H

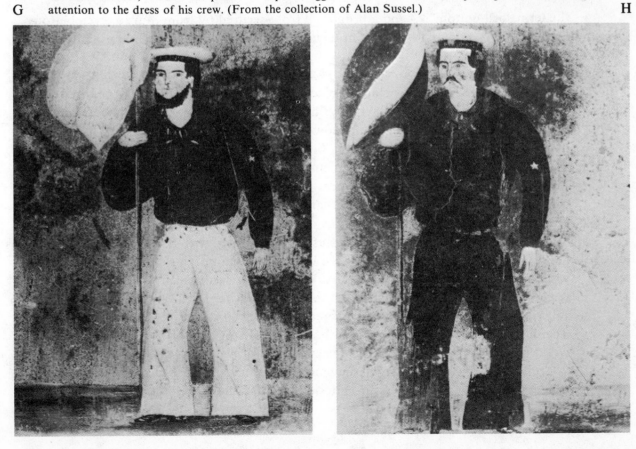

Fig. 179. Rear view of seaman with musket, 1861. "Sailor on Sentry" by Alfred Waud. (From Library of Congress.)

Fig. 180. Petty officer in summer dress, 1862, equipped for shore duty. He wears the seaman's blue cloth jacket over a blue frock. His trousers are blue.

the term "bell bottom" — and a broad fall front secured by from four to seven buttons across the top. Apparently, fly-front trousers were also issued, at least during the Civil War.

●*Black varnished hat*. Worn since the War of 1812, this traditional dress hat was on its way out in the 1850's. It was made of black glazed (japanned) straw or tarpaulin, with a low crown and wide brim. A black silk ribbon (without lettering), 1.125 inches wide, was fastened around the crown and hung down the back. This hat was abolished in 1866 and its place as the dress hat taken by the blue cloth cap.

Fig. 177

●*White straw or "sennit" hat*. Similar in pattern to the black hat, above, and also fitted with a black ribbon. It was, of course, the warm weather headdress, worn on dress occasions. It lasted somewhat longer than the black hat, not being abolished until after 1872.

Fig. 179
Fig. 181

●*Blue cloth cap*. This is the headdress usually associated with the seaman and the one almost universally worn during the Civil War. It was made of thick blue cloth with a low, wide, soft crown; it had no visor. At first it was strictly a service hat, "worn by the crew at sea, except on holidays or at muster." About the time of the Civil War it was given a black silk ribbon, on which it became customary to letter in gilt or yellow the name of the wearer's ship, and thereafter became the seaman's dress cap. In warm weather the cap could be given a white linen cover, fastened by a draw string.

Apparently it was customary to sew some sort of an insigne on top of these blue caps in order to prevent snipers aloft from shooting their own men. This often took the form of a star or many-pointed sun.

Fig. 181. Petty officer and seamen aboard a monitor; drill with a boat howitzer, 1863-1865.

Fig. 182. Powder monkey (ordinary seaman) in jacket, worn over a blouse.

Fig. 183. Seaman in overcoat. (By Michael J. McAfee, after photograph.)

•*Working suit*. This comprised a canvas duck "jumper" and pair of overalls. The jumper resembled the frock but its collar was plain canvas and there were no cuffs. The overalls were straight and full and probably had a fly front. It was usual to wear the jumper over the overalls. The working suit was introduced by the regulations of 1869, but somewhat similar garments in blue and white had been worn earlier.

•*Black silk neckerchief*. A square-shaped piece of silk, probably three feet on a side, worn underneath the collar of the frock. Its wear by this time was traditional and surrounded by various myths.

•*Undershirt*. Red flannel undershirts were widely worn during the period of the Civil War and perhaps at other times. Underwear was never referred to in naval dress regulations, and it is not possible to determine the degree to which red or other colors were employed.

•*Shoes*. Black shoes, of a low cut, were part of the regular clothing issue, but no information has been found on their pattern.

•*Foul weather gear*. Dress regulations make no mention of overcoats or the like for petty officers and seamen, although it is apparent that they could be worn in bad weather. Possibly some of the higher ranks wore overcoats of officers' pattern, but the pea jacket was the obvious garment for most. This medium length, double-breasted overcoat, made of coarse navy blue woolen cloth, had been in common use with mariners for over a century and probably formed part of a seaman's issue of clothing. Some examples reached down to the seaman's knees.

Fìg. 184. Variations in the design of seamen's work blouses, 1861-1865. Note also the use of fly-front trousers. (By Michael J. McAfee from photographs.)

Insignia

The insignia worn by both naval officers and seamen changed frequently and in some cases radically during this period. Since it will be clearer to present these changes graphically, our remarks in the text will be confined to generalities.

The eagle and foul anchor was the closest to a general naval device that can be found in this period. It was used on all buttons and on the officers' belt plate. This last was a two-part buckle of brass which, with a black morocco belt, was worn by all ranks of officer. It remained regulation throughout our period.

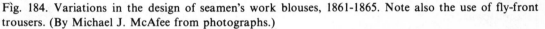

Fig. 186

In 1852 there was no grade in the navy above that of captain, although a captain in command of a squadron was, by courtesy, called "commodore." Below this the ranks of officers were: commander, lieutenant, master, passed midshipman, and midshipman. These were the sea (later called "line") officers. There were also civil (later called "staff") officers, as mentioned above, who might or might not in 1852 have been accorded a relative rank with sea officers. One of the complicating features of naval insignia in this period was the gradual assimilation of the various classes and ranks of civil officer into the naval hierarchy.

The need for a rank higher than captain was obvious to naval men by 1852, but less so to others. To many men of influence in those days the name "admiral" sounded like a title of nobility and not until 1862 did Congress authorize the establishment of the rank of rear admiral. Meanwhile (in 1857), as a temporary expedient, certain captains were breveted "flag officers" to afford them higher command. The Senior Captain of the Navy and commanders-in-chief of squadrons were allowed extra stars on their epaulets and shoulder straps in 1852, but no new insignia were provided with the flag officer brevet.

Various other changes were made in the officers' rank structure: new ranks were created, others eliminated, and several titles were changed. To clarify these alterations (at the risk of oversimplification) it would be well to explain the titles of rank and function as used in the navy during the period 1852-1872. First are the commissioned officers of the line:

Admiral *(grade created for Farragut, 25 July 1866)*
Vice Admiral *(grade created 21 December 1864, Farragut being the first to hold it)*
Rear Admiral *(grade created 16 July 1862)*
Flag Officer *(title created 16 January 1857 to avoid use of the term "Admiral")*
Commodore *(courtesy title until 16 July 1862, when the grade was formally created)*
Captain
Commander
Lieutenant Commander *(grade created 16 July 1862)*
Lieutenant
Master *(grade existed throughout period; originally had been "Sailing Master." Became a commissioned officer in 1862 and after the period changed to Lieutenant Junior Grade)*
Ensign *(title for Passed Midshipman after 16 July 1862)*
Passed Midshipman *(Midshipman who had passed his examination for promotion to Lieutenant; called "Ensign" after 1862 although term continued in use)*
Midshipman *(grade given undergraduates at the U.S. Naval Academy; not strictly in the line of the navy in the latter part of the period)*
Master
Master's Mate
Shipped or Rated Master's Mate *(usually a warrant officer)*

The officers of the staff come next. When holding a relative rank (as all did by 1865), this rank (shown in parentheses) often depended upon length of service and was not reflected in their title, although it could be in their insignia:

Surgeon of the Fleet *(Commodore; title created 1846)*
Surgeon *(Lieutenant Commander — Captain)*
Passed Assistant Surgeon *(Lieutenant)*
Assistant Surgeon *(Master)*
Fleet Paymaster *(Captain; title by 1863)*

Paymaster *(called Purser before 1860; Lieutenant Commander — Captain)*
Assistant Paymaster *(Master)*
Fleet Engineer *(Captain; created by 1863)*
Chief Engineer *(Lieutenant Commander — Captain)*
1st Assistant Engineer *(Master)*
2nd Assistant Engineer *(Ensign)*
3rd Assistant Engineer *(Midshipman or warrant officer)*
Naval Constructor *(Lieutenant Commander — Captain)*
Assistant Naval Constructor *(Master)*
Chaplain *(Lieutenant Commander — Commander)*
Professor of Mathematics *(Lieutenant Commander — Commander)*
Secretary *(Lieutenant)*
Clerk *(Midshipman or warrant officer)*

(The chiefs of bureaus in the staff corps ranked with commodores.)

There were the warrant officers, all of the same grade: boatswains and gunners, together with carpenters and sailmakers (who were classed as staff officers after 1863).

Following these were the petty officers, those of the line being roughly in order of rank:

Master-at-arms
Boatswain's Mates
Gunner's Mates
Seamen Gunners
Chief or Signal Quartermaster
Cockswain to Commander-in-chief
Captains of Forecastle
Quartermasters
Cockswains
Captains of Tops (three kinds)
Captains of Afterguard
Quarter-Gunners
2nd Captains of Forecastle
2nd Captains of Tops (three kinds)

Petty officers of the staff comprised another list, with relative ranks interwoven with the list above:

Yeomen
Surgeon's Stewards (later called Apothecaries)
Paymaster's Stewards (later called Paymaster's Writers)
Masters of the Band
Schoolmasters
Ship's Writers
Carpenter's Mates
Armorers
Sailmaker's Mates

Painters
Coopers
Armorer's Mates
Ship's Corporals
Captains of Hold
Ship's Cooks
Bakers
Machinists (created about 1869)

Finally, there were various ranks and duties among the other crew members that were recognized by titles:

Seamen
Ordinary Seamen
1st Class Firemen

2nd Class Firemen
Landsmen
Coal Heavers
Boys

The devices worn by the different ranks and ratings are illustrated. It will be observed that their use falls into four stages. That from 1852 to 1862 counted heavily on distinctions in clothing to mark the rank and function of officers; insignia on the whole were limited and unsystematic, and stressed the difference between line and staff as strongly as they did between grades. Petty officers were given an "eagle and anchor" device with a star over it — worn on the right arm by the six higher grades and on the left by the others — but that was the only insigne worn by enlisted men. It is possible that some petty officers wore only the star.

The Civil War, as has been said, forced the navy to expand the number of ranks, give staff officers greater recognition, and standardize clothing. This led to a more systematic plan of rank insignia. Some changes, like the orders of 8 February 1861 affecting engineers, came early; the most important order was that of 31 July 1862, which widely revised both uniforms and insignia of line officers.

The system of rank insignia established in 1862 lasted only a year, until 23 May 1863, at which time a change in officers' sleeve devices was ordered and the star established for line officers. This new system remained in effect until 1866, when the entire question of uniforms and insignia was restudied and new regulations were issued on 1 December.

The final stage began in 1866 and continued through the end of the period with which we are here concerned. By that time both naval uniforms and insignia had developed much closer to what they are today; officers wore a standardized uniform, as did enlisted men, and virtually all ranks and ratings were marked by a device of one sort or another.

Buttons.

Navy buttons came in three sizes: large (.875 inch); medium (.7 inch); small (.575 inch). All were brass and bore an eagle-on-anchor device, above three barely perceptible cannon balls and surrounded by thirteen stars, within a rope circle. This design was introduced in 1852 and, with minor variations, continued in use for many years after our period. Some buttons worn by enlisted men were made of bone or of hard rubber (with "U.S.N.", three stars, and an anchor).

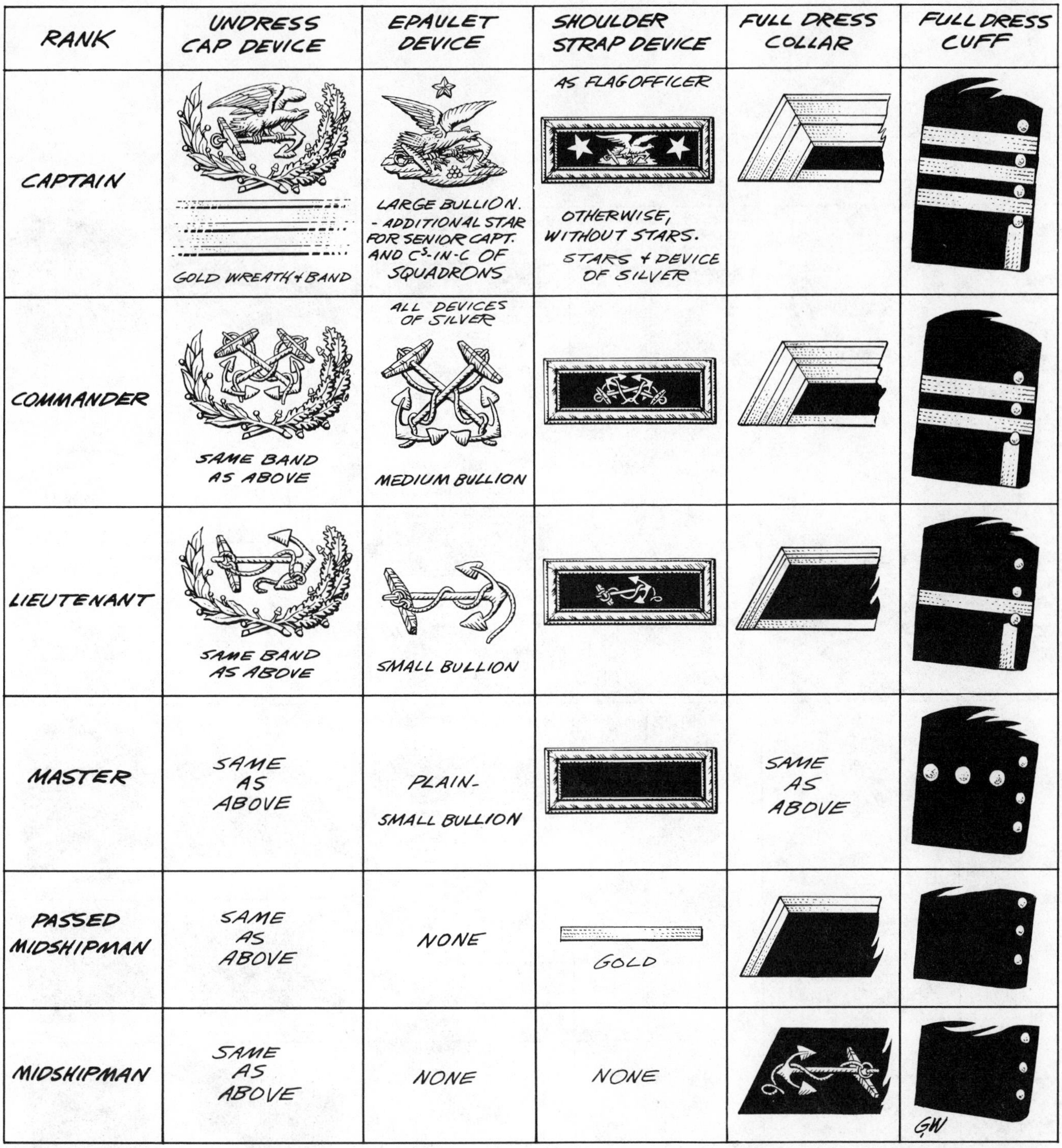

RANK	UNDRESS CAP DEVICE	EPAULET DEVICE	SHOULDER STRAP DEVICE	FULL DRESS COLLAR	FULL DRESS CUFF
CAPTAIN	GOLD WREATH + BAND	LARGE BULLION. - ADDITIONAL STAR FOR SENIOR CAPT. AND Cs-IN-C OF SQUADRONS	AS FLAG OFFICER / OTHERWISE, WITHOUT STARS. STARS + DEVICE OF SILVER		
COMMANDER	SAME BAND AS ABOVE	ALL DEVICES OF SILVER / MEDIUM BULLION			
LIEUTENANT	SAME BAND AS ABOVE	SMALL BULLION			
MASTER	SAME AS ABOVE	PLAIN- SMALL BULLION		SAME AS ABOVE	
PASSED MIDSHIPMAN	SAME AS ABOVE	NONE	GOLD		
MIDSHIPMAN	SAME AS ABOVE	NONE	NONE		

Fig. 185-a. Rank insignia, sea or line officers, 1852-1862.

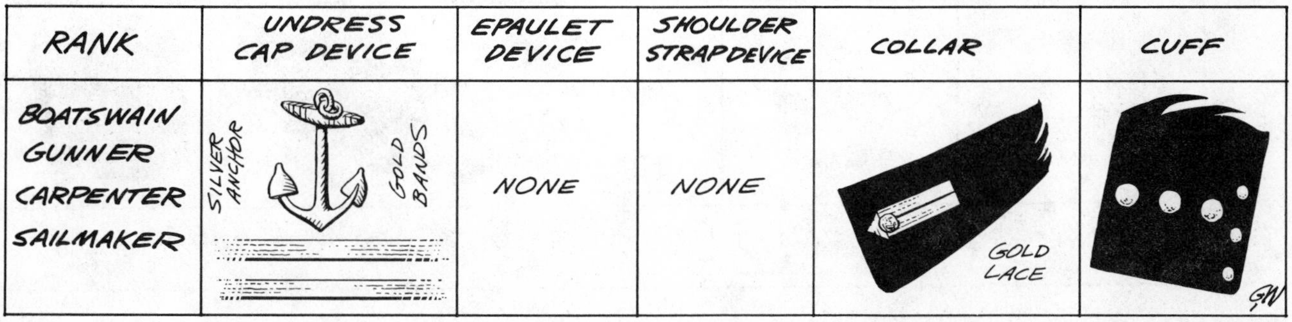

RANK	UNDRESS CAP DEVICE	EPAULET DEVICE	SHOULDER STRAP DEVICE	COLLAR	CUFF
BOATSWAIN GUNNER CARPENTER SAILMAKER	SILVER ANCHOR / GOLD BANDS	NONE	NONE	GOLD LACE	

Fig. 185-b. Rank insignia, warrant officers, 1852-1862.

542

RANK	UNDRESS CAP DEVICE	EPAULET DEVICE	SHOULDER STRAP DEVICE	FULL DRESS COLLAR	FULL DRESS CUFF *
SURGEON	A. IN USE FROM 1847 TO 1852. CHANGED ON 24 SEPTEMBER TO:	FOR SENIOR SURGEONS, A SILVER ROSETTE ABOVE LETTERS 𝔐𝔇 MEDIUM BULLION FOR 12 YEARS SERVICE, SMALL FOR LESS. ON 24 SEPTEMBER 1852, DEVICE CHANGED TO:	OVER 12 YRS. SERVICE NO ACORNS FOR LESS THAN 12 YRS. SERVICE. 24 SEPTEMBER 1852 DEVICE CHANGED TO:		
PASSED ASSISTANT SURGEON				SAME AS ABOVE	SAME AS ABOVE
ASSISTANT SURGEON	B. PLACED ABOVE LACE BAND.	SMALL BULLION FOR PASSED AND ASSISTANT SURGEONS.	PASSED ASSISTANT FOR ASSISTANT, THE SAME, BUT WITHOUT BARS.	SAME AS ABOVE	SAME AS ABOVE
PURSER	FROM 1852 — PRIOR TO 1852, SAME WREATH AS A.; 𝔓𝔇 IN CENTER	𝔓𝔇 1847 TO 1852. CHANGED 24 SEPT. TO: MEDIUM BULLION REGARDLESS OF YEARS OF SERVICE.	OVER 12 YRS. SERVICE NO OAK LEAVES FOR LESS. DEVICE FROM 1852		
CHAPLAIN	1847-1852, SAME WREATH AS A., BUT WITH NO CENTER DEVICE. FROM 1852, SAME WREATH AS B.	NONE	NONE		
PROFESSOR AND SECRETARY	SAME AS A., NO CENTER DEVICE	NONE	NONE		
CLERK	SAME AS ABOVE	NONE	NONE		

*UNDRESS CUFFS (SURGEONS & PURSERS ONLY), AUGUST, 1856: TWO 3/4" GOLD STRIPES.

GW

Fig. 185-c. Rank insignia, civil or staff officers, 1852-1864.

RANK	UNDRESS CAP DEVICE	EPAULET DEVICE	SHOULDER STRAP DEVICE	FULL DRESS COLLAR	FULL DRESS CUFF
CHIEF ENGINEER	SILVER ANCHOR	ON SILVER STRAP, HAVING A SOLID (SMOOTH) CRESCENT. SMALL BULLION		WREATH AND WHEEL OF GOLD. SILVER ANCHOR	
FIRST ASSISTANT ENGINEER	SAME AS ABOVE	NONE	NONE	SAME AS ABOVE.	SAME AS ABOVE, BUT ONE LESS LARGE BUTTON.
SECOND ASSISTANT ENGINEER		NONE	NONE		
THIRD ASSISTANT ENGINEER		NONE	NONE		SAME AS ABOVE.

Fig. 185-d. Rank insignia, engineer officers, 1852-1861.

RANK	UNDRESS CAP DEVICE	EPAULET DEVICE	SHOULDER STRAP DEVICE	FULL DRESS COLLAR	UNDRESS CUFF
CHIEF ENGINEER	SILVER DEVICE GOLD WREATH.	PLAIN	OVER 12 YEARS SERVICE / FOR LESS THAN 12 YEARS, NO ACORNS.	½ INCH LACE (GOLD)	15 YEARS, SAME AS CAPTAIN. / 5 YEARS, SAME AS COMMANDER. / LESS THAN 5 YEARS, SAME AS LT. COMMANDER.
FIRST ASSISTANT ENGINEER	SAME AS ABOVE	NONE	1861-1862 ONLY	SAME AS ABOVE	SAME AS MASTER
SECOND ASSISTANT ENGINEER		NONE	1861-1862 ONLY		SAME AS ENSIGN
THIRD ASSISTANT ENGINEER		NONE	NONE		SAME AS MIDSHIPMAN.

CHAPLAINS, PROFESSERS OF MATHEMATICS, COMMODORE'S SECRETARIES AND CLERKS EMPLOYED THE CAP DEVICE SHOWN ABOVE. CUFFS FOR ALL EXCEPT CHAPLAINS TO BEAR THREE SMALL NAVAL BUTTONS ON THE SLASH; THE CHAPLAIN'S TO BE PLAIN. NO OTHER DESIGNATING BADGES WERE AUTHORIZED UNTIL 1864. SEE CHARTS F. AND J.

Fig. 185-e. Rank insignia, engineer and staff officers, 1861-1864.

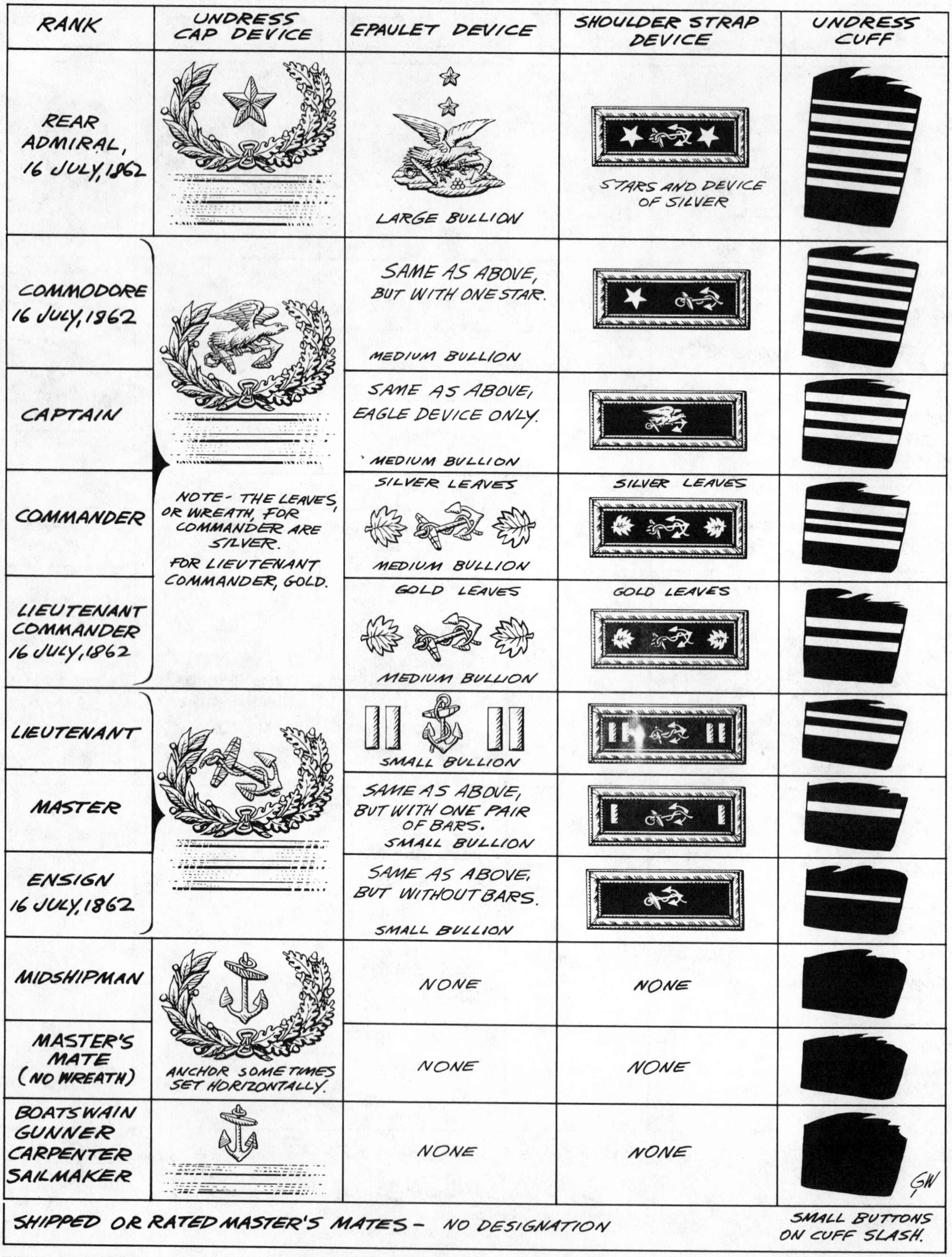

544

RANK	UNDRESS CAP DEVICE	EPAULET DEVICE	SHOULDER STRAP DEVICE	UNDRESS CUFF
REAR ADMIRAL, 16 JULY, 1862		LARGE BULLION	STARS AND DEVICE OF SILVER	
COMMODORE 16 JULY, 1862		SAME AS ABOVE, BUT WITH ONE STAR. MEDIUM BULLION		
CAPTAIN		SAME AS ABOVE, EAGLE DEVICE ONLY. MEDIUM BULLION		
COMMANDER	NOTE- THE LEAVES, OR WREATH, FOR COMMANDER ARE SILVER. FOR LIEUTENANT COMMANDER, GOLD.	SILVER LEAVES MEDIUM BULLION	SILVER LEAVES	
LIEUTENANT COMMANDER 16 JULY, 1862		GOLD LEAVES MEDIUM BULLION	GOLD LEAVES	
LIEUTENANT		SMALL BULLION		
MASTER		SAME AS ABOVE, BUT WITH ONE PAIR OF BARS. SMALL BULLION		
ENSIGN 16 JULY, 1862		SAME AS ABOVE, BUT WITHOUT BARS. SMALL BULLION		
MIDSHIPMAN		NONE	NONE	
MASTER'S MATE (NO WREATH)	ANCHOR SOMETIMES SET HORIZONTALLY.	NONE	NONE	
BOATSWAIN GUNNER CARPENTER SAILMAKER		NONE	NONE	
SHIPPED OR RATED MASTER'S MATES - NO DESIGNATION				SMALL BUTTONS ON CUFF SLASH.

Fig. 185-f. Rank insignia, line and warrant officers, 1862-1864.

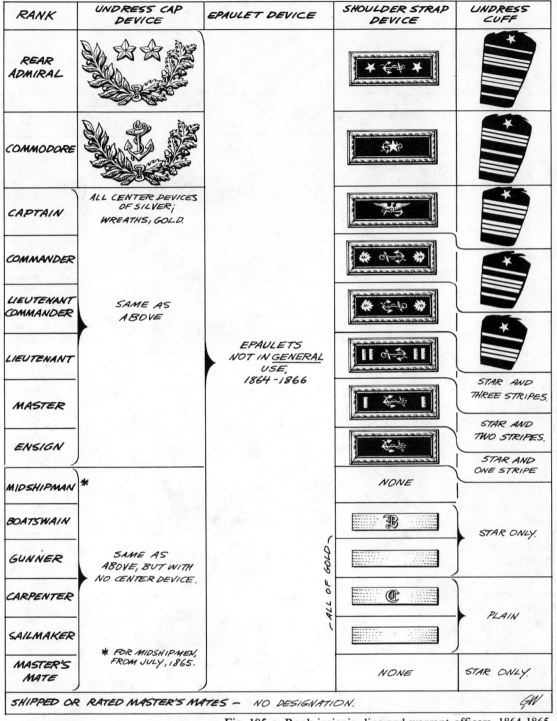

RANK	UNDRESS CAP DEVICE	EPAULET DEVICE	SHOULDER STRAP DEVICE	UNDRESS CUFF
REAR ADMIRAL				
COMMODORE				
CAPTAIN	ALL CENTER DEVICES OF SILVER; WREATHS, GOLD.	EPAULETS NOT IN GENERAL USE, 1864-1866		
COMMANDER				
LIEUTENANT COMMANDER	SAME AS ABOVE			
LIEUTENANT				
MASTER				STAR AND THREE STRIPES.
ENSIGN				STAR AND TWO STRIPES.
MIDSHIPMAN *			NONE	STAR AND ONE STRIPE
BOATSWAIN				STAR ONLY.
GUNNER	SAME AS ABOVE, BUT WITH NO CENTER DEVICE.			
CARPENTER				PLAIN
SAILMAKER				
MASTER'S MATE	* FOR MIDSHIPMEN, FROM JULY, 1865.		NONE	STAR ONLY.

(ALL OF GOLD)

SHIPPED OR RATED MASTER'S MATES — NO DESIGNATION.

Fig. 185-g. Rank insignia, line and warrant officers, 1864-1865.

RANK DESIGNATION FOR VICE ADMIRAL (ADMIRAL FARRAGUT ONLY), FROM JANUARY, 1865

UNDRESS CAP DEVICE	SHOULDER STRAP DEVICE	UNDRESS CUFF	OVERCOAT COLLAR*

* FROM DECEMBER, 1863, ALL OFFICERS WERE TO WEAR INDICATION OF RANK ON THE POINTS OF THE OVERCOAT COLLAR, THE DESIGN TO BE TAKEN FROM THE SHOULDER STRAPS. LIEUTENANTS AND MASTERS BARS WERE TO BE SILVER, AND ENSIGNS, HAVING NO SHOULDER STRAPS, WERE TO HAVE THE FRONT EDGE BOUND WITH NARROW GOLD CORD.

Fig. 185-g-1. Rank insignia, vice admiral, 1865.

RANK	UNDRESS CAP DEVICE	SHOULDER STRAP DEVICE	UNDRESS CUFF SAME AS CHART E, BUT WITHOUT STAR.
CHIEF OF BUREAU OF MEDICINE AND SURGERY			SAME AS FOR COMMODORE.
FLEET SURGEON AND SURGEON OVER 15 YEARS SERVICE.	SAME AS ABOVE		SAME AS FOR CAPTAIN.
SURGEON OVER 5 YEARS SERVICE.			SAME AS FOR COMMANDER.
SURGEON UNDER 5 YEARS SERVICE.		THE SAME BUT WITH LEAVES OF GOLD.	SAME AS FOR LIEUTENANT COMMANDER.
PASSED ASSISTANT SURGEON		THE SAME BUT WITH TWO PAIRS OF GOLD BARS.	SAME AS FOR LIEUTENANT
ASSISTANT SURGEON		THE SAME BUT WITH ONE PAIR OF GOLD BARS.	SAME AS FOR MASTER.
CHIEF OF BUREAU OF PROVISIONS AND CLOTHING	 SAME WREATH AS ABOVE	 GOLD SPRIG.	SAME AS FOR COMMODORE
FLEET PAYMASTER, OVER 15 YEARS SERVICE.	SAME AS ABOVE		SAME AS FOR CAPTAIN
PAYMASTER, OVER 5 YEARS SERVICE.			SAME AS FOR COMMANDER
PAYMASTER, UNDER 5 YEARS SERVICE		THE SAME, BUT WITH GOLD LEAVES.	SAME AS FOR LIEUTENANT COMMANDER
ASSISTANT PAYMASTER		THE SAME BUT WITH ONE PAIR OF GOLD BARS	SAME AS FOR MASTER.
CHIEF OF BUREAU OF STEAM ENGINEERING	 SAME WREATH AS ABOVE.	 GOLD LEAVES	SAME AS FOR COMMODORE
FLEET ENGINEERS AND CHIEF ENGINEER, OVER 15 YEARS SERVICE.	SAME AS ABOVE.		SAME AS FOR CAPTAIN
CHIEF ENGINEER OVER 5 YEARS SERVICE.			SAME AS FOR COMMANDER.

Fig. 185-h. Rank insignia, staff officers, 1864-1866.

RANK	UNDRESS CAP DEVICE	SHOULDER STRAP DEVICE	UNDRESS CUFF SAME AS CHART E, WITHOUT STAR.
CHIEF ENGINEER, UNDER 5 YEARS SERVICE		SAME DEVICE AS PRECEDING, BUT WITH GOLD LEAVES	SAME AS FOR LIEUTENANT COMMANDER
FIRST ASSISTANT ENGINEER	SAME AS PRECEDING.	SAME DEVICE, BUT WITH TWO GOLD BARS.	SAME AS FOR MASTER
SECOND ASSISTANT ENGINEER		SAME DEVICE, NO ADDITIONS	SAME AS FOR ENSIGN.
THIRD ASSISTANT ENGINEER		NONE	PLAIN
CHIEF OF BUREAU OF CONSTRUCTION	SILVER  SAME WREATH AS ABOVE.	GOLD  SPRIG	SAME AS FOR COMMODORE
NAVAL CONSTRUCTOR OVER TWENTY YEARS SERVICE			SAME AS FOR CAPTAIN
NAVAL CONSTRUCTOR OVER TWELVE YEARS SERVICE.	SAME AS ABOVE		SAME AS FOR COMMANDER
NAVAL CONSTRUCTOR UNDER 12 YEARS SERVICE		SAME AS ABOVE, BUT WITH GOLD LEAVES.	SAME AS FOR LIEUTENANT COMMANDER
ASSISTANT NAVAL CONSTRUCTOR		SAME AS ABOVE, BUT WITH TWO GOLD BARS.	SAME AS FOR MASTER
CHAPLAIN OVER 12 YEARS SERVICE	SILVER  SAME WREATH AS ABOVE		SAME AS FOR COMMANDER
CHAPLAIN UNDER 12 YEARS SERVICE	SAME AS ABOVE	SAME AS ABOVE BUT, WITH GOLD LEAVES	SAME AS FOR LIEUTENANT COMMANDER
PROFESSOR OF MATHEMATICS UNDER 12 YEARS SERVICE.	SILVER LETTER, GOLD DISC  SAME WREATH AS ABOVE		SAME AS FOR COMMANDER
PROFESSOR OF MATHEMATICS UNDER 12 YEARS SERVICE	SAME AS ABOVE	SAME AS ABOVE, BUT WITH GOLD LEAVES.	SAME AS FOR LIEUTENANT COMMANDER
SECRETARY	SILVER  SAME WREATH AS ABOVE		SAME AS FOR MASTER
CLERK	WREATH ONLY	NONE	NONE

Fig. 185-i. Rank insignia, staff officers, 1864-1866.

548

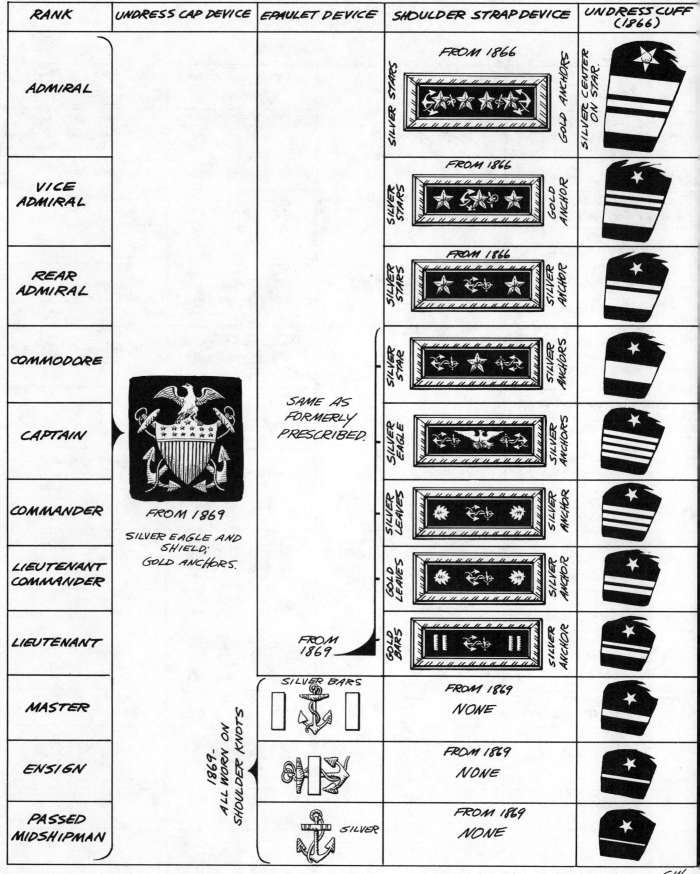

RANK	UNDRESS CAP DEVICE	EPAULET DEVICE	SHOULDER STRAP DEVICE	UNDRESS CUFF (1866)
ADMIRAL			FROM 1866 — SILVER STARS — GOLD ANCHORS	SILVER CENTER ON STAR.
VICE ADMIRAL			FROM 1866 — SILVER STARS — GOLD ANCHOR	
REAR ADMIRAL			FROM 1866 — SILVER STARS — SILVER ANCHOR	
COMMODORE			SILVER STAR — SILVER ANCHORS	
CAPTAIN	FROM 1869 — SILVER EAGLE AND SHIELD; GOLD ANCHORS.	SAME AS FORMERLY PRESCRIBED.	SILVER EAGLE — SILVER ANCHORS	
COMMANDER			SILVER LEAVES — SILVER ANCHOR	
LIEUTENANT COMMANDER			GOLD LEAVES — SILVER ANCHOR	
LIEUTENANT		FROM 1869	GOLD BARS — SILVER ANCHOR	
MASTER		SILVER BARS	FROM 1869 NONE	
ENSIGN		1869 – ALL WORN ON SHOULDER KNOTS	FROM 1869 NONE	
PASSED MIDSHIPMAN		SILVER	FROM 1869 NONE	

Fig. 185-j. Rank insignia, line officers, 1866-1872.

GW

RANK	UNDRESS CAP DEVICE	EPAULET DEVICE, 1869	SHOULDER STRAP DEVICE	FULL DRESS COLLAR DEVICE	UNDRESS CUFF FROM 1869
SURGEON, OVER 12 YEARS SERVICE (COMMANDER)		SILVER		FROM 1869 COMPARABLE TO THAT PRESCRIBED FOR LINE OFFICERS *	
SURGEON, LESS THAN 12 YEARS (LIEUTENANT)		GOLD			
PASSED ASS'T. SURGEON (MASTER)		NONE	NONE	NONE	
ASSISTANT SURGEON (ENSIGN)		NONE	NONE	NONE	
PAYMASTER, OVER 12 YEARS SERVICE (COMMANDER)	SAME AS LINE OFFICERS.	GOLD LEAVES SILVER DEVICE		COMPARABLE TO THAT PRESCRIBED FOR LINE OFFICERS	
PAYMASTER LESS THAN 12 YEARS (LIEUTENANT)		GOLD BARS SILVER DEVICE	SAME DEVICE, BUT WITH TWO PAIRS OF GOLD BARS.		
PASSED ASS'T. PAYMASTER (MASTER)		NONE	NONE	NONE	
ASSISTANT PAYMASTER (ENSIGN)		NONE	NONE	NONE	
CHIEF ENGINEER, OVER 12 YEARS SERVICE (COMMANDER)		SILVER		COMPARABLE TO THAT PRESCRIBED FOR LINE OFFICERS	
CHIEF ENGINEER LESS THAN 12 YRS. (LIEUTENANT)		SAME AS ABOVE	SAME DEVICE, BUT WITH TWO PAIRS OF GOLD BARS.		
FIRST ASS'T. ENGINEER (MASTER)		NONE	NONE	NONE	
SECOND ASS'T. ENGINEER (ENSIGN)		NONE	NONE	NONE	
THIRD ASS'T. ENGINEER (MIDSHIPMAN)		NONE	NONE	NONE	
SECRETARY TO ADMIRAL AND VICE ADMIRAL		NONE		NONE	

* SEE CHART A.

GW

Fig. 185-k. Rank insignia, staff officers, 1866-1872.

RANK	CAP DEVICE	COLLAR DEVICE		SLEEVE DEVICE
BOATSWAINS AND GUNNERS			NONE	NOTE - SEAMEN GUNNERS WERE ENTITLED TO WEAR ON BOTH SLEEVES, IN FRONT, HALFWAY BETWEEN WRIST AND ELBOW, THE CROSSED GUNS BADGE SURMOUNTED BY A STAR — AS WELL AS THE P.O. BADGE.
CARPENTERS AND SAILMAKERS	SAME AS ABOVE		NONE	NOTE - THE LETTER A, FOR APPRENTICE; W, FOR SHIP'S WRITERS AND S, FOR SHIP'S SCHOOL-MASTERS WERE AUTHORIZED FOR SLEEVE WEAR BY THOSE OCCUPYING SUCH POSITIONS.
MASTER-AT-ARMS				WORN ON BOTH SLEEVES AT THE POSITION CORRESPONDING TO THE GOLD STAR ON THE OFFICER'S SLEEVE — PETTY OFFICER BADGE WORN ON BOTH SLEEVES ABOVE THE ELBOW.
PETTY OFFICERS AND FIREMEN FIRST CLASS	NONE	NOT NECESSARILY BADGES OF RANK, THE COLLARS, OF BLUE DENIM, AND CUFFS OF THE SAME WERE, NEVERTHELESS, DISTINCTIVE. THE WRIST STRIPES PARTICULARLY SUGGESTING CLASS DISTINCTION.		THIS BADGE, PRIOR TO 1866, WAS THE SOLE DEVICE WHICH DESIGNATED ALL PETTY OFFICERS. IT WAS WORN BY BOATSWAIN'S, GUNNER'S CARPENTERS AND SAILMAKER'S MATES, SHIP'S STEWARDS, AND SHIP'S COOKS ON THE RIGHT SLEEVE ABOVE THE ELBOW. OTHER PETTY OFFICERS WORE IT ON THE LEFT SLEEVE.
SIGNAL QUARTERMASTER AND QUARTERMASTER	NONE			WORN ON BOTH SLEEVES, IN FRONT, HALF-WAY BETWEEN THE WRIST AND ELBOW. PETTY OFFICER'S BADGE (WITHOUT STAR) ON LEFT SLEEVE, BELOW ELBOW.
CAPTAINS OF TOPS	NONE	PETTY OFFICERS.		WORN ON RIGHT OR LEFT SLEEVE (FOR PORT OR STARBOARD WATCH), IN FRONT, HALFWAY BETWEEN WRIST AND ELBOW. P.O. BADGE ALSO, ON RIGHT SLEEVE, ABOVE ELBOW.
GUNNERS MATE AND QUARTER GUNNERS	SAME AS MASTER-AT-ARMS, BUT MATES ONLY	SEAMEN.		WORN ON BOTH SLEEVES, IN FRONT, BY MATES, AND ON ONE SLEEVE ONLY BY QUARTER GUNNERS; THE SLEEVE DETERMINED BY WHICH (AS ABOVE). P.O. BADGE ON RIGHT SLEEVE.
CARPENTERS MATES	NONE	ORDINARY SEAMEN AND FIREMEN 2ª CLASS.		BOTH SLEEVES, HALFWAY BETWEEN WRIST AND ELBOW. P.O. BADGE ON LEFT SLEEVE ABOVE ELBOW, WITHOUT STAR.
SAILMAKERS MATES	NONE	LANDSMEN, COAL-HEAVERS AND BOYS.		BOTH SLEEVES, AS ABOVE. P.O. BADGE ON LEFT SLEEVE ONLY, ABOVE ELBOW, BUT WITHOUT STAR.
COCKSWAINS TO C-IN-C AND CAPTAINS OF FORECASTLE	NONE			CAPTAINS OF FORECASTLE ONLY; IN FRONT, ON RIGHT OR LEFT SLEEVE (ACCORDING TO WATCH).
COCKSWAINS TO COMMANDERS OF VESSELS AND BOATSWAINS MATES	NONE	SAME AS ABOVE		BOATSWAIN ONLY; IN FRONT, ON RIGHT OR LEFT SLEEVE (ACCORDING TO WATCH).
MACHINIST	SAME AS MASTER-AT-ARMS			ON BOTH SLEEVES. P.O. BADGE ON LEFT SLEEVE, ABOVE ELBOW.

Fig. 185-1. Rank insignia, petty officers and seamen, 1852-1872.

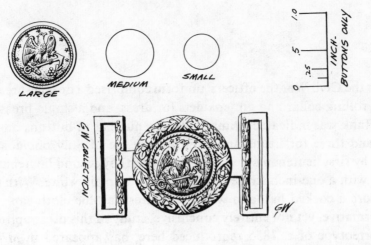

Fig. 186. Naval buttons and officer's belt plate.

Revenue-Marine (Revenue Cutter Service)

The commencement of our period found the Revenue-Marine (later to become the U.S. Coast Guard) at a low point in its career. Returned to the Treasury Department following the War with Mexico, its fleet had shrunk to eight cutters and its administration had become dissipated among local seaport politicians. One of the few bright spots of these years was the launching of the steam cutter *Harriet Lane,* a highly successful vessel destined to lead the service out of the age of sail.

The Civil War brought the Revenue-Marine again under navy control and with this came widespread action and a substantial increase in vessels. All the while the cutters did not lose sight of their older mission of revenue protection. In 1863 it became known by law as the Revenue Cutter Service, although the new designation does not seem to have been generally used for some years thereafter. Following the War, the Revenue-Marine returned to direct Treasury Department control, where it remained a civilian agency.

Documentary and graphic evidence of the dress of Revenue-Marine officers, petty officers, and seamen of our early years is unfortunately scarce, although it grows more plentiful by the Civil War period. In general it can be said that their uniforms, arms, and accouterments resembled those found in the navy; only in insignia was there a marked distinction. But the relatively small size of the Revenue-Marine, the nature of its vessels, and the wide differences in peacetime between its duties and those of the navy did lead to certain differences in dress which must be borne in mind.

There were no officers above the grade of captain in the Revenue-Marine, and only three grades below: those of first, second and third lieutenant. There was no service academy to produce midshipmen. Engineers were the only staff officers; revenue cutters, like merchant vessels, did not carry surgeons, chaplains, or paymasters, and required nothing like the number and complexity of crew members of a frigate, sloop, or even ironclad. Furthermore, in small crews it was not as necessary to indicate a man's specialty by insignia as it was on a larger vessel.

Prior to the Civil War the officers' uniform comprised a double-breasted navy blue tail coat with rolling collar and gilt epaulets for dress, and a single-breasted frock coat for undress. Rank was indicated primarily by the number of buttons on the cuffs (four for captains and three for lieutenants) and by the use of only one epaulet (on the right shoulder) by first lieutenants and one (on the left) by second lieutenants. Trousers were navy blue with a one-inch stripe of black braid, or plain white. With the dress uniform, officers wore a cocked hat, and with the undress, a blue cloth cap.

An informative, yet not entirely conclusive, study of this dress uniform, as pictured in the daguerreotype of c. 1855 reproduced here, has appeared in *Military Collector & Historian* and is cited below.

Fig. 187

Chief engineers wore a first lieutenant's uniform without the epaulet but with the "Treasury Arms" embroidered in gold on each side of the collar. Assistant engineers apparently wore the uniform of a third lieutenant (i.e., without epaulets) but with the same collar device.

There is much that is uncertain about these earlier uniforms. By 1862 the tail coat had been given up and the basic officer's upper garment for all ranks became a navy blue double-breasted frock coat with rolling collar, two rows of nine Revenue-Marine buttons down the front, and four on the skirts in rear; plain navy blue pants; and a blue cloth "Navy cap" with 1½ inch gold lace band. On this coat the officer wore plain gold epaulets for full dress and shoulder straps for undress. Prior to 1862 his sword was probably of a distinctive model (Peterson, 172-174); after that year and until nearly the end of our period it was by regulation of navy pattern.

Rank was indicated on the cuffs of this coat by gold lace stripes or large Revenue-Marine buttons, and on the shoulder straps by bars of gold lace. The gold embroidered cap device was a foul anchor superimposed over a shield within a wreath, and the same foul anchor and shield appeared on shoulder straps, and on buttons and belt buckles. Engineer officers were not authorized epaulets; their cap devices varied with their rank, as illustrated in the accompanying chart, as did the devices on their shoulder straps.

In 1864 the Treasury Department (General Order, 20 August) introduced half-inch gold lace stripes on the cuffs of the frock coat to indicate rank: four for captains, three for first lieutenants, two for second, and a single stripe for third (a rank recently introduced). Above these stripes was a one-inch "National shield." Engineer officers wore similar stripes corresponding to the last three grades; their cap device now became "a wheel within a wreath . . . worked in gold" for all ranks.

Enlisted men of the Revenue-Marine — so far as can be told from the scanty evidence — wore essentially the same clothing as those of the navy, especially when serving under naval command; this same applies to insignia. They must also have carried naval weapons and accouterments, although mention will be made below of a distinctively marked Revenue-Marine single-shot pistol.

Fig. 187. Revenue-Marine officer, c. 1855, full dress. (From daguerreotype of Henry Harwood Key in Maryland Historical Society.)

Firearms

The navy's requirements for muskets and rifles differed greatly from that of the army, so far as they related to those used by seamen. The weapons of Marines, on the other hand, closely followed army patterns. Since the sailor rarely had to carry his supply of ammunition on his person, the advantage of lighter weight cartridges did not apply. Because of the short range at which naval actions calling for long arms were fought, accuracy was less important than shock power, and the crowded conditions demanded weapons that were shorter than the usual musket. Finally, there was always the problem of salt water to be met. "Sea service" arms, therefore, were often tinned or covered with leather.

The patterns of shoulder weapons provided by the Navy Department in the 1850's and even the 1860's are far from clear. Some small arms were provided by the War Department or manufactured at its armories, but just what the models were and in what quantity they were supplied is difficult to say.

The navy had for some years prior to our period been experimenting with breech-loading and repeating arms. As early as 1841 it ordered some Jenks breechloading percussion rifles, a caliber .54 weapon with the "mule-ear" side-hammer and an overall length of 52.5 inches. The Jenks had a bayonet stud under the barrel to take a socket bayonet. Both the rifle and the bayonet were stamped "USN". How many were purchased and how long they were kept in use is uncertain.

Experimental orders were also placed about the same time with Samuel Colt for rifled repeating carbines as well as for revolvers, described later. The carbines were used in the Seminole War and 100 more were ordered in 1845. That some were still in use in the 1850's is suggested by the statement that two men "with revolving rifles slung across their shoulders" escorted Commodore Perry when he landed in Japan in 1853.

The Model 1842 musket was used during almost the entire period we cover in this book. When the army adopted its line of caliber .58 rifled arms in 1855, the navy, under the influence of Lieutenant John A. Dahlgren, decided to retain the caliber .69. Specifications were drawn up which ultimately led to the manufacture under contract of a distinctive rifle by Eli Whitney, described below.

•*Whitney Navy Rifle, Model 1861 ("Plymouth")*. Percussion, cal .69, deeply rifled, 50 in. overall. Barrel finished bright; blued steel furniture and lock. Lock marked with large spread eagle, flag and martial trophies, "US" and "WHITNEY-VILLE", plus the date. Used a brass-handled, 22 in. saber bayonet, or the Dahlgren knife bayonet. The latter was 16.5 in. overall, brass mounted with walnut grips and a wide 1.5-in. blade; it was sometimes called a "bowie" bayonet. Its black leather scabbard was brass mounted.

•*Sharps & Hankins Breechloading Navy Cartridge Rifle, Model 1861*. During the Civil War the navy procured about 500 of this single-shot breechloader (in addition to a far larger number of Sharps & Hankins breechloading carbines). Cal .52, using No. 56 Sharps & Hankins rim-fire cartridge. Rifled with 6 grooves, overall length 47.6 in. Brass butt plate; all other furniture iron. Browned barrel; receiver, operating lever, and hammer case-hardened in mottled colors. Sling swivels on middle band and under stock.

Central hammer; loaded by unlocking and depressing trigger guard. Leaf rear sight, moveable and graduated to 800 yards. Marked on receiver "SHARPS/&/HANKINS/ PHILADA." and "SHARPS/PATENT/1859."

Brass-handled saber bayonet, 25 in. overall, marked "COLLINS & CO." and year, and numbered serially with the rifle.

•*Sharps & Hankins Breechloading Cartridge Carbine, Model 1862.* Described on pages 164, 165. The barrels of navy carbines were covered with leather to protect them from corrosion by salt air. Over 6,000 were delivered to the Navy Department.

Following the Civil War the navy conducted a series of tests to decide upon a breechloading arm for the naval service. The weapon adopted was the Remington and arrangements were made to manufacture it at the Springfield Armory on a royalty basis to E. Remington & Sons.

•*U.S. Navy Rifle, Model 1870, Remington.* Breechloading with Remington rolling block action, using a cal .50 center-fire copper army cartridge. Overall length 48.625 in.; rifled with three broad grooves. All metal bright (except the receiver, which was case-hardened in mottled colors) for Marines, and browned for ship's company. Receiver marked with an eagle, "USN" and "SPRINGFIELD", plus the date. Used a 20 in. blade bayonet with fish-scale grips, brass handle decorated with navy ordnance device; bayonet stud under the barrel. Blade front sight and slide-leaf rear sight. Total of 22,000 made during 1870-1871, of which 10,000 were rejected and sold due to faulty sighting arrangement.

During the period 1845 to about 1860 the Navy Department purchased a considerable number of smoothbore, percussion, single-shot pistols of the U.S. Model 1842 (see page 167). This was a cal .54 weapon, 14 in. overall, with bright barrel and brass mountings, and a swivel ramrod. These pistols were made by various contractors, including Henry Aston, H. Aston & Co. and Ira N. Johnson; and they were also produced at the Springfield Armory. All were marked with the maker's name and date on the lock plate. Those designed for the navy were stamped with an anchor or "U.S.N.", usually on the barrel. These pistols were designed primarily for use by seamen and were kept on the arms racks aboard ship. They were used throughout the Civil War period.

The same is true of the U.S. Model 1842 pistols made under contract by N.P. Ames (see page 167). This was a much shorter weapon (11.75 in. overall), with lacquer-browned barrel, case-hardened lock and hammer, and brass mountings. It was also cal .54, but had what was called a "box-lock," the hammer being inside the lock plate to facilitate handling when carried inside a sailor's belt. Naval pistols were stamped "USN" together with the maker's name and date; a small lot for the Revenue-Marine were stamped "USR."

In 1845 the War Department placed an order for the navy for "100 boarding pistols, 5-charged each $25.00, including appendages." These were the first revolvers ordered for naval use; they were Model 1839 Colts of the Paterson model, and apparently only 50 were delivered. Other experimental orders followed, eventually leading to the design of the Colt navy percussion revolver, Model 1851. This was a six-shot, cal .36 weapon, single-action, 13 in. overall, with blued barrel, cylinder, and trigger. It was the first of a long line of cal .36 belt revolvers, made by Colt and other manufacturers, that bore the name "navy." The name, of course, designated a type and size of pistol and did not mean that the weapons were used exclusively in naval service or were intended for such use. The navy also purchased Colts of army model 1860 and navy models of 1861 or 1862, as well as Whitneys, Remingtons, and Starrs.

Many naval officers favored the revolver as the weapon to be carried by sailors in boarding operations, and many Model 1851 Colts were fitted with shoulder stocks (some with canteens in the butt) to facilitate their use in action. Yet to what degree the issue revolver equaled in numbers aboard ship the single-shot pistol is open to question. Their far greater expense, the comparative rarity of the employment of any sort of pistol, and the hostility of some ordnance officers to repeating weapons must have held down their numbers. The cal .36 holster revolver, however, was the weapon of the naval officer, used by him in actions at sea and on land.

Despite the use of the revolver by seamen during the war, the navy returned to the single-shot pistol after it was over. There were two models:

•*U.S. Single-Shot Navy Pistol, Model 1866, Remington.* Cal .50, breechloading, using a rim-fire metallic cartridge. Overall length 13.25 in. Blued barrel, other external parts case-hardened. It had the characteristic Remington rolling block and a sheath-trigger (no trigger guard). Marked on the receiver "REMINGTON ILION N.Y. U.S.A. PAT. MAY 3d NOV. 15th 1864, APRIL 17, 1866" and on the barrel with an anchor. The sheath-trigger was found to be dangerous and a new model followed.

•*U.S. Single-Shot Navy Pistol, Model 1867, Remington.* Cal .50, breechloading, using a center-fire metallic cartridge. It differed from the Model 1866 chiefly in having a regular oval trigger guard. In all, 6,500 of these two models were furnished to the navy.

Swords, Dirks and Knives

In 1852 the Navy Department adopted a new pattern sword for all officers which continued in use throughout our period and is still in use today with minor variations. It was well illustrated in the 1852 dress regulations, together with its scabbard, sword knots, and the belt on which it was worn. The blade was slightly curved and etched on its obverse with floral decorations, a circle of stars, and a foul anchor under the national shield. The hilt was brass and the grips were made of fish skin bound with twisted gilt wire. Overall length 34 inches. Its most distinctive feature was a pattern of oak leaves and acorns, plus the raised letters "USN", set into the quillon. The scabbard was usually of black leather, mounted with gilded brass. Most distinctive were its brass carrying rings, made to resemble twisted ropes, and its drag cast in the form of a dolphin (Peterson No. 138).

Fig. 162

Naval outfitters offered for sale several non-regulation varieties of this sword. Most were made along the general lines of the regulations but were more decorative or provided scabbards of solid silver or sharkskin. An English design (Peterson No. 139) sold by W.H. Horstmann & Co. had an eagle-head pommel, a considerably embellished blade, and a half-basket guard carrying an eagle and anchor design.

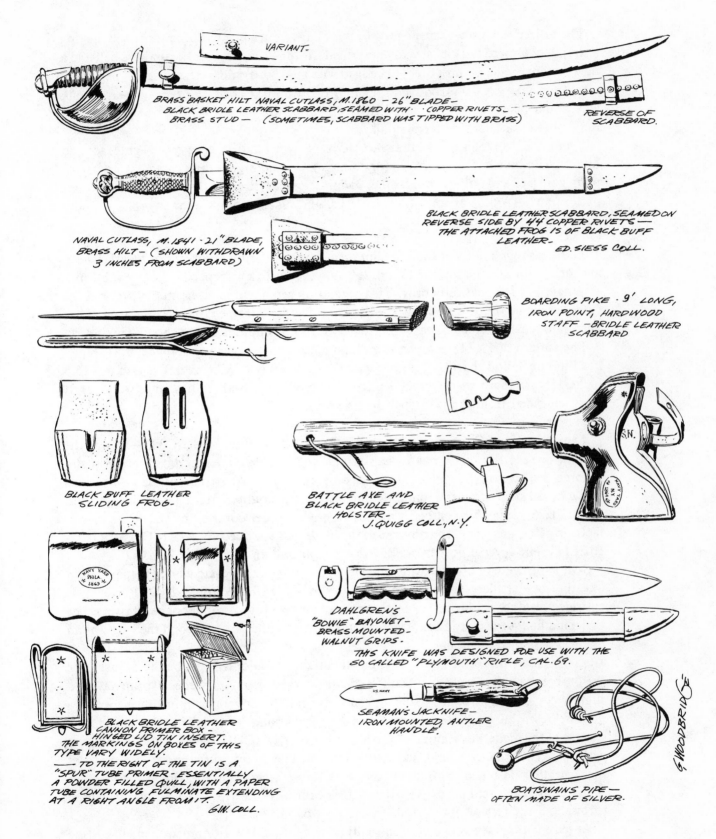

BRASS "BASKET" HILT NAVAL CUTLASS, M.1860 - 26" BLADE -
BLACK BRIDLE LEATHER SCABBARD, SEAMED WITH COPPER RIVETS,
BRASS STUD — (SOMETIMES, SCABBARD WAS TIPPED WITH BRASS)

VARIANT.

REVERSE OF SCABBARD.

NAVAL CUTLASS, M.1841 - 21" BLADE,
BRASS HILT — (SHOWN WITHDRAWN
3 INCHES FROM SCABBARD)

BLACK BRIDLE LEATHER SCABBARD, SEAMED ON
REVERSE SIDE BY 44 COPPER RIVETS —
THE ATTACHED FROG IS OF BLACK BUFF
LEATHER —
ED. SIESS COLL.

BOARDING PIKE · 9' LONG,
IRON POINT, HARDWOOD
STAFF — BRIDLE LEATHER
SCABBARD

BLACK BUFF LEATHER
SLIDING FROG.

BATTLE AXE AND
BLACK BRIDLE LEATHER
HOLSTER -
J.QUIGG COLL, N.Y.

BLACK BRIDLE LEATHER
CANNON PRIMER BOX -
HINGED LID TIN INSERT.
THE MARKINGS ON BOXES OF THIS
TYPE VARY WIDELY.
— TO THE RIGHT OF THE TIN IS A
"SPUR" TUBE PRIMER - ESSENTIALLY
A POWDER FILLED QUILL, WITH A PAPER
TUBE CONTAINING FULMINATE EXTENDING
AT A RIGHT ANGLE FROM IT.
G.W. COLL.

DAHLGREN'S
"BOWIE" BAYONET -
BRASS MOUNTED -
WALNUT GRIPS.
THIS KNIFE WAS DESIGNED FOR USE WITH THE
SO CALLED "PLYMOUTH" RIFLE, CAL. 69.

SEAMAN'S JACKNIFE -
IRON MOUNTED, ANTLER
HANDLE.

BOATSWAINS PIPE -
OFTEN MADE OF SILVER.

G.WOODBRIDGE

Fig. 188. Naval arms accouterments.

The officer's sword was suspended by two slings from a black leather waist belt, having a round, two-piece buckle, already described. In 1869 this became the undress belt and a new pattern, made of dark blue silk, edged with gold cord, and bearing various designs in gold embroidery, was introduced for full dress. Admirals' belts carried a pattern of oak leaves and acorns, while those of subordinate officers carried stripes of gold thread indicating rank, eight patterns in all.

From 1852 to 1866 there were two patterns of sword knot: a cord type of gold lace and bullion with blue lines interwoven for commanders and higher ranks, and a strap type of plain gold lace and bullion for all other commissioned officers. All officers wore the latter pattern after 1866. Warrant officers, clerks, and mates did not wear sword knots, and chaplains did not wear swords.

Dirks.

The dress regulations of 1852 did not mention the wearing of dirks, nor had they been authorized for anyone since 1813. In 1869, however, a dirk was specified for wear by midshipmen, but for boat duty only. This regulation remained in effect until 1876, but the extent to which the dirk was worn during these few years is open to much question. It has been said that hundreds of early photographs of midshipmen fail to show a single dirk.

The pattern dirk of 1869 had a straight, undecorated, single-edged blade, brass eagle-head pommel, and sharkskin grips covered with brass wire. The overall length was 15.5 inches. Its scabbard was of black leather with a brass tip and fittings, and two rings. It was suspended from the waist belt like a sword.

Cutlasses.

Fig. 188

The cutlass supplied seamen from 1852 to about the time of the Civil War was the pattern of 1841. Its blade was wide, straight, and double-edged, and its brass grip and pommel were cast in the same mold as the foot artillery sword, pattern of 1833. The guard was a broad strip of brass expanding into a wide, flat counter guard. Overall length was about 26.25 inches. The cutlass was manufactured under contract by the Ames Manufacturing Company, and the obverse of the blade was stamped "N.P. AMES/SPRING-FIELD". The reverse bore "USN" with the year and an inspector's initials.

Scabbards were of black leather and came in two types. One had a brass throat and tip like the foot artillery sword, and the other, designed by Admiral D.D. Porter, was entirely of leather held together on the reverse side by a row of copper or brass rivets. The first kind had a brass stud for attachment to a frog, while on the second the frog was an integral part of the scabbard.

Fig. 188

●*Pattern 1860 Cutlass.* A new model naval cutlass was adopted just before or just after the outbreak of the Civil War. It differed considerably from its predecessor in having a slightly curved, single-edged blade; in being longer (32 in. overall); in having grips and a pommel resembling those of the cavalry saber; and a solid, brass half-basket guard. The reverse of the blade was stamped "Made by/AMES CO./CHICOPEE", and the obverse with "U.S.N.", the date, and inspector's initials. The common scabbard was made of black leather fastened with a long row of brass rivets and bearing a brass stud. Apparently some scabbards were given brass throats and tips. This cutlass was used throughout the rest of our period (Peterson, No. 53).

At least two ornate versions of this cutlass were used, the differences lying in cutting the letters "USN" out of the brass guard and adding floral designs to the guard or to the brass mountings of the scabbard (Peterson, Nos. 140 and 141.) Apparently such cutlasses were available for sale to commissioned, warrant, and chief petty officers.

Seamen's Knives.

If the use of the dirk is uncertain in this period, that of the clasp knife by sailors is well established. All seamen concerned with ropes and rigging required a knife, and its possession was an accepted fact despite the obvious danger such possession by unruly seamen implied. Most sailors carried clasp knives and those on merchant vessels and whalers as a rule bought their own. This was probably true with naval seamen as well, at least up to the time of the Civil War when the first identifiable clasp knife was issued by the navy. This was a true jackknife with a 3.75-inch blade folding into an antler handle. The blade had an almost rounded point and was stamped "U.S. NAVY"; the handle was fitted with a brass staple to take a lanyard. The knife was made in Sheffield, England, and supplied to the navy through an American jobber.

Fig. 188

To reduce the lethal potential of the seaman's knife its point could be squared, and a jackknife with such a point was issued by the navy, although this seems to have occurred after 1872.

Pikes and Battle-axes

Crew members normally served aboard ship without belts or sidearms of any kind. When action was expected they were served out weapons and accouterments according to the duties they were expected to perform, and the men found their other implements in well rehearsed locations near their battle stations. We will not describe the numerous implements used in the exercise of the ship's guns since only one or two were carried on the persons of the crew. Men working in powder magazines wore a "magazine-dress," a simple worsted shirt reaching to the knees, and shoes made wholly of cotton canvas or buckskin, or no shoes at all.

Naval *Ordnance Instructions* carried detailed descriptions of the duties, arms, and accouterments of seamen detailed for boarding an enemy ship, or repelling boarders from one. Normally only a portion of a gun's crew was designated for this duty, but in emergencies all hands might be called on deck to fight off an enemy. Rattles, about 12 inches long with two-inch ratchets, were used to call boarders.

Boarding parties, during the Civil War at least, carried swords, revolvers and breechloading rifles, and wore cartridge boxes. In resisting boarders the pike was added to the list, and if the ship's arms racks contained muskets, these, too, were passed out.

Another important man during combat was the Fireman assigned to most guns' crews. His was the job of putting out fires caused by enemy action and for this purpose he was given a fire-bucket and carried a "battle-axe" in a case attached to the belt around his waist.

●*Boarding-pike.* Hardwood staff, 8.5-9 feet overall, with iron point having long side-straps. Most pikes were enlarged at the bottom by a ferrule about an inch thick. Pikes

Fig. 188

were sometimes painted white, or white with red point. Points were kept encased in protective black bridle-leather scabbards, about 11 inches long with a cord at the open end. Scabbards were stamped at navy yards and the example inspected carried in an oval: "NAVY YARD/N.Y./1863" with two anchors.

•*Battle-axe*. Iron head with hickory haft; overall length c. 20 in. Axe head was single-bitted, 4.25-in. blade, with hammer head; lower side notched twice. Haft bored for thong. Some axes were stamped on head "U.S.N." or with other markings including a maker's name.

Axe sheath was made of black bridle leather, shaped to fit head of axe, with strap and stud to secure axe and loop on rear to slide on waist belt. Stamped by the producing navy yard as, for example, "NAVY YARD/N.Y./1864" with two anchors.

Accouterments

Fig. 189

The officer's sword belt has already been described. It did not change in pattern throughout our period, except through the adoption of a full dress pattern in 1869. It was worn, with the sword, on all occasions of ceremony but not to the extent that prevailed in the army. On the prospect of action officers added a revolver holster and perhaps a revolver cartridge pouch to the sword belt.

The accouterments worn by petty officers and crew, and even the way they were to be worn, were specified in some detail for different duties such as boarding, boat duty, and shore duty. Shore parties that anticipated being away from their ship or base overnight were supplied with other accouterments like haversacks, canteens, and blanket rolls.

•*Waist belt*. White and later black buff leather (grained leather was supposed to become stiff and horny when exposed to the sea air), 2 in. wide, 40-44 in. long; standing loop and

Fig. 189

eyelet holes at one end and brass hook riveted to other. A japanned iron buckle was adopted about 1862, and it would seem that some belts were given oval brass plates after the Civil War. This belt was worn by "Captains of guns and boarders, as well as by small-arms men and the crews of field-howitzers." The frogs and boxes to hold arms and ammunition, except at first the musket cartridge box, were fitted with vertical loops permitting them to be slipped onto this belt.

•*Primer box*. Black bridle leather, rectangular in shape, inside dimensions 3.2x1.75x2.8

Fig. 189

in. Single tin insert with hinged lid. Single flap attached by 1-in. billet to brass button on bottom. Belt on rear, 2 in. wide. Stamped usually with navy yard designation inside oval; sometimes with "USN" in oval, c. 2.5 in. wide. Worn on front of the belt by captains of guns, and of field and boat howitzers.

Cartridge Boxes.

•*Navy Musket Cartridge Box*. Black bridle leather, double flaps, no usual implement pocket. Inside dimensions 7.2x1.6x5.8 in. Two tin inserts, each with one lower and two upper compartments, the latter of unequal size, holding 40 caliber-.69 paper cartridges. Embossed "USN" in oval on outer flap, 3.5 in. wide. Stamped on inside flap, in clipped

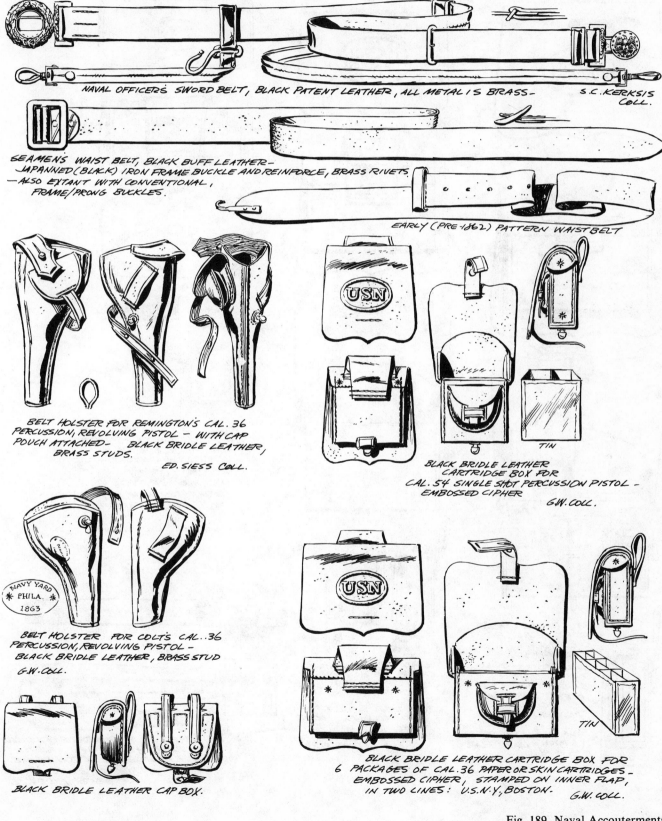

NAVAL OFFICERS SWORD BELT, BLACK PATENT LEATHER, ALL METAL IS BRASS.

S.C. KERKSIS COLL.

SEAMEN'S WAIST BELT, BLACK BUFF LEATHER — JAPANNED (BLACK) IRON FRAME BUCKLE AND REINFORCE, BRASS RIVETS. — ALSO EXTANT WITH CONVENTIONAL, FRAME/PRONG BUCKLES.

EARLY (PRE-1862) PATTERN WAISTBELT

BELT HOLSTER FOR REMINGTON'S CAL. 36 PERCUSSION, REVOLVING PISTOL — WITH CAP POUCH ATTACHED — BLACK BRIDLE LEATHER, BRASS STUDS.

ED. SIESS COLL.

BLACK BRIDLE LEATHER CARTRIDGE BOX FOR CAL. 54 SINGLE SHOT PERCUSSION PISTOL — EMBOSSED CIPHER

G.W. COLL.

NAVY YARD PHILA. 1863

BELT HOLSTER FOR COLT'S CAL. 36 PERCUSSION, REVOLVING PISTOL — BLACK BRIDLE LEATHER, BRASS STUD

G.W. COLL.

BLACK BRIDLE LEATHER CAP BOX.

BLACK BRIDLE LEATHER CARTRIDGE BOX FOR 6 PACKAGES OF CAL. 36 PAPER OR SKIN CARTRIDGES — EMBOSSED CIPHER, STAMPED ON INNER FLAP, IN TWO LINES: U.S.N.Y., BOSTON.

G.W. COLL.

Fig. 189. Naval Accouterments.

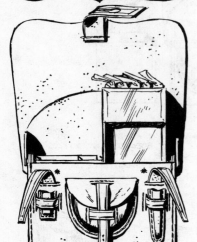

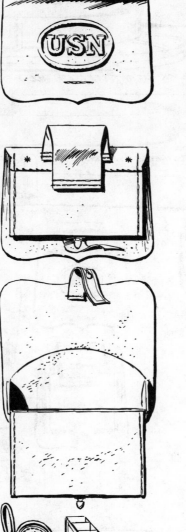

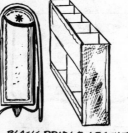

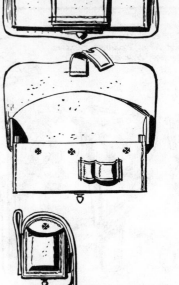

BLACK BRIDLE LEATHER CARTRIDGE BOX FOR SHARPS & HANKINS NAVY CARBINE, CAL. 52 RIMFIRE, AND MAY VERY WELL HAVE BEEN USED WITH ANY OTHER SIMILAR TYPE CARTRIDGES.

MARKED ON INSIDE FLAP:

U.S.N.Y. BOSTON   G.W. COLL.

BLACK BRIDLE LEATHER CARTRIDGE BOX FOR CAL. 69 PAPER CARTRIDGES —
SMALL POCKETS FOR CONE KEY AND PICK, BALL SCREW AND WIPER. FLEECE LINED CAP POUCH. EMBOSSED CIPHER

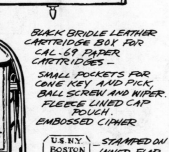

U.S.N.Y. BOSTON — *STAMPED ON INNER FLAP.*

A. KRAUSE COLL.

BLACK BRIDLE LEATHER CARTRIDGE BOX FOR COLT'S REVOLVING CARBINE, CAL. 56.

EMBOSSED CIPHER — NO IMPLEMENT POCKET.

NAVY YARD N.Y. 1863 — *STAMPED ON INNER FLAP.*

G.W. COLL.

BATTLE (TO QUARTERS) RATTLE. OF WOOD, BRASS SCREWS — WHEN RAPIDLY ROTATED, THE ACTION OF THE HARDWOOD 'SPRINGS' INDEXING AGAINST THE TEETH OF THE GEARS, PRODUCES A LOUD, IRRITATING RATTLE —

Fig. 190. Naval Accouterments.

rectangle: "U.S.N.Y./BOSTON".

Suspended from a black buff leather shoulder belt, 1.5 in. wide, ending in brass hooks for fastening to a vertical loop on rear. Actually, during the Civil War these boxes were produced without the shoulder belt and were worn on the waist belt.

Percussion cap pocket of light upper leather sewed to front of box under flaps, 4.5x2.5 in. Pocket for ball screw and wiper sewn on right of cap pocket; one for cone key and cone pick sewn on left.

Used with Model 1842 musket and Whitney navy rifle, both caliber-.69.

●*Navy Carbine Cartridge Box.* Black bridle leather, double flaps, no implement pocket. Inside dimensions 6.4x1.3x3.7 in. Single tin insert divided into two lower and five upper compartments, holding 40 caliber-.69 paper cartridges. Embossed "USN" in oval 3.5 in. wide on outer flap; examples observed stamped "NAVY YARD/N.Y." and date on inner flap. Single wide, vertical loop on rear to fit waist belt. Used for Colt revolving carbine cartridges.

Fig. 189, 190

●*Sharps & Hankins Navy Carbine Box.* Black bridle leather, double flaps, loop for tools sewn to front of box under flaps. Inside dimensions 6.1x2x2.5 in. Probably fitted with wooden insert bored for 20 cartridges; it could hold packaged cartridges. Single vertical loop on rear. Stamped on inside flap, in clipped rectangle: "U.S.N.Y./BOSTON". Embossed with "USN" in oval, 3.5 in. wide, on outer flap.

●*Cartridge Box for Navy Rifle, Model 1870, Remington,* Black bridle leather, single flap. Inside dimensions uncertain. Upper edge of box reinforced by copper strip riveted to inside. No insert used during normal exercises; wooden block fitted inside to preserve shape when not holding packaged cartridges. Embossed on flap with "USN" in large-sized oval. Single vertical loop on rear.

●*Navy Pistol Cartridge Box.* Black bridle leather, double flaps, cap pouch sewn to box under flaps. Inside dimensions 2.75x1x3 in. Single tin insert divided in half vertically. Embossed on outer flap with small "USN" in oval, and stamped on inner flap by navy yard, with year, in oval. Single vertical loop on rear. Made for caliber-.54 cartridges.

●*Navy Revolver Cartridge Box.* Black bridle leather, double flaps, cap pouch sewn to box under flaps. Inside dimensions 5x1x2.5 in. Single tin insert divided into six equal compartments, each capable of holding one package of caliber-.36 combustible revolver cartridges. Embossed on outer flap with small "USN" in oval, and stamped on inner flap inside clipped rectangle "U.S.N.Y./BOSTON." Single vertical loop on rear.

●*Navy Cap Pouch.* Black bridle leather, double flaps, inside dimensions 2.6x2.25 in. (same as U.S. Army regulation). Lined with sheepskin inside and fitted with cone pick. Embossed with small "USN" in oval on outer flap. Two vertical loops on rear. Example noted made by R. Nece.

Pistol Frogs.

The Navy called the holster, along with other accouterments, a "frog." *Ordnance Instructions* for 1852 and 1866 described only one pattern, for the single-shot pistol, but there were at least four other patterns of pistol-frogs made for revolvers. All frogs had features in common: they were bottomless scabbards shaped to fit a specific model of weapon, with a single belt loop and a strap to retain the pistol. The frog for the pistol was made of black buff leather, others used bridle leather. Most, if not all, bore the usual

564

navy-yard stamp in an oval. The several types were:

• *Frog for caliber-.54 pistol.* Had a pocket of thin leather to hold three cartridges and a cap pocket.

• *Frog for Remington navy revolver.* Longer than the others, being c. 8 in. overall. Had a cap pocket sewn to outside.

• *Frog for Colt navy revolver.* About 5.5 in. overall; no pockets.

• *Frog for Starr navy revolver.* Similar to Colt frog but wider at bottom and opened in front 2 in.

• *Frog for Whitney navy revolver.* Similar to Colt frog but cut out in a semi-circle at bottom.

Fig. 188 ### Sword and Bayonet Frogs.

Unless the cutlass scabbard had a frog attached to it, it was hung on the waist belt by a separate frog of black buff leather with a pocket notched to accept the brass stud on the scabbard. A very similar frog held the bayonet scabbard for the Plymouth Rifle.

• *Dahlgren Knife Bayonet Frog.* Similar to other frogs but wider at the base. Example noted was stamped on the outside of the loop, in an oval, "NAVY YARD/PHILA/ 1863".

• *Socket Bayonet Scabbard.* Black bridle leather, overall length 19.3 in. Brass ferrule and tip, brass stud.

• *Saber Bayonet Scabbard.* Black bridle leather, overall length 20.9 in. Brass ferrule and tip, brass stud.

Flags

U.S. naval flags fall into several categories, only a few of which will be treated here. First, there was the national ensign — the Stars and Stripes — which every ship carried in several sizes and hoisted at different positions for different occasions. There was the jack which consisted of the union of the national ensign and which was flown from the jack staff at the bow of the vessel when moored. Next came naval signal flags which, with lights, were used for communication between vessels. Then there were general purpose flags hoisted to issue an order or to indicate something was happening or going to happen, as a ship taking on powder, or under quarantine, or recalling its boats. Naval landing parties did not normally carry flags, although one of the ship's ensigns could be extemporized. Apparently there were no true colors aboard a ship except what the Marine guard might have had — that is, silken national or organizational flags; all naval flags appear to have been made of bunting in this period.

In addition to the flags above, there existed a series of designating flags and pennants which indicated the rank of the commander of a vessel or of a group of vessels, and the vessel (flag-ship) on which the commander was located. In a sense, these flags became personal symbols, something like the army headquarters flags of the Civil War, but they always remained indications of rank rather than insignia of some specific squadron or division. The system governing these flags changed three times during our period.

Years before the 1850's a long, narrow pennant, the commission pennant, or sometimes called a "coach-whip," had become the mark of a naval captain, or of an officer of lower rank when in command of a vessel of war. Near the staff it was blue with a line of white stars; beyond that it had two stripes, red over white. Such a flag was never carried by merchantmen and hence the narrow pennant symbolized the authority of a naval vessel.

A captain who had been placed in command of a fleet or squadron, and by courtesy was called a "commodore," was entitled "to wear" (that is, to hoist on one of the masts of his flag-ship) a "broad pennant." This was a forked flag (burgee) with slightly converging top and bottom. It was normally blue and contained the same number of white stars as the union of the national ensign. However, should two or more squadrons come together, only the senior commodore wore this blue pennant; the next in rank hoisted a similar one of red, while the lowest ranking commodore used a white pennant with blue stars.

In 1857 Congress directed that captains in command of squadrons be designated "flag-officers." This introduced a plain square blue flag, the size of the jack, to designate such officers. Further to designate seniority, orders specified wearing this flag on different masts. In 1861, plain red and white flags were prescribed for junior flag-officers who found themselves in the presence of seniors. Such was the system used throughout the Civil War, the square flag being carried on by admirals once the rank had been created.

The admiral's square flag was required to be rectangular in February 1865. Two months later a new edition of navy regulations was approved which, with further changes in 1866, altered and regularized the system of flags.

From 1866 to 1869 four rectangular blue flags were authorized:

Secretary of Navy: 4 white stars and a white anchor

Admiral: 4 white stars

Vice Admiral: 3 white stars

Rear Admiral: 2 white stars

A blue pennant with one white star was prescribed for a commodore, and red and white versions of the rear admiral's flag and the pennant were used to denote relative seniority. A new triangular pennant was established for commanders of divisions. It came in different colors to denote specific divisions and was worn by officers below the rank of commodore at the mainroyal masthead, alongside their narrow pennant.

Late in 1869 came a radically new and unpopular system which was to last six years. The jack was adopted as the Secretary of the Navy's flag, while admirals and commodores were given rectangular flags or pennants of seven red stripes on white, bearing a system of red stars. Again the mast on which the flag was worn indicated seniority, while an elaborate system of triangular pennants was devised to indicate division and squadron commanders. With this our period closes.

SOURCES

U.S., Navy Dept., *Regulations for the Government of the United States Navy, 1865,* GPO, Washington, D.C., 1865.

-----, *Regulations for the Uniform & Dress of the Navy and Marine Corps of the United States . . .,* Lippincott, Grambo and Co., Philadelphia, 1852.

-----, *Uniforms for Officers of the United States Navy as Prescribed in General Order of the Secretary of the Navy, July 31, 1862,* Tomes, Son & Melvain, 6 Maiden Lane, New York, 1863. To this at least 3 "appendices" were added showing changes.

-----, *Regulations for the Uniform of the Navy of the United States, 28 January 1864.* Reprinted in Schuyler, Hartley & Graham's *Illustrated Catalog,* New York, 1864.

-----, *Regulations for the Uniform and Equipment of the United States Navy,* Pollard & Leighton, No. 6 Court Street, Boston, 1866.

-----, *Uniform for the United States Navy, Prepared under Direction of the Secretary of the Navy,* GPO, Washington, D.C., 1869.

-----, *Ordnance Bureau, Ordnance Instructions for the United States Navy,* 1st ed., Washington, D.C., 1852. A 2nd ed. was published 1860; a 3rd ed., 1864; and a 4th ed., 1866.

James C. Tily, *The Uniforms of the United States Navy,* New York, 1964.

Robert H. Rankin, *Uniforms of the Sea Services: A Pictorial History,* Annapolis, Md., 1962.

Company of Military Historians, "Military Uniforms in America," plates 70, 126, 143, 181, all by H. Charles McBarron, Jr. Still other plates by McBarron have appeared in U.S. Navy Dept., "Uniforms of the United States Navy, 1776-1898," Washington, D.C., 1966.

Geo. Henry Preble, *Origin and History of the American Flag, . . .,* new ed., 2 vols., Philadelphia, 1917.

Naval Sketches of the War in California . . ., New York, 1939. The colored drawings of Gunner William H. Meyers, 1846-1847.

Narrative of the Expedition of an American Squadron to the China Seas and Japan, Performed in the Years 1852, 1853, and 1854, . . ., 3 vols., Washington, D.C., 1856, vol. I.

Captain A.T. Mahan, *From Sail to Steam: Recollections of Naval Life,* New York, 1907.

Stephen H. Evans, *The United States Coast Guard, 1790-1915 . . .,* Annapolis, Md., 1949.

Howard V.L. Bloomfield, *The Compact History of the United States Coast Guard,* New York, 1966.

George B. Keester, "Naval Dirks in the Collection of the United States Naval Academy Museum," in *Military Collector & Historian,* VIII, 31-34.

Robert H. McCauley, Jr., "A U.S. Revenue Marine Officer's Uniform, ca. 1855," in *Military Collector & Historian,* XXVI, 21-23.

Harold L. Peterson, *American Knives . . .,* New York, 1958.

-----, *The American Sword, 1775-1945 . . .,* New Hope, Pa., 1954.

A.W. Lindert, "U.S. Naval Martial Sidearms, 1775-1875," in *The Gun Report,* August, 1971.

This chapter has been read in draft by Captain James C. Tily USN, Ret., and has benefited greatly from his comments. Valuable assistance came from the late Lt. Col. John H. Magruder, III, Col. F. Brooke Nihart, Ernest D. Laube, Francis A. Lord, and Henry A. Vadnais, Jr. of the Naval Historical Center.

CHAPTER 14

★ *U.S. MARINE CORPS* ★

The Marine Corps in 1851 comprised some 1300 officers and men, about half of whom were at sea in small detachments. There they performed much the same duties as had generations of Marines before them: guard duty aboard ship, service as sharpshooters and in repelling boarders, heading landing operations, and furnishing a show of color on special occasions such as Commodore Perry's negotiations in Japan. Ashore, the Corps provided the guards for the principal navy yards and stations.

At the outbreak of the Civil War the Marine Corps was augmented, but far from enough to meet the calls made upon it. At no time did its strength exceed 3900, with which it had to provide detachments for a constantly increasing number of naval vessels. By this time it had become the practice to assign a division of guns aboard ship to Marines. At sea and as elements of landing forces the Marines played a gallant if minor role in the Civil War; in land combat the record of the Corps was slight and brought it no great fame.

The Corps supplied much of its own clothing and accouterments, which more than often differed from corresponding army items. Service aboard ship made different demands upon equipage than service on land — the effects of salt water and coal smoke were especially serious. Marines, like sailors, served under more rapidly changing and extreme weather conditions than soldiers; as a result the Corps employed distinctive warm weather clothing, and guards on sea-going vessels were issued special gear for foul weather and extreme cold.

The uniform specified for the Marine Corps in 1851 and worn until 1859 was essentially that prescribed in 1839, and much like that worn by the army throughout the 1840's. For dress, officers wore a dark blue, double-breasted tail coat faced and piped with scarlet, having "slashed flaps" or loops of gold lace on the cuffs and skirts, with larger loops on the collar. Rank was indicated by the number of loops on the cuffs, and the size of the bullion of the gilt epaulets, described later under insignia.

Fig. 191

Trousers were of dark blue cloth with a 1.75-inch scarlet stripe in winter, and plain white linen drilling in summer. Officers of captain's rank and above wore a chapeau bras, from 8.5 to 10 inches high, with black silk cockade, gold lace loop, and crimson and gold tassels. To its top was fitted a scarlet cock-feathers plume. The plume of the

Fig. 191. Captain, U.S. Marine Corps. 1854.
Michael J. McAfee after regulations.

Fig. 192. U.S. Marine Corps. Private, full dress, 1852-
1859. His cap is black with red pompon, brass device and
a chinstrap looped up. His coatee is dark blue piped red
with yellow lace and buttons; brass shoulder scales with
red fringe. His trousers are light blue. He wears white
belts with brass plates; black cartridge box and cap
pouch. He carries a U.S. M1842 percussion musket, cal
.69. Based on descriptions and photographs.

Commandant, Marine Corps, was of "red and white cock feathers, equally divided from tip to stem." Subalterns wore a black beaver cap, reinforced with leather, with a modified bell crown. Although a wide octagonal cap plate was illustrated in the *Regulations* published in 1852, it seems never to have been adopted. Subalterns continued to wear the brass rectangular plate with clipped corners, bearing an eagle and anchor device, that is illustrated in the *U.S. Military Magazine.* The cap had a brass scale chinstrap and red cock-feathers plume.

Enlisted Marines, except musicians, wore a similar tail coat, double-breasted for sergeant majors and quartermaster sergeants, single-breasted for others. It had scarlet *Fig. 192* piping, but yellow worsted lace binding was substituted for gold lace on the collar, cuffs, and skirts and yellow worsted epaulets took the place of the officer's pattern in all but the top grades. Rank, again, was indicated by the number of loops on the cuffs and the style of the epaulets. Sergeants major, quartermaster sergeants, drum and fife majors wore the same epaulets as lieutenants with a gold fringe substituted for bullion. Sashes were worn by first sergeants and the top pay grades. Pants were "light sky blue" cloth in winter and "white linen or cotton" in summer, and non-commissioned officers wore 1.5-inch dark blue stripes edged with scarlet on the former. The dress hat was similar to the black beaver cap worn by subalterns except it carried a red pompon and a cut-out brass eagle.

A distinctive feature of the Marine dress uniform was the scarlet cloth coat of all musicians. It had white linings, collar, and turnbacks, was cut like that of other enlisted *Plate III* Marines—double-breasted for drum and fife majors, single-breasted for other musicians.

The fatigue uniform for all officers except subalterns was a dark blue frock coat, closely resembling the navy pattern, double-breasted with ten buttons in each row. The *Fig. 193* frock coat for subalterns was single-breasted and had a stand-up collar like that worn in the army. With this were worn dark blue pants without stripes and a dark blue forage cap (called "fatigue cap" in the regulations) similar to the army pattern used in 1851. The blue cloth shoulder straps worn on this coat, and the gold "foul anchor" cap device are described below.

Officers were also authorized a dark blue cloth or kerseymere shell or mess jacket, lined with white shalloon, having a stand-up collar edged with gold lace (c. .375-inch wide) and one false row of 16 small Marine buttons. This jacket was fastened with hooks and eyes down the front and its bottom and front were edged with the same gold lace as the collar. A high-pointed cuff was also formed of the same lace. In summer a white linen shell jacket of similar design, but without buttons or lace, was substituted. This shell jacket, one of the most distinctive garments worn in the Corps, survives with modifications in the evening dress jacket of today.

Enlisted Marines wore a sky blue kersey fatigue uniform similar to that of the army, but without binding. On the shell jacket of this uniform sergeants wore two diagonal stripes of yellow worsted lace on each arm below the elbow; corporals had single stripes. The forage caps were dark blue, similar to the army pattern. Non-commissioned officers were authorized the same dark blue and scarlet pants stripes worn with the dress uniform.

The enlisted man's shirt was made of red flannel and remained such until 1859, when the color was changed to blue. To judge from paintings, however, red shirts remained in vogue into the Civil War era. Shirts of white cotton were also issued for warm weather use.

The Marine Corps blanket, authorized in 1859 and probably issued before that time, was made of gray wool, 7x5.5 feet in size, with black letters "U.S.M.", 4 inches high placed in the center.

The 1859 Uniform

On 6 January 1859 Brevet Brigadier General Archibald Henderson died; he had fought aboard the *Constitution* in 1815 and for 39 years had been Commandant of the Marine Corps. Two months before he died he convened a board of officers to revise its uniform, and one of the first acts of his successor was to transmit its findings to the Navy Department. These were approved on 24 January 1859 and put into practice at once.

Fig. 194

The Marine dress regulations of 1859 remained in effect with only slight modification until 1875. They did away with the tail coat, giving everyone for full dress (except musicians) a double-breasted frock coat of dark blue cloth with a skirt extending three-fourths of the distance from the top of the hip to the bend of the knee. The system of gold lace collar and cuff loops, piped with scarlet, was carried over from the old uniform coat, and lieutenants, captains, and field officers continued to be distinguished by the number of loops on their cuffs.

All officers save the Commandant had eight large-sized buttons in each row, evenly spaced, plus six on the back of the skirt. The Commandant was authorized to place his buttons in pairs. He and all field officers continued to wear a "chapeau (French Pattern)" for dress, although its shape was considerably lowered (5.5 inches in rear); its feather plume now lay along the top rather than standing upright. Trousers were normally sky blue with a .375-inch scarlet welt; officers "*not* serving in line with troops" were allowed dark blue pants with the same welt. White linen pants were worn by all hands in warm weather.

The dress cap worn by company officers was made of black cloth and of black felt for men, reinforced with leather and bearing a large yellow metal plate. The officer's pompon was of gold net, the enlisted Marine's of red worsted. The same three patterns of gold epaulets being worn were continued in use, except that silver insignia of rank and a silver Corps device were added to the straps.

We have said that enlisted men, except musicians, also wore a blue double-breasted frock coat. This had seven large Marine buttons on each row and six on the back of the skirt; scarlet piping on collar, cuffs, and skirt pockets; and loops on collar and cuffs of yellow worsted half-inch lace. Rank was indicated by the use of two or three loops on the

Fig. 193. U.S. Marine Corps. Harper's Ferry, Virginia, October 1859. The officer is wearing a dark blue cap, M 1839 U.S. Army forage, with gilt device; a dark blue coat with brass buttons; light blue trousers with scarlet strips; black shoes and crimson sash. He is armed with a M 1851 foot officer's sword with black, brass mounted scabbard; the sword belt is black with brass plate and fittings. The sergeant in foreground wears the army type forage cap; overcoat is the marine pattern of blue-gray with new, 1859 pattern rank designation: yellow chevrons (2), and brass buttons; light blue trousers with red welt; white belts with brass plates and black cartridge box and cap pouch. The remaining Marines: two at left without overcoats wear old army fatigue jackets of light blue but without lace; the others wear marine overcoats and are similarly armed and equipped, i.e. M 1842 percussion muskets, white belting and black cartridge boxes and cap pouches, brass buttons and plates. Figure wearing M 1859 forage cap is an army officer. Based on descriptions and contemporary woodcut.

FIRST SERGEANT,
1859-1892.

OFFICERS'
UNDRESS,
1859-

LIEUTENANT,
FULL DRESS, 1861.

DRUM MAJOR, 1860

Fig. 194. *First Sergeant, 1859-1872.* He wears a black cap with red pompon, a brass device with silver letter "M"; dark blue coat with scarlet piping and yellow lace, yellow chevrons piped scarlet; dark red crimson worsted sash; light blue trousers with scarlet cord; and 1851 foot officer's sword (private purchase). *Officer, undress, 1859.* His cap is dark blue with gold device; dark blue jacket with gold lace trim and brass buttons; light blue trousers with scarlet welt. *Lieutenant, full dress, 1861.* He wears a chapeau bras with gold trim and red and white (?) feathers; dark blue coat with gold and scarlet trim, gold epaulets; crimson sash; light blue trousers with scarlet welt; and black sword belt with brass fittings and old pattern plate. *Drum Major, 1860.* He wears a black fur "busby" with red bag and yellow tassel and red pompon; scarlet coat with white and yellow trim, yellow metal shoulder scales with red fringe (?) and yellow buttons; light blue trousers with red cord; crimson sash; white gloves; baton is brass mounted on wooden staff with gold cords; and 1851 foot officers sword. Based on photographs, woodcuts and descriptions.

cuffs, as before; chevrons were also worn on both arms, above the elbow, of yellow silk lace on a scarlet ground, points up. Full worsted epaulets were given up in favor of brass scales with yellow worsted bullion fringes. White cotton gloves were worn on parade.

Enlisted men's trousers were sky blue kersey, plain for most but with a narrow scarlet cord for sergeant majors, quartermaster sergeants, the drum major, and chief musicians. Enlisted men also were given white linen pants in warm weather.

The drum major, chief musicians, and musicians wore a frock coat of "scarlet cochineal dyed cloth," double-breasted and cut like other enlisted men's; the collar, cuff loops, and skirt pockets piped with white. The two top grades wore three cuff loops, others wore two. The dress cap and trousers were the same as other enlisted men. The drum major was given a distinctive hat of black astrakhan lambskin with a black leather chinstrap, red pompon and bag, the latter bearing a gold cord and tassel.

The undress uniform of the Corps also comprised a dark blue frock coat with full skirts, plain collar, and buttons only on the cuffs. Officers' coats were of cloth and double-breasted, 3 small buttons on each cuff, 4 large on the back of the skirt, and 8 in each front row. Enlisted men wore single-breasted kersey coats, 2 small buttons on each cuff, 2 large on the rear, and 7 large in front. The bottom of the collar of this coat was piped with scarlet. Musicians wore this same coat for undress without special insignia.

Fig. 197

With the undress coat officers wore a new device, the gold cord shoulder knot described below. Enlisted men's shoulders were plain, but NCO's wore the same chevrons as in full dress. The pants of both officers and men were sky blue as for dress, and both wore a dark blue cloth "fatigue cap" of chasseur pattern with a straight visor. The cap ornament until 1868 was a bugle, embroidered in gold on a red cloth patch for officers and of brass for the men, with an old English "M" in the center in white metal. Enlisted men's caps were plain, but those for officers had three rows of narrow black silk braid down four sides plus, for the first time, the 4-lobed knot called a "quatrefoil" which today is one of the more distinctive features of a Marine officer's uniform.

In warm weather on ship board officers were allowed a frock coat of white linen, cut like the undress coat, with which the gold shoulder knots were worn. This is the only instance of this garment among military dress of the period, although linen coats were frequently worn by civilians in warm climates. It appears to have replaced the white linen shell jacket.

Fig. 195

Officers were now authorized a "fatigue jacket" which differed from the earlier shell jacket in being buttoned rather than hooked down the front and in being a generally more serviceable garment. It was, however, lined with scarlet and edged all around with half-inch gold lace. Liberties seem to have been taken with its ornamentation, for in some photographs the pointed cuff braid extends twelve inches or more up the arm.

Fig. 194

The 1859 regulations introduced the "fatigue sack" for enlisted men aboard sea-going vessels. It was made of dark blue flannel, "open half way down front" and buttoning with four small Marine buttons. This was in reality a blouse or shirt worn outside the pants, about six inches shorter than the frock coat. NCO's wore their chevrons on it, and it was customary to wear a white cotton shirt underneath. This was the garment worn for formations at sea or in port in warm weather, and by shore parties.

Fig. 198

Enlisted Marines were issued twelve white cotton and eight blue flannel shirts every

Fig. 195. U.S. Marine Officer wearing white undress frock coat and trousers, 1860. Based on regulations.

Fig. 197. 2nd Lieutenant A.W. Ward, U.S. Marine Corps, 1865. Michael J. McAfee from photograph.

Fig. 196. *U.S. Marine Drummer, 1863.* He wears a dark blue cap with red top and band, yellow quarterfoil and brass lyre device, black visor and chin strap; blue-gray marine overcoat with brass buttons; light blue trousers (stripe ?); white drum sling with black heart; and drum (unknown). From a photograph.

Fig. 198. *U.S. Marine Corps. Sergeant, fatigue dress (Korea) 1871.* He wears a dark blue cap with brass and silver device; dark blue flannel blouse with yellow chevrons, piped red; light blue trousers with red stripe; white belts with brass plate; canteen, haversack as U.S. Army; and gray blanket roll. He carried a U.S. M1861 rifled musket and non-regulation sword with brass hilt and black scabbard with brass mountings. From photographs.

four years. They were also allowed one "over-coat" of "blue grey mixture." It was single-breasted with seven large Marine buttons, had 5-inch turn-over cuffs and a button-on cape that came down to the upper edge of the cuff. Chevrons were worn on the cuffs of the overcoat.

A "great coat" was also issued, but only to sea-going Marines for wear on certain prescribed occasions. Whether or not it differed materially from the overcoat has not been determined.

Fig. 196

The overcoat prescribed for officers in 1859 was the dark blue "cloak coat" given army officers in 1851. The frogs and braiding were identical, including those on the cuffs which showed rank. The Commandant wore five cuff braids as prescribed for army general officers.

Insignia

The various devices of the Marine Corps underwent frequent change during 1851-1872 and not until the last years of the period did the Corps receive its now celebrated globe and foul anchor emblem.

Fig. 199

The dress cap worn by subalterns in 1851 carried a brass or gilt plate bearing an eagle on a foul anchor device. Enlisted Marines wore a cut-out brass eagle on their dress caps.

The forage cap device for officers, established in 1840, was a foul anchor within a wreath, embroidered in gold. Enlisted Marines wore a somewhat similar wreath enclosing the old English letters "USM", apparently of brass.

In 1859 these insignia were given up and the Corps adopted the light infantry bugle, it is said, in recognition of its association with the British Corps of Royal Marines which in 1855 had been designated a "Light Corps" because of its increasing combat service ashore. In all cases the bugle was yellow metal and had inside its ring an old English letter "M" in white metal.

The new dress cap was given a brass plate about four inches high representing the national shield within a floral border, all within a half wreath; on the center of the shield appeared the bugle device. Both officers and men wore this insignia, but in different qualities. The national shield and wreath were worn until 1875 when a smaller version of the shield alone was prescribed; it was 2.875 inches high. The bugle, however, was replaced by the globe and foul anchor device in 1868. Forage caps carried the bugle device alone, on a red background, embroidered for officers and in metal for the men, until 1868 when the caps also were given the globe and anchor.

The officer's waist belt plate before 1859 was rectangular and of brass, bearing the letters "USM" within a wreath; after 1859 it became the standard model prescribed for army officers in 1851. At this same time, as will be seen, the Corps adopted the regulation army pattern foot officer's sword, and the change to the army sword belt plate was probably a corollary of the change.

Enlisted men's waist belt plates were not distinctively marked during our entire period. All enlisted men, however, wore the round army-issue eagle shoulder belt plate during the 1850's and later. As noted below under accouterments, white cross belts continued in use through the Civil War.

Insignia of Rank and Function

Rank was indicated, either generally or specifically, as follows in this period (special Commandant's uniform excepted):

	To 1859	1859-1876
Officers, full dress	a. Number of loops on cuffs b. Size of epaulet fringes c. Aiguilettes for staff officers d. Type of hat	a. Number of loops on cuffs b. Size of epaulet fringes and rank devices on epaulet straps c. Type of hat
EM, full dress	a. Single or double-breasted coat b. Number of loops on cuffs c. Type of epaulet and size of fringe d. Addition of aiguillettes and sash e. Chevrons (after 1852)	a. Number of loops on cuffs b. Chevrons c. Size of epaulet fringe d. Addition of sash
Officers, undress	a. Single or double-breasted coat b. Rank devices on shoulder straps	a. Rank devices and number of cords on shoulder knots
EM, undress	a. Arm stripes	a. Chevrons b. Addition of sash
Officers, overcoat (probably same as undress)		a. Braid on sleeves
EM, overcoat	a. none	a. Chevrons on cuffs

The loops worn on the cuffs at different times were made of .5-inch gold lace for officers and yellow worsted lace for men. The rule prior to 1859 was:

Field officers, sergeants major, quartermaster sergeants,
 drum and fife majors: 4 loops
Captains, staff officers, sergeants: 3 loops
Other officers and men: 2 loops

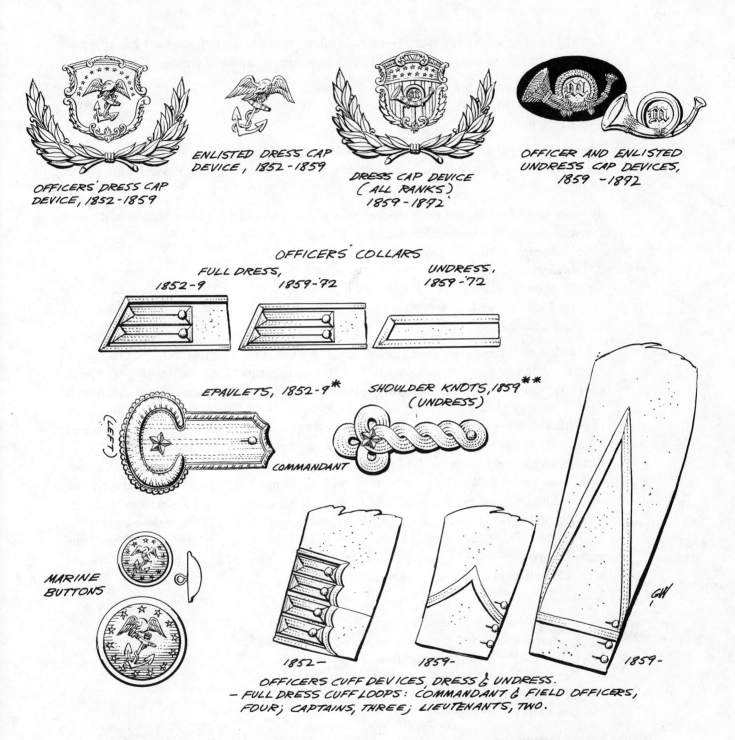

OFFICERS' DRESS CAP
DEVICE, 1852-1859

ENLISTED DRESS CAP
DEVICE, 1852-1859

DRESS CAP DEVICE
(ALL RANKS)
1859-1872

OFFICER AND ENLISTED
UNDRESS CAP DEVICES,
1859 -1872

OFFICERS' COLLARS

FULL DRESS,
1852-9

1859-'72

UNDRESS,
1859-'72

EPAULETS, 1852-9 *

SHOULDER KNOTS, 1859 **
(UNDRESS)

(LEFT)

COMMANDANT

MARINE
BUTTONS

1852-

1859-

1859-

OFFICERS CUFF DEVICES, DRESS & UNDRESS.
— FULL DRESS CUFF LOOPS: COMMANDANT & FIELD OFFICERS,
FOUR; CAPTAINS, THREE; LIEUTENANTS, TWO.

* OFFICERS' EPAULETS. SUBSEQUENT TO 1859, THE BADGE OF RANK WAS MOVED TO THE
STRAP, AND ITS PLACE WITHIN THE CRESCENT WAS TAKEN BY THE BUGLE HORN
DEVICE. RANK BADGES SAME AS BELOW. — FOR FRINGE WIDTHS, SEE TEXT.

** SHOULDER KNOTS. COMMANDANT, AS SHOWN; COLONEL, 4 BRAIDS, SILVER SPREAD-EAGLE;
LT. COLONEL, 4 BRAIDS, SILVER LEAF; MAJOR, 4 BRAIDS, PLAIN; CAPTAIN, 3 BRAIDS, 2 SILVER
BARS; 1ST LIEUTENANT, 3 BRAIDS, 1 SILVER BAR; 2D LIEUTENANT, 3 BRAIDS, PLAIN.

Fig. 199a. U.S. Marine Corps Insignia.

In 1859 the higher NCO's were given only three loops and all other men got two. The officers' epaulets were of the U.S. Navy pattern and the fringe sizes were:

Field officers: 3.5 inches long, .5 inch wide
Captains, staff officers: 2.5 inches long, .25 inch wide
Lieutenants: 2.5 inches long, .125 inch wide

These same epaulets were retained after 1859; however, a bugle of solid silver containing the letter "M" was placed within the crescent and the following rank devices were added to the strap:

Commandant: Silver embroidered star if a general officer, otherwise as colonel
Colonel: Silver embroidered eagle
Lieutenant Colonel: Silver embroidered leaf
Major: Nothing
Captain: 2 silver embroidered bars
1st Lieutenant: 1 silver embroidered bar
2nd Lieutenant: Nothing

Enlisted men's epaulets were somewhat more unusual. The top four NCO's before 1859 wore epaulets of "the same pattern as those for Lieutenants" only with a "fringe of gold" instead of bullion. Presumably this meant a fringe with strands about .0625 inch wide. The other enlisted Marines wore yellow worsted with fringe about .25 inch wide. In 1859 fringed brass scales were prescribed for all enlisted men. These scales are illustrated in the 1859 dress regulations; and differed in size from the army pattern with 2.5-inch straps as against 2 inches for the latter. But a more important distinction lay in the fact that these scales had removable yellow worsted fringes fastened to a separate plate attached underneath the crescent. The fringe was 3.5 inches long with bullion .375 inch wide for higher ranking sergeants, .25 for sergeants, and .0625 for corporals and privates.

The officers' shoulder straps and shoulder knots both carried rank devices. The straps worn before 1859 were of navy pattern, 1x4 inches in size, of dark blue cloth bordered with .25-inch gold embroidery. The devices were:

Colonel: Silver embroidered eagle
Lieutenant Colonel: Gold embroidered "flower" or leaf
Major: Silver embroidered "flower" or leaf
Captain: 2 silver embroidered bars at each end
1st Lieutenant: 1 silver embroidered bar at each end
2nd Lieutenant: Nothing

The shoulder knots authorized in 1859 were 7 - 7.25 inches long, being twisted straps of 3 or 4 fine gold cords, .1875 inch diameter, ending in a clover leaf, with a small Marine button at the other end. Rank was indicated by the number of cords plus the same rank devices as found on the straps of the epaulet:

Commandant and field officers: 4 cords
Captains and under: 3 cords

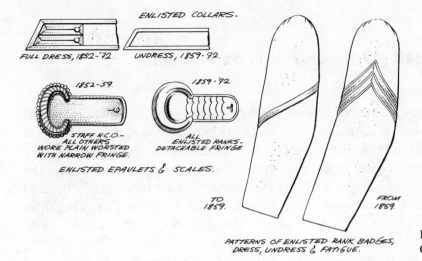

ENLISTED COLLARS.

FULL DRESS, 1852-'72.   UNDRESS, 1859-'72.

1852-59.   1859-'72.

STAFF N.C.O.-
ALL OTHERS
WORE PLAIN WORSTED
WITH NARROW FRINGE.

ALL
ENLISTED RANKS-
DETACHABLE FRINGE

ENLISTED EPAULETS & SCALES.

TO
1859.

FROM
1859.

PATTERNS OF ENLISTED RANK BADGES,
DRESS, UNDRESS & FATIGUE.

Fig. 199b. U.S. Marine Corps Insignia.

Marine Corps insignia for NCO's was especially interesting. Before 1859, for fatigue, they wore diagonal "stripes" of yellow worsted lace, as already mentioned. These were about 6 inches long, placed below the elbow and inclining toward it. They were essentially the same as the "half chevrons" in the army, except as to color. The 1859 dress regulations introduced the chevron for use on both dress and fatigue clothing, with points up in both cases and placed above the elbow. Chevrons were made of .5-inch yellow silk or worsted lace on scarlet ground or piped in scarlet as follows:

Sergeant Major: 3 bars and an arc (silk)
"Quarter Master" Sergeant: 3 bars and a tie (silk)
Drum Major: 3 bars and a tie, with a star in the center (silk)
1st Sergeant: 3 bars and a lozenge (worsted)
Sergeant: 3 bars (worsted)
Corporal: 2 bars (worsted)

The same chevrons were worn on the cuffs of the overcoat.

Aiguillettes worn on the right shoulder were the mark of the staff officer before 1859, and they were also worn by staff sergeants on the left shoulder. Apparently the former were of army pattern, made of gold cord; the latter were "of yellow silk, with gilt tags." Aiguillettes were not worn after 1859 until musicians re-adopted them in 1875.

The officer's sash was of crimson silk net with bullion fringe ends, passing twice around the body and tied on the left hip. It was worn by an officer of the day over his right shoulder. Until 1859 all higher ranking sergeants wore the same sash with a plain fringe, while the orderly (first) sergeant had one of red worsted. After 1859 all sergeants of these grades were given red worsted sashes. A new sash, of buff silk net, was introduced in 1859 for the Commandant alone. Sashes were not worn for fatigue duties.

The braiding on officers' overcoats has already been mentioned.

Buttons

The Marine Corps button is illustrated in the Lippincott, Grambo edition of the 1839 dress regulations. It came in two sizes, about .55 and .8 inch, and was described as "gilt, convex, with eagle, anchor, and stars, raised border." With minor variation it continued throughout the period, and for much longer.

Small Arms and Accouterments

Arms

Enlisted Marines in this period were issued regulation army shoulder arms, the Model 1842 musket in the beginning, changing to the Model 1855 rifle musket prior to the Civil War and the Model 1863 in 1864. However, they did not necessarily take shoulder arms aboard ship. There does not seem to have been anything like a standard firearm for the Marine officer. One, at least, carried a Model 1855 pistol-carbine throughout the Civil War. Others carried the Colt revolver, navy model. About 1870 the Corps began to receive a breech-loading rifle musket, probably the U.S. Navy rifle, Model 1870, Remington. Musket slings were of black leather.

Fig. 191

Since the 1820's Marine officers had worn a distinctive curved sword with a Mameluke hilt. The pattern carried in 1851 (Peterson, *American Sword,* No. 144) was relatively plain and undecorated, not quite 37 inches overall, with a slightly curved blade, ivory grips shaped in the Mameluke style, secured by two star-shaped rivets. The pommel was pierced for a crimson and gold sword knot with bullion tassel. The scabbard was brass with a high median ridge on each side; it had both a stud for frog attachment and two carrying rings, and was suspended from a two-inch white buff leather belt by means of a sliding frog. The belt buckle is described under insignia.

Fig. 193

This sword was given up in 1859 on the recommendation of a board of officers who felt the army sword with its leather scabbard was more efficient. As a result Marine officers were authorized the Model 1850 foot officer's sword which was worn until 1875, when the Mameluke hilt was restored. As Commandant, Brig. Gen. Jacob Zeilin wore an army staff and field officer's sword, Model 1860 during the Civil War, but this seems to have been the sole exception.

With the army sword the Marine officer wore either a black leather belt of army pattern with the army regulation plate, or he used the older white leather belt with the same plate. The latter was more common and customary for dress. The sword knot from 1859 to 1875 had a gold lace strap with gold bullion tassel — apparently the army pattern.

In general, Marine NCO's and musicians wore the same swords as infantry until 1859. Thereafter the NCO's wore the army foot officer's sword, Model 1850, with a leather rather than sharkskin grip and with a frog stud on the scabbard instead of rings. Musicians continued to wear Model 1840 musician's or NCO's swords.

Accouterments

Enlisted Marines, except the higher grades of NCO, wore 2.25-inch white buff leather cross belts and a somewhat narrower waist belt of the same material. The cartridge box was suspended on the right from one shoulder belt, the bayonet scabbard on the left from another, and the cap pouch rode on the waist belt. This arrangement appears to have been employed for parade and dress purposes throughout our period. The army regulation eagle-pattern breastplate was worn with these belts. The waist belt plate was rectangular, brass, slightly convex, and without device. NCO's and musicians who were authorized swords wore them in white buff leather frogs, sliding on the waist belt after 1859. Prior to that NCO's probably wore double-frogged shoulder belts.

Some time after 1855 and before 1859 the Marine Corps authorized "white waist belts of the French pattern, with the French clasp and knapsack sliding slings." This belt was a version of the Model 1855 sword bayonet belt, based on the *chasseurs a pied* pattern. It did not at once replace the older belts and there is some question whether it was worn at all.

Enlisted Marines wore a distinctive knapsack:

• *"U.S.M." Double-Bag Knapsack.* Two sections attached by 3-in. canvas strip, of black painted canvas. Front section was an envelope 14.5x13x3 in., with short flap fastened by 3 buttons. Rear section (14.5x16 in.) formed into a container by 2 vertical flaps, tied with thongs. Four leather loops sewn to outside of front, two on each side through which pass two russet straps (1 in. wide) encircling knapsack and buckling at bottom; sewn to those straps near top and bottom of knapsack are two carrying straps, also buckling at bottom. An adjustable breast strap slides on carrying straps. No blanket roll straps.

This knapsack carried "U.S.M." in an oval on the rear. Dress regulations prescribed an outer knapsack covering of black cow-skin; to what extent this was worn has not been discovered.

The haversack and canteen were of army pattern, and this was also the case with other accouterments, although a great deal of irregularity must have prevailed.

Colors and Flags

Marine commands carried national colors similar to those of the infantry, but no regimental colors or standards were used by the Corps until the 20th century. After the Mexican War certain citizens of the District of Columbia presented the Corps with a special flag bearing the legend: "From Tripoli to the Halls of the Montezumas." How this flag was carried, if carried at all, is not known. The colors used in the Mexican War and at First Manassas are now in the Marine Corps Museum, Quantico, Va.

SOURCES

Regulations for the Uniform & Dress of the Navy and Marine Corps of the United States..., Lippincott, Grambo, and Co., Philadelphia, 1852. Illustrated edition containing the dress regulations of 1 July 1839.
Regulations for the Uniform & Dress of the Marine Corps of the United States, October, 1859..., Charles Desilver, Philadelphia, 1859. Illustrated edition containing the dress regulations of 24 January 1859.
Clyde H. Metcalf, *A History of the United States Marine Corps,* New York, 1939.
Colonel Robert H. Rankin , *Uniforms of the Sea Services: A Pictorial History,* Annapolis, Md., 1962. (Naval regulations and instructions cited under "U.S. Navy.")
We are greatly indebted to the late Lt. Col. John H. Magruder, III, U.S.M.C.R., Brig. General E. H. Simmons, Col. F. Brooke Nihart, and to other members of his staff, for their help in preparing this chapter.

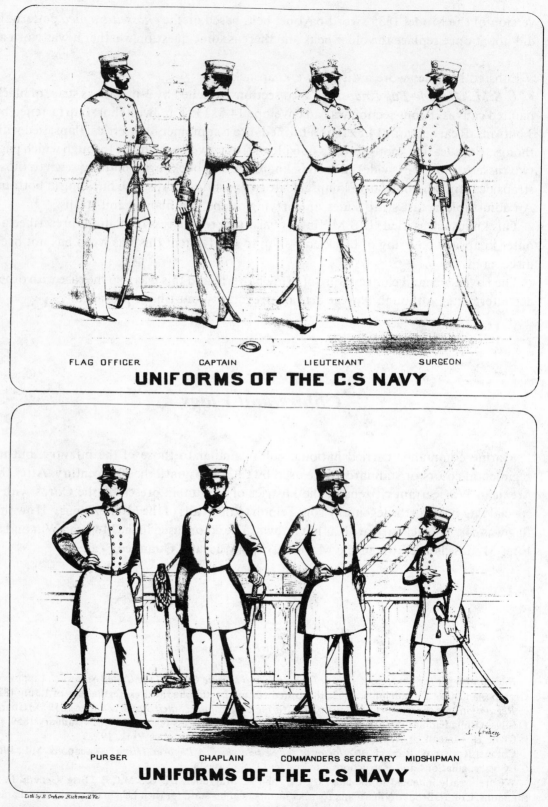

FLAG OFFICER   CAPTAIN   LIEUTENANT   SURGEON

UNIFORMS OF THE C.S NAVY

PURSER   CHAPLAIN   COMMANDERS SECRETARY   MIDSHIPMAN

UNIFORMS OF THE C.S NAVY

Lith by B Graham Richmond Va.

Fig. 200 (above) and 201 (below). Page from original regulations, *Uniform and Dress of the Navy of the Confederate States,* Richmond, Va. (Reproduced from Riling-Halter facsimile of 1952.)

CHAPTER 15

★

CONFEDERATE STATES NAVY AND MARINE CORPS

The Confederate States Navy Department, and with it the navy, was established by an act of the Confederate Congress which was passed on 20 February 1861 and signed by the President on 21 February. A Marine Corps was provided for in a budget of 12 March 1861, but not approved until an act of 16 March 1861. The establishment was enlarged and improved by several later acts, especially that of 21 April 1862, when the rank of admiral was created. By November of 1863, the enlisted strength of the navy was 2,700 and as of 28 April 1864, it had 753 officers of all grades.

In most details its organization, ranks, and functions corresponded to those of the U.S. Navy. In the Navy Department an Office of Provision and Clothing—for some while under Paymaster John de Bree and later James A. Semple—handled the procurement and issue of clothing and some accouterments. Weapons, on the other hand, were handled by the Office of Ordnance and Hydrography.

The navy was at first entirely a regular establishment, but in April 1863 a "Volunteer Navy" was added to include and give official recognition to ships and men engaged in privateering but was evidently little, if at all, used. A month later Secretary of the Navy Stephen R. Mallory succeeded in having an act passed by the Confederate Congress which established the "Provisional Confederate Navy." For a year the provisional navy had only nine commissioned officers, all of whom had been appointed one grade above their rank in the regular navy or were commissioned from civil life. In June of 1864, however, almost every officer in the regular navy, with the exception of a few captains and commanders, was assigned to the provisional navy.

In June 1864 all enlisted men and officers of the regular navy were transferred to the provisional navy. So far as clothing and insignia were concerned, there was no distinction between these three forces except the gilt letters "V.N." on the officers' caps of the volunteer navy.

In July 1863 the C.S.S. *Patrick Henry* was converted into a school ship with 50 midshipmen and anchored off Drewry's Bluff on the James River. In the fall of that year the Confederate States Naval Academy was formally opened with a regular staff of instructors and an authorized strength of 106 students.

At the end of the Civil War, in 1865, the naval personnel in the vicinity of Richmond, Va., were formed into a provisional battalion under Commodore John R. Tucker and distributed in the fortifications at Drewry's Bluff, and in Batteries Brooke, Wood, and Semmes. The organization was called variously Tucker's Naval Battalion or the Naval Brigade.

Fig. 200, 201

The only known regulations covering the dress of the Confederate Navy are those cited below. Their date is not known, but some time in early 1862 seems logical. They were clearly based upon the U.S. Navy dress regulations of 1852 which in places they copied word for word. There were, however, several marked differences:

1. All references to dress uniforms were omitted, and hence they specified no tail coats, epaulets, cocked hats, or stripes on the pants. The only uniform prescribed was the "undress." Indeed, no dress uniforms were known to have been worn by Confederate naval officers.

2. In place of "navy blue" the Confederate regulations everywhere substituted "gray" or "steel gray." As we will see below, blue uniforms were worn by both officers and crew under certain circumstances, but gray was, by 1862, the prescribed color, together with white in warm weather. Surviving records and actual uniforms make it clear that any shade of gray was acceptable.

3. A considerably different system of rank insignia was adopted, although it followed much the same complicated pattern as the U.S. regulations.

Officers' Dress

The first uniforms worn by Confederate naval officers were blue and these seem to have been worn through 1861 at least. Presumably the change to gray occurred following the issue of the dress regulations cited below, but of this we cannot be certain. A photograph taken in New Orleans about May 1861 of Commander Raphael Semmes and his staff shows all in U.S. regulation naval frock coats and epaulets; even the lieutenant of Marines wears the blue dress coat of the U.S. Marines. The only difference was a new system of rank insignia on the cuffs. When Midshipman James M. Morgan joined his ship at Baton Rouge, La., in July 1861, he found that "all the naval officers wore the blue uniforms of the United States Navy which they had brought South with them, and kicked like steers when they were afterwards compelled to don the gray, contemptuously demanding to know, 'Who had ever seen a gray sailor, no matter what nationality he served?' " He himself wore blue and his photograph is included in *Recollections of a Rebel Reefer,* from which the quotation is taken.

Blue, as will be noted later, lasted well into the Civil War, at least for service and off duty dress. Lieutenant George Gift of the C.S.S. *Gaines,* then at Mobile, Ala., was informed by his fiancee that he looked elegant in his "dark blue flannel suit"; this was in September 1863.

A good overall picture of Confederate naval officers' dress may be gained from the account of the capture of the *Atlanta,* given in the *Providence Journal* of 17 June 1863:

[The officers who surrendered] are in what I suppose should be called uniform, but it's rather a hard-looking uniform. It is of the universal gray, and bears the devices pertaining to each particular rank, in gilt lace or red cord embroidery, and to some extent resembles our own method of naval uniform trimming. The rank of the executive officer is signified by a gilt shoulder-strap filled with blue, with a single star, like a brigadier-general. A commander has two stars, and so on.

Most of their coat-buttons are our own naval buttons, with a frequent sprinkling of army buttons among them, especially on the cuffs. Some of them have buttons with the coat-of-arms of Virginia, South Carolina, or some other State, upon them. They have a button of their own adoption, an anchor with crossed cannon, but it is not generally worn yet. Most of the uniforms look "home-made" enough, and are faded and rusty.

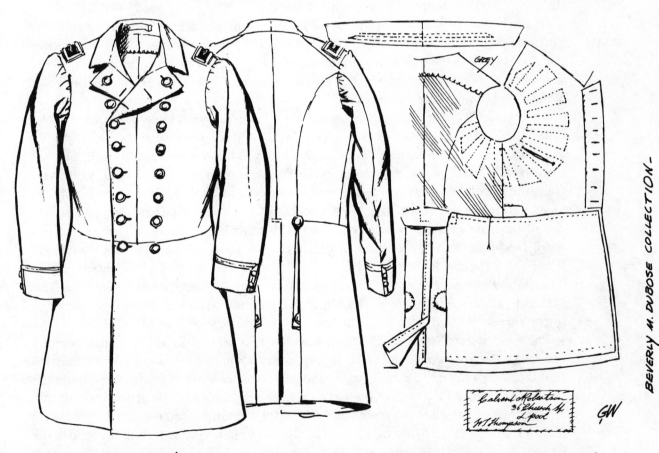

BEVERLY M. DuBOSE COLLECTION

C.S. NAVY OFFICER'S FROCK COAT OF ENGLISH MANUFACTURE. CADET GREY CLOTH, BREAST AND BACK LINED WITH GREY-BROWN SATEEN, SKIRTS WITH BLACK SATEEN. BULLION AND BLACK SHOULDER STRAPS ON GREY PATCHES, GOLD CUFF BRAID, GILT "C.S.N." BUTTONS (FIRMIN & SONS, 153 STRAND, LONDON, & 13 CONDUIT ST.). THIS COAT WAS OWNED AND WORN BY W.T. THOMPSON, CHIEF ENGINEER, C.S.S. FLORIDA.
— BUTTONS ARRANGED IN TWO ROWS OF NINE EACH.

Fig. 202. Sketch of original officer's coat made in England. George Woodbridge from specimen.

Photographs showing some of these men in confinement later at Fort Warren bear out the variety of their dress.

Fig. 202 The coat specified in 1862 was a frock "of steel grey cloth," double-breasted except for chaplains, professors, secretaries, and clerks. It had nine buttons in each row (the single-breasted style varied in this regard), the rows being 4.5 inches apart at the top, 2.5 at the waist line. There was a rolling collar which was worn buttoned up for dress and turned back into lapels otherwise. Shoulder straps and a special system of braid on the cuffs indicated rank. We will return to the cuff braid under "Insignia," but it should be mentioned that cuffs were supposed to be slashed and fastened with four small buttons. Flag Officer Franklin Buchanan's coat (in the Maryland Historical Society) has four such buttons; incidentally, these are Virginia buttons while the large ones on his coat front bear the Maryland device. Naval officers' coats were cut in the full-sleeved style of the day, with four buttons on the rear of the skirts.

Fig. 203 Officers wore a steel gray cloth or white linen single-breasted vest with nine small buttons, and full pants of the same two materials. Their cap was gray and of the same pattern as worn in the U.S. Navy. Black waterproof covers were commonly worn. White straw hats were used "in summer or in tropical climates." These had a 6-inch crown and a 3.5-inch brim, and bore no decoration.

Fig. 204 Officers also were permitted to wear jackets, of steel gray cloth or white linen, double-breasted with rolling collar. These were, in fact, frock coats cut off at the waist line. No gray jackets have survived and it appears that blue was the accepted jacket color. The one worn by C. Lucian Jones, Paymaster of the *Tallahassee* (in the U.D.C. Hall, Savannah, Ga.) is made of dark blue homespun and is single-breasted with six medium-sized C.S. naval buttons. It has no insignia. With this is displayed a dark blue cloth vest and a naval cap of the same color. For what it is worth, Master's Mate I. Dutton Graves wrote in April 1864 that "blue jackets and white pants, you know, are regular sailor style . . ." Finally, Lieutenant Robert D. Minor's jacket (in the Museum of the Confederacy) is blue, double-breasted, with U.S. artillery buttons and a .75-inch stripe of gold braid on each cuff, about 1.5 inches from the edge. It has a standing collar and was worn buttoned to the throat. He had it on when he was shot in an open boat in March 1862.

The Confederate States naval officer's overcoat, as prescribed in 1862, was a roomier version of the frock coat, with skirts falling to about 3 inches below the knees. It carried shoulder straps but no lace on its cuffs, and had no cape. An interesting example of such an overcoat, once Flag Officer Buchanan's, is also in the Maryland Historical Society.

Fig. 203 The dress of passed midshipmen and of midshipmen presented no especially unusual features. Midshipman Morgan, already quoted, was photographed while attached to the Cruiser *Georgia* in 1863. His uniform is that illustrated in naval dress regulations with three exceptions: he wears seven buttons in each row on his coat instead of the nine prescribed, no "strip of gold lace" is visible on his shoulders, and no "foul anchor without wreath" is visible on his cap. Morgan's cap may have been blue. One worn by Midshipman William Augustus Lee aboard the *Patrick Henry*, possibly as late as 1863, has survived and is made of blue cloth.

As with Confederate army officers, naval and Marine Corps officers were authorized to draw clothing by an act approved in January 1865.

Fig. 203. C.S. Navy, 1862-1865. Petty officer, lieutenant, captain (in overcoat), lieutenant, chief engineer (under 12 years), midshipman, seaman.

Fig. 204. *C.S. Navy, Paymaster.* He wears all dark blue: jacket and vest of "homespun" with brass buttons; gold device and lace on cap, black strap and visor; white shirt with black cravat. From uniform worn by Paymaster C. Lucian Jones in U.D.C. Hall, Savannah, Ga.

Petty Officers' and Seamen's Dress

Among the earliest uniforms for seamen ordered by the C.S. Navy Department were those which Captain James D. Bulloch, Naval Agent, was instructed in May 1861 to purchase in England. Three months later Bulloch reported he had secured "the entire amount of clothing for seamen and marines" and was sending the goods on. All items were "to be similar to the clothing used in the British Navy without any designating marks."

The items purchased by Bulloch included:

Cloth or cassinette pants	Shoes
Cloth jumpers	Woolen socks
Cloth round jackets	Blankets
Duck pants	Blue cloth caps
Blue flannel overshirts	Pea jackets
Blue flannel undershirts	Barnesley shirting frocks
Blue flannel underdrawers	Black silk handkerchiefs

At this time the C.S. Navy was employing 500 seamen and seeking authority for 500 more; Bulloch had been ordered to secure 1,000 sets of uniforms. From the start, then, the navy attempted to furnish clothing in kind, as distinct from the army system.

It is apparent that much British naval clothing reached the Confederacy and was issued, since a list of supplies furnished the crew of the *Savannah* in December 1861 included "English clothing." Indeed some of the clothing issued after October of that year sound like imported items: "blue flannel undershirts, blue caps, blue cloth trousers" (to the *Raleigh*); "blue pea jackets," etc. (to the *Georgia*); "blue satinet trousers" (for the *Savannah*); etc.

Gray flannel overshirts began to appear on the records of issues late in 1861, but it was not until well into 1863 that notations like "grey wool jackets," "grey wool pants," or "grey caps" were entered with any frequency. It seems safe to say that blue woolen garments formed the basis of the Confederate seaman's winter wardrobe throughout 1862.

The naval dress regulations of 1862 prescribed the same items of outside clothing for Confederate seamen as were worn in the U.S. Navy, the difference lying in the color. Jackets and trousers were to be of gray cloth, frocks (jumpers) were gray wool with white duck cuffs and collars lined with blue cotton cloth, "stitched round with thread." "Thick grey caps without visors" were worn by the crew at sea. Otherwise, in their white clothing, black hats and neckerchiefs, and straw hats the men of the two navies were dressed much the same.

By 1863 the Navy Department's Office of Provision and Clothing, under Paymaster John de Bree, was experiencing the same shortages as his colleagues in the Army's Quartermaster Department. Mills manufacturing cloth were monopolized by the army, foreign purchase was becoming increasingly uncertain, and purchases on the open market in competition with speculators meant paying exhorbitant prices. Contracts let

Fig. 205. Unidentified ambrotype of two men possibly Confederate seamen. Note the inverted anchor belt plate worn by seaman on left. Collection of Michael J. McAfee.

to John Fraser & Co.; Gautherin & Girard, of Paris; Crewshaw & Co.; G.R. Ghiselin & Co.; and others produced small amounts of cloth, ready-made clothing, shoes, blankets, and other items, but never enough and rarely of good quality.

Most Confederate seamen's clothing was made from goods bought in the South and manufactured into "plain but substantial clothing" at Richmond, Savannah, and Mobile. There was little uniformity and complaints about quantity and materials were numerous. To meet the always desperate need for shoes, an establishment was operated in Mobile where they were made of canvas.

As mentioned above, the individual garments were similar to naval clothing worn in the North which has already been described. Doubtless many sailors dressed in whatever they could get, at least for most of the time, and must have resembled the merchant seamen of their day. Yet now and then the Confederate sailor put on a fancy general muster like that aboard the *Alabama* when she signed on her first crew. Lieutenant Arthur Sinclair describes in his memoirs the "bronzed, stalwart, well-seasoned set ·of fellows, who now . . . have exchanged their nondescript rags for our paymaster's nobby blue-and-white uniforms [and] look as promising as any set of men that ever went to sea."

Insignia

A ship in full sail seems to have been the first general device considered by the C.S. Navy, but this was abandoned later in the war for a device that bore a foul anchor imposed on crossed-cannon. The evidence for this, however, is purely circumstantial.

No regulations have been found governing Confederate naval officers' sword belt buckles, although at least four versions exist. All are the round, two-piece, cast brass variety. It is believed that the earliest pattern bore the letters "CN" within a wreath, and that this was replaced in 1863 by one having a foul anchor on which the letters "CSN" *Fig. 206* were imposed. Both patterns are in Battle Abbey, Richmond, Va. A third two-piece buckle, bearing the letters "CSN" alone, has been reported.

Sometime in 1863, or perhaps earlier, a buckle was manufactured in England to be worn with a special C.S. naval officer's sword. The maker is believed to have been Robert Mole of Birmingham. The buckle bore the foul anchor on crossed-cannon device (which also appeared on the blade and counterguard of the sword) within a wreath of cotton and tobacco leaves.

The Confederate petty officer and seaman, so far as is known, wore no distinctive belt buckle or general service device of any kind.

Officers of the volunteer navy were prescribed uniforms similar to those worn by "corresponding grades in the regular Navy, with the addition of the letters V.N., plain gilt, three-quarters of an inch long on the front of the cap" (Instructions of 19 June 1863).

Fig. 207 a, b, c From the scanty sources available it appears that officer's rank was indicated prior to 1862 by the use of the U.S. Navy system with a modification of the cuff device. To the .75-

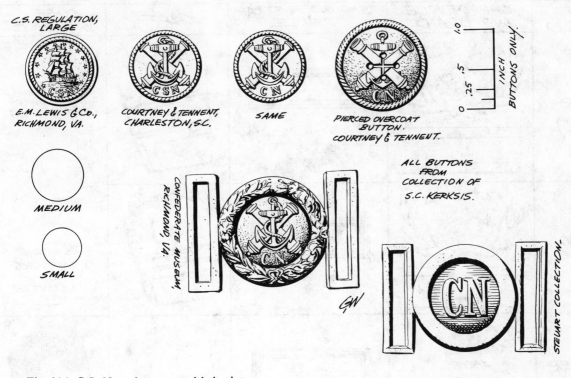

Fig. 206. C.S. Navy buttons and belt plates.

inch gold braid that encircled the cuff (1 for lieutenants, 2 for commanders, etc.) was added a single loop top and bottom, on the center of the sleeve. Presumably this loop was merely sewn on over the older lace. Shoulder straps, epaulets and other devices remained essentially as worn in the "Old Service" on, as has been said, blue uniforms.

The 1862 uniform regulations designated the rank and function of an officer by an elaborate system which included shoulder straps, cuff braid and buttons, device and braid on the cap, and to a limited extent the pattern of the coat. So far as is known, it was not altered during the period of the war.

Pictures and even descriptions of Confederate seamen are rare indeed, and we have next to no idea what insignia of rank or function they wore. Chief petty officers were prescribed a device "embroidered in black silk on the right sleeve of their gray jackets above the elbow in front, a foul anchor of not more than three inches length." The same device, embroidered in blue, was worn on white frocks. Other petty officers, except officers' stewards and yeomen, wore the same on the left sleeve.

An "honorable discharge badge" was prescribed in the 1862 *Naval Regulations* (page 144) which is surprisingly like this petty oficer's device. It also was a foul anchor, 2.5 inches in length, of blue or white embroidery, worn on the left sleeve above the elbow. Each additional honorable discharge gained the wearer a star, .5 inch high.

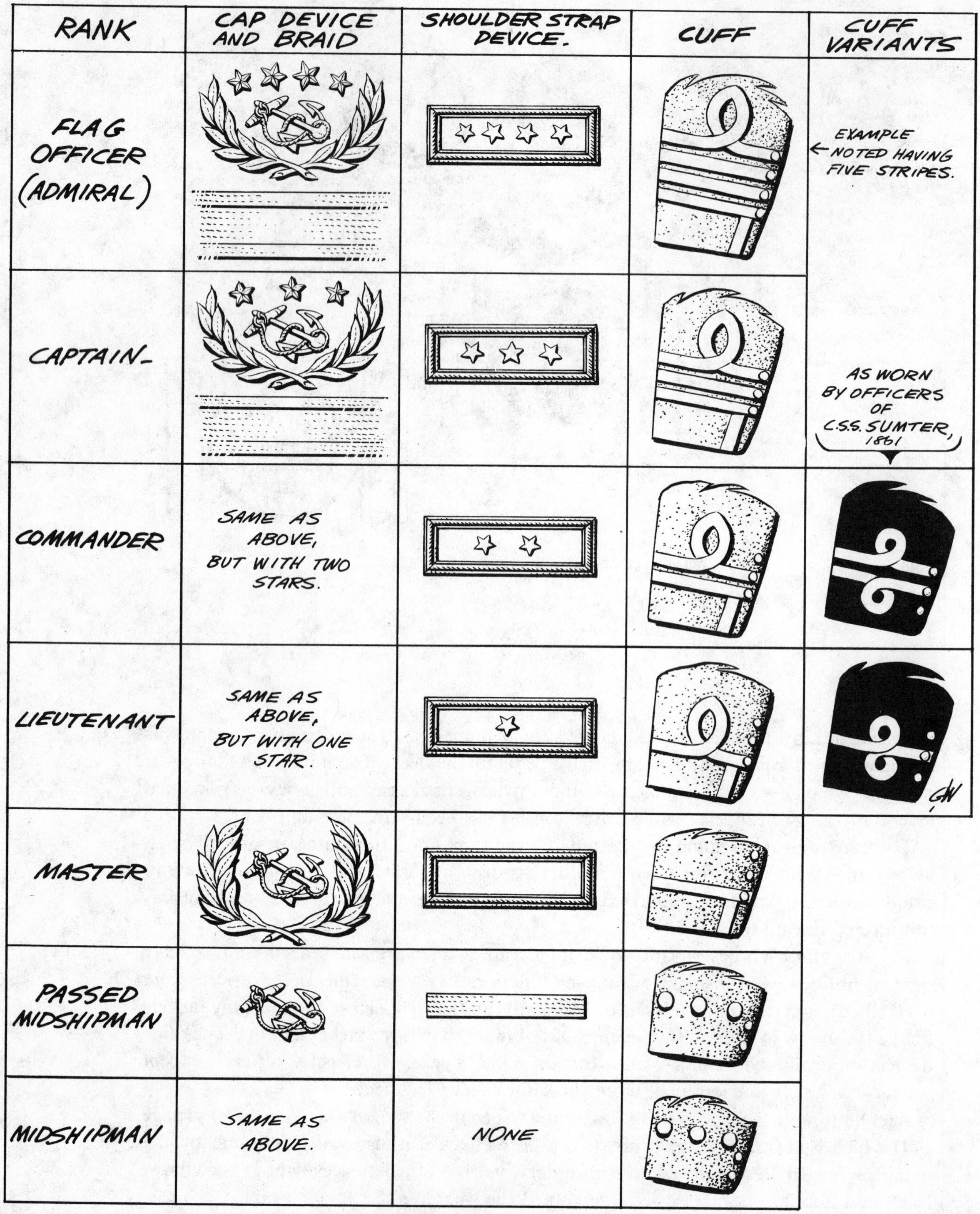

RANK	CAP DEVICE AND BRAID	SHOULDER STRAP DEVICE.	CUFF	CUFF VARIANTS
FLAG OFFICER (ADMIRAL)				← EXAMPLE NOTED HAVING FIVE STRIPES.
CAPTAIN				AS WORN BY OFFICERS OF C.S.S. SUMTER, 1861
COMMANDER	SAME AS ABOVE, BUT WITH TWO STARS.			
LIEUTENANT	SAME AS ABOVE, BUT WITH ONE STAR.			
MASTER				
PASSED MIDSHIPMAN				
MIDSHIPMAN	SAME AS ABOVE.	NONE		

Fig. 207a. C.S. Navy Rank Designation.

RANK OR FUNCTION-	CAP DEVICE	SHOULDER STRAP DEVICE-	CUFF
SURGEON, OVER 12 YEARS SERVICE.	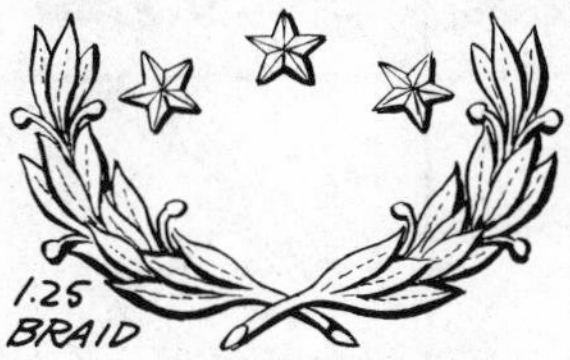 1.25 BRAID	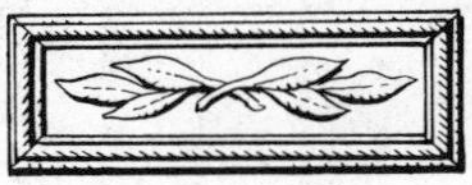 BLUE CLOTH BASE	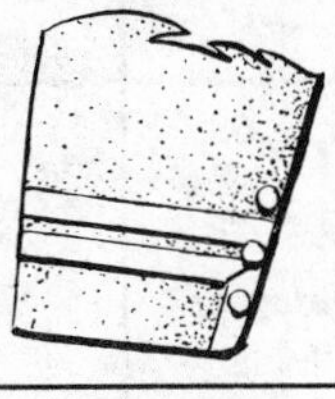
SURGEON, UNDER 12 YEARS SERVICE.	SAME AS ABOVE, BUT WITH TWO STARS.	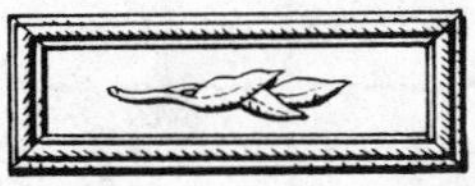 BLUE CLOTH BASE	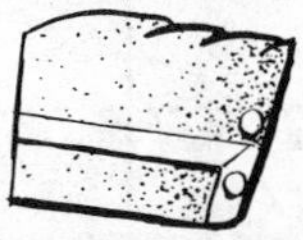
PASSED ASSISTANT SURGEON.	SAME AS ABOVE, BUT WITH ONE STAR.	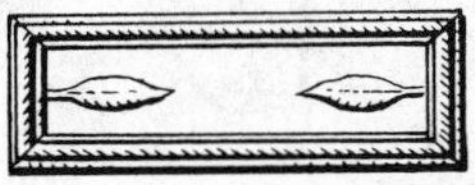 BLUE CLOTH BASE	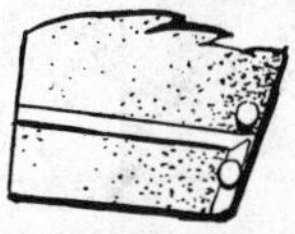
ASSISTANT SURGEON.	SAME AS ABOVE, BUT WREATH ONLY.	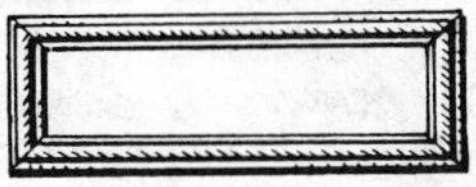 BLUE CLOTH BASE	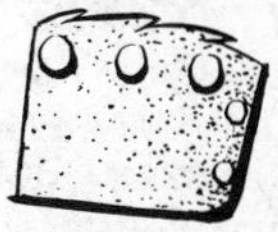 GW
PAYMASTER, OVER 12 YEARS SERVICE.	SAME AS SURGEON (THREE STARS).	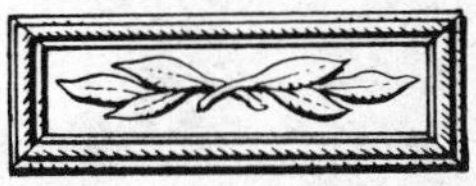 DARK GREEN CLOTH BASE	SAME AS SURGEON (OVER 12 YRS.)
PAYMASTER, UNDER 12 YEARS SERVICE	SAME AS SURGEON (TWO STARS).	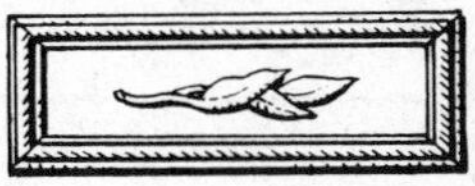 DARK GREEN CLOTH BASE	SAME AS SURGEON (UNDER 12 YRS.)
ASSISTANT PAYMASTER	SAME AS PASSED ASSISTANT SURGEON (ONE STAR)	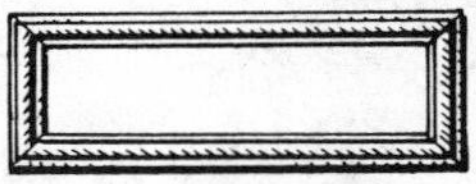 DARK GREEN CLOTH BASE	SAME AS PASSED ASSISTANT SURGEON.
CHIEF ENGINEER, OVER 12 YEARS SERVICE	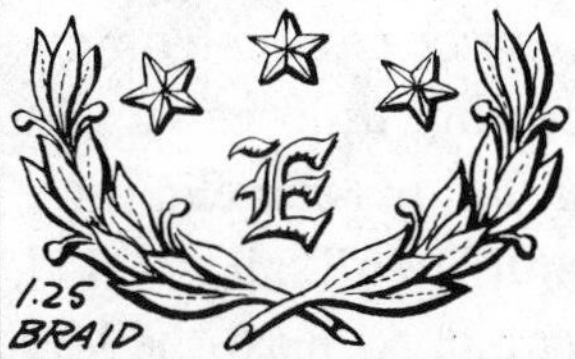 1.25 BRAID	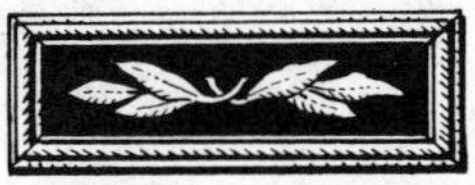 DARK BLUE CLOTH BASE	SAME AS SURGEON (OVER 12 YRS.)
CHIEF ENGINEER, UNDER 12 YEARS SERVICE	SAME AS ABOVE, BUT WITH TWO STARS	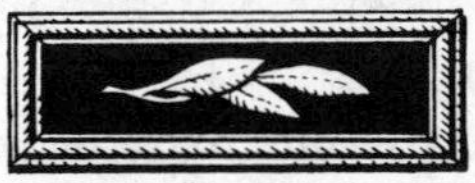 DARK BLUE CLOTH BASE	SAME AS SURGEON (UNDER 12 YRS).
FIRST ASSISTANT ENGINEER	SAME AS ABOVE, BUT WITH ONE STAR.	NONE	SAME AS PASSED ASSISTANT SURGEON.
SECOND & THIRD ASSISTANT ENGINEERS	SAME AS ABOVE, BUT WREATH AND LETTER ONLY.	NONE	SAME AS ASSISTANT SURGEON

Fig. 207b. C.S. Navy Rank Designation.

RANK OR FUNCTION	CAP DEVICE	SHOULDER STRAP DEVICE	CUFF, OR SLEEVE	COLLAR-
CHAPLAIN PROFESSOR SECRETARY CLERK	NONE	NONE	PLAIN	PLAIN
WARRANT OFFICERS	NONE	NONE		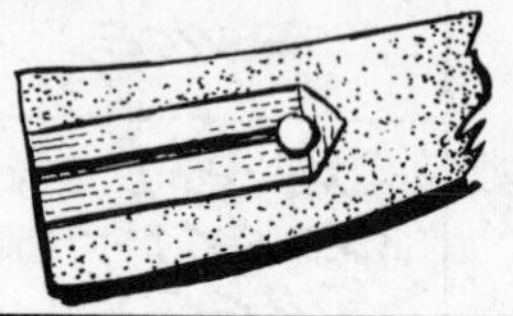

PETTY OFFICERS SLEEVE DEVICE OF BLACK SILK EMBROIDERY FOR WINTER, BLUE FOR SUMMER. WORN ON RIGHT SLEEVE BY BOATSWAIN'S, GUNNER'S, CARPENTER'S, SAILMAKER'S MATES AND SHIP'S STEWARDS, AND SHIP'S COOKS. WORN ON LEFT SLEEVE BY ALL OTHER PETTY OFFICER'S EXCEPT OFFICER'S STEWARDS AND YEOMEN. ALL PETTY OFFICERS AND CREWMEN WERE TO HAVE COLLARS AND CUFFS OF WHITE DUCK, LINED WITH BLUE COTTON, ADDED TO THEIR GREY FROCK (JUMPER).

ABOVE ELBOW, IN FRONT.

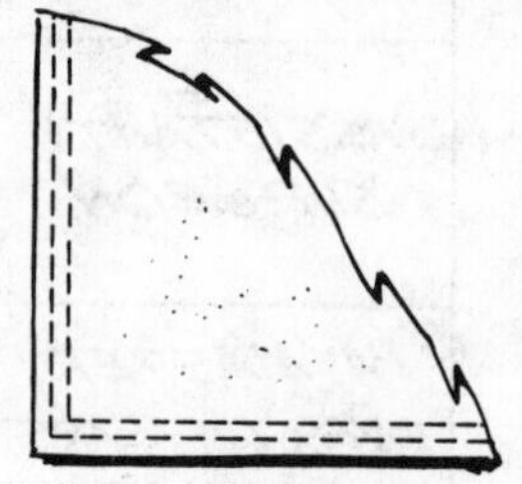

WHITE CANVAS DUCK COLLAR WITH COLORED STITCHING.

Fig. 207c. C.S. Navy Rank Designation.

Buttons

An idea of the miscellany of buttons worn can be gained from the *Providence Journal* account above, and this is borne out by surviving uniforms.

The button specified in the naval dress regulations came in three sizes (although only two sizes are found today) and represented a ship in full sail, "C.S.N." below, and 13 stars around the other sides, all within a ring of cable. At least the large size (c. 1 inch) was made in brass by E.M. Lewis & Co. of Richmond, Va. The rarity of this button suggests its manufacture was limited.

Fig. 206

The most common naval button, which exists in brass in four sizes, has an upright foul anchor imposed on crossed-cannon barrels, muzzles up, with "CSN" below, all within a ring of cable. The sizes were 1,.9,.75, and .65 inch. All were made in England, apparently by Firmin & Son, of London, for S. Isaacs Campbell & Co., and Southern importing firms.

A version of the same button, made of black composition for enlisted seamen and of 1.3 inch diameter, was sold by Courtney & Tennant of Charleston, S.C. It was a 4-hole, sew-through type (Manton's Patent) having the anchor and crossed-cannon, but with "CN" below. From a letter of Commander James H. North, in England, it appears that this button was designed and ordered in April 1863.

Small Arms and Accouterments

Firearms

Probably the first small arms ordered for the new C.S. Navy were those listed by the Secretary in his May 1861 instructions to Commander Bulloch: 1000 navy revolvers and 1000 "navy carbines" or "sea service rifles," with fixed ammunition and caps, plus a supply of cutlasses. In time, apparently, these were secured and shipped to America, but we can only guess what types they were. The revolvers were probably Kerrs, caliber .38, and the rifles, the Enfield short model or musketoon. All were being made at the London Armoury with whom Bulloch had established contact. Of the cutlasses ordered he wrote that they were "identical with those used in the British Navy and can be shipped upon the end of the rifle as a bayonet."

The statement above has value only in suggesting the kind of weapons sought by the Navy Department. Doubtless a variety of shoulder arms and navy revolvers were put to use on the Confederate privateers and men-of-war. Returns of small arms aboard captured Confederate vessels include "rifled muskets," "Springfield muskets," and "Maynard rifles" among many other types of weapons. One type specifically designed for the service can be identified:

Wilson Breechloading rifle. Made in England. Caliber .54, 49 in. overall. All brass furniture except for barrel bands, which were iron. Elevated rear sight. Lock plate stamped with a crown and date, and breech block stamped "T. Wilson's Patent" and proofmarks.

This was a "sea-service" model and was fitted to take an Enfield Navy cutlass bayonet (see below). Probably only a few of these rifles were imported.

Swords and Cutlasses.

No sword was specifically prescribed for naval oficers, so far as is now known, but two general types have been identified as having been widely worn, the first mentioned to such an extent that it has been called a "regulation" pattern.

Fig. 208

• *C.S. Naval Officer's Sword (Robert Mole?).* Straight blade chased with designs of cotton, tobacco, Confederate flag, and naval insignia, some of which are repeated on the counterguard. Gold-plated brass hilt with pommel and backstrap in the form of a sea monster, sharkskin grips bound with gilt wire. Reverse of counterguard hinged. Overall length 36 in. Most examples are stamped "Mole" (believed to be the maker, Robert Mole of Birmingham, England) on blade and counterguard, and "Courtney & Tennant, Charleston, S.C." on ricasso. Others marked "Firmin & Sons . . . London" on ricasso.

• *C.S. Naval Officer's Sword (L. Haiman & Bro., etc.).* Almost straight blade etched with various designs but including either "C.S." or "C.S.A." Brass guard and pommel, sometimes gold-plated, resembling the U.S. naval officer's sword, Model 1852, except for an elaborately designed counterguard. About 33 in. overall; leather grips bound with gilt wire. Metal scabbard with brass mountings, sometimes covered with black leather. Some blades marked with name of L. Haiman & Bro., Columbus, Ga.

• *C.S. Naval Cutlass (Old Ames Type).* Imitation of the U.S. Model 1841 cutlass, about 27 in. overall, with cast brass grip and broad strip of brass for the guard. Made by Thomas, Griswold & Co. and Cook & Bro., both of New Orleans, La., and other makers. Scabbard of leather with brass throat and tip. The original frog and belt of one example

596

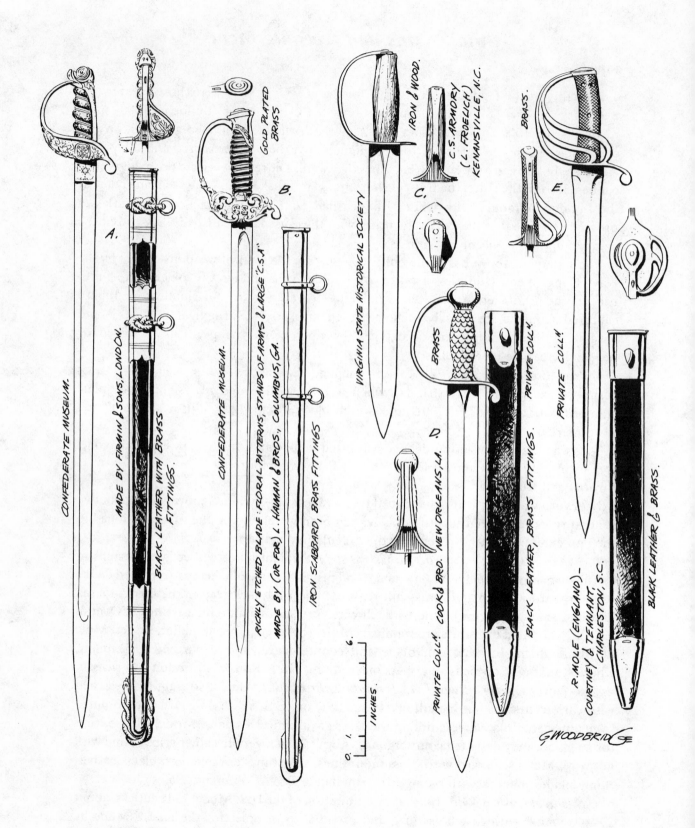

CONFEDERATE MUSEUM.

MADE BY FIRMIN & SONS, LONDON.

BLACK LEATHER WITH BRASS FITTINGS.

A.

GOLD PLATED BRASS

B.

CONFEDERATE MUSEUM.

RICHLY ETCHED BLADE: FLORAL PATTERNS, STANDS OF ARMS & LARGE "C.S.A."

MADE BY (OR FOR) L. HAIMAN & BROS., COLUMBUS, GA.

IRON SCABBARD, BRASS FITTINGS

VIRGINIA STATE HISTORICAL SOCIETY

IRON & WOOD.

C.

C.S. ARMORY (L. FROELICH) KENANSVILLE, N.C.

D.

BRASS

PRIVATE COLL. COOK & BRO. NEW ORLEANS, LA.

BLACK LEATHER, BRASS FITTINGS.

PRIVATE COLL.

BRASS.

E.

PRIVATE COLL.

R. MOLE (ENGLAND) - COURTNEY & TENNANT, CHARLESTON, S.C.

BLACK LEATHER & BRASS.

0 1 6

INCHES

G.WOODBRIDGE

Fig. 208. *C.S. Naval Swords and Cutlasses.*

survive, made of cotton webbing, leather-mounted and fastened in front by a hook. This was probably the most commonly used cutlass, so far as the use of any cutlass can be said to have been common.

• *C.S. Naval Cutlass (Mole's British Type)*. Same grip and guard as the Enfield Cavalry Saber, Pattern 1853 (see page 457), and made by the same English manufacturer, Robert Mole of Birmingham. Straight, 20-in., double-edged blade of the classic Roman pattern. Imported by Courtney & Tennant of Charleston, S.C., whose name was on the blade.

Several other patterns of cutlass were manufactured in the Confederacy. One, probably made by Froelich & Co., Kenansville, N.C., resembled the U.S. Starr cutlass of 1861. Another, by Cook & Bro., had a solid, half-basket guard like the U.S. Model 1860, but differed in all other details. Still others were rough products of local blacksmiths, not always identifiable as cutlasses.

• *Enfield Navy Cutlass Bayonet*. Slightly curved blade, 33 in. overall, steel half-basket guard and checkered leather grips. Spring catch to engage lug on right side of the barrel of an Enfield short rifle or Wilson breechloading rifle. Leather scabbard with iron mountings with stud to engage frog.

Article 43 of the C.S. *Navy Regulations* states: "The use of sheath-knives on board ship is strictly forbidden. Jack-knives shall be worn with lanyards and in fobs."

Flags

The overall story of the Confederate flag has already been given (Chapter XI). This section will be confined to a brief review of the flags used in the Confederate naval service.

We remind the reader that it was the general practice of navies in the mid-19th century to display the national flag, or a modification of it, as the naval ensign, and also to display a jack, which in America was the canton or union of the ensign. The former was flown at the gaff of a steam sloop ship or from the mainmast of a ram type ship; the jack flew from the foremast when at anchor. This practice was followed by the Confederacy.

There were numerous other naval flags, as described in the section on the U.S. Navy, but about their use on Confederate ships we can do little more than surmise. The C.S. *Navy Regulations* of 1862 strongly suggest, however, that the systems used closely corresponded to those of the U.S. service of the period, especially as regards the general signal flags and those indicating command.

• *Naval Ensign, 1861 Pattern*. This was the so-called stars and bars with somewhat narrower dimensions than used on land. The ensign of the C.S. gunboat *Ellis*, captured in February 1862, was 2.25 feet hoist by 4.4 feet fly (Naval Academy Museum). It had 3 rows of 4 large stars each. The ensign of the schooner *Sue* was 4.45x6 feet, with 6 stars in a circle; that of the steamer *Beaufort* was only 34x34 inches (both in N.Y. State Military Collection).

• *Naval Jack, 1861 Pattern*. Dark blue rectangular flag with 7 or more white stars, probably arranged in different patterns. The jack of the C.S. ram *Atlanta* had its 7 stars arranged in a circle and was 4.5x5.7 feet (Naval Academy Museum). This jack was captured in June 1863. It will be observed that, except for the number of its stars, the C.S. naval jack was the same as the U.S. pattern.

● *Naval Ensign, 1863 Pattern.* This was the white national flag adopted on 1 May 1863. Union warships observed and reported its use off Newport News as early as 12 May. One captured on the C.S. ram *Atlanta* in June of that year was 5.8x12.5 feet in dimensions, while another taken from a blockade runner off Wilmington was 9.25x17.7 feet (both Naval Academy Museum).

● *Naval Jack, 1863 Pattern.* The canton of the 1863 national flag was the battle flag adopted by the Army of Northern Virginia and, as such, became the new pattern jack. One such flag captured aboard the C.S. ram *Albemarle* in October 1864 was 6.5x8.15 feet. The double use of this flag has caused some confusion but the naval version can be readily distinguished by its far larger size (battle flags rarely exceeded 4x4 feet) and its more rectangular proportions. The C.S. Navy never hoisted the battle flag as an ensign, its sole naval use being as a jack. Furthermore, despite one mislabelled example said to have been hoisted on the "Merrimac" in 1862, there is no evidence that it was used at sea before May 1863.

● *Naval Ensign, 1865.* This would have been the 1863 ensign with a broad red bar across its fly end and possibly different proportions. However, there is no evidence that this ensign was ever issued to or hoisted aboard a Confederate vessel.

Confederate States Marine Corps

The Confederate Marine Corps was established at the same time and by the same acts as the Navy, to comprise a battalion of six companies commanded by a major. In May 1861 it was expanded to include enough men and officers for ten companies, but remained a "Corps" commanded by a colonel, Lloyd J. Beall. Actually no more than six companies were ever raised during the four years of its existence, and by October 1864 its aggregate strength had dropped to 539 men and officers. The Corps never served as a unit, being used as provisional commands, as small detachments aboard ship, as guards at naval stations and yards, and in coastal fortifications. A Camp of Instruction was maintained at Drewry's Bluff, Va. At the very end of the war Marine elements served with the army in Semmes' and Tucker's Naval Brigades.

Fig. 210

No regulations governing the Confederate Marine uniform have been found and probably none were ever published. A "description of marine clothing," said to have been sent to the naval agent in England in May 1861 to assist him in purchasing early uniforms for the Corps, has not been located, but in all likelihood it was a generalized statement which can be reconstructed in the main. It seems probable that the uniform of the U.S. Marine Corps served as the general model with two significant changes: gray was substituted for dark blue and jackets were prescribed instead of frock coats for ordinary dress. Other differences were the result of circumstances rather than planning.

SECOND LIEUTENANT,
NOV. 1862 - FEB. 1863
(HENRY M. DOAK)

FIRST
LIEUTENANT
1862 - 1865.
(FRANCIS H.
CAMERON)

PRIVATE,
CAPT. VAN BENTHUYSEN'S
COMPANY, FLORIDA,
1861.

FIRST LIEUTENANT
COMMANDING MARINE GUARD,
C.S.S. SAVANNAH, 1861.
(HENRY L. GRAVES)

G.WOODBRIDGE

Fig. 209. *C.S. Marine Corps. 2nd Lieutenant, 1862 (Doak):* gray cap with gold lace; gray coat with gold lace; light blue trousers with gold or red welt; brass hilted sword and black belt with brass plate. *1st Lieutenant, 1861-1862 (Cameron):* gray or blue cap; dark blue coat with gold lace; light blue trousers; and black belt with brass plate. *1st Lieutenant 1861-1862 (Graves):* blue or gray cap with gold lace; gray coat with dark blue edging, gold rank designation on collar, gold knots with the loops having red centers, brass U.S.M.C. buttons; sky blue trousers with dark blue stripe; scarlet sash; and brass hilted sword with black leather, brass mounted scabbard. *Private, Florida, 1861:* straw hat, blue flannel shirt; dark blue trousers; standard, or common, types accouterments; and Enfield pattern rifled musket. From photographs and contemporary descriptions and surviving specimens.

Fig. 209

The dress uniform worn by Lieutenant Henry L. Graves, who commanded the Marine guard on the C.S.S. *Savannah*, has been preserved (Atlanta Historical Society). It consists of a cadet gray frock coat with a low standing collar of the army pattern and two rows of buttons, quite widely spaced over the chest, narrowing top and bottom. Insignia of rank are sewn on the collar, which is edged top and bottom with a .125-inch piping of black cord; the plain, pointed cuffs have a similar edging. An interesting feature of the uniform is the presence of a pair of gold lace shoulder knots on a red base, much like the knots worn by Marine officers in the North. (These probably do not belong to this uniform. See Donnelly, *History of the CSMC*.) The pants are sky blue with a .25-inch black stripe. The cap is missing; it could well have been the blue pattern, regulation for infantry, or a gray forage model. The buttons are those issued the "Old Corps," the U.S. Marines.

Photographs of other Marine officers do not entirely substantiate this uniform, but the differences are hardly to be wondered at considering the trouble to which these men must have been put to equip themselves. Some wore gray naval frock coats with rolling collars and shoulder straps, while others had bare shoulders and the army's gold braid cuff loops. Some letters written by Lieutenant Graves, mentioned above, have come down to us and indicate his everlasting struggle to keep properly clothed and the latitude in style and even color permitted. By 1863 Graves was wearing or considering for wear such diverse garments as a gray sack coat, a coat and pants "of a sort of blue flannel," and vests of white linen and black cassimere.

Gray sack coats, white linen pants, gray cloth pants and gray jackets were all worn by Confederate Marine officers. For dress they had crimson sashes and black leather belts. Whether there was a distinctive dress cap is still an open question.

Enlisted men of the Corps were authorized for dress the following items for a four-year enlistment:

2 Uniform coats	1 Uniform cap
1 Pair of epaulettes or counter straps	3 Pompons
8 Pair linen overalls	16 Shirts
4 Pair woolen overalls	2 Stocks
24 Pair brogans	8 Pair socks

And for fatigue and other purposes:

4 Fatigue jackets	8 Flannel shirts
6 Fatigue overalls	2 Blankets
3 Fatigue caps	2 Knapsacks
5 Linen jackets	1 Great coat

Information on the cut and character of these garments and accouterments is conflicting and unquestionably the supply was irregular in all respects. Yet it is apparent that by late 1863, at least, the C.S. Marine uniform was distinctive. The Corps' Quartermaster on 7 December of that year warned against civilians and soldiers of the army wearing Marine clothing which, he said, "is readily known by its material and style." Captain Van Benthuysen's company at Pensacola during the summer of 1861 was issued at diverse times: blue pants, blue flannel shirts, white pants, and white shirts or jumpers. On 20

Fig. 210. C.S. Navy and Marine Corps. *Tucker's Naval Battalion, April 6 to 9, 1865.* Mixed force of C.S. Sailors and Marines wearing C.S. naval and marine clothing: blue, gray, brown-gray, light blue, etc. From contemporary descriptions and uniform regulations.

October 1861 this same company received: 5 pairs sergeant's jean pants, 4 pairs corporal's jean pants, 91 pairs private's pants, 5 sergeant's satinett frock coats, 4 corporal's frock coats, 91 private's frock coats, 100 leather stocks, and 100 forage caps. The earlier issues were probably retained for fatigue use.

It is probable that the C.S. Marine dress uniform was based on that prescribed for the U.S. Marine Corps, with appropriate differences: gray double-breasted frock coat with medium blue or black collar and cuffs and yellow worsted epaulets; white linen or cotton, or sky blue cloth pants (with stripes of two widths, for sergeants and for corporals); and a medium blue dress cap with red pompon.

The fatigue dress was similar to that of the Confederate infantry with dress pants worn on occasions. A black waterproof cap cover was often added at sea. Flannel shirts of blue or gray, or white cotton shirts were sometimes worn as outer garments; and white linen or cotton jackets saw service for musters in warm weather.

• *Insignia.* No insignia distinctive of the C.S. Marine Corps have been identified. There is mention in a clothing receipt roll of June 1864 of "eagles and rings," suggesting cap devices, but these could have been captured items. The surviving officer's coat has U.S. Marine buttons but the probability is that C.S. naval buttons were more common.

• *Small Arms and Accouterments.* The earliest record of equipment specifically ordered for the Corps listed "1000 waist belts, black leather (such as used in British service), with cartridge box, cap box, and bayonet scabbard, attached by means of slides; 1000 knapsacks, such as used in British service, with straps to connect with the waist belt; 20 bugles, with extra mouth pieces; and 20 swords for noncommissioned officers, with shoulder belts." In the main, however, arms varied from station to station, although Enfields were apparently popular.

In the account of the surrender of the *Atlanta,* quoted in part above, is contained the statement that the "Marine officer has a sword, and a fine one it is, with equipments, made by Firman & Sons, 153 Strand and 13 Conduit Street, London."

SOURCES

C.S. Navy Dept., *Uniform and Dress of the Navy of the Confederate States,* [Richmond, Va., 1862?], plates. Reprinted 1952 by Ray Riling; reprinted 1960 in a revised edition with one plate colored and introduction by Richard Harwell, stating what is known about this rare pamphlet and other information of value.

Official Records of the Union and Confederate Navies in the War of the Rebellion, 30 vols., Washington, D.C., 1894-1927. The most useful material will be found in series 2, vol. II.

C.S., Navy Dept., *Regulations for the Navy of the Confederate States,* Richmond, Va., 1862.

Ralph W. Donnelly, "Uniforms and Equipment of Confederate Marines," in *Military Collector & Historian,* IX, 1-7.

J. Thomas Scharf, *History of the Confederate States Navy from Its Organization to the Surrender of Its Last Vessel . . .,* 2nd ed., Albany, N.Y. 1894.

Joseph T. Durkin, S.J., *Stephen R. Mallory: Confederate Navy Chief,* Chapel Hill, N.C., 1954.

William G. Gavin, *Accouterment Plates: North and South, 1861-1865 . . .,* Philadelphia, Pa., 1963.

Alphaeus H. Albert, *Record of American Uniform and Historical Buttons . . ., 1775-1968,* Hightstown, N.J., 1969.

William A. Albaugh, III, *Confederate Edged Weapons,* New York, 1960.

Claud E. Fuller and Richard D. Steuart, *Firearms of the Confederacy . . .,* Huntington, West Virginia, 1944.

W. Adolphe Roberts, *Semmes of the Alabama,* New York, 1938.

Arthur Sinclair, *Two Years on the Alabama,* Boston, 1896.

James Morris Morgan, *Recollections of a Rebel Reefer,* New York, 1917.

This chapter is based in part upon material in Record Group 45, National Archives, and in the Naval Historical Center. The section of naval flags owes much to a study prepared and graciously made available by Dr. George B. Keester, one time Curator, U.S. Naval Academy Museum. The work on the C.S. Marine Corps, *op. cit.,* by Ralph W. Donnelly, is the starting point for the study of this field. This section of the manuscript was read by Mr. Donnelly and Robert K. Krick and we have profited greatly from their comments and criticisms.